KB264439

해설로 짜는 전략의 적용,

해설주의 토익 실전 모의고사 LC

해설주의 토익 실전 모의고사 LC 5회분

지은이 백형식
초판 1쇄 인쇄 2018년 3월 9일
초판 1쇄 발행 2018년 3월 23일

발행인 박효상 **총괄이사** 이종선 **편집장** 김현 **기획 · 편집** 김효정, 김설아 **디자인** 김보연
표지디자인 물질과비물질 **조판** 조영라
마케팅 이태호, 이전희 **관리** 김태옥

종이 월드페이퍼 **인쇄 · 제본** 현문자현

출판등록 제10-1835호 **발행처** 사람in **주소** 121-839 서울시 마포구 양화로 11길 14-10 (서교동) 4F
전화 02) 338-3555(代) **팩스** 02) 338-3545
E-mail saramin@netsgo.com **Homepage** www.saramin.com

책값은 뒤표지에 있습니다.
파본은 바꾸어 드립니다.

ⓒ 백형식 2018

ISBN
978-89-6049-660-6 14740
978-89-6049-658-3 (세트)

사람이 중심이 되는 세상, 세상과 소통하는 책 사람in

해설주의 토익
실전 모의고사 LC

백형식 저

사람In
saram in.com

TOEIC을 준비하는 학습자들은 느끼지 못하겠지만 사실 신토익이 시행되고 문제 유형이 여러 면에서 변화를 거쳐 왔습니다. 그 와중에 수많은 교재들이 서점가를 점령했고 그 교재들에 포함되어 있는 상당수의 문제들이 사실은 과거 "뉴토익" 시절에 사용 되었던 문제들의 재탕인 것이 현실입니다.

이제 변화하던 여러 가지 유형 틀이 확립되었지만 아직도 변화된 유형조차 반영하지 못한 교재들이 버젓이 베스트셀러로 팔리고 있다는 현실이 너무나 안타깝습니다.

모의고사란 실전과 같은 경험을 제공해 줄 수 있어야만 하기에 최신 기출문제의 구성을 그대로 담아내야만 합니다. 그리고 해설에는 문제를 풀이하는 데 필요한 필수적인 비법들을 제공해줘야 합니다.

청취력이 약한 사람이 단시간에 청취력을 향상시킬 수 있는 기적은 존재하지 않습니다. 오늘 여러분의 듣기 실력과 이번 달 말에 여러분의 듣기 실력 즉 '청취력'에는 큰 변화가 생기지 않습니다. 그러나 단기간에 LC점수가 필요한 것이 현실입니다. "토익은 기술이다"라는 말이 있듯이 문제를 풀이할 때 필요한 기술들이 있습니다. 좀더 쉽게 답을 맞추기 위한 팁들이라고 볼 수 있습니다. 이러한 다양한 노하우를 해설에 담아 냈습니다. 듣기 실력이 없어도 답을 찾는 기술이 존재합니다.

본서는 모의고사에 오랜 기간 동안 분석한 실전 팁들을 최대한 담아냈습니다. 제시한 팁들을 활용하여 최단 기간에 점수 향상을 이룰 수 있을 것이라 믿습니다.

기출문제와 유형 및 난이도를 정확히 맞춘 모의고사를 토익커 여러분들께 제공해 드릴 수 있게 되어 기쁘게 생각합니다.

여러분 모두 토익의 고민에서 빨리 탈출하시기를 기원하며….

백형식 드림

문제지

해설지

신토익 문제 구성
한눈에 보기

PART 1

	신토익	구토익
유형	사진 묘사	사진 묘사
문항수	총 6문항	총 10문항

사진을 묘사하는 4개의 보기가 등장하는 유형 유지

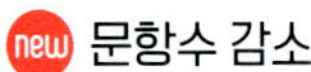 문항수 감소

PART 2

	신토익	구토익
유형	질의 응답	질의 응답
문항수	총 25문항	총 30문항

질문에 대한 적절한 응답을 찾는 유형은 유지

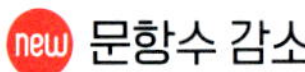 문항수 감소

PART 3

	신토익	구토익
유형	짧은 대화	짧은 대화
문항수	13개 대화(대화당 3문항) 총 39문항	10개 대화(대화당 3문항) 총 30문항

3명의 화자가 대화를 나누는 신유형 추가

대화와 문항수 증가

PART 4

	신토익	구토익
유형	설명문	설명문
문항수	10개 설명문(설명문당 3문항) 총 30문항	10개 설명문(설명문당 3문항) 총 30문항

제시된 정보를 참고하는 신유형 추가

PART 5

	신토익	구토익
유형	단문 공란 채우기	단문 공란 채우기
문항수	총 30문항	총 40문항

단문에 있는 공란에 적절한 단어/표현을 채우는 유형 유지

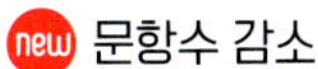 문항수 감소

PART 6

	신토익	구토익
유형	장문 공란 채우기	장문 공란 채우기
문항수	총 16문항	총 12문항

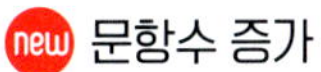 문제 형태 변화

문항수 증가

PART 7

	신토익	구토익
유형	단일 지문	단일 지문
문항수	10개 단일 지문 지문당 2–4문항 총 29문항	9개 단일 지문 지문당 2–5문항 총 28문항
유형	이중 지문	이중 지문
문항수	2개 세트 지문 세트당 5문항 총 10문항	4개 세트 지문 세트당 5문항 총 20문항
유형	삼중 지문	
문항수	3개 세트 지문 세트당 5문항 총 15문항	
문항수	총 54문항	총 48문항

신유형인 삼중 지문 유형 추가

기존 독해 문제 풀이 방식 유지

문항수 증가

실전 풀이

44. What does the man think about the interview?
(A) He did very well.
(B) He did poorly.
(C) He was well-prepared.
(D) He had a great time.

45. How did the woman find out BK's interview style?
(A) She had an interview with BK Corporation.
(B) She had heard from other interviewees.
(C) She read a business magazine.
(D) She has contacted the personnel department.

46. What is the woman trying to do?
(A) Comfort the man
(B) Critique the man's performance
(C) Persuade the man to keep his current job
(D) Provide the man with an analysis of his interview

47. What are the speakers talking about?
(A) Accounting work
(B) The availability of a job
(C) The lack of personnel
(D) The new secretary

48. According to the woman, why isn't she able to hire the man?
(A) She has already filled the position.
(B) She believes he lacks work experience.
(C) She thinks he is overqualified.
(D) She doesn't think he has the right education.

49. What information does the woman give the man?
(A) He is eligible for a discount.
(B) He is required to have previous work experience.
(C) He can apply for another job.
(D) He should submit additional documents.

50. What is the woman likely
(A) Attend a board meetir
(B) Talk to some executives
(C) Make a decision to laur
(D) Complete a loan appl

51. What does the man men joint venture proposal?
(A) It will be reviewed by week.
(B) It will reduce costs to
(C) It will be beneficial to
(D) It will encourage more the industry.

52. What is the woman's cor situation?
(A) There are strict govern
(B) Raising funds for the ver
(C) The industry is very c
(D) Both companies seer unsound.

53. What are the speakers ma
(A) A business meeting
(B) A product order
(C) A sales conference
(D) An advertising campa

54. What does the man impl "Anything else"?
(A) He wants the woman deadline.
(B) He wants to invite the w
(C) He wants to the wom meeting.
(D) He wants the woman to

55. What will the woman pro week?
(A) Attend a conference
(B) Hire new employees
(C) Arrange a meeting
(D) Take a vacation

Questions 38-40 refer to the following conversation.

M　How's it going, Grace? [38] I hear that the seminar has been canceled. That must be a relief for you.

W　I am quite glad. We had to cancel it, though. [39] We couldn't find enough speakers with sufficient experience in the field.

M　Well, we are working with some cutting-edge technology. [40] I can contact some of my old professors and see if they would like to speak.

W　That would be great, actually. I am organizing a committee, and our goal is to have the seminar sometime in winter.

M　[40] OK. I'll send them an e-mail. Also, I'll ask around at some other companies.

1. 스크립트 해석 및 단서 확인

해당 스크립트 해석 및 문제의 단서를 통하여 지문을 분석한다.

문제 해설

실외 전경을 배경으로 2인 이상이 등장하는 사진이므로 사람들의 공통동 통된 동작이나 강조가 되는 동작이 없을 경우 외모적 특성 순서로 분석하 경을 구성하는 주요 요소들의 위치와 상태 또는 배열 형태를 살펴보는 승객들이 비행기에서 내리는 행동, 비행기가 활주로에 착륙한 상태, 그리 제공하는 차량들이 위치하고 있는 상태에 집중해야 하며, 이 중 비행기에 을 '비행기 등에서 내리다'의 뜻을 지닌 disembark를 사용하여 묘사하고

2. 문제 해설

해당 문제에 대한 깊이 있고 적확한 해설을 통해 출제 의도를 이해한다.

토익 분석

선택의문문에서 두 가지 선택 사항 중 하나를 고르는 것이 아닌 새로운 변 또한 비중이 높은 정답 유형임을 알아 둬야 한다. (B)는 선택의문문 장했고, 질문에서는 'leave; 남겨 두다'를 쓰고 대답에는 '떠나다'라고 써 (C)는 전형적인 권유, 제안 질문에 대한 답변으로 오답이다. 이 문제에서 트는 선택의문문은 Yes/No 답변이 불가하다는 것과 thanks but 구문 대한 답변이라는 것이다.

3. 토익 분석

해당 문제의 출제 경향을 포함한 전반적인 신토익 문제 경향 및 풀이법을 파악한다.

Part 1
기출 표현 총정리

보다, 읽다_사람

look into

- she is looking into a glass case.
- she is looking into a store window.

들다, 잡다_사람

hold

- A man is holding a piece of wood.
- Some people are holding onto a railing.

복사하다_사람

copy

- A woman is copying a document.

걷다_사람

walk along

- One of the men is walking along the water.
- He is walking along the shore.

일하다_사람

work at

- The man is working at a desk.

서 있다_사람

stand

- Some men are standing near a building.
- One of the men is standing on a ladder.

앉다_사람

sit

- They are sitting at a wooden table.
- They are sitting around a conference table.

착용하다_사람

wear

- A woman is wearing a pair of gloves.
- A woman is wearing a jacket.

기다리다_사람

wait

- Some people are waiting in a lobby.
- Some people are waiting in line at a ticket counter.

멈추다_사물

stop at / stopped near

- The train is stopped at the station.
- A vehicle is stopped at the traffic signal.
- A cyclist is stopped near some benches.

싣다, 담다_사람

load

- Some movers are loading a vehicle with furniture.
- A man is loading cart with laundry.

내려오다_사람

step down

- A woman is stepping down from a train.

먹다_사람

have a snack / have a meal

- They're having a snack near the water.
- She's having a meal.

손을 뻗다_사람

reach

- She's reaching over her desk.
- One of the women is reaching for a bottle.

치워진_사물

be cleared of

- The counter has been cleared of objects.

말하다_사람

speak to

- A man is speaking to a group of people.

놓여 있다(위치)_사물

be placed on

- A potted plant has been placed on the floor.
- A floral arrangement has been placed on a table.

진열된_사물

be on display

- Some vegetables are on display in the store.
- Some jewelry is on display.

설치되다_사물

be set up
- Two computers are set up next to each other.
- There are chairs set up in front of a building.

기대어 있다_사람

lean against
- A man is leaning against a wall.
- Some bicycles are leaning against a fence.

줄지어져 있다_사물

be lined up
- Picnic tables are lined up in a row.
- Some shopping carts have been lined up against a wall.

걸려 있다, 매달려 있다_사물

be propped against
- A whiteboard is propped against the wall.
- Some artwork is propped against the sofa.

펼쳐져 있다_사물

be spread out
- Some papers are spread out on a table.
- A newspaper has been spread out on the carpet.

수리되다_사물

be repaired, be examined
- Some tracks are being repaired.
- A light fixture is being repaired.
- A piece of equipment is being examined.

보다, 읽다_사람

examine
- She's examining some clothing.

불이 밝혀진_사물

be illuminated
- The sitting area is illuminated by floor lamps.

주차되다_사물

be parked
- A truck is being parked in a garage.
- Some bicycles have been parked along a railing.

걸려있다, 매달려있다_사물

be mounted
- Some decorations have been mounted on the wall.
- A bicycle has been mounted on the front of a bus.

요리(준비하다)_사람

prepare
- She's preparing some food.

청소하다(닦다)_사람

wipe
- A man is wiping a counter.
- A woman's wiping a car window with a cloth.

보다, 읽다_사람

read
- She's reading under an umbrella.
- She's reading over his shoulder.

가리키다_사람

point at(toward)
- A woman is pointing toward a boat.
- A man is pointing at a screen.

놓여 있다(위치)_사물

be on
- A laptop computer is on a desk.
- Some computers are on a table.

마주하다_사람

face
- The armchairs are facing the paintings.
- He's facing some computer monitors.

마주하다_사람

face away(등지다)
- They're facing away from each other.

실려 있다_사물

be loaded
- A bicycle has been loaded onto a truck.
- Shopping bags are being loaded into a car.

탑승하다_사람

board
- Passengers are boarding a train.
- Some people are boarding an airplane.

진열된_사물

be being displayed
- The mattress is being displayed in a store window.
- Some clothing is being displayed.

옮기다, 나르다_사람

carry
- A woman is carrying some trays.
- A woman's carrying a jacket over her arm.

열다_사람 / 열려 있다_사물

open
- One woman is opening a notebook.
- A woman's holding a door open.
- A door has been left open.

청소하다(쓸다)_사람

sweep
- A man is sweeping a walkway.
- Leaves are being swept out of the road.
- A garden path is being swept.

내려오다_사람

descend
- Some people are descending some stairs.

놓여 있다(위치)_사물

be above
- There are cabinets above a computer monitor.

담긴_사물

be put in
- Flowers have been put in a vase.

보다, 읽다_사람

look at
- One of the women is looking at some files.
- A woman is looking at clothing.

꺼내다, 내리다_사람

take down
- A woman is taking cookware down from a display.

위로 몸을 숙이다_사람

lean over
- Some people are leaning over a railing.
- They're leaning over some boxes.

듣다_사람

listen
- An audience is listening to a lecturer.
- Some people are listening to a presentation.

비어 있다_사물

unoccupied
- An office is unoccupied.
- The benches are occupied.

팔다_사람

sell
- Some vendors are selling merchandise.
- They're selling merchandise at a street fair.

일을 수행하다_사람

carry out
- Park maintenance work is being carried out.

앉다_사람

seat
- Some people are seated in a circle.
- Some travelers are seated in a waiting area.

내려오다_사람

step off
- One of the hikers is stepping off a bridge.

요리(썰다)_사람

cut
- A man is cutting some food.

확인하다_사람

check
- He's checking his phone.

통화하다_사람

talk on
- A man is talking on the phone.

들여다보다_사람

look in
- One woman is looking in her bag.
- She is looking in a drawer.

타이핑하다_사람

type on
- A man's typing on a keyboard.

고르다, 선택하다_사람

choose

- He's choosing some vegetables.

걸려 있다, 매달려 있다_사물

hang

- Some people are hanging up a picture.
- Some hanging flower baskets decorate a window.

가득 차다_사물

be filled with

- A file drawer has been filled with folders.
- A basket has been filled with items.

자전거 타다_사람

cycle

- He's cycling in a city.
- Some cyclists are riding past a building.

놓여 있다(위치)_사물

be arranged

- Plants are arranged on tables.
- Some chairs have been arranged on a beach.

휴식을 취하다_사람

rest

- Some people are resting by a stream.
- He's resting against a lamppost.
- Some people are resting on the steps.

끌다, 당기다_사람

pull

- He's pulling a cart.
- A man is pulling a cart of boxes.

고르다, 선택하다_사람

select

- A woman is selecting some fruit.

기대어 있다_사람

lean forward

- The woman is leaning forward to touch a notepad.

건너다(길, 다리)_사람

cross

- Some people are crossing a road.
- Some pedestrians are crossing the street.

나눠주다, 분배하다_사람

distribute

- Some printed materials are being distributed to a class.
- One of the men is distributing papers.

줄지어져 있다_사물

be lining

- Trees are lining both sides of a street.

놓여 있다(위치)_사물

be located

- Some buildings are located near a hill.

질문이나 보기를 정확히 이해하지 못해서 찍어야 한다면 꼭 사용해 보세요.

100% 정답인 표현들 - 질문에 관계없이 들리면 무조건 답

모른다 : I don't know, I have no idea, I'm not sure, I haven't heard, I haven't been told.

내가 알기로는 아니다 : Not that I know of.

상황에 따라 다른다 : depend

결정되지 않았다 : It hasn't been decided(=announced)

오늘 결정될 것이다 : It will be decided(=announced) today.
물어봐라(확인해봐라), 물어보겠다(확인해 보겠다) : I'll check~, I'll ask~, let me
check~, Let me ask~, You should ask~, You should check~.

99% 정답 표현

"But"이 포함된 보기

질문에서 들렸던 발음과 비슷한 발음의 단어가 포함되지 않았다는 전제하에 보기에
But이 들린다면 99% 정답이다.

90% 정답

의문문 형태의 보기 (반문표현)

질문에서 들렸던 발음과 비슷한 발음의 단어가 포함되지 않았다는 전제하에 보기가
의문문 형태라면 90% 이상 정답률을 갖는다.

질문 유형별 답 찾기

Know-how를 이야기 하기 전에 몇 가지 기본 규칙을 먼저 기억하자.

1. 3개의 질문 중 첫 번째 질문은 거의 대화의 초반부 지문 속에 답이 등장한다.
2. 3개의 질문 중 두 번째 질문은 답의 위치를 대화의 내용으로 파악해야 한다.
3. 3개의 질문 중 세 번째 질문은 거의 대화의 후반부 지문 속에 답이 등장한다.
4. 대화 흐름의 기본은 사건이 초반부에 터지고 후반부로 가면서 해결책이 제시된다.
   과거에서 미래로 흘러간다.
5. 답의 위치를 짐작할 수 없을 경우는 언제나 반전 표현 / 제안(요청) 표현 / 의도(미
   래 행동) 표현 / 키워드를 활용한다. 답의 위치를 알 수 없는 상황에서 이 표현들이
   등장하면서 답을 제시해주는 경우가 대부분이다. 따라서 이 표현들을 듣는 연습을
   해야 한다.

암기 포인트! - 언제나 정답을 이끌어 주는 중요한 힌트 `정답 5형제!`

1. 반전 표현

But, I'm sorry, Actually, So, I'm afraid, Unfortunately, however, also 등

2. 요청 표현

명령문 (Please + 동사원형), Could you~, Can you~, I want you to~, I need you to~ 등

3. 제안 표현

You / We should~, You / We could~, You / We can~, You'd better, Let~, Do you mind~, Would you like me to~?, Do you want me to~?, How about~?, Why don't you~? 등이 등장하며, 이때 요청 / 제안의 답을 자주 이끄는 동사로는 ask, suggest, recommend, invite, advise, request, require 등이 있다.

4. 의도 표현

I'd like to~, I want to~, I need to~가 가장 많이 사용되며 미래 행동 표현인 I'll~, I'm going to~, I must(should, have to) ~도 의도 문제에 답으로 등장한다.

5. 미래 행동 표현

I'll~, I'm going to~, I must (should, have to)~, I'd like to~, I want to~, I need to~ 등이 등장한다.

키워드

질문 속의 명사가 동사보다 좋다. 시간 관련 표현, 숫자, 고유명사, 최상급 표현들은 항상 우선 순위 키워드로 사용된다. 또한 질문 속에 나오는 전치사 about 뒤의 명사도 좋은 키워드로 활용된다. 고유명사 키워드는 처음 등장 후에는 다양한 대명사로 대체된다는 것도 기억하자.

추가

항상 대화 전반적으로 등장하는 문두 시점 또는 기간 표현, 문두 부사, 부사구, If 가정법 문장, also 또한 중요한 포인트니 놓치지 말자.

유형 1. 전화 메시지 남기기

서두

상대방 이름, 자기 소개(이름, 직책, 부서, 회사, 회사 업종, 회사 위치 정보)

전화 건 목적(일반적인 전화 메시지의 경우)

I'm calling + 전화목적

전화 건 목적(회신하는 전화 메시지의 경우)

I've received~, I'm returning~, I'm calling back~과 같은 표현이 약간의 부대 설명을 이끈다. 부대 설명에는 상대방이 요청한 사항, 상대방이 언급한 문제점, 요청사항 등이 등장하며 이후 반전 표현과 전화 목적이 나온다.

세부사항

키워드, 반전 표현, 부사구 등

반전 표현

However, By the way, So, I'm afraid, Unfortunately, I'm sorry, Actually, But 등

키워드

질문 속의 명사가 동사보다 좋다. 시간 관련 표현, 숫자, 고유 명사, 최상급 표현들은
항상 우선 순위 키워드로 사용된다. 또한 질문 속에서 전치사 about 뒤의 명사도 좋은
키워드로 활용된다. 질문 속에 존재하는 if절 문장의 내용은 최고의 키워드이다.

부사구

Most of all, In addition to~, Also, Lastly, Finally 등

Offer / Ask / Suggest 유형 문제 등장

정보 요청 방법, 주문 방법, 연락 방법 등이 등장하며 답의 형태는 다음과 같다.
- If 가정법 (To 동사원형, For 명사) + available, free of charge, complimentary,
  discount, coupon, special offer, given, provided, offered 등의 표현
- If 가정법 (To 동사원형, For 명사) + Please 명령문 형태의 문장 또는 ask, suggest,
  recommend, invite, urge, encourage, advise, require 등의 동사들로 답을 이끄는 문
  장들
- If 가정법 (To 동사원형, For 명사), 요청하는 내용의 Could you~, Can you~, You /
  We should~, You / We could~, You / We can~, Let~ 등

유형 2. 자동 응답 메시지

서두

You've reached~, Thank you for calling + 녹음주체(업체명에서 청자 정보와 업종, 위
치 정보 등을 찾을 수 있음)

녹음 목적

생략될 경우가 많지만 나온다면 보통 영업 시간 안내나 가게 이전 또는 몇 주년 기념
식에 따른 세일 안내가 나온다.

부재 중 이유

- 상담원이 바쁘다는 내용이면 대기 시간 및 대기 순서 등장
- 영업 시간이 끝났음
- 사무실 부재 중

세부사항

- 작은 회사의 경우는 예약 방법, 영업 시간 안내
- 큰 회사의 경우는 주로 할인율, 할인 품목, 할인 기간, 할인 장소 듣기와 같은 sale 관련 이벤트 내용

Offer / Ask / Suggest 유형 문제 등장

정보 요청 방법, 주문 방법, 연락 방법 등이 등장하며 답의 형태는 다음과 같다.

- If 가정법 (To 동사원형, For 명사) + available, free of charge, complimentary, discount, coupon, special offer, given, provided, offered 등의 표현
- If 가정법 (To 동사원형, For 명사) + Please 명령문 형태의 문장 또는 ask, suggest, recommend, invite, urge, encourage, advise, require 등의 동사들로 답을 이끄는 문장들
- If 가정법 (To 동사원형, For 명사), 요청하는 내용의 Could you~, Can you~, You / We should~, You / We could~, You / We can~, Let~ 등

유형 3. 제품 or 회사광고

서두

의문문 또는 가정법 등이 자주 등장하며 이 부분에서 청자와 광고 대상을 유추해야 할 때가 많다.

광고대상

- 광고하는 상품명이나 홍보하려는 회사명 등장
- 제품명이 나올 경우는 바로 다음 세부 정보로 이어져 제품 특징을 열거
- 회사 이름이나 가게 이름이 나올 경우는 가게 이전이나 몇 주년 기념 등으로 세일 유무를 알리고, 세부 정보에서 세일에 관한 세부 사항이 열거되며 세일은 언제나 시작이나 끝을 알리는 시점이나 기간이 등장

키워드

제품의 특징이나 업체만의 차이점, 장점 그리고 업체의 경우 세일에 관한 내용이 등장하며 세일 관련 내용이 등장할 때는 날짜나 기간 표현이 중요하다. 여기서 특히 세부 정보 부분에서는 반전 표현이나 부사구가 답을 찾는데 유용하다.

마무리

구입 방법, 신청 방법, 정보 요청 방법 등이 등장

Offer/ Ask / Suggest 유형 문제 등장

정보 요청 방법, 주문 방법, 연락 방법 등이 등장하며 답의 형태는 다음과 같다.

- If 가정법 (To 동사원형, For 명사) + available, free of charge, complimentary, discount, coupon, special offer, given, provided, offered 등의 표현
- If 가정법 (To 동사원형, For 명사) + Please 명령문 형태의 문장 또는 ask, suggest, recommend, invite, urge, encourage, advise, require 등의 동사들로 답을 이끄는 문장들
- If 가정법 (To 동사원형, For 명사), 요청하는 내용의 Could you~, Can you~, You / We should~, You / We could~, You / We can~, Let~ 등

유형 4. 공지 글

환영인사

대체로 Welcome to~, Thank you for~ 등으로 시작하는 초반부 이벤트명이나 장소명에서 청자와 이벤트의 목적, 개최 시기 등의 정보를 얻는다.

화자소개

This is~, My name is~, I'm~ 등으로 시작하는 화자의 이름과 부서 및 직책 등이 제시된다.

주제문

알림 사항 즉 글의 목적이나 공지의 내용이 등장한다. announce, present, introduce, inform, remind, report, let you know와 같은 동사들과 I'd like to~, I'm here to~, I want to~, I need to~, I will~, I'm going to~, I must(should / have to)~ 등의 표현들이 답을 이끈다.

중반부

서론에 등장한 주제문에 대한 부연 설명이 이루어지는 부분으로 세부 정보를 찾는 문제가 등장한다. 세부 정보를 찾는 문제는 질문 속의 키워드를 이용하거나 반전 표현 (However, By the way, So, I'm afraid, Unfortunately, I'm sorry, Actually, But 등) 또는 글의 흐름을 잠시 끊어주는 부사구들이 답을 제시해 준다.

키워드

질문 속의 명사가 동사보다 좋다. 시간 관련 표현, 숫자, 고유 명사, 최상급 표현들은 항상 우선 순위 키워드로 사용된다. 또한 질문 속에서 전치사 about 뒤의 명사도 좋은 키워드로 활용된다. 질문 속에 존재하는 if절 문장의 내용도 최고의 키워드이다.

부사구

Most of all, In addition to~, Also, Lastly, Finally 등

Offer / Ask / Suggest 유형 문제 등장

정보 요청 방법, 주문 방법, 연락 방법 등이 등장하며 답의 형태는 다음과 같다.

- If 가정법 (To 동사원형, For 명사) + available, free of charge, complimentary, discount, coupon, special offer, given, provided, offered 등의 표현

- If 가정법 (To 동사원형, For 명사) + Please 명령문 형태의 문장 또는 ask, suggest, recommend, invite, urge, encourage, advise, require 등의 동사들로 답을 이끄는 문장들

- If 가정법 (To 동사원형, For 명사), 요청하는 내용의 Could you~, Can you~, You / We should~, You / We could~, You / We can~, Let~ 등

유형 5. 지시사항(여행, 관광, 견학)

서두

장소 힌트(Welcome to~, Thank you for~ 등)로 시작하거나 화자 소개(This is~, My name is~, I'm~ 등)로 시작하며 이때 화자는 가이드나 (공장) 직원인 경우가 대부분이다.

주제문

소요 시간, 주의 사항 등이 언급(주의 사항은 "~을 하기 전에"와 같은 지점 표현이 자주 사용된다)되며 공연장이라면 '전화기를 꺼두세요', 박물관이나 전시장이라면 '사진 찍지 마세요', 동물원이라면 '먹이 주지 마세요' 등과 같은 주의 사항이 언급된다.

세부정보

여행 일정 소개(first, next, then, after, following, finally, lastly 등)의 표현에 유의하며 듣는다. lastly와 finally는 특히 중요하다.

Offer / Ask / Suggest 유형 문제 등장

정보 요청 방법, 주문 방법, 연락 방법 등이 등장하며 답의 형태는 다음과 같다.

- If 가정법 (To 동사원형, For 명사) + available, free of charge, complimentary, discount, coupon, special offer, given, provided, offered 등의 표현

- If 가정법 (To 동사원형, For 명사) + Please 명령문 형태의 문장 또는 ask, suggest, recommend, invite, urge, encourage, advise, require 등의 동사들로 답을 이끄는 문장들

- If 가정법 (To 동사원형, For 명사), 요청하는 내용을 담은 Could you~, Can you~, You / We should~, You / We could~, You / We can~, Let~ 등

마지막

다음 행동이 언급되며 시간 표현이나 let's, why don't we 등과 같은 제안 표현이 자주
등장한다.

유형 6. 공항 안내 방송 (공항, 버스터미널, 기차역 공통)

서두

청자와 장소 힌트 제공(Attention! passengers. ~)

알림 사항

문제점과 원인이 등장하며 문제점은 언제나 교통수단의 결항(cancel), 지연(delay),
악천후(inclement, deteriorating, poor weather conditions), due to icy runway,
accident 등이 등장한다. 바로 이 부분에서 공항인지 버스터미널인지 또는 기차역인
지 알 수 있다.

세부사항

주제문에서 언급된 문제점으로 인해 초래된 변동 사항들이 언급이 된다. 키워드 찾기
문제 등이 등장한다. 물론 반전 표현과, 부사구, 시점 표현은 언제나 중요하다.

Offer / Ask / Suggest 유형 문제 등장

등장한 문제가 생겼고 그로 인해 여러 가지 변동사항이 생겨서 손님들에게 불편을 끼
쳐 미안하다는 말이 자주 나오며 답의 형태는 다음과 같다.
- If 가정법 (To 동사원형, For 명사) + available, free of charge, complimentary,
  discount, coupon, special offer, given, provided, offered 등의 표현
요청 부분으로 환불이나 시간 변경에 대한 내용이 언급되는 경우
- If 가정법 (To 동사원형, For명사), 요청하는 내용의 Could you~, Can you~, You /
  We should~, You / We could~, You / We can~, Let~ 등

유형 7. 기내방송

서두

- 환영 인사 (Welcome aboard + 비행편 이름)로 시작하는데 이 부분에서 비행기라
  는 것을 알 수 있다.
- 기장의 안내 멘트의 경우에는 기장의 신분을 밝히고 이름을 제시한다.

세부 내용

기내 방송은 글의 목적, 즉 주제문에 대해 다양한 비행 정보를 제공한다. 목적지, 출발지, 날씨, 총 소요 시간, 현지 날씨에 대한 정보를 제공하며 주로 'We're scheduled (planning) to arrive (land) in 목적지 in about 예상시간'의 형식으로 등장한다. Local time, weather와 관련한 각종 키워드를 활용하는 문제 역시 빈출 유형이다.

주의사항

- 도착 방송이라면 안전 벨트(fasten your seat belt), 세관 보고서(fill out customs declaration card), 개인 소지품(personal belongings and effects)에 관한 주의 사항들을 언급한다. 필요 시 승무원을 호출하라는 멘트 또한 자주 나온다. '다음에 또 이용해 주세요'라는 안내방송으로 끝난다.
- 이륙 방송이라면 각종 전자기기 전원을 끄고, 안전벨트를 하고, 좌석을 세우고, 도움이 필요하면 역시 승무원을 불러달라고 한다. 이륙 후 스낵 및 음료를 제공한다는 안내 방송이 나오고 끝난다.

유형 8. 일기예보

하루 치 일기예보의 경우

청자 힌트(라디오 청취자 또는 TV 시청자)

방송명 및 진행자 소개를 통해 방송의 종류와 방송 시간 등의 정보를 알 수 있다.

날씨 관련

- 과거 날씨 및 피해 상황
- 지금 현재 날씨 및 Ask / Suggest 문제 유형의 경우 : if 가정법, Please + 동사 원형으로 정답 등장
- 앞으로의 날씨 변화 및 Ask / Suggest 문제 유형의 경우 : if 가정법, Please +동사원형으로 정답 등장

다음 방송 정보

다음 방송 시간, 다음 방송 내용을 보여주는 Stay tune, now. Let's~, We'll be back~, I'll be back~과 같은 표현들이 이끈다.

일주일 치 일기 예보의 경우

청자 힌트(라디오 청취자 또는 TV 시청자)

방송명 및 진행자 소개를 통해 방송의 종류와 방송 시간 등의 정보를 알 수 있다.

날씨 관련

- 월요일부터 주말까지의 일기 소개(요일 가지고 날씨 찾기, 날씨 표현 가지고 요일 찾기 문제가 주로 등장)
- 주말까지의 날씨 소개가 끝나고 난 후 Ask / Suggest 문제 유형의 경우 : if 가정법, Please + 동사원형으로 정답 등장. 이 경우에는 주로 주말에 날씨가 좋을 경우 가족과 피크닉 또는 공원에 가라는 내용이 나온다.

다음 방송 정보

다음 방송 시간, 다음 방송 내용을 보여주는 Stay tune, now. Let's~, We'll be back~, I'll be back~과 같은 표현들이 이끈다.

유형 9. 교통 방송

서두

- 청자힌트 (Attention, drivers!)의 경우 교통 방송이기에 운전자들을 대상으로 방송한다.
- 진행자 이름과 방송명이 등장하는데 이로써 방송 시간 및 방송 종류 등을 알 수 있다.

주제문

문제점과 원인이 등장하며 주요 내용은 날씨 때문에 도로 사정이 좋지 않다, 사고가 나서 도로가 밀린다, 특정 이벤트 때문에 도로가 밀린다, 공사 때문에 도로가 밀린다 등의 내용이 나온다.

변동사항

키워드 찾기 문제가 등장한다. 도로명이나 시간 표현 등을 키워드로 이용한 문제가 자주 나온다.

Ask / Suggest 문제

if 가정법, Please + 동사원형으로 정답이 등장하며 주로 대중 교통(public transportation)을 이용해라, 다른 길(alternate route)을 찾아라, 우회(detour)해라 등의 내용이 온다.

다음 방송 정보

다음 방송 시간이나 다음 방송 내용을 보여주는 Stay tune, now. Let's~, We'll be back~, I'll be back~과 같은 표현들이 이끈다.

유형 10. 초대 손님이 나오는 방송

서두

- 방송명 및 진행자 소개가 나온다.
- 초대 손님 소개(인물 소개) : 이름 등으로 간략하게 인물 소개를 한다. 인물 소개는
  초대 손님의 이름이 먼저 나오고, 이름 뒤에는 직업이나 직책 등이 언급된다. 대체
  로 유명한 음악가와 같은 예술인, 영화 배우, 운동 선수 등이 자주 소개된다.

세부 사항

- 초대 손님의 경력 소개가 이루어진다. 언제부터 커리어를 시작했고 어떻게 성공하
  게 되었는지를 이야기한다. 이때 키워드를 이용하거나 시점 표현 및 반전 표현을 이
  용해 답을 찾도록 한다.
- 초대 손님이 오늘 무엇을 하게 될지에 대한 미래 행동이 언급된다. 보통의 경우, 성
  공 스토리를 들려주기 위해 나왔다라고 하거나 질문 답변 시간을 갖거나 특정 주제
  에 대해 강의를 한다.

다음 방송 정보

다음 방송 시간이나 다음 방송 내용을 보여주는 Stay tune, now. Let's~, We'll be
back~, I'll be back~과 같은 표현들이 이끈다.

유형 11. 인물 소개글 및 연설문

서두

- 청자 힌트 등장
- 화자 소개 및 인물 소개는 보통 회사 내에서 이루어지며 This is~, My name is~,
  I'm~으로 시작한다.

주제문

- 인물 소개 및 구체적인 장소 힌트가 등장한다.
- 좋은 소식의 경우는 I'm happy(proud, pleased) to introduce (announce, present,
  inform, report, remind, let you know) + 신규직원 또는 초대연사의 순으로 표현
- 나쁜 소식의 경우는 I'm sorry to/ I regret to/ I am saddened to announce + 은퇴직
  원 또는 특정인물의 순으로 표현. 이름 뒤엔 간략한 소개 문장이 나오는데 주로 직
  업, 직책, 근무 회사 등의 정보가 언급된다.

인물 경력 소개

시간 순으로 소개되는데 이 부분이 키워드 찾기 문제가 된다. 주로 시점이나, 지역, 반
전, 부사구를 이용해 답을 찾는다.

지원동기, 인품소개

다음 행동 언급

시점 표현(~하기 전에), 시간 표현(Now, tonight~), 제안 표현(Let~), He is here to~,
He would like to~ 등이 답을 이끈다. 보통의 경우, 연설을 하거나, 연설 전후에 식사
를 하거나, 자료를 같이 보거나, 질문에 답변하는 시간이 나올 것이다.

ACTUAL TEST
1

LISTENING TEST

In the Listening test, you will be asked to demonstrate how well you understand spoken English. The entire Listening test will last approximately 45 minutes. There are four parts, and directions are given for each part. You must mark your answers on the separate answer sheet. Do not write your answers in your test book.

Part 1

Directions: For each question in this part, you will hear four statements about a picture in your test book. When you hear the statements, you must select the one statement that best describes what you see in the picture. Then find the number of the question on your answer sheet and mark your answer. The statements will not be printed in your test book and will be spoken only one time.

Sample Answer

Example

Statement (C), "Two monitors are set up next to each other," is the best description of the picture, so you should select answer (C) and mark it on your answer sheet.

1.

2.

Go on to the next page.

3.

4.

5.

6.

Go on to the next page.

7. Mark your answer on your answer sheet.

8. Mark your answer on your answer sheet.

9. Mark your answer on your answer sheet.

10. Mark your answer on your answer sheet.

11. Mark your answer on your answer sheet.

12. Mark your answer on your answer sheet.

13. Mark your answer on your answer sheet.

14. Mark your answer on your answer sheet.

15. Mark your answer on your answer sheet.

16. Mark your answer on your answer sheet.

17. Mark your answer on your answer sheet.

18. Mark your answer on your answer sheet.

19. Mark your answer on your answer sheet.

20. Mark your answer on your answer sheet.

21. Mark your answer on your answer sheet.

22. Mark your answer on your answer sheet.

23. Mark your answer on your answer sheet.

24. Mark your answer on your answer sheet.

25. Mark your answer on your answer sheet.

26. Mark your answer on your answer sheet.

27. Mark your answer on your answer sheet.

28. Mark your answer on your answer sheet.

29. Mark your answer on your answer sheet.

30. Mark your answer on your answer sheet.

31. Mark your answer on your answer sheet.

PART 3

Directions: You will hear some conversations between two or more people. You will be asked to answer three questions about what the speakers say in each conversation. Select the best response to each question and mark the letter (A), (B), (C), or (D) on your answer sheet. The conversations will not be printed in your test book and will be spoken only one time.

32. Where is the conversation taking place?
(A) At a library
(B) At an airport
(C) At a theater
(D) At a zoo

33. Why does the woman apologize?
(A) All the first-class seats are booked.
(B) The flight has been delayed.
(C) Some seats are unavailable.
(D) Meals aren't provided on the flight.

34. What will the man most likely do next?
(A) Book a ticket for the next flight
(B) Upgrade his seat
(C) Send an e-mail
(D) Complete a form

35. Why does the man say, "I need to show him the report today"?
(A) To request a document from the woman
(B) To ask for help on a project
(C) To invite the woman to a meeting
(D) To show the result of a test

36. What does the woman say about the test group?
(A) It didn't affect the test result.
(B) It was changed after the test.
(C) It was not arranged yet.
(D) It had fewer people than expected.

37. What will the man discuss next time?
(A) Hiring a new employee
(B) Complaining to a client
(C) Arranging more tests
(D) Adding a new facility

38. According to the man, what has happened?
(A) A vacation schedule has been updated.
(B) A committee has been formed.
(C) A seminar has been canceled.
(D) An office protocol has changed.

39. What problem does the woman mention?
(A) A budget was not sufficient.
(B) There weren't enough speakers.
(C) She could not find a location.
(D) Her project was not ready.

40. What does the man offer to do?
(A) Finish a coworker's project
(B) Cancel a vacation
(C) Attend a conference
(D) Contact some professionals

41. What do the men imply about the business?
(A) It was recently formed.
(B) It is becoming successful.
(C) It extended its product line.
(D) It opened a new factory.

42. What does the woman want to do?
(A) Improve a production process
(B) Train some employees
(C) Revise a budget
(D) Continue an expansion

43. What do the men suggest doing?
(A) Opening a new branch
(B) Getting more contracts
(C) Relocating the business
(D) Canceling a meeting

Go on to the next page.

44. Why is the woman calling?
(A) To make a reservation
(B) To cancel a dinner
(C) To ask about a menu
(D) To extend an invitation

45. What does the man ask for?
(A) A phone number
(B) An e-mail address
(C) A shipping address
(D) A name

46. Why does the woman say, "That's a good question"?
(A) She is upset about service.
(B) She is unsure about a menu.
(C) She is excited about a meal.
(D) She is sure she will be on time.

47. What department does the woman work in?
(A) Shipping
(B) Customer Service
(C) Technical Support
(D) Product Development

48. What does the man ask for?
(A) Information on refunds
(B) The location of a store
(C) An exchange for a defective item
(D) A way to repair a technical problem

49. What does the woman offer to do?
(A) Send video files
(B) Arrange an exchange for a product
(C) Transfer a call
(D) Reduce a price

50. What does the man ask about the job?
(A) How much it pays
(B) When he can start
(C) If there is vacation leave
(D) Whether it is still available

51. What problem does the woman mention about the job?
(A) It involves frequent traveling.
(B) It is in an inconvenient location.
(C) Its salary is quite low.
(D) It requires a lot of overtime.

52. What does the man mean when he says, "I can't be too picky"?
(A) He will not apply for the job.
(B) He does not have many options.
(C) He has many job offers.
(D) He is moving to a new house.

53. Which department does the woman most likely work for?
(A) Payroll
(B) Accounting
(C) Technical Support
(D) Product Development

54. What problem does the woman say she has?
(A) Some calculations aren't right.
(B) She has limited time.
(C) Her computer is not working properly.
(D) Some information is currently unavailable.

55. What does the man suggest the woman do?
(A) Call the software engineers
(B) Examine the formulas
(C) Search the Internet for help
(D) Start over from the beginning

56. Why is the man interviewing the woman?
(A) She is a popular program producer.
(B) She won a prestigious design award.
(C) She created her own product.
(D) She developed a new management method.

57. What has happened to the woman?
(A) Her program has become a hit.
(B) Her business has been successful.
(C) Her company has been sold.
(D) Her family has made donations.

58. What is the woman interested in doing?
(A) Helping revive smaller companies
(B) Keeping hair in good condition
(C) Purchasing a new innovative product
(D) Launching a beauty business

59. What is the man interested in?
(A) Internal communication
(B) Management skills
(C) Productivity growth
(D) Customer satisfaction

60. What does the man want the woman to do?
(A) Explain the content of the lecture in depth
(B) Conduct experiments at his company
(C) Temporarily work at his company
(D) Go to his company for a lecture

61. What does the woman offer to do?
(A) Postpone the date of her lecture
(B) Test a product for customers
(C) Send her colleague in her place
(D) Visit the man's company to give a presentation

Model	Price	Weight
Evotech 200	$699	2.2 kg
Orchard X4	$799	1.7 kg
Blitz P Series	$1299	1.1 kg
Rockware III	$999	2.9 kg

62. Where does the man most likely work?
(A) At an airport
(B) At a travel agency
(C) At a car dealership
(D) At an electronics store

63. What is indicated about the woman?
(A) She recently started a new job.
(B) She has won a journalism award.
(C) She has traveled to several countries.
(D) She has never owned a laptop computer.

64. Look at the graphic. What computer model will the woman most likely choose?
(A) Evotech 200
(B) Orchard X4
(C) Blitz P Series
(D) Rockware III

Go on to the next page.

Company	Print Quality	Price (per page)
Office Club	Black & White	5 cents
Paper Factory	Black & White	6 cents
Print Solutions	Color	9 cents
National Express	Color	12 cents

65. What does the woman request that the man do?
(A) Make some repairs
(B) Train new workers
(C) Conduct an interview
(D) Prepare some materials

66. What problem does the man mention?
(A) Some employees have not arrived.
(B) Some prices have recently increased.
(C) Some office equipment is malfunctioning.
(D) Some manuals were delivered to the wrong location.

67. Look at the graphic. Which company will the man most likely choose?
(A) Office Club
(B) Paper Factory
(C) Print Solutions
(D) National Express

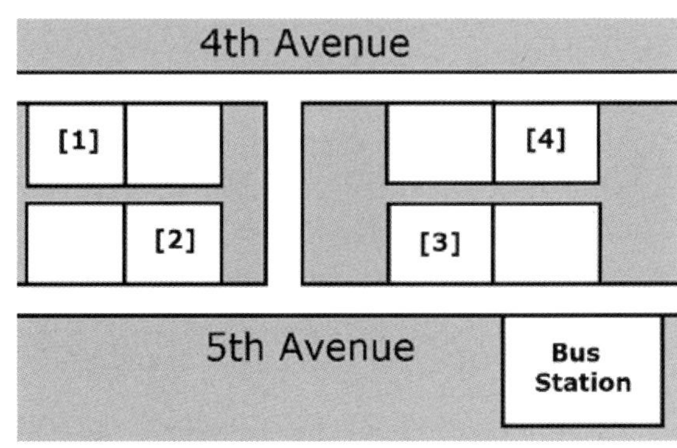

68. Who most likely is the woman?
(A) A bank employee
(B) A tour guide
(C) A bus driver
(D) A tourist

69. What problem does the woman mention?
(A) She has lost her map.
(B) She is unable to find an ATM.
(C) She cannot access her bank account.
(D) She needs to exchange money.

70. Look at the graphic. In which position is the bank located?
(A) [1]
(B) [2]
(C) [3]
(D) [4]

PART 4

Directions: You will hear some talks given by a single speaker. You will be asked to answer three questions about what the speaker says in each talk. Select the best response to each question and mark the letter (A), (B), (C), or (D) on your answer sheet. The talks will not be printed in your test book and will be spoken only one time.

71. What is different about Papa Diego Pizza?
(A) It offers free side menus.
(B) It uses organic ingredients only.
(C) It doesn't provide delivery.
(D) It uses a very special recipe.

72. What is the purpose of the advertisement?
(A) To ask about an item
(B) To promote a new menu
(C) To ask about the new branch on Sutton Street
(D) To inform customers of a special offer

73. How can people get a free pizza?
(A) By ordering one for pickup
(B) By buying a new type of pizza
(C) By visiting another branch
(D) By calling earlier than other customers

74. What does the speaker say the survey is about?
(A) Commuting methods
(B) Public transportation
(C) Popular attractions
(D) Voluntary services

75. What kind of survey is the speaker talking about?
(A) A face-to-face survey
(B) A telephone survey
(C) An Internet-based survey
(D) A mail survey

76. Which is one of the purposes of Goodride?
(A) To promote the concept of carpooling
(B) To reduce fuel consumption
(C) To increase the city's water supply
(D) To ease the city's traffic congestion

77. Who is the intended audience of the announcement?
(A) Museum visitors
(B) Library users
(C) Store customers
(D) Office employees

78. According to the speaker, what time does the facility close?
(A) At 7:00 A.M.
(B) At 9:40 P.M.
(C) At 9:55 P.M.
(D) At 10:00 P.M.

79. What does the speaker ask the listeners to do?
(A) Refrain from taking pictures
(B) Prepare to leave the building
(C) Make some purchases
(D) Reshelve some library materials

80. Who most likely is the speaker?
(A) An event organizer
(B) A restaurant owner
(C) A new club member
(D) A local politician

81. According to the speaker, where will dinner be served?
(A) On a boat
(B) In the garden area
(C) At a restaurant
(D) At the speaker's house

82. What does the speaker mean when he says, "Let's make this a day to remember"?
(A) The event should be very enjoyable.
(B) The listeners should take many photos.
(C) There are many details to memorize.
(D) The listeners have visited the place before.

Go on to the next page.

83. Why does the speaker congratulate the listener?
(A) The listener was recently hired.
(B) The listener has announced his retirement.
(C) The listener finalized a business contract.
(D) The listener was awarded a bonus.

84. What does the speaker imply when he says, "We expect great things from you"?
(A) He wants the listener to work harder.
(B) He is impressed with the listener.
(C) He knows the listener has a difficult job.
(D) He wants the listener to submit some documents.

85. What is the listener invited to do?
(A) Test a product
(B) Join a luncheon
(C) Attend a conference
(D) Enroll in a course

---

86. Who most likely are the listeners?
(A) Stockbrokers
(B) New employees
(C) Computer experts
(D) Software developers

87. What does the speaker say happened on Friday?
(A) There was a power outage.
(B) There were equipment failures.
(C) The stock market suffered a sharp decline.
(D) Some broken computers were repaired.

88. What will probably happen on Sunday?
(A) All transactions will be stopped.
(B) All of the computers will be replaced.
(C) A new system will be installed.
(D) End-of-the-week tasks will be performed.

89. What is the report mainly about?
(A) A new electric iron
(B) A business decision
(C) A bestselling newspaper
(D) The power of the Internet

90. According to the speaker, what is CradlePoint?
(A) An online media site
(B) A home appliance retailer
(C) A well-known publication
(D) An Internet service provider

91. How have some customers reacted to the beta version?
(A) They haven't been interested.
(B) They have been quite negative.
(C) They have responded favorably.
(D) They have showed mixed responses.

---

92. What is the main purpose of the festival?
(A) A local food festival
(B) A musical performance
(C) A famous carnival
(D) A visiting celebrity

93. What problem does the speaker mention?
(A) Tickets are selling out.
(B) The weather will be unfavorable.
(C) The traffic will be bad.
(D) Some events will be canceled.

94. Why does the speaker say, "You'd better get on it"?
(A) The event needs more participants.
(B) She is requesting help.
(C) The listeners should act quickly.
(D) The tickets are too expensive.

Tour Packages (Thailand)	
3 nights 4 days	$659
4 nights 5 days	$729
5 nights 6 days	$829
6 nights 7 days	$879

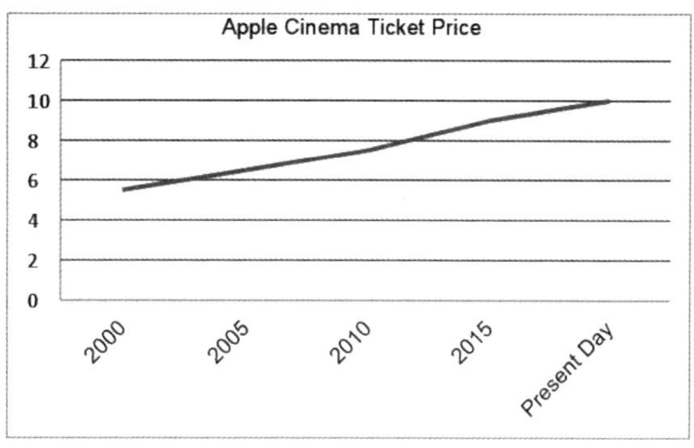

95. Why is the man calling?
(A) To inquire about travel options
(B) To complain about a price
(C) To confirm a decision
(D) To change a travel itinerary

96. Look at the graphic. How long will the man most likely stay in Thailand?
(A) 4 days
(B) 5 days
(C) 6 days
(D) 7 days

97. What does the speaker intend to do tomorrow?
(A) Send his credit card details
(B) Visit a business
(C) Cancel a payment
(D) Begin his vacation

98. What is the speaker discussing?
(A) A company expansion
(B) The hiring of staff
(C) A decline in business
(D) The relocation of a cinema

99. What does the speaker say happened last weekend?
(A) A new business opened.
(B) A cinema was closed down
(C) A movie was released.
(D) An advertisement was published.

100. Look at the graphic. What ticket price does the speaker recommend?
(A) $5.50
(B) $6.50
(C) $7.50
(D) $9.00

This is the end of the Listening test. Turn to Part 5 in your test book.

ACTUAL TEST 1

01. B	21. A	41. B	61. D	81. C
02. B	22. B	42. D	62. D	82. A
03. D	23. A	43. B	63. A	83. C
04. B	24. C	44. A	64. B	84. B
05. A	25. B	45. D	65. D	85. B
06. D	26. C	46. B	66. C	86. C
07. B	27. A	47. B	67. C	87. B
08. A	28. B	48. D	68. D	88. D
09. A	29. C	49. C	69. D	89. B
10. C	30. C	50. D	70. B	90. A
11. B	31. B	51. C	71. B	91. C
12. B	32. B	52. B	72. D	92. A
13. A	33. A	53. B	73. A	93. A
14. C	34. D	54. A	74. A	94. C
15. A	35. A	55. B	75. C	95. C
16. C	36. D	56. C	76. D	96. C
17. A	37. C	57. B	77. B	97. B
18. B	38. C	58. B	78. D	98. C
19. A	39. B	59. A	79. B	99. A
20. B	40. D	60. C	80. A	100. C

ACTUAL TEST

2

LISTENING TEST

In the Listening test, you will be asked to demonstrate how well you understand spoken English. The entire Listening test will last approximately 45 minutes. There are four parts, and directions are given for each part. You must mark your answers on the separate answer sheet. Do not write your answers in your test book.

Part 1

Directions: For each question in this part, you will hear four statements about a picture in your test book. When you hear the statements, you must select the one statement that best describes what you see in the picture. Then find the number of the question on your answer sheet and mark your answer. The statements will not be printed in your test book and will be spoken only one time.

Sample Answer

Example

Statement (C), "Two monitors are set up next to each other," is the best description of the picture, so you should select answer (C) and mark it on your answer sheet.

1.

2.

Go on to the next page.

3.

4.

5.

6.

Go on to the next page.

7. Mark your answer on your answer sheet.

8. Mark your answer on your answer sheet.

9. Mark your answer on your answer sheet.

10. Mark your answer on your answer sheet.

11. Mark your answer on your answer sheet.

12. Mark your answer on your answer sheet.

13. Mark your answer on your answer sheet.

14. Mark your answer on your answer sheet.

15. Mark your answer on your answer sheet.

16. Mark your answer on your answer sheet.

17. Mark your answer on your answer sheet.

18. Mark your answer on your answer sheet.

19. Mark your answer on your answer sheet.

20. Mark your answer on your answer sheet.

21. Mark your answer on your answer sheet.

22. Mark your answer on your answer sheet.

23. Mark your answer on your answer sheet.

24. Mark your answer on your answer sheet.

25. Mark your answer on your answer sheet.

26. Mark your answer on your answer sheet.

27. Mark your answer on your answer sheet.

28. Mark your answer on your answer sheet.

29. Mark your answer on your answer sheet.

30. Mark your answer on your answer sheet.

31. Mark your answer on your answer sheet.

PART 3

Directions: You will hear some conversations between two or more people. You will be asked to answer three questions about what the speakers say in each conversation. Select the best response to each question and mark the letter (A), (B), (C), or (D) on your answer sheet. The conversations will not be printed in your test book and will be spoken only one time.

32. Where does the man most likely work?
(A) At a travel agency
(B) At a restaurant
(C) At a hotel
(D) At an airline

33. Why is the woman calling?
(A) To make a formal complaint
(B) To inquire about a package tour
(C) To find out more about food options
(D) To request a time change

34. What does the man offer the woman?
(A) A refund on a ticket
(B) A voucher for a hotel
(C) A discount on an upgrade
(D) A complimentary meal

35. What is the woman still waiting to receive?
(A) A sales report
(B) A work schedule
(C) Some project guidelines
(D) Some contact information

36. What does the man recommend the woman do?
(A) Come in to work early
(B) Come by a manager's office
(C) Visit a Web site
(D) Make an appointment

37. What does the man say will happen this afternoon?
(A) Some new employees will be hired.
(B) A staff meeting will take place.
(C) A new server will be installed.
(D) A deadline will be chosen.

38. What are the speakers discussing?
(A) A new advertisement
(B) A company celebration
(C) An overseas excursion
(D) A restaurant's grand opening

39. What problem does the man mention?
(A) A guest list is incomplete.
(B) A deadline cannot be met.
(C) A venue is fully booked.
(D) A date has been changed.

40. What will the woman most likely do next?
(A) Visit a restaurant
(B) Call a friend
(C) E-mail a manager
(D) Review a menu

41. What time is the train now expected to depart?
(A) At 8:00 A.M.
(B) At 9:00 A.M.
(C) At 10:00 A.M.
(D) At 11:00 A.M.

42. Why are the speakers concerned?
(A) They are at the wrong station.
(B) They are waiting for another passenger.
(C) They lost their bus tickets.
(D) They will be late for a meeting.

43. What will the man most likely do next?
(A) Reschedule a meeting
(B) Call for a taxi
(C) Take another train
(D) Go to a bus station

Go on to the next page.

44. What does the man want to do?
(A) Obtain a membership
(B) Start a subscription
(C) Purchase a book
(D) Join a club

45. What does the woman ask the man to do?
(A) Complete some paperwork
(B) Take a tour of the building
(C) Show some identification
(D) Print out a document

46. Why does the woman say, "Great"?
(A) She is pleased about opening hours.
(B) She is impressed with the man's qualifications.
(C) She agrees with the man's suggestion.
(D) She can proceed with a process.

47. Where is the conversation most likely taking place?
(A) At a grocery store
(B) At an electronics store
(C) At an auto shop
(D) At a hardware store

48. What does the woman say she needs?
(A) Items in various colors
(B) Overnight delivery
(C) Products in different sizes
(D) A product warranty

49. Why does the woman thank the man?
(A) He giftwrapped her purchases.
(B) He gave her a complimentary item.
(C) He provided her with a discount.
(D) He arranged for a free delivery.

50. Who most likely are the speakers?
(A) Tour guides
(B) Company employees
(C) Real estate agents
(D) College professors

51. Who are the speakers talking about?
(A) Prospective employees
(B) Advertising experts
(C) New college students
(D) Corporate executives

52. According to the woman, what is the purpose of the event?
(A) Cost reduction
(B) Social responsibility
(C) Career development
(D) Aggressive advertising

53. According to the woman, what will happen this weekend?
(A) A party will take place.
(B) An office will be renovated.
(C) New computers will be delivered.
(D) New furniture will be installed.

54. What does the woman ask the men to do?
(A) Throw away some trash
(B) Pack up some files
(C) Unplug their computers
(D) Attend a meeting

55. What do the men suggest about the flooring?
(A) It can be easily damaged.
(B) It will be replaced.
(C) It needs to be cleaned.
(D) It was recently installed.

56. Why is Ms. Johansson not in the office now?
  - (A) She forgot about an appointment.
  - (B) She went out for lunch.
  - (C) She is stuck in traffic.
  - (D) She was fired yesterday.

57. What does the man want to do?
  - (A) Try some sandwiches
  - (B) Submit an application
  - (C) Go get some food for lunch
  - (D) Call Ms. Johansson immediately

58. When does the woman tell the man to come back?
  - (A) In ten minutes
  - (B) In thirty minutes
  - (C) In an hour
  - (D) Tomorrow

59. Where does the woman want to go?
  - (A) To an airport
  - (B) To a bus station
  - (C) To a shopping mall
  - (D) To a hotel

60. Who is the woman talking to?
  - (A) A store clerk
  - (B) A bus driver
  - (C) A tour guide
  - (D) A supervisor

61. What does the man advise the woman to do?
  - (A) Purchase a ticket
  - (B) Visit a shopping mall
  - (C) Wait for an express bus
  - (D) Take a taxi

Color	Flat	Curved
Standard Black	Available	Available
Mirrored Black	Unavailable	Available
Glossy White	Unavailable	Available
Matte White	Available	Unavailable

62. What are the speakers mainly discussing?
  - (A) Television repair
  - (B) Grand opening
  - (C) Return policy
  - (D) Office renovation

63. What benefit does the woman mention?
  - (A) An office will be more conveniently located.
  - (B) Clients will be impressed.
  - (C) An area will be easier to clean.
  - (D) Customers will be served more quickly.

64. Look at the graphic. What color of TV will the woman most likely order?
  - (A) Standard Black
  - (B) Mirrored Black
  - (C) Glossy White
  - (D) Matte White

Go on to the next page.

Glee Market **Special Summer Promotion**	
Total Purchase Amount	Discount
$10-$50	5%
$50-$100	10%
$100-$200	15%
$200+	20%

Class	Instructor's Availability
Dance Aerobics	Weekdays
Step Aerobics	Weekdays and Weekends
Traditional Yoga	Weekends
Hot Yoga	Weekdays and Weekends

65. What is the main purpose of the woman's call?
(A) To cancel a transaction
(B) To return a phone call
(C) To complain about a product
(D) To purchase some merchandise

66. What problem does the man mention?
(A) An order cannot be processed.
(B) An item is currently unavailable.
(C) A delivery will arrive later than usual.
(D) A Web site is not working properly.

67. Look at the graphic. What discount will the woman receive?
(A) 5%
(B) 10%
(C) 15%
(D) 20%

68. What are the speakers mainly discussing?
(A) The opening of a business
(B) The price of some machinery
(C) The location of a fitness center
(D) The training of new employees

69. What benefit does the woman mention?
(A) The staff has lots of experience.
(B) There is a variety of equipment.
(C) There is a discounted membership.
(D) The hours of operation will be extended.

70. Look at the graphic. Which class will the woman most likely open?
(A) Dance Aerobics
(B) Step Aerobics
(C) Traditional Yoga
(D) Hot Yoga

PART 4

Directions: You will hear some talks given by a single speaker. You will be asked to answer three questions about what the speaker says in each talk. Select the best response to each question and mark the letter (A), (B), (C), or (D) on your answer sheet. The talks will not be printed in your test book and will be spoken only one time.

---

71. Who are the listeners?
(A) Regular office workers
(B) Conference participants
(C) Repair technicians
(D) Company trainees

72. What does the speaker emphasize?
(A) That the data should be entered correctly
(B) That employees should skillfully handle office equipment
(C) That the side that will be sent must be face down
(D) That employees must turn off every computer when leaving the office

73. What is already programmed into the machine?
(A) The mechanism of transmission
(B) The area code of the city
(C) The number of the receiver
(D) The telephone numbers of main clients

74. What caused the traffic delay on the Thomas Jefferson Bridge?
(A) A car accident
(B) Maintenance work
(C) Road closures
(D) Poor weather conditions

75. What does the speaker recommend doing?
(A) Taking an alternate route
(B) Allowing extra time for travel
(C) Using public transportation
(D) Staying indoors

76. What will the listeners probably hear next?
(A) A commercial
(B) A sports report
(C) A weather report
(D) A music program

77. Why is the speaker calling?
(A) To decline a job offer
(B) To inform a customer of a problem
(C) To postpone an interview
(D) To accept an invitation to speak at a convention

78. What does the speaker plan to do next Monday?
(A) Conduct some interviews
(B) Pack things up for a move
(C) Preside over an event
(D) Go to a convention center

79. What does the speaker ask the listener to do?
(A) Make travel arrangements
(B) Review some workshop materials
(C) Bring a computer monitor
(D) Provide his preference for a presentation method

---

80. What is the purpose of the talk?
(A) To describe a foundation's history
(B) To request financial aid
(C) To introduce a new employee
(D) To describe a process

81. According to the speaker, what does the foundation hope to do next year?
(A) Alter an ad campaign
(B) Make a larger profit
(C) Enlarge its operation
(D) Open a local store

82. Why does the woman say, "Give it a thought"?
(A) To request that the listeners consider something
(B) To encourage questions from the listeners
(C) To remind the listeners to return something
(D) To introduce a new speaker

Go on to the next page.

83. Where does the speaker most likely work?
(A) At a wedding hall
(B) At a bakery
(C) At a clothing store
(D) At a car rental agency

84. Why does the speaker say, "You have my word"?
(A) To ask the listener to meet
(B) To request some advice
(C) To reassure the listener
(D) To express gratitude

85. What does the speaker offer to do?
(A) Apply a discount
(B) Pick out additional items
(C) Replace a product
(D) Change an appointment

86. What is the purpose of the talk?
(A) To welcome a new employee
(B) To outline seminar topics
(C) To introduce a speaker
(D) To discuss new strategies

87. Who most likely is Jonathan Fielder?
(A) A leading CEO
(B) An advertising expert
(C) A renowned journalist
(D) A software designer

88. Why does the speaker say, "Please keep that in mind"?
(A) To make sure the listeners pick up a schedule
(B) To request that the listeners take their seats
(C) To remind the listeners to follow instructions
(D) To check that the listeners know where a room is

89. Who most likely is the speaker?
(A) An auto engineer
(B) A marketing expert
(C) A sales manager
(D) A company president

90. According to the speaker, what is the new goal of the company?
(A) To develop a new product
(B) To hold more technology patents
(C) To expand its domestic market share
(D) To be a leader in the world market

91. How does the speaker suggest the goal be accomplished?
(A) By launching a new product
(B) By stepping up marketing promotions
(C) By conducting customer surveys
(D) By recruiting qualified research and development personnel

92. What most likely is Ms. Beckinsale's profession?
(A) Reporter
(B) Radio announcer
(C) Journalism professor
(D) Television producer

93. Who selected Ms. Beckinsale as journalist of the year?
(A) Mr. Walter
(B) Her peers
(C) Her college classmates
(D) The Association of Newspapers

94. What are the listeners asked to do?
(A) Nominate some candidates
(B) Sign up for a subscription
(C) Attend an awards ceremony
(D) Give a warm welcome

Ryan Carter Records U.S. Album Sales (in millions)	
Desperate Love	4.4
Songs for Someone	3.8
Save the Last Dance	2.5
Electric Carnival	1.1

Department Relocation	Date
Monday, June 6	Sales
Wednesday, June 8	Human Resources
Friday, June 10	Customer Service
Monday, June 13	Marketing

95. What is the speaker mainly discussing?
(A) An upcoming concert
(B) A radio competition
(C) A singer's career
(D) A sale at a music store

96. What instrument does Ryan Carter play?
(A) Guitar
(B) Piano
(C) Violin
(D) Drums

97. Look at the graphic. Which album was released this year?
(A) Desperate Love
(B) Songs for Someone
(C) Save the Last Dance
(D) Electric Carnival

98. What does the speaker say about the Lifeson Building?
(A) It is conveniently located.
(B) It is currently unoccupied.
(C) It includes modern amenities.
(D) It has recently been expanded.

99. Look at the graphic. When will the accounting department move?
(A) On June 6
(B) On June 8
(C) On June 10
(D) On June 13

100. What will happen on June 15?
(A) A new branch will be opened.
(B) An office space will be renovated.
(C) Staff will attend a meal.
(D) Equipment will be installed.

This is the end of the Listening test. Turn to Part 5 in your test book.

01. D	21. C	41. B	61. D	81. C
02. A	22. A	42. D	62. D	82. A
03. B	23. A	43. B	63. B	83. C
04. C	24. A	44. A	64. C	84. C
05. D	25. A	45. C	65. D	85. B
06. C	26. C	46. D	66. C	86. C
07. A	27. A	47. D	67. B	87. B
08. B	28. B	48. C	68. A	88. C
09. A	29. A	49. C	69. B	89. D
10. B	30. B	50. B	70. B	90. D
11. C	31. C	51. A	71. D	91. B
12. B	32. D	52. A	72. C	92. A
13. C	33. D	53. D	73. B	93. B
14. A	34. C	54. B	74. B	94. D
15. B	35. C	55. A	75. A	95. C
16. C	36. B	56. C	76. A	96. B
17. A	37. B	57. C	77. C	97. C
18. A	38. B	58. C	78. C	98. B
19. B	39. C	59. D	79. D	99. B
20. B	40. B	60. B	80. B	100. C

ACTUAL TEST

3

LISTENING TEST

In the Listening test, you will be asked to demonstrate how well you understand spoken English. The entire Listening test will last approximately 45 minutes. There are four parts, and directions are given for each part. You must mark your answers on the separate answer sheet. Do not write your answers in your test book.

Part 1

Directions: For each question in this part, you will hear four statements about a picture in your test book. When you hear the statements, you must select the one statement that best describes what you see in the picture. Then find the number of the question on your answer sheet and mark your answer. The statements will not be printed in your test book and will be spoken only one time.

Sample Answer

Example

Statement (C), "Two monitors are set up next to each other," is the best description of the picture, so you should select answer (C) and mark it on your answer sheet.

1.

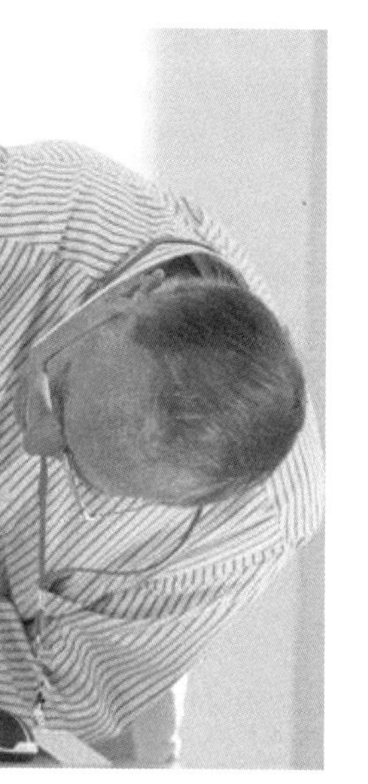

2.

Go on to the next page.

3.

4.

5.

6.

Go on to the next page.

PART 2

Directions: You will hear a question or statement and three responses spoken in English. They will not be printed in your test book and will be spoken only one time. Select the best response to the question or statement and mark the letter (A), (B), or (C) on your answer sheet.

7. Mark your answer on your answer sheet.

8. Mark your answer on your answer sheet.

9. Mark your answer on your answer sheet.

10. Mark your answer on your answer sheet.

11. Mark your answer on your answer sheet.

12. Mark your answer on your answer sheet.

13. Mark your answer on your answer sheet.

14. Mark your answer on your answer sheet.

15. Mark your answer on your answer sheet.

16. Mark your answer on your answer sheet.

17. Mark your answer on your answer sheet.

18. Mark your answer on your answer sheet.

19. Mark your answer on your answer sheet.

20. Mark your answer on your answer sheet.

21. Mark your answer on your answer sheet.

22. Mark your answer on your answer sheet.

23. Mark your answer on your answer sheet.

24. Mark your answer on your answer sheet.

25. Mark your answer on your answer sheet.

26. Mark your answer on your answer sheet.

27. Mark your answer on your answer sheet.

28. Mark your answer on your answer sheet.

29. Mark your answer on your answer sheet.

30. Mark your answer on your answer sheet.

31. Mark your answer on your answer sheet.

PART 3

Directions: You will hear some conversations between two or more people. You will be asked to answer three questions about what the speakers say in each conversation. Select the best response to each question and mark the letter (A), (B), (C), or (D) on your answer sheet. The conversations will not be printed in your test book and will be spoken only one time.

32. What are the speakers talking about?
(A) A business course
(B) An information event
(C) A meeting schedule
(D) A confidential document

33. What topic is the woman interested in?
(A) Time management
(B) Data analysis
(C) Efficient communication skills
(D) Supply chain management

34. What does the man say he will deliver to the woman?
(A) Several papers about value chain analysis
(B) Copies of the speakers' slides
(C) A guest speaker's contact information
(D) A complete set of conference presentations

35. What does the man compare for the woman?
(A) Two cap colors and designs
(B) Some of the customer bases
(C) Discounts for bulk orders
(D) Cap personalization options

36. What is the woman concerned about?
(A) The changed logo and slogan
(B) The total production costs
(C) The availability of several sizes
(D) The time schedule for the completion of her order

37. What does the man ask the woman to do?
(A) E-mail him some documents
(B) Choose a logo design
(C) Send him some picture files
(D) Make a down payment

38. What type of business is the man calling?
(A) A movie theater
(B) An opera house
(C) An art gallery
(D) A history museum

39. What information does the woman ask for?
(A) The man's travel arrangements
(B) The man's credit card details
(C) The man's age
(D) The man's preferred date

40. What will the man most likely do next?
(A) Fill out a form
(B) Pick up a brochure
(C) Give his credit card information
(D) Visit a Web site

41. What are the speakers mainly discussing?
(A) An office relocation
(B) An office layout
(C) An office supplies order
(D) Office equipment

42. What problem does the woman mention?
(A) The work will be too complicated to handle alone.
(B) She will go on a business trip next week.
(C) The company might be legally liable for an accident.
(D) She does not want to work overtime.

43. What is the man's concern?
(A) He has too many boxes to carry.
(B) He does not like his work.
(C) He has a deadline to meet.
(D) He doesn't have a laptop computer.

Go on to the next page.

44. What does the man think about the interview?
(A) He did very well.
(B) He did poorly.
(C) He was well-prepared.
(D) He had a great time.

45. How did the woman find out BK's interview style?
(A) She had an interview with BK Corporation.
(B) She had heard from other interviewees.
(C) She read a business magazine.
(D) She has contacted the personnel department.

46. What is the woman trying to do?
(A) Comfort the man
(B) Critique the man's performance
(C) Persuade the man to keep his current job
(D) Provide the man with an analysis of his interview

47. What are the speakers talking about?
(A) Accounting work
(B) The availability of a job
(C) The lack of personnel
(D) The new secretary

48. According to the woman, why isn't she able to hire the man?
(A) She has already filled the position.
(B) She believes he lacks work experience.
(C) She thinks he is overqualified.
(D) She doesn't think he has the right education.

49. What information does the woman give the man?
(A) He is eligible for a discount.
(B) He is required to have previous work experience.
(C) He can apply for another job.
(D) He should submit additional documents.

50. What is the woman likely going to do?
(A) Attend a board meeting
(B) Talk to some executives about a proposal
(C) Make a decision to launch a joint venture
(D) Complete a loan application

51. What does the man mention about the joint venture proposal?
(A) It will be reviewed by the board next week.
(B) It will reduce costs to a great extent.
(C) It will be beneficial to both companies.
(D) It will encourage more joint ventures in the industry.

52. What is the woman's concern about the situation?
(A) There are strict government regulations.
(B) Raising funds for the venture will be tough.
(C) The industry is very competitive.
(D) Both companies seem financially unsound.

53. What are the speakers mainly discussing?
(A) A business meeting
(B) A product order
(C) A sales conference
(D) An advertising campaign

54. What does the man imply when he says, "Anything else"?
(A) He wants the woman to push back a deadline.
(B) He wants to invite the woman somewhere.
(C) He wants to the woman to extend a meeting.
(D) He wants the woman to give more details.

55. What will the woman probably do next week?
(A) Attend a conference
(B) Hire new employees
(C) Arrange a meeting
(D) Take a vacation

56. What kind of business do the speakers most likely work for?
(A) A publishing company
(B) A financial firm
(C) A pharmaceutical company
(D) A healthcare service provider

57. What does the man mention about the retiree market?
(A) It is extremely competitive.
(B) It has been somewhat underserved.
(C) It has been saturated.
(D) The regulatory hurdles are high.

58. What does the woman suggest the man do?
(A) Start his own company
(B) Try hard to finalize the deal
(C) Write a new business proposal
(D) Conduct more market research

59. Why does the woman congratulate the man?
(A) He started his own business.
(B) He received a promotion.
(C) He won a prize.
(D) He was nominated for an award.

60. What does the man suggest the woman do?
(A) Meet him for a meal
(B) Apply for a new job
(C) Work with him on a project
(D) Write a reference letter

61. What does the woman imply when she says, "I'll come up with something"?
(A) She will deliver something to the man.
(B) She will make a suggestion.
(C) She will give the man directions.
(D) She will bring a gift for the man.

62. What is the main topic of the conversation?
(A) A job interview
(B) A recruitment event
(C) A workshop
(D) An advertisement

63. When will the women meet with their manager?
(A) Later today
(B) Tomorrow morning
(C) Tomorrow afternoon
(D) In a few days

64. What does a woman mean when she says, "Stop by then"?
(A) She wants the man to refrain from doing something.
(B) She is giving an invitation to the man.
(C) She is asking about the man's opinion.
(D) She is inquiring about the man's plans.

Go on to the next page.

Walking Trails – Selby Mountain Park	
Birch Trail	3.5 kilometers
Oak Trail	5.5 kilometers
Evergreen Trail	7.5 kilometers
Valley Trail	11 kilometers

Regis Health Clinic
Resident Doctors

Room 1 – Dr. Torville
Room 2 – Dr. Brand
Room 3 – Dr. Owler
Room 4 – Dr. Mooney

65. Where is the conversation taking place?
(A) In a vehicle
(B) In a parking lot
(C) In an information office
(D) In a bus terminal

66. What problem does the man mention?
(A) He forgot some equipment.
(B) He lost his rucksack.
(C) He hurt his leg.
(D) He does not have much time.

67. Look at the graphic. Which trail will the speakers probably choose?
(A) The Birch Trail
(B) The Oak Trail
(C) The Evergreen Trail
(D) The Valley Trail

68. Who most likely is the woman?
(A) A physician
(B) A pharmacist
(C) A clinic patient
(D) A receptionist

69. What does the woman ask for?
(A) A prescription
(B) An appointment schedule
(C) An identification card
(D) A credit card

70. Look at the graphic. Which room will the man go to next?
(A) Room 1
(B) Room 2
(C) Room 3
(D) Room 4

PART 4

Directions: You will hear some talks given by a single speaker. You will be asked to answer three questions about what the speaker says in each talk. Select the best response to each question and mark the letter (A), (B), (C), or (D) on your answer sheet. The talks will not be printed in your test book and will be spoken only one time.

71. According to the speaker, what is the study mainly about?
(A) The effects of a new medicine
(B) The effects of organic food
(C) The effects of exercise on health
(D) The effects of sleeping patterns

72. For how long will participants be involved?
(A) One month
(B) Three months
(C) Twelve months
(D) Thirty-six months

73. What will participants do monthly?
(A) Visit the doctor
(B) Complete an online survey
(C) E-mail a report
(D) Perform some exercises

74. What is the speaker calling to discuss?
(A) An appointment problem
(B) A new medical treatment
(C) An accounting mistake
(D) An unpaid balance

75. Who most likely is the speaker?
(A) A receptionist
(B) A physical therapist
(C) A professional athlete
(D) A patient

76. What is the listener offered as compensation?
(A) A free session
(B) A cash reward
(C) Complimentary gifts
(D) A discount

77. Where does the speaker most likely work?
(A) At a local newspaper
(B) At a bookstore
(C) At an office supplies store
(D) At a print shop

78. Why does the speaker say, "This might be your last chance"?
(A) To encourage the listener to buy an item
(B) To inform the listener of a decision
(C) To request that the listener send a payment
(D) To notify the listener that a store is closing

79. What does the speaker offer to do?
(A) Provide directions
(B) Place another order
(C) Give a discount
(D) Recommend new printers

80. Who is this message intended for?
(A) Bank investors
(B) Customers
(C) Bank personnel
(D) Weather reporters

81. According to the speaker, what caused the closures?
(A) Road resurfacing
(B) Building construction
(C) Adverse weather
(D) A national holiday

82. How does the speaker say the information will be shared?
(A) By personal phone calls
(B) By electronic mail
(C) By text messages
(D) By social networking services

Go on to the next page.

83. What industry does the speaker most
    likely work in?
    (A) Cable TV service
    (B) Sports marketing
    (C) Personal finance
    (D) Food production

84. What does the speaker say will happen on
    Wednesday?
    (A) The office will open late.
    (B) Food will be shared.
    (C) Some new packages will be released.
    (D) The Fishbone Grill will provide lunch.

85. According to the speaker, how can
    employees win the competition?
    (A) By working the most hours
    (B) By making the most creative product
    (C) By enrolling the most customers
    (D) By receiving the most
        recommendations

86. What kind of company does the speaker
    work for?
    (A) A marketing firm
    (B) A furniture design firm
    (C) An advertisement agency
    (D) An Internet service company

87. According to the speaker, what will be
    different for this project?
    (A) It will look flashier.
    (B) It will look more casual.
    (C) It will look more professional.
    (D) It will be more appropriate for social
        media.

88. What does the speaker ask the listeners to
    do before the next meeting?
    (A) Respond to a survey
    (B) Send related information
    (C) E-mail a proposal
    (D) Work additional hours

89. What is the purpose of the talk?
    (A) To discuss a problem
    (B) To explain a process
    (C) To introduce a speaker
    (D) To give a schedule of events

90. Why does the speaker say, "You'll not
    believe your ears"?
    (A) He thinks a talk will be surprising.
    (B) He believes the volume is too loud.
    (C) He is recommending a radio broadcast.
    (D) He advises using the provided
        headphones.

91. What is the audience invited to do after
    the talk?
    (A) Enjoy some refreshments
    (B) Enter a prize raffle
    (C) Meet the speaker
    (D) Sign up for a newsletter

Late Night Festival Schedule	
DJ Momo	August 2
DJ Doom	August 10
DJ Chan	August 16
DJ Summer	September 4

Passenger	Carly Fine	
Flight	**Seat**	**Gate**
KA816	3B	I19
Boarding Zone	3	

92. What problem does the speaker mention?
(A) A road needs to be repaired.
(B) An artist is unavailable.
(C) The venue is overbooked.
(D) Wrong information was announced.

93. Look at the graphic. According to the speaker, which DJ's performance will be rescheduled?
(A) DJ Momo
(B) DJ Doom
(C) DJ Chan
(D) DJ Summer

94. What does the speaker recommend the listeners do?
(A) Get a refund
(B) Call for questions
(C) Reschedule an appointment
(D) Check an e-mail

95. What is the announcement about?
(A) A flight delay
(B) A boarding zone change
(C) A plane problem
(D) A lost child

96. Look at the graphic. Which number should Carly Fine pay attention to now?
(A) KA816
(B) I19
(C) 3B
(D) 3

97. What will the speaker announce later?
(A) Where to get a coupon
(B) How to get to the nearest hotel
(C) Why the flight was delayed
(D) When the boarding will start

Go on to the next page.

| **Flora's Restaurant** |
| **- Set Lunch Menu -** |
| <u>Appetizer</u> |
| Blue Crab Cakes |
| <u>Main Dish</u> |
| Poached Salmon |
| <u>Side Dish</u> |
| Greek Salad |
| <u>Dessert</u> |
| Cherry Cheesecake |

98. Who most likely is the speaker?

(A) A restaurant owner

(B) A head chef

(C) A food critic

(D) A waiter

99. What problem does the speaker mention?

(A) Service was very slow.

(B) A dish was served cold.

(C) Staff members were impolite.

(D) An item was unavailable.

100. Look at the graphic. Which menu item was featured in a magazine?

(A) Blue Crab Cakes

(B) Poached Salmon

(C) Greek Salad

(D) Cherry Cheesecake

This is the end of the Listening test. Turn to Part 5 in your test book.

ANSWER

01. B	21. A	41. A	61. B	81. C
02. D	22. B	42. C	62. D	82. B
03. B	23. C	43. C	63. B	83. A
04. C	24. C	44. B	64. B	84. B
05. B	25. B	45. C	65. A	85. C
06. C	26. C	46. A	66. C	86. C
07. B	27. B	47. B	67. B	87. C
08. A	28. A	48. A	68. D	88. B
09. B	29. B	49. C	69. C	89. C
10. C	30. B	50. B	70. B	90. A
11. B	31. C	51. C	71. C	91. D
12. C	32. B	52. B	72. C	92. A
13. A	33. D	53. D	73. B	93. C
14. B	34. B	54. D	74. A	94. B
15. C	35. D	55. A	75. B	95. C
16. B	36. D	56. B	76. D	96. D
17. A	37. C	57. B	77. C	97. A
18. C	38. D	58. C	78. A	98. C
19. C	39. C	59. B	79. D	99. D
20. B	40. D	60. A	80. C	100. D

ACTUAL TEST

4

1.

2.

Go on to the next page.

3.

4.

5.

6.

Go on to the next page.

7. Mark your answer on your answer sheet.

8. Mark your answer on your answer sheet.

9. Mark your answer on your answer sheet.

10. Mark your answer on your answer sheet.

11. Mark your answer on your answer sheet.

12. Mark your answer on your answer sheet.

13. Mark your answer on your answer sheet.

14. Mark your answer on your answer sheet.

15. Mark your answer on your answer sheet.

16. Mark your answer on your answer sheet.

17. Mark your answer on your answer sheet.

18. Mark your answer on your answer sheet.

19. Mark your answer on your answer sheet.

20. Mark your answer on your answer sheet.

21. Mark your answer on your answer sheet.

22. Mark your answer on your answer sheet.

23. Mark your answer on your answer sheet.

24. Mark your answer on your answer sheet.

25. Mark your answer on your answer sheet.

26. Mark your answer on your answer sheet.

27. Mark your answer on your answer sheet.

28. Mark your answer on your answer sheet.

29. Mark your answer on your answer sheet.

30. Mark your answer on your answer sheet.

31. Mark your answer on your answer sheet.

PART 3

Directions: You will hear some conversations between two or more people. You will be asked to answer three questions about what the speakers say in each conversation. Select the best response to each question and mark the letter (A), (B), (C), or (D) on your answer sheet. The conversations will not be printed in your test book and will be spoken only one time.

32. What has the woman recently done?
(A) Trained some staff
(B) Moved overseas
(C) Started a new job
(D) Requested a promotion

33. What problem does the woman mention?
(A) Her workspace is untidy.
(B) Her Internet connection is slow.
(C) Her supervisor is inexperienced.
(D) Her salary was paid late.

34. Why does the man say, "Oh, you don't say"?
(A) He is surprised by the information.
(B) He thinks the woman is exaggerating.
(C) He misheard the woman's response.
(D) He would like to discuss something in more detail.

35. What is the man mainly looking for in a car?
(A) Design originality
(B) Interior space
(C) Market value
(D) Fuel efficiency

36. According to the woman, what is currently being offered to car buyers?
(A) A gift certificate
(B) A partial refund
(C) Free auto insurance
(D) A zero-percent loan

37. Why does the man ask the woman to show another car model?
(A) He wants a luxury car.
(B) He wants a stylish urban car.
(C) He wants a less expensive car.
(D) He wants a car in a smaller size.

38. Where does the woman work?
(A) At a restaurant
(B) At a theater
(C) At a health food store
(D) At a fitness center

39. Why does the man say, "Are you serious"?
(A) To show appreciation
(B) To express disbelief
(C) To agree with a statement
(D) To change the topic

40. What will the man probably do next?
(A) Make a delivery
(B) Refund an order
(C) Visit a supplier
(D) Make a phone call

41. Where does the man work?
(A) At a post office
(B) At an airline
(C) At a diplomatic institution
(D) At a retailer

42. What is the woman worried about?
(A) Exceeding a budget
(B) Arriving late for an interview
(C) Being unable to visit
(D) Failing to get a visa

43. What does the woman ask the man about?
(A) A registration procedure
(B) An expiration date
(C) A delivery time
(D) A service fee

Go on to the next page.

44. What problem does the woman mention?
(A) The repair costs are too high.
(B) An item she purchased is not working
properly.
(C) Her repair request has not been
processed yet.
(D) Her product is too complicated to operate.

45. Why does the man need to know the
purchase date?
(A) To record the incident
(B) To check out the inventory
(C) To find out the average life span of the
product
(D) To determine if the woman can get her
money back

46. Why does the woman say she doesn't
remember when she bought the product?
(A) She has a poor memory.
(B) She didn't check her e-mail.
(C) She received it as a gift.
(D) She lost her receipt.

---

47. According to the man, what did the
company do?
(A) Hired some new staff members
(B) Expanded its business
(C) Moved its headquarters to Europe
(D) Took over a smaller one

48. What will happen at the company soon?
(A) Several branches in Europe will be closed.
(B) Some volunteers will be needed for a
corporate event.
(C) A large personnel reshuffle will take place.
(D) Some employees will hand in transfer
requests.

49. Why might the woman want to transfer to
another branch office?
(A) She doesn't get along with some of her
colleagues.
(B) She is interested in classical European
culture.
(C) She can get paid more and receive
better benefits.
(D) She wants to work under competent
direction.

50. What does the man say will take place in a
month?
(A) A talent show
(B) A client meeting
(C) A product launch
(D) A career fair

51. What does the woman say she is
concerned about?
(A) The duration of the event
(B) The location of the show
(C) The size of the booth
(D) The number of participants

52. What will the woman do next?
(A) Make a suggestion
(B) Check the stock
(C) Print out some posters
(D) Talk to a manager

---

53. What is the man's problem?
(A) He has a scheduling conflict.
(B) He was not notified of a policy change.
(C) He is unable to access some
information.
(D) He is confused about a message he
received.

54. Why does the man say, "I don't know what
to say"?
(A) To explain his worries about giving a
speech
(B) To express his gratitude
(C) To show his frustration
(D) To ask the women for their opinion

55. What will the speakers likely do next?
(A) Go to a restaurant
(B) Check a schedule
(C) Attend a ceremony
(D) Shop for some clothing

---

56. Why does the woman talk to the man?
(A) To sublease her house
(B) To discuss some tenants' complaints
(C) To renew a rental agreement
(D) To inform him about some available housing

57. Why is the man looking for a new place to live?
(A) He started a new job.
(B) He has a long commute.
(C) His lease will expire soon.
(D) The apartment where he currently lives is very old.

58. What does the woman suggest that the man do?
(A) Contact a real estate agent
(B) Look for a different house on Lloyd Street
(C) Search through the company's online database
(D) Take a tour of a new apartment

59. Where most likely does the conversation take place?
(A) In a supermarket
(B) In a fitness center
(C) In a sporting goods store

60. What is the woman's problem?
(A) She was sent the wrong items.
(B) The items she wants are not available.
(C) She was charged too much.
(D) She is in the wrong place.

61. What does the woman ask the man to do?
(A) Reorder some items
(B) Make a delivery
(C) Call a manager
(D) Give her a discount

Sureshot Bicycles	
Sureshot Sierra	$430
Sureshot Trek	$460
Sureshot Glide	$490
Sureshot Blizzard	$520

62. Where are the speakers planning to go?
(A) To a beach
(B) To a mountain
(C) To an amusement park
(D) To a historical site

63. What is the woman concerned about?
(A) A travel schedule
(B) A bicycle route
(C) A weather forecast
(D) A work deadline

64. Look at the graphic. Which bicycle will the man probably purchase?
(A) Sureshot Sierra
(B) Sureshot Trek
(C) Sureshot Glide
(D) Sureshot Blizzard

Go on to the next page.

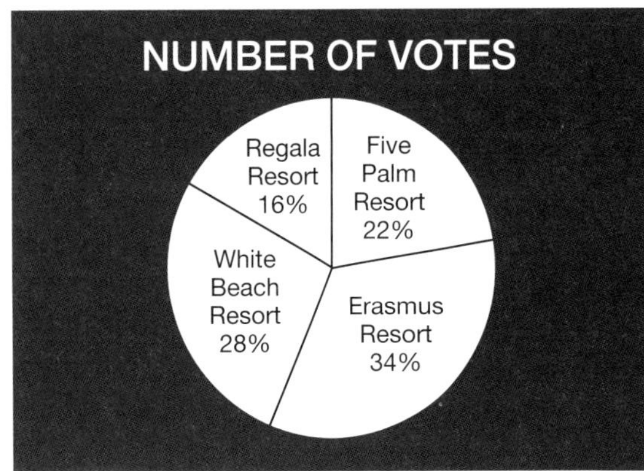

Dundee Public Library
1st Floor – General Books Section
2nd Floor – Reference Section
3rd Floor – DVDs & CDs
4th Floor – Journals & Periodicals

65. What department do the speakers work in?
(A) Accounting
(B) Marketing
(C) Personnel
(D) Sales

66. Look at the graphic. Which resort will the man probably choose?
(A) Regala Resort
(B) Five Palm Resort
(C) White Beach Resort
(D) Erasmus Resort

67. What will the woman do next?
(A) Announce plans to the staff
(B) Check a flight schedule
(C) Visit a travel agency
(D) Reserve some rooms

68. What is the conversation mainly about?
(A) Borrowing a book
(B) Replacing a lost library card
(C) Applying for a position
(D) Obtaining a membership

69. What does the man ask the woman to do?
(A) Pay a fee
(B) Return some materials
(C) Photocopy a document
(D) Fill out a form

70. Look at the graphic. Which floor will the woman probably go to next?
(A) The first floor
(B) The second floor
(C) The third floor
(D) The fourth floor

PART 4

Directions: You will hear some talks given by a single speaker. You will be asked to answer three questions about what the speaker says in each talk. Select the best response to each question and mark the letter (A), (B), (C), or (D) on your answer sheet. The talks will not be printed in your test book and will be spoken only one time.

71. Where is this speech probably being given?
(A) At a new-hire training session
(B) At a retirement dinner
(C) At a press conference
(D) At a charity fundraiser

72. What products does the Beagle Corporation probably manufacture?
(A) Vehicles
(B) Microwaves
(C) Ceramic objects
(D) Semiconductor chips

73. How long has the Beagle Corporation been in business?
(A) 18 years
(B) 32 years
(C) 42 years
(D) 60 years

74. According to the speaker, how is the weather outside?
(A) It's sunny.
(B) It's windy.
(C) It's cloudy.
(D) It's rainy.

75. Which expense will the money raised be used to cover?
(A) Medical services
(B) Housing
(C) Toy presents
(D) Transportation

76. Who is Susan Kang?
(A) A donor
(B) A charity organizer
(C) A performer
(D) A guest speaker

77. Who most likely is Ms. McGowan?
(A) A language specialist
(B) A public speaking trainer
(C) A radio show host
(D) A relationship therapist

78. What is the main topic of Ms. McGowan's talk?
(A) How to find a business partner
(B) How to become a psychologist
(C) How to avoid divorce
(D) How to communicate better

79. According to the speaker, which is the most critical to successful relationships?
(A) Understanding human psychology
(B) Showing respect for the opposition
(C) Listening to other people's opinions
(D) Winning the favor of one's colleagues

80. What information should the listeners look for on a Web site?
(A) Driving directions
(B) An event schedule
(C) Ticket costs
(D) A tour itinerary

81. Why is the event at Lavender Bistro expected to be popular?
(A) A new menu item will be launched.
(B) The restaurant has received good reviews.
(C) A competition will be held.
(D) An advertising campaign was successful.

82. Why does the speaker say, "Lavender Bistro rarely has an empty table"?
(A) To criticize the layout of a local restaurant
(B) To praise the food served at a business
(C) To advise listeners to choose a different venue
(D) To recommend making a reservation

Go on to the next page.

83. What are the listeners scheduled to do?
(A) Sample some foods
(B) Test out some machines
(C) Perform some repairs
(D) Survey some customers

84. What does the speaker imply when she says, "you shouldn't be afraid to speak your mind here"?
(A) The listeners should discuss an issue among themselves.
(B) The listeners can leave the room whenever necessary.
(C) The listeners will listen to a talk by an expert.
(D) The listeners should feel free to say negative things.

85. What are the listeners asked to do next?
(A) Review some guidelines
(B) Go to another room
(C) Complete a form
(D) Change their clothes

86. What is the announcement about?
(A) A productivity increase
(B) A new computer course
(C) A change in business hours
(D) New performance management software

87. What are the employees asked to do tomorrow?
(A) Use a new program
(B) Install a new computer system
(C) Turn off their computers
(D) Gather statistics on productivity

88. According to the speaker, why should the technical support team be contacted?
(A) To have them develop new software
(B) To submit criticism
(C) To discuss some creative ideas with them
(D) To report problems with the computer network

89. What kind of business does the speaker probably work for?
(A) A courier service
(B) A supermarket
(C) A restaurant
(D) A kitchen appliance manufacturer

90. What do some customers want the business to offer?
(A) Options that vary
(B) Gourmet recipes
(C) Longer business hours
(D) Better customer service

91. What will the listeners probably do next?
(A) Fill out a questionnaire
(B) Sample some products
(C) Enter a cooking contest
(D) Ask for a discount

92. Why does the speaker say, "Benton Boulevard is under construction right now"?
(A) To complain about noise
(B) To recommend public transportation
(C) To explain a delay
(D) To suggest a different route

93. What does the speaker say about the amusement park?
(A) It is not currently operational.
(B) It will close early today.
(C) It has been open for three months.
(D) It has won awards.

94. Whom does the speaker introduce as a special guest?
(A) A business owner
(B) A journalist
(C) An architect
(D) An investor

MON	TUE	WED	THU	FRI	SAT
Radio Interview		Studio Session		CD Launch Party	

95. Look at the graphic. On which day does the speaker want to schedule the live performance?
(A) Tuesday
(B) Wednesday
(C) Thursday
(D) Saturday

96. What did the speaker send to the listener?
(A) A map
(B) Interview questions
(C) A contract
(D) Concert tickets

97. What does the speaker apologize for?
(A) The performance fee
(B) The busy schedule
(C) The location of a business
(D) The cancelation of an event

98. Who gave a press conference today?
(A) A local celebrity
(B) A community group leader
(C) A council member
(D) A company president

99. Look at the graphic. Which building will be affected by the first road closure?
(A) The train station
(B) The bank
(C) The art gallery
(D) The hospital

100. What information does the speaker say can be found on the Web site?
(A) Directions to a building
(B) Details about an event
(C) A construction schedule
(D) A feedback form

This is the end of the Listening test. Turn to Part 5 in your test book.

01. D	21. C	41. C	61. A	81. C
02. D	22. A	42. C	62. B	82. D
03. C	23. A	43. D	63. C	83. B
04. A	24. B	44. B	64. A	84. D
05. C	25. A	45. D	65. C	85. D
06. D	26. C	46. D	66. C	86. D
07. C	27. B	47. B	67. D	87. A
08. A	28. C	48. C	68. D	88. B
09. B	29. B	49. D	69. D	89. C
10. B	30. C	50. D	70. C	90. A
11. A	31. C	51. C	71. B	91. B
12. C	32. C	52. D	72. B	92. C
13. A	33. D	53. A	73. C	93. A
14. A	34. A	54. B	74. D	94. C
15. A	35. D	55. A	75. B	95. A
16. C	36. B	56. D	76. C	96. C
17. A	37. D	57. B	77. D	97. B
18. A	38. D	58. C	78. D	98. D
19. B	39. B	59. C	79. C	99. A
20. A	40. D	60. B	80. B	100. C

LISTENING TEST

In the Listening test, you will be asked to demonstrate how well you understand spoken English. The entire Listening test will last approximately 45 minutes. There are four parts, and directions are given for each part. You must mark your answers on the separate answer sheet. Do not write your answers in your test book.

Part 1

Directions: For each question in this part, you will hear four statements about a picture in your test book. When you hear the statements, you must select the one statement that best describes what you see in the picture. Then find the number of the question on your answer sheet and mark your answer. The statements will not be printed in your test book and will be spoken only one time.

Sample Answer

Ⓐ Ⓑ Ⓒ ⬤ 

Example

Statement (C), "Two monitors are set up next to each other," is the best description of the picture, so you should select answer (C) and mark it on your answer sheet.

1.

2.

Go on to the next page.

3.

4.

5.

6.

Go on to the next page.

7. Mark your answer on your answer sheet.

8. Mark your answer on your answer sheet.

9. Mark your answer on your answer sheet.

10. Mark your answer on your answer sheet.

11. Mark your answer on your answer sheet.

12. Mark your answer on your answer sheet.

13. Mark your answer on your answer sheet.

14. Mark your answer on your answer sheet.

15. Mark your answer on your answer sheet.

16. Mark your answer on your answer sheet.

17. Mark your answer on your answer sheet.

18. Mark your answer on your answer sheet.

19. Mark your answer on your answer sheet.

20. Mark your answer on your answer sheet.

21. Mark your answer on your answer sheet.

22. Mark your answer on your answer sheet.

23. Mark your answer on your answer sheet.

24. Mark your answer on your answer sheet.

25. Mark your answer on your answer sheet.

26. Mark your answer on your answer sheet.

27. Mark your answer on your answer sheet.

28. Mark your answer on your answer sheet.

29. Mark your answer on your answer sheet.

30. Mark your answer on your answer sheet.

31. Mark your answer on your answer sheet.

PART 3

Directions: You will hear some conversations between two or more people. You will be asked to answer three questions about what the speakers say in each conversation. Select the best response to each question and mark the letter (A), (B), (C), or (D) on your answer sheet. The conversations will not be printed in your test book and will be spoken only one time.

32. What does the man want to do?
(A) Use a moving service
(B) Rent a house
(C) Visit a property
(D) Purchase an office building

33. Who most likely is the woman?
(A) A property manager
(B) An architect
(C) A travel agent
(D) An office worker

34. What does the woman advise the man to do?
(A) Look at a map
(B) Make a quick decision
(C) Start a meeting without her
(D) Take his key to the security office

35. What does the man offer to do?
(A) Attend a meeting
(B) Fix a device
(C) Call the office
(D) Get a laptop

36. Why does one woman need a laptop?
(A) To work on a project
(B) To check a schedule
(C) To send an e-mail
(D) To make an appointment

37. What does Susan offer to do?
(A) Explain how to send an e-mail
(B) Make an appointment with the clients
(C) Buy a laptop computer
(D) Forward an e-mail

38. Where does the man most likely work?
(A) At a taxi company
(B) At a furniture store
(C) At a hotel
(D) At a restaurant

39. What is the purpose of the woman's call?
(A) To make a complaint
(B) To cancel a request
(C) To inquire about a bill
(D) To arrange transportation

40. What does the woman plan to do this afternoon?
(A) Practice an instrument
(B) View a photography exhibit
(C) Visit a sports venue
(D) Meet a friend

41. What does the man apologize for?
(A) Sending an order to the wrong location
(B) Making an error in a document
(C) Forgetting to bring some items
(D) Being late for an appointment

42. What will happen at the store on Saturday?
(A) A staff party will be held.
(B) New employees will start working.
(C) A delivery will be made.
(D) A sale will begin.

43. What will the man likely do next?
(A) Clean a warehouse
(B) Deliver some items
(C) Pick up some goods
(D) Make a phone call

Go on to the next page.

44. Who is the man?
(A) A restaurant manager
(B) A waiter
(C) A business owner
(D) A caterer

45. What does the man inquire about?
(A) Getting a discount on his meal
(B) Reserving a table
(C) Using a catering service
(D) Interviewing the chef

46. What does the woman offer to do?
(A) Make a recommendation
(B) Create a price list
(C) Waive a fee
(D) Attend an event

47. Why is the woman calling the man?
(A) To apologize for an error
(B) To get an update on a client
(C) To ask for his e-mail address
(D) To praise him for some work he did

48. According to the man, what should be prepared by May 17?
(A) Some floor plans
(B) Some performance evaluations
(C) Some presentation slides
(D) Some catalogues

49. What is the woman asked to do?
(A) Reschedule the meetings
(B) Deliver a presentation
(C) Hire an assistant
(D) Contact the supervisor

50. Why is the woman calling?
(A) To ask about membership costs
(B) To request an interview
(C) To contact a manager
(D) To schedule a meeting

51. What does the woman imply when she says, "I have good timing then"?
(A) She can stay longer than expected.
(B) She can take advantage of a new deal.
(C) She has a very busy schedule.
(D) She plans to revisit another time.

52. What does the man recommend?
(A) Visiting the Web site
(B) Contacting other locations
(C) Taking a tour
(D) Attending a luncheon

53. Why is the man calling?
(A) To confirm a reservation
(B) To get information about an event
(C) To register employees for a workshop
(D) To apply for a sales position

54. According to the woman, what does the man have to do?
(A) Visit an information booth
(B) Sign up online
(C) Provide an account number
(D) Verify an e-mail address

55. What does the woman request?
(A) Contact information
(B) The names of attendees
(C) The address of a company
(D) Application forms

56. What are the women asked to do?
(A) Order some materials
(B) Call some clients
(C) Submit a report
(D) Attend a meeting

57. Why does the woman say, "Let me see when I'm free"?
(A) She is offering a service for no charge.
(B) She is checking her availability.
(C) She wants to know about some costs.
(D) She would like to change her work shift.

58. What does the man say he will send the woman?
(A) A client's contact details
(B) An inventory report
(C) An event schedule
(D) A product catalog

59. Who most likely is the man?
(A) A mechanic
(B) An attorney
(C) An exterminator
(D) A landscaper

60. Why does the man apologize?
(A) There was a payment error.
(B) A scheduled visit didn't occur.
(C) He is cancelling a contract.
(D) The store is closing early.

61. What does the man offer the woman?
(A) A free item
(B) A discount
(C) A membership
(D) A gift certificate

ART GALLERY MAP

HALL 1	HALL 2
Paintings	Sculptures
HALL 3	HALL 4
Photographs	Drawings

62. Look at the graphic. In which hall will the man meet the artist?
(A) Hall 1
(B) Hall 2
(C) Hall 3
(D) Hall 4

63. What will happen at the gallery this evening?
(A) An art class will be held.
(B) A talk will be given.
(C) An exhibition will begin.
(D) A performance will take place.

64. Why does the woman suggest using the west door?
(A) It is the only unlocked door.
(B) It is less crowded.
(C) It is next to a gift shop.
(D) It is the closest entrance.

Go on to the next page.

www.magazineportal.com/categories

Magazine Categories

1 - Sports and
    Fitness
2 - Entertainment and
    Culture
3 - Computers and
    Technology
4 - Cooking and
    Home Improvement

1	2
Visitors must return ID tags before leaving	**Please do not touch equipment**
3	4
Safety goggles must be worn at all times	**Visitors must report to the security office**

65. What project is the man busy doing?
(A) Preparing a room
(B) Filing some documents
(C) Updating a Web site
(D) Contacting patients

66. Look at the graphic. Which category will the man most likely search?
(A) Category 1
(B) Category 2
(C) Category 3
(D) Category 4

67. Why does the woman recommend buying magazines from Magazine Portal?
(A) The magazines are high quality.
(B) The patients enjoy them the most.
(C) The Web site has the largest selection.
(D) The business receives a discount.

68. Look at the graphic. Which sign does the man refer to?
(A) Sign 1
(B) Sign 2
(C) Sign 3
(D) Sign 4

69. Why is the man at the construction site?
(A) To pick up some materials
(B) To perform an inspection
(C) To install some equipment
(D) To interview for a job

70. What does the woman give to the man?
(A) An ID tag
(B) A parking permit
(C) Safety goggles
(D) A site map

PART 4

Directions: You will hear some talks given by a single speaker. You will be asked to answer three questions about what the speaker says in each talk. Select the best response to each question and mark the letter (A), (B), (C), or (D) on your answer sheet. The talks will not be printed in your test book and will be spoken only one time.

71. What is the speaker advertising?
(A) A new residential complex
(B) A shopping mall
(C) An architectural firm
(D) An athletic complex

72. What benefit does the speaker mention?
(A) A clean environment
(B) Discounts at local restaurants
(C) Access to exclusive facilities
(D) Special prices on memberships

73. According to the advertisement, what is located in downtown Kensington?
(A) A golf course
(B) Luxury accommodations
(C) Animal amenities
(D) An underground shopping center

74. What led to the increase in sales?
(A) Low prices
(B) Booming exports
(C) Successful advertising
(D) High quality

75. According to the speaker, what has the company decided to do?
(A) Post a job advertisement
(B) Remove the old inventory
(C) Employ temporary workers
(D) Pay bonuses to employees

76. What are the listeners instructed to do if they want to work overtime?
(A) Sign up first
(B) Submit an application
(C) Talk to the plant manager
(D) Go to the registration desk

77. Where does the talk most likely take place?
(A) At a factory
(B) At a tourist information center
(C) At a science museum
(D) At a research facility

78. Why does the speaker say, "It'll take at least three hours"?
(A) To tell the listeners to be prepared
(B) To apologize for a schedule change
(C) To arrange a meeting time
(D) To correct some details

79. According to the speaker, what should the listeners keep in their hands?
(A) Their guide books
(B) Their ID tags
(C) Their notepads
(D) Their security keycards

80. According to the message, what happened two days ago?
(A) Some items were discontinued.
(B) An order was placed online.
(C) New products arrived at the store.
(D) Internet transactions were cancelled.

81. Why does the speaker say she cannot process Mr. Kyle's order now?
(A) She lost his order form.
(B) The computer system is out of order.
(C) An item is currently out of stock.
(D) He hasn't paid for his purchase yet.

82. What does the speaker want Mr. Kyle to know?
(A) An alternative product is available.
(B) The pricing information was not accurate.
(C) His order has just been processed.
(D) Some products are being offered at discounted prices.

Go on to the next page.

83. According to the speaker, what caused the project delay?
(A) A land shortage
(B) Weather conditions
(C) Insufficient funds
(D) Some mechanical problems

84. What does the speaker propose the city do to continue the project?
(A) Raise property taxes
(B) Use profits from events
(C) Hold a fundraising event
(D) Recruit volunteers for the project

85. What is required to proceed with the speaker's proposal?
(A) A vote from all residents
(B) A review by the government
(C) The approval of the mayor
(D) A majority vote by the council members

86. Who most likely are the listeners?
(A) Telephone operators
(B) Sales representatives
(C) Repair technicians
(D) Advertising managers

87. What is the purpose of the talk?
(A) To announce a new work policy
(B) To introduce new staff members
(C) To explain a workshop schedule
(D) To describe some customer complaints

88. What does the speaker imply when she says, "There is a café just across the road"?
(A) The listeners are wrong about there being no coffee shops.
(B) The listeners might have difficulty finding a location.
(C) The listeners should have lunch at the café.
(D) The listeners will meet in the café at the end of the day.

89. What is the talk mainly about?
(A) Meetings with clients
(B) Reports about marketing strategy
(C) Plans on expanding a working area
(D) The efficiency of documentation

90. What will the listeners probably do this Friday?
(A) Reorganize the office area
(B) Move to third floor
(C) Arrange a client meeting
(D) Attend a workshop

91. What does the speaker think the designers will like?
(A) The choice of programs to use
(B) The wide space for documents
(C) The decreased workload
(D) The technical support service

92. Why is the speaker calling?
(A) To register for a convention
(B) To ask for help with a task
(C) To inquire about an ad campaign
(D) To get some directions

93. What does the speaker imply when she says, "It wasn't my idea"?
(A) She understands a change is inconvenient.
(B) She thinks the listener should be proud.
(C) She is pleased that the team is communicating well.
(D) She wants the listener to suggest some options.

94. What does the speaker ask the listener to do?
(A) Place an advertisement
(B) Contact the company chairman
(C) Hold a staff meeting
(D) Request a display table

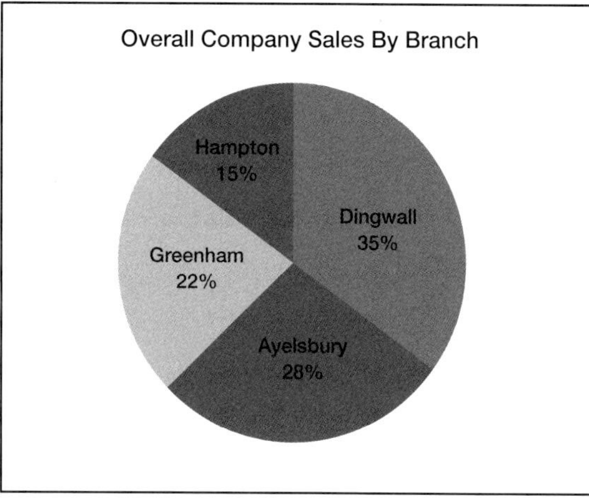

95. What problem does the speaker mention?
(A) A road will be temporarily closed.
(B) Inclement weather is expected.
(C) A guest speaker is unavailable.
(D) Some equipment has been damaged.

96. Look at the graphic. According to the speaker, which film showing will be postponed?
(A) Golden Years
(B) A Brief Romance
(C) The Outlaw
(D) Space Quest III

97. What does the speaker recommend the listeners do?
(A) Request a refund
(B) Visit a Web site
(C) Contact an event organizer
(D) Attend a different event

98. According to the speaker, what was mentioned in the memo?
(A) The company will release new products.
(B) Employees must attend a training session.
(C) Sales are lower than expected.
(D) Some managers have been promoted.

99. What problem does the speaker mention?
(A) A competitor has increased its market share.
(B) An advertising campaign was unsuccessful.
(C) Customers have complained about a product.
(D) Production costs have increased.

100. Look at the graphic. Which branch may be closed?
(A) Hampton
(B) Dingwall
(C) Ayelsbury
(D) Greenham

This is the end of the Listening test. Turn to Part 5 in your test book.

01. B	21. A	41. C	61. B	81. C
02. A	22. C	42. D	62. B	82. A
03. B	23. C	43. D	63. A	83. C
04. C	24. A	44. C	64. D	84. B
05. D	25. C	45. C	65. A	85. D
06. A	26. C	46. A	66. B	86. C
07. B	27. C	47. A	67. D	87. C
08. A	28. C	48. A	68. D	88. C
09. C	29. A	49. D	69. B	89. C
10. A	30. A	50. A	70. D	90. A
11. B	31. C	51. B	71. A	91. B
12. A	32. B	52. C	72. C	92. B
13. B	33. A	53. C	73. C	93. A
14. A	34. B	54. B	74. C	94. D
15. C	35. D	55. A	75. C	95. A
16. B	36. C	56. D	76. A	96. B
17. A	37. A	57. B	77. D	97. B
18. C	38. C	58. B	78. A	98. C
19. B	39. D	59. C	79. B	99. B
20. B	40. C	60. B	80. B	100. D

1

★★★ 2인 이상 + 등장인물의 동작 파악

(A) 비행기가 곧 활주로에 착륙하려고 한다.
(B) 몇몇 탑승객들이 비행기에서 내리고 있다.
(C) 탑승객들이 머리 위 짐칸에서 가방을 내리고 있다.
(D) 비행기들이 공항에 줄지어 늘어서 있다.

어휘 be about to + 동사원형 막~하려던 참이다, 곧 ~할 것이다 land 땅, 육지, ~에 착륙하다 runway 활주로 disembark from ~에서 내리다 aircraft 비행기 overhead bin 머리 위 선반(짐칸) be lined up in a row 줄지어 늘어서다

(A) An airplane is about to land on the runway.
(B) Some passengers are disembarking from the aircraft.
(C) Passengers are unloading the bags from the overhead bins.
(D) Airplanes are lined up in a row at the airport.

문제 해설

실외 전경을 배경으로 2인 이상이 등장하는 사진이므로 사람들의 공통된 행동을 먼저 파악한 후 공통된 동작이나 강조가 되는 동작이 없을 경우 외모적 특징 순서로 분석해야 한다. 그 이후에 실외 전경을 구성하는 주요 요소들의 위치와 상태 또는 배열 형태를 살펴보는 것이 적절하다. 그러므로 탑승객들이 비행기에서 내리는 행동, 비행기가 활주로에 착륙한 상태, 그리고 비행기 주변에 서비스를 제공하는 차량들이 위치하고 있는 상태에 집중해야 하며, 이 중 비행기에서 내리는 탑승객들의 동작을 '비행기 등에서 내리다'의 뜻을 지닌 disembark를 사용하여 묘사하고 있는 (B)가 정답이 된다.

토익 분석

무엇보다 비행기는 막 착륙하려는 찰나가 아니라 이미 활주로에 착륙한 상태이므로 is about to land on the runway가 부적절하다는 점에 주의해야 하며, 또한 disembark from은 교통수단에서 내리는 행동을 표현하는 고난이도 표현이므로 꼭 기억해 둬야 한다. overhead bin(=overhead compartment)은 LC뿐 아니라 PART 5에서 복합 명사로 많이 출제되었던 표현이다.

2

★★★ 풍경 + 전체 상태 파악

(A) 모든 건물들의 모습이 동일하다.
(B) 도시의 스카이라인이 구름에 가려져 있다.
(C) 몇몇 고층 건물들이 해안선 근처에 위치하고 있다.
(D) 건물들이 서로 멀리 떨어져 있다.

어휘 identical 동일한 모습을 지닌, 똑같은 skyline 스카이라인 be obscured by ~에 의해 가려지다 be located near ~의 근처에 위치하다 shoreline 해변, 해안선 be far apart from ~로부터 멀리 떨어져 있다

(A) All of the buildings are identical.
(B) The city skyline is obscured by clouds.
(C) Some tall buildings are located near the shoreline.
(D) The buildings are far apart from one another.

문제 해설

풍경 사진이므로 사진의 중심부에서 사진의 측면 방향으로 이동하면서 사진을 구성하는 주요 요소들의 위치와 상태 혹은 배열 형태를 파악해야 할 필요가 있다. 그러므로 무엇보다 다양한 모습과 크기의 건물들과 고층 건물들의 상층부가 구름에 가려진 상태를 언급하는 표현이 정답으로 제시될 가능성이 높으며, 이 중 도시의 스카이라인이 구름에 가려 있는 모습을 정확하게 묘사하고 있는 (B)가 정답임을 알 수 있다.

토익 분석

사진 문제에서 보기에 All이 등장하는 보기의 경우 대부분은 오답으로 활용되는 경우가 많다는 것과 (C)번 보기에서와 같이 the shoreline(해안가)과 같은 사진 속에 등장하지 않는 사물 등이 등장하는 보기는 우선적으로 소거해야 한다.

3

(A) Some vehicles are parked behind the dumpster.
(B) A person is transporting some building materials.
(C) Some vehicles are waiting for the light to change.
(D) The garbage bin is being emptied.

문제 해설

두 사람과 사람 주변의 사물이 중심인 사진이므로 사진 속 인물의 행동과 외모적 특징 그리고 사람 주변의 주요 사물의 위치와 상태 및 배열 형태에 집중해야 할 필요가 있다. 그러므로 한 남자가 쓰레기통을 비우는 행동, 길가에 트럭 한 대가 주차된 상태, 그리고 도로에 자동차들이 운행 중인 상태와 연관된 표현이 정답으로 제시될 가능성이 높으며, 이 중 쓰레기통을 비우고 있는 사람의 동작을 표현하고 있는 (D)가 정답이 된다.

토익 분석

쓰레기통 옆에 트럭 한 대가 주차가 된 것은 맞지만 차량 여러 대가 쓰레기통 뒤에 주차가 된 상황은 옳지 않으며 Some vehicles are waiting for the light to change와 같은 추측성 보기는 토익에서 가장 즐겨 사용하는 오답용 보기로 주의해야 한다. 이과 같은 표현은 교차로가 강조되고 차량들이 신호 대기 중임이 명확한 사진이어야 한다.

★★ 2인 이상 + 등장인물의 동작 파악

(A) 몇몇 차량들이 쓰레기통 뒤에 주차가 되어 있다.
(B) 한 사람이 건축 자재를 운반하고 있다.
(C) 몇몇 차량들이 신호등이 바뀌기를 기다리고 있다.
(D) 쓰레기통이 비워지고 있다.

어휘 vehicle 차량 transport ~을 운반하다, ~을 수송하다 garbage bin 쓰레기통 empty 비워진, ~을 비우다

4

(A) Both of the telephones are in use.
(B) A man is talking on a pay phone.
(C) There are some people waiting in line.
(D) A man is working on the construction site.

문제 해설

한 남자와 보행자들 그리고 공중전화라는 사물이 등장하고 있는 사진이므로 사진 속 남자의 행동 및 외모적 특징을 파악한 후 공중전화의 위치와 상태 및 배열 형태에 집중해야 한다. 그리고 보행자들의 행동 역시 파악해야 한다. 남자가 공중전화를 사용하여 통화 중인 행동 그리고 두 대의 공중전화가 나란히 위치하고 있는 배열 상태와 관련된 표현 그리고 보행자들이 걷고 있는 동작이 정답으로 제시될 가능성이 높으며, 이 중 남자가 공중전화로 통화 중인 동작을 설명하고 있는 (B)가 정답임을 알 수 있다.

토익 분석

사물의 경우, (A)처럼 사물의 상태는 정확하게 묘사하고 있으나 사물의 수를 부적절하게 언급하는 방식의 오답도 자주 제시되고 있으므로 이에 주의해야 할 필요가 있다. (D)에서 사용된 work의 경우 walk와 함께 유사 발음으로 오답용 보기를 구성할 때 자주 활용된다.

★★ 2인 이상 + 등장인물의 동작 파악

(A) 전화기 두 대가 모두 사용 중이다.
(B) 한 남자가 공중전화를 통해 얘기하고 있다.
(C) 사람들이 줄 서 기다리고 있다.
(D) 한 남자는 공사장에서 작업을 하고 있다.

어휘 be in use 사용되다 pay phone 공중전화
wait in line 줄을 서서 기다리다 work on 작업을 하다

★★ 2인 이상 + 풍경

(A) 횡단보도는 보행자로 복잡하다.
(B) 몇몇 자동차들이 신호등에서 좌회전을 하고 있다.
(C) 건물 한쪽에 위치한 현수막이 철거되고 있다.
(D) 사람들이 아치형 문을 향해 가고 있다.

어휘 crosswalk 횡단보도 pedestrian 보행자
make a left turn at ~에서 좌회전하다 banner 현수막
head toward ~를 향해 가다 archway 아치 형태 입구

(A) The crosswalk is crowded with pedestrians.
(B) Some cars are making a left turn at a traffic signal.
(C) The banner is being removed from the side of the building.
(D) People are heading toward the entrance of the archway.

문제 해설

도로 풍경을 배경으로 2인 이상 등장하는 사진이므로 사람들의 공통된 행동 및 외모적 특징부터 파악한 이후에 사람들이 각기 달리 취하는 행동과 실외 풍경을 구성하는 주요 사물들의 위치와 상태 및 배열 형태에 집중해야 한다. 그러므로 횡단보도를 건너는 많은 보행자들의 행동, 시내 도로를 주행하는 자동차들의 움직임 그리고 여러 건물들이 도로를 따라 위치하고 있는 배열 형태에 초점을 맞춰야 하며, 이 중 횡단보도에 건너가는 많은 보행자들의 동작을 정확하게 묘사하고 있는 (A)가 정답이다.

토익 분석

사람들이 걸어가는 사진이지만 사진 속에 the archway가 등장하지 않기에 (D)는 소거해야 한다. 사진 속에 등장하지 않는 사물이나 동작이 들리는 보기는 가장 먼저 소거해야 한다는 점을 명심하고 (B)와 같이 명확하지 않은 추측성 보기들에 주의해야 한다. 사진은 언제나 객관적인 정확한 사실만을 묘사한다는 점을 기억해야 한다.

★★ 2인 이상 + 등장인물의 동작 파악

(A) 그들은 사진첩을 보고 있다.
(B) 그들은 물 옆에 서 있다.
(C) 그들은 필름을 현상하고 있다.
(D) 그들은 외부에서 자신들의 사진을 찍고 있다.

어휘 look through ~을 훑어보다, ~을 통해 보다, ~을 자세히 조사하다 photo album 사진첩 get sth p.p. ~이 ~되도록 하다 develop ~을 인화하다 have sth p.p. ~이 ~되도록 하다 outdoors 외부에서, 바깥에서

(A) They are looking through a photo album.
(B) They are standing next to the water.
(C) They are getting some film developed.
(D) They are having their photograph taken outdoors.

문제 해설

전형적인 2인 중심의 사진이므로 사진 속 인물들의 공통된 행동 및 외모적 특징부터 파악하는 것이 순서이다. 따라서 두 사람이 서로 휴대 전화를 바라보는 행동, 휴대 전화를 이용하여 두 사람의 사진을 촬영하고 있는 행동, 그리고 남자가 선글라스를 착용한 상태를 묘사하는 표현이 정답으로 제시될 가능성이 높으며, 이 중 스스로 사진 촬영하고 있는 행동을 묘사하고 있는 (D)가 정답이다.

토익 분석

두 사람이 무엇을 바라보고 있지만, 앨범을 보는 것은 아니므로 (A)는 오답이고 사진을 찍는 동작에서 연상 가능한 film과 develop을 사용한 (C)는 혼동용 보기이다. 또한, 사진 속에 '물가'는 등장하지 않기에 (B)역시 오답이다.

7

How long have you been waiting for a table?
(A) It's about nine pages long.
(B) I just got here myself.
(C) About eight miles.

문제 해설

자리가 나기를 얼마 동안 기다렸는지 묻는 How long~ 의문문으로, 이에 지금 막 도착했음을 밝히며 간접적으로 기다린 시간이 얼마 되지 않고 있음을 언급하고 있는 (B)가 정답이다.

토익 분석

How long은 기간뿐 아니라 "길이나, 분량"도 물어볼 수 있다는 것을 기억해야 한다. (A)와 (C)는 바로 이점을 이용한 오답 보기로 각각 분량과 길이를 이용한 오답 보기가 된다. How long 질문 중 주의해야 할 대표적인 유형의 문제이다.

★★ 직접의문문 How long

테이블이 나기를 얼마 동안 기다리셨나요?
(A) 약 9페이지 분량이요.
(B) 저는 이곳에 막 도착했어요.
(C) 대략 8마일 정도예요.

어휘 wait for ~를 기다리다 get here 이곳에 도착하다

8

Should I give this budget report to you or leave it on Mr. Cyrus's desk?
(A) You can give it to me.
(B) Yes, you can leave on Monday.
(C) Thanks, but I can manage myself.

문제 해설

이 보고서를 Cyrus 씨의 책상 위에 두어야 하는지, 아니면 상대방에게 줘야 하는지 묻는 선택의문문으로, 이에 자신에게 달라고 대답하는 (A)가 정답이다.

토익 분석

선택의문문에서 두 가지 선택 사항 중 하나를 고르는 것이 아닌 새로운 의견을 제시하는 유형의 답변 또한 비중이 높은 정답 유형임을 알아 둬야 한다. (B)는 선택의문문에서 나오지 않는 Yes가 등장했고, 질문에서는 'leave; 남겨 두다'를 쓰고 대답에는 '떠나다'라고 써서 함정이 포함된 오답이다. (C)는 전형적인 권유, 제안 질문에 대한 답변으로 오답이다. 이 문제에서 기억할 두 가지 중요 포인트는 선택의문문은 Yes/No 답변이 불가하다는 것과 thanks but 구문은 무조건 권유, 제안 질문에 대한 답변이라는 것이다.

★★★ 선택의문문

이 보고서를 Cyrus 씨의 책상 위에 두어야 하나요, 아니면 당신한테 드려야 할까요?
(A) 저한테 주세요.
(B) 네, 당신은 월요일에 출발할 수 있어요.
(C) 고맙습니다만, 저 스스로 처리할 수 있어요.

어휘 budget report 예산 보고서 leave 떠나다, ~에 무엇을 두다

9

You should fill out these forms in duplicate.
(A) Do you happen to have a pen I can use?
(B) We are supposed to wear formal attire.
(C) I'm looking for someone to fill in for me tomorrow.

★★★ 평서문 – 권유, 제안, 요청

당신은 이 서류들을 두 통 작성해 주셔야 합니다.
(A) 혹시 제가 빌려 쓸 수 있는 펜이 있으신가요?
(B) 저희는 정장을 착용하기로 되어 있어요.
(C) 저는 내일 저 대신 근무해 줄 사람을 찾고 있어요.

어휘 fill out 작성하다 in duplicate 두 통으로
be supposed to + 동사원형 ~하기로 되어 있다
formal attire 정장 fill in ~를 대신해서 일을 하다

문제 해설

평서문 형태지만 이 서류들을 두 통씩 작성해 줄 것을 당부하는 권유, 제안, 요청 문장이다, 이에 자신이 빌려 쓸 수 있는 펜이 있는지 반문하며, 우회적으로 상대가 바라는 대로 서류를 두 통씩 작성할 것임을 밝히고 있는 (A)가 정답이다.

토익 분석

(B)는 질문의 form과 유사한 발음의 formal을 이용한 유사 발음 어휘 함정이 포함된 오답이며, (C)는 질문의 fill을 중복하여 제시하는 동일 어휘 함정이 등장하는 오답이라 할 수 있다. PART 2에서는 질문 속에서 들렸던 발음과 유사한 단어들을 활용한 오답 보기가 함정으로 활용된다는 점을 기억해야 한다.

10

★★ 부가의문문

공항 서틀버스가 20분마다 출발하지요, 그렇지 않나요?
(A) 편도 표는 2달러예요.
(B) 네, 저희는 백화점에서 근무해요.
(C) 아니요, 30분마다 운행해요.

어휘 depart 출발하다 a one-way ticket 편도 티켓

The airport shuttle departs every twenty minutes, doesn't it?

(A) $2 for a one-way ticket.
(B) Yes, we work at the department store.
(C) No, it runs every thirty minutes.

문제 해설

공항 서틀버스가 20분마다 출발하는지 여부를 확인하는 부가의문문으로, 이에 그렇지 않다는 부정 답변 No와 함께 30분마다 출발한다며 상대가 잘못 알고 있는 사실을 정확하게 알려 주고 있는 (C)가 정답이다.

토익 분석

편도 표의 가격을 언급하고 있는 (A)는 How much 의문문에 적합한 내용이자 질문의 bus에서 연상이 가능한 ticket을 이용한 연상 어휘 오답이며, (B) 역시 공항 서틀버스의 배차 간격이 20분임을 뜻하는 Yes란 긍정 답변과 백화점에서 근무한다는 부연 설명이 서로 관련 없는 내용으로 구성되어 있을 뿐만 아니라 질문에 등장한 depart의 파생어 department를 이용한 파생어 오답이라 할 수 있다.

11

★★ 일반의문문

5월에 저희 신상품에 대한 새로운 광고 캠페인을 시행할 예정인가요?
(A) 물론이에요, 함께 점심 식사를 하지요.
(B) 네, 현재로서는 계획이 그렇습니다.
(C) 아니요, 저는 그것이 매우 효과적인 광고 전략이라 생각해요.

어휘 launch ~을 시행하다 advertising campaign 광고 캠페인 effective 효과적인 advertising strategy 광고 전략

Are we going to launch our new advertising campaign for the new product in May?

(A) Sure, let's have lunch together.
(B) Yes, that's the plan for now.
(C) No, I think it's a very effective advertising strategy.

문제 해설

5월에 신상품에 대한 새로운 광고 캠페인을 시행할 계획인지 여부를 묻는 일반의문문으로 이에 그 계획이 사실임을 뜻하는 Yes란 답변에 이어 현재로서는 계획이 그렇다는 부연 설명을 언급하고 있는 (B)가 정답이다.

토익 분석

(A)는 그 계획이 사실임을 의미하는 Sure란 답변과 함께 점심 식사를 하자고 권고하는 부연 설명이 서로 무관한 내용이자 질문의 launch와 유사한 발음을 지닌 lunch를 이용한 유사 발음 어휘 오답이며, (C)는 그 계획이 사실이 아님을 뜻하는 부정 답변 No와 그것이 매우 효과적인 광고 전략이라는 부연 설명이 모순되었고, 질문의 advertising이 중복 제시된 동일 어휘 오답이기도 하다.

12

I heard there is a strike at the Detroit chemical plant.

(A) In fact, it couldn't be better.
(B) Yes, but management gave in to the union yesterday.
(C) No, I watched a baseball game on television.

문제 해설

Detroit의 화학 공장에서 파업이 발생했다는 정보를 전달하고 있는 평서문으로 이에 파업이 사실임을 인정하는 긍정 답변 Yes에 이어 경영진이 어제 노조에 양보함으로써 사태가 해결되었다는 추가 정보를 제공하고 있는 (B)가 정답이다.

토익 분석

(A)는 파업에 대해 이 이상 좋을 수 없다는 비논리적 답변을 제시하고 있는 오답이며, (C)는 파업 발생을 부정하는 No라는 답변과 TV로 야구 경기를 관람했다는 부연 설명이 서로 무관한 내용이자 질문의 strike를 통해 연상할 수 있는 baseball을 이용한 연상 어휘 오류가 포함된 오답이다. 사실 이 문제의 경우 청취 실력이 약할 경우 오답 보기의 뜻을 정확히 파악하기 쉽지 않다. 하지만 보기에 but이 등장할 경우 정답 확률이 99%라는 것을 기억한다면 (B)가 정답이 된다는 것을 어렵지 않게 파악할 수 있다.

★★★ 평서문

저는 Detroit의 화학 공장에서 파업이 발생했다고 들었어요.
(A) 사실, 이 이상 좋을 수 없네요.
(B) 네, 하지만 경영진이 어제 노조에 양보했어요.
(C) 아니요, 저는 야구 경기를 TV로 관람했어요.

어휘 strike 파업 chemical plant 화학 공장 in fact 사실은 couldn't be better 이 이상 좋을 수 없다, 아주 좋다 management 경영진 gave in to ~에 양보하다 union 노조

13

Excuse me. Could you please push the tenth floor button for me?

(A) Sure. Isn't there a clinic that recently moved in there?
(B) No, my office is on the fifth floor.
(C) Yes, I have a handful of documents.

문제 해설

10층 버튼을 눌러 줄 수 있는지 여부를 묻는 권유, 제안, 요청 의문문으로 이를 수락하는 Sure라는 답변에 이어 10층에는 최근 입주한 클리닉이 있지 않은지 반문하며 사실을 확인하고 있는 (A)가 정답이다.

토익 분석

(B)는 10층 버튼을 눌러줄 수 없다는 부정 답변 No와 자신의 사무실이 5층에 있다는 부연 설명이 서로 무관한 내용으로 구성된 오답이며, 또한 floor를 중복 사용한 오답 유형이다. (C)는 10층 버튼을 눌러 주겠다는 Yes란 긍정 답변과 제 손 한가득 서류가 있다는 부연 설명이 서로 모순되는 내용으로 구성된 오답이라 할 수 있다. 이 문제 역시 보기 구성이 쉽지 않은 고난이도 문제에 해당하지만, PART 2에서 질문과 관계없이 보기 문장이 '의문문' 형태인 반문 표현일 경우 정답 확률이 90% 이상이라는 사실을 기억해 둔다면 (A)가 어렵지 않게 정답임을 예상할 수 있다.

★★★ 의문문 – 권유, 제안, 요청

실례합니다. 저 대신 10층 버튼을 눌러 주시겠어요?
(A) 물론이에요, 그곳은 최근에 입주한 클리닉이 있지 않나요?
(B) 아니요, 제 사무실은 5층이에요.
(C) 네, 제 손 한가득 서류들이 있어서요.

어휘 push the tenth floor button 10층 버튼을 누르다 clinic 의료원 recently 최근에 move in ~에 들어가다, ~에 입주하다 handful 손 한가득

14

★★★ 일반의문문

당신이 제게 새로운 본사 건물을 구경시켜 주실 건가요?
(A) 네, 그건 정말 인상적인 공연이었어요.
(B) 아니요, Thompson 씨가 새로운 프로젝트를 담당하고 있어요.
(C) 물론이에요. 10분 뒤에 로비에서 만나요.

어휘 show sb around ~에게 ~을 구경시켜 주다
headquarters 본사 impressive 인상적인
performance 공연, 실적, 경기 head 머리, 수장, ~을 책임지다, ~을 담당하다, ~로 향하다

Will you show me around the new company headquarters?

(A) Yes, it was an impressive performance.
(B) No, Mr. Thompson is heading the new project.
(C) Sure, let's meet in the lobby in ten minutes.

문제 해설

상대방이 새로운 본사 건물을 구경시켜 줄 것인지 여부를 묻는 일반의문문으로, 이를 수락하는 Sure 이라는 답변에 이어 10분 뒤 로비에서 만날 것을 권고하고 있는 (C)가 정답이다.

토익 분석

(A)는 새로운 본사 건물을 구경시켜 주겠다는 Yes란 긍정 답변과 정말 인상적인 공연이었다는 부연 설명이 서로 연관성이 없는 내용이자 질문의 show를 통해 연상할 수 있는 performance를 이용한 연상 어휘 오답이 되겠으며, (B)는 새로운 본사 건물을 구경시켜 줄 수 없다는 No라는 부정 답변과 Thompson 씨가 새로운 프로젝트 담당자임을 밝히는 부연 설명이 서로 무관한 내용이자 질문에 등장한 headquarters의 일부 어휘인 head의 파생어 heading을 이용한 오답이다. PART 2에서 질문 속에 사용된 단어와 형태나 발음 일부분이 중복되는 단어가 사용되는 보기는 대체로 오답용 혼동 보기임을 기억해야 한다.

★★★ 평서문

제가 만약 제 차를 노상에 주차하면, 주차 위반 딱지를 받을 수도 있어요.
(A) 이 건물 뒤에 무료로 주차할 수 있어요.
(B) 네, 저희는 종종 근처 공원으로 산책을 가요.
(C) 저는 인터넷으로 제 표를 주문했어요.

어휘 parking ticket 주차 위반 딱지 at the rear of ~의 뒤에 go for a walk 산책을 가다 nearby 근처의, 근처에 있는 over the Internet 인터넷으로

If I park my car on the street, I might get a parking ticket.

(A) You can park for free at the rear of this building.
(B) Yes, we often go for walks in a nearby park.
(C) I ordered my ticket over the Internet.

문제 해설

만약 노상 주차를 하게 되면 자신이 주차 위반 딱지를 받을 수 있다는 문제점을 제기하는 평서문으로 이에 건물 뒤편에 무료 주차가 가능하다며 해결책을 제시하고 있는 (A)가 정답이다.

토익 분석

(B)는 노상 주차로 인해 주차 위반 딱지를 받을 수 있다는 점을 인정하는 Yes란 긍정 답변과 종종 근처 공원으로 산책을 간다는 부연 설명이 서로 연관성이 없는 내용이자 질문의 park를 반복하여 제시하는 동일 어휘 함정이 포함된 오답이며, (C)는 인터넷을 통해 표를 주문했다는 내용으로 질문의 ticket을 중복하여 들려주는 동일 어휘 오답일 뿐 이는 노상 주차로 인해 주차 위반 딱지를 받을 수 있다는 문제점에 대한 해결책이 될 순 없다. 여기서 주의할 점은 PART 2의 질문 속에 사용된 단어가 보기에 중복 사용되어 오답이 될 경우에는 대체로 그 단어가 '다의어'로 의미가 바뀌어 사용된다는 점이다. 예를 들어 'Park; 주차하다, 공원'과 같이 두 가지 의미를 지녀 질문에서는 '주차하다'의 뜻이고 보기에서는 '공원'의 의미로 사용될 경우 오답이 되는 것이다. 간혹 보기에 Park가 중복되었음에도 정답이 되는 경우는 질문과 보기에서 같은 의미로 활용된 경우가 된다.

16

Did you fully read over the new contract?

(A) Sorry. I didn't bring a pen with me.
(B) Yes, I'll contact her this afternoon.
(C) Yes, but there are some clauses I don't understand.

문제 해설

새로운 계약서를 읽어 봤는지 여부를 묻는 일반의문문으로 이에 새로운 계약서를 읽어 봤음을 뜻하는 Yes란 답변에 이어 이해할 수 없는 몇몇 조항들이 있다는 문제점을 제시하고 있는 (C)가 정답이다.

토익 분석

(A)는 미안하다고 사과하는 Sorry라는 답변과 펜을 가지고 오지 않았다는 부연 설명이 서로 연관성이 없는 내용으로 오답이며, (B) 역시 새로운 계약서를 읽었음을 뜻하는 Yes란 답변과 그녀에게 오후에 연락할 것이란 부연 설명이 서로 상관없는 내용으로 구성되었을 뿐만 아니라 질문의 contract와 유사한 발음의 contact를 이용한 유사 발음 어휘 오답이라 할 수 있다. 이 문제에서 유용한 팁은 PART 2 문제는 but이 사용되는 보기는 질문 속에서 들린 단어가 중복 사용되지 않는다면 정답 확률이 99% 된다는 점이다. 유용한 포인트니 반드시 기억하자.

★★★ 일반의문문

새로운 계약서를 모두 읽어 보셨나요?
(A) 미안해요. 제가 펜을 가져오질 않았어요.
(B) 네, 오늘 오후에 그녀에게 연락해 볼게요.
(C) 네, 하지만 제가 이해할 수 없는 몇몇 조항들이 있더라고요.

어휘 contact ~에게 연락하다 clause 조항

17

Will this parcel reach New York by the end of the week?

(A) No, it'll arrive early next week.
(B) Yes, I think New York is a great city.
(C) You can pick it up in the baggage claim area.

문제 해설

소포가 주말까지 New York에 도착할 수 있는지 여부를 묻는 일반의문문이다. 이에 소포가 주말까지 도착할 수 없음을 뜻하는 No라는 부정 답변에 이어 다음 주 초에 도착할 것이란 부가 정보를 제시하고 있는 (A)가 정답이다.

토익 분석

(B)는 소포가 주말까지 도착할 것을 뜻하는 Yes란 긍정 답변과 New York이 대단한 도시라는 부연 설명이 서로 무관한 내용이자 질문의 New York을 중복하여 들려주는 동일 어휘 오답이며, 수하물 인수 지역에서 가져갈 수 있다고 대답하는 (C) 역시 질문에 적절하지 않은 내용의 답변이자 질문의 parcel을 통해 연상할 수 있는 pick up과 baggage claim area를 이용한 연상 어휘 오답이다.

★★ 일반의문문

이 소포가 이번 주말까지 New York에 도착할 수 있을까요?
(A) 아니요, 다음 주 초에 도착할 겁니다.
(B) 네, New York은 대단한 도시라 생각해요.
(C) 당신은 수하물 인수 지역에서 그것을 가져갈 수 있어요.

어휘 parcel 소포 reach ~에 도착하다, ~에 도달하다
baggage claim area 수하물 인수 지역

18

It was a great first day, and we're looking forward to the rest of the trip.

(A) He is one of the most famous movie stars.
(B) You'll have even more fun tomorrow.
(C) Yes, I should get some rest.

★★ 평서문

정말 재미있었던 첫째 날이었고요. 저희는 남은 여행도 기대가 큽니다.
(A) 그는 가장 유명한 영화배우 중 한 명이에요.
(B) 내일은 더 재미있을 겁니다.
(C) 네, 저는 휴식을 취해야 합니다.

어휘 look forward to ~를 기대하다, ~를 바라다
get some rest 휴식을 취하다

재미있었던 첫날이고 남은 여행도 기대가 크다는 의견 및 기대를 밝히고 있는 평서문으로 이에 내일은 더 재미있을 것이라며 우회적으로 첫날이 재미있었음을 동의함과 동시에 이후 일정이 더 즐거울 것이란 정보를 언급하고 있는 (B)가 정답이다.

토익 분석

(A)의 경우 질문 속에 사람 이름이나 직책이 등장하지 않았기 때문에 인칭 대명사인 he가 사용될 수 없으므로 오답이다. (C)는 첫날이 재미있었음을 인정하는 Yes란 긍정 답변은 좋았으나 휴식을 취해야 한다고 말하는 내용은 질문과 상관없는 내용이다. 또한 질문의 rest(나머지-휴식)를 중복하여 제시하는 동일 어휘 함정이 포함된 오답이 되겠다. 이 문제의 핵심이자 PART 2에서 많이 활용되는 팁은 질문 속에 사람 이름이나 직책이 들리지 않았다면 he, she, her, him이 들리는 보기는 무조건 오답이라는 것이다.

19

★★★ 권유, 제안, 요청

점심을 사다 먹을까요?
(A) 그래요, 요리하고 싶지 않군요.
(B) 죄송하지만, 자리가 있습니다.
(C) 그렇지만 그녀는 너무 바빠요.

어휘 takeout 음식 등을 주문해서 가지고 가는 것
be taken 차지가 되다

Should we order takeout for lunch?

(A) Yes, I don't feel like cooking.
(B) Sorry, this is taken.
(C) But she is so busy.

문제 해설

일반의문문 형태지만 점심을 사다 먹자고 제안하는 '권유, 제안, 요청' 유형의 질문이다. 이에 대해 긍정 답변과 더불어 음식하기 싫으니 사다 먹자고 우회적으로 답변하는 (A)가 정답이다.

토익 분석

(B)는 질문 속에 사용된 take out의 일부분인 take를 활용한 혼동 보기가 되며 (C)는 but이 등장하여 정답 확률이 높았지만, 질문에서 사람 이름이나 직책명이 들리지 않았기에 she가 사용될 수 없다는 것이 오답의 이유가 된다.

20

★★★ 부정의문문

새로운 사무실을 흰색으로 색칠하는 것이 낫지 않을까요?
(A) 아니요, 그녀는 아주 유명한 예술가예요.
(B) 네, 그게 좋아 보이겠네요.
(C) 네, 이미 그를 만났어요.

어휘 rather 오히려, 차라리, 다소 famous 유명한
look good ~이 좋아 보이다

Wouldn't you rather paint the new office white?

(A) No, she is a very famous artist.
(B) Yes, that would look good.
(C) Yes, I already met him.

문제 해설

새로운 사무실을 흰색으로 도색 하는 것에 대해 묻는 질문에 대해 Yes라는 답변에 이어 그게 좋아 보일 것 같다는 생각을 밝히고 있는 (B)가 정답이다.

토익 분석

(A)는 도색 하는 것에 반대하는 부정 답변 No와 그녀가 유명한 예술가라는 부연 설명은 서로 관련이 없는 내용이고, 질문에 언급되지 않은 특정한 여자를 지칭하는 she라는 인칭 대명사가 등장하는 대명사 오류가 포함된 오답이다. (C) 역시 질문 속에 지칭하는 대상이 존재하지 않음에도 him을 사용한 오답 보기다.

21

Do you plan on flying or driving home for the Christmas holiday?

(A) It's cheaper to go by car.
(B) I think it's a national holiday.
(C) Yes, I plan on going to England.

문제 해설

연휴에 비행기를 타고 집으로 갈 것인지 혹은 자동차를 타고 갈 것인지 묻는 선택의문문으로 이에 차를 몰고 가는 것이 저렴하다며 간접적으로 자동차를 선택하고 있는 (A)가 정답이다.

토익 분석

(B)는 질문의 holidays의 파생어인 holiday를 이용하고 있는 오답일 뿐 국경일임을 뜻하는 내용은 교통수단의 선택과 무관한 내용이며, (C) 역시 선택의문문에서 선호되지 않는 Yes란 답변이 등장하고 있을 뿐만 아니라 질문의 plan on을 반복하여 들려주는 동일 어휘 함정 및 질문의 flying에서 연상이 가능한 England를 이용한 연상 어휘 함정이 복합적으로 등장하는 오답이다.

★★★ 선택의문문

크리스마스 연휴를 맞아 비행기를 타고 집으로 가시나요, 아니면 자동차를 몰고 가시나요?
(A) 차로 몰고 가는 것이 더 저렴해요.
(B) 국가 공휴일인 걸로 알고 있어요.
(C) 네, 저는 영국으로 갈 계획이에요.

어휘 plan on V-ing ~할 계획이에요 national holiday 국경일

22

How did you assemble this chair?

(A) More than an hour.
(B) There was a manual in the box.
(C) It was quite expensive.

문제 해설

의자를 어떻게 조립했는지 방법을 묻는 how 직접의문문에 대해 상자 안에 있던 매뉴얼을 제시하며 질문에 대한 답을 한 (B)가 정답이다.

토익 분석

(A)는 기간으로 기간을 묻는 how long 질문에 대한 답변으로 적합하다. (C)는 상태를 묻는 how 질문에 대한 답변으로 적당하다. 이 문제의 포인트는 how 문제의 경우 방법을 묻는 것인지 상태를 묻는 것인지 빠르게 구별해 내는 능력이 중요하다는 점이다.

★ 직접의문문 how

이 의자를 어떻게 조립하셨나요?
(A) 한 시간 넘게요.
(B) 상자 안에 설명서가 있었어요.
(C) 아주 비쌌어요.

어휘 assemble 조립하다 manual 설명서, 매뉴얼

23

Aren't you meeting Ms. Park at the airport?

(A) The flight's been delayed.
(B) I couldn't meet the deadline.
(C) It is not portable.

문제 해설

Park 씨를 공항에서 만나는 것 아니냐고 확인하는 질문이다. 비행기가 지연되어 만나지 못한다고 우회적으로 부정을 하는 (A)가 정답이다.

★★ 일반의문문

Park 씨를 공항에서 만나시는 것 아닌가요?
(A) 비행기가 지연되었어요.
(B) 제가 마감일을 맞추지 못했어요.
(C) 그것은 휴대용이 아니에요.

어휘 delay 지연시키다 meet the deadline 마감 기한을 맞추다 portable 휴대용의

(B)는 질문 속에 사용된 meet(만나다)를 meet(기한 등을 맞추다)로 중복 사용한 혼동 오답 보기다.
(C)는 질문 속에 사용된 airport의 일부분인 port를 변형한 portable을 사용한 유사 발음 함정을 이용한 오답이다.

24

★★ 평서문

제가 지원서를 출력해야 합니다
(A) 그 파일들은 이미 분류가 되었어요.
(B) 그것은 3일 이내에 구성될 것입니다.
(C) 몇 개의 사본이 필요하신지요?

어휘 print out 출력하다 application form 지원서
sort out 분류하다, 정리하다 copy 사본

I need to print out some application forms.

(A) The files are already sorted out.
(B) It'll be formed within three days.
(C) How many copies do you need?

문제 해설

지원서를 출력해야 함을 말하는 평서문이지만 실제 의도는 출력을 부탁하는 권유, 제안, 요청 유형의 문제이다. 이에 대해 몇 부가 필요하냐고 반문하는 (C)가 정답이 된다.

토익 분석

(A)는 application form(지원서)에서 연상 가능한 file을 이용한 연상 단어 오류를 포함한 오답이며 (B)는 질문 속에 사용된 application form의 일부분인 form을 동사로 활용한 미끼용 오답 보기다. PART 2의 경우 다의어를 다른 의미로 중복 사용하여 오답을 만드는 것이 일반적인 패턴임을 기억해야 한다. 또한, 암기해 두면 두고두고 유용한 포인트 중 하나로 PART 2에서 질문과 관계없이 보기가 '의문문'의 형태로 구성되어 있을 경우 정답 확률이 90% 이상이 된다. 물론 질문 속에 사용된 단어를 이용한 오답용 중복 단어가 있을 경우를 제외한 경우에만 해당한다.

25

★★ 직접의문문

이 프로그램에 어떻게 등록을 하나요?
(A) 금요일까지 등록이 가능합니다.
(B) Smith 씨에게 문의해 보세요.
(C) 그럼요, 당신의 이름을 적으셔야 합니다.

어휘 register for 등록하다, 신청하다 write down 적다, 쓰다

How should I register for this program?

(A) Registration is opened till Friday.
(B) You'd better ask Mr. Smith.
(C) Sure, you should write your name down.

문제 해설

등록 방법을 묻는 how 직접의문문에 대하여 Smith 씨에게 문의하라고 우회적으로 모른다는 사실을 밝히는 (B)가 정답이다.

토익 분석

(A)의 경우 질문에 사용된 register for를 변형한 registration을 활용한 오답 보기가 된다. (C)의 경우 Sure는 주로 '권유, 제안, 요청' 유형에 대한 답변으로 적합하므로 오답임을 알 수 있다. 이 문제에서 기억하면 도움이 될 포인트는 바로 '누구에게 물어봐라, ~을 확인해 봐라'와 같은 내용의 보기는 PART 2에서 정답 확률이 거의 100%임을 기억하자. 질문과 보기를 이해하지 못했을 경우 일한 내용의 보기가 등장한다면 주저하지 말고 정답으로 선택하자.

26

Can't we get better seats than these?

(A) We'll be sitting here.
(B) I reserved them last Monday.
(C) Sorry, the front rows are fully booked.

문제 해설

더 좋은 좌석을 요청하는 질문에 대해 좌석들이 이미 예약이 찼다고 밝히는 (C)가 정답이다.

토익 분석

(A) 질문 속의 seat의 유사 발음인 sit을 활용한 유사 발음 오류를 이용한 오답이다. (B)의 경우 seat에서 연상 가능한 reserve를 이용한 연상 단어 오류이다. 권유, 제안, 요청 질문에 대한 부정 답변의 경우 I'm sorry, I'm afraid, No thanks, 긍정 but ~. 구문을 이용한다는 것 역시 암기해 둬야 한다.

★★ 권유, 제안, 요청 유형

이 좌석들보다 좀 더 좋은 자리를 얻을 수 없을까요?
(A) 우리는 이곳에 앉을 것입니다.
(B) 제가 지난 월요일에 예약했습니다.
(C) 죄송합니다, 앞줄은 전부 예약이 꽉 찼습니다.

어휘 reserve 예약하다 fully 완전히 be booked 예약이 된

27

Why did Mr. Kim leave this area blank?

(A) I'm sure it was a mistake.
(B) Yes, he left already.
(C) This is a prohibited area.

문제 해설

왜 근무 지역을 지키지 않고 비워 두었냐는 질책성 질문에 대하여 실수로 그랬을 것이라고 핑계를 대는 (A)가 정답이다.

토익 분석

(B) 질문에 사용된 leave는 근무 지역을 비워 두었다는 의미로 사용된 단어지만 이를 변형하여 '퇴근하다'의 의미로 left 사용한 오답 보기가 된다. (C)의 경우 질문 속에 this area를 변형하여 중복 사용한 오답 보기가 된다. PART 2에서 질문 속에 사용된 '덩어리 단어'를 일부만 사용하거나 분리해서 사용하는 보기는 대체로 오답 보기임을 기억해야 한다.

★ 직접의문문

Kim 씨는 왜 이 담당 구역을 비워 뒀나요?
(A) 실수였을 거라고 생각해요.
(B) 네, 그는 이미 떠났습니다.
(C) 이 지역은 금지 구역입니다.

어휘 leave sth blank (장소)를 비워 두다 leave 떠나다 prohibit 금지하다

28

Are you still working on the computer?

(A) Do you want to go for a walk?
(B) You go ahead.
(C) He is working for Ms. Lee.

문제 해설

상대방에게 컴퓨터 사용이 끝났는지 묻는 일반의문문에 대해 '사용하세요'라고 우회적으로 모두 사용했음을 말하는 (B)가 정답이 된다.

★ 일반의문문

그 컴퓨터를 계속 사용하는 것인가요?
(A) 산책하러 가실래요?
(B) 사용하세요.
(C) 그는 Lee 씨를 위해 일을 합니다.

어휘 work on 작업하다 go for a walk 산책하러 가다 work for ~를 위해 일하다, ~에 소속되어 근무하다

(A)는 PART 2에서 정답으로 자주 등장하는 의문문 형태를 취하고 있지만, work의 유사 발음인 walk를 사용한 오답 보기가 된다. (C)의 경우 질문 속에 사람 이름이나 직책이 등장하지 않았으므로 He가 누구를 지칭하는지 알 수 없기에 오답이다. PART 2에서 질문 속에 '사람 이름이나 직책'이 들리지 않았다면 'he, she, her, him'이 등장하는 보기는 무조건 오답 처리해야 한다는 것을 기억하자.

29

★★★ 평서문

저는 지출 보고서를 받지 못했습니다.
(A) 그것은 출장이었습니다.
(B) 네, 그것들은 비쌌어요.
(C) 제가 최대한 빨리 넘겨 드릴게요.

어휘 expense report 지출 보고서　hand over 건네주다

I didn't get the expense report yet.

(A) It was a business trip.
(B) Yes, they were expensive.
(C) I'll hand it over as soon as possible.

문제 해설

지출 보고서를 받지 못했다는 평서문이다. 평서문이지만 실제로 지출 보고서를 달라는 요청에 가깝다. 이에 대해 최대한 빨리 주겠다고 답한 (C)가 정답이다.

토익 분석

(A)는 목적이나 이유를 묻는 질문에 대한 답변으로 적합하며 (B)는 질문 속에 사용된 expense의 변형단어인 expensive를 활용한 오답 보기가 된다.

30

★ 직접의문문

이 프로젝트의 책임자가 누구인가요?
(A) 그 배터리가 충전되지 않았어요.
(B) B 회의실에서요.
(C) 아직 결정되지 않았어요.

어휘 be in charge of ~에 대해 책임을 지다　charge 충전하다

Who's in charge of this project?

(A) The battery isn't charged.
(B) In Conference Room B.
(C) We haven't decided yet.

문제 해설

책임자가 누구인지 묻는 who 직접의문문에 대해 아직 결정되지 않아 알 수 없다고 답한 (C)가 정답이다.

토익 분석

(A)는 질문 속에 be in charge에 사용된 다의어 charge를 다른 의미로 중복 사용한 오답이 된다. (B)는 명확하게 where 질문에 답변임을 알 수 있다. 암기해야 할 또 하나의 중요 포인트는 PART 2 보기에 '결정되지 않았다'는 내용이 등장할 경우 질문에 관계없이 정답이 된다는 점을 기억해 두면 매우 유용하다.

31

How did yesterday's meeting go?

(A) I went there by taxi.
(B) I also missed it.
(C) I'm meeting Mr. White.

문제 해설

미팅의 결과를 묻는 how 직접의문문이다. how go만 듣고 어떻게 갔는지 교통수단이 등장한 (A)를 선택하게끔 의도된 문제이다. how did sth go는 무엇이 어땠는지 결과를 묻는 질문이다. 이에 대해 자신도 참석을 못해 모른다고 답한 (B)가 정답이다.

토익 분석

(A)는 how질문 중 '교통수단'을 묻는 질문에 대한 답변으로 적합하다. (C)는 질문 속에 사용된 meeting을 중복 사용한 오답이다.

★★★ 직접의문문

어제 미팅이 어떻게 되었나요?
(A) 택시로 갔습니다.
(B) 저도 참석을 못했습니다.
(C) 저는 White 씨를 만납니다.

어휘 how did sth go ~결과가 어떻게 되었나요?
miss 불참하다, 놓치다

남 안녕하세요. [32] Miami 행 제일 빠른 비행기 편을 예약하고 싶습니다. 일등석이면 좋겠습니다.

여 [33] 죄송합니다. 저녁 7시 비행기 좌석이 좀 남았는데 [33] 일등석 좌석은 없습니다. .

남 유감이군요. 그렇다면 예약 가능한 좌석 중 선택을 해야겠군요. 비행 중 기내식이 제공되나요?

여 네, 추가 비용 10달러를 내시면 점심을 드실 수 있습니다. 무료 기내식을 즐기시려면 [34] 저희 항공사 멤버십에 가입하기 위한 서류를 작성하시면 됩니다.

남 그것 좋군요. [34] 지금 제가 등록하겠습니다.

Questions 32-34 refer to the following conversation.

M Hi, [32] I'd like to book a ticket for the earliest flight to Miami. It'd be great if I could get a first-class seat.

W [33] I'm sorry. We do have some seats left for the 7 P.M. flight, [33] but we don't have any more first-class seats available.

M That's too bad. Then I'll just have to choose from the seats that are available. Are any meals provided during the flight?

W You can have lunch if you pay an extra $10. If you want to enjoy complimentary meals on our flights, [34] you can fill in a form to sign up for our airline membership.

M That sounds good. [34] Let me sign up right now.

어휘 book a ticket 표를 예약하다 first-class seat 일등석 available 이용 가능한 provide a meal 식사를 제공하다 complimentary 무료의 sign up for 신청하다, 가입하다

32

★ 도입부 정보

대화가 이루어지는 장소는 어디인가?
(A) 도서관에서   (B) 공항에서
(C) 극장에서   (D) 동물원에서

어휘 take place 개최되다

토익 분석

대화가 이루어지는 장소와 정보는 대화 초반부에 장소 관련 단어들이 힌트로 등장한다

Where is the conversation taking place?

(A) At a library   **(B) At an airport**
(C) At a theater   (D) At a zoo

문제 해설

첫 번째 남자 대화에서 'I'd like to book a ticket for the earliest flight.'와 first-class seat에서 공항임을 예상할 수 있다. 따라서 (B)가 정답이다.

33

★★ 문제점

여자가 사과하는 이유는 무엇인가?
(A) 모든 일등석 좌석 예약이 찼다.
(B) 비행편이 지연되었다.
(C) 일부 좌석들이 이용 가능하다.
(D) 기내식이 제공되지 않는다.

어휘 apologize 사과하다

토익 분석

문제점은 주로 반전 표현 및 의도를 나타내는 표현들이 답을 제시한다. 여자의 첫 번째 대화에서 'I'm sorry.'와 but이 답의 힌트이다.

Why does the woman apologize?

(A) All the first-class seats are booked.
(B) The flight has been delayed.
(C) Some seats are unavailable.
(D) Meals aren't provided on the flight.

문제 해설

여자가 사과하는 이유는 뭔가 문제가 생겼기 때문임을 알 수 있으며 Part 3에서 문제점은 언제나 대화 속 초반부에 힌트가 등장한다. but 뒤에 이어지는 문장에서 we don't have any more first-class seats available이라고 말하고 있으므로 (A)가 정답이 된다.

34

★★ 미래 행동

남자가 다음에 할 행동은 무엇인가?
(A) 다음 비행 편을 예약한다.
(B) 좌석을 업그레이드한다.
(C) 이메일을 보낸다.
(D) 서류를 작성한다.

어휘 book a ticket 표를 예약하다

토익 분석

미래 행동을 묻는 문제로 대개 대화문의 후반부에 답이 등장한다. 요청, 제안 표현인 You can~이 정답 힌트이다.

What will the man most likely do next?

(A) Book a ticket for the next flight   (B) Upgrade his seat
(C) Send an e-mail   **(D) Complete a form**

문제 해설

남자가 무엇을 할지 상대방의 대화에서 힌트가 제시되고 있다. 여자의 대화에서 you can과 같은 전형적인 요청, 제안 힌트(you can fill in the form to sign up for our airline membership)가 답을 제시하고 있다. 이에 대해 남자가 바로 가입을 하겠다(Let me sign up right now)고 동의를 했다. 따라서 서류를 작성하겠다고 답한 (D)가 정답이 된다.

Questions 35-37 refer to the following conversation.

M Hi, Anne. I got your message saying that you'll finish the report tomorrow. [35] But I have a meeting with Joseph today, and… I need to show him the report today.

W Well, it's almost done. However, I'm not quite sure about the analysis of our test group on the report. It mentions that only twelve teenagers will be volunteering for the test. [36] That won't be enough for us to gather any data with this test group. We'll need to make some changes.

M Oh, why wasn't I informed of this? There isn't much time left to make any changes to the project. [37] I'll have to talk about that change being implemented in our second test. We'll have to run the test with this limited number, and then conduct a second test to get more data.

어휘 get the message 메시지를 받다 analysis 분석 mention 언급하다 volunteer 자원하다 gather data 데이터를 수집하다 inform 알리다 implement 이행하다 limited 제한된

남 안녕하세요, Anne. 당신이 내일 보고서를 마무리할 거라는 메시지를 제가 받았어요. [35] 그런데 오늘 제가 Joseph과 미팅을 진행할 예정인데… 제가 Joseph에게 오늘 그 보고서를 보여 줘야 해서요.

여 거의 마무리가 되어가요. 그러나 그 보고서에 저희 실험 그룹에 대한 분석 부분은 확실치가 않아요. 오직 십대 12명만 테스트에 지원할 거라 하는데, [36] 이 하나의 실험군에서 얻을 수 있는 데이터가 충분하지 않을 듯 해요. 저희는 약간의 조정이 필요합니다.

남 오, 왜 제가 이 사실에 대해 통보받지 못했죠? 이 프로젝트를 조정하기에는 시간적 여유가 없습니다. [37] 두 번째 테스트에서 조정하는 것에 관해 얘기해야 할 것 같습니다. 제한된 인원으로만 이번 실험을 시행해야만 합니다 그리고 더 많은 데이터를 얻기위해 두 번째 실험을 시행 할 수 밖에요.

35

Why does the man say, "I need to show him the report today"?

(A) To request a document from the woman
(B) To ask for help on a project
(C) To invite the woman to a meeting
(D) To show the result of a test

문제 해설

남자는 여자가 내일까지 보고서 마무리할 것을 아는 상태에서 오늘 Joseph과의 미팅에서 보고서를 보여 줘야 한다고 했다. 즉 보고서를 하루 당겨 보여달라고 요청하는 상황으로 정답은 (A)가 된다.

★★★ 맥락 파악

왜 남자는 "I need to show him the report today."라고 말하는가?
(A) 여자로부터 서류를 요청하기 위하여
(B) 프로젝트에 도움을 요청하기 위하여
(C) 여자를 미팅에 초대하기 위하여
(D) 실험 결과를 보여 주기 위하여

어휘 request 요청하다

토익 분석

앞뒤 문장의 흐름(flow)을 정확히 파악해야만 한다. 반전 표현 **but**이 힌트이다.

36

What does the woman say about the test group?

(A) It didn't affect the test result.   (B) It was changed after the test.
(C) It was not arranged yet.   **(D) It had fewer people than expected.**

문제 해설

세부 정보를 찾는 문제로 여자의 대사 키워드에 test group과 반전 표현인 however를 유의해서 봐야 한다. 이어지는 문장인 'That won't be enough for us to gather any data with this test group. We'll need to make some changes.'에서 하나의 그룹에서 수집할 수 있는 데이터가 충분치 않다고 말하고 있으므로 예상한 것보다 부족한 인원이라는 것을 유추해 볼 수 있다. 따라서 (D)가 정답이 된다.

★★ 세부 정보 찾기

여자가 실험 그룹에 대해 뭐라고 말하고 있나?
(A) 실험 결과에 영향을 미치지 않았다.
(B) 실험 이후에 변경됐다.
(C) 아직 준비되지 않았다.
(D) 예상했던 것보다 적다.

어휘 affect 영향을 미치다 arrange 준비하다

토익 분석

세부 정보 찾기는 키워드를 활용하는 문제이다. 키워드는 **Test group**이며 반전 표현 **however** 역시 중요 힌트이다.

37

What will the man discuss next time?

(A) Hiring a new employee   (B) Complaining to a client
(C) Arranging more tests   (D) Adding a new facility

문제 해설

대화 후반부 남자 대화 속에 미래 행동의 답변을 이끄는 표현인 I'll이 답을 제시하고 있다. 'I'll have to talk about that change being implemented in our second test.'에서 남자가 다음 테스트에 변화를 주는 것에 대해 얘기한다 했으니 더 많은 실험을 준비한다고 말한 (C)가 정답이 된다.

★★ 미래 행동

남자는 이후 무엇을 논의할 것인가?
(A) 새로운 직원을 채용하는 것
(B) 고객에게 불만을 표하는 것
(C) 더 많은 실험을 준비하는 것
(D) 새로운 설비를 추가하는 것

어휘 complain 불만을 표하다 facility 시설, 기관

토익 분석

미래 행동을 묻는 문제로 대화문의 후반부에 답이 제시된다. I'll이 정답 힌트이다.

남 어떻게 지내요, Grace? [38] 제가 듣기로는 세미나가 취소되었다고 하던데요. 당신에게는 분명 안심이 되는 일일 거예요.

여 저는 상당히 기뻐요. 우리는 그 행사를 취소해야 했어요. [39] 업계에서 풍부한 경험이 있는 연설자들을 충분히 찾을 수가 없었어요.

남 저, 우리는 최첨단의 기술을 가지고 일하고 있어요. [40] 제가 예전에 저를 가르쳐 주셨던 교수님들께 연락해서 연설을 하실 수 있는지 알아봐 드릴 수 있어요.

여 실은, 그렇게 되면 좋을 거 같아요. 제가 위원회를 조직하고 있는데, 목표가 세미나를 겨울 중에 개최하는 거예요.

남 [40] 알겠어요. 제가 교수님들께 이메일을 보낼게요. 그리고 다른 회사에도 이리저리 알아볼게요.

Questions 38-40 refer to the following conversation.

M How's it going, Grace? [38] I hear that the seminar has been canceled. That must be a relief for you.

W I am quite glad. We had to cancel it, though. [39] We couldn't find enough speakers with sufficient experience in the field.

M Well, we are working with some cutting-edge technology. [40] I can contact some of my old professors and see if they would like to speak.

W That would be great, actually. I am organizing a committee, and our goal is to have the seminar sometime in winter.

M [40] OK. I'll send them an e-mail. Also, I'll ask around at some other companies.

어휘 relief 안심, 안도 though (문장 끝이나 중간에서) 하지만 sufficient (능력이) 충분한 field 업계, 분야 cutting-edge 최첨단의 contact ~에게 연락하다 professor 교수 see if ~인지 알아보다 organize ~을 조직하다 committee 위원회 ask around 이리저리 알아보다

38

★ 주제, 목적

남자의 말에 따르면, 무슨 일이 있었는가?
(A) 휴가 일정이 업데이트되었다.
(B) 위원회가 구성되었다.
(C) 세미나가 취소되었다.
(D) 사무실 규정이 변경되었다.

어휘 form 구성되다, 형성되다 protocol 규정, 규약

토익 분석

지문의 첫 번째 문제에서 발생한 사건을 묻는 것은 주제, 목적 문제이다. 언급된 남자의 첫 번째 대화문에 집중하자.

According to the man, what has happened?

(A) A vacation schedule has been updated.
(B) A committee has been formed.
(C) A seminar has been canceled.
(D) An office protocol has changed.

문제 해설

남자의 말에서 무슨 일이 있었는지를 파악하는 첫 번째 질문이므로 대화 초반부에 제시되는 남자 대사를 중점적으로 파악해야 한다. 남자는 대화를 시작하면서 'I hear that the seminar has been canceled.'라는 말로 세미나가 취소된 것에 대해 언급하고 있으므로 (C)가 정답이 된다.

39

★★ 문제점

여자는 무슨 문제점을 언급하는가?
(A) 예산이 충분하지 않다.
(B) 연설자가 충분하지 않았다.
(C) 위치를 찾을 수 없었다.
(D) 자신의 프로젝트가 준비되지 않았다.

어휘 budget 예산 sufficient 충분하다 location 위치, 지점

토익 분석

대화 중반부에서 문제점과 관련해 여자가 언급하는 부정적인 정보에 집중하자.

What problem does the woman mention?

(A) A budget was not sufficient.
(B) There weren't enough speakers.
(C) She could not find a location.
(D) Her project was not ready.

문제 해설

여자는 대화 중반부에 'We couldn't find enough speakers with sufficient experience in the field.'라는 말로 충분한 연설자를 찾지 못했다고 알리고 있으므로 이에 대해 언급한 (B)가 정답이다.

40

★★★ 요청제안

남자는 무엇을 제안하는가?
(A) 동료 직원의 프로젝트를 끝내겠다.
(B) 자신의 휴가를 취소하겠다.
(C) 콘퍼런스에 참석하겠다.
(D) 몇몇 전문가들에게 연락하겠다.

어휘 coworker 동료 attend 참여하다 professional 전문가

토익 분석

요청 제안 문제는 주로 후반부에 힌트가 있다. 'I can~, If 가정법' 문장이 정답 힌트이다.

What does the man offer to do?

(A) Finish a coworker's project   (B) Cancel a vacation
(C) Attend a conference   **(D) Contact some professionals**

문제 해설

남자가 하겠다고 말한 일을 묻는 질문으로, 대화 후반부에 제시된다. 남자는 I can contact some of my old professors and see if they would like to speak라고 말한 후 대화 마지막에 'OK. I'll send them an e-mail. Also, I'll ask around at some other companies.'라며 자신이 교수들에게 연락하겠다고 말하고 있으며, 이를 '전문가'를 뜻하는 'professionals'로 바꿔 말한 (D)가 정답이다.

Questions 41-43 refer to the following conversation with three speakers.

W It's great to finally sit down with members of our European branch. Has business been going well?

M1 [41] Indeed it has. We have contracts with suppliers in several different countries, and the trade agreements have been benefitting us.

M2 Tony is right. Opening the corporation for international business was surely a good move. I look forward to growing the business.

W I'm glad to hear it. It may be too soon to propose, but [42] based on your success, I want to start drawing up plans to also expand in Asia.

M1 That's maybe a little too ambitious. [43] I think we should concentrate on our European operations for a while.

M2 [43] Yes. For now, I believe it would be better to just secure more contracts in Europe and the United States.

여 마침내 우리 유럽 지사의 직원들과 함께하게 돼서 기뻐요. 사업은 잘되어 가고 있나요?

남1 [41] 사실 잘되고 있습니다. 여러 다른 국가에 있는 공급 업체와 계약을 맺은 상태이고, 사업 협정이 우리에게 혜택이 되어 왔어요.

남2 Tony의 말이 맞아요. 해외 사업을 위해 회사를 여는 것은 분명 좋은 계기였어요. 저는 사업이 성장해 나가길 고대하고 있어요.

여 그 얘기를 들으니 기쁘네요. 제안을 하기에는 너무 이른 것일 수도 있지만, [42] 여러분의 성공을 기반으로 저는 아시아에서도 사업을 확장하는 계획을 그려 보는 걸 시작해 보고 싶어요.

남1 그건 어쩌면 조금 많이 의욕이 지나친 일 같아요. [43] 제 생각에 우리는 한동안은 유럽에서의 사업에 집중해야 해요.

남2 [43] 네. 현재로서는, 유럽과 미국에서 더 많은 계약을 확보하는 게 더 나은 일이라고 생각해요.

어휘 branch 지사, 지점 go well 잘 되어 가다 indeed 사실은 contract 계약(서) supplier 공급업체 trade agreement 사업 협정, 무역 협정 benefit ~에게 혜택이 되다 corporation 기업 surely 분명 move 움직임 look forward to -ing ~하기를 고대하다 too A to do ~하기에는 너무 A하다 propose 제안하다 based on ~을 기반으로 draw up a plan 계획을 세우다 expand 확장하다 ambitious 의욕이 넘치는 concentrate on ~에 집중하다 operation 사업, 경영 for now 지금으로선, 당분간은 secure ~을 확보하다

41

What do the men imply about the business?

(A) It was recently formed.   **(B) It is becoming successful.**
(C) It extended its product line.   (D) It opened a new factory.

문제 해설

키워드 business가 제시되는 대화에서 'Indeed it has. We have contracts with suppliers in several different countries, and the trade agreements have been benefiting us.'라는 말로 여러 회사와 계약도 맺고 잘 진행되는 것을 알리므로 이를 'successful'이라는 말로 표현한 (B)가 정답이다.

★★★ 암시 추론

남자들은 회사에 관해 무엇을 암시하는가?
(A) 최근에 설립되었다.   (B) 성공하고 있다.
(C) 제품 라인을 확대했다.   (D) 새로운 공장을 열었다.

어휘 recently 최근에 form ~을 설립하다, 구성하다 successful 성공적인 extend ~을 확대하다, 늘이다

토익 분석

암시 추론 문제로 질문 속에 키워드가 제시되는 경우가 많다. 질문 속에 언급된 business가 키워드이다.

42

What does the woman want to do?

(A) Improve a production process   (B) Train some employees
(C) Revise a budget   **(D) Continue an expansion**

문제 해설

여자가 원하는 일을 묻는 두 번째 문제이므로 대화 중반부에서 의도 표현을 여자 대화에서 듣는다 '~ based on your success, I want to start drawing up plans to also expand in Asia.'라는 말로 다른 지역으로도 사업을 확장하는 계획에 대해 언급하고 있으므로 (D)가 정답임을 알 수 있다.

★★★ 의도 파악

여자는 무엇을 하고 싶어 하는가?
(A) 생산 절차를 개선하는 일 (B) 직원들을 교육하는 일
(C) 예산을 수정하는 일   (D) 사업 확장을 지속하는 일

어휘 improve ~을 개선하다 revise ~을 수정하다 budget 예산 expansion 확대, 확장

토익 분석

의도, 미래 행동 표현인 I want to가 힌트이다.

43

What do the men suggest doing?

(A) Opening a new branch   **(B) Getting more contracts**
(C) Relocating the business   (D) Canceling a meeting

문제 해설

남자들이 제안하는 일을 묻는 세 번째 질문으로 대화 후반부에 남자 대화에서 요청 제안 표현을 들어야 한다. 'I believe it would be better to just secure more contracts in Europe and the United States.'라는 말로 더 많은 계약을 따내는 것이 우선시되는 일이라고 알리고 있으므로 (B)가 정답이다.

★★ 요청, 제안

남자들은 무엇을 제안하는가?
(A) 새로운 지사를 여는 일 (B) 더 많은 계약을 따내는 일
(C) 회사를 이전하는 일   (D) 회의를 취소하는 일

어휘 relocate ~을 이전하다 cancel ~을 취소하다

토익 분석

요청 제안 문제는 주로 후반부에 힌트가 나온다. 이 문제는 it would be better가 정답 힌트이다.

여 안녕하세요. [44] 제가 아까 아침에 전화했었는데, 제가
  통화한 남자분이 말하기를 오늘 저녁 시간이 바쁘지
  만 빈 테이블이 있을 거라고 했어요. 제가 나중에 다
  시 전화하기를 권해 주셨어요.

남 일부 예약 취소가 있었기 때문에 예약을 도와 드릴
  수 있습니다. [45] 어느 분 성함으로 예약해 드릴까요?

여 Quinn이라는 이름으로 예약해 주세요. 7시에 6명이
  앉을 수 있는 자리로 해 주시겠어요?

남 네. 고객님의 예약이 확정되었음을 알려 드리게 되어
  기쁩니다. 일행분들과 함께 특별 메뉴에서 주문하실
  건가요? 그러시다면, 제공되는 양이 제한됩니다.

여 [46] 좋은 질문이네요. 다른 사람들에게 물어보고 다시
  전화 드릴게요.

Questions 44-46 refer to the following conversation.

W Good afternoon. [44] I called earlier in the morning, and the man I spoke
   to said that you were busy tonight but there might be an open table. He
   suggested that I call back again later.

M We have had some cancellations, so we should be able to make the
   reservation. [45] What name should I put the reservation under?

W Please reserve it under the name Quinn. Can I get a table for six people at
   7 P.M.?

M Yes. I'm happy to tell you that your reservation has been confirmed. Will
   your party be ordering from the special menu? If so, supply is limited.

W [46] That's a good question. I will ask the others and call you back.

어휘 open table 빈 테이블 suggest that 제안하다 cancellation 취소 make a reservation 예약하다 put the
reservation under A A라는 이름으로 예약하다 reserve ~을 예약하다 confirm 확인하다 party 일행 supply 제공
(량) limited 제한된

44

★★ 주제, 목적

여자는 왜 전화를 거는가?
(A) 예약을 하기 위해
(B) 저녁 식사를 취소하기 위해
(C) 메뉴에 관해 물어보기 위해
(D) 초청장을 발송하기 위해

어휘 extend an invitation 초청장을 보내다

토익 분석

전화한 사람의 첫 번째 대화에 목적이 등장, I called와 반
전 표현 but이 정답 힌트이다.

Why is the woman calling?

(A) To make a reservation
(B) To cancel a dinner
(C) To ask about a menu
(D) To extend an invitation

문제 해설

여자는 'I called earlier in the morning, and the man I spoke to said you were busy tonight,
but there might be an open table. He suggested that I call back again later.'라는 말로 다시 전
화를 거는 이유를 설명하고, 자리 예약 목적으로 (A)가 정답임을 알 수 있다.

45

★ 요청, 제안

남자는 무엇을 요청하는가?
(A) 전화번호   (B) 이메일 주소
(C) 배송 주소   (D) 이름

어휘 shipping 운송, 배송

토익 분석

요청 제안 문제는 주로 후반부에 힌트가 나온다. 단순 정
보를 요청하는 경우이므로 의문문이 정답 힌트이다.

What does the man ask for?

(A) A phone number   (B) An e-mail address
(C) A shipping address   **(D) A name**

문제 해설

남자가 요청하는 일을 묻는 질문으로 대화 중반부에 남자는 예약이 가능하다는 말과 함께 'What
name should I put the reservation under?'라는 말로 예약하는 사람의 이름을 묻고 있으므로 (D)
가 정답이다.

46

★★★ 맥락 파악

여자는 왜 "That's a good question"이라고 말하는가?
(A) 서비스에 대해 화가 나 있다.
(B) 메뉴에 대해 확실하지 않다.
(C) 식사에 대해 기뻐하고 있다.
(D) 제시간에 갈 것이라는 점을 확신하고 있다.

어휘 upset 화가 난, 기분 나쁜 be unsure about ~에 대
해 불확실하다 on time 제시간에, 제때

토익 분석

후반부 여자 대화에 집중하여 흐름을 파악한다. 반전 표
현 대신 단골 답변 표현인 'I will~'이 힌트를 제시한다.

Why does the woman say, "That's a good question"?

(A) She is upset about service.   **(B) She is unsure about a menu.**
(C) She is excited about a meal.   (D) She is sure she will be on time.

문제 해설

여자가 말하는 "That's a good question."라는 표현이 대화에서 어떤 의미로 사용되었는지 묻는 질
문이다. 여자는 대화 후반부에 남자가 메뉴를 선택하는 질문에 대해 'That's a good question. I will
ask the others and call you back.'라고 답하고 있다. 바로 뒤에 이어지는 말로 보아 지금 바로 확실
히 결정할 수 없어 다른 사람들에게 물어봐야 하는 상황임을 알 수 있으므로 (B)가 정답이 된다.

Questions 47-49 refer to the following conversation.

W　⁴⁷ Customer service center. Anna Henderson speaking. How may I help you?

M　Hello, Ms. Henderson. ⁴⁸ I recently purchased a digital camcorder from your store, but I'm having some problems with it. When I try to use the video function, I get an error message on the display screen. I can save videos on the camcorder, but when I try to transfer them to my computer, the files are deleted. Could you advise me on how to fix this problem?

W　Well, several customers have experienced similar problems, so we should be able to help you. ⁴⁹ Please hold a moment while I put you through to our Technical Support Department.

여　⁴⁷ 고객 서비스 센터의 Anna Henderson입니다. 어떻게 도와 드릴까요?

남　안녕하세요, Henderson씨. ⁴⁸ 저는 최근에 당신의 상점에서 디지털 캠코더를 구입했습니다. 그런데 그것에 약간의 문제가 있어요. 캠코더에 비디오를 저장할 수 있는데, 그것들을 컴퓨터로 옮기려고 하면, 파일들이 삭제가 됩니다. 이 문제를 해결하는 방법을 저에게 알려 주시겠어요?

여　글쎄요, 일부 고객님들이 유사한 문제를 겪으셔서, 저희가 고객님을 도와 드릴 수 있습니다. ⁴⁹ 제가 저희 기술지원 부서로 연결해 드리는 동안 잠시 기다려 주세요.

어휘 function 기능　transfer ~을 보내다, ~을 환승하다　delete ~을 삭제하다　experience 겪다　put sby through to ~를 ~로 연결시켜 주다

47

What department does the woman work in?

(A) Shipping　　　　　　　　(B) **Customer Service**
(C) Technical Support　　　　(D) Product Development

문제 해설

여자가 근무하는 부서에 대한 질문으로 대화 초반부 여자의 근무 부서가 직접적으로 언급되는 부분이나 그것을 유추할 수 있는 관련 어휘가 제시되는 부분에 집중하는 것이 중요하다. 여자는 대화 시작과 함께 Customer service center. Anna Henderson speaking이라고 말하며 자신이 고객 서비스 센터에서 근무하고 있음을 직접적으로 밝히고 있다. 따라서 정답은 (B)가 된다.

★ 도입부 정보

여자가 근무하는 부서는 어디인가?
(A) 배송
(B) 고객 서비스
(C) 기술 지원
(D) 제품 개발

어휘 department 부사　shipping 배송

토익 분석

대화가 이루어지는 장소는 대화 초반부에 장소나 직업 관련 단어들이 힌트로 등장한다.

48

What does the man ask for?

(A) Information on refunds
(B) The location of a store
(C) An exchange for a defective item
(D) **A way to repair a technical problem**

문제 해설

남자가 요청하는 것에 관한 질문이므로 남자의 대화 내용에서 제시되는 남자의 요구 사항을 노려 들어야 할 필요가 있다. 따라서 남자가 여자에게 'Could you advise me on how to fix this problem?'라고 말하며 자신이 구매한 제품에서 발생한 결함을 수리할 방법을 알려 달라고 요구하는 부분을 통해 정답은 (D)임을 알 수 있다.

★★ 요청, 제안

남자가 요청하는 것은 무엇인가?
(A) 환불 정보
(B) 상점의 위치
(C) 불량품의 교환
(D) 기술적인 문제를 수리하는 방법

어휘 refund 환불　defective 결함이 있는

토익 분석

요청 제안 문제는 주로 후반부에 힌트가 나온다. 요청 표현인 Could you~?가 정답 힌트이다.

49

What does the woman offer to do?

(A) Send video files　　　　　(B) Arrange an exchange for a product
(C) **Transfer a call**　　　　　(D) Reduce a price

문제 해설

여자의 제안 사항에 대해 묻는 마지막 질문이므로 후반부 여자의 대화 내용에서 여자가 남자에게 제안하는 내용이 나오는 부분에 집중하되 동사를 놓치지 않도록 주의해야 한다. 여자는 대화 말미에서 남자에게 'Please hold on a moment while I put you through to our Technical Support Department.'이라고 말하며 잠시만 대기하면 기술 지원부와 연결해 줄 것을 밝히고 있으므로 정답은 (C)가 된다.

★★★ 요청, 제안

여자가 제안하는 것은 무엇인가?
(A) 영상 파일을 전송하기
(B) 해당 제품의 교환을 주선하기
(C) 담당자에게 전화 연결하기
(D) 가격 할인하기

어휘 offer 제안하다　reduce 할인하다

토익 분석

요청 제안 문제는 주로 후반부에 힌트가 나온다. 요청 표현인 Please 명령문이 힌트로 사용되었다.

남　안녕하세요. ⁵⁰ 이번 주 초에 귀사의 웹 사이트에 게시되었던 공석에 관해 전화 드렸습니다. 이미 그 자리가 채워졌나요?

여　몇몇 면접자가 있기는 했지만, 여전히 지원서를 받는 중입니다. 저희는 적합한 경력을 지닌 분이 필요해요. 인사 업무에 대한 경력이 있으신가요?

남　네. 저는 지난 8년 동안 **Maple Ridge Financial** 사의 인사부에서 근무해 왔습니다만, 제가 이사를 하기 때문에 새로운 직장이 필요합니다.

여　아, 잘될 것 같네요. ⁵¹ 하지만 알아 두셔야 할 게 있어요. 저희는 신입 수준의 연봉밖에 제공하지 않습니다. 그래도 관심이 있으신가요?

남　⁵² 음, 그런 것 같습니다. 저는 곧 일을 시작해야 합니다. 까다롭게 선택할 수 없어요.

Questions 50-52 refer to the following conversation.

M　Hello. ⁵⁰ I am calling about the opening that was posted on your Web site earlier in the week. Have you filled the position yet?

W　We have had a few interviews, but we are still accepting applications. We need someone with adequate experience. Do you have a background in human resources?

M　Yes. I have been working in the HR department of Maple Ridge Financial for the past 8 years, but I am moving and need a new job.

W　Oh, that sounds great. ⁵¹ There is one thing you should know, though. We can only offer a starting-level salary. Are you still interested?

M　⁵² Well, I suppose so. I will need to start working soon. I can't be too picky.

어휘 opening 공석, 빈자리 post ~을 게시하다 fill (자리 등) ~을 채우다 position 직책, 일자리 accept ~을 받아들이다, 접수하다 application 지원(서), 신청(서) adequate 적합한 experience 경력, 경험 background 경력, 배경 human resources 인사(부) though (문장 끝이나 중간에서) 하지만 offer ~을 제공하다 starting level 신입 수준의 interested 관심 있는 I suppose so 그렇게 생각합니다 picky 까다로운

50

★★ 세부 정보

남자는 일자리에 관해 무엇을 물어보는가?
(A) 급여가 얼마인지　(B) 언제 시작할 수 있는지
(C) 휴가가 있는지　(D) 여전히 지원 가능한지

어휘 vacation leave 휴가 whether ~인지 아닌지 available 이용 가능한

토익 분석

세부 정보 찾기는 키워드를 활용한다. **job**이 키워드로 이와 연관된 **opening**과 **position**이 정답 힌트이다.

What does the man ask about the job?

(A) How much it pays　　(B) When he can start
(C) If there is vacation leave　　**(D) Whether it is still available**

문제 해설

남자가 일자리에 관해 무엇을 물어보는지를 파악하도록 요구하는 첫 번째 질문이므로 대화 초반부에서 중점적으로 언급하는 핵심 내용을 파악하는 것이 관건이다. 대화를 시작하면서 남자는 'I am calling about~the position yet?'라는 말로 공고를 낸 자리가 채워졌는지를 묻고 있으므로 (D)가 정답이 된다.

51

★★★ 문제점

여자는 일자리와 관련해 무슨 문제점을 언급하는가?
(A) 빈번한 출장을 포함하고 있다.
(B) 편리하지 않은 곳에 위치해 있다.
(C) 연봉이 꽤 낮다.　(D) 많은 추가 근무를 필요로 한다.

어휘 involve ~을 포함하다 frequent 빈번한 inconvenient 불편한 require ~을 필요로 하다 overtime 추가 근무, 야근

토익 분석

여자 대화에서 문제점을 찾는다. 빈출 정답 힌트; **you should, we can**이 사용된 점을 눈여겨 봐야 한다.

What problem does the woman mention about the job?

(A) It involves frequent traveling.　　(B) It is in an inconvenient location.
(C) Its salary is quite low.　　(D) It requires a lot of overtime.

문제 해설

여자가 언급하는 문제점을 파악하도록 요구하는 두 번째 질문이므로 대화 중반부에서 문제점과 관련해 여자가 언급하는 부정적인 정보에 집중해 들어야 한다. 여자는 대화 중반부에 'There is one thing~still interested?'라는 말로 한 가지 알아 두어야 할 점에 대해 언급한 후 그것이 매우 낮은 수준의 연봉임을 알리고 있으므로 (C)가 정답이다.

52

★★★ 맥락 파악

남자가 "I can't be too picky"라고 말할 때 무엇을 의미하는가?
(A) 그 일자리에 지원하지 않을 것이다.
(B) 선택권이 많지 않다.
(C) 많은 채용 제안을 받았다.
(D) 새로운 주택으로 이사할 것이다.

어휘 apply for ~에 지원하다 option 선택(할 수 있는 것) job offer 채용 제안

토익 분석

제시된 표현의 의도를 묻는 맥락문제의 경우 앞뒤 문장의 흐름(flow)을 정확히 파악해야만 한다.

What does the man mean when he says, "I can't be too picky"?

(A) He will not apply for the job.　　**(B) He does not have many options.**
(C) He has many job offers.　　(D) He is moving to a new house.

문제 해설

남자가 말하는 "I can't be too picky"라는 표현이 대화 속에서 어떤 의미로 사용되었는지를 묻는 세 번째 질문이므로 대화 후반부에 제시되는 남자의 말을 통해 해당 표현을 확인할 수 있어야 한다. 이때 앞뒤에 함께 제시되는 말들을 통해 의미의 흐름을 파악해 정답을 찾아야 한다. 남자는 대화 마지막에 'Well, I suppose so. I will need to start working soon. I can't be too picky.'라는 말로 대화를 마무리하고 있는데, 빨리 일을 시작해야 한다고 말하는 것으로 보아 가능한 한 빨리 일자리를 찾아야 하는 상황임을 알 수 있다. 따라서 선택권이 많지 않다는 의미로 쓰인 (B)가 정답이 된다.

Questions 53-55 refer to the following conversation.

W [53] Jason, I'm having trouble with the June budget. [54] When I enter the numbers into the spreadsheet, the totals don't add up correctly.

M Are you working from the finalized May file?

W Yes, so everything should come out right. Not much has changed since last month. Any idea what the problem might be?

M Sometimes you can manipulate a formula without realizing it. [55] Perhaps you should look at all the formulas and make sure they are set up right. If that doesn't fix it, then send it to me, and I'll play around with it.

어휘 have trouble with ~하는 데 어려움이 있다 enter ~로 들어가다, ~을 입력하다 add up ~을 더하다 finalized 마무리가 된, 최종의 come out ~이 나오다, ~이 출시되다 manipulate ~을 조작하다, ~을 조종하다 play around with ~과 놀다, ~을 손보다

여 [53] Jason 씨, 6월 예산 작업을 하는 데 어려움이 있어요. [54] 제가 스프레드시트에 숫자를 입력하면 총계가 정확하게 계산되지 않아요.

남 마무리가 된 5월 자료부터 작업하고 있나요?

여 네, 그래서 모든 수치가 정확하게 나와야 해요. 지난 달 이후로 바뀐 것이 거의 없어서요. 문제가 발생하는 이유에 대해 생각나는 것이 있나요?

남 간간히 인식하지 못한 상태에서 입력 공식을 조작할 수도 있어요. [55] 모든 입력 공식들을 한 번 살펴보고 그것이 제대로 되어 있는지 확인해 봐야 할 것 같네요. 그래도 제대로 문제점이 수정되지 않는다면, 제게 한 번 보내 보세요. 그러면 제가 그걸 손보도록 할게요.

53

Which department does the woman most likely work for?

(A) Payroll
(B) Accounting
(C) Technical Support
(D) Product Development

★ 도입부 정보

여자는 어느 부서에서 근무할 것 같은가?
(A) 급여
(B) 회계
(C) 기술 지원
(D) 제품 개발

어휘 payroll 급여 accounting 회계

토익 분석

여자가 근무하는 장소는 여자의 첫 번째 대화에 집중한다.

문제 해설

여자의 근무 부서를 유추하는 질문이므로 대화 전반부에서 여자의 근무 부서가 직접적으로 언급되는 부분 혹은 여자의 근무 부서를 추측할 수 있을 만한 관련 어휘나 표현이 제시되는 부분에 집중해야 한다. 대화 시작과 함께 여자가 Jason, I'm having trouble with the June budget이라고 말하며 6월 예산 작업의 어려움을 토로하는 부분을 통해 여자는 회계 부서에서 근무 중임을 가늠할 수 있으므로 정답은 (B)가 된다.

54

What problem does the woman say she has?

(A) Some calculations aren't right.
(B) She has limited time.
(C) Her computer is not working properly.
(D) Some information is currently unavailable.

★★ 문제점

여자는 어떠한 문제점을 언급하고 있는가?
(A) 계산이 정확하지 않다.
(B) 그녀는 시간의 제약을 받고 있다.
(C) 그녀의 컴퓨터가 제대로 작동하지 않는다.
(D) 일부 정보를 현재 사용할 수가 없다.

어휘 calculation 계산 properly 제대로 unavailable 불가능한

토익 분석

이 문제의 경우 여자 대화에서 trouble 이라는 문제점을 언급하는 직접적인 힌트가 되는 단어가 제시되었다.

문제 해설

여자의 문제점을 묻고 있으므로 대화 전반부 여자의 대화 내용에서 등장하는 문제점을 주의 깊게 들어야 한다. 여자는 대화 초반 When I enter the numbers into the spreadsheet, the totals don't add up correctly이라고 말하며 스프레드시트에 숫자를 입력하면 총계가 정확하게 계산되지 않는다는 문제점을 언급하고 있으므로 정답은 (A)임을 알 수 있다. 문제점은 언제나 대화 초반부에 언급된다는 사실을 기억해야 한다.

55

What does the man suggest the woman do?

(A) Call the software engineers
(B) Examine the formulas
(C) Search the Internet for help
(D) Start over from the beginning

★★ 요청, 제안

남자가 여자에게 제안하는 것은 무엇인가?
(A) 소프트웨어 공학자에게 연락한다.
(B) 공식들을 검사한다.
(C) 인터넷 검색을 통해 도움을 받는다.
(D) 처음부터 다시 시작한다.

어휘 examine 조사, 검사하다 formula 공식

토익 분석

요청, 제안 문제이므로 you should라는 정답 힌트가 사용되었다.

문제 해설

남자가 여자에게 제안하는 내용을 묻는 마지막 질문이므로 대화 후반부 남자의 대화 내용에서 동사를 중심으로 여자에게 제안하는 내용을 파악하는 데 집중해야 한다. 남자는 대화 말미에서 여자에게 'Perhaps you should look at all the formulas and make sure they are set up right.'라고 말하며 모든 공식들을 살펴보고 그 공식들에 이상이 없는지 확인해 볼 것을 제안하고 있다. 그러므로 정답은 (B)가 된다.

남　오늘 아침 저희 쇼에 출연해 주신 것에 감사합니다, **Connor** 씨. ^{56,57} 당신의 혁신적인 모발 관리 제품인 **Silk Shine**이 지난달에 출시된 이후로, 엄청난 매출을 기록하고 있습니다. 성공의 비결이 무엇이라 생각하십니까?

여　안녕하세요, 그리고 오늘 쇼에 초청해 주셔서 감사드립니다. 저는 The Morning Brew Talk Show!의 오랜 팬이었습니다. 아시다시피, 제가 모발 관리 산업 분야에서 20년이 넘는 경험을 갖고 있고 Silk Shine을 디자인하는데 수년의 시간을 보냈습니다. 기본적으로 제품 자체가 좋아서 잘 팔린다는 생각이 드네요.

남　⁵⁷ 당신은 창고에서 사업을 시작해서, 현재는 미국 내에 몇몇 제조 공장들과 대략 800개 정도의 지점들을 보유하고 있습니다. 이런 빠른 성공이 당신의 인생에 어떠한 영향을 미쳤나요?

여　⁵⁸ 저는 사람들이 자신의 모발을 관리할 수 있도록 도와주는 일에 굉장히 열정적으로 임했고, 이에 대한 긍정적 반응은 제겐 일종의 축복과도 같습니다. 빠른 변화이긴 하지만 제 가족과 저는 공인으로서 그리고 성공적인 사업가로서의 삶에 아주 잘 적응해 가고 있습니다.

Questions 56-58 refer to the following conversation.

M　Thank you for joining us on our show this morning, Ms. Connor. ^{56,57} Since your revolutionary hair-care product, Silk Shine, was released last month, you have had record-breaking sales. What do you attribute your success to?

W　Good morning, and thank you for having me. I've always been a fan of The Morning Brew Talk Show! You know, I have over 20 years' experience in the hair-care industry and have spent several years designing Silk Shine. I think the product basically sells itself!

M　⁵⁷ You started in your garage, and now you own several factories and about 800 branches in the U.S. How has the whirlwind of success affected your life?

W　⁵⁸ I am passionate about helping people take care of their hair and am just blessed to have received such positive responses. My family and I are adjusting to our new lives as public figures and successful business owners quite well even though it has been a fast transition.

어휘 revolutionary 혁신적인　hair-care product 모발 관리 제품　release ~을 출시하다　record-breaking 기록적인　attribute A to B A는 B에 기인하다　basically 기본적으로　itself 그 자체, 바로 그것　garage 창고, 차고　whirlwind 회오리바람, 빠른　affect ~에 영향을 미치다　passionate 열정적인　be blessed 신성한　positive 긍정적인　response 답변, 대응　adjust to ~에 적응하다　public figure 공인　quite 매우, 꽤　transition 변천, 과도기, 변화

56

★★★ **주제, 목적**

남자가 여자를 인터뷰하는 이유는 무엇인가?
(A) 그녀는 유명한 경제학자이다.
(B) 그녀는 저명한 디자인상을 수상했다.
(C) 그녀는 자신만의 제품을 제작했다.
(D) 그녀는 새로운 관리 기법을 개발했다.

어휘 prestigious 명망 있는, 일류의　method 기법

토익 분석

인터뷰의 목적은 대화문의 주제, 목적을 묻는 문제로 대화 첫 번째 문장에 결정적인 힌트가 등장한다.

Why is the man interviewing the woman?
(A) She is a popular program producer.　(B) She won a prestigious design award.
(C) She created her own product.　(D) She developed a new management method.

문제 해설

여자를 인터뷰하는 이유에 대해 묻는 첫 번째 질문이므로 대화 초반부 남자의 대화 내용에서 제시되는 인터뷰 이유에 초점을 맞춰야 한다. 대화 초반 남자가 Since your revolutionary~record-breaking sales라고 말하며 여자의 혁신적인 모발 관리 제품이 큰 성공을 거두고 있다고 언급하는 부분을 통해 인터뷰를 하게 되었음을 알 수 있다. 따라서 정답은 (C)가 된다.

57

★★ **암시 추론**

여자에게 어떠한 일이 발생했는가?
(A) 그녀의 프로그램이 성공을 거뒀다.
(B) 그녀의 사업이 성공하였다.
(C) 그녀의 회사가 매각되었다.
(D) 그녀의 가족은 기부를 했다.

어휘 hit n. 인기　center of interest 관심의 중심(대상)

토익 분석

암시 추론 문제의 경우 질문 속에 키워드가 제시되는 경우가 많지만 이 문제의 경우 키워드가 없기에 대화를 전반적으로 이해해야만 한다.

What has happened to the woman?
(A) Her program has become a hit.　**(B) Her business has been successful.**
(C) Her company has been sold.　(D) Her family has made donations.

문제 해설

여자에게 그간 발생한 일에 대해 묻는 질문으로 대화 초반 남자가 Since your revolutionary~record-breaking sales라고 말하며 여자의 혁신적인 모발 관리 제품이 큰 성공을 거두고 있다고 언급하는 부분, 그리고 이후 남자가 You started~in the U.S.라고 이야기하는 부분을 통해 그간 시도한 여자의 사업이 상당히 성공적이었음을 알 수 있다. 따라서 정답은 (B)가 된다.

58

★★★ **의도 파악**

여자는 무엇을 하는 것에 관심이 있는가?
(A) 중소기업 회생에 도움을 주는 것
(B) 모발을 좋은 상태로 유지하는 것
(C) 혁신적인 신제품을 구매하는 것
(D) 미용 사업을 시작하는 것

어휘 revive 회생하다　innovative 혁신적인

토익 분석

이 문제의 경우 I am passionate about이 사용되었다.

What is the woman interested in doing?
(A) Helping revive smaller companies　**(B) Keeping hair in good condition**
(C) Purchasing a new innovative product　(D) Launching a beauty business

문제 해설

여자가 관심을 갖고 있는 것에 관해 묻는 마지막 질문이므로 대화 후반부 여자의 대화 내용에서 제시되고 있는 여자의 관심 분야를 노려 들어야 할 필요가 있다. 대화 후반부에서 여자는 I am passionate about helping people take care of their hair라고 이야기하며 자신은 사람들의 모발 관리에 도움을 주는 것에 열성적임을 밝히고 있다. 그러므로 정답은 (B)가 된다.

Questions 59-61 refer to the following conversation.

M Hi. I was one of the attendees at your lecture today. [59] I think your experiments are very interesting, especially the one on the effects of clear communication between coworkers.

W Yes, people seem to always be surprised by how much productivity increases just by adopting highly effective internal communication practices.

M It seems obvious, but I didn't expect it to be that high. But the actual numbers were astonishingly high. [60] I wonder if you could come to my company and become a consultant in human resources for a while.

W I am honored, but I'm afraid my schedule is tight for the next few months. [61] Instead, I could go to your company and give a lecture on communication like I did today.

어휘 attendee 참석자 experiment 실험 especially 특히 effect 효과 coworker 직장 동료 be surprised by ~에 의해 놀라다 productivity 생산성 working environment 근무 환경 obvious 분명한, 명백한 that 그렇게나 actual 실질적인, 사실적인 astonishingly 놀랍게도 consultant 자문, 고문 human resources 인사 분야 for a while 한동안

남 안녕하세요, 저는 오늘 당신의 강연을 들었던 참석자입니다. [59] 저는 당신의 실험들에 관해 큰 흥미를 느끼고 있는데, 그중 특히 직장 동료들 사이에서의 명확한 의사소통이 주는 효과에 관한 실험에 눈길이 갑니다.

여 네, 사람들이 매우 효율적인 내부 의사소통 방식을 선택함으로써 생산성이 얼마나 향상되는지에 대해 항상 놀라워하는 것 같습니다.

남 네, 저도 생산성의 향상이 그렇게까지 높을 것이라 고려하지 못했던 것은 분명합니다. 그렇지만 실질적인 수치가 놀라울 정도로 높더군요. [60] 저는 귀하께서 저희 회사로 오셔서 인사 분야에서 한동안 고문 역할을 해 주실 수 있는지 궁금합니다.

여 영광입니다만, 제 일정이 향후 몇 달간은 굉장히 빡빡합니다. [61] 대신 제가 귀사로 가서 오늘과 같이 의사소통에 관한 강연을 해 드리도록 하겠습니다.

59

What is the man interested in?

(A) Internal communication　　(B) Management skills
(C) Productivity growth　　(D) Customer satisfaction

문제 해설

남자가 관심이 있는 것을 묻는 첫 번째 질문이므로 대화 초반 남자의 대화 내용에서 제시되는 남자의 관심 사항에 집중해야 한다. 남자는 대화 시작과 함께 'I think your experiments~between coworkers.'라고 말하며 직장 동료들 사이에서의 명확한 의사소통이 주는 효과에 관한 실험에 대한 큰 관심을 보이고 있다. 이를 통해 남자는 회사 내부의 의사소통에 대한 관심이 크다는 점을 알 수 있으므로 정답은 (A)가 된다.

★★ 의도 파악

남자가 관심이 있는 것은 무엇인가?
(A) 조직 내부의 의사소통　(B) 경영 기법
(C) 생산성 증대　　(D) 고객 만족도

어휘 be interested in 에 관심이 있는 remarkable 뛰어난 productivity 생산성 improve 향상 시키다

토익 분석

의도를 묻는 첫 번째 문제는 질문 속 남자 또는 여자의 첫 번째 문장에 답이 제시된다.

60

What does the man want the woman to do?

(A) Explain the content of the lecture in depth
(B) Conduct experiments at his company
(C) Temporarily work at his company
(D) Go to his company for a lecture

문제 해설

남자가 여자에게 원하는 것을 묻고 있으므로 남자의 대화 내용에서 제시되는 관련 단서를 동사 중심으로 파악하는 것이 중요하다. 대화 후반부에서 남자는 여자에게 'I wonder if~for a while.'라고 말하며 자신의 회사로 와서 인사 분야에서 한동안 고문 역할을 해 줄 수 있는지 궁금하다고 묻는다. 이를 통해 남자는 여자가 자신의 회사에서 인사 분야에 대해 도움을 주길 원한다는 점을 알 수 있으므로 정답은 (C)가 된다.

★★★ 요청, 제안

남자는 여자가 무엇을 하길 원하는가?
(A) 강연 내용에 대해 좀 더 깊이 있게 설명하는 것
(B) 그의 회사에서 여자가 실험을 행하는 것
(C) 임시로 남자의 회사에서 근무하는 것
(D) 강연을 위해 그의 회사를 방문하는 것

어휘 in depth 심도 있게 conduct 시행하다

토익 분석

요청 제안 문제는 주로 후반부에 힌트가 나온다. 빈출 정답 힌트인 I wonder if you could가 답을 제시한다.

61

What does the woman offer to do?

(A) Postpone the date of her lecture　(B) Test a product for customers
(C) Send her colleague in her place
(D) Visit the man's company to give a presentation

문제 해설

여자가 제안하는 것을 묻는 마지막 질문이므로 대화 후반부 여자의 대화 내용에서 등장하는 여자의 제안 사항을 사전에 대비하고 노려 들어야 할 필요가 있다. 따라서 대화 종료 직전 여자가 남자에게 'Instead, I could go to your company and give a lecture on communication like I did today.'라고 말하며 남자의 회사로 가서 오늘과 같이 의사소통에 관한 강연을 해 주겠다고 제안하는 부분을 통해 정답은 (D)임을 알 수 있다.

★★ 요청, 제안

여자가 남자에게 제안하는 것은 무엇인가?
(A) 강연 일자를 연기하는 것
(B) 고객을 위해 제품을 시험하는 것
(C) 그 자리에 그녀의 동료를 보내는 것
(D) 남자의 회사를 방문해서 강의하는 것

어휘 postpone 연기하다 colleague 동료

토익 분석

요청, 제안 문제는 주로 후반부에 힌트가 나온다. 답을 이끄는 조합으로 I could가 사용되었다.

여 안녕하세요, 아까 통화한 사람인데요. ⁶² 제가 일을 위해 컴퓨터가 필요해서, 하나를 고르기 위해 왔습니다.

남 아, Sandra Miller 씨군요. 저희는 현재 구매 가능한 여러 모델을 보유하고 있기 때문에, 꼭 알맞은 것을 찾으실 거라고 확신합니다.

여 ⁶³ 저, 제가 막 기자로 일을 시작했기 때문에, 출장 갈 때 가져갈 수 있도록 휴대가 가능한 것이 필요할 거 같아요.

남 노트북이 손님께서 필요로 하시는 부분을 충족시켜 드릴 거 같네요. 가격이 중요하다는 점은 확실하겠지만, 무게에 대해서는 어떻게 생각하세요?

여 저, 가격은 크게 걱정하는 부분이 아니에요. 하지만 ⁶⁴ 천 달러보다 많이 지출하고 싶지는 않아요. 하지만 무게는 2킬로그램 미만이어야 해요.

남 알겠습니다. 저희 모델들 중에서 가장 인기 있는 것들을 담은 목록이 여기 있는데, 이 제품들은 모두 현재 재고가 있습니다.

모델	가격	무게
Evotech 200	699달러	2.2 kg
Orchard X4	799달러	1.7 kg
Blitz P Series	1,299달러	1.1 kg
Rockware III	999달러	2.9 kg

Questions 62-64 refer to the following conversation and list.

W Hi, we spoke earlier on the phone. ⁶² I need a computer for work, and I'm here to pick one out.

M Ah, you must be Sandra Miller. We have several models available now, so I'm sure you'll find one that's right for you.

W ⁶³ Well, I just began working as a journalist, so I'll need something portable so that I can take it with me when I travel.

M It sounds like a laptop would meet your needs. I'm sure the price is important to you, but how about the weight?

W Well, the price isn't a huge concern for me. But ⁶⁴ I'd rather not spend more than a thousand dollars. The weight has to be under two kilograms, though.

M I see. Here is a list of our most popular models. All of them are currently in stock.

Model	Price	Weight
Evotech 200	$699	2.2 kg
Orchard X4	$799	1.7 kg
Blitz P Series	$1299	1.1 kg
Rockware III	$999	2.9 kg

어휘 on the phone 전화상으로 pick out ~을 고르다 have A available A가 구매 가능하다 several 여러 가지의, 여럿의 be right for ~에게 적합하다, 알맞다 journalist 기자 portable 휴대가 가능한 It sounds like ~인 것 같다 meet ~을 충족하다 needs 필요(로 하는 것) weight 무게 huge 큰, 엄청난 concern 걱정, 우려 I'd rather (not) ~하는(하지 않는) 편이 낫다 more than ~가 넘는 though (문장 끝이나 중간에서) 하지만 popular 인기 있는 currently 현재 in stock 재고가 있는

62

★ 도입부 정보

남자는 어디에서 일하고 있을 가능성이 가장 큰가?
(A) 공항에서
(B) 여행사에서
(C) 자동차 판매 대리점에서
(D) 전자 제품 매장에서

어휘 dealership 판매 대리점

토익 분석

근무 장소는 대화의 첫 번째 문장에 집중한다.

Where does the man most likely work?

(A) At an airport
(B) At a travel agency
(C) At a car dealership
(D) At an electronics store

문제 해설

남자의 근무 장소에 대해 유추할 것을 요구하는 첫 번째 질문이므로 대화 초반부에서 남자가 하는 일과 관련해 직접적으로 언급되는 부분, 혹은 이를 추측할 수 있을 만한 관련 어휘가 제시되는 부분에 집중해야 한다. 대화를 시작하면서 여자가 'I need a computer for work, and I'm here to pick one out.'라는 말로 자신이 필요한 컴퓨터 때문에 왔다고 알리고 있으므로 컴퓨터를 판매하는 장소로 (D)가 알맞다.

63

What is indicated about the woman?

(A) She recently started a new job.
(B) She has won a journalism award.
(C) She has traveled to several countries.
(D) She has never owned a laptop computer.

문제 해설

여자에 대해 알 수 있는 점을 찾도록 요구하는 두 번째 질문이므로 대화 중반부에서 여자가 언급하는 정보를 파악해 각 보기의 내용과 비교해 풀어야 한다. 대화 중반부에 여자는 자신이 필요한 장비를 언급하면서 'Well, I just began working as a journalist'라는 말로 이제 막 기자로서 일을 시작한 것에 대해 알리고 있으므로 이를 다른 말로 바꿔 표현한 (A)가 정답이다.

★★★ 암시 추론

여자에 대해 알 수 있는 것은 무엇인가?
(A) 최근에 새로운 직장에서 일을 시작했다.
(B) 저널리즘 상을 받았다.
(C) 여러 나라에 출장 갔었다.
(D) 노트북 컴퓨터를 가져 본 적이 없다.

어휘 recently 최근에 journalism 저널리즘 award 상 own ~을 소유하다, 갖고 있다

토익 분석

암시 추론 문제의 경우 질문 속에 키워드가 제시되는 경우가 많지만 이 문제의 경우 키워드가 없기에 여자의 대화에 집중해야 한다.

64

Look at the graphic. What computer model will the woman most likely choose?

(A) Evotech 200
(B) Orchard X4
(C) Blitz P Series
(D) Rockware III

문제 해설

질문에서 묻는 내용과 관련해 대화 속에 제시된 단서를 바탕으로 도표의 정보를 함께 확인해 정답을 찾아야 하는 문제이다. 이때 각 보기에 제시된 내용 외의 정보가 대화 속에서 단서로 제시될 것이므로 이에 집중해 대화를 들어야 한다. 각 보기에 제품명이 쓰여 있으므로 도표에 함께 제시된 가격 및 무게 정보에 집중해 들어야 한다. 여자는 대화 후반부에 'I'd rather not spend more than a $1,000. The weight has to be under two kilograms, though.'라는 말로 자신이 원하는 조건을 밝히고 있는데, 천 달러 미만이면서 2킬로그램이 되지 않는 제품을 말하고 있으므로 도표에서 이 조건에 부합하는 것은 (B)임을 알 수 있다.

★★ 그래픽

도표를 확인하시오. 여자는 어떤 컴퓨터 모델을 선택할 가능성이 가장 큰가?
(A) Evotech 200
(B) Orchard X4
(C) Blitz P Series
(D) Rockware III

토익 분석

그래픽 문제는 간접 정보를 찾아야 한다. 표에는 모델, 가격, 무게의 정보를 담고 있다. 모델을 찾기 위해서 간접 정보인 가격이나 무게 정보를 들어야 한다.

여 Paul, [65] 각 신입 사원들을 위해 교육 설명서 사본을 제공해 줘야 해요. 이 일이 확실히 완료되도록 해 주실 수 있으세요?

남 할 수 있어요. 하지만 [66] 사무실에 있는 복사기가 오늘 아침에 작동을 멈춰서 이틀이나 지나야 수리될 거예요.

여 저도 알고 있어요. 하지만 이 근처에 인쇄해 주는 곳이 몇 군데 있잖아요.

남 선택권이 있는 것은 좋은 일이죠. 하지만 어느 곳을 선택해야 하나요?

여 저, 설명서 안에 들어 있는 대부분의 도표들은 컬러로 코드화되어 있어서 [67] 컬러로 된 사본이 필요해요. 하지만 가능한 한 많은 비용을 절약하도록 해야 하기도 해요.

남 알겠어요. 한 군데를 선택해서 오늘 오후에 주문하겠습니다.

회사	인쇄 품질	가격 (페이지 당)
Office Club	흑백	5센트
Paper Factory	흑백	6센트
Print Solutions	컬러	9센트
National Express	컬러	12센트

Questions 65-67 refer to the following conversation and list.

W Paul, [65] we need to provide each new employee with a copy of the training manual. Could you make sure that gets done?

M I can do that. But [66] the copy machine in our office stopped working this morning, and it won't be repaired for a couple of days.

W I'm aware of that. But there are a few print shops around here.

M It's good to have some options. But which shop should I choose?

W Well, most of the diagrams in the manual are color-coded, [67] so we need color copies. But we should also try to save as much money as we can.

M I understand. I'll pick one of the companies and place an order this afternoon.

Company	Print Quality	Price (per page)
Office Club	Black & White	5 cents
Paper Factory	Black & White	6 cents
Print Solutions	Color	9 cents
National Express	Color	12 cents

어휘 provide A with B A에게 B를 제공하다 a copy of ~의 사본, ~ 1부 training 교육 manual 설명서, 지침서 make sure that 확실히 ~하다, ~하는 것을 확실히 해 두다 get done 완료되다 stop -ing ~하는 것을 멈추다 work (기계 등이) 작동되다 repair ~을 수리하다 be aware of ~을 알고 있다, 인지하다 around ~의 주변에 option 선택(할 수 있는 것) choose ~을 선택하다 most of 대부분의 diagram 도표 as much A as one can 가능한 한 많은 A pick ~을 고르다 place an order 주문하다

65

★★ 요청, 제안

여자는 남자가 무엇을 해야 한다고 요청하는가?
(A) 수리 작업을 해야 한다.
(B) 신입 직원들을 교육해야 한다.
(C) 면접을 실시해야 한다.
(D) 자료를 준비해야 한다.

어휘 make a repair 수리하다 conduct ~을 실시하다 prepare ~을 준비하다 material 자료, 재료

토익 분석

요청 제안 문제는 주로 후반부에 힌트가 나온다. 의도 표현인 we need to와 요청 표현인 Could you가 정답 힌트이다.

What does the woman request that the man do?

(A) Make some repairs
(B) Train new workers
(C) Conduct an interview
(D) Prepare some materials

문제 해설

여자가 요청하는 일을 묻는 첫 번째 질문이므로 대화 초반부에 여자의 말에서 제시되는 요청 관련 표현을 바탕으로 단서를 파악하는 것이 관건이다. 여자는 대화를 시작하면서 남자에게 'we need to provide each new employee with a copy of the training manual. Could you make sure that gets done?'라는 말로 특정 문서의 사본을 준비해 줄 것을 요청하고 있으므로 이를 '자료'를 뜻하는 'materials'로 바꿔 해당 상황에 대해 언급한 (D)가 정답이다.

66

What problem does the man mention?

(A) Some employees have not arrived.
(B) Some prices have recently increased.
(C) Some office equipment is malfunctioning.
(D) Some manuals were delivered to the wrong location.

★★ 문제점

남자는 언급한 문제점은 무엇인가?
(A) 일부 직원이 도착하지 않았다.
(B) 일부 가격이 최근에 올랐다.
(C) 일부 사무용 장비가 고장 나 있다.
(D) 일부 설명서가 엉뚱한 곳으로 배송되었다.

어휘 arrive 도착하다 recently 최근에 increase 오르다, 증가하다 equipment 장비 malfunction (기계 등이) 제대로 작동하지 않다, 오작동하다

토익 분석

문제점은 주로 반전 표현이 답을 제시한다. 반전 표현 but이 사용되었다.

문제 해설

남자가 언급하는 걱정거리를 파악하도록 요구하는 두 번째 질문이므로 대화 중반부에서 걱정하는 일과 관련해 남자가 언급하는 정보에 집중해 들어야 한다. 여자의 요청 사항을 들은 남자는 대화 중반부에 'But our copy machine in our office stopped working this morning, and it won't be repaired for a couple of days.'라는 말로 복사기가 고장 나 있어서 수리를 해야 한다고 말하고 있으므로 (C)가 정답이다.

67

Look at the graphic. Which company will the man most likely choose?

(A) Office Club
(B) Paper Factory
(C) Print Solutions
(D) National Express

★★ 그래픽

도표를 확인하시오. 남자는 어느 회사를 선택할 가능성이 가장 큰가?
(A) Office Club
(B) Paper Factory
(C) Print Solutions
(D) National Express

토익 분석

그래픽 문제는 간접 정보를 들어야 한다. 표에는 회사, 인쇄품질, 가격 정보가 있다. 인쇄품질이나 가격 정보를 가지고 답을 찾아야 한다.

문제 해설

질문에서 묻는 내용과 관련해 대화 속에 제시된 단서를 바탕으로 도표의 정보를 함께 확인해 정답을 찾아야 하는 문제이다. 이때 각 보기에 제시된 내용 외의 정보가 대화 속에서 단서로 제시될 것이므로 이에 집중해 대화를 들어야 한다. 각 보기에 회사명이 쓰여 있으므로 도표에 함께 제시된 가격 및 인쇄 상태 정보에 집중해 대화를 들어야 한다. 여자는 대화 후반부에 'so we need color copies. But we should also try to save as much money as we can.'라는 말로 선택 조건을 제시하고 있는데, 컬러이면서 가격이 낮은 것을 말하고 있으므로 도표에서 이 조건에 부합하는 것이 (C)임을 알 수 있다.

남 실례합니다, 제가 좀 도와 드릴까요? 길을 좀 잃으신 것 같아서요.

여 네, 부탁드려요! [68] 제가 관광을 하려고 이 도시를 방문 중인데, 은행을 꼭 찾아야 해요.

남 오, 괜찮으신가요? 아무런 문제가 없으시길 바라요.

여 괜찮습니다. [69] 저는 그저 달러를 파운드로 바꿔야 해서요. 공항에서 하는 걸 깜빡했어요.

남 은행은 여기서 그렇게 멀지 않아요. [70] 버스 정류장 밖으로 나가시면, 왼쪽으로 돌아서 5번가를 따라 걸어가세요. 4번가로 이어지는 거리가 보이겠지만 그 길로 가지 마시고요. 5번가를 따라 계속 직진하시면 오른쪽에 은행을 찾으실 수 있어요.

여 정말 감사합니다! 당신의 도움이 아니면 저는 길을 잃었을 거예요.

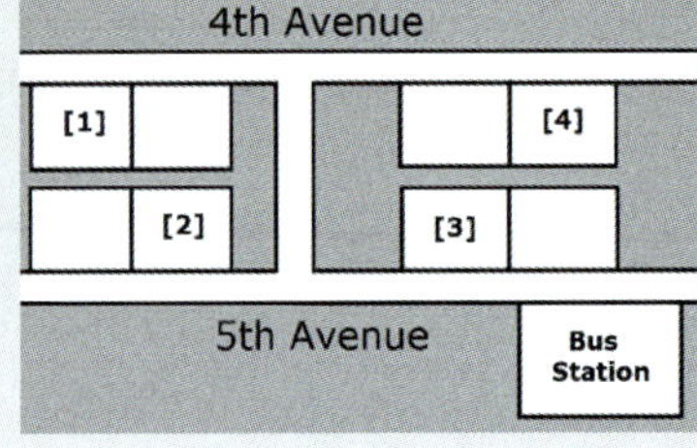

Questions 68-70 refer to the following conversation and map.

M Excuse me, can I help you? You look a little lost.

W Yes, please! [68] I'm visiting the city for some sightseeing, but I really need to find a bank.

M Oh, is everything OK? I hope you haven't had any trouble.

W Everything is fine. [69] I just need to change some dollars into pounds. I forgot to do it at the airport.

M The bank isn't far from here. [70] When you exit the bus station, turn left and walk along Fifth Avenue. You'll see a street that leads to Fourth Avenue, but don't take that. Keep going straight along Fifth and you'll see the bank on your right.

W Thanks a lot! I'm sure I would've gotten lost without your help.

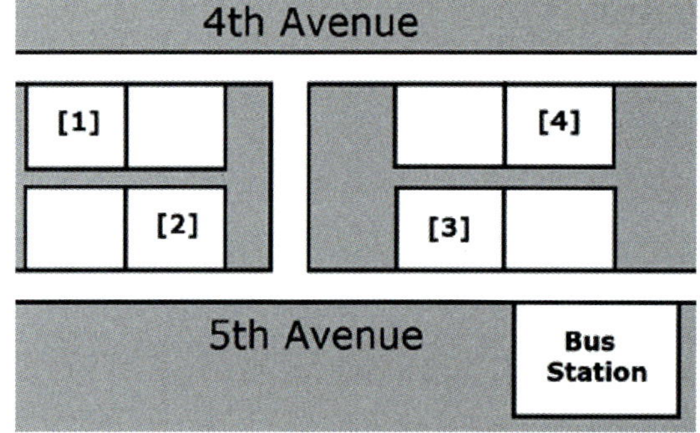

어휘 look 형용사 ~한 것처럼 보이다 a little 조금, 약간 lost 길을 잃은 sightseeing 관광 change A into B A를 B로 바꾸다 forget to do ~하는 것을 잊다 far from ~에서 멀리 있는 exit ~에서 나가다 turn left 왼쪽으로 돌다 along (거리 등) ~을 따라 lead to (길 등이) ~로 이어지다 take (거리에서) ~로 들어서다 keep -ing 계속 ~하다 go straight 직진하다 on one's right 오른쪽에 would have p.p. ~했었을 것이다 without ~가 아니었다면

68

★ 도입부 정보

여자는 누구일 가능성이 가장 큰가?
(A) 은행 직원
(B) 여행 가이드
(C) 버스 기사
(D) 관광객

어휘 employee 직원

토익 분석

대화 속 등장인물들의 직업을 묻는 도입부 정보 찾기 문제는 대화 초반부에 장소나 직업 관련 단어들이 힌트로 등장한다

Who most likely is the woman?

(A) A bank employee
(B) A tour guide
(C) A bus driver
(D) A tourist

문제 해설

여자의 신분에 대해 유추할 것을 요구하는 첫 번째 질문이므로 대화 초반부에서 여자가 하는 일과 관련해 직접적으로 언급되는 부분, 혹은 이를 추측할 수 있을 만한 관련 어휘가 제시되는 부분에 집중해야 한다. 대화 초반부에 여자는 'I'm visiting the city for some sightseeing'라는 말로 자신의 신분을 밝히고 있으므로 관광객을 뜻하는 (D)가 정답임을 알 수 있다.

69

What problem does the woman mention?

(A) She has lost her map.
(B) She is unable to find an ATM.
(C) She cannot access her bank account.
(D) She needs to exchange money.

문제 해설

여자가 언급하는 문제점을 파악하도록 요구하는 두 번째 질문이므로 대화 중반부에서 문제점과 관련해 여자가 언급하는 부정적인 정보에 집중해 들어야 한다. 여자는 대화 중반부에 'I just need to change some dollars into pounds. I forgot to do it at the airport.'라는 말로 자신이 하지 못한 일을 언급하고 있는데, 달러를 파운드로 바꾸는 일을 '환전하다'라는 의미로 쓰이는 'exchange money'로 바꿔 제시한 (D)가 정답이다.

★★★ 문제점

여자는 무슨 문제점을 언급하는가?
(A) 갖고 있던 지도를 잃어버렸다.
(B) 현금 자동 지급기를 찾을 수 없다.
(C) 자신의 은행 계좌를 이용할 수 없다.
(D) 환전을 해야 한다.

어휘 be unable to do ~할 수 없다 ATM 현금 자동 지급기 access ~을 이용하다, ~에 접근하다 account 계좌 exchange money 환전하다

토익 분석

여자 대화에 집중한다. 의도 표현 중 하나인 I (just) need to가 중요한 단서를 제시하고 있다.

70

Look at the graphic. In which position is the bank located?

(A) [1]
(B) [2]
(C) [3]
(D) [4]

문제 해설

질문에서 묻는 내용과 관련해 대화 속에 제시된 단서를 바탕으로 도표의 정보를 함께 확인해 정답을 찾아야 하는 문제이다. 지도가 도표로 제시되어 있으므로 대화에서 언급되는 출발점과 위치 관련 표현에 집중해 들어야 한다. 남자는 대화 후반부에 'When you exit the bus station, turn left and walk along Fifth Avenue. You'll see a street that leads to Fourth Avenue, but don't take that. Keep going straight along Fifth and you'll see the bank on your right.'라는 말로 위치를 알려 주고 있는데, 버스 정류장에서 출발해 5번가를 따라 직진하다가 나오는 4번가로 연결되는 길로 가지 말고 계속 직진하면 오른쪽에 은행이 있다고 알리고 있으므로 (B) [2]가 정답이다.

★★★ 그래픽

두 표를 확인하시오. 어느 곳에 은행이 위치해 있는가?
(A) [1]
(B) [2]
(C) [3]
(D) [4]

어휘 located 위치하다

토익 분석

지도가 제시되는 그래픽 문제의 경우 대화 중 제시되는 길안내 표현들을 듣고 정확한 위치를 찾는 문제이다.

남　Papa Diego Pizza! [71] 저희는 오직 유기농 재료만을 사용하는 Los Angles 도심에 있는 유일한 피자 가게입니다. 저희가 절대 음식을 두고 장난치지 않는다는 점을 믿으셔도 됩니다! [72] 이번 일주일 동안만, 저희는 Sutton 가에 위치한 또 다른 지점의 개장을 축하하기 위한 판촉 행사를 벌이고 있습니다. [73] 만약 여러분이 지금 대형 피자를 주문하면, 또 다른 피자를 무료로 받으실 수 있습니다. 하지만 이 행사는 오직 직접 오셔서 피자를 수령하는 경우에만 해당됩니다. 저희에게 연락을 주시는 최초 100명의 고객님들에게는 원하시는 사이드 메뉴 또한 무료로 드립니다. 전화기를 들고 555-1234로 연락을 주십시오.

Questions 71-73 refer to the following advertisement.

M　Papa Diego Pizza! [71] We are the only pizza store in downtown Los Angeles that offers only organic ingredients. You can be assured that we don't joke around about food! [72] For this week only, we are offering promotions to celebrate another branch opening on Sutton Street. [73] If you order a large pizza right now, you can get another one for free. However, this offer is only for pick-up orders. For the first one hundred customers that call us, we'll throw in a free side menu of your choice as well! What are you waiting for? Pick up the phone and give us a call at 555-1234.

어휘 organic 유기농의　ingredient 재료, 성분　assure ~을 보장하다, ~을 확신하다　joke around ~에 대해 농담하다　promotion 판촉, 홍보　celebrate ~을 축하하다　pick-up 수령　throw in ~을 무료로 주다

71

★ 도입부 정보

Papa Diego Pizza가 다른 점은 무엇인가?
(A) 무료 사이드 메뉴를 제공한다.
(B) 유기농 재료만을 사용한다.
(C) 배달 서비스를 제공하지 않는다.
(D) 아주 특별한 요리법을 사용한다.

어휘 ingredient 재료　provide 제공하다

토익 분석

광고지문에서 업체에 관한 정보는 지문의 도입부에 업체명과 함께 언급된다.

What is different about Papa Diego Pizza?

(A) It offers free side menus.
(C) It doesn't provide delivery.
(B) It uses organic ingredients only.
(D) It uses a very special recipe.

문제 해설

Papa Pizza의 차이점에 대해 묻는 질문이므로 지문의 도입부에서 Papa Pizza를 소개하며 남다른 장점이나 특징을 언급하는 내용이 제시되는 부분에 집중해야 한다. 따라서 화자가 지문 시작과 함께 'We are the only pizza shop in downtown Los Angeles that offers only organic ingredients.' 이라고 말하며 Papa Pizza가 오직 유기농 재료만을 사용하는 Los Angles 도심에 있는 유일한 피자 가게임을 알리는 부분을 통해 정답은 (B)임을 알 수 있다.

72

★★ 광고 목적

광고의 목적은 무엇인가?
(A) 제품에 관해 문의하기 위해서
(B) 새로운 메뉴를 판촉하기 위해서
(C) Sutton 가에 있는 새로운 지점에 관해 문의하기 위해서
(D) 고객들에게 특별 판촉 행사를 전달하기 위해서

어휘 purpose 목적　promote 홍보하다　inform 알리다

토익 분석

광고의 목적은 도입부 상품 또는 업체 소개가 이루어진 후 답이 제시된다. 업체 광고의 경우 신규 지점 오픈이나 업체 이전 등을 축하하기 위해 할인을 제공하는 경우가 일반적이다.

What is the purpose of the advertisement?

(A) To ask about an item
(B) To promote a new menu
(C) To ask about the new branch on Sutton Street
(D) To inform customers of a special offer

문제 해설

광고의 목적은 지문 초반부의 업체 소개 다음 문장에 제시된다. 따라서 화자가 'For this week only, we are offering promotions to celebrate another branch opening on Sutton Street.'라고 말하며 Sutton 가에 위치한 또 다른 지점의 개장을 축하하기 위한 판촉 행사를 진행 중임을 밝히는 부분을 통해 광고 전화의 목적은 고객에게 판촉 행사를 알리기 위함임을 알 수 있으므로 정답은 (D)가 된다.

73

★★ 요청, 제안

사람들이 무료 피자를 얻을 수 있는 방법은 무엇인가?
(A) 직접 피자를 수령하는 주문을 한다.
(B) 새로운 피자를 구매한다.
(C) 다른 지점을 방문한다.
(D) 다른 고객들보다 먼저 연락한다.

어휘 branch 지점

토익 분석

청자의 행동은 언제나 화자의 요청, 제안에 의해 이루어진다. 이 문제 역시 요청 표현인 if~, you can~.이 힌트이다.

How can people get a free pizza?

(A) By ordering one for pickup
(C) By visiting another branch
(B) By buying a new type of pizza
(D) By calling earlier than other customers

문제 해설

무료 피자를 얻는 방법은 화자가 제시해 준다. 지문 중반부에서 'If you order a large pizza right now, you can get another one for free.'라고 말하며 대형 피자를 주문하면 무료 피자를 얻을 수 있음을 밝히고 있으며 이어서 However, this offer is only for pickup orders라고 이야기하며 직접 와서 피자를 수령해가는 주문에 국한해서만 혜택이 제공됨을 밝히고 있다. 따라서 정답은 (A)가 된다.

Questions 74-76 refer to the following recorded message.

M   Now through September 30, [74, 75] the Oakland City Department of Transportation and Tourism is conducting a 3-minute online survey on how you get to work. Complete it, and you might win one of a hundred $80 Telegraph Shopping Mall gift cards! Simply visit our Web site at www.oaklandcity.ca.gov and click on the Goodride Program Annual Survey. [76] Goodride is the city's program to decrease the number of vehicle trips and to help reduce traffic congestion and air pollution. Survey results will be used to analyze commuting trends in the city. Please visit our Web site or call us at 354-4740 or 339-2797 to learn more about the survey. Thank you.

어휘 Department of Transportation and Tourism 교통 관광국 conduct ~을 행하다 online survey 인터넷 설문 조사 get to work 출근하다 complete ~을 완성하다 simply 단순히, 간단하게 annual survey 연간 설문 조사 survey results 설문 조사 결과 be used to ~하는 데 이용되다 analyze ~을 분석하다

남   지금부터 9월 30일까지 [74, 75] Oakland시의 교통관광국에서는 여러분께서 출근할 때 이용하는 교통수단에 대한 3분간의 인터넷 설문 조사를 실시합니다. 설문지를 작성하시고 100장의 80달러 Telegraph 쇼핑몰 선물카드를 경품으로 타세요. 저희 홈페이지 www.oaklandcity.ca.gov를 방문해서 간단히 Goodride Program Annual Survey를 클릭하세요. [76] Goodride는 차량 이동 횟수를 감소시켜 교통 정체 현상과 공기 오염을 완화시키는데 도움을 주는 Oakland 시의 프로그램입니다. 설문 조사 결과는 시에서 통근 교통수단의 추세를 분석하는데 사용될 것입니다. 저희 설문 조사에 대한 더 많은 정보를 알고 싶으시면 저희 홈페이지를 방문해 주시거나 354-4740 또는 339-2797번으로 연락하세요. 감사합니다.

74

What does the speaker say the survey is about?

(A) Commuting methods   (B) Public transportation
(C) Popular attractions   (D) Voluntary services

문제 해설

the survey의 목적에 대해 묻는 질문이므로, the survey라는 키워드를 활용해야 한다 지문 초반부에서 the Oakland City Department of Transportation and Tourism is conducting a 3-minute online survey on how you get to work라고 이야기하며 이 설문 조사가 통근 방법과 관련된 설문 조사임을 밝히는 부분을 통해 정답은 (A)임을 알 수 있다.

★★ 세부 정보

화자는 설문 조사가 무엇과 관련이 있다고 언급하는가?
(A) 통근 수단   (B) 대중교통
(C) 인기 관광지   (D) 자원봉사 서비스

어휘 commute 통근 attraction 명소 voluntary 자발적인

토익 분석

세부 정보 찾기는 키워드를 활용하는 문제이다. Survey가 키워드이다.

75

What kind of survey is the speaker talking about?

(A) A face-to-face survey   (B) A telephone survey
(C) An Internet-based survey   (D) A mail survey

문제 해설

survey의 방식에 관해 묻는 질문이므로 역시 survey를 키워드로 답을 찾아야 한다. 74번 문제와 같은 문장이나 이어지는 문장에 답이 제시될 것임을 알 수 있다. 화자가 지문 초반부에서 the Oakland City Department of Transportation and Tourism is conducting a 3-minute online survey on how you get to work라고 이야기하는 부분을 통해 이 설문 조사는 3분짜리 인터넷 설문 조사임을 알 수 있으므로 정답은 (C)가 된다.

★ 세부 정보

화자는 어떤 방식의 설문 조사를 언급하고 있는가?
(A) 대면 설문 조사   (B) 전화 설문 조사
(C) 인터넷 설문 조사   (D) 우편 설문

어휘 face-to-face 대면하는 based 기반하는

토익 분석

역시 survey라는 키워드를 활용하는 세부 정보 찾기 문제이다.

76

Which is one of the purposes of Goodride?

(A) To promote the concept of carpooling   (B) To reduce fuel consumption
(C) To increase the city's water supply   **(D) To ease the city's traffic congestion**

문제 해설

Goodride의 목적 중 한 가지를 묻는 질문이므로 지문에서 Goodride가 키워드로 등장하는 부분을 중심으로 해당 목적을 파악하는 것이 현명하다. 따라서 화자가 Goodride is the city's program to decrease the number of vehicle trips and to help reduce traffic congestion and air pollution이라고 말하는 부분을 통해 Goodride의 목적은 자동차로 이동하는 것을 감소시켜 궁극적으로는 교통 체증과 공기 오염을 감소시키는 것임을 알 수 있다. 그러므로 정답은 (D)가 된다.

★★★ 세부 정보

Goodride의 목적 중 한 가지는 무엇인가?
(A) 카풀 제도의 개념을 널리 알리기 위해서
(B) 연료 소비량을 감소시키기 위해서
(C) 시의 물 공급량을 증가시키기 위해서
(D) 시의 교통 체증을 완화시키기 위해서

어휘 concept 개념 fuel 연료 consumption 소비 water supply 상수도 congestion 혼잡

토익 분석

Goodride를 키워드로 답을 찾는 세부 정보 찾기 문제이다.

여 ⁷⁷ 도서관을 이용하시는 분들께 안내 말씀 드립니다. ⁷⁸ 현재 시각은 저녁 9시 40분이며, 도서관은 20분 후, 10시에 문을 닫습니다. 여러분이 대출하셔야 할 도서는 도서관 대출 창구로 가지고 와 주십시오. 아울러 여러분이 빌린 모든 참고 자료들은 도서관을 떠나기 전 3층에 있는 도서관 대출 창구로 반납해 주시기 바랍니다. 도서관 폐장 15분 전에 벨이 울릴 것이며 이는 책을 읽던 분들은 독서를 멈추고 바로 떠나 주셔야 함을 의미하는 신호가 되겠습니다. 도서관 자료를 이용하시던 분은 그 자료를 테이블 위에 놔두시면 도서관 사서들이 원래 있던 위치로 가져다 놓을 것이니 절대 직접 원래 있던 곳으로 가져다 놓지 마십시오. 복사기는 도서관이 폐장 5분 전에 전원이 차단될 예정입니다. ⁷⁹ 떠나실 때는 소지품을 꼭 챙겨 주시길 바랍니다. 도서관은 내일 오전 7시에 다시 개장합니다. Manchester 공공 도서관을 방문해 주셔서 감사 드립니다.

Questions 77-79 refer to the following announcement.

W ⁷⁷ **Attention, library patrons.** ⁷⁸ **It is now 9:40 P.M., and the library will be closing in 20 minutes, at 10 o'clock.** Please bring any books that need to be checked out to the circulation desk. In addition, return all reference materials you have borrowed to the circulation desk on the third floor before you leave the library. A bell will be rung fifteen minutes before closure, which is the signal for readers to stop working immediately and to leave. You should leave the materials on the tables for the librarian to reshelve and not reshelve the books yourselves. Photocopiers will be switched off five minutes before closing. ⁷⁹ **Please ensure that you take all your belongings with you when you leave.** The library will open tomorrow at 7 A.M. Thank you for visiting the Manchester Public Library.

어휘 check out ~을 계산하다, ~을 대출하다 circulation desk 도서관 대출 창구 reference materials 참고 자료 signal 신호, 암호 immediately 바로, 즉시 materials 자료, 재료 reshelve (도서나 자료를) 원래 자리하던 책장에 두다 photocopier 복사기 switch off ~의 전원을 차단하다 ensure ~을 확실하게 하다 belongings 소지품

77

★★ 도입부 정보 – 청자

안내문이 의도하는 청자는 누구인가?
(A) 박물관 방문자들　　(B) 도서관 이용자들
(C) 상점 고객들　　(D) 사무실 직원들

어휘 announcement 발표, 공지

토익 분석

청자를 찾는 문제로 첫 번째 지문이 시작하자 마자 들리는 '환영 인사' 부분에서 답을 찾는 쉬운 유형이다.

Who is the intended audience of the announcement?

(A) Museum visitors　　　**(B) Library users**
(C) Store customers　　　(D) Office employees

문제 해설

안내문의 청자를 묻는 첫 번째 질문으로 지문 초반부에서 청자에 대해 직접적으로 언급하는 부분이나 청자의 정체를 가늠할 수 있을 만한 관련 어휘를 중심으로 청취해야 한다. 따라서 화자가 지문 시작과 함께 바로 Attention, library patrons이라고 말하며, 이 안내문의 청자가 도서관 이용자임을 직접적으로 밝히는 부분을 통해 정답은 (B)임을 알 수 있다.

78

★★ 세부 정보

화자에 따르면, 이 시설은 몇 시에 문을 닫는가?
(A) 오전 7시　　　(B) 오후 9시 40분
(C) 오후 9시 55분　　(D) 오후 10시

어휘 facility 시설

토익 분석

세부 정보 찾기는 키워드를 활용하는 문제이다. 일반적으로 키워드는 명사를 사용하지만, 영업시간 관련 문제는 언제나 동사 open/close와 같은 단어가 키워드로 활용된다.

According to the speaker, what time does the facility close?

(A) At 7:00 A.M.　　　(B) At 9:40 P.M.
(C) At 9:55 P.M.　　　**(D) At 10:00 P.M.**

문제 해설

키워드 close를 활용하는 문제로 시설이 폐장하는 구체적인 시각이 지문에서 제시될 것임을 사전에 알 수 있다. 화자는 지문 초반부에서 'It is now 9:40 P.M., so the library will be closing in 20 minutes, at 10 o'clock.'라고 말하며 현재 저녁(오후) 9시 40분이며 20분 뒤, 즉, 정확히 10시에 도서관을 폐장할 것임을 밝히고 있다. 따라서 정답은 (D)가 된다.

79

★★★ 요청, 제안

청자가 요청 받는 것은 무엇인가?
(A) 사진 촬영을 하지 말 것
(B) 건물을 떠날 준비를 할 것
(C) 구매한 상품에 대한 가격을 지불할 것
(D) 도서관 자료들을 제자리에 가져다 놓을 것

어휘 refrain 자제 make a purchase 구매하다

토익 분석

청자의 행동은 언제나 화자의 요청, 제안에 의해 이루어진다. Please 명령문과 You should 로 시작하는 요청, 제안 표현들이 힌트이다.

What does the speaker ask the listeners to do?

(A) Refrain from taking pictures　　**(B) Prepare to leave the building**
(C) Make some purchases　　　(D) Reshelve some library materials

문제 해설

화자가 청자에게 요청, 제안을 할 때 사용하는 명령문들을 들어야 한다. 여러 개의 명령문 문장들이 들리므로 보기와 비교 작업을 해야 하는 어려운 문제이다. 1. Please bring any books that need to be checked out, 2. You should leave the materials on the tables, 3. Please ensure that you take all your belongings with you when you leave. 마지막에 언급된 세 번째 명령문에서 떠날 때는 개인 소지품을 확실하게 챙길 것을 요청하고 있다. 문닫을 시간이 되었기에 정시에 떠나야 한다는 것을 알 수 있다. 따라서 정답은 (B)임을 알 수 있다.

Questions 80-82 refer to the following talk.

M   Hello! I am happy to welcome you all to the 10th Annual Yacht Club Extravaganza. **80 My name is Nick Galloway, as many of you know, and I will be hosting our adventure.** Before we disembark, we will spend the afternoon here at the yacht club. We will have a meet and greet session in the garden area. New members can look around and get comfortable. Later, **81 we will have an early dinner at a nearby beachside restaurant.** For your meal, you can choose between beef or fish. After that, we will set out on the sea for our evening cruise. **82 Let's make this a day to remember!**

어휘 annual 연례의 host ~을 진행하다 disembark 내리다 session (특정 활동을 위한) 시간, 프로그램 get comfortable 편안하게 있다 meal 식사 set out 출발하다, 떠나다 cruise 크루즈 여행 make A B A를 B로 만들다

남 안녕하세요! 제10회 연례 **Yacht Club Extravaganza**에 오신 여러분 모두를 환영할 수 있어 기쁩니다. 많은 분들께서 아시다시피 **80 제 이름은 Nick Galloway**이며, 여러분들께서 즐기실 모험을 진행할 것입니다. 내리시기 전에, 이곳 요트 클럽에서 오후 시간을 보낼 것입니다. 우리는 정원 구역에서 서로 인사를 하는 시간을 가질 것입니다. 신입 회원들께서는 주변을 둘러보시면서 편안하게 계실 수 있습니다. 이후에, **81 근처의 해변에 있는 레스토랑에서 이른 저녁 식사를 할 예정입니다.** 식사 메뉴로, 소고기 요리 또는 생선 요리 중에서 선택하실 수 있습니다. 그 후에는, 저녁 크루즈 여행을 위해 바다로 떠날 것입니다. **82 오늘을 기억에 남을 만한 하루로 만들어 봅시다!**

80

Who most likely is the speaker?

(A) An event organizer (B) A restaurant owner
(C) A new club member (D) A local politician

문제 해설

화자의 신분에 대해 유추할 것을 요구하는 첫 번째 질문이므로 담화 초반부에서 화자가 하는 일과 관련해 직접적으로 언급되는 부분, 혹은 이를 추측할 수 있을 만한 관련 어휘가 제시되는 부분에 집중해야 한다. 담화 초반부에 행사 참여에 대한 감사 인사를 한 남자는 곧이어 'My name is Nick Galloway, as many of you know, and I will be hosting our adventure.'라는 말로 자신이 하는 일을 알리고 있는데, 행사와 관련해 동사 'host'는 진행 또는 주최하는 것을 의미하므로 (A)가 정답이 된다.

★★ 도입부 정보 – 화자

화자는 누구일 가능성이 가장 큰가?
(A) 행사 조직자 (B) 레스토랑 주인
(C) 신입 회원 (D) 지역 정치인

어휘 organizer (행사 등의) 조직자 politician 정치인

토익 분석

회자 정보는 '환영 인사' 다음에 this is, I'm, my name is, I'll be와 같은 표현들이 이름이나 직책과 함께 제시된다.

81

According to the speaker, where will dinner be served?

(A) On a boat (B) In the garden area
(C) At a restaurant (D) At the speaker's house

문제 해설

저녁 식사가 제공되는 장소를 파악하도록 요구하는 두 번째 질문이므로 담화 중반부에 언급되는 저녁 식사 장소 관련 정보에 집중해 들어야 한다. 키워드로 dinner가 사용된 'we will have an early dinner at a nearby beach side restaurant.'라는 문장에서 저녁 식사는 레스토랑에서 한다는 것을 알 수 있으므로 (C)가 정답이다.

★ 세부 정보

화자의 말에 따르면, 어디에서 저녁이 제공될 것인가?
(A) 보트 위에서
(B) 정원 구역에서
(C) 레스토랑에서
(D) 화자의 집에서

토익 분석

세부 정보 찾기는 키워드를 활용하는 문제이다. 키워드로 dinner가 활용되었다.

82

What does the speaker mean when he says, "Let's make this a day to remember"?

(A) The event should be very enjoyable.
(B) The listeners should take many photos.
(C) There are many details to memorize.
(D) The listeners have visited the place before.

문제 해설

화자가 말하는 "Let's make this a day to remember"라는 표현이 담화 속에서 어떤 의미로 사용되었는지를 묻는 질문으로 앞뒤에 제시되는 말들을 통해 의미의 흐름을 파악해 정답을 찾아야 한다. 화자는 문두 시점 표현인 Later와 After that를 활용하여 행사 진행 순서를 설명한 후에 담화 마지막에 가서 해당 표현을 사용하면서 담화를 마무리하고 있으므로 해당 표현이 말 그대로 의미하는 '오늘을 기억에 남을 만한 하루로 만들어 보자'라는 말은 즐거운 행사가 될 것임을 의미하므로 그에 대해 언급한 (A)가 정답이다.

★★★ 맥락 파악

화자가 "Let's make this a day to remember"라고 말할 때 무엇을 의미하는가?
(A) 행사 일정이 매우 즐거울 것이다.
(B) 청자들이 사진을 많이 찍어야 한다.
(C) 외워야 할 많은 상세 정보가 있다.
(D) 청자들이 해당 장소를 방문한 적이 있다.

어휘 details 상세 정보 memorize ~을 외우다

토익 분석

'반전 표현과 문두에 부사구나 시점 표현'이 중요하다. 이 문제는 Later와 After that을 사용하여 정답 힌트를 제시했다.

남 여보세요. Mark Conroy 씨이신가요? 저는 회사의 사
장인 Max Sitwell입니다. 83 Tri-State Bank와의 계약
을 체결한 것에 대해 개인적으로 감사 드리고 싶습니
다. 이 새로운 사업은 우리 회사가 성장하고 진정으
로 최고의 회사들 중의 하나로 우뚝 서는 데 도움이
될 것입니다. 84 더욱이, 사업 파트너들과 저는 귀하
의 전문가적인 태도와 날카로운 사업 감각에 대해 매
우 깊은 인상을 받았습니다. 우리는 귀하로부터 뛰어
난 일들을 기대하고 있습니다. 그러므로 우리 Lowell
Attorneys의 사업 파트너들과 저는 귀하를 승진시켜
드리고자 합니다. 85 축하의 의미로, 다음 주 금요일
정오에 Grand Estates Country Club에서 열리는 오찬
행사에 귀하를 초대하고자 합니다. 참석이 가능하신
지 답신 전화를 주셔서 제게 알려 주시기 바랍니다.

Questions 83-85 refer to the following telephone message.

M   Hello. Is this Mark Conroy? This is Max Sitwell, the president of the firm.
83 I would like to personally thank you for securing the contract with Tri-
State Bank. This new business will help our firm grow and truly stand out
as one of the best. 84 Furthermore, the partners and I were very impressed
with your professional attitude and sharp business sense. We expect great
things from you. Therefore, the partners and I here at Lowell Attorneys
would like to give you a promotion. 85 As a means of celebrating, I am
inviting you to a luncheon at Grand Estates Country Club next Friday at
noon. Please respond and let me know if you are available.

어휘 firm 회사 would like to do ~하고자 하다 personally 개인적으로 secure ~을 확보하다, 얻다 contract 계약
help A do A가 ~하는 것을 돕다 truly 진정으로 stand out 두드러지다, 돋보이다 furthermore 더욱이, 게다가 be
impressed with ~에 깊은 인상을 받다 attitude 태도 sharp 날카로운 expect ~을 기대하다, 예상하다 therefore 그
러므로, 따라서 promotion 승진 as a means of ~의 수단으로 celebrate 축하하다, 기념하다 luncheon 오찬

83

★★ 주제, 목적

화자는 왜 청자를 축하하는가?
(A) 청자가 최근에 채용되었다.
(B) 청자가 자신의 은퇴를 발표했다.
(C) 청자가 사업 계약을 최종 마무리 지었다.
(D) 청자가 보너스를 받았다.

어휘 recently 최근에 retirement 은퇴 finalize ~을 마무
리 짓다

토익 분석

주제, 목적은 지문의 도입부에 환영 인사 I'll, I'm here to,
I would like to, I want to, I need to와 같은 표현들로 답이
제시된다. 이 문제의 경우 I would like to가 정답 힌트이다.

Why does the speaker congratulate the listener?
(A) The listener was recently hired.
(B) The listener has announced his retirement.
(C) The listener finalized a business contract.
(D) The listener was awarded a bonus.

문제 해설

화자가 왜 축하 인사를 하는지 파악하도록 요구하는 첫 번째 질문이므로 담화 초반부 주제문에서
축하 인사와 함께 언급하는 이유에 집중해 들어야 한다. 담화 시작 부분에 'I would like to~Tri-
State Bank.'라는 말로 감사 인사와 함께 한 회사와 계약을 체결한 것을 밝히고 있으므로 이를 '마무
리 짓다'라는 의미로 쓰이는 동사 'finalize'로 바꿔 해당 상황을 언급한 (C)가 정답이 된다.

84

★★★ 맥락 파악

화자가 "We expect great things from you"라고 말할 때
무엇을 암시하는가?
(A) 청자가 더 열심히 일해 주기를 원하고 있다.
(B) 청자에게 깊은 인상을 받았다.
(C) 청자가 어려운 일을 하고 있다는 것을 알고 있다.
(D) 청자가 서류를 제출해 주기를 원하고 있다.

어휘 submit ~을 제출하다 document 문서, 서류

토익 분석

앞뒤 문장의 흐름을 파악해야만 하는 문제이다. '반전 표
현과 문두에 부사구나 시점 표현'이 중요하며 문두 부사
Furthermore을 이용한 문제이다.

What does the speaker imply when he says, "We expect great things from you"?
(A) He wants the listener to work harder.
(B) He is impressed with the listener.
(C) He knows the listener has a difficult job.
(D) He wants the listener to submit some documents.

문제 해설

화자가 말하는 "We expect great things from you"라는 표현이 담화 속에서 어떤 의미로 사용
되었는지를 묻는 두 번째 질문이므로 담화 중반부에 제시되는 화자의 말을 통해 해당 표현을 확
인할 수 있어야 하며, 이때 앞뒤에 함께 제시되는 말들을 통해 의미의 흐름을 파악해 정답을 찾
아야 한다. 화자는 담화 중반부에 문두 부사 Furthermore를 활용하여 힌트를 제시하고 있다.
'Furthermore~great things from you.'라는 말로 상대방으로부터 깊은 인상을 받은 이유를 언급
하면서 해당 표현을 덧붙이고 있으므로 (B)가 정답이 된다는 것을 알 수 있다.

85

★★ 요청, 제안

청자는 무엇을 하도록 요청 받는가?
(A) 제품을 테스트해 볼 것   (B) 오찬에 함께 할 것
(C) 콘퍼런스에 참석할 것   (D) 강좌에 등록할 것

어휘 attend ~에 참석하다 enroll in ~에 등록하다

토익 분석

ask, invite, insist, offer 등의 요청 제안 동사들이 정답 힌트를
제시해 준다. 이 문제는 invite와 please 명령문이 힌트이다.

What is the listener invited to do?
(A) Test a product   **(B) Join a luncheon**
(C) Attend a conference   (D) Enroll in a course

문제 해설

청자가 요청 받는 일을 묻는 세 번째 질문이므로 담화 후반부에 화자의 말에서 제시되는 요청 관련 표현
을 바탕으로 단서를 파악하는 것이 관건이다. 담화 후반부에 화자는 요청, 제안 문제의 정답 힌트인invite
을 사용하여 답을 제시하고 있다 'As a means of celebrating~if you are available.' 오찬 행사에 초
대한다는 말과 함께 이와 관련해 답변을 달라고 요청하고 있으므로 (B)가 정답임을 알 수 있다.

Questions 86-88 refer to the following talk.

W [88] Thank you, everyone, for being willing to come in and work on a Saturday. I know you all have plans for your weekends, so your sacrifice is greatly appreciated. As you are well aware, [87] our computer network completely shut down on Friday, leaving the whole company unable to handle the important end-of-the-week work that needed to be completed. [86] We need to work tirelessly today to get the network up and running properly [88] so that when the stockbrokers come in to work tomorrow, they will be able to get caught up on the work that should have been done on Friday. If all of you do your jobs, Monday should start without a hitch!

여 [88] 토요일임에도 출근하셔서 작업을 해 주시는 여러 분께 감사 드립니다. 여러분 모두 주말 계획이 있다는 점을 알고 있기에 여러분의 주말을 희생하고 근무해 주시는 점에 무척 고마울 따름입니다. 여러분도 잘 아시고 계시듯이, [87] 지난 금요일 우리 컴퓨터 네트워크가 작동하지 않아 전사적으로 처리되어야 할 필요가 있는 중요한 주말 업무들이 이뤄지지 않는 상황에 직면하고 있습니다. [86] 우리는 오늘 헌신적으로 작업을 해서 컴퓨터 네트워크를 제대로 가동시켜야 합니다. [88] 그래서 내일 주식 중개인들이 출근하면 금요일에 처리되었어야 할 밀린 업무를 따라잡을 수 있도록 해야 합니다. 만약 모든 사람들이 작업을 잘 해 내면, 월요일부터는 순조롭게 업무를 시작할 수 있을 겁니다.

어휘 be willing to do ~할 의지가 있다 come in 출근하다 sacrifice 희생 be aware ~을 인식하다 shut down ~을 폐쇄하다, ~을 닫다 whole 전체의 complete ~을 완료하다 work tirelessly 꾸준히 노력하다 properly 알맞게 stock broker 중개인 catch up on ~을 따라잡다 should have V(p.p.) ~했었어야 한다 without a hitch 문제없이, 큰 무리 없이

86

Who most likely are the listeners?

(A) Stockbrokers
(B) New employees
(C) Computer experts
(D) Software developers

문제 해설

청자들의 정체를 유추해야 하는 질문이므로 지문에서 청자들의 정체를 추측할 수 있을 만한 관련 어휘나 표현이 등장하는 부분에 집중해야 한다. 따라서 화자가 지문 중반부에서 We need to~properly라고 말하며 열심히 작업하여 컴퓨터 네트워크 시스템이 제대로 작동할 수 있도록 해야 한다고 이야기하는 부분을 통해 청자들은 바로 컴퓨터 전문가들임을 알 수 있으므로 정답은 (C)가 된다.

★★★ 도입부 정보 – 청자

청자들은 누구일 것 같은가?
(A) 주식 중개인들
(B) 최근에 입사한 직원들
(C) 컴퓨터 전문가들
(D) 소프트웨어 개발자들

어휘 expert 전문가 developer 개발업자

토익 분석

청자를 찾는 문제로 자기소개 문장 뒤 주제문 이후 제시되는 문장에서 유추해야 하는 어려운 유형의 문제이다. 'you 또는 we'가 들어가는 문장에 힌트가 나오게 된다. 이 문제는 We need to 가 중요 힌트이다.

87

What does the speaker say happened on Friday?

(A) There was a power outage.
(B) There were equipment failures.
(C) The stock market suffered a sharp decline.
(D) Some broken computers were repaired.

문제 해설

금요일에 발생한 일들에 대해 묻고 있으므로 지문에서 키워드 Friday란 시점이 등장하는 부분을 중심으로 단서를 파악해야 한다. 화자는 청자에게 작업 지시를 내리는 과정에서 our computer network completely shut down on Friday라고 말하는 부분을 통해 금요일에는 회사의 컴퓨터 네트워크가 완전히 작동을 중단했음을 밝히고 있다. 그러므로 금요일에는 장비의 오작동이 있었음을 알 수 있으므로 정답은 (B)가 된다.

★★ 세부 정보

화자는 금요일에 어떠한 일이 발생했었다고 언급하는가?
(A) 정전이 있었다.
(B) 장비의 오작동이 있었다.
(C) 주식 시장에서 주가 폭락이 발생했다.
(D) 몇몇 고장 난 컴퓨터들이 수리되었다.

어휘 outage 정전 sharp 급격한 decline 하락, 폭락 repair 수리하다

토익 분석

Friday를 키워드로 답을 찾는 세부 정보 찾기 문제이다.

88

What will probably happen on Sunday?

(A) All transactions will be stopped.
(B) All of the computers will be replaced.
(C) A new system will be installed.
(D) End-of-the-week tasks will be performed.

문제 해설

일요일에 이뤄질 일에 대해 묻는 마지막 질문이므로 지문에서 키워드 Sunday란 시점이 제시되는 부분을 중심으로 단서를 파악해야 할 필요가 있다. 다만 지문에서는 화자가 직접적으로 일요일이란 시점을 언급하는 부분이 등장하지 않는다는 점에서 문제 풀이의 어려움이 뒤따르고 있다. 화자는 지문 말미에서 청자들에게 so that~on Friday라고 말하며 주식 중개인들이 내일 출근해서 금요일에 처리했어야 했던 업무들을 따라잡을 수 있도록 해야 한다는 부분, 그리고 지문 초반 화자가 Thank you, everyone, for being willing to come in and work on a Saturday라고 이야기하며 작업을 하러 출근한 오늘이 토요일임을 밝히고 있으므로 내일은 곧 일요일임을 알 수 있다. 그러므로 궁극적으로 일요일에 이뤄질 일은 바로 주식 중개인들이 밀린 업무를 처리하는 것임을 파악할 수 있으므로 정답은 (D)가 된다.

★★★ 미래 행동

일요일에는 무엇이 이뤄질 것 같은가?
(A) 모든 거래가 정지될 것이다.
(B) 모든 컴퓨터들이 교체될 것이다.
(C) 새로운 시스템이 설치될 것이다.
(D) 주말 업무가 처리될 것이다.

어휘 transaction 거래, 매매 replace 교체되다 install 설치하다 task 일, 과업

토익 분석

Sunday를 키워드로 활용하는 세부 정보 문제지만 문두에 제시된 Saturday와 지문 후반부 Tomorrow를 이용해 Sunday를 알아내야 한다.

남 지면에 출력된 신문의 하락과 인터넷이 지속적인 성
    장으로 인해, 이러한 부류의 합병이 일어날 수밖에
    없었습니다. [89, 90] New York Gazette와 인터넷 언론인
    CradlePoint는 어제 최초의 전 세계적인 디지털 신문
    을 출간하기 위해 합병할 것이라 발표하였습니다. 매
    일 세 가지 형태의 신문이 출시될 것이며, 대중들의
    관심이 많이 쏠리는 세계적인 사건에 대한 정기적인
    업데이트가 이뤄질 것이라고 합니다. 많은 세부 사항
    들은 여전히 해결되어야 하지만, [91] 시험판은 이미 신
    문에 대해 호평을 한 500명의 확인되지 않은 고객들
    에게 배포되었다고 합니다.

Questions 89-91 refer to the following news report.

M With the decline of the printed newspaper and the continual boom of
   the Internet, a merger like this one was bound to happen. [89, 90] The *New York
   Gazette* and Internet media site CradlePoint announced yesterday that they
   will join forces to create the first global digital newspaper. There will be
   three editions released every day, with regular updates on world events
   of mass interest. While many details have yet to be ironed out, [91] the beta
   version has already been rolled out to five hundred select customers, who
   have shared nothing but positive feedback.

어휘 decline 하락, ~이 하락하다, ~을 거절하다 continual 지속적인 boom 성장, 호황 merger 합병 be bound to
do ~할 수밖에 없다, 반드시 ~하다 release ~을 출시하다 mass interest 큰 관심, 대중의 관심 have yet to do 여전
히 ~해야 한다, 아직 ~하지 못하다 iron out ~을 해결하다, ~을 다리미질 하다 roll out to ~에게 나가다, ~에게 출
시되다, ~에게 양산되다 nothing but 오직, 단지 positive 긍정적인

89

★★★ 주제, 목적

보도문은 무엇에 관한 것인가?
(A) 새로운 전기다리미
(B) 사업적 결정
(C) 판매 부수가 높은 신문
(D) 인터넷의 파급력

어휘 decision 결정

토익 분석

주제, 목적은 지문의 도입부에 등장하며 특히 뉴스나 보
도 등과 같은 지문은 정보를 전달하기 위해 announce 같
은 '알리다'의 의미를 지닌 동사가 힌트로 제시된다.

What is the report mainly about?

(A) A new electric iron   **(B) A business decision**
(C) A bestselling newspaper   (D) The power of the Internet

문제 해설

보도문의 주제에 관한 첫 번째 질문이므로 지문 초반부에서 집중적으로 언급되는 중심 소재를 파
악하는 것이 바람직하다. 화자는 지문 초반부에서 The New York Gazette and Internet media site
CradlePoint announced yesterday that they will join forces to create the first global digital newspaper
라고 말하며 New York Gazette와 인터넷 언론인 CradlePoint가 어제 최초의 전 세계적인 디지털 신
문을 출간하기 위해 합병할 것이라 발표했음을 보도하고 있다. 그러므로 이를 통해 보도문의 주제는 두
회사 간의 사업적 결정이라 할 수 있으므로 정답은 (B)가 된다.

90

★★ 세부 정보

화자에 따르면, CradlePoint는 무엇인가?
(A) 인터넷 미디어   (B) 가전제품 유통업체
(C) 유명한 출판업체   (D) 인터넷 서비스 업체

어휘 appliance 가전제품 retailer 판매점, 소매업
publication 출판업

토익 분석

세부 정보 찾기는 키워드를 활용하는 문제이다. 고유명사
CradlePoint가 키워드이다.

According to the speaker, what is CradlePoint?

(A) An online media site   (B) A home appliance retailer
(C) A well-known publication   (D) An Internet service provider

문제 해설

CradlePoint의 정체에 관한 질문이므로 지문에서 화자가 키워드 CradlePoint를 언급하는 부분
을 중심으로 이에 대한 정체와 관련된 정보를 파악해야 한다. 따라서 화자가 지문 초반부에서 The
New York Gazette and Internet media site CradlePoint announced yesterday that they will
join forces to create the first global digital newspaper라고 말하는 부분을 통해 CradlePoint는 인
터넷 미디어임을 알 수 있으므로 정답은 (A)가 된다.

91

★★ 세부 정보

시험판에 대한 고객들의 반응은 어떠한가?
(A) 고객들은 무관심을 보인다.
(B) 고객들은 상당히 부정적인 반응을 보인다.
(C) 고객들은 호의적인 반응을 보인다.
(D) 그들은 긍정과 부정이 뒤섞인 반응을 보인다.

어휘 negative 부정적인 favorably 호의적인 response
반응, 대답

토익 분석

the beta version이 키워드로 활용된 세부 정보 찾기 문제
이다.

How have some customers reacted to the beta version?

(A) They haven't been interested.
(B) They have been quite negative.
(C) They have responded favorably.
(D) They have showed mixed responses.

문제 해설

the beta version에 대한 고객의 반응을 묻는 마지막 질문이므로 지문 말미에서 키워드 the beta
version이 포함 된 문장을 노려 들어야 한다. 화자는 지문 종료 직전 the beta version has already
been rolled out to five hundred select customers, who have shared nothing but positive
feedback이라고 말하며 시험판이 이미 500명의 고객에게 배포되었으며 이들은 모두 시험판에 대
해 긍정적인 반응을 보여주고 있음을 밝히고 있다. 그러므로 정답을 (C)임을 알 수 있다.

Questions 92-94 refer to the following talk.

W   It's that time of year again! [92] The Columbus Food Festival will be held at various locations along State Street from July 8 to July 10. The bulk of activity will take place at the Central Plaza where some of the nation's most impressive chefs will give cooking demonstrations, culinary lessons, and even free samples. [93] Please be aware, though, that you will need to pre-order tickets for the main events, and they are close to selling out. [94] You'd better get on it! Also, a smaller craft beer festival will take place outside of West Station. Jackio's Brewery, the main sponsor, is selling a combo ticket for both events. It can be purchased online or from any participating vendor.

여   일 년 중 그때가 다시 돌아왔습니다! [92] Columbus Food Festival이 7월 8일부터 10일까지 State Street를 따라 위치한 다양한 곳에서 열릴 예정입니다. 대부분의 행사가 Central Plaza에서 열릴 것이며, 이곳에서는 전국에서 가장 인상적인 요리사들 중의 몇 분께서 요리 시연회와 요리 강습을 열고 심지어 무료 시식 요리까지 제공해 드릴 것입니다. [93] 하지만 주요 행사에 대한 입장권을 미리 주문하셔야 할 필요가 있으며 매진 임박이라는 점에 유의하시기 바랍니다. [94] 어서 구입하시기 바랍니다! 또한, 소규모 수제 맥주 축제가 West Station 바깥 구역에서 열릴 것입니다. 주요 후원사인 Jackio's Brewery가 이 두 가지 행사에 대한 콤보 입장권을 판매하고 있습니다. 입장권을 온라인으로 또는 행사에 참가하는 판매업체를 통해 구입하실 수 있습니다.

어휘 be held at ~에서 열리다, 개최되다 various 다양한 location 지점, 위치 along (거리 등) ~을 따라 the bulk of 대부분의 activity 활동 take place (행사 등이) 열리다, 개최되다 impressive 인상적인 demonstration 시연(회) culinary 요리의, 음식의 be aware that ~임에 유의하다 though (문장 중간이나 끝에서) 하지만 pre-order ~을 미리 주문하다, 선주문하다 be close to 거의 ~하게 되다, ~하기 직전이다 had better ~하는 편이 낫다 get on ~을 시작하다 craft 수제의 outside of ~의 바깥에 both 둘 다 participating 참여하는 vendor 판매업체, 판매업자

92

What is the main purpose of the festival?

(A) A local food festival   (B) A musical performance
(C) A famous carnival   (D) A visiting celebrity

문제 해설

지문의 도입부에서 The Columbus Food Festival will be held at various locations along State Street from July 8 to July 10. 이라고 행사명과 더불어 목적, 장소, 기간 등에 정보가 제시되고 있다. 행사의 이름에서 행사가 음식과 관련된 것임을 알 수 있다. 따라서 (A)가 정답이 된다.

★ 도입부 정보 – 행사목적

축제의 목적은 무엇인가?
(A) 지역 음식 축제   (B) 뮤지컬 공연
(C) 유명 카니발   (D) 방문 예정인 유명 인사

어휘 visiting 방문하는 celebrity 유명 인사

토익 분석

행사의 목적은 지문의 첫 문장 환영 인사와 함께 등장하는 행사명에 답이 제시된다.

93

What problem does the speaker mention?

(A) Tickets are selling out.   (B) The weather will be unfavorable.
(C) The traffic will be bad.   (D) Some events will be canceled.

문제 해설

화자가 언급하는 문제점을 파악하도록 요구하는 두 번째 질문이므로 담화 중반부에서 문제점과 관련해 화자가 언급하는 부정적인 정보에 집중해 들어야 한다. Please be aware, though, that you will need to pre-order tickets for the main events, and they are close to selling out. 명령문 +you need to 의 요청, 제안 문장으로 문제점이 언급되고 있다. 입장권이 거의 매진되어 미리 구입하도록 알리고 있으므로 (A)가 정답임을 알 수 있다.

★★ 문제점

화자는 무슨 문제점을 언급하고 있는가?
(A) 입장권이 매진되고 있다.
(B) 날씨가 좋지 않을 것이다.
(C) 교통 상황이 좋지 않을 것이다.
(D) 일부 행사가 취소될 것이다.

어휘 sell out 매진되다 unfavorable 좋지 못한, 호의적이지 않은 traffic 교통(량) cancel ~을 취소하다

토익 분석

문제점은 주로 도입부 주제문에 제시되지만 이 문제의 경우 '요청, 제안' 정답 힌트로 문제점을 상기 시킨 유형이다.

94

Why does the speaker say, "You'd better get on it"?

(A) The event needs more participants.   (B) She is requesting help.
(C) The listeners should act quickly.   (D) The tickets are too expensive.

문제 해설

화자가 말하는 "You'd better get on it"라는 표현이 담화 속에서 어떤 의미로 사용되었는지를 묻는 세 번째 질문이므로 담화 후반부에 제시되는 화자의 말을 통해 해당 표현을 확인할 수 있어야 하며, 이때 앞뒤에 함께 제시되는 말들을 통해 의미의 흐름을 파악해 정답을 찾아야 한다. 화자는 담화 후반부에 'you will need to pre-order tickets for the main events, and they are close to selling out. You'd better get on it!'라고 말하면서 입장권이 매진되고 있으니 미리 구입해야 한다는 점에 유의하라는 말 다음에 해당 표현을 사용하고 있으므로 빨리 조처를 해 입장권을 구입하도록 권하고 있음을 알 수 있다. 따라서 (C)가 정답이 된다.

★★★ 맥락 파악

화자는 왜 "You'd better get on it"라고 말하는가?
(A) 행사에 더 많은 참가자들이 필요하다.
(B) 화자가 도움을 요청하고 있다.
(C) 청자들이 빠르게 행동으로 옮겨야 한다.
(D) 입장권이 너무 비싸다.

어휘 participant 참가자 request ~을 요청하다

토익 분석

'제시된 특정 문장'의 의도를 파악하는 유형으로 앞뒤 문장의 흐름을 파악해야만 하는 문제이다.

남 여보세요, 저는 **Sam Huckabee**입니다. 제가 오늘 태
국으로 가는 여행 패키지에 관해 이야기하기 위해 아
까 귀하의 여행사에 갔었습니다. [95, 96] 저와 얘기한 직
원이 네 가지 패키지를 보여 주었지만, 그때는 어느
여행으로 해야 할지 확실하지 않았습니다. 저, 생각
해 봤는데, 829달러의 비용이 드는 것으로 하고 싶
습니다. 오늘 저와 얘기를 나눈 직원이 신용카드 대
신에 현금으로 비용을 지불하면 할인을 받을 수 있을
거라고 알려 주어서 [97] 이를 처리하기 위해 내일 아침
에 귀하의 사무실로 다시 찾아갈 예정입니다. 도와주
셔서 감사 드리며, 내일 뵙겠습니다.

여행 패키지 (태국)	
3박 4일	659달러
4박 5일	729달러
5박 6일	829달러
6박 7일	879달러

Questions 95-97 refer to the following telephone message and list.

M Hello, this is Sam Huckabee calling. I was in your travel agency earlier today to speak about some tour packages for Thailand. [95, 96] The travel agent showed me four packages, but I wasn't sure which one to take at the time. Well, I've thought about it, and I'd like to take the one that costs $829. The agent I spoke with today informed me that I'd receive a discount if I paid in cash rather than by credit card, [97] so I'll come back to your office tomorrow morning to take care of that. Thanks for your help, and I'll see you tomorrow.

Tour Packages (Thailand)	
3 nights 4 days	$659
4 nights 5 days	$729
5 nights 6 days	$829
6 nights 7 days	$879

어휘 travel agency 여행사 travel agent 여행사 직원 at the time 그때, 그 당시에 cost ~의 비용이 들다 inform A that A에게 ~라고 알리다 receive ~을 받다 discount 할인 in cash 현금으로 rather than ~보다는 차라리 take care of ~을 처리하다

95

★★★ 전화 목적

남자는 왜 전화를 거는가?
(A) 선택 가능한 여행에 관해 문의하기 위해
(B) 가격에 대해 불평하기 위해
(C) 자신의 결정을 확인해 주기 위해
(D) 여행 일정을 변경하기 위해

어휘 inquire about ~에 관해 문의하다 option 선택(할 수 있는 것) complain about ~에 대해 불평하다 confirm ~을 확인해 주다 decision 결정 itinerary 여행 일정(표)

토익 분석

전화 목적은 상대방의 이름을 부르고 본인 소개를 하는 문장 다음에 답이 등장한다. 반전 표현 But과 의도 표현인 I'd like to가 힌트를 제시했다.

Why is the man calling?

(A) To inquire about travel options
(B) To complain about a price
(C) To confirm a decision
(D) To change a travel itinerary

문제 해설

남자가 전화를 거는 이유를 묻는 첫 번째 질문이므로 담화 초반부에서 전화 용건과 관련해 중점적으로 언급하는 핵심 내용을 파악하는 것이 관건이다. 남자는 담화 초반부에 'The travel agent showed me four packages, but I wasn't sure which one to take at the time. Well, I've thought about it, and I'd like to take the one that costs $829.'라는 말로 상담을 하던 당시에는 확실히 결정을 못했지만, 지금 자신이 생각한 부분을 알리겠다고 말하고 있으므로 '결정을 확인해 주기 위해'라는 의미로 쓰인 (C)가 정답임을 알 수 있다.

96

Look at the graphic. How long will the man most likely stay in Thailand?

(A) 4 days
(B) 5 days
(C) 6 days
(D) 7 days

문제 해설

질문에서 묻는 내용과 관련해 담화 속에 제시된 단서를 바탕으로 도표의 정보를 함께 확인해 정답을 찾아야 하는 문제이다. 이때 각 보기에 제시된 내용 외의 정보가 담화 속에서 단서로 제시될 것이므로 이에 집중해 담화를 들어야 한다. 각 보기에 기간이 제시되어 있으므로 이와 함께 도표에 제시된 가격 정보에 집중해 들어야 한다. 화자는 담화 중반부에 'I'd like to take the one that costs $829.'라는 말로 자신이 결정한 여행 패키지의 가격을 알리고 있으므로 도표에서 이에 해당하는 기간인 (C)가 정답이 된다.

★★ 그래픽

도표를 확인하시오. 남자는 태국에 얼마나 오래 머물 가능성이 가장 큰가?
(A) 4일
(B) 5일
(C) 6일
(D) 7일

토익 분석

제시된 표는 여행 기간과 가격 정보를 포함한다. 기간을 찾기 위해서는 지문에서 가격 정보를 들어내야 한다.

97

What does the speaker intend to do tomorrow?

(A) Send his credit card details
(B) Visit a business
(C) Cancel a payment
(D) Begin his vacation

문제 해설

화자가 내일 계획하는 일을 파악하도록 요구하는 세 번째 질문이므로 담화 후반부에서 '내일'이라는 시점 표현과 함께 언급되는 일에 집중해 들어야 한다. so I'll come back to your office tomorrow morning to take care of that.라는 말로 내일 아침에 방문하여 일을 처리하겠다고 말하고 있으므로 (B)가 정답이다.

★★ 미래 행동

화자는 내일 무엇을 할 계획인가?
(A) 자신의 신용카드 정보를 보낼 것이다.
(B) 업체를 방문할 것이다.
(C) 지불 비용을 취소할 것이다.
(D) 자신의 휴가를 시작할 것이다.

어휘 details 상세 정보 cancel ~을 취소하다 payment 지불 비용

토익 분석

미래 행동 문제는 언제나 지문의 가장 마지막 문장에서 시점 표현, 제안 또는 각종 반전 표현이 등장하여 힌트를 제공한다. 이 문제는 반전 표현 So와 미래 행동 표현인 I'll이 힌트를 제시한다.

여 [98] 회의 안건 중의 첫 번째는 감소하고 있는 고객들의 수에 대한 문제입니다. 우리는 왜 요즘 점점 더 적은 사람들이 우리 극장을 찾고 있는지에 대해 알아봐야 하는데, 우리의 수익에 정말로 큰 타격을 입히고 있기 때문입니다. 여러분 모두가 아시다시피, [99] 지난 주에 Richmond Boulevard에 대형 멀티플렉스 극장이 문을 열었으며, 이는 도시 내의 우리 지역에서 가장 큰 경쟁사가 될 것입니다. 그곳은 이미 매우 인기가 있는 것으로 나타났습니다. 따라서 저는 우리 극장으로 고객들을 유치할 수 있는 몇 가지 방법에 대해 이야기하고자 합니다. [100] 우선, 저는 2010년의 가격으로 입장권 가격을 낮추고자 합니다. 저는 이렇게 하는 것이 경쟁사로부터 고객들을 다시 찾아 오는 데 크게 도움이 될 것으로 생각합니다.

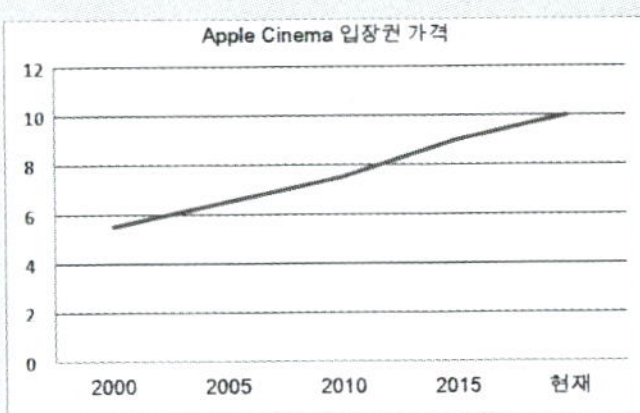

Questions 98-100 refer to the following talk and graph.

W [98] The first thing on our meeting agenda is the issue of the falling number of customers. We need to find out why fewer people are coming to our cinema these days, because it is really hurting our profits. As all of you know, [99] a large multiplex theater opened on Richmond Boulevard last weekend, and it will be our main rival in this part of the city. It's already proven to be very popular. So, I'm going to speak to you about a few ways we can attract people to our cinema. [100] First of all, I'd like to lower our ticket price back to the 2010 price. I think it will really help us to win customers back from our competitor.

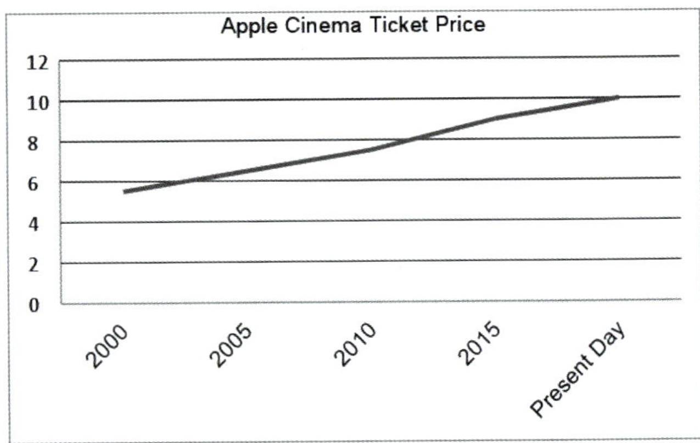

어휘 agenda 안건, 의제 issue 문제, 사안 the falling number of 감소하는 ~의 숫자 find out ~을 알아내다, 확인하다 hurt one's profits 수익에 타격을 입히다 prove to be ~한 것으로 드러나다, 밝혀지다 popular 인기 있는 attract ~을 끌어들이다, 유치하다 first of all 우선, 먼저 lower ~을 낮추다 help A to do A가 ~하도록 돕다 win ~을 얻다, 받다 competitor 경쟁사

98

★★ 주제, 목적

화자는 무엇에 관해 이야기하고 있는가?
(A) 사업의 확장
(B) 직원 채용
(C) 사업의 하락
(D) 극장의 위치 이전

어휘 expansion 확장, 확대 hiring 채용 decline 축소, 감소 relocation 위치 이전

토익 분석

주제, 목적은 지문의 도입부에 등장한다. 의도 표현인 We need to가 힌트를 제시했다.

What is the speaker discussing?
(A) A company expansion
(B) The hiring of staff
(C) A decline in business
(D) The relocation of a cinema

문제 해설

담화의 주제를 묻는 첫 번째 질문이므로 담화 초반부에서 중점적으로 언급하는 핵심 내용을 파악하는 것이 관건이다. 담화를 시작하면서 화자는 'The first thing on our meeting agenda is the issue of the falling number of customers. 'We need to' find out why fewer people are coming to our cinema these days, because it is really hurting our profits.'라는 말로 고객이 줄어드는 문제가 있어서 그에 대한 원인을 파악해야 한다고 알리고 있으므로 이를 '축소, 감소'를 뜻하는 'decline'으로 제시한 (C)가 정답이다.

99

What does the speaker say happened last weekend?

(A) A new business opened.
(B) A cinema was closed down
(C) A movie was released.
(D) An advertisement was published.

문제 해설

키워드 last weekend이 등장 하는 문장을 노려 들어야 한다. 화자는 담화 중반부에 'a large multiplex theater opened on Richmond Boulevard last weekend'라는 말로 지난주에 새로운 극장이 문을 열었다고 알리고 있으며, 이를 '업체, 회사' 등을 의미하는 'business'로 바꿔 해당 상황에 대해 말한 (A)가 정답이 된다.

★ 세부 정보

화자는 지난주에 무슨 일이 있었다고 말하는가?
(A) 새로운 업체가 문을 열었다.
(B) 한 극장이 문을 닫았다.
(C) 한 영화가 개봉되었다.
(D) 광고가 발간되었다.

어휘 close down 문을 닫다, 폐업하다 release ~을 출시하다, 공개하다 advertisement 광고 publish ~을 발간하다, 출판하다

토익 분석

세부 정보 찾기는 키워드를 활용하는 문제로 last weekend가 키워드이다.

100

Look at the graphic. What ticket price does the speaker recommend?

(A) $5.50
(B) $6.50
(C) $7.50
(D) $9.00

문제 해설

질문에서 묻는 내용과 관련해 담화 속에 제시된 단서를 바탕으로 도표의 정보를 함께 확인해 정답을 찾아야 하는 문제이다. 이때 각 보기에 제시된 내용 외의 정보가 담화 속에서 단서로 제시될 것이므로 이에 집중해 담화를 들어야 한다. 각 보기에 비용 정보가 제시되어 있으므로 도표에서 이와 함께 제시된 정보, 즉 과거의 연도에 집중해 들어야 한다. 화자는 담화 후반부에 가격을 낮추는 일과 관련해 'First of all, I'd like to lower our ticket price back to the 2010 price'라는 말로 2010년의 가격으로 변경하겠다고 알리고 있으므로 도표에서 해당 시기의 가격인 (C)가 정답이다.

★★ 그래픽

도표를 확인하시오. 화자는 어느 입장권 가격을 추천하는가?
(A) 5.50달러
(B) 6.50달러
(C) 7.50달러
(D) 9달러

어휘 recommend 추천하다

토익 분석

그래프는 가격과 연도 정보를 담고 있다. 가격을 찾기 위해서는 지문에서 연도 정보를 들어야 한다. 문두 부사구 First of all과 의도 표현인 I'd like to가 정답 힌트를 제시했다.

해설서

1

★★★ 2인 중심 + 사물

(A) 남자는 창문 밖 풍경을 내다보고 있다.
(B) 남자는 대화를 하며 손동작을 하고 있다.
(C) 그들은 식사를 같이하고 있다.
(D) 그들은 테이블을 사이에 두고 마주 보고 앉아 있다.

어휘　gaze out 밖을 내다보다　scenery 풍경, 경치
gesture with one's hands 손짓을 하다　sit across sth from
each other ~을 사이에 두고 마주 보고 앉다

(A) The man is gazing out at the scenery.
(B) The man is gesturing with his hands while talking.
(C) They are having a meal together.
(D) They are sitting across the table from each other.

문제 해설

두 사람이 등장하고 있는 사진이므로 사진 속 남녀의 공통된 행동 및 외모적 특징을 살펴본 후, 이들의 개별적 행동과 외모적 특징을 파악해야 하며, 이어서 사물들의 위치와 상태에 초점을 맞춰야 할 필요가 있다. 그러므로 남녀가 마주 보고 착석한 상태, 남녀가 서로 바라보고 있는 행동, 남녀가 서로 대화를 하는 행동, 여자가 손짓하는 모습, 그리고 남녀 사이에 위치한 테이블과 그 위에 놓인 물건들에 집중해야 하며, 이 중 테이블을 사이에 두고 서로 마주 보고 착석한 상태를 묘사하고 있는 (D)가 정답이다.

토익 분석

사람이 여러 명인 사진은 주어를 바꾸거나 주어의 수를 가지고 혼동 보기를 만드는 경우가 많다는 것을 기억해야 한다. (B)는 주어가 여자가 와야 하는데 남자로 바꿔 만든 혼동 보기다.

2

★★ 2인 이상 + 실외 전경

(A) 버스는 탑승객들을 태우기 위해 정차해 있다.
(B) 몇몇 탑승객들은 배낭을 들어 올리고 있다.
(C) 버스 안의 대부분 좌석에는 사람들이 착석해 있다.
(D) 몇몇 사람들은 길을 건너가기 위해 줄 서 있다.

어휘　passenger 탑승객　board 게시판, ~에 탑승하다
backpack 배낭　seat 좌석　be lined up ~가 줄지어 있다
cross the street 길을 건너다

(A) The bus has stopped for passengers to board.
(B) Some passengers are picking up their backpacks.
(C) Almost all of the seats on the bus are taken.
(D) Some people are lined up to cross the street.

문제 해설

실외 전경을 배경으로 두 사람 이상 등장하는 사진이므로 사람들의 동일한 행동과 외모적 특징 그리고 실외 전경을 구성하는 주요 사물인 버스 상태를 파악하는 것이 중요하다. 따라서 사람들이 줄을 지어 서 있는 동작과 몇몇 사람들이 가방을 메고 있는 상태, 그리고 인도 옆에 버스가 정차된 상태에 집중해야 하며, 이 중 탑승객을 태우기 위해 정차된 버스의 상태를 묘사하고 있는 (A)가 정답이다.

토익 분석

(B)와 (D)처럼 사람들의 행동과 매치 되는 사물이나 장소를 의도적으로 잘못된 조합으로 구성된 보기와 같이 상태는 정확하게 묘사하되, 그들의 부수적인 행동이나 관련 사물을 달리 표현하여 오답을 유도하는 유형의 함정에 주의해야 한다.

3

(A) A group of people are engaged in a conversation.
(B) Some people are shielded from the sun.
(C) Beach umbrellas are casting shadows on the sand.
(D) All chairs in a seating area are occupied.

(A) 한 무리의 사람들이 대화를 나누고 있다.
(B) 몇몇 사람들은 햇볕을 피하고 있다.
(C) 비치파라솔들이 모래 위에 그림자를 드리우고 있다.
(D) 좌석이 배치된 곳의 모든 의자가 점유되어 있다.

어휘 be engaged in ~에 종사하다, ~에 관여하다, ~에 집중하다 be shielded from ~로부터 피하다, ~로 부터 보호를 받다 cast shadows on ~에 그림자를 드리우다

문제 해설

실외 전경을 배경으로 두 사람 이상 등장하는 사진이므로 사람들의 동일한 행동과 외모적 특징 그리고 실외 전경을 구성하는 주요 사물의 위치와 상태를 파악해야 한다. 따라서 몇몇 사람들이 파라솔 아래 의자에 앉아서 햇볕을 피하고 있는 상태, 파라솔 그림자를 드리우는 상태에 초점을 맞춰야 하며, 이 중 몇몇 사람들이 파라솔 아래에서 햇볕을 피하고 있는 상태를 묘사하고 있는 (B)가 정답이다.

토익 분석

(C)는 역시 그림자를 드리우고 있다는 표현은 맞지만, 짝을 이루는 장소(모래 위)가 오답으로 등장했다. (D)는 모든 좌석이 아니라 일부 좌석이라 했어야 한다. 보통 Part 1의 보기 중에 all이 등장할 경우 대체로 오답으로 출제된다.

4

(A) They are sweeping a concrete floor.
(B) A man is trimming some bushes.
(C) They are raking the leaves into a pile.
(D) A woman is mowing the lawn.

(A) 그들은 콘크리트 바닥을 쓸고 있다.
(B) 남자는 관목을 다듬고 있다.
(C) 그들은 잎사귀를 긁어모아 더미를 만들고 있다.
(D) 여자는 잔디를 깎고 있다.

어휘 sweep ~을 쓸다 trim ~을 자르다, ~을 다듬다 rake 갈퀴, ~을 긁어모으다 pile 더미, ~을 쌓다 mow 잔디 등을 깎다

문제 해설

실외 전경을 배경으로 두 사람이 등장하고 있으므로 사람들의 공통 행동과 외모적 특징 그리고 실외 전경을 구성하는 주요 사물의 위치와 상태에 집중해야 함이 옳다. 그러므로 남녀가 갈퀴를 쥐고 갈퀴질을 하는 행동, 긴팔 상의와 긴 바지를 착용하고 있는 상태, 낙엽이 쌓여 있는 상태가 중요하다. 이 중 남녀가 잎사귀를 모아 쌓아 놓는 행동을 묘사하고 있는 (C)가 정답이다.

토익 분석

(A)는 빗자루를 가지고 쓸고 있는 동작이 보이지 않는다 (B)의 경우 가위 등을 가지고 가지치기를 하는 듯한 상황에서 사용되는 표현이다. (D) 역시 정원에서 잔디를 깎는 상황에서 사용되는 mow를 활용한 오답이다. 사진 속에 보이지 않는 사물이나 동작은 우선 소거하는 것이 답을 찾는 과정의 첫 단계임을 기억해야 한다. 정원과 관련된 표현들로 mow(잔디 깎다), rake(낙엽을 긁어모으다), plant(심다), water, sprinkle(물 주다)과 같은 표현들은 빈출 표현이므로 기억해야 한다.

5

★★ 1인 중심 + 실내 전경

(A) 한 명의 도서관 이용자가 책장들 옆을 걸어가고 있다.
(B) 몇몇 선반 부품들이 조립되고 있다.
(C) 많은 책이 선반 위에 쌓여지고 있다.
(D) 도서관에 몇몇 책장들이 여러 줄로 배열되어 있다.

어휘 library patron 도서관 이용자 shelving unit 선반 부품 assemble ~을 조립하다 bookshelves 책장 be lined up in rows 여러 줄로 나란히 배열되다 stack 쌓다

(A) A library patron is walking by the bookshelves.
(B) Some shelving units are being assembled.
(C) Many books are being stacked on the shelf.
(D) Bookshelves have been lined up in rows in the library.

문제 해설

실내 전경을 배경으로 한 사람이 등장하는 사진이므로 그 사람의 행동과 외모적 특징 그리고 실내 전경을 구성하는 주요 사물인 책장과 등의 위치와 상태를 파악하는 것이 중요하다. 따라서 도서관 내부 책상 옆에서 카트를 밀고 가는 사람의 행동, 책으로 가득 찬 책장들의 상태, 그리고 줄지어 있는 책장들을 묘사하는 표현에서 정답이 제시될 가능성이 높으며, 이 중 책장들이 줄지어 배열된 상태를 설명하고 있는 (D)가 정답이다.

토익 분석

횡대, 종대, 원형, 또는 반원형으로 배열된 사람들이나 사물들의 모습이 등장하는 경우 이를 묘사하는 정답이 자주 제시되는 경향이 있음을 알아 두도록 한다. 그리고 사물이 주체인 문장에 being 등장한다면 대체로 사람의 동작이 포함되어야 한다는 것도 기억하자.

6

★★ 3인 중심 + 실외 전경

(A) 그들은 모두 손을 잡고 있다.
(B) 그들은 재킷을 착용하고 있다.
(C) 그들은 물가 옆을 산책하고 있다.
(D) 그들은 해변을 따라 개를 산책시키고 있다.

어휘 put on ~을 착용하고 있다(동작) stroll 걷다, 산책하다 past ~을 지나 the body of water 수역, 물 walk 걷다, ~을 걷게 하다, ~을 산책시키다 along the shore 해변을 따라

(A) They are all holding hands.
(B) They are putting on jackets.
(C) They are strolling past the body of water.
(D) They are walking their dogs along the shore.

문제 해설

실외 전경을 배경으로 세 명의 사람이 등장하는 사진이므로 사람들의 공통된 행동과 외모적 특징과 해변의 상태에 집중해야 할 필요가 있다. 따라서 사람들이 나란히 해변을 산책하는 행동, 재킷을 착용하고 있는 상태, 그리고 해변에 파도가 치는 모습과 관련된 표현에서 정답이 제시될 가능성이 높으며, 이 중 해변을 걷는 사람들의 동작을 명확하게 설명하고 있는 (C)가 정답이다.

토익 분석

사람의 경우, 사람의 옷차림이나 장신구 착용 여부는 정확하게 묘사하되, 수 일치를 달리하여 오답을 유도하는 유형의 함정과 또는 착용한 상태를 나타내는 wearing/have s/t on과 같은 표현들과 입어 보는 동작을 설명하는 put on/try on을 반대로 사용한 혼동 보기들에 주의해야 한다. (A) 손을 잡고 있는 사람도 있지만 all 모두는 아니기에 수 일치를 활용한 오답이다. (B) 옷을 입는 동작을 설명하는 put on이 혼동 포인트다.

7

Who is going to attend the retirement party?

(A) Everybody from our department, I believe.
(B) It will be held at the ballroom.
(C) He's not going to make it there on time.

문제 해설

은퇴 파티 행사에 참석하는 사람이 누구인지를 묻는 Who 직접의문문에 대해 부서의 모든 사람이라는 말로 Who에 대해 직접적으로 답변한 (A)가 정답이다.

토익 분석

(B)는 질문에 제시된 party와 관련지을 수 있는 ballroom이라는 단어를 통해 혼동을 유발하는 보기로 Who가 아닌 Where로 묻는 질문에 적합한 답변이다. (C)는 질문에서 확인할 수 없는 He를 언급한 답변이며, Who보다는 참석 여부에 초점을 맞춘 오답이다.

★★ 직접의문문 Who

은퇴 파티에 누가 참석할 건가요?
(A) 저희 부서 사람들 모두가 참석할 것 같아요.
(B) 무도회장에서 개최될 거예요.
(C) 그는 그곳에 제때 가지 못할 거예요.

어휘 attend ~에 참석하다 retirement 은퇴 department 부서 be held at ~에 열리다 ballroom 무도회장 make it there 그곳으로 가다 on time 제때

8

How should I address you?

(A) No, it wasn't difficult to find.
(B) Call me Dr. Smith.
(C) That's the correct address.

문제 해설

어떻게 상대방의 호칭을 불러야 하는지를 묻는 How 직접의문문이므로 자신을 부르는 방법을 알려주는 (B)가 정답이다. How 의문문의 경우 방법을 묻는 것인지, 아니면 정도를 묻는 것인지를 구별하는 것이 중요하다. 참고로, address가 동사로 쓰일 때는 '연설하다, (문제 등을) 다루다, ~의 호칭을 부르다' 등과 같은 여러 의미로 잘 쓰인다는 것을 기억해 두는 것이 좋다.

토익 분석

(A)는 의문사로 시작되는 의문문에 어울리지 않는 No로 시작되는 답변이므로 오답이며, (C)의 경우 질문에서 동사로 사용된 address가 지니는 다른 의미(주소)를 활용해 혼동하게 만드는 오답이다.

★★★ 직접의문문 how

어떻게 당신의 호칭을 불러야 할까요?
(A) 아니요, 찾는 게 어렵지 않았어요.
(B) Smith 박사라고 부르세요.
(C) 그것이 올바른 주소에요.

어휘 address v. ~의 호칭으로 부르다 n. 주소 difficult to find 찾기 어려운 correct 올바른, 정확한

9

Who should I submit this application to?

(A) Didn't I tell you last time?
(B) Thanks, but I'm not interested.
(C) You should apply it twice a day.

★★ 직접의문문 who

누구에게 신청서를 제출해야 할까요?
(A) 내가 지난번에 말해 주지 않았나요?
(B) 고맙지만 저는 관심 없어요.
(C) 하루에 두 번 발라야 합니다.

어휘 submit A to B A를 B에게 제출하다 application 신청서, 지원서 last time 지난번에 interested 관심이 있는 apply ~을 바르다, 적용하다 twice a day 하루에 두 번

문제 해설

신청서를 누구에게 제출해야 하는지를 묻는 Who 의문문이지만, 직접적으로 그 대상을 알려 주는 대신 자신이 지난번에 알려 주지 않았는지를 되묻는 (A)가 정답이다. 이렇게 의문사에 해당되는 직접적인 대답 대신 특정 조건이나 방법을 되묻는 방식의 답변이 정답으로 제시되는 경우가 많다는 것도 알아 두는 것이 좋다.

토익 분석

(B)는 감사의 인사로 시작하는 답변인데, 질문을 받는 사람이 보일 수 있는 반응으로 적절하지 않으며, (C)는 application과 발음이 유사한 apply를 활용해 혼동을 유발하는 오답 보기이다. apply는 자동사로 '신청하다, 지원하다'를 의미하며, 타동사로 '~을 바르다, 적용하다'라는 의미로 쓰인다.

10

★★ 평서문

이 복사기들은 너무 낡았어요. 새것을 사야 할 것 같습니다.
(A) 네, 그것들은 테이블 바로 옆에 있어요.
(B) 알겠어요, 공급업체에 연락할게요.
(C) 맞아요, 커피가 너무 진해요.

어휘 copy machine 복사기 obsolete 낡은, 구식의 right (강조) 바로 next to ~ 옆에 contact ~에게 연락하다 supplier 공급업체 strong (맛, 향 등이) 진한, 강한

These copy machines are obsolete. We should buy new ones.

(A) Yes, they are right next to the table.
(B) OK, I'll contact our supplier.
(C) Right, this coffee is too strong.

문제 해설

복사기가 낡아서 새것을 구입해야 한다고 제안하는 내용의 평서문에 대해 긍정을 뜻하는 OK와 함께 공급업체에 연락하겠다는 말로 구입 의사를 나타내는 (B)가 정답이다.

토익 분석

(A)는 긍정을 나타내는 Yes로 답변이 시작되고 있지만, 뒤에 이어지는 말이 구입과 관련된 것이 아닌 위치를 알려 주는 말이므로 어울리지 않는다. (C)도 동의를 나타내는 Right로 답변이 시작되고 있지만, copy와 발음을 혼동할 수 있는 coffee를 활용한 오답 보기로 전혀 어울리지 않는 엉뚱한 대답이다.

11

★★★ 선택의문문

제품 샘플들을 전부 검사해 보셨나요, 아니면 제가 검토해 볼까요?
(A) 네, 제가 나중에 당신 사무실로 건너갈 수 있어요.
(B) 그는 잘하고 있는 것 같아요.
(C) 제가 거의 다 끝마쳤어요.

어휘 look through ~을 검사하다, 쭉 훑어보다 go over ~을 검토하다 come over to ~로 건너가다 do alright 잘 하고 있다 be almost done 거의 끝마치다

Have you looked through all the product samples or should I go over them?

(A) Yes, I can come over to your office later.
(B) I think he is doing alright.
(C) I'm almost done.

문제 해설

상대방이 제품 샘플들을 모두 검사해 봤는지를 확인함과 동시에, 그렇지 않을 경우 자신이 해야 하는지를 묻는 선택의문문이므로 이에 대해 자신이 거의 끝마쳤다는 말로 대답하는 (C)가 정답이다.

토익 분석

(A)는 상대방의 사무실로 건너갈 수 있다는 의미를 나타내는 말로, 제품 샘플 검사와는 전혀 관련 없는 대답이며 go over와 연관성 있게 들리는 come over를 활용한 오답이다. (B)는 대상을 알 수 없는 he에 대해 언급하는 대답으로 I think와 doing 등의 단어로 인해 자신이 하고 있다는 말처럼 들리게 만드는 혼동 보기이다.

12

How did you learn about the position?

(A) He is teaching at a local community college.
(B) Mr. Kim in accounting told me.
(C) I'll post it on the board.

문제 해설

특정 직책에 대해 어떻게 알게 되었는지를 묻는 How 의문문에 대해 특정 인물의 이름을 언급하면서 그 사람이 자신에게 말해 주었음을 알리는 (B)가 정답이다. 방법을 묻는 How 의문문의 경우, 그 방법을 아는 사람의 이름이나 장소 등을 말하는 답변이 정답으로 제시될 수 있다는 점을 알아 두어야 한다.

토익 분석

(A)는 질문에 언급된 the position으로 인해 혼동할 수 있는 보기로, 자신이 알게 된 방법이 아닌 He의 상황에 대해 말하는 오답 보기이다. (C)는 position과 일부분 유사하게 들리는 post를 활용한 오답 보기인데다 질문에서 과거시제 did로 묻는 것과 달리 미래의 일을 말하는 will을 사용해 어울리지 않는 반응이다.

★★ 직접의문문 how

이 직책에 대해 어떻게 아셨나요?
(A) 그는 지역 전문 대학에서 강의합니다.
(B) 회계부의 Kim 씨가 말해 줬습니다.
(C) 제가 게시판에 그것을 게시할 거예요.

어휘 learn about ~에 대해 알다 local 지역의, 현지의 community college 전문 대학 accounting 회계(부) post ~을 게시하다 board 게시판

13

Can I see you either on Monday or Tuesday?

(A) I had a wonderful time yesterday.
(B) I've already seen it.
(C) Let me check my schedule.

문제 해설

월요일과 화요일 중의 하루에 상대방을 만날 수 있는지를 묻는 선택의문문에 대해 직접적으로 하루를 선택하는 대신 일정을 먼저 확인해 보겠다는 말로 대답하는 (C)가 정답이다.

토익 분석

특정 요일에 만날 수 있는지를 묻는 것은 앞으로 있을 일과 관련된 것이므로 (A)와 같이 과거시제 동사로 즐거운 시간을 보냈다고 말하는 것은 어울리지 않는다. (B)도 마찬가지로, 현재 완료 시제 동사를 통해 과거의 경험을 말하는 내용이므로 질문에서 묻는 일과 시점이 맞지 않는 오답이다.

★★ 선택의문문

월요일이나 화요일 중에서 하루 뵐 수 있을까요?
(A) 저는 어제 아주 좋은 시간을 보냈습니다.
(B) 저는 그것을 이미 봤습니다.
(C) 제 스케줄을 좀 확인해 볼게요.

어휘 either A or B A 또는 B 둘 중의 하나 have a wonderful time 아주 즐거운 시간을 보내다 Let me do 제가 ~할게요

14

It's so cold here.

(A) Do you want me to close the window?
(B) I don't know why she called.
(C) Yes, with some ice, please.

★★ 평서문

이곳이 아주 춥군요.
(A) 창문을 닫아 드릴까요?
(B) 그녀가 전화를 왜 했는지 모르겠어요.
(C) 네, 얼음을 좀 넣어 주세요.

어휘 want A to do A가 ~하기를 원하다 call 전화를 걸다 with some ice 얼음을 넣어서

이곳이 아주 춥다는 의미의 평서문에 대해 추운 것을 해결할 수 있는 방법으로 <u>창문을 닫기를 원하는지를 묻는</u> (A)가 정답이다.

토익 분석

(B)는 <u>cold와 발음이 같은 called를 활용한 오답</u>으로, 특정 공간이 춥다는 의견을 말하는 것과 전혀 관련 없는 '전화를 거는 일'을 의미하므로 어울리지 않는 반응이다. (C)의 경우 <u>cold와 연관성 있게 들리는 ice를 언급하는 오답</u>인데, with some ice라는 말은 음료를 주문하는 상황에서 할 수 있는 말이므로 상대방이 춥다고 말한 것에 대한 반응으로 어울리지 않는다.

15

★★ 권유, 제안, 요청 유형

커피나 한잔하면서 이야기합시다.
(A) 그는 아주 말이 많아요.
(B) 좋아요, 그런데 곧 회사로 돌아가야 합니다.
(C) 저는 오늘 점심을 싸 오지 않았어요.

어휘 over (음료, 식사 등) ~하면서 talkative 말이 많은, 수다스러운 get back to ~로 돌아가다 bring ~을 가져오다

Let's talk over a cup of coffee.

(A) He is so talkative.
(B) Sure, but I have to get back to work soon.
(C) I didn't bring my lunch today.

문제 해설

커피 한잔하면서 이야기를 나눠 보자고 제안하는 말에 대해 긍정을 나타내는 <u>Sure와 함께 회사로 곧 돌아가야 한다는 말</u>로 오래 있을 수는 없다는 의미를 나타내는 (B)가 정답이다.

토익 분석

(A)의 경우 상대방의 제안에 대한 자신의 의견이 아닌 He에 대한 생각을 말하는 보기이므로 핵심에서 벗어난 답변이다. (C)는 <u>coffee와 연관성 있게 들리는 lunch를 활용한 오답</u>으로, 상대방의 제안에 대한 수락 또는 거절 등 자신의 의견을 말하는 대답이 아니므로 어울리지 않는다.

16

★★ 직접의문문 why

왜 Goodman 씨가 갑자기 일을 그만두셨나요?
(A) 음, 잘 하셨네요.
(B) 그는 그 직장에 꽤 만족했어요.
(C) 누가 알겠어요?

어휘 quit ~을 그만두다 all of a sudden 갑자기 do a good job 잘 해내다 quite 꽤, 상당히 be satisfied with ~에 만족하다 Who knows? 누가 알겠어요?, 아무도 모른다

Why did Mr. Goodman quit the job all of a sudden?

(A) Well, you did a good job.
(B) He was quite satisfied with the job.
(C) Who knows?

문제 해설

Goodman 씨가 갑자기 일을 그만둔 이유를 묻는 Why 의문문에 대해 <u>아무도 알 수 없다는 의미</u>에 해당되는 말로 답변하는 (C)가 정답이다.

토익 분석

(A)는 질문에 포함된 job이 반복 사용된 답변으로, 질문에서 말하는 Goodman 씨가 아닌 상대방이 일을 잘 한 것에 대한 칭찬에 해당되는 말이므로 어울리지 않는 반응이다. (B)도 job이 반복 사용되었고 Goodman 씨를 지칭하는 것으로 생각할 수 있는 <u>대명사 He가 언급되었지만, 일에 상당히 만족했다는 말이므로 질문에서 말하는 '일을 갑자기 그만둔 것'의 이유로 맞지 않는 반응</u>이다.

17

Do you know where the copy machine is?

(A) It should be on the second floor.
(B) I can mail you some copies.
(C) I know where the coffee maker is.

문제 해설

Do you know where ~?로 시작하는 일반의문문은 Where 의문문과 같다. 따라서 특정 장소를 언급하는 말로 답변하는 (A)가 정답이다. Do you know로 시작되는 의문문은 그다음에 이어지는 의문사에 집중하는 것이 중요하다.

토익 분석

(B)는 copy의 복수형인 copies를 활용한 혼동 보기로, 복사기의 위치가 아닌 사본을 우편으로 전송하는 방법을 알리는 말이므로 질문의 핵심에서 벗어난 답변이다. (C)는 copy와 발음이 유사하게 들리는 coffee를 활용해 혼동을 유발하는 답변으로, 위치와 관련된 말이지만 복사기가 아닌 커피 메이커와 관련된 말이므로 반드시 주의해 오답 처리해야 하는 보기이다.

★★ 일반의문문

복사기가 어디에 있는지 아세요?
(A) 2층에 있을 겁니다.
(B) 제가 사본들을 우편으로 보내 드릴 수 있어요.
(C) 저는 커피 메이커가 어디에 있는지 알고 있어요.

어휘 copy machine 복사기 on the second floor 2층에
mail ~을 우편으로 보내다

18

What time do you usually get off work?

(A) It depends on the situation.
(B) I normally take public transportation.
(C) I work out every day.

문제 해설

일반적으로 얼마나 늦게 퇴근하는지를 묻는 것에 대해 정확한 시점 대신 상황에 따라 다르다는 말로 답변하는 (A)가 정답이다. How late로 시작되는 의문문은 '얼마나 늦게 ~하는지'를 묻는 것이므로 시점과 관련된 표현이 나올 수도 있다는 점에 유의해야 한다.

토익 분석

(B)는 usually와 동일한 의미로 사용되는 normally를 활용해 일반적으로 반복되는 일을 말하고 있지만, 대중교통을 이용한다는 의미로 방법을 말하는 내용이므로 어울리지 않는 반응이다. (C)는 work의 다른 의미를 활용한 답변으로 work out은 '운동하다'라는 뜻으로 사용되는 표현이므로 질문의 핵심에서 벗어난 오답이다.

★★★ 직접의문문 how late

보통 몇 시에 퇴근하세요?
(A) 상황에 따라 달라요.
(B) 난 대체로 대중교통을 이용해요.
(C) 난 매일 운동을 합니다.

어휘 get off work 퇴근하다 depend on ~에 따라 다르다,
~에 달려 있다 situation 상황 normally 일반적으로, 보통
public transportation 대중교통 work out 운동하다

19

Who's leading the workshop this Friday?

(A) I'll bring some reading materials.
(B) Isn't it the new guy from the head office?
(C) Mr. Romero lives in a loft.

★★ 직접의문문 who

이번 주 금요일에 누가 워크숍을 진행하나요?
(A) 제가 읽을거리를 가져갈게요.
(B) 본사에서 온 그 새로운 남자 아닌가요?
(C) Romero 씨는 맨 위층에 살아요.

어휘 lead ~을 이끌다, 진행하다 bring ~을 가져오다
material 자료, 재료 head office 본사 loft 맨 위층, 다락

금요일에 있을 워크숍을 진행하는 사람이 누구인지를 묻는 Who 의문문에 대해 본사에서 오는 새로운 직원이 아닌지를 되묻는 (B)가 정답이다.

토익 분석

(A)는 질문에 포함된 leading과 발음이 유사한 reading을 활용한 오답으로, 워크숍 진행을 맡은 사람이 아닌 읽을거리(reading materials)를 가져가겠다는 말이므로 어울리지 않는 반응이다. (C)는 Who에 해당되는 사람 이름이 언급되기는 하지만 워크숍 진행과 관련 없는 거주 공간을 알리는 답변이므로 오답이다.

20

★★★ 부가의문문

우리 회사의 새로운 휴대 전화가 내일 공개됩니다, 그렇지 않나요?
(A) 아니요, 당신은 그것을 갱신해야 합니다.
(B) 네, 일반 대중들에게 그것을 보여 주게 되어 흥분됩니다.
(C) 제게 2시에 전화 주세요.

어휘 unveil ~을 공개하다　renew ~을 갱신하다　be excited to do ~해서 흥분되다, 들뜨다　the public 일반 대중들　phone ~에게 전화하다

Our new mobile phone is being unveiled tomorrow, isn't it?

(A) No, you need to renew it.
(B) Yes, I'm excited to show it to the public.
(C) Please phone me at 2 o'clock.

문제 해설

새로운 휴대 전화가 내일 공개되는 것이 맞는지 확인하는 부가의문문이므로 긍정을 나타내는 Yes와 함께 휴대 전화기를 it으로 지칭해 그것을 보여 줄 수 있게 되어 흥분된다는 생각을 말하는 (B)가 정답이다.

토익 분석

(A)는 부정을 나타내는 No로 답변이 시작되지만, 뒤에 이어지는 내용이 제품 공개가 아닌 '갱신'과 관련된 내용이므로 부가의문문에서 말하는 핵심에서 벗어난 오답이다. (C)는 phone의 다른 의미(전화하다)를 활용한 오답으로 제품 공개와는 관련 없는 전화 거는 시점을 알리는 말이므로 어울리지 않는 반응이다.

21

★★★ 평서문

저는 이 책상이 조립 전 상태로 출시된다고 들었어요.
(A) 네, 저는 생산 조립 라인에서 근무해요.
(B) 저는 세 명이 앉을 테이블을 예약하고 싶습니다.
(C) 아니요, 하지만 자세한 설명서로 인해 조립이 어렵진 않을 겁니다.

어휘 preassembled 조립 전 상태의　production line 생산 조립 라인　reserve ~을 예약하다, ~을 비축하다　step-by-step 단계별　instructions 설명, 설명서　allow ~을 허용하다　easy assembly 쉬운 조립

I heard this desk will come preassembled.

(A) Yes, I work on the production line.
(B) I'd like to reserve a table for three.
(C) No, but the step-by-step instructions allow for easy assembly.

문제 해설

책상이 조립되지 않은 상태로 출시된다고 들었다며 사실 관계를 확인하고 있는 평서문으로 이에 실제로는 그렇지 않다는 부정 답변 No에 이어 설명서를 보고 직접 조립해야 한다는 사실을 전달하고 있는 (C)가 정답이다.

토익 분석

(A)는 책상이 조립 전 상태로 출시된다는 사실에 동의하는 Yes란 긍정 답변과 자신이 생산 조립 라인에서 근무한다는 부연 설명이 서로 무관한 내용이자 질문의 assembled를 통해 연상할 수 있는 생산 조립 라인, 즉, production line을 이용한 연상 어휘 오답이 된다. 세 명이 앉을 테이블 예약을 원하는 (B) 또한 책상이 조립 전 상태로 출시되는지 여부를 알 수 없는 내용이자 질문의 desk와 유사어 관계인 table을 등장시킨 오답이 된다. 사실 이 문제의 경우 보기의 내용이 파악되지 않아도 (C)가 but을 포함한 보기로 정답 확률이 높은 보기라는 것만 알아도 답을 골라낼 수 있다. Part 2에서 유사 발음이나 유사 형태의 단어만 중복 사용되지 않는다면 but을 포함한 보기는 정답 확률이 99%이다.

22

Shouldn't we stop investing in the company struggling financially?

(A) Let's just wait a few more weeks.
(B) Yes, it is selling well.
(C) No, at the fundraiser last week.

문제 해설

재정적으로 고전하는 회사에 대한 투자를 중단해야 할지 여부를 묻는 부정의문문으로, 이에 몇 주만 더 기다려 볼 것을 권고하며 우회적으로 상대 의견에 부정적 반응을 보이는 (A)가 정답이다.

토익 분석

(B)는 질문의 sales의 유사 발음인 sell을 활용한 유사 발음 오답이며, (C) 또한 회사에 투자 중단에 반대하는 No라는 부정 답변과 지난주의 기금 마련 행사를 언급하고 부연 설명이 서로 무관한 내용을 구성되었을 뿐만 아니라 질문의 investing에서 연상할 수 있는 fund를 이용한 연상 어휘 오답이다.

★★★ 권유, 제안, 요청 유형

재정적으로 어려움을 겪고 있는 그 회사에 대한 투자를 중단해야 하지 않을까요?
(A) 몇 주만 더 기다려 봅시다.
(B) 네, 그것은 잘 팔려요.
(C) 아니요, 지난주에 있었던 기금 마련 행사에서요.

어휘 invest in ~에 투자하다 struggle 투쟁하다, 몸부림치다, 고전한다 fundraiser 기금 마련, 기금 모집

23

Why don't you leave right after dinner?

(A) No, that would be too late.
(B) I'll take her out to dinner tonight.
(C) I had to stay up all night.

문제 해설

저녁 식사 이후에 떠날 것을 권유하고 있는 Why don't you 유형의 권유의문문으로 이에 저녁 식사 이후에 떠나는 것을 부정하는 No라는 답변에 이어 그때 떠나면 너무 늦다는 부연 설명을 제시하고 있는 (A)가 정답이다.

토익 분석

(B)는 질문의 dinner를 반복하여 들려주는 동일 어휘 함정이 내포되었고 누구를 지칭하는지 알 수 없는 대명사 her를 사용한 오답이며 (C)는 why 질문에 대한 답변으로 적절하며 질문의 after dinner에서 연상 가능한 night를 활용한 오답이다.

★★★ 권유, 제안, 요청 유형

저녁 식사 이후에 바로 떠나시는 것이 어때요?
(A) 아니요, 그때면 너무 늦을 것 같아요.
(B) 저는 오늘 밤에 그녀를 데리고 저녁 식사를 하러 갈 겁니다.
(C) 저는 밤새 깨어 있어야만 했어요.

어휘 right after ~직후에 take sby out to dinner ~를 데리고 저녁 식사를 하러 가다 stay up 깨어 있다

24

Please let me know if you need to make an appointment with Dr. Smith.

(A) Thanks but I'm OK.
(B) The point is very simple.
(C) It was a little disappointing.

★★ 권유, 제안, 요청 유형

Smith 박사님과의 예약이 필요하시다면 저에게 알려 주세요.
(A) 고맙지만 전 괜찮습니다.
(B) 핵심은 아주 간단해요.
(C) 조금 실망스러웠습니다.

어휘 make an appointment with ~와의 예약을 하다 disappointing 실망스러운

Smith 박사와의 예약이 필요하면 알려달라는 권유, 제안, 요청 질문에 대해 고맙지만 괜찮다고 답한 (A)가 정답이다. 'thanks but~' 은 무조건 권유, 제안, 요청 질문에 대한 답변이라는 것도 기억해야 한다.

토익 분석

(B)는 상대 이야기에 부적합한 내용이자 질문의 appointment의 일부와 동일한 발음 함정을 이용한 오답이다. (C)는 역시 질문 속에 사용된 appointment의 유사 형태 단어인 disappointing을 반복 사용한 오답이다.

25

★★★ 일반의문문

복사기가 왜 갑자기 작동을 멈췄는지 아시나요?
(A) 전기 플러그가 꽂혀 있나요?
(B) 오늘 밤에 집에 걸어가야 하기 때문입니다.
(C) 네, 제가 커피를 끓일 거예요.

어휘 copy machine 복사기 stop -ing ~하는 것을 멈추자 work (기계 등이) 작동되다 all of a sudden 갑자기 plug in ~의 전기 플러그를 꽂다 walk home 집에 걸어가다 brew ~을 끓이다

Do you know why the copy machine stopped working all of a sudden?

(A) Is it plugged in?
(B) Because I have to walk home tonight.
(C) Yes, I'll brew some coffee.

문제 해설

Do you know why ~?로 시작되는 의문문은 Why 의문문과 같으며, 복사기가 작동을 멈춘 이유를 묻는 것에 대해 기계 작동과 관련해 먼저 확인해야 하는 '전기 플러그'가 꽂혀 있는지를 되묻는 (A)가 정답이다.

토익 분석

(B)는 why의 답변에 해당하는 because로 시작되는 답변이지만 집으로 걸어간다는 의미이므로 어울리지 않는 반응이며, working과 발음이 유사한 walk를 활용한 오답이므로 발음에 반드시 주의해야 한다. (C)는 copy와 발음이 유사한 coffee를 활용한 혼동 보기로, 복사기의 작동 여부와 전혀 관련 없는 커피를 언급한 오답이다.

26

★★★ 평서문

점검 담당자가 내일 방문하실 예정입니다.
(A) 방문 시간이 곧 종료될 것입니다.
(B) 아뇨, 저는 그것들을 본 적이 없습니다.
(C) 다음 주에 이곳으로 오시기로 되어 있지 않나요?

어휘 inspector 점검 담당자, 조사관 visiting hours 방문 시간 over 종료된, 끝난 be supposed to do ~하기로 되어 있다

The inspector will be visiting tomorrow.

(A) Visiting hours will be over soon.
(B) No, I haven't seen them.
(C) Isn't he supposed to be here next week?

문제 해설

점검 담당자가 내일 방문할 예정이라는 의미를 나타내는 평서문에 대해 inspector를 he로 지칭해 다음 주에 오기로 되어 있는 것이 아닌지를 확인하기 위해 되묻는 (C)가 정답이다.

토익 분석

(A)는 visiting이 반복 사용된 답변으로, 점검 담당자의 방문 일정과 관련 없는 방문 시간의 종료 시점을 언급하는 오답이다. (B)는 부정을 나타내는 No로 답변이 시작되고 있지만, 뒤에 이어지는 말에 포함된 them이 가리키는 대상을 알 수 없으므로 어울리지 않는 반응이다.

27

Who will be responsible for organizing the event?

(A) It hasn't been decided yet.
(B) There were many participants.
(C) He is a newcomer.

문제 해설

행사를 조직하는 일을 맡는 사람이 누구인지를 묻는 Who 의문문에 대해 특정 인물을 언급하는 대신 '아직 결정되지 않았다'는 말로 알 수 없다는 의미를 나타내는 (A)가 정답이다. 이렇게 '아직 결정되지 않았다, 잘 모르겠다, ~가 알고 있다' 등과 같이 회피성의 답변들은 정답 가능성이 높은 보기들이다.

토익 분석

(B)는 event와 연관성 있게 들리는 participants를 활용한 오답으로, 행사 조직 책임자가 아닌 참가자들의 규모와 관련된 답변이므로 어울리지 않는 반응이다. (C)는 누군지 알 수 없는 He를 언급해 신입이라는 정보를 제공하는 답변이므로 마찬가지로 질문의 핵심에서 벗어난 오답이다.

★★★ 직접의문문 who

누가 그 행사를 조직하는 일을 책임지고 있나요?
(A) 아직 결정되지 않았습니다.
(B) 많은 참가자가 있습니다.
(C) 그는 신입입니다.

어휘 be responsible for ~을 책임지고 있다 organize ~을 조직하다, 준비하다 decide ~을 결정하다 yet 아직 participant 참가자 newcomer 신입

28

What should I do with these application forms?

(A) Our firm is financially sound.
(B) Forward them to the personnel.
(C) It shouldn't be a problem.

문제 해설

지원서를 갖고 자신이 해야 하는 일이 무엇인지를 묻는 What 의문문에 대해 application forms를 them으로 지칭해 인사부로 전송하라고 알려 주는 (B)가 정답이다.

토익 분석

(A)는 application과 연관성 있게 들리는 내용으로 회사의 재정적 상태를 언급하는 말이므로 질문의 의도에 맞지 않는 답변이다. (C)는 '문제가 되지 않을 것'이라는 의미로서 상대방을 안심시키는 상황에 할 수 있는 말이므로 어울리지 않는 반응이다.

★★ 직접의문문 what

이 지원서들을 가지고 제가 뭘 해야 하나요?
(A) 우리 회사는 재정적으로 안정적인 곳입니다.
(B) 그것들을 인사부로 전송해 주세요.
(C) 그건 문제가 되지 않을 겁니다.

어휘 application form 지원서, 신청서 financially 재정적으로 sound 안정된, 견실한 forward A to B A를 B로 전송하다 personnel 인사(부), 직원들

29

I really enjoyed the meal last night.

(A) I'm glad you liked it.
(B) Who's going to join us for dinner?
(C) It will be the best course of action.

★★★ 평서문

저는 어젯밤에 정말 맛있게 식사를 했습니다.
(A) 마음에 드셨다니 기쁩니다.
(B) 누가 우리와 함께 저녁 식사를 할 예정이죠?
(C) 그것이 가장 좋은 조치 방법일 거예요.

어휘 meal 식사 be going to do ~할 예정이다 join ~와 함께하다 the best course of action 가장 좋은 조치 방법

어젯밤에 맛있게 식사를 했다는 말에 대해 the meal을 it으로 지칭해 그것을 마음에 들어 해서 기쁘다는 말로 답변하는 (A)가 정답이다.

토익 분석

(B)는 meal과 연관성 있게 들리는 dinner를 활용한 오답 보기로, enjoyed라는 과거시제 동사로 말하는 과거의 일과 달리 be going to do라는 미래시제 표현으로 말하고 있으므로 서로 시제가 맞지 않는 답변이다. (C) 또한 미래를 나타내는 will이 포함된 답변으로, meal과 관련성 있게 들리는 course를 활용한 오답이다.

30

★★ 부가의문문

신입 직원들은 아직 안전 설명서를 받지 않았죠, 그렇죠?
(A) 금고에 보관하시면 됩니다.
(B) 이미 갖고 있는 것이 분명합니다.
(C) 영수증을 보여 주셔야 합니다.

어휘 receive ~을 받다 manual 설명서, 안내서 keep ~을 보관하다 safe 금고 present ~을 보여 주다, 제시하다 receipt 영수증

The new employees haven't received the safety manual, right?

(A) You can keep them in the safe.
(B) I'm sure they already have.
(C) You need to present the receipt.

문제 해설

신입 직원들이 안전 관련 설명서를 받았는지를 확인하기 위한 부가의문문에 대해 new employees를 they로 지칭해 이미 갖고 있을 거라고 알리는 (B)가 정답이다.

토익 분석

(A)는 safety와 발음이 유사한 safe를 활용한 오답으로, 신입 직원들이 안전 관련 설명서를 받았는지의 여부와 관련 없는 물품 보관 위치를 알리는 말이므로 어울리지 않는 답변이다. (C)는 received와 발음이 유사한 receipt를 활용한 오답으로, 영수증을 제시해야 한다는 말은 물품 교환이나 반품 등을 하는 상황에서 사용할 수 있는 말이다.

31

★★ 직접의문문 how many

우리가 지난달에 얼마나 많은 자동차를 판매했나요?
(A) 모든 것이 세일 중입니다.
(B) 네, 저에게 세 부의 추가 사본이 있습니다.
(C) 수치를 확인해 봐야 할 겁니다.

어휘 How many ~? 얼마나 많은 ~? on sale 세일 중인 extra 추가의, 여분의 will have to do ~해야 할 것이다 figure 수치, 숫자

How many cars did we sell last month?

(A) Everything is on sale.
(B) Yes, I have three extra copies.
(C) I will have to check the figures.

문제 해설

얼마나 많은 자동차를 판매했는지 묻는 How many 의문문에 대해 직접적인 수량을 말해 주는 대신 수치를 확인해 봐야 알 수 있다는 의미를 나타내는 말로 답변하는 (C)가 정답이다.

토익 분석

(A)는 sell과 연관성 있게 들리는 on sale을 활용한 오답으로, 질문에서 과거를 나타내는 did와 함께 묻는 지난달의 판매 수량이 아닌 현재 시제 동사를 활용해 현재의 상황을 말하는 답변이므로 어울리지 않는다. (B)는 의문사 의문문에 어울리지 않는 Yes로 답변하는 오답이다.

Questions 32-34 refer to the following conversation.

M [32] Good morning, and thanks for calling Iron Air. This is Ed. How may I help you?

W Hello, this is Mary Young. [33] I have two tickets booked for the flight to Paris on Thursday at 6:40 P.M., but my husband and I can't make it for that time. I was wondering if we could change it to the 9:55 plane.

M OK, Ms. Young. We have some seats available for 9:55 P.M., but they are not together. Is that OK?

W We would really prefer to sit together. Are there any other options?

M Well, [34] I can move you up to first class and give you a 50% discount for being such a valued customer. How does that sound?

W That would be great. Thank you so much.

어휘 have A p.p. A가 ~되게 하다 book v. ~을 예약하다 make it 가다, 도착하다 I was wondering if ~인지 궁금합니다 available 이용 가능한 prefer to do ~하는 것을 선호하다 option 선택 가능한 것 move A up to B A를 B로 상향 조정해 주다 give A a discount for B A에게 B에 대해 할인해 주다 such a 이렇게, 이러한 valued 소중한

남 [32] 안녕하세요, Iron Air에 전화 주셔서 감사합니다. 저는 Ed입니다. 무엇을 도와 드릴까요?

여 안녕하세요, 저는 Mary Young입니다. [33] 목요일 오후 6시 40분에 파리로 가는 항공편 탑승권을 2장 예약했는데, 제 남편과 제가 그 시간에 맞춰 갈 수 없어서요. 9시 55분 비행기로 변경할 수 있는지 궁금합니다.

남 알겠습니다. Young 씨. 오후 9시 55분에 이용 가능하신 좌석이 좀 기는 하지만 함께 붙어 있는 좌석은 아닙니다. 괜찮으시겠어요?

여 저희는 정말로 함께 앉고 싶어요. 다른 선택 사항은 없나요?

남 저, [34] 일등석으로 상향 조정하고 이렇게 소중한 고객이 되어 주신 것에 대해 50%를 할인해 드릴 수 있습니다. 이렇게 하는 것은 어떠신가요?

여 좋을 것 같아요. 정말 감사합니다.

32

Where does the man most likely work?

(A) At a travel agency (B) At a restaurant
(C) At a hotel **(D) At an airline**

문제 해설

남자가 근무하는 장소에 대해 유추할 것을 요구하는 첫 번째 질문이므로 대화 초반부에서 남자의 근무 장소가 직접적으로 언급되는 부분, 혹은 이를 추측할 수 있을 만한 관련 어휘가 제시되는 부분에 집중해야 한다. 남자는 대화를 시작하면서 'Good morning, and thanks for calling Iron Air.'라는 말로 회사의 명칭을 포함해 인사말을 전하고 있으며, 뒤이어 여자가 항공권 변경에 대해 문의하는 내용을 통해서도 남자의 근무지를 유추할 수 있으므로 (D)가 정답임을 알 수 있다. 남자가 직접 항공권 변경 및 관련 업무를 진행하는 상황이므로 (A)와 혼동하지 않도록 주의해야 한다.

★ 도입부 정보

남자는 어디에서 일하고 있을 가능성이 있는가?
(A) 여행사에서
(B) 레스토랑에서
(C) 호텔에서
(D) 항공사에서

어휘 travel agency 여행사

토익 분석

남자의 직업은 남자의 첫 번째 대화 문장에서 답을 찾을 수 있다.

33

Why is the woman calling?

(A) To make a formal complaint (B) To inquire about a package tour
(C) To find out more about food options **(D) To request a time change**

문제 해설

여자가 전화를 거는 목적을 묻는 두 번째 질문이므로 대화 중반부에서 들을 수 있는 여자의 말에서 중점적으로 언급되는 핵심 내용을 파악하는 것이 관건이다. 여자는 자신이 원하는 바를 'I have two tickets booked for the flight to Paris on Thursday at 6:40 P.M., but my husband and I can't make it for that time. I was wondering if we could change it to the 9:55 plane.'라고 알리고 있으며, 이 말의 핵심은 시간을 변경하는 것이므로 (D)가 정답임을 알 수 있다.

★★ 주제, 목적

여자는 왜 전화를 거는가?
(A) 정식 항의를 하기 위해
(B) 패키지여행에 관해 문의하기 위해
(C) 선택 가능한 음식에 관해 더 알아보기 위해
(D) 시간 변경을 요청하기 위해

어휘 make a complaint 항의하다, 불평하다 formal 정식의, 공식의 inquire about ~에 관해 문의하다

토익 분석

요청, 제안 표현 중 하나인 If you could~, 가 정답 힌트로 제시되었다.

34

What does the man offer the woman?

(A) A refund on a ticket (B) A voucher for a hotel
(C) A discount on an upgrade (D) A complimentary meal

문제 해설

남자가 제공하는 것을 묻는 마지막 문제이므로 대화 후반부에서 들을 수 있는 남자의 말에서 자신이 해 주겠다고 제안하는 내용에 집중해야 한다. 남자는 대화 후반부에 'I can move you up to first class and give you a 50% discount for being such a valued customer. How does that sound?'라는 말로 좌석 등급을 올리고 이에 대해 50% 할인을 제공해 줄 수 있다고 말한 뒤에 이것이 어떤지를 묻고 있으므로 (C)가 정답임을 알 수 있다.

★★ 요청, 제안

남자는 여자에게 무엇을 제공하는가?
(A) 티켓에 대한 환불
(B) 호텔에서 사용 가능한 쿠폰
(C) 등급 상향 조정에 대한 할인
(D) 무료 식사

어휘 refund on ~에 대한 환불 voucher 쿠폰, 상품권 discount on ~에 대한 할인 complimentary 무료의

토익 분석

대표적인 요청, 제안 표현인 I can~이 힌트로 사용된다.

여 안녕하세요, [35] Bill. 제가 월간 진행 상황 업데이트를 작성하려고 노력 중인데, 새로운 가이드라인을 아직 받지 못했어요. 당신은 받았어요?

남 어제 받기로 되어 있었는데, 아직 아무 얘기도 듣지 못했어요. [36] 팀장님 사무실로 가서 물어보는 게 어때요?

여 그러려고 해 봤는데, 팀장님 비서가 그러는데 오전 중에는 자리를 비우신다고 하더라고요.

남 알겠어요. [37] 저, 점심시간 이후에 열리는 회의까지 기다려 봅시다. 부서 전체가 그곳에 참석할 거예요.

여 좋은 생각이에요. 거기서 봐요.

Questions 35-37 refer to the following conversation.

W   Hey, Bill. [35] I'm trying to write the monthly status update but haven't been given the new guidelines yet. Have you received them?

M   We were supposed to get them yesterday, but I haven't heard anything. [36] Why don't you go to the manager's office and ask her?

W   I tried, but her secretary said she's away during the morning.

M   OK. [37] Well let's just wait until the meeting after lunch. The whole department will be there.

W   Good idea. I'll see you there.

어휘 status (진행) 상황 receive ~을 받다 be supposed to do ~하기로 되어 있다, ~할 예정이다 Why don't you ~? ~하는 게 어때요? secretary 비서 away 부재중인, 자리를 비운

35

★★ 세부 정보

여자는 무엇을 받기 위해 여전히 기다리는 중인가?
(A) 매출 보고서
(B) 근무 일정표
(C) 프로젝트 가이드라인
(D) 연락처

어휘 sales 매출, 판매(량) contact information 연락처

토익 분석

여자 대화에서 답을 찾는 세부 정보 문제. 반전 표현인 but 이 결정적인 힌트를 제시했다.

What is the woman still waiting to receive?

(A) A sales report
(B) A work schedule
(C) Some project guidelines
(D) Some contact information

문제 해설

여자가 받기 위해 기다리는 것을 묻는 첫 번째 질문이므로 대화 초반부에서 여자가 뭔가를 받는 일과 관련해 언급하는 내용을 파악하는 것이 관건이다. 여자는 대화를 시작하면서 'I'm trying to write the monthly status update but haven't been given the new guidelines yet.'라는 말로 자신이 작성 중인 문서와 관련된 가이드라인을 아직 받지 못했다고 알리고 있으므로 이를 'project guidelines'라는 말로 표현한 (C)가 정답이다.

36

★ 요청, 제안

남자는 여자가 무엇을 하도록 권하는가?
(A) 일찍 출근할 것
(B) 팀장의 사무실에 들를 것
(C) 웹 사이트를 방문할 것
(D) 약속을 잡을 것

어휘 sales 매출, 판매(량) contact information 연락처

토익 분석

남자 대화에서 요청, 제안 표현 찾기. Why don't you~가 정답 힌트로 사용된다.

What does the man recommend the woman do?

(A) Come in to work early
(B) Come by a manager's office
(C) Visit a Web site
(D) Make an appointment

문제 해설

남자가 여자에게 권하는 일을 파악하도록 요구하는 두 번째 문제이므로 대화 중반부에서 제시되는 남자의 말에서 제안이나 권고 등과 관련된 표현과 함께 언급되는 정보를 파악해야 한다. 남자는 대화 중반부에 'Why don't you ~?'를 활용한 제안 표현을 통해 'Why don't you go to the manager's office and ask her?'라는 말로 부서장 사무실로 가서 물어보라고 제안하고 있으므로 이를 'Come by a manager's office'로 바꿔 표현한 (B)가 정답이다.

37

★★ 미래 행동

남자는 오늘 오후에 무슨 일이 있을 것이라고 말하는가?
(A) 신입 직원들이 채용될 것이다.
(B) 직원회의가 열릴 것이다.
(C) 새로운 서버가 설치될 것이다.
(D) 마감 시한이 정해질 것이다.

어휘 take place 일어나다, 발생되다 install ~을 설치하다 deadline 마감시한 choose ~을 정하다, 선택하다

토익 분석

미래 행동 문제로 남자의 가장 마지막 문장에 정답이 등장한다. 요청, 제안 표현인 let's~와 this afternoon때 paraphrase한 after lunch가 정답 힌트이다.

What does the man say will happen this afternoon?

(A) Some new employees will be hired.
(B) A staff meeting will take place.
(C) A new server will be installed.
(D) A deadline will be chosen.

문제 해설

남자가 오늘 오후에 있을 일로 언급하는 것을 찾도록 요구하는 마지막 질문이므로 대화의 후반부에서 '오늘 오후'를 나타내는 시점 표현과 함께 제시되는 정보에 집중해 들어야 한다. 남자는 대화 후반부에 'Well let's just wait until the meeting after lunch. The whole department will be there.'라는 말로 오후 시간을 가리키기 위해 '점심 식사 후'라는 시점 표현을 활용해 전체 부서가 모이는 회의가 있음을 알리고 있으므로 이를 직원회의가 열린다는 말로 바꿔 표현한 (B)가 정답이다.

Questions 38-40 refer to the following conversation.

W   Hi, Phil. ³⁸ What's happening with the invitations for this year's company Christmas party?

M   Well, we haven't printed them out yet, as we may have run into a problem with the usual restaurant. ³⁹ It seems they don't have any tables for our party on the eighteenth.

W   Oh, really? But we've always managed to book the party room.

M   Not this time. I guess we contacted them too late this year. What should we do?

W   Well, it's too late to cancel the party, so ⁴⁰ I'll give my friend a call right now. She has a new Italian restaurant downtown that we could go to instead.

M   That sounds like a good plan. Let me know how you get on.

어휘 print out ~을 인쇄하다 may have p.p. ~했을 수도 있다 run into ~와 맞닥뜨리다 usual 평상시의, 보통의 manage to do 어떻게든 ~하다 book v. ~을 예약하다 contact ~에게 연락하다 too 형용사 to do ~하기에는 너무 …한 cancel ~을 취소하다 give A a call A에게 전화하다 downtown ad. 시내에 있는 instead 그 대신 let A know A에게 알리다 get on ~를 해 나가다, 꾸려 나가다

여   안녕하세요, Phil. ³⁸ 올해의 사내 크리스마스 파티 초청장에 무슨 일이 생긴 거죠?

남   저, 아직 인쇄를 하지 못했는데, 우리가 보통 이용하던 레스토랑에 문제가 생긴 것 같아요. ³⁹ 18일에 열리는 우리 파티에 필요한 테이블이 전혀 없는 것 같아요.

여   아, 정말이에요? 하지만 우리는 항상 어떻게든 파티룸을 예약해 왔잖아요.

남   이번엔 아니에요. 제 생각에는 올해는 너무 늦게 연락한 것 같아요. 어떻게 하죠?

여   음, 파티를 취소하기에는 너무 늦었으니까 ⁴⁰ 제가 친구에게 지금 바로 전화해 볼게요. 우리가 대신 갈 만한 새로운 이탈리안 레스토랑을 그 친구가 시내에서 운영하고 있어요.

남   좋은 계획인 것 같아요. 어떻게 되어 가는지 제게 알려 주세요.

38

What are the speakers discussing?

(A) A new advertisement   **(B) A company celebration**
(C) An overseas excursion   (D) A restaurant's grand opening

문제 해설

대화의 주제를 묻는 첫 번째 질문이므로 대화 초반부에서 중점적으로 언급하는 핵심 내용을 파악하는 것이 관건이다. 대화를 시작하면서 여자가 'What's happening with the invitations for this year's company Christmas party?'라는 말로 회사의 크리스마스 파티에 필요한 초청장에 대해 묻고 있으므로 이 행사에 대해 기념행사를 뜻하는 'company celebration'으로 바꿔 표현한 (B)가 정답이다.

★ 주제, 목적

화자들은 무엇에 관해 이야기하고 있는가?
(A) 새로운 광고   (B) 회사의 기념행사
(C) 해외여행   (D) 레스토랑 개장식

어휘 advertisement 광고 celebration 기념행사, 축하 행사 excursion 여행, 야유회

토익 분석

대화의 주제는 첫 번째 문장에 집중한다.

39

What problem does the man mention?

(A) A guest list is incomplete.   (B) A deadline cannot be met.
(C) A venue is fully booked.   (D) A date has been changed.

문제 해설

남자의 문제점에 대해 묻는 두 번째 질문이므로 대화 중반부에 언급되는 남자의 말에서 들을 수 있는 부정적인 내용을 파악하는 것이 관건이다. 남자는 행사를 개최할 장소와 관련해 'It seems they don't have any tables for our party on the eighteenth.'라는 말로 예약 가능한 테이블이 없는 것 같다는 문제점을 언급하고 있으므로 이에 대해 언급한 (C)가 정답이다. 예약할 자리가 없는 것에 대해 정답 보기에서는 'fully booked'라는 말로 바꿔 표현하고 있다.

★★ 문제점

남자는 무슨 문제점을 언급하는가?
(A) 초대 손님 목록이 완료되지 않았다.
(B) 마감 시한이 충족될 수 없다.
(C) 한 장소에 예약이 완전히 찼다.
(D) 날짜가 변경되었다.

어휘 incomplete 완료되지 않은 meet a deadline 마감 기한을 충족하다 venue (행사 등의) 개최 장소 fully 완전히, 모두 booked 예약된

토익 분석

남자의 문제점은 남자의 초반부 대화 문장에 제시된다.

40

What will the woman most likely do next?

(A) Visit a restaurant   **(B) Call a friend**
(C) E-mail a manager   (D) Review a menu

문제 해설

여자의 추후 행동을 묻는 마지막 질문이며, 이에 대한 단서는 대화 후반부 또는 최종 화자의 말에서 제시되는 경우가 일반적이다. 여자는 대화 후반부에 자신들이 원했던 장소를 예약할 수 없는 상황과 관련해 'I'll give my friend a call right now. She has a new Italian restaurant downtown that we could go to instead.'라는 말로 레스토랑을 운영하는 자신의 친구에게 전화를 걸어 해결 방법을 찾아보려 하고 있으므로 (B)가 정답임을 알 수 있다.

★★ 미래 행동

여자는 곧이어 무엇을 할 가능성이 가장 큰가?
(A) 레스토랑을 방문한다.
(B) 자신의 친구에게 전화한다.
(C) 부서장에게 이메일을 보낸다.
(D) 메뉴를 확인한다.

어휘 review ~을 확인하다, 검토하다

토익 분석

미래 행동이므로 여자의 마지막 대화 문장에 집중한다. 미래 행동 답변을 이끄는 대표적인 힌트인 I'll이 사용된다.

남 ⁴¹ 여러분, 오전 8시 기차가 1시간 정도 지연될 거라고 막 공지됐어요.
여1 아, 너무 안 좋네요. ⁴² 우리가 9시에 출발하면, 고객 사무실에 11시까지 절대로 도착할 수 없을 거예요.
남 ⁴² 제 생각도 그래요. 기다리고 있을 여유가 없어요.
여2 당신 말이 맞아요. 그렇게 되면 우리 쪽 사람들이 전문적인 것으로 보이지 않을 거예요. 차량을 렌트할 시간이 충분한가요?
여1 그렇지 않을 거예요. ⁴³ 약간 비싸기는 하겠지만, 택시를 부를 수 있어요.
남 ⁴³ 좋은 생각이에요. 지금 바로 할게요.

Questions 41-43 refer to the following conversation with three speakers.

M ⁴¹ Hey guys, they just announced that the 8:00 A.M. train will be delayed by one hour.
W1 Oh, that's too bad. ⁴² If we leave at nine, we'll never get to our client's office by 11.
M ⁴² That's what I'm thinking. We can't afford to wait.
W2 You're right. That'll look unprofessional on our part. Is there enough time to rent a car?
W1 I don't think so. ⁴³ It will be a little expensive, but we could call a cab.
M ⁴³ Good idea. I'll do that now.

어휘 announce that ~라고 공지/발표하다 by (정도) ~만큼, (기한) ~까지 get to ~로 가다, ~에 도착하다 can't afford to do ~할 여유가 없다 unprofessional 전문적이지 않은 on one's part ~의 측에서 enough 충분한 rent ~을 대여하다 a little 약간, 조금 cab 택시

41

★★ 세부 정보

현재 기차는 몇 시에 출발할 것으로 예상되는가?
(A) 8시에
(B) 9시에
(C) 10시에
(D) 11시에

어휘 expect 예상하다 depart 출발하다

토익 분석

세부 정보 문제로 키워드 train을 활용해야 한다.

What time is the train now expected to depart?

(A) At 8:00 A.M.　　　　**(B) At 9:00 A.M.**
(C) At 10:00 A.M.　　　　(D) At 11:00 A.M.

문제 해설

기차가 출발할 것으로 예상되는 시간을 묻는 첫 번째 문제이므로 대화 시작 부분에서 기차 출발 시간과 관련된 정보를 파악해야 한다. 이때 특정 이유와 함께 기존의 시간이 변경되는 상황에 대해 알리는 경우가 많으므로 주의해야 한다. 대화를 시작하는 남자가 'Hey guys, they just announced that the 8:00 A.M. train will be delayed by one hour.'라는 말로 변경 시간을 알리고 있는데, 8시에서 1시간이 지연된 것이므로 (B)가 정답임을 알 수 있다.

42

★★★ 문제점

화자들은 왜 걱정하고 있는가?
(A) 엉뚱한 역에 와 있다.
(B) 다른 탑승객을 기다리고 있다.
(C) 버스표를 잃어버렸다.
(D) 회의에 늦을 것이다.

어휘 concerned 걱정하는, 우려하는 passenger 탑승객

토익 분석

대화의 문제점은 초반부에 제시된다. if가정법~이 정답을 제시하고 있다. 가정법 문장은 언제나 중요한 힌트를 제시한다.

Why are the speakers concerned?

(A) They are at the wrong station.　　(B) They are waiting for another passenger.
(C) They lost their bus tickets.　　**(D) They will be late for a meeting.**

문제 해설

화자들이 걱정하는 이유를 묻는 두 번째 질문이므로 대화 중반부에서 화자들이 특정 문제점과 함께 걱정이나 우려 등을 나타내는 표현을 통해 언급하는 정보를 파악해야 한다. 열차 출발 시간이 변경되었다는 말을 들은 여자들 중의 한 명이 'If we leave at 9:00, we'll never get to our client's office by 11:00.'라는 말로 고객과 만나는 시간에 맞춰 갈 수 없을 것에 대해 언급하자 남자도 곧바로 'That's what I'm thinking. We can't afford to wait.'라고 동의하고 있으므로 화자들은 회의에 늦을까 걱정하고 있음을 알 수 있다. 따라서 이와 같은 문제점에 대해 언급한 (D)가 정답이다.

43

★★ 미래 행동

남자는 곧이어 무엇을 할 가능성이 가장 큰가?
(A) 회의 일정을 재조정할 것이다.
(B) 택시를 부를 것이다.
(C) 다른 기차를 탈 것이다.
(D) 버스 정류장으로 갈 것이다.

어휘 reschedule ~의 일정을 재조정하다 take (교통수단) ~을 타다

토익 분석

미래 행동이므로 남자의 마지막 대화에 I'll~ 형태로 정답이 제시된다. 상대방 여자 대화에 반전 표현 but과 요청 제안 표현인 we could가 힌트를 제시했다.

What will the man most likely do next?

(A) Reschedule a meeting　　　　**(B) Call for a taxi**
(C) Take another train　　　　(D) Go to a bus station

문제 해설

남자의 추후 행동을 묻는 마지막 질문이며, 이에 대한 단서는 대화 후반부 또는 최종 화자의 말에서 제시되는 경우가 일반적이다. 대화의 후반부에 한 여자가 'It will be a little expensive, but we could call a cab.'이라는 말로 택시를 부르자고 제안하는 것에 대해 'Good idea. I'll do that now.'라는 말로 자신이 지금 바로 부르겠다고 알리고 있으므로 (B)가 정답이 된다.

Questions 44-46 refer to the following conversation.

W Welcome to the Newport Community Center. How can I help you?
M ⁴⁴ Hi, I'm new to the area and would like to get a membership card for this library. What do I have to do?
W Well, it's pretty simple. ⁴⁵ Do you have a driver's license or another piece of ID with a picture? ⁴⁶ Then I can start entering your details into the computer.
M ⁴⁶ Yes, I do. Here's my driver's license.
W ⁴⁶ Great. Your membership card will be ready in a few minutes. You can use our facilities and come back to pick it up later. Oh, I should warn you that our printer is not working at the moment, but it will be fixed on Tuesday.

어휘 be new to ~에 새로 이사 오다 would like to do ~하고 싶다 driver's license 운전면허증 ID (= identification) 신분증 then 그러면 enter A into B A를 B에 입력하다 details 세부 사항 warn A that A에게 ~라고 알리다. 주의를 주다 work (기계가) 작동하다 at the moment 현재 pick up ~을 가져가다, 가져오다

여 Newport Community Center에 오신 것을 환영합니다. 무엇을 도와 드릴까요?
남 ⁴⁴ 안녕하세요, 저는 이 지역에 새로 이사를 와서 이 도서관의 회원 카드를 발급받고 싶습니다. 뭘 해야 하나요?
여 저, 아주 간단합니다. ⁴⁵ 운전면허증이나 사진이 들어 있는 다른 신분증이 있으신가요? ⁴⁶ 그러면 컴퓨터에 귀하의 상세 정보를 입력하는 일을 시작할 수 있습니다.
남 ⁴⁶ 네, 있어요. 여기 제 운전면허증입니다.
여 ⁴⁶ 좋습니다. 귀하의 회원 카드는 몇 분 후에 준비가 될 겁니다. 저희 시설을 이용하시고 회원 카드를 가지러 잠시 후 돌아 오시기 바랍니다. 그리고 저희 프린터가 고장 났다는 것을 알려드려야겠군요. 목요일에 수리가 될 겁니다.

44

What does the man want to do?

(A) Obtain a membership　　(B) Start a subscription
(C) Purchase a book　　(D) Join a club

문제 해설

남자가 하고 싶어 하는 일에 관해 묻는 첫 번째 질문이므로 대화 초반부에서 제시되는 남자의 말에서 자신이 원하는 일과 관련해 언급하는 정보를 파악해야 하는 문제이다. 남자는 대화 초반부에 'Hi, I'm new to the area and would like to get a membership card for this library. What do I have to do?'라는 말로 회원 카드를 받고 싶다는 말로 자신이 원하는 것을 알리고 있으므로 이를 '회원 자격을 얻는 것'이라는 말로 바꿔 제시한 (A)가 정답이다.

★ **의도 파악**

남자는 무엇을 하고 싶어 하는가?
(A) 회원 자격을 얻는 것
(B) 정기 구독을 시작하는 것
(C) 책을 구입하는 것
(D) 클럽에 가입하는 것

어휘 obtain ~을 얻다 subscription (정기) 구독, (서비스 등의) 가입 purchase ~을 구입하다

토익 분석

남자의 의도는 남자 첫 번째 대화문에 집중해야 한다. 의도 표현인 (I) would like to~가 힌트를 제시하고 있다.

45

What does the woman ask the man to do?

(A) Complete some paperwork　　(B) Take a tour of the building
(C) Show some identification　　(D) Print out a document

문제 해설

여자가 남자에게 요청하는 것이 무엇인지를 묻는 두 번째 문제이므로 대화의 중반부에서 들을 수 있는 여자의 말에서 요청 표현과 함께 제시되는 정보에 집중해 들어야 한다. 여자는 대화 중반부에 'Do you have a driver's license or another piece of ID with a picture?'라는 말로 사진이 들어 있는 신분증이 있는지 묻고 있으므로 신분증을 보여 달라고 요청하고 있음을 알 수 있다. 따라서 (C)가 정답이 된다.

★★ **요청, 제안**

여자는 남자가 무엇을 하도록 요청하는가?
(A) 서류 작업을 완료하는 것　　(B) 건물을 견학하는 것
(C) 신분증을 제시하는 것　　　(D) 문서를 출력하는 것

어휘 complete ~을 완료하다 paperwork 서류 작업 take a tour of ~을 견학하다 print out ~을 출력하다

토익 분석

여자 대화에서 요청, 제안 힌트 문장을 찾아야 한다. 명령문과 의문문이 가장 흔한 힌트 문장으로 이 문제의 경우 Do you have~? 의문문이 힌트 표현이다.

46

Why does the woman say, "Great"?

(A) She is pleased about opening hours.
(B) She is impressed with the man's qualifications.
(C) She agrees with the man's suggestion.
(D) She can proceed with a process.

문제 해설

여자가 말하는 "Great"이라는 표현이 대화 속에서 어떤 의미로 사용되었는지를 묻는 세 번째 질문이므로 대화 후반부에 제시되는 여자의 말을 통해 해당 표현을 확인할 수 있어야 하며, 이때 앞뒤에 함께 제시되는 말들을 통해 의미의 흐름을 파악해 정답을 찾아야 한다. 여자는 대화의 맨 마지막에 해당 표현을 사용하고 있다. 이는 앞서 'Then I can start entering your details into the computer.'라는 말로 신분증 정보를 입력할 수 있다고 말하는 것에 대해 남자가 그의 신분증을 제시하는 것에 대한 반응으로 사용한 말이므로 회원 가입 절차를 진행할 수 있다는 의미를 나타내는 (D)가 정답임을 알 수 있다.

★★★ **맥락 파악**

여자는 왜 "Great"라고 말하는가?
(A) 영업시간에 대해 만족하고 있다.
(B) 남자의 자격 요건에 깊은 인상을 받았다.
(C) 남자의 제안에 동의하고 있다.
(D) 절차를 진행할 수 있다.

어휘 pleased 만족한, 기쁜 be impressed with ~에 깊은 인상을 받다 qualification 자격 요건 agree with ~에 동의하다 suggestion 제안 proceed with ~을 진행하다 process 절차, 과정

토익 분석

대화의 흐름을 파악해야 한다 결정적인 힌트는 요청, 제안 표현들 중 하나인 (Then) I can~ 이 제시되고 있다.

남 됐습니다, 고객님, 고객님의 제품에 대한 계산을 마쳤습니다. 오늘 제가 도와 드릴 다른 일은 또 없으신가요?
여 실은, [47, 48] 새 드릴 날이 좀 필요해요. 이 제품은 어디에서 찾을 수 있죠?
남 [47] 4번 통로에 전동 드릴과 공구 벨트 사이에 있습니다. 어느 사이즈를 찾고 계신가요?
여 흠. [48] 다양한 사이즈가 필요해요. 제가 이전에 사용하던 세트를 최근에 잃어버렸어요.
남 알겠습니다, 그럼 진열된 Craftworks 16개들이 세트를 구매하는 건 어떠세요? [49] 재고가 너무 많은 세트라서 반값에 드릴 수 있는데, 고객님께서 오늘 이미 꽤 많이 비용을 지불하셔서요.
여 [49] 그것 잘됐네요. 정말 감사합니다. 지금 가서 가져올게요.
남 별말씀을요. 돌아오시는 대로 다른 제품에 추가해 드리겠습니다.

Questions 47-49 refer to the following conversation.

M   OK, ma'am, I've finished ringing up your goods. Is there anything else I can help you with today?

W   Actually, [47, 48] I need some new drill bits. Where can I find those?

M   [47] There are some in aisle 4 between the power drills and tool belts. Which size are you looking for?

W   Hmm. [48] I'll need a variety of sizes. I recently lost my previous set.

M   OK, why don't you get the Craftworks 16-piece set on display? [49] We have too many sets in stock, so I'll give it to you for half price, as you have spent quite a bit already today.

W   [49] That's wonderful! Thank you so much. I'll go and get it now.

M   No problem. I'll add it to your other goods once you get back.

어휘 finish -ing ~하는 것을 마치다 ring up ~을 계산하다 goods 제품, 상품 help A with B A가 B하는 것을 돕다 drill bit 드릴 날 find ~을 찾아내다 aisle 통로, 복도 tool belt 공구 벨트 look for ~을 찾다 a variety of 다양한 recently 최근에 previous 이전의 on display 진열 중인 have A in stock A를 재고로 갖고 있다 half price 반값 quite a bit 꽤 많이 add A to B A를 B에 추가하다 once 일단 ~하면 get back 돌아오다

47

★★ 도입부 정보

대화가 어디에서 일어나고 있을 가능성이 가장 큰가?
(A) 식료품 매장에서　　(B) 전자 제품 매장에서
(C) 자동차 매장에서　　(D) 공구점에서

어휘 take place 벌어지다 grocery store 식료품점

토익 분석

장소 힌트는 대화의 첫 번째 문장과 최대 두 번째 문장에 힌트가 반드시 등장한다.

Where is the conversation most likely taking place?

(A) At a grocery store　　(B) At an electronics store
(C) At an auto shop　　**(D) At a hardware store**

문제 해설

대화 장소에 관해 묻는 첫 번째 질문이므로 대화 초반부에서 대화 장소를 직접적으로 밝히는 부분 혹은 대화 장소를 유추할 수 있는 단서가 제시되는 부분에 집중해야 한다. 대화 초반부에서 언급되는 제품 명칭들, 즉 new drill bits, power drills and tool belts 등의 정보를 통해 화자들이 대화를 나누는 장소가 (D)임을 알 수 있다.

48

★★ 의도 파악

여자는 무엇이 필요하다고 말하는가?
(A) 다양한 색상의 제품　　(B) 익일 배송
(C) 다양한 사이즈의 제품　　(D) 제품 품질 보증

어휘 various 다양한 overnight delivery 익일 배송 warranty 품질 보증(서)

토익 분석

여자의 의도를 나타내는 힌트 표현인 I need (to)와 I'll이 결합되어 사용되었다.

What does the woman say she needs?

(A) Items in various colors　　(B) Overnight delivery
(C) Products in different sizes　　(D) A product warranty

문제 해설

여자가 필요로 하는 것을 밝히는 내용에 대해 묻는 두 번째 질문이므로 대화 중반부에서 언급되는 여자의 말에서 자신이 필요로 하는 것을 알리는 부분에 집중해 들어야 한다. 여자는 제품 사이즈에 대해 묻는 남자의 말에 'Hmm. I'll need a variety of sizes.'라고 대답하고 있으므로 다양한 사이즈로 된 제품이 필요하다는 것을 알 수 있으므로 (C)가 정답이 된다.

49

★★★ 암시 추론

여자는 왜 남자에게 감사해 하는가?
(A) 자신의 구입 제품을 선물용으로 포장해 주었다.
(B) 자신에게 무료 제품을 주었다.
(C) 자신에게 할인을 제공해 주었다.
(D) 무료 배송을 준비해 주었다.

어휘 giftwrap ~을 선물용으로 포장해 주다 purchase n. 구매 제품 complimentary (=free) 무료의 provide A with B A에게 B를 제공해 주다 arrange for ~을 준비하다

토익 분석

남자 후반부 대화에 반전 표현 So, 의도나 미래 행동 힌트인 I'll~이 사용되어 힌트를 제시하고 여자의 후반부 대화에서 키워드 thank you가 등장했다.

Why does the woman thank the man?

(A) He giftwrapped her purchases.
(B) He gave her a complimentary item.
(C) He provided her with a discount.
(D) He arranged for a free delivery.

문제 해설

여자가 감사하는 이유를 묻는 마지막 문제이므로 대화 후반부에 여자의 말에서 언급되는 '감사 표현'에 앞서 남자가 말하는 내용을 파악하는 것이 관건이다. 대화 후반부에 남자는 여자의 제품 구매와 관련해 'We have too many sets in stock, so I'll give it to you for half price, as you have spent quite a bit already today.'라는 말로 반값에 제공하겠다고 알리고 있고 이에 대해 여자가 감사하고 있으므로 할인을 뜻하는 'discount'로 바꿔 해당 대화 상황에 대해 언급한 (C)가 정답이다.

Questions 50-52 refer to the following conversation.

M [51] Who are those people lined up in front of our office building? They are young and look like students, but they are all quite well-dressed.

W [51] They are all college students who will graduate this semester. [50] Today is our company's open house for recruiting talent.

M Really? This is the first time I heard about it! [51] I don't think the company has ever held such an event before. Whose idea was it?

W It was the personnel department's suggestion. [52] They concluded it would be cheaper than running year-round ads in the media.

어휘 line up 줄을 서다 quite 꽤 well-dressed 옷을 잘 차려입은 graduate 졸업하다 semester 학기 open house 오픈 하우스, 일반 공개일 recruit ~을 채용하다 talent 인재, 재능, 소질 hold an event 행사를 주최하다 Personnel Department 인사부 suggestion 제안 run an ad (advertisement) 광고를 내다 year-round 1년 내내

남 [51] 우리 사무실 건물 앞에 줄 서 있는 저 사람들은 누구인가요? 모두 다 학생같이 어려 보이는데 모두 정장 차림이네요.

여 [51] 전부 이번 학기에 졸업하는 대학생들이에요. [50] 오늘이 인재들을 채용하고자 마련한 회사의 오픈 하우스 행사 날이거든요.

남 그래요? 저는 그 행사에 대해 처음 듣네요! [51] 제가 알기론 회사에서 이전엔 이런 행사를 하지 않았던 걸로 알고 있습니다. 누구의 생각이었나요?

여 이 행사는 인사부에서 제안한 겁니다. [52] 방송 매체에 1년 내내 광고를 내는 것보다 이 행사가 광고비를 더 절감할 수 있다는 결론을 내린 겁니다.

50

Who most likely are the speakers?

(A) Tour guides

(B) Company employees

(C) Real estate agents

(D) College professors

문제 해설

화자들의 신분을 유추해야 하는 첫 번째 질문이므로 대화 전반부에서 화자의 정체를 추측할 수 있을 만한 관련 어휘 및 표현에 집중해야 한다. 여자가 'Today is our company's open house for recruiting talent.'라는 말로 소속 회사에서 인재 채용을 위한 행사가 있음을 밝히는 부분을 통해 화자들은 회사에 근무하는 직원들임을 유추할 수 있으므로 (B)가 정답이다.

★ 도입부 정보

화자들은 누구일 것 같은가?

(A) 관광 가이드　　　　(B) 회사 직원

(C) 부동산 중개업자　　(D) 대학교수

어휘 real estate agent 부동산 중개업자 professor 교수

토익 분석

직업은 언제나 대화의 첫 번째 문장이나 두 번째 문장에 힌트가 제시된다.

51

Who are the speakers talking about?

(A) Prospective employees　　(B) Advertising experts

(C) New college students　　(D) Corporate executives

문제 해설

화자들이 집중적으로 언급하고 있는 대상자의 정체를 묻고 있으므로 대화에서 화자들이 말하는 특정인의 정보에 집중해야 할 필요가 있다. 남자는 대화 시작과 함께 여자에게 특정 사람들에 대해 묻자 여자가 'They are all college students who will graduate this semester. Today is our company's open house for recruiting talent.'라는 말로 대학 졸업생들이 회사의 인재 채용을 위한 행사에 왔음을 알리고 있다. 따라서 취업 준비를 하는 사람들임을 알 수 있으므로 '잠재 직원'을 뜻하는 (A)가 정답이다.

★★ 주제, 목적

화자들은 누구에 관해 이야기하고 있는가?

(A) 잠재 직원들　　　(B) 광고 전문가들

(C) 대학 신입생들　　(D) 회사 임원들

어휘 prospective 잠재적인, 유망한 expert 전문가 executive 임원

토익 분석

초반부 대화에 대화의 주제가 제시된다.

52

According to the woman, what is the purpose of the event?

(A) Cost reduction　　(B) Social responsibility

(C) Career development　　(D) Aggressive advertising

문제 해설

행사의 목적을 묻는 마지막 질문이므로 대화 후반부에 제시되는 행사 관련 정보를 노려 들어야 한다. 대화 말미에 여자는 남자에게 'They concluded it would be cheaper than running year-round ads in the media.'라고 이야기하며 매체를 통한 광고보다 이러한 행사가 비용이 더 적게 소요된다는 점을 언급하고 있다. 따라서 이를 통해 비용을 아끼는 것이 행사의 목적임을 알 수 있으므로 (A)가 정답이다.

★★ 세부 정보

여자에 따르면, 행사의 목적은 무엇인가?

(A) 비용 절감

(B) 사회적 책임

(C) 경력 개발

(D) 적극적 광고 활동

어휘 reduction 감소, 절감 responsibility 책임 development 개발, 발전 aggressive 적극적인, 공격적인

토익 분석

마지막 문제는 후반부에 답이 제시된다. 후반부 여자 대화에 집중한다.

여 여러분, 안녕하세요. ⁵³ 이번 주에 우리가 새로운 책
    상들과 의자들을 우리 사무실에 들여놓는다는 것을
    다시 한 번 알려 드립니다.
남1 오, 거의 잊을 뻔했네요. 사무실을 개선할 때가 되었
     죠.
남2 일을 간단히 처리하기 위해 우리가 할 수 있는 게 있
     나요?
여 ⁵⁴ 네. 두 분 모두 각자의 문서를 모두 확인해 보고 상
    자에 넣어 주셨으면 합니다.
남1 좋은 생각이에요. 사무실을 바꾸는 동안 중요한 것을
     잃어버리고 싶지 않아요. 사실, 저는 바닥이 약간 걱
     정돼요.
남2 맞아요. ⁵⁵ 진짜 목재로 되어 있어서 조금이라도 긁히
     면 완전히 망가질 거예요.
여 알겠어요, 제가 배송하시는 분들께 조심해 달라고 얘
    기할게요.

Questions 53-55 refer to the following conversation with three speakers.

W   Hi, guys. ⁵³ Just a reminder that this is the weekend we will be getting new
     desks and chairs put in our offices.
M1   Oh, I almost forgot. It's about time we upgrade.
M2   Is there anything we can do to simplify the process?
W   ⁵⁴ Yes. I'd like you both to go through all of your documents and put them
     into boxes.
M1   Good idea. We don't want to lose anything important during the change.
     Actually, I'm a little worried about the floor.
M2   Right. ⁵⁵ It's genuine hardwood, and any scratches would completely ruin it.
W   OK, I'll tell the delivery guys to be careful.

어휘 Just a reminder that ~라는 점을 다시 한 번 알려 드립니다 get A p.p. A가 ~되게 하다 It's about time (that)
~할 때가 되다 simplify ~을 간단히 하다 go through ~을 확인/검토하다 document 문서, 서류 put A into B A를 B
에 넣다 lose ~을 잃어버리다 actually 사실, 실은 a little 약간, 조금 be worried about ~에 대해 걱정하다 genuine
진짜의, 진품의 hardwood 목재 scratch 긁힘, 스크래치 completely 완전히 ruin ~을 망가뜨리다

53

★★ 세부 정보

여자의 말에 의하면, 이번 주말에 무슨 일이 있을 것인가?
(A) 파티가 열릴 것이다.
(B) 사무실이 개조될 것이다.
(C) 새로운 컴퓨터들이 배송될 것이다.
(D) 새로운 가구가 설치될 것이다.

어휘 take place 열리다, 개최되다 renovate ~을 개조하
다, 보수하다 deliver ~을 배송하다 install ~을 설치하다

토익 분석

여자의 초반부 대화에서 키워드 **weekend**를 이용하는 문제
이다.

According to the woman, what will happen this weekend?

(A) A party will take place.

(B) An office will be renovated.

(C) New computers will be delivered.

(D) New furniture will be installed.

문제 해설

여자의 말에서 확인할 수 있는 이번 주말에 있을 일을 파악하도록 요구하는 첫 번째 질문이므
로 대화 초반부에서 제시되는 여자의 말에 집중해야 한다. 여자는 대화를 시작하면서 'Just a
reminder~our offices.'라는 말로 주말에 새로운 책상과 의지가 사무실에 들어온다고 알리고 있으
므로 이를 'New furniture'로 바꿔 표현해 '새로운 가구가 설치된다'라고 언급한 (D)가 정답이다.

54

★★ 요청, 제안

여자는 남자에게 무엇을 하도록 요청하는가?
(A) 쓰레기를 버릴 것   (B) 문서를 정리할 것
(C) 컴퓨터의 플러그를 뺄 것 (D) 회의에 참석할 것

어휘 throw away ~을 버리다 pack up (짐 등) ~을 꾸리다
unplug 플러그를 빼다 attend ~에 참석하다

토익 분석

여자 대화에서 요청, 제안 힌트 표현을 들어야 한다.
I want you to 의 변형인 **I'd like you to ~**를 이용하여 정답
을 제시했다.

What does the woman ask the men to do?

(A) Throw away some trash   **(B) Pack up some files**

(C) Unplug their computers   (D) Attend a meeting

문제 해설

여자가 요청하는 것을 파악하는 두 번째 질문이므로 대화 중반부에 제시되는 여자의 말에서 요청이
나 부탁 등을 나타내는 표현과 함께 언급되는 정보를 파악해야 한다. 여자는 대화 중반부에 'I'd like
you to ~'라는 요청 표현을 이용해 'I'd like you~into boxes.'와 같이 요청하고 있는데, 문서를 확인
해 상자에 넣어 정리하도록 요청하고 있으므로 (B)가 정답임을 알 수 있다.

55

★★★ 세부 정보

남자들은 바닥재에 관해 무슨 말을 하는가?
(A) 쉽게 손상될 수 있다.   (B) 교체될 수 있다.
(C) 청소되어야 한다.   (D) 최근에 설치되었다.

어휘 easily 쉽게 damaged 손상된 replace ~을 교체하
다 recently 최근에

토익 분석

세 번째 문제로 후반부 남자들의 대화에서 키워드
flooring을 활용한다. 반전 표현 **Actually**와 키워드 **floor**가
힌트를 제시한다.

What do the men suggest about the flooring?

(A) It can be easily damaged.   (B) It will be replaced.

(C) It needs to be cleaned.   (D) It was recently installed.

문제 해설

남자들이 바닥재에 관해 말하는 내용에 대해 묻는 세 번째 질문이므로 대화의 후반부에 집중해야
한다. 대화 후반부에 남자들 중의 한 명이 'Actually, I'm a little worried about the floor.' 바닥이
걱정된다'고 말을 꺼내자 다른 남자가 이에 대해 'It's genuine hardwood, and any scratches would
completely ruin it.'라는 말로 그 이유에 해당하는 내용을 덧붙이고 있다. 이는 손상되기 쉬운 상태
라는 것을 의미하므로 (A)가 정답이 된다.

Questions 56-58 refer to the following conversation.

M   Excuse me. I'm here to meet Ms. Johansson. I was contacted by her about a job offer last week. She told me to meet her here at one o'clock today.

W   You must be Mr. Anderson. Thanks for coming here. Unfortunately, [56] Ms. Johansson isn't in the building right now. She's caught in traffic at the moment. She said she'll be here in thirty minutes, but perhaps she'll be here a little earlier if she's lucky. Would you mind waiting for a while?

M   Not at all. [58] Do you mind if I come back in thirty minutes then? [57] I haven't eaten lunch yet, so I'd like to go outside and eat something.

W   Sure, you are more than welcome to do that. [58] Why don't you come back in an hour? I'll tell Ms. Johansson about the situation. Besides, she needs to catch up with other work, too. By the way, if you like sandwiches, you should try Joe's Sandwiches downstairs.

어휘 contact ~에게 연락하다 job offer 채용 제안 tell A to do A에게 ~하라고 말하다 be caught in traffic 교통 체증에 갇히다 Would you mind -ing? ~하시겠습니까? for a while 잠깐 동안 then 그럼, 그렇다면 be more than welcome to do 얼마든지 ~해도 좋다 besides 게다가 catch up with ~을 따라잡다 by the way (화제 전환) 그런데 downstairs 아래층에

남   실례합니다, 저는 Johansson 씨를 만나러 왔습니다. 지난주에 그분에서 채용 제안 차 제게 연락을 하셨습니다. 오늘 1시에 이곳에서 면접을 보자고 하셔서요.

여   그렇다면 당신이 Anderson 씨이군요. 와주셔서 감사합니다. 안타깝게도, [56] Johansson 씨께서 지금 구내에 안 계십니다. 현재 교통 체증에 갇혀 있으세요. 이곳에 30분 후에 도착할 것이라고 하셨는데 운이 좋으면 이보다 조금 일찍 도착하실 수 있다고 하셨어요. 잠시 기다려 주시겠어요?

남   물론입니다. [58] 그럼 제가 30분 뒤에 다시 와도 괜찮을까요? [57] 아직 점심 식사를 못 해서, 나가서 식사하고 싶은데요.

여   물론입니다. 얼마든지 그렇게 하셔도 됩니다. [58] 그러면 한 시간 뒤에 오시는 건 어떠세요? 제가 Johansson 씨께 이 상황에 대해 말씀을 드리겠습니다. 게다가 처리해야 할 다른 업무도 있으시고 해서요. 그건 그렇고, 샌드위치를 좋아하시면, 아래층에 있는 Joe's Sandwiches에 한 번 가 보세요.

56

Why is Ms. Johansson not in the office now?

(A) She forgot about an appointment.   (B) She went out for lunch.
(C) She is stuck in traffic.   (D) She was fired yesterday.

문제 해설

Johansson 씨가 사무실에서 없는 이유에 대해 묻는 첫 번째 질문이므로 대화 초반부에서 Johansson 씨가 사무실에 없는 상황과 함께 그 이유가 제시될 것임을 예상하고 대화를 들어야 한다. 대화 초반부에 여자가 'Ms. Johansson isn't in the building right now. She's caught in traffic at the moment.' 라는 말로 교통 체증에 갇혀 있는 상황임을 언급하고 있으므로 (C)가 정답이다.

★★ 세부 정보

왜 Johansson 씨가 현재 사무실에 없는가?
(A) 약속을 잊었나.   (B) 점심 식사를 위해 외출했다.
(C) 교통 체증에 갇혀 있다. (D) 어제 해고되었다.

어휘 forget about ~을 잊다 appointment 약속, 예약 fire ~을 해고하다

토익 분석

세부 정보 문제이기에 키워드를 찾아야 한다. Ms. Johansson이 키워드로 힌트를 제시하고 있다.

57

What does the man want to do?

(A) Try some sandwiches   (B) Submit an application
(C) Go get some food for lunch   (D) Call Ms. Johansson immediately

문제 해설

남자가 원하는 것을 묻는 두 번째 질문이므로 대화 중반부에 남자가 바람이나 희망 사항을 언급하는 부분을 파악해야 한다. 대화 중반부에 남자가 'I haven't eaten lunch yet, so I'd like to go outside and eat something.'이라는 말로 점심을 먹지 않아서 나가서 식사하고 싶어함을 밝히고 있으므로 (C)가 정답이다. 대화 중에 여자가 샌드위치를 추천하는 부분이 있는데, 이는 여자의 추천일 뿐 남자가 원하는 것은 아니므로 (A)를 잘못 고르지 않도록 주의해야 한다.

★★ 의도 파악

남자는 무엇을 하고 싶어 하는가?
(A) 샌드위치를 먹기   (B) 지원서를 제출하기
(C) 나가서 점심 식사하기
(D) Johansson 씨에게 즉시 연락하기

어휘 submit ~을 제출하다 application 지원서, 신청서 immediately 즉시

토익 분석

남자 대화에 집중해서 의도 답변을 이끄는 힌트를 찾아야 한다. 반전 표현 so와 대표적인 의도 표현인 I'd like to~가 정답을 제시하고 있다.

58

When does the woman tell the man to come back?

(A) In ten minutes   (B) In thirty minutes
(C) In an hour   (D) Tomorrow

문제 해설

남자가 돌아오는 시점에 대해 묻는 마지막 질문이므로 대화 후반부에서 남자가 돌아오는 시점이 언급되는 부분이 있음을 예상하고 들어야 한다. 대화 후반부에 남자는 'Do you mind if I come back in 30 minutes then?'라고 말하며 30분 뒤에 돌아와도 되는지 묻고 있지만, 여자가 곧이어 'Why don't you come back in an hour?'이라는 말로 한 시간 뒤에 돌아올 것을 권하고 있다. 따라서 결과적으로 남자는 한 시간 뒤에 올 것임을 유추할 수 있으므로 (C)가 정답이다.

★★ 요청, 제안

여자가 남자에게 언제 돌아오라고 말하고 있나?
(A) 10분 후   (B) 30분 후
(C) 한 시간 후   (D) 내일

어휘 probably 아마도 come back 돌아오다

토익 분석

여자의 후반부 대화에서 요청, 제안 표현 중 하나인 Why don't you~가 정답을 제시하고 있다.

여 안녕하세요. ⁵⁹ 제가 Hamilton Hotel로 가려고 하는데
    요. 이 버스가 맞는 방향으로 가는 건가요?
남 죄송하지만, 그쪽으로 가지 않습니다. ⁶⁰ 이 버스는
    공항으로 가는 급행 버스입니다.
여 알겠습니다. 도와주셔서 감사합니다.
남 별말씀을요. 204번 버스를 타실 것을 권해 드리겠
    지만, 이 정류장에는 한 시간에 한 번 밖에 오지 않는
    데다 막 떠났네요.
여 오, 저는 그렇게 오래 기다릴 수 없어요. 곧 누군가를
    만나야 해서요.
남 ⁶¹ 그러시면, 택시를 타셔야겠네요. 버스보다 그렇게
    더 많이 비싸지도 않을 겁니다. 길 맞은편에 있는 쇼
    핑몰 앞에서 택시 타는 곳을 찾을 수 있습니다.
여 잘됐네요. 정말 감사합니다.

Questions 59-61 refer to the following conversation.

W   Hello, ⁵⁹ I'd like to get to the Hamilton Hotel. Is this bus going in the correct direction?

M   Sorry, I don't go that way. ⁶⁰ This bus is an express bus to the airport.

W   OK, thanks for the help.

M   No problem. I would suggest taking the 204 bus, but it only comes to this stop once an hour and it just left.

W   Oh, I can't wait that long. I have to meet someone soon.

M   ⁶¹ In that case, you should take a taxi. It won't be much more expensive than the bus. You can find a taxi stand in front of the shopping mall across the street.

W   Great. Thanks a lot.

어휘 would like to do ~하고 싶다 get to ~로 가다 correct 맞는, 올바른 direction 방향 suggest -ing ~하기를 제안하다 once an hour 한 시간에 한 번 in that case 그러시다면, 그런 경우에는 expensive 비싼 pick A up A를 차로 태우다 in front of ~의 앞에 across ~의 맞은편에

59

★ 의도 파악

여자는 어디로 가기를 원하는가?
(A) 공항으로   (B) 버스 정류장으로
(C) 쇼핑몰로   (D) 호텔로

어휘 take place 열리다, 개최되다 renovate ~을 개조하다, 보수하다 deliver ~을 배송하다 install ~을 설치하다

토익 분석

여자의 의도를 묻는 문제는 여자의 초반부 대화문(첫 번째)에서 의도 답변을 이끄는 힌트 표현들에 집중한다. I'd like to~가 정답 힌트로 사용되었다.

Where does the woman want to go?

(A) To an airport
(B) To a bus station
(C) To a shopping mall
(D) To a hotel

문제 해설

여자가 가기를 원하는 장소를 묻는 첫 번째 문제이므로 대화 초반부에서 '이동 및 목적지' 등과 관련해 제시되는 정보에 집중해 들어야 한다. 여자는 대화를 시작하면서 'I'd like to get to the Hamilton Hotel.'라는 말로 특정 호텔에 가고 싶다고 알리고 있으므로 (D)가 정답이다.

60

★★ 도입부 정보

여자는 누구에게 얘기하고 있는가?
(A) 매장 점원   (B) 버스 기사
(C) 투어 가이드   (D) 상사

어휘 clerk 점원 supervisor 상사, 책임자

토익 분석

직업은 대화의 첫 번째 또는 두 번째 문장에 반드시 힌트가 등장한다.

Who is the woman talking to?

(A) A store clerk   **(B) A bus driver**
(C) A tour guide   (D) A supervisor

문제 해설

여자가 대화를 나누는 상대방의 신분에 대해 유추할 것을 요구하는 두 번째 질문이므로 대화 중반부에서 상대방의 직업이나 특정 업무와 관련해 추측할 수 있을 만한 관련 어휘가 제시되는 부분에 집중해야 한다. 대화 중반부에 남자는 여자의 문의 사항을 들은 후 'This bus is an express bus to the airport.'라는 말로 대답하고 있으므로 남자는 버스 기사인 것으로 추측할 수 있다. 따라서 (B)가 정답이 된다.

61

★ 요청, 제안

남자는 여자가 무엇을 하도록 권하는가?
(A) 티켓을 구입할 것   (B) 쇼핑몰을 방문할 것
(C) 급행 버스를 기다릴 것 (D) 택시를 탈 것

어휘 purchase ~을 구입하다

토익 분석

세 번째 문제이므로 남자 후반부 대화에서 요청, 제안의 힌트 표현을 찾아야 한다. You should~가 정답 문장을 제시하고 있다.

What does the man advise the woman to do?

(A) Purchase a ticket   (B) Visit a shopping mall
(C) Wait for an express bus   **(D) Take a taxi**

문제 해설

남자가 권하는 것을 파악하도록 요구하는 세 번째 질문이므로 대화 후반부에 제시되는 남자의 말에서 제안이나 권고 등을 나타내는 표현과 함께 언급되는 정보를 파악해야 한다. 대화 후반부에 남자는 'In that case, you should take a taxi. It won't be much more expensive than the bus.'라는 말로 택시를 탈 것을 권하면서 탈 수 있는 곳을 알려 주고 있으므로 (D)가 정답이다.

Questions 62-64 refer to the following conversation and list.

M   Good morning, Chloe. [62] The remodeled office looks much better now. It's so much brighter!

W   Yeah, I'm very pleased with the changes. [63] New clients will have a better first impression now.

M   They will be even more impressed once we get the new television. Have you picked one out at Best One Electronics yet?

W   I have seen some of the choices. Should it have a flat screen or a curved screen?

M   [64] Let's spend some extra money and buy a curved-screen TV. I don't want the TV to be black, though. Let's be unique and get a white one!

W   I agree. I'll look at what's available and place an order this afternoon.

Color	Flat	Curved
Standard Black	Available	Available
Mirrored Black	Unavailable	Available
Glossy White	Unavailable	Available
Matte White	Available	Unavailable

어휘 remodeled 개조/보수된 be pleased with ~에 대해 기쁘다 first impression 첫인상 even (비교급 수식) 훨씬 impressed 깊은 인상을 받은 once 일단 ~하면 pick out ~을 고르다 flat 평평한 curved 곡선의 extra 추가/별도의 though (문장 끝이나 중간에서) 하지만, 그러나 unique 독특하게 agree 동의하다 available 구매 가능한 place an order 주문하다 standard 일반의, 표준의 unavailable 구매 불가능한

남   좋은 아침이에요, **Chloe.** [62] 개조 공사가 끝난 사무실이 지금 훨씬 더 좋아 보여요. 아주 훨씬 더 밝네요!

여   네, 바꾸니까 정말 기뻐요. [63] 이제 새로운 고객들이 더 나은 첫인상을 받게 될 거예요.

남   일단 우리가 새로운 **TV**를 사면 고객들이 훨씬 더 깊은 인상을 받게 될 거예요. 혹시 **Best One Electronics**에서 이미 한 대 골라 두셨나요?

여   몇 가지 선택 가능한 것들을 봐 뒀어요. 평면 화면이어야 하나요, 아니면 곡선 화면이어야 하나요?

남   [64] 추가 비용을 써서 곡선 화면으로 된 **TV**를 구입합시다. 하지만 검은색으로 된 **TV**는 아니었으면 좋겠어요. 독특하게 백색으로 된 것을 구입해요!

여   동의해요. 무엇이 구매 가능한지 보고 오늘 오후에 주문할게요.

색상	평면	곡선
Standard Black	구매 가능	구매 가능
Mirrored Black	구매 불가능	구매 가능
Glossy White	구매 불가능	구매 가능
Matte White	구매 가능	구매 불가능

62

What are the speakers mainly discussing?

(A) Television repair
(B) Grand opening
(C) Return policy
(D) Office renovation

문제 해설

대화의 주제를 묻는 첫 번째 질문이므로 대화 초반부에서 중점적으로 언급하는 핵심 내용을 파악하는 것이 관건이다. 대화를 시작하는 남자가 'The remodeled office looks much better now. It's so much brighter!'라는 말로 개조된 사무실의 특성에 대해 언급하고 있으므로 (D)가 정답임을 알 수 있다.

★ **주제, 목적**

화자들은 주로 무엇에 관해 이야기하고 있는가?
(A) TV 수리
(B) 개장
(C) 교환 규정
(D) 사무실 개조

어휘 repair ~을 수리하다 move into ~로 이사하다

토익 분석

주제는 대화의 시작 부분에 제시된다.

★★ 세부 정보

여자는 무슨 이점을 언급하고 있는가?
(A) 사무실이 더 편리한 곳에 위치할 것이다.
(B) 고객들이 깊은 인상을 받을 것이다.
(C) 한 구역이 청소하기 더 쉬워질 것이다.
(D) 고객들이 더 빠르게 서비스를 제공받을 것이다.

어휘 conveniently located 편리하게 위치한 serve ~에게 서비스를 제공하다

토익 분석

키워드가 존재하지 않기 때문에 여자 대화에 집중하며 긍정적인 의견을 제시하는 부분을 찾아내야 한다.

What benefit does the woman mention?

(A) An office will be more conveniently located.
(B) Clients will be impressed.
(C) An area will be easier to clean.
(D) Customers will be served more quickly.

문제 해설

여자가 언급하는 좋은 점에 대해 묻는 두 번째 질문이므로 여자의 말에서 들을 수 있는 장점 등에 집중해 들어야 한다. 여자는 대화에 'New clients will have a better first impression now.'라는 말로 앞으로 발생할 좋은 효과에 대해 언급하고 있는데, 이는 고객들이 좋은 첫인상을 받을 것이라는 뜻이므로 (B)가 정답임을 알 수 있다.

★★★ 그래픽

도표를 확인하시오. 여자는 무슨 TV 색상을 주문할 가능성이 클 것인가?
(A) Standard Black
(B) Mirrored Black
(C) Glossy White
(D) Matte White

어휘 mirrored 거울이 달린, 거울 같은 glossy 광이 나는 matt 무광의

토익 분석

제시된 표에 색상과 형태 정보가 제시되어 있다. 대화에 제시되는 모양 정보가 결정적인 힌트가 된다. 요청, 제안 표현인 let's~와 의도 표현인 I (don't) want to가 정답을 제시한다.

Look at the graphic. What color of TV will the woman most likely order?

(A) Standard Black
(B) Mirrored Black
(C) Glossy White
(D) Matte White

문제 해설

질문에서 묻는 내용과 관련해 대화 속에 제시된 단서를 바탕으로 도표의 정보를 함께 확인해 정답을 찾아야 하는 문제이다. 이때 각 보기에 제시된 내용 외의 정보가 대화 속에서 단서로 제시될 것이므로 이에 집중해 대화를 들어야 한다. 각 보기에 제품의 색상이 쓰여 있으므로 이와 함께 도표에 제시된 TV 화면의 특징 및 구매 가능 여부에 집중해 들어야 한다. 남자는 대화 후반부에 'Let's spend some extra money and buy a curved-screen TV. I don't want the TV to be black, though. Let's be unique and get a white one!'라는 말로 '곡선 화면으로 되어 있으며 흰색인 것'을 구매 조건으로 언급하고 있는데, 도표에서 흰색으로 된 두 가지 중에서 곡선 화면으로 구매 가능한 것이 'Glossy White'이므로 (C)가 정답이다.

Questions 65-67 refer to the following conversation and information.

W ⁶⁵ Hello, I was browsing the Glee Market Web site, and I'd like to buy three of the wooden kitchen chairs that are on sale for $30.

M Alright. ⁶⁶ Normally our customers receive their orders in two business days, but it might take a little longer right now because of our current promotion.

W That's fine. But I have a question about the promotion. Since the chairs are already marked down, can I still receive the additional discount?

M Sure. Every order we process is eligible for the promotion. The more you spend, the more you save.

W ⁶⁷ OK, so my total price will be $90 before the additional discount is applied.

M That's correct. It looks like you're going to save quite a bit of money today.

Glee Market
Special Summer Promotion

Total Purchase Amount	Discount
$10-$50	5%
$50-$100	10%
$100-$200	15%
$200+	20%

어휘 browse ~을 훑어보다, 둘러 보다 wooden 목재의 on sale 할인 중인 normally 일반적으로 order 주문(품) in + 시간 ~ 후에 take ~의 시간이 걸리다 a little 약간, 조금 longer 더 긴, 더 오랜 current 현재의 promotion 판촉 행사 be marked down 할인되다, 인하되다 additional 추가의 process ~을 처리하다 be eligible for ~에 해당되다, ~에 대한 자격이 있다 The more A, the more B 더 많이 A할수록, 더 많이 B하다 apply ~을 적용하다 correct 맞는, 옳은 quite a bit of 꽤 많이, 상당히 많이

여 ⁶⁵ 여보세요, 제가 Glee Market 웹 사이트를 훑어봤는데, 30달러에 할인 판매 중인 목재 주방 의자 3개를 구입하려고 합니다.

남 알겠습니다. ⁶⁶ 보통 저희 고객들께서는 주문품을 영업일 이틀 후에 받으시지만, 현재 진행 중인 저희 판촉 행사 때문에 지금은 시간이 조금 더 걸릴 수도 있습니다.

여 그건 괜찮아요. 그런데 판촉 행사에 대해서 질문이 있어요. 그 의자들이 이미 가격이 할인됐는데, 여전히 추가 할인을 받을 수 있나요?

남 물론입니다. 저희가 처리하는 모든 주문품은 판촉 행사에 해당됩니다. 더 많이 구입하실 수록 더 많이 절약하실 수 있습니다.

여 ⁶⁷ 알겠어요. 그럼 추가 할인이 적용되기 전에 제 총액은 90달러가 되겠네요.

남 맞습니다. 오늘 꽤 많은 금액을 절약하시게 되는 것 같네요.

Glee Market
여름 판촉 행사

총 구매 금액	할인율
10-50달러	5%
50-100달러	10%
100-200달러	15%
200달러 이상	20%

65

What is the main purpose of the woman's call?

(A) To cancel a transaction
(B) To return a phone call
(C) To complain about a product
(D) To purchase some merchandise

문제 해설

여자가 전화를 거는 목적을 묻는 첫 번째 질문이므로 대화 초반부에서 중점적으로 언급하는 용건과 관련된 핵심 내용을 파악하는 것이 관건이다. 여자는 대화를 시작하면서 'Hello, I was browsing the Glee Market Web site and I'd like to buy three of the wooden kitchen chairs that are on sale for $30.'라는 말로 의자 제품 3개를 구입하려는 의사를 밝히고 있으므로 상품 구입이 주목적임을 알 수 있다. 따라서 (D)가 정답이 된다.

★★ 주제, 목적

여자가 전화를 거는 주목적은 무엇인가?
(A) 거래를 취소하는 것
(B) 전화에 응답하는 것
(C) 제품에 대해 불평하는 것
(D) 상품을 구입하는 것

어휘 cancel ~을 취소하다 transaction 거래 (내역) reply to ~에 응답하다 complain about ~에 불평하다 merchandise 상품

토익 분석

여자의 전화 목적은 여자의 첫 번째 대화문에 I'm calling과 같은 표현이나 의도 표현으로 답이 등장한다. I'd like to가 정답 힌트를 제시했다.

★★ 문제점

남자는 무슨 문제점을 언급하는가?
(A) 주문이 처리될 수 없다.
(B) 한 제품이 현재 구매될 수 없다.
(C) 배송이 평소보다 늦게 도착할 것이다.
(D) 웹 사이트가 제대로 작동하지 않고 있다.

어휘 item 제품, 품목 unavailable 구매할 수 없는 delivery 배송(품) arrive 도착하다 than usual 평소보다 work 작동하다 properly 제대로, 적절히, 알맞게

토익 분석

남자의 문제점은 남자의 초반부 대화에 반전 표현으로 답이 제시된다. but이 정답 힌트로 사용되었다.

What problem does the man mention?

(A) An order cannot be processed.

(B) An item is currently unavailable.

(C) A delivery will arrive later than usual.

(D) A Web site is not working properly.

문제 해설

남자가 언급하는 문제점이 무엇인지를 묻는 문제이므로 남자의 말에서 문제점을 나타내는 정보에 집중해 들어야 한다. 대화 초반부에 남자는 'Normally our customers receive their orders in two business days, but it might take a little longer right now because of our current promotion.' 라는 말로 특정 행사로 인해 배송이 평소보다 조금 더 시간이 걸릴 수도 있음을 알리고 있으므로 이에 대해 언급한 (C)가 정답이 된다.

★★ 그래픽

도표를 확인하시오. 여자는 어느 할인율을 적용 받을 것인가?
(A) 5%
(B) 10%
(C) 15%
(D) 20%

어휘 receive 받다

토익 분석

제시된 표에는 구매 금액과 할인율에 대한 정보가 포함되어 있다. 할인율을 찾기 위해서는 대화 중 구매 금액에 관한 정보를 들어야 한다. 반전 표현 so 역시 중요한 힌트를 제시하고 있다.

Look at the graphic. What discount will the woman receive?

(A) 5%

(B) 10%

(C) 15%

(D) 20%

문제 해설

질문에서 묻는 내용과 관련해 대화 속에 제시된 단서를 바탕으로 도표의 정보를 함께 확인해 정답을 찾아야 하는 문제이다. 이때 각 보기에 제시된 내용 외의 정보가 대화 속에서 단서로 제시될 것이므로 이에 집중해 대화를 들어야 한다. 각 보기에 비율이 제시되어 있으므로 도표에서 이와 함께 쓰여 있는 가격 정보에 집중해 들어야 한다. 대화 마지막 부분에 여자가 자신의 가격 정보를 'OK, so my total price will be $90 before the additional discount is applied.'라고 알리고 있으므로 도표에 90달러에 해당하는 할인 비율로 제시된 (B)가 정답이다.

Questions 68-70 refer to the following conversation and list.

M   Hello, Kelly. Did you notice that the machines have been added to the weight room? They are brand new.

W   Yes, they're really nice. [68, 69] When our fitness center finally opens, our members will be impressed with all of the different types of equipment we have.

M   I hope so. But we're not finished yet. We need to open a fitness class, and I have a few applications right here.

W   Alright. But what kind of class should we open? Yoga has been pretty popular over the past few years.

M   Our members might want something more exciting than yoga, [70] so let's open an aerobics class. And it should meet on weekends.

W   Sure. I'll look through the applications and arrange for interviews.

Class	Instructor's Availability
Dance Aerobics	Weekdays
Step Aerobics	Weekdays and Weekends
Traditional Yoga	Weekends
Hot Yoga	Weekdays and Weekends

어휘 notice that ~임을 알고 있다 add A to B A를 B에 추가하다 weight room 체력 단련실 brand new 완선히 새로운 be impressed with ~에 깊은 인상을 받다 equipment 장비 finished 끝난 application 지원(서) pretty 아주, 매우 over the past few years 지난 몇 년 동안 aerobics 에어로빅 on weekends 주말마다 look through ~을 살펴보다 arrange for ~을 준비하다

남   안녕하세요, **Kelly**. 체력 단련실에 기구들이 추가되었다는 것을 알고 계셨어요? 완전히 새로운 것들이에요.

여   네, 정말로 좋은 것들이에요. [68, 69] 우리 피트니스 센터가 마침내 문을 열면 우리가 보유하고 있는 모든 다른 종류의 장비에 대해 회원들이 깊은 인상을 받을 거예요.

남   그러길 바라요. 하지만 아직 끝나지 않았어요. 우리는 피트니스 강좌를 개설해야 하는데, 여기 몇몇 지원서들을 가져 왔어요.

여   알겠어요. 하지만 무슨 종류의 강좌를 개설해야 하죠? 요가가 지난 몇 년 동안 아주 인기가 있었어요.

남   우리 회원들은 요가보다 더 흥미로운 뭔가를 원할 수도 있기 때문에 [70] 에어로빅 강좌를 개설합시다. 그리고 매주 주말에 진행하는 거예요.

여   좋아요. 제가 지원서들을 살펴보고 면접을 준비할게요.

강좌	강사 활용 시간
Dance Aerobics	매주 주중
Step Aerobics	매주 주중 및 주말
Traditional Yoga	매주 주말
Hot Yoga	매주 주중 및 주말

68

What are the speakers mainly discussing?

(A) The opening of a business
(B) The price of some machinery
(C) The location of a fitness center
(D) The training of new employees

문제 해설

대화의 주제를 묻는 첫 번째 질문이므로 대화 초반부에서 중점적으로 언급하는 핵심 내용을 파악하는 것이 관건이다. 새로운 기구들이 추가되었다는 말을 들은 여자가 대화 초반부에서 'When our fitness center finally opens, our members will be impressed with all of the different types of equipment we have.'라는 말로 피트니스 센터가 새롭게 문을 열게 되는 상황에 대해 언급하고 있으므로 이를 '업체의 개장'이라는 말로 바꿔 표현한 (A)가 정답이다.

★★ 주제, 목적

화자들은 주로 무엇을 논의하고 있는가?
(A) 업체의 개장
(B) 기기의 가격
(C) 피트니스 센터의 위치
(D) 신입 직원 교육

어휘 machinery 기기, 기구, 장비 location 위치, 지점 training 교육

토익 분석

주제는 대화 첫 번째 문장과 두 번째 문장 중 반드시 답이 나온다.

★★★ 암시 추론

여자는 무슨 이점을 언급하는가?
(A) 직원들이 경험이 많다.
(B) 다양한 장비가 있다.
(C) 할인된 회원권이 있다.
(D) 운영 시간이 늘어날 것이다.

어휘 a variety of 다양한 discounted 할인된 hours of operation 운영 시간, 영업시간

토익 분석

특별한 키워드가 없는 문제이므로 여자 대화를 전반적으로 파악해야 하는 문제이다.

What benefit does the woman mention?

(A) The staff has lots of experience.
(B) There is a variety of equipment.
(C) There is a discounted membership.
(D) The hours of operation will be extended.

문제 해설

여자가 이점으로 언급하는 내용을 파악하도록 요구하는 두 번째 질문이므로 대화 중반부에서 여자가 언급하는 장점 또는 긍정적인 정보를 확인해 내야 한다. 대화 중반부에 여자는 'our members will be impressed with all of the different types of equipment we have'라는 말로 회원들이 깊은 인상을 받게 된다는 말로 좋은 점에 대해 언급하고 있으며, 그 근거로 모든 종류의 다른 장비들을 제시하고 있으므로 (B)가 정답이다.

70

★★ 그래픽

도표를 확인하시오. 여자는 무슨 강좌를 개설할 가능성이 가장 큰가?
(A) Dance Aerobics
(B) Step Aerobics
(C) Traditional Yoga
(D) Hot Yoga

어휘 traditional 전통

토익 분석

강좌와 강사 시간에 관한 정보가 제시되어 있다. 강좌를 찾기 위해서 대화에서 '강사 시간'에 관한 정보를 찾아야만 한다. 반전 표현 So와 요청, 제안 표현인 let's, it should 가 정답 표현을 제시했다.

Look at the graphic. Which class will the woman most likely open?

(A) Dance Aerobics
(B) Step Aerobics
(C) Traditional Yoga
(D) Hot Yoga

문제 해설

질문에서 묻는 내용과 관련해 대화 속에 제시된 단서를 바탕으로 도표의 정보를 함께 확인해 정답을 찾아야 하는 문제이다. 이때 각 보기에 제시된 내용 외의 정보가 대화 속에서 단서로 제시될 것이므로 이에 집중해 대화를 들어야 한다. 각 보기에 강좌 이름이 제시되어 있으므로 도표에서 이와 함께 표기된 시간 정보에 귀 기울여 들어야 한다. 대화 후반부에 남자가 'so let's open an aerobics class. And it should meet on weekends.'라는 말로 주말에 모이는 에어로빅 강좌를 개설하자고 알리고 있으므로 이 조건에 부합하는 것으로 (B)가 정답이 된다.

Questions 71-73 refer to the following instructions.

W [71] Hello, new interns! I'm going to explain how this fax machine works. [72] Basically, the paper you want to fax must be inserted into the top face down. Make sure the side you want to fax is facing down because that is the side that will be sent. [73] The local area code is already programmed in the machine, so all you have to do is dial the number and press the send button. If you want to send it out of the local area, you must remember to erase the area code that is in there and replace it with the area code of the city you are sending it to. Once it is sent, you will hear a beep.

여 [71] 안녕하세요, 신입 수습 직원 여러분! 저는 이 팩스기의 조작법을 설명해 드리고자 합니다. [72] 기본적으로, 팩스로 보내야 하는 종이는 앞면이 아래를 향하도록 넣어야 합니다. 보내고자 하는 면이 반드시 아래로 향하도록 해야 하는데, 그 이유는 아래로 향하는 면이 보내지기 때문입니다. [73] 팩스기에 이미 우리 지역 번호가 입력되어 있으므로 그냥 번호를 입력하시고 전송 버튼을 누르시면 됩니다. 만약 우리 지역의 외부로 팩스를 보내시려면, 팩스기에 있는 지역 번호를 지우시고 보내시고자 하는 도시의 지역 번호로 바꾸어 입력하셔야 합니다. 일단 전송이 되고 나면, 삐 소리의 발신음을 듣게 되실 겁니다.

어휘 work (기계 등이) 작동되다 basically 기본적으로 fax n. 팩스, 팩스기 v. ~을 팩스로 보내다 insert ~을 삽입하다 face down 윗면이 아래를 향하는 상태 make sure (that) 반드시 ~하다 local area code 지역 번호 erase ~을 지우다 replace A with B A를 B로 바꾸다, A를 B로 교체하다 once 일단 ~하면, ~하자마자

71

Who are the listeners?

(A) Regular office workers (B) Conference participants
(C) Repair technicians **(D) Company trainees**

문제 해설

청자의 정체를 파악해야 하는 첫 번째 질문이므로 담화 초반부에 직책이나 특정 업무 등과 관련해 제시되는 정보를 통해 청자의 정체를 파악해야 한다. 담화를 시작하면서 화자가 대상자들에게 'Hello, new interns!'라고 인사말을 건네는 부분을 통해 청자는 회사의 수습 직원임을 알 수 있으므로 interns와 같은 의미에 해당되는 보기인 (D)가 정답이다.

★★ 도입부 정보 – 청자

청자들은 누구인가?
(A) 정규 사무직원들 (B) 회의 참석자들
(C) 수리 기술자들 (D) 회사 수습 직원들

어휘 regular 정규의 participant 참가자 repair 수리 trainee 교육받는 사람

토익 분석

청자 정보는 99% 지문의 첫 문장에 환영 인사 부분에 등장한다.

72

What does the speaker emphasize?

(A) That the data should be entered correctly
(B) That employees should skillfully handle office equipment
(C) That the side that will be sent must be face down
(D) That employees must turn off every computer when leaving the office

문제 해설

화자가 중요하다고 강조한 내용을 묻는 두 번째 질문이므로 담화 중반부에 화자가 특별히 강조하는 중요 사항이 제시될 것임을 예상하고 들어야 한다. 화자는 담화 중반부에 'Basically, the paper you want to fax must be inserted from the top face down.'이라고 말하며 기본적으로 자신이 팩스를 보내고자 하는 면이 아래를 향하도록 해야 한다고 밝히고 있다. 뒤이어 'Make sure the side you want to fax is facing down because that is the side that will be sent.'라고 말하며 다시 한 번 자신이 팩스를 보내고자 하는 면이 아래쪽을 향해야 한다는 점을 강조하고 있다. 따라서 팩스를 보내고자 하는 면이 아래로 향해야 한다는 점을 언급한 (C)가 정답이다.

★★★ 암시 추론

화자는 무엇이 중요하다고 강조하고 있는가?
(A) 자료가 정확하게 입력되어야 하는 것
(B) 직원들이 사무기기를 능숙하게 다루는 것
(C) 보내는 면이 아래쪽을 향하도록 하는 것
(D) 직원들이 퇴근할 때 모든 컴퓨터의 전원을 끄는 것

어휘 emphasize ~을 강조하다 correctly 정확히 skillfully 능숙하게 handle ~을 다루다, 처리하다 leave ~에서 나가다, 떠나다

토익 분석

대화문에서 뭔가 강조하기 위해서는 명령문이나 요청, 제안 형태의 표현이 등장한다. 조동사 must와 명령문 Make sure ~를 사용해 정답을 제시했다.

73

What is already programmed into the machine?

(A) The mechanism of transmission **(B) The area code of the city**
(C) The number of the receiver (D) The telephone numbers of main clients

문제 해설

기계에 이미 입력된 것을 묻는 마지막 질문이므로 담화 후반부에 already programmed와 관련된 내용이 제시되는 부분을 중심으로 단서를 파악하는 것이 중요하다. 화자가 담화 후반부에 'The local area code is already programmed in the machine.'이라는 말로 팩스기에 이미 자신들이 있는 곳의 지역 번호가 입력되어 있는 상태임을 밝히고 있으므로 (B)가 정답이다.

★★ 세부 정보

기계에 이미 입력된 것은 무엇인가?
(A) 전송 작동 원리 (B) 도시의 지역 번호
(C) 수신자의 번호 (D) 주요 고객들의 전화번호

어휘 mechanism 원리, 방법 transmission 전송 receiver 수신자

토익 분석

키워드를 활용하는 세부 정보 문제로 질문 속에 사용된 programmed가 키워드가 된다.

남 훌륭한 지역 뉴스 보도에 감사 드립니다, Stacy 기자. 자, 이제는 지역 교통 소식을 전해 드리겠습니다. 9월 13일 월요일 오늘 교통 상황은 Thomas Jefferson 다리를 제외한 모든 구간이 매우 원활해 보입니다. **74** 현재 진행 중인 도로 보수 공사로 인해 다리의 북쪽과 남쪽으로 향하는 양방향 모두 교통 정체 현상이 발생하고 있습니다. **75** 이 강을 건널 계획이신 운전자 분들은 대신 St. George 다리나 Franklin 다리를 이용하시는 것이 좋겠습니다. **76** 다음 순서로, 광고를 들으신 후에 Harry 기자가 오늘의 날씨를 전해 드리겠습니다.

Questions 74-76 refer to the following report.

M Thank you, Stacy, for that wonderful local news report. Now, to our local traffic report. The traffic on this Monday, September 13, is looking very smooth throughout the city except on the Thomas Jefferson Bridge. **74** The ongoing road repairs there have cars backed up in both the northbound and southbound lanes. **75** Motorists planning to cross the river are advised to take the St. George Bridge or the Franklin Bridge. **76** Next, it's time for Harry with the day's weather report after this commercial.

어휘 traffic report 교통 소식 look + 형용사 ~하게 보이다 smooth 원활한, 순조로운 throughout ~ 전역에 걸쳐 except ~를 제외하고 ongoing 진행 중인 have A p.p. A가 ~되게 하다 back up ~가 밀리다, ~를 정체시키다 both A and B A와 B 둘 다 northbound 북행의 southbound 남행의 motorist 운전자 plan to do ~할 계획이다 be advised to do ~하도록 권장되다, ~하는 것이 좋다 weather report 일기 예보 commercial 광고 (방송)

74

★ 세부 정보

무엇이 오늘 Thomas Jefferson Bridge의 교통 체증을 초래했는가?
(A) 교통사고
(B) 유지 관리 작업
(C) 도로 폐쇄
(D) 악천후

어휘 cause ~을 초래하다 delay 지연, 지체 accident 사고 maintenance 유지 관리 closure 폐쇄

토익 분석

Thomas Jefferson Bridge를 키워드로 답을 찾는 세부 정보 문제이다. 교통방송에서 문제점은 주제문에 등장한다.

What caused the traffic delay on the Thomas Jefferson Bridge?
(A) A car accident
(B) Maintenance work
(C) Road closures
(D) Poor weather conditions

문제 해설

교통 체증의 원인을 묻는 첫 번째 질문이므로 담화 시작 부분에 교통 정체 현상과 그 원인이 제시될 것임을 예상하고 들을 수 있다. 담화 초반부에 교통 체증을 언급한 후에 'The ongoing road repairs there have cars backed up in both the northbound and southbound lanes.'라는 말로 도로 보수 공사로 인해 다리의 양방향 모두 교통 정체 현상이 발생되고 있다고 알리고 있으므로 보수 공사를 유지 관리 작업으로 바꿔 표현한 (B)가 정답이다.

75

★★ 요청, 제안

화자는 무엇을 하도록 추천하고 있는가?
(A) 대체 경로를 이용할 것
(B) 이동에 더 많은 시간을 할애할 것
(C) 대중교통을 이용할 것
(D) 실내에 머무를 것

어휘 alternate 대체의 route 경로 allow ~을 할애하다, 감안하다 travel 이동 public transportation 대중교통 indoors 실내에

토익 분석

요청, 제안의 답을 이끄는 빈출 힌트 표현을 찾아야 한다. advise가 힌트 표현으로 활용되었다.

What does the speaker recommend doing?

(A) Taking an alternate route
(B) Allowing extra time for travel
(C) Using public transportation
(D) Staying indoors

문제 해설

화자의 추천 사항에 대해 묻는 두 번째 질문이므로 지문에서 화자의 말에서 권고 사항과 관련된 표현이 제시되는 부분에서 단서를 찾아야 한다. 담화 중반부에 화자가 'Motorists planning to cross the river are advised to take the St. George Bridge or the Franklin Bridge.'라는 말로 Thomas Jefferson 다리를 건너려는 운전자들은 St. George 다리나 Franklin 다리를 대신 이용하도록 권하고 있으므로 (A)가 정답이다.

76

★★★ 미래 행동

청자들은 다음으로 무엇을 듣게 될 것 같은가?
(A) 상업 광고
(B) 스포츠 뉴스
(C) 일기 예보
(D) 음악 프로그램

어휘 commercial a. 상업의 n. 광고

토익 분석

방송에서 미래 행동은 무조건 마지막 문장에 등장한다. 시점 표현인 next와 after가 결정적인 힌트 표현이다.

What will the listeners probably hear next?
(A) A commercial
(B) A sports report
(C) A weather report
(D) A music program

문제 해설

청자들이 다음으로 듣게 될 것을 묻는 마지막 질문이므로 담화 후반부에 특히 집중해 방송 순서를 명확히 파악해야 한다. 화자는 담화 마지막에 'Next, it's time for Harry with the day's weather report after this commercial.'이라는 말로 광고 후에 일기 예보를 듣게 될 것이라고 알리고 있으므로 (A)가 정답이다. weather report와 commercial이 함께 언급되는 상황에서 그 순서를 빠르게 파악하는 것이 중요하다.

Questions 77-79 refer to the following telephone message.

W Hi, Ms. Hwang. This is Sunny Ha. [77, 78] Thank you for considering me for the job. However, I won't be able to make it next Monday since I will be attending a four-day workshop in San Diego. [78] I've been asked to lead the workshop, so I don't think I can be excused from it. [77] However, I will be available for an interview next Friday since I'll be back from the workshop next Thursday. When we talked on the phone last week, you asked me to bring my portfolio with me. [79] I wonder if you prefer it on paper or on screen. If you don't mind, I'd love to present my portfolio on a screen since much of my work is in video form.

여 안녕하세요, Hwang 씨. 저는 Sunny Ha라고 합니다. [77, 78] 직책에 대해 저를 고려해 주셔서 감사 드립니다. 그러나 제가 San Diego에서 4일간 열리는 워크숍에 참석해야 하는 관계로 다음 주 월요일에 갈 수 없습니다. [78] 제가 워크숍을 진행하도록 요청을 받아서 자리를 비울 수 없을 것 같습니다. 하지만 다음 주 목요일에 워크숍을 끝내고 돌아오기 때문에 [77] 다음 주 금요일에는 면접을 볼 시간이 있을 것입니다. 지난주에 전화로 이야기를 나눴을 때, 제게 포트폴리오를 가져오도록 요청하셨습니다. [79] 귀하께서 종이로 된 것을 선호하시는지, 아니면 화면상으로 보시는 것을 선호하시는지 궁금합니다. 괜찮으시다면, 제 작업물의 대부분이 영상 형태이기 때문에 제 포트폴리오를 화면을 통해 보여 드리고 싶습니다.

어휘 consider ~을 고려하다 be able to do ~할 수 있다 make it 가다, 도착하다 since ~이므로 attend ~에 참석하다 be asked to do ~하도록 요청받다 lead ~을 이끌다, 진행하다 be excused from ~에서 빠지다 available (사람이) 시간이 나는 ask A to do A에게 ~하도록 요청하다 portfolio (구직 시 제출하는) 포트폴리오, 작품집 wonder if ~인지 궁금하다 present ~을 보여 주다, 제시하다 video form 영상 형태, 비디오 형식

77

Why is the speaker calling?

(A) To decline a job offer   (B) To inform a customer of a problem

(C) To postpone an interview

(D) To accept an invitation to speak at a convention

문제 해설

전화를 건 이유를 묻는 문제는 담화 주제를 묻는 것과 같으므로 담화가 시작되는 초반부에 집중해 단서를 찾아야 한다. 화자는 담화 시작 부분에 'Thank you for~workshop in San Diego.'라는 말로 다음 주 월요일에 출장을 가야 하는 관계로 면접에 참석할 수가 없음을 밝히고 있다. 뒤이어 'However, I will be available for an interview next Friday'라는 말로 다른 날로 면접을 볼 수 있는지를 확인하는 내용이 있으므로 면접 일정을 연기하는 것이 목적임을 알 수 있다. 따라서 이에 해당되는 보기인 (C)가 정답이다.

★★★ 전화 목적

화자가 연락을 한 이유는 무엇인가?
(A) 채용 제의를 거절하기 위해서
(B) 고객에게 문제점을 알리기 위해서
(C) 면접을 연기하기 위해서
(D) 컨벤션에서의 연설 초청을 수락하기 위해서

어휘 decline ~을 거절하다 inform A of B A에게 B를 알리다 postpone ~을 연기하다 accept ~을 받아들이다

토익 분석

전화 목적은 메시지의 주제문에 해당한다. 특히 주제문의 However와 같은 반전 표현은 결정적인 힌트를 제시한다.

78

What does the speaker plan to do next Monday?

(A) Conduct some interviews   (B) Pack things up for a move

(C) Preside over an event   (D) Go to a convention center

문제 해설

화자가 다음 주 월요일에 할 일에 관한 질문이므로 next Monday라는 미래 시점이 제시되는 부분을 중심으로 단서를 파악하는 것이 옳다. 화자는 담화 초반부에 'However~workshop in San Diego.'라는 말로 다음 주 월요일에 있을 워크숍으로 인해 출장을 가야 한다는 사실을 언급한 직후, 'I've been asked to lead the workshop'이라고 말하며 그 워크숍을 자신이 진행해야 함을 밝히고 있다. 따라서 '행사를 주재한다'는 의미로 쓰인 (C)가 정답이다.

★★ 세부 정보

화자는 다음 주 월요일에 무엇을 할 계획인가?
(A) 면접을 실시한다.   (B) 이사를 위해 짐을 꾸린다.
(C) 행사를 주재한다.   (D) 컨벤션 센터로 간다.

어휘 conduct ~을 실시하다 pack thing up 짐을 꾸리다 preside over (행사 등) ~을 주재하다

토익 분석

next Monday가 키워드로 활용된 세부 정보 문제이다. 반전 표현인 however역시 답을 찾는데 있어 중요한 힌트가 되었다.

79

What does the speaker ask the listener to do?

(A) Make travel arrangements   (B) Review some workshop materials

(C) Bring a computer monitor

(D) Provide his preference for a presentation method

문제 해설

화자의 요청 사항에 대해 묻는 마지막 질문이므로 지문 후반부에 제시되는 요청 관련 표현을 중심으로 단서를 찾아야 한다. 화자는 담화 마지막에 'I wonder if you prefer it on paper or on a screen.'이라고 말하며 자신의 작품을 지면으로 볼 것인지 아니면 화면을 통해서 볼 것인지 궁금하다고 언급한 직후, 'If you don't mind~video form.'라는 말로 영상 형태로 봐주길 우회적으로 요청하고 있다. 따라서 화자는 청자가 작품을 어떠한 방식으로 보길 원하는지 알고 싶어 하는 것이므로 (D)가 정답이다.

★★ 요청, 제안

화자는 청자에게 무엇을 하도록 요청하는가?
(A) 출장 일정을 잡는 일 (B) 워크숍 자료를 검토하는 일
(C) 컴퓨터 모니터를 가지고 오는 일
(D) 원하는 발표 방식을 알려 주는 일

어휘 make travel arrangements 출장 일정을 잡다 material 자료, 재료 preference 선호(하는 것)

토익 분석

요청, 제안 문제의 대표적인 힌트 표현 중 하나인 if가정법 ~, I'd like(love) to 문장이 답이 제시하고 있다.

여 여러분 안녕하세요, 그리고 연례 *Farmdale Corporation* 연회에 참석해 주셔서 감사합니다. 오늘 밤의 주 연설자를 모시기 전에, **80 우리 Fresh Food for Kids Foundation에 기부금을 내시도록 요청 드리는 시간을 갖고자 합니다.** 이곳은 자선 단체로, Cincinnati 전역에 있는 저소득의 불우한 아이들이 신선하고 건강에 좋은 음식을 매일 이용할 수 있도록 하는 곳입니다. **81 내년까지, 우리는 주변에 있는 여러 주로 활동을 확대하기를 바라고 있습니다. 82 이와 같은 훌륭한 대의에 대해 여러분께서 내주시는 단 1달러라도 진심으로 감사하게 여길 것입니다. 한 번 생각해 보시기 바랍니다.** 그럼 이제, *Farmdale*의 *Donald Humphries* 대표님을 소개해 드리겠습니다.

Questions 80-82 refer to the following talk.

W   Hello everyone, and thank you for attending the annual Farmdale Corporation banquet. Before we get to the main speaker of the night, **80 I'd like to take a moment to ask that you donate some money to the Fresh Food for Kids Foundation.** It is a charity that gives low-income, impoverished children across Cincinnati access to fresh, healthy meals every day. **81 By next year, we hope to spread our operation to neighboring states. 82 We would really appreciate every dollar you can spare for this great cause. Give it a thought.** And now, I'd like to introduce the President of Farmdale, Mr. Donald Humphries.

어휘 attend ~에 참석하다 annual 연례의 banquet 연회 get to the main speaker 주 연설자를 소개하다, 만나다 take a moment to do ~할 시간을 잠시 갖다 donate ~을 기부하다 charity 자선 단체 low-income 저소득의 impoverished 불우한, 빈곤한 across ~의 전역에서 give A access to B A가 B를 이용할 수 있게 하다 spread out one's operation 활동/운영을 확대하다 neighboring 주변/인근의 appreciate ~에 감사하다 spare (시간, 돈 등) ~을 할애하다, 내다 cause 대의 (명분) give it a thought 한 번 생각해 보다 introduce ~을 소개하다

80

★★ 주제, 목적

담화의 목적은 무엇인가?
(A) 재단의 역사를 설명하는 것
(B) 재정적인 도움을 요청하는 것
(C) 신입 직원을 소개하는 것   (D) 절차를 설명하는 것

어휘 describe ~을 설명하다 request ~을 요청하다 aid 지원, 도움 process 절차, 과정

토익 분석

의도 표현과 '알리다'의 의미를 지니는 동사들이 답을 제시한다. 의도 표현 I'd like to가 결정적인 힌트이다.

What is the purpose of the talk?

(A) To describe a foundation's history   **(B) To request financial aid**
(C) To introduce a new employee   (D) To describe a process

문제 해설

담화의 목적을 묻는 첫 번째 질문이므로 담화 초반부에서 중점적으로 언급하는 핵심 내용을 파악하는 것이 관건이다. 화자는 담화 초반부에서, 본격적인 행사를 진행하기에 앞서 하려는 일을 'I'd like to~Kids Foundation.'라는 말로 알리고 있는데, 이 말의 핵심은 돈을 기부하도록 요청하는 것이므로 이를 'financial aid'라는 말로 바꿔 제시한 (B)가 정답이 된다.

81

★★ 세부 정보

화자의 말에 따르면, 재단은 내년에 무엇을 하기를 희망하는가?
(A) 광고 캠페인을 변경하는 일
(B) 더 많은 수익을 올리는 일
(C) 활동을 넓히는 일
(D) 지역 매장을 여는 일

어휘 alter ~을 변경하다 make a profit 수익을 내다

토익 분석

next year가 키워드로 활용된 세부 정보 찾기 문제이다.

According to the speaker, what does the foundation hope to do next year?

(A) Alter an ad campaign   (B) Make a larger profit
(C) Enlarge its operation   (D) Open a local store

문제 해설

재단이 내년에 하기를 희망하는 일을 묻는 두 번째 질문이므로 담화 중반부에서 '내년'이라는 미래 시점 표현과 함께 언급하는 핵심 내용을 파악하는 것이 관건이다. 화자는 담화 중반부에 'By next year~neighboring states.'라는 말로 내년까지 하려는 일을 알리고 있는데, 인근에 있는 다른 주로 활동 영역을 넓히는 것에 대해 밝히고 있으므로 이에 대해 언급한 (C)가 정답이 된다.

82

★★★ 맥락 파악

여자는 왜 "Give it a thought"이라고 말하는가?
(A) 청자들에게 뭔가를 고려하도록 요청하기 위해
(B) 청자들이 질문을 하도록 권하기 위해
(C) 청자들에게 뭔가를 반납하도록 상기시키기 위해
(D) 새로운 연설자를 소개하기 위해

어휘 consider ~을 고려하다 encourage ~을 권하다, 장려하다 remind A to do A가 ~하도록 상기시키다

토익 분석

제시된 표현의 전후 문장을 이해하여 흐름을 파악해야만 한다.

Why does the woman say, "Give it a thought"?

(A) To request that the listeners consider something
(B) To encourage questions from the listeners
(C) To remind the listeners to return something
(D) To introduce a new speaker

문제 해설

화자가 말하는 "Give it a thought"라는 표현이 담화 속에서 어떤 의미로 사용되었는지를 묻는 세 번째 질문이므로 담화 후반부에 제시되는 이 표현 및 앞뒤에 함께 제시되는 말들을 통해 의미의 흐름을 파악해 정답을 찾아야 한다. 화자는 담화 후반부에 'We would really appreciate every dollar you can spare for this great cause.'라는 말로 적은 돈이라도 감사할 것이라고 알린 후에 해당 표현을 사용하고 있으므로 기부를 하는 것에 대해 고려해 보라는 의미로 쓰였음을 유추할 수 있다. 따라서 이와 같은 맥락에 해당하는 의미를 지닌 (A)가 정답이 된다.

Questions 83-85 refer to the following talk.

M ⁸³ Hello. This is Tom Hopkins at Hopkins and Sons Attire calling you back about the tuxedo rental you inquired about earlier today. First of all, thank you for choosing us to provide your wedding day attire. We have the jacket, vest, and pants ready to be fitted. Regrettably, there was a problem with our supplier, and the shoes will not arrive for another three days. ⁸⁴ We will be ready to do the fitting by Friday. You have my word. I noticed on your order, though, that you have not yet picked out your bowtie or handkerchief. ⁸⁵ If you would like, I could arrange a display of various bowties and handkerchiefs that would match nicely with your tuxedo. I look forward to seeing you in a few days.

남 ⁸³ 안녕하세요. 저는 Hopkins and Sons Attire의 Tom Hopkins이며, 귀하께서 오늘 아까 문의하셨던 턱시도 대여에 대해 답신 전화 드립니다. 우선, 귀하의 결혼식 의복을 제공해 드릴 수 있도록 저희를 선택해 주신 것에 대해 감사 드립니다. 저희는 재킷과 조끼, 그리고 바지를 맞춰 준비해 드릴 수 있습니다. 유감스럽게도, 저희 공급업체에 문제가 있어서 앞으로 3일 동안은 신발은 도착하지 않을 것입니다. ⁸⁴ 금요일까지 의복을 가봉해 드리도록 준비할 것입니다. 약속 드릴 수 있습니다. 하지만 저는 귀하의 주문에서 나비넥타이와 손수건을 아직 고르지 않으셨다는 점을 알게 되었습니다. ⁸⁵ 괜찮으시다면, 귀하의 턱시도와 훌륭하게 어울릴 만한 다양한 나비넥타이와 손수건들을 보여 드릴 수 있게 준비할 수 있습니다. 며칠 후에 뵙기를 기대합니다.

어휘 call A back A에게 답신 전화를 하다 tuxedo 턱시도 rental 대여 inquire about ~에 대해 문의하다 first of all 우선 provide ~을 제공하다 attire 의복 vest 조끼 have A ready A를 준비하다 fit ~에 맞추다, 어울리다 regrettably 유감스럽게도 supplier 공급업체 fitting (옷의) 가봉 though (문장 끝이나 중간에서) 하지만 You have my word 약속 드립니다 notice that ~임을 알게 되다 arrange ~을 준비하다, 마련하다 display 보여 주는 일 various 다양한 match with ~에 어울리다 nicely 훌륭히, 멋지게 look forward to -ing ~하기를 고대하다

83

Where does the speaker most likely work?

(A) At a wedding hall
(B) At a bakery
(C) At a clothing store
(D) At a car rental agency

문제 해설

화자의 근무 장소를 유추할 것을 요청하는 첫 번째 질문이므로 담화 초반부에서 언급되는 소개 인사와 함께 직접적으로 언급되는 회사명이나 부서명, 혹은 화자가 하는 일을 추측할 수 있을 만한 관련 어휘가 제시되는 부분에 집중해야 한다. 화자는 담화를 시작하면서 인사말을 먼저 전한 후 'Hello~wedding day attire.'라는 말로 상대방이 문의했던 턱시도 대여와 관련해 전화했다고 말하면서 결혼식 의복과 관련해 자신이 속한 회사를 선택한 것에 감사하고 있으므로 (C)가 정답임을 알 수 있다.

★★ 도입부 정보 – 화자

화자는 어디에서 근무하고 있을 가능성이 가장 큰가?
(A) 결혼식장
(B) 제과점
(C) 의류 매장
(D) 렌터카 지점

어휘 ask A to do A에게 ~하도록 요청하다

토익 분석

근무 장소는 지문의 도입부에서 장소 관련 정보를 찾는다. 특히 회사명이 등장하는 경우가 많다. at Hopkins and Sons Attire가 결정적인 힌트이다.

84

Why does the speaker say, "You have my word"?

(A) To ask the listener to meet
(B) To request some advice
(C) To reassure the listener
(D) To express gratitude

문제 해설

화자가 말하는 'You have my word'라는 표현이 담화 속에서 어떤 의미로 사용되었는지를 묻는 두 번째 질문이므로 담화 중반부에 제시되는 이 표현 및 앞뒤에 함께 제시되는 말들을 통해 의미의 흐름을 파악해 정답을 찾아야 한다. 화자는 담화 중반부에 신발 제품은 이용 가능하지 않다는 정보와 함께 'We will be ready to do the fitting by Friday.'라는 말로 금요일까지 의복을 가봉하는 일을 준비하겠다고 알리면서 'You have my word.'라는 표현을 사용하고 있는데, 이는 특정 시점까지 자신이 말한 일을 완료하겠다는 것을 강조하려는 뜻을 나타낸다. 즉 약속의 의미로 사용된 표현이므로 이를 '청자를 안심시키기 위해'라는 의미로 바꿔 표현한 (C)가 정답이 된다.

★★★ 맥락 파악

화자는 왜 "You have my word"라고 말하는가?
(A) 청자에게 만나도록 요청하기 위해
(B) 조언을 요청하기 위해
(C) 청자를 안심시키기 위해
(D) 감사의 뜻을 표현하기 위해

어휘 request ~을 요청하다 reassure ~을 안심시키다 express ~을 표현하다 gratitude 감사(하는 마음)

토익 분석

두 번째 질문의 답은 지문 중반부에 등장하며 의도 또는 미래 행동 표현 중 하나인 we(I) will~이 힌트를 제시하고 있다.

85

What does the speaker offer to do?

(A) Apply a discount
(B) Pick out additional items
(C) Replace a product
(D) Change an appointment

문제 해설

화자가 해 주겠다는 의도를 나타내는 일이 무엇인지를 묻는 세 번째 문제이므로 담화의 후반부에서 화자가 언급하는 제안 관련 표현과 함께 제시되는 정보를 파악해야 한다. 화자는 담화 후반부에 'If you would like, I could ~'이라는 말로 정중하게 제안을 하는 의미를 나타내는 표현을 사용해 'If you would like~with your tuxedo.'라는 말로 턱시도에 어울릴 만한 다양한 나비넥타이와 손수건 제품을 준비해 두겠다고 알리고 있으므로 이를 '추가 제품을 고르는 일'이라는 말로 바꿔 제시한 (B)가 정답이다.

★★ 요청, 제안

화자는 무엇을 하겠다고 하는가?
(A) 할인을 적용하는 일 (B) 추가 물품들을 고르는 일
(C) 제품을 교체하는 일 (D) 약속을 변경하는 일

어휘 additional 추가의 replace ~을 교체하다

토익 분석

요청, 제안 힌트 표현들 중 if 가정법~, I could~가 결정적인 단서를 제시한다.

여 **86** 신사 숙녀 여러분, 저는 여러분 모두가 오늘 저녁
의 기조연설자 Jonathan Fielder를 맞이할 준비가 되
셨기를 바랍니다. **87** 이분은 획기적인 성과와 함께,
우리 세대를 위해 단독으로 광고 전략을 재정립해 오
신 분입니다. 이와 같은 이유로, 이분이 작업하신 것
은 현재 몇몇 최고의 브랜드들에 대한 상업 광고에서
보실 수 있습니다. 자, 이분은 자신이 갖고 있는 지식
을 우리와 함께 나눌 준비가 되셨습니다. Jonathan
Fielder 씨께서 업계에서 25년이 넘는 기간 동안 터
득해 오신 것을 우리에게 말씀해 주실 것이며, 또한
규칙을 깰 수 있는 용기를 찾아 광고계에 새로운 것
을 전할 수 있는 방법에 대해서도 말씀해 주실 것입
니다. **88** 질문이 있으신 분은, 발표 후에 있을 질의응
답 시간에 Fielder 씨에게 해 주시기 바랍니다. 이 점
을 명심해 주십시오.

Questions 86-88 refer to the following talk.

W **86** Ladies and gentlemen, I hope you are all ready for this evening's keynote speaker, Jonathan Fielder. **87** With his groundbreaking work, he has single-handedly redefined advertising strategies for this generation. As such, his work can be seen in commercials for some of today's top brands. Now, he is ready to share some of his knowledge with us. Mr. Jonathan Fielder will tell us what he has learned from over twenty-five years in the industry, and also how to find the courage to break the rules and give the advertising world something new. **88** If you have any questions, please ask him during the question and answer session that will be held after his presentation. Please keep that in mind.

어휘 be ready for ~에 대한 준비가 되다 keynote speaker 기조연설자 groundbreaking 획기적인 single-handedly 단독으로, 혼자서 redefine ~을 재정립하다 strategy 전략 generation 세대 as such 그러한 이유로 commercial 광고 방송, 상업 광고 share ~을 공유하다 knowledge 지식 industry 업계 how to do ~하는 법 courage 용기 advertising world 광고계 question and answer session 질의응답 시간 be held (행사 등) ~이 열리다, 개최되다

86

★★ 주제, 목적

담화의 목적은 무엇인가?
(A) 신입 사원들을 환영하는 것
(B) 세미나 주제들을 개괄적으로 설명하는 것
(C) 연설자를 소개하는 것
(D) 새로운 전략들을 논의하는 것

어휘 outline ~을 개괄적으로 설명하다

토익 분석

주제문은 도입부 환영 인사 바로 다음 문장에 등장한다.

What is the purpose of the talk?

(A) To welcome a new employee (B) To outline seminar topics
(C) To introduce a speaker (D) To discuss new strategies

문제 해설

담화의 목적을 묻는 첫 번째 질문이므로 담화 초반부에서 중점적으로 언급하는 핵심 내용을 파악하는 것이 관건이다. 화자는 담화를 시작하면서 'Ladies and gentlemen~keynote speaker.'라는 말로 행사의 기조연설자를 맞이할 준비가 되었기를 희망하는 말과 함께 해당 연설자가 어떤 사람인지를 알리고 있으므로 (C)가 정답임을 알 수 있다.

87

★★★ 세부 정보

Jonathan Fielder는 누구일 가능성이 가장 큰가?
(A) 선구적인 대표 이사 (B) 광고 전문가
(C) 유명 저널리스트 (D) 소프트웨어 디자이너

어휘 leading 주요한 expert 전문가 renowned 유명한

토익 분석

인물 소개는 언제나 소개하는 인물의 이름이 언급되는 문장과 남자는 he, 여자는 she로 받아주는 문장들을 들어야 한다. Jonathan Fielder가 키워드다.

Who most likely is Jonathan Fielder?

(A) A leading CEO **(B) An advertising expert**
(C) A renowned journalist (D) A software designer

문제 해설

'Jonathan Fielder'라는 사람의 신분에 대해 유추할 것을 요구하는 두 번째 질문이므로 담화 중반부에서 이 사람이 하는 일과 관련해 직접적으로 언급되는 부분, 혹은 이를 추측할 수 있을 만한 관련 어휘가 제시되는 부분에 집중해야 한다. 화자는 담화 중반부에 해당 인물과 관련해 'With his groundbreaking~generation.'라는 말로 광고 전략을 재정립한 사람이라고 소개하고 있으므로 광고를 전문으로 하는 사람임을 알 수 있다. 따라서 이를 '광고 전문가'라는 말로 바꿔 표현한 (B)가 정답이 된다.

88

★★★ 맥락 파악

화자는 왜 "Please keep that in mind"라고 말하는가?
(A) 청자들이 반드시 일정표를 가져가도록 하기 위해
(B) 청자들이 자리에 앉도록 요청하기 위해
(C) 청자들이 안내 사항을 따르도록 상기시키기 위해
(D) 청자들이 방이 있는 곳을 아는지 확인하기 위해

어휘 make sure (that) 반드시 ~하다, 꼭 ~하다 request that ~하도록 요청하다 remind A to do A가 ~하도록 상기시키다 instructions 안내/지시 사항

토익 분석

요청, 제안의 힌트 문장인 'If가정법~, please명령문~'형태의 문장이 단서를 제시하고 있다.

Why does the speaker say, "Please keep that in mind"?

(A) To make sure the listeners pick up a schedule
(B) To request that the listeners take their seats
(C) To remind the listeners to follow instructions
(D) To check that the listeners know where a room is

문제 해설

화자가 말하는 "Please keep that in mind"라는 표현이 담화 속에서 어떤 의미로 사용되었는지를 묻는 세 번째 질문이다. 이 표현을 그대로 해석해 보면, '그것을 마음속에 유지하라'라는 의미를 나타내는데, 이는 무언가를 꼭 기억해 주기를 알릴 때 사용하는 표현이며, 후반부에 'If you have any questions~presentation.'라는 말과 함께 해당 표현을 사용하는 것으로 담화를 마치고 있으므로 화자가 언급하는 안내 사항을 꼭 기억하도록 강조하는 표현임을 알 수 있다. 따라서 이를 '안내 사항을 따르도록 상기시키기 위해'라는 말로 바꿔 표현한 (C)가 정답이 된다.

Questions 89-91 refer to the following speech.

M   Good afternoon, everyone. [89] I'm greatly honored to head the Gaby Tire Corporation. Gaby Tire is the world's second largest tire maker and currently has a 31% market share of the world tire market. [89] As your new president, [90] I plan to obtain a 50% slice of the world tire market over the next two years and hope to achieve a position of leadership in the industry. After months of experiments, our company has developed a new tire that won't slip on water and snow. We have applied for patents on the technology in 120 countries, including the United States, China, South Korea, Japan, and Australia. Not only do we have a new product to present, but we also have new technology that is exclusive to our company. [91] In order to be at the top of the market, we will implement marketing plans for our new product more aggressively for the rest of the year and provide active support for exports.

어휘 be honored to do ~하게 되어 영광이다 greatly 대단히, 매우 currently 현재 market share 시장 점유율 obtain ~을 획득하다 slice 부분 achieve ~을 달성하다 industry 업계 experiment 실험 slip 미끄러지다 apply for ~에 지원/신청하다 patent 특허 including ~을 포함해 exclusive 독점적인 in order to do ~하기 위해 implement ~을 시행하다 aggressively 적극적으로, 공격적으로 the rest of ~의 나머지 support 지원 export 수출(품)

89

Who most likely is the speaker?

(A) An auto engineer   (B) A marketing expert
(C) A sales manager   **(D) A company president**

문제 해설

화자의 정체를 유추하는 질문으로 지문 초반부에서 화자의 직책이나 업무적인 특징 등과 관련된 정보를 찾는 것이 관건이다. 담화 초반부에 'I'm greatly honored to head the Gaby Tire Corporation'이라고 말하며 자신이 Gaby 타이어 사를 이끈다고 언급하는 부분, 뒤이어 'As your new president'이라는 말로 회사의 신임 사장임을 직접적으로 밝히는 부분을 통해 (D)가 정답임을 알 수 있다.

★ 도입부 정보 – 화자

화자는 누구일 것 같은가?
(A) 자동차 엔지니어   (B) 마케팅 전문가
(C) 영업부장   (D) 회사의 사장

어휘 expert 전문가

토익 분석

자기소개 문장을 이끄는 대표 표현 중 하나인 I'm~이 이끄는 문장이 단서를 제시했다.

90

According to the speaker, what is the new goal of the company?

(A) To develop a new product   (B) To hold more technology patents
(C) To expand its domestic market share   **(D) To be a leader in the world market**

문제 해설

회사의 새로운 목표에 대해 묻는 두 번째 질문이므로 담화 중반부에서 회사의 목표나 계획 등이 제시될 것임을 예상하고 들어야 한다. 화자는 담화 중반부에 'I plan to~in the industry.'라고 말하며 향후 2년간 세계 타이어 시장에서의 점유율을 50% 선으로 끌어 올리고 업계 선두 업체가 되길 바란다는 새로운 목표를 제시하고 있으므로 (D)가 정답임을 알 수 있다. 국내 시장이 목표가 아니므로 (C)는 오답이다.

★★ 세부 정보

화자에 따르면, 회사의 새로운 목표는 무엇인가?
(A) 신제품을 개발하는 것
(B) 더 많은 기술 관련 특허를 보유하는 것
(C) 국내 시장 점유율을 확대하는 것
(D) 세계 시장의 선도 업체가 되는 것

어휘 develop ~을 개발하다 hold ~을 보유하다 expand ~을 확대/확장하다 domestic 국내의

토익 분석

화자는 회사의 목표를 연설문의 본론 부분에서 언급한다.

91

How does the speaker suggest the goal be accomplished?

(A) By launching a new product **(B) By stepping up marketing promotions**
(C) By conducting customer surveys
(D) By recruiting qualified research and development personnel

문제 해설

화자가 목표를 달성하는 방법으로 제안한 내용을 묻는 마지막 질문이므로 담화 후반부에서 목표 달성을 위한 구체적인 방법이 제시되는 부분에 집중해야 한다. 화자는 담화의 마지막에 'In order to~support for exports.'라는 말로 더 적극적으로 마케팅에 임하고 수출을 적극적으로 지원할 것임을 밝히고 있다. 따라서 마케팅 활동을 강화한다는 의미로 쓰인 (B)가 정답이다. 중반부에 함께 제시되는 출시할 신제품이 있다는 내용은 회사의 상황을 언급하는 것이므로 오답이다.

★★★ 세부 정보

화자는 목표가 어떻게 달성되어야 한다고 제안하는가?
(A) 신제품을 출시함으로써
(B) 마케팅 활동을 강화함으로써
(C) 고객 설문 조사를 실시함으로써
(D) 자격을 갖춘 연구 개발 인력을 모집함으로써

어휘 accomplish 달성/완성하다 launch ~을 출시하다 step up ~을 강화하다 conduct ~을 실시하다

토익 분석

의도, 미래 행동 표현: We(I) will~ 문장이 단서를 제시한다.

남 안녕하세요, 저는 **Steve Walter**입니다. [92] 오늘 저녁에 언론계에서 이룬 업적에 우리가 경의를 표하고자 하는 분은 **Alice Beckinsale** 씨입니다. 저는 항상 언론인들이 문제를 진단하고 사회의 미래 진로에 대한 방향을 설정할 수 있는 여론 주도자들이라 생각해 왔기 때문에 우리가 그녀에게 이 상을 수여하는 것이 적합하다고 여깁니다. [93] 그녀는 최근에 권위 있는 언론인 협회에 의해 올해의 언론인으로 선정되었는데, 뛰어난 활동 중에 만들어 낸 중요한 업적을 인정받아 같은 동료 언론인들의 결정을 통해 선정되었습니다. [92] **Beckinsale** 씨가 대학 졸업 직후 저희 신문사로 처음 일자리를 구하러 왔을 때, 저는 그녀의 눈에서 결단력을 보았고, 훌륭한 언론인이 될 것임을 알았습니다. 제가 옳았다고 말할 수 있게 되어 더없이 자랑스럽습니다. [94] **Alice Beckinsale** 씨에게 큰 박수를 보내주십시오.

Questions 92-94 refer to the following introduction.

M   Good evening. I'm Steve Walter. [92] The person we are honoring for her achievements in journalism this evening is Alice Beckinsale. I have always thought journalists are opinion leaders who can diagnose problems and set directions for future courses of society, so it seemed appropriate that we grant her this award. [93] She was recently selected as the journalist of the year by a prestigious journalist society, where she was handpicked by her colleagues in recognition of the important work she has produced in her fantastic career. [92] When Ms. Beckinsale first came out of college and came to my newspaper company about a job, I saw the determination in her eyes and knew she would make a great journalist. I couldn't be prouder to say I was right. [94] Please give a round of applause to Alice Beckinsale.

어휘 honor A for B B에 대해 A에게 경의를 표하다, 영예를 주다 achievement 업적 journalist 언론인 opinion leader 여론 주도자 diagnose ~을 진단하다 set directions for ~에 대한 방향을 정하다 seem + 형용사 ~한 것 같다 appropriate 적합한, 알맞은 grant A B A에게 B를 주다, 수여하다 recently 최근에 be selected as ~로 선택/선정되다 prestigious 권위 있는 handpick ~을 손수 따다, ~을 손수 주의해서 고르다 colleague 동료 in recognition for ~에 대해 인정을 받은 come out of college 대학을 졸업하다 determination 결단력, 단호함 couldn't be 비교급 가장 ~하다 give A a round of applause A에게 큰 박수를 보내다

92

★★ 세부 정보

Beckinsale 씨의 직업은 무엇일 것 같은가?
(A) 기자
(B) 라디오 아나운서
(C) 언론학 교수
(D) TV 프로그램 제작자

어휘 profession 직업 professor 교수

토익 분석

인물 소개 글에서 특정 인물의 직업 등을 묻는 문제는 그 사람의 이름이 키워드로 활용된다. **Beckinsale** 가 들리는 문장에 단서가 나온다.

What most likely is Ms. Beckinsale's profession?

(A) Reporter
(B) Radio announcer
(C) Journalism professor
(D) Television producer

문제 해설

Beckinsale 씨의 직업을 유추해야 하는 첫 번째 질문이므로 담화 초반부에서 Beckinsale 씨의 직업을 추측할 수 있을 만한 관련 어휘나 표현이 제시되는 부분에 집중해야 한다. 화자가 담화 초반부에서 'The person we are~Alice Beckinsale.'이라고 알리는 부분에서 언론인임을 먼저 알 수 있고, 'When Ms. Beckinsale~about a job'이라고 알리는 부분에서 Beckinsale 씨가 신문사 기자임을 유추할 수 있다. 따라서 (A)가 정답임을 알 수 있다.

93

★★ 세부 정보 – 사람

누가 Beckinsale 씨를 올해의 언론인으로 선정했는가?
(A) Walter 씨
(B) 그녀의 동료들
(C) 그녀의 대학 동창들
(D) 신문 연합

어휘 peer 동료 (직원) association 협회

토익 분석

인물 소개글에는 소개하는 사람의 이름 초반부에 한번 제시되고 그 다음부터는 대명사 he, she를 사용한다. **Beckinsale** 를 받아 주는 She가 나오는 문장들을 들어야 한다.

Who selected Ms. Beckinsale as journalist of the year?

(A) Mr. Walter
(B) Her peers
(C) Her college classmates
(D) The Association of Newspapers

문제 해설

Beckinsale 씨를 올해의 언론인으로 선정한 사람에 대해 묻는 두 번째 질문이므로 담화 중반부에서 올해의 언론인, 즉 the journalist of the year가 등장하는 부분을 중심으로 선정 주체를 파악해야 한다. 담화 중반부에 화자가 'She was recently~her colleagues'라는 말로 같은 업계의 동료들이 손수 올해의 언론인으로 선정했음을 밝히고 있으므로 colleagues와 동일한 의미에 해당되는 (B)가 정답이다.

94

★★ 화자의 요청 사항

청자들은 무엇을 하도록 요청 받는가?
(A) 몇몇 후보들을 추천할 것
(B) 구독을 신청할 것
(C) 시상식에 참석할 것
(D) 따뜻하게 환영해 줄 것

어휘 nominate ~을 지명하다 candidate 후보자, 지원자 sign up for ~을 신청하다 subscription (정기) 구독 give a warm welcome ~을 따뜻하게 환영하다

토익 분석

요청, 제안 문제에 대한 대표적인 힌트 표현인 Please 명령문~이 답을 제시하고 있다.

What are the listeners asked to do?

(A) Nominate some candidates
(B) Sign up for a subscription
(C) Attend an awards ceremony
(D) Give a warm welcome

문제 해설

화자의 요청 사항에 대해 묻는 마지막 질문이므로 담화 후반부에서 화자가 말하는 요청 표현을 중심으로 단서를 파악해야 한다. 화자는 담화 마지막에 'Please give a round of applause to Alice Beckinsale.'라고 말하며 Beckinsale 씨에게 큰 박수를 보내도록 요청하고 있다. 이는 청자들이 Beckinsale 씨를 따뜻하게 환영해 주길 바라는 것으로 이와 같은 의미에 해당되는 (D)가 정답이다.

Questions 95-97 refer to the following radio broadcast and list.

M Good evening, listeners! I'm Jack Hoult, and I'll be your host on WKT Rock Radio for the next ninety minutes. 95 Today's special guest is the internationally popular singer, Ryan Carter. Ryan started off as a member of the boy band Four Seasons, but later launched a solo career. 96 He's enjoyed great success, and he has received much praise for his singing and piano playing. His four albums have each sold over one million copies, and his first album, *Desperate Love*, sold over four million. 97 His newest album, released earlier this year, has already sold two point five million copies. Now, let's welcome Ryan to the studio.

Ryan Carter Records U.S. Album Sales (in millions)	
Desperate Love	4.4
Songs for Someone	3.8
Save the Last Dance	2.5
Electric Carnival	1.1

어휘 host 진행자, 주최자 internationally 세계적으로 popular 인기 있는 start off as ~로서 경력을 시작하다 later 나중에 launch ~을 시작하다 enjoy great success 대단한 성공을 거두다 receive much praise 극찬을 받다 million 백만의 over …가 넘는 release ~을 출시하다 sales 판매(량)

남 청취자 여러분, 안녕하세요! 저는 Jack Hoult이며, 앞으로 90분 동안 WKT Rock Radio에서 여러분의 진행자가 되어 드릴 것입니다. 95 오늘의 특별 게스트는 세계적으로 유명한 가수인 Ryan Carter 씨입니다. Ryan 씨는 보이 그룹인 Four Seasons의 일원으로 시작했지만, 이후에 솔로로서의 경력을 시작했습니다. 96 Ryan 씨는 대단한 성공을 거두어 왔으며, 노래 및 피아노 연주에 대해 극찬을 받아 왔습니다. Ryan 씨가 출시한 네 개의 앨범들은 각각 1백만 장이 넘게 판매됐으며, 첫 번째 앨범인 Desperate Love는 4백만 장이 넘게 판매되었습니다. 97 올해 초에 출시된 최신 앨범은 이미 2백 50만 장이 판매되었습니다. 자, Ryan 씨를 스튜디오로 모시겠습니다.

Ryan Carter 레코드 미국 앨범 판매량 (단위, 백만 장)	
Desperate Love	4.4
Songs for Someone	3.8
Save the Last Dance	2.5
Electric Carnival	1.1

95

What is the speaker mainly discussing?

(A) An upcoming concert
(B) A radio competition
(C) A singer's career
(D) A sale at a music store

문제 해설

담화의 주제를 묻는 첫 번째 질문이므로 담화 초반부에서 중점적으로 언급하는 핵심 내용을 파악하는 것이 관건이다. 화자는 담화를 시작하면서 자신을 소개하는 인사를 먼저 한 후 'Today's special guest is the internationally popular singer, Ryan Carter. Ryan started off as a member of the boy band, Four Seasons, but later launched a solo career.'라는 말로 방송 게스트로 나올 가수가 어떤 경력을 지니고 있는지 알리고 있으므로 (C)가 정답임을 알 수 있다.

★★ 주제, 목적

화자는 주로 무엇에 대해 이야기하고 있는가?
(A) 다가오는 콘서트
(B) 라디오 경연 대회
(C) 한 가수의 경력
(D) 음반 매장의 할인 행사

어휘 upcoming 다가오는 competition 경연대회 sale 할인 행사

토익 분석

지문 도입부에 자기소개 문장 다음이 주제문이다. I'm~으로 시작한 자기소개 문장이 주제문이 다음에 나올 것이라는 힌트를 주고 있다.

★★ 세부 정보

Ryan Carter는 무슨 악기를 연주하는가?
(A) 기타
(B) 피아노
(C) 바이올린
(D) 드럼

어휘 instrument 악기

토익 분석

인물 소개글에서 사람의 이름은 키워드로 활용 되지만 지문 초반부에 이름이 한 번 소개된 후에는 **he, she**와 같은 대명사가 사용된 문장을 들어야 한다. 키워드 **Ryan Carter**를 받는 **he**로 시작한 문장이 힌트를 제시했다.

What instrument does Ryan Carter play?

(A) Guitar
(B) Piano
(C) Violin
(D) Drums

문제 해설

Ryan Carter라는 사람이 다루는 악기에 대해 묻는 두 번째 문제이므로 담화 중반부에서 언급되는 특정 악기와 관련된 정보에 집중해 들어야 한다. 화자는 담화 중반부에 해당 인물을 대명사 he와 his를 사용해 지칭하면서 'He's enjoyed great success, and he has received much praise for his singing and piano playing.'라는 말로 노래 및 피아노 연주에 대해 격찬을 받아 왔다고 알리는 것으로 볼 때 (B)가 정답이 된다.

★★★ 그래픽

도표를 확인하시오. 올해 어느 앨범이 출시되었는가?
(A) Desperate Love
(B) Songs for Someone
(C) Save the Last Dance
(D) Electric Carnival

어휘 desperate 절망적인, 자포자기의

토익 분석

제시된 표에는 앨범 이름과 판매량이 제시되었기에 앨범을 찾기 위해서는 지문에 언급되는 '판매량' 관련 정보에 집중해야 한다.

Look at the graphic. Which album was released this year?

(A) Desperate Love
(B) Songs for Someone
(C) Save the Last Dance
(D) Electric Carnival

문제 해설

질문에서 묻는 내용과 관련해 담화 속에 제시된 단서를 바탕으로 도표의 정보를 함께 확인해 정답을 찾아야 하는 문제이다. 이때 각 보기에 제시된 내용 외의 정보가 담화 속에서 단서로 제시될 것이므로 이에 집중해 담화를 들어야 한다. 각 보기에 앨범 제목이 제시되어 있으므로 이와 함께 언급된 판매량 수치가 담화에 제시될 것임을 예상하고 들어야 하며, 질문에 '올해'라는 특정 시점이 언급되어 있으므로 해당 시점 표현과 함께 화자가 판매량 수치를 말할 것임을 알 수 있다. 화자는 담화 후반부에 'His newest album, released earlier this year, has already sold two point five million copies.'라는 말로 올해 초에 출시된 새 앨범이 2백 50만 장이 판매되었다고 했으므로 이 판매량에 해당하는 앨범인 (C)가 정답이 된다.

Questions 98-100 refer to the following excerpt from a meeting and schedule.

W The most important item on the meeting agenda is our firm's upcoming relocation to the Lifeson Building. 98 At the moment, there are no tenants in the Lifeson Building, and our company will be the first one. We plan to relocate our main departments one at a time, starting with the sales department on Monday, June 6. You can take a look at the schedule I distributed at the start of the meeting. 99 Although it's not listed, the accounting department will move on the same day as the HR department. 100 After we are all settled into the new workspace, we'll have a celebration dinner. This will take place on June 15, and all employees are welcome.

Department Relocation Date	
Monday, June 6	Sales
Wednesday, June 8	Human Resources
Friday, June 10	Customer Service
Monday, June 13	Marketing

어휘 item 안건 agenda 의제 firm 회사 upcoming 곧 있을 relocation (위) 이전 at the moment 현재 tenant 입주자 relocate 이전하다 one at a time 한 번에 하나씩 take a look at ~을 한 번 보다 distribute ~을 나눠 주다 at the start of ~가 시작될 때 although ~이기는 하지만 listed 목록에 있는, 기재된 accounting department 회계부 be settled into ~에 정착하다 workspace 근무 장소 celebration 기념행사 take place (행사 등이) 열리다, 개최되다

여 회의 의제에서 가장 중요한 안건은 곧 우리 회사가 **Lifeson Building**으로 위치를 이전한다는 것입니다. 98 현재, **Lifeson Building**에는 입주한 회사가 없는 상태이므로 우리 회사가 첫 번째가 될 것입니다. 우리는 한 번에 하나씩 주요 부서들을 옮길 계획이며, 6월 6일, 월요일에 영업부부터 시작할 것입니다. 회의가 시작될 때 제가 나눠 드린 일정표를 확인해 보실 수 있습니다. 99 목록에는 들어 있지 않지만, 회계부는 인사부와 같은 날에 이전할 것입니다. 100 새로운 업무 공간에 모두 자리를 잡은 후에는, 기념 만찬 행사를 할 예정입니다. 이 행사는 6월 15일에 열릴 것이며, 모든 직원을 환영합니다.

부서별 이전 날짜	
6월 6일, 월요일	영업부
6월 8일, 수요일	인사부
6월 10일, 금요일	고객 서비스부
6월 13일, 월요일	마케팅부

98

What does the speaker say about the Lifeson Building?

(A) It is conveniently located.
(B) It is currently unoccupied.
(C) It includes modern amenities.
(D) It has recently been expanded.

문제 해설

화자가 Lifeson Building에 대해 언급하는 정보를 찾도록 요구하는 첫 번째 질문이므로 담화 초반부에 해당 명칭과 함께 제시되는 정보에 집중해 들어야 한다. 화자는 담화를 시작하면서 해당 건물 이름과 함께 'At the moment, there are no tenants in the Lifeson Building'이라고 알리고 있는데, 이는 그 건물에 입주해 있는 회사가 없다는 의미이므로 이를 'currently unoccupied'라는 표현으로 바꿔 제시한 (B)가 정답이 된다.

★ 세부 정보

화자는 Lifeson Building에 대해 무슨 말을 하는가?
(A) 편리한 곳에 위치해 있다.
(B) 현재 비어 있는 상태이다.
(C) 현대적인 편의 시설을 포함하고 있다.
(D) 최근에 확장되었다.

어휘 conveniently located 편리한 곳에 위치한 currently 현재 unoccupied 비어 있는 amenities 편의시설

토익 분석

세부 정보 문제로 키워드 Lifeson Building를 활용하는 문제이다.

★★★ 그래픽

도표를 확인하시오. 회계부는 언제 이전할 것인가?
(A) 6월 6일에
(B) 6월 8일에
(C) 6월 10일에
(D) 6월 13일에

어휘 move 이전, 이동

토익 분석

표에 이전 날짜와 부서명의 정보가 제시되어 있다. 이전 날짜를 찾기 위해서는 지문에서 부서명에 대한 정보를 들어야 한다.

Look at the graphic. When will the accounting department move?

(A) On June 6
(B) On June 8
(C) On June 10
(D) On June 13

문제 해설

질문에서 묻는 내용과 관련해 담화 속에 제시된 단서를 바탕으로 도표의 정보를 함께 확인해 정답을 찾아야 하는 문제이다. 이때 각 보기에 제시된 내용 외의 정보가 담화 속에서 단서로 제시될 것이므로 이에 집중해 담화를 들어야 한다. 각 보기에 날짜가 쓰여 있으므로 도표에 이와 함께 제시된 정보인 부서명과 관련된 정보를 담화에서 파악해 내야 한다. 담화 중반부에 화자는 회계부와 관련해 'Although it's not listed, the accounting department will move on the same day as the HR department.'라는 말로 인사부와 같은 날에 옮긴다고 알리고 있으므로 도표에서 인사부가 이전하는 날짜로 표기된 (B)가 정답이 된다.

★★ 세부 정보

6월 15일에 무슨 일이 있을 것인가?
(A) 새로운 지사가 문을 열 것이다.
(B) 사무 공간이 개조될 것이다.
(C) 직원들이 식사 자리에 참석할 것이다.
(D) 장비가 설치될 것이다.

어휘 branch 지사, 지점 renovate ~을 개조하다 attend ~에 참석하다 equipment 장비 install ~을 설치하다

토익 분석

세부 정보 문제로 키워드인 June 15만 들으면 쉽게 답을 찾을 수 있는 문제이다.

What will happen on June 15?

(A) A new branch will be opened.
(B) An office space will be renovated.
(C) Staff will attend a meal.
(D) Equipment will be installed.

문제 해설

질문에 제시된 '6월 15일'이라는 특정 날짜에 있을 일을 묻는 마지막 문제이므로 담화 후반부에서 이 날짜 표현과 함께 언급되는 일과 관련된 정보에 집중해 들어야 한다. 화자는 담화를 마무리하면서 'After we are all settled into the new workspace, we'll have a celebration dinner. This will take place on June 15, and all employees are welcome.'라는 말로 기념 저녁 만찬 행사가 열릴 예정인데 그 날짜가 '6월 15일'이라고 알리고 있으므로 (C)가 정답임을 알 수 있다.

1

★★ 1인 중심 + 사람 동작

(A) 그는 컴퓨터 모니터를 들어 올리고 있다.
(B) 그는 천으로 모니터를 닦고 있다.
(C) 그는 창틀을 박박 문지르고 있다.
(D) 그는 안경을 써보고 있다.

어휘 wipe ~을 닦다 cloth 천, 옷감, 행주 scrub 문지르다 windowsill 창틀 try on 입어보다, 써보다

(A) He is lifting the computer monitor.
(B) He is wiping the monitor with a cloth.
(C) He is scrubbing the windowsill.
(D) He is trying on a pair of glasses.

문제 해설

1인 중심의 사진이므로 남자의 행동과 옷차림이나 장신구 착용과 관련된 외모적 특징에 집중해야 하며 아울러 사람이 특정 도구나 기기와 함께 등장하는 경우 이를 이용한 행동을 표현하는 정답이 자주 제시되므로 이 부분에 초점을 맞춰야 할 필요가 있다. 그러므로 남자가 안경을 착용하고 있는 상태, 남자가 천을 가지고 모니터 화면을 닦는 행동이 정답 포인트가 된다. 이 중 남자가 천으로 모니터를 닦고 있는 동작을 표현한 (B)가 정답이라 할 수 있다.

토익 분석

사진 속에 없는 동작. 사물이 등장하는 보기는 무조건 소거한다. 소거법을 적용하여 (A), (C)를 소거해 낸다. (D)의 경우 주의해야 할 함정 보기다. 뭔가를 착용하는 동작은 put on을 사용하며, 가게에서 물건을 착용해 보는 경우는 try on을 사용한다. try on이 오답 함정이다.

2

★★ 2인 이상 + 사물 동작

(A) 남자가 주문을 받고 있다.
(B) 남자들이 테이블 주변에 착석해 있다.
(C) 모든 사람이 유리잔을 들고 있다.
(D) 액체가 유리잔에 부어지고 있다.

어휘 take an order 음식 주문을 받다 liquid 액체

(A) A man is taking an order.
(B) Men are sitting around the table.
(C) All of people are holding glasses.
(D) Some liquid is being poured into a glass.

문제 해설

2인 이상 등장하는 사진이므로 이들의 공통된 행동과 개별적 행동, 그리고 외모적 특징을 살펴본 후, 이들의 개별적 행동과 외모적 특징을 파악해야 하며, 이어서 사물의 위치와 상태에 집중하는 것이 적절하다. 한 남자가 병에 든 음료를 잔에 따르는 행동과 손님들이 착석해 있는 상황을 고려해야 한다. 이 중 남자가 잔에 음료를 따르는 행동을 사물 주어 입장에서 수동태로 표현한 (D)가 정답이다.

토익 분석

보통 사람이 여럿 등장하는 문제는 혼동 보기를 만들 때 항상 주어의 수를 가지고 장난을 치는 경우가 많다. (C)와 (B)가 바로 그 예다. (C)는 all of people이 오답 포인트고 (B)는 Men are가 오답이 되는 이유다. 항상 여러 명이 등장하는 문제에서 혼동 보기가 등장할 것을 대비해 주어의 수를 명확히 확인하는 습관이 필요하다.

3

(A) The woman is opening the car door.
(B) The woman is sitting behind the steering wheel.
(C) One of the people is seated in the rear of the car.
(D) The woman has both her hands on the steering wheel.

(A) 여자가 차 문을 열고 있다.
(B) 여자가 운전대 뒤에 착석해 있다.
(C) 한 사람이 자동차의 뒷좌석에 착석해 있다.
(D) 여자가 두 손을 운전대 위에 올리고 있다.

어휘 steering wheel 운전대 rear 뒤의

문제 해설

2인 중심의 사진이지만 남자의 모습은 사진에서 거의 보이지 않고 있으므로 여자의 행동과 옷차림이나 장신구 착용과 관련된 외모적 특징을 살펴본 후 여자 주변 사물의 위치와 상태를 파악하는 것이 바람직하다. 그러므로 여자가 운전대를 쥐고 있고, 키를 받기 위해 손을 뻗고 있는 행동 그리고 차 안에 앉아 있는 동작에 집중해야 한다. 이 중 여자가 운전대 뒤에 착석해 있는 상태를 표현하고 있는 (B)가 정답이라 할 수 있다.

토익 분석

사람의 동작 위주의 문제에서 여러 가지 동작이 느껴지는 경우 가장 흔하게 오답을 만드는 방식은 동사와 잘못된 장소나 사물의 조합을 짝짓는 것이다. 여자는 사진에서 운전석에 앉아 있지 뒷좌석에 앉아 있지 않기에 (C)는 오답이다. 그리고 여자는 한쪽 손만 핸들을 잡고 있으므로 (D)도 오답이다. 항상 수 일치, 동사와 올바른 사물의 조합을 신경 써야 한다.

4

(A) She is resting her arm on the table.
(B) She is laying a cushion on the sofa.
(C) She is lying on her side.
(D) She is adjusting a seat.

(A) 그녀는 테이블에 팔을 올리고 쉬고 있다.
(B) 그녀는 쿠션을 소파 위에 놓고 있다.
(C) 그녀는 측면으로 누워 있다.
(D) 그녀는 좌석을 조정하고 있다.

어휘 rest the arm on the table 테이블 위에 파일 올리고 쉬다 lie ~에 눕다 lay 두다, 놓다 adjust ~을 조작하다, ~을 조절하다

문제 해설

1인 중심의 사진이므로 여자의 행동과 옷차림이나 장신구 착용과 관련된 외모적 특징을 살펴본 후 여자 주변 사물의 위치와 상태를 파악하는 것이 바람직하다. 그러므로 여자가 소파 위에 누워 있는 상태, 여자가 팔을 이마에 올리고 있는 행동과 관련된 정답이 제시될 가능성이 높으며, 이 중 여자가 소파 위에 측면으로 누워있는 모습을 정확하게 설명하고 있는 (C)가 정답이다.

토익 분석

사진 문제에서 유사 발음은 자주 활용되는 혼동 보기 포인트다. lying (눕다)과 laying (놓다)은 유사 발음으로 주의해야 한다.

★★ 1인 중심 + 사람 동작

(A) 그는 다림판을 잡고 있다.
(B) 셔츠가 테이블 위에서 접히고 있다.
(C) 선반 위에 옷들이 차곡차곡 쌓이고 있다.
(D) 그는 세탁기에 빨래를 채우고 있다.

어휘 ironing board 다림질 판 fold ~을 접다 stack ~을
쌓다 load A with B A에 B를 싣다 washing machine 세
탁기 laundry 세탁물, 빨래, 세탁소

(A) He is holding an ironing board.
(B) A shirt is being folded on the table.
(C) Some clothes are being stacked on a shelf.
(D) He is loading the washing machine with laundry.

문제 해설

실내 정경을 배경으로 한 사람이 등장하는 사진이므로 남자의 행동과 외모적 특징과 실내 정경의
주요 사물인 옷(빨래)들의 위치와 상태에 초점을 맞춰야 한다. 그러므로 남자가 수건을 개고 있는
행동, 남자 주변에 수건이 쌓여 있는 상태와 관련된 표현이 정답으로 제시될 것임을 가늠할 수 있으
며, 이 중 남자가 수건을 접는 동작을 사물 주어로 수동진행형으로 언급하고 있는 (B)를 정답으로
골라야 한다.

토익 분석

사진 문제에서 자주 활용되는 유사 발음이 등장했다. hold와 fold는 빈출 조합으로 꼭 기억해 둬야
한다. (A)는 fold가 아닌 hold를 활용한 혼동 보기가 된다. (C)의 경우 역시 주의할 보기다. 사물 주
어일 경우 행동이 동반되지 않는다면 being 형태가 사용될 수 없다.

★★ 사물 + 사물 위치

(A) 몇몇 사람들이 서로 옆에 서 있다.
(B) 몇몇 차량들이 차고 안에 주차되어 있다.
(C) 몇몇 자전거들이 거치대에 묶여 있다.
(D) 한 남자가 트럭을 도로에서 운전 중이다.

어휘 garage 차고 be secured to ~에 묶이다, ~에 단단
히 고정되다, ~에 안전하게 보관되다 rack 거치대

(A) Some people are standing next to each other.
(B) Some vehicles are parked in the garage.
(C) Some bicycles are secured to a rack.
(D) A man is driving a truck on the street.

문제 해설

실외 정경을 배경으로 중앙에 자전거와 몇몇 사람들이 배경에 작게 나오는 사진이므로 먼저 실외
정경의 주요 사물인 자전거의 위치와 상태에 집중하는 것이 순서라 할 수 있다. 그러나 대개 배경에
사람들이 있을 때 걷고 있는 한 남자의 명확한 행동을 유심히 봐야 한다. 몇몇 자전거들이 거치대에
묶여 있는 상태를 명확하게 묘사하고 있는 (C)가 정답이다.

토익 분석

배경 속에 희미한 사람, 사람은 중요한 요소가 아님을 기억하자. 항상 사진 속에 초점이 맞아 있는
것에 집중을 한다.

7

Why can't we use the restroom on the third floor?

(A) We need some rest.
(B) It's currently under maintenance.
(C) I think you should use the elevator.

문제 해설

3층에 있는 화장실을 사용하지 못하는 이유를 묻는 Why 직접의문문으로, 이에 현재 화장실이 수리 중이라는 구체적인 이유를 제시하고 있는 (B)가 정답이다.

토익 분석

휴식이 필요하다고 언급하고 있는 (A)는 3층 화장실을 사용할 수 없는 이유와 무관한 내용이자 질문의 rest를 중복하여 들려주는 동일 어휘 함정이 포함된 오답이며, 엘리베이터를 사용하도록 권고하는 (C)는 질문의 third floor를 통해 연상할 수 있는 elevator를 이용한 연상 어휘 오답으로 How 직접의문문 중 '방법'을 묻는 질문에 답변으로 적합하다.

★★ 직접의문문

3층에 있는 화장실을 사용할 수 없는 이유가 뭔가요?
(A) 저희는 휴식이 필요해요.
(B) 현재 수리 중에 있어요.
(C) 엘리베이터를 사용하셔야 합니다.

어휘 restroom 화장실 rest 휴식 currently 현재 maintenance 수리, 보수, 유지 elevator 엘리베이터

8

Could you give me some feedback on our new advertising strategies?

(A) Yes, but I can't go over them until next week.
(B) Some advertisements in the local papers.
(C) No, I already ordered some.

문제 해설

새로운 광고 전략에 대한 의견을 줄 수 있는지 여부를 묻는 Could 조동사로 시작하는 일반의문문으로 권유, 제안, 요청 유형이다. 이에 광고 전략에 대한 의견을 제공할 것이나 그 전략을 다음 주에 검토할 것임을 밝히는 제한적 긍정 답변의 (A)가 정답이다.

토익 분석

지역 신문의 몇몇 광고를 지칭하고 있는 (B)는 새로운 광고 전략에 대한 의견을 제공할 것인지 여부와 관련이 없는 내용이자 advertising과 advertisements라는 파생어들을 이용한 파생어 오답이며, what 직접의문문에 답변으로 적합하다. (C)는 새로운 광고 전략에 대한 의견을 제공할 수 없다는 부정 답변 No와 이미 약간 주문했다는 부연 설명이 서로 무관한 내용으로 구성된 오답이 되겠다. Part 2에서 질문 속에 들린 단어가 중복 사용되지 않는다는 전제하에 보기 문장에 but이 포함된 경우 정답 확률이 99%라는 점을 기억해 두면 질문과 답을 이해하지 못했을 때 아주 유용하다.

★★★ 권유, 제안, 요청 유형

새로운 광고 전략에 대한 의견을 주실 수 있겠어요?
(A) 물론이에요, 하지만 다음 주나 되어야 검토할 수가 있어요.
(B) 지역 신문에 나온 몇몇 광고들이요.
(C) 아니요, 저는 이미 약간 주문했어요.

어휘 feedback on ~에 대한 의견 go over ~을 검토하다

9

Would you like me to pick you up at the airport?

(A) Yes, I picked up the phone.
(B) That would be very helpful.
(C) The first flight departs at 7:30 A.M.

★★ 권유, 제안, 요청 유형

공항에서 제가 귀하께 차편을 제공해 주길 원하십니까?
(A) 네, 제가 전화를 받았어요.
(B) 그러면 아주 큰 도움이 될 겁니다.
(C) 첫 비행기는 오전 7시 30분에 출발해요.

어휘 pick up ~을 차에 태우다, ~을 들어 올리다, ~을 구매하다 helpful 도움이 되는 depart 출발하다

공항에서 자신이 차편을 제공해 주길 원하는지 여부에 대해 묻는 'Would you like sby to 동사원형' 형태의 대표적인 빈출 Would 조동사로 시작하는 일반의문문으로 권유, 제안, 요청 유형이다. 이에 큰 도움이 될 것이라며 우회적으로 차편을 제공해 주도록 요청하고 있는 (B)가 정답이다.

토익 분석

(A)는 차편을 원하는 Yes란 긍정 답변과 자신이 전화를 받았다는 부연 설명이 서로 관련이 없는 내용이자 질문의 pick up과 파생어 관계인 picked up을 통한 파생어 오답이며 첫 비행기 일정을 언급하고 있는 (C)는 When 의문문에 적절한 내용이자 질문의 airport와 관련이 있는 flight를 이용한 연상 어휘 오답이라 할 수 있다.

10

★★★ 평서문

대규모 수리는 시행하기 전에 관리실로부터 허가를 받아야 해요.
(A) 네, 그것들은 대규모 공사 중입니다.
(B) 다 수리하는데 2주에서 3주 정도가 소요될 겁니다.
(C) 오, 저는 몰랐어요. 알려 주셔서 감사합니다.

어휘 get permission from ~로부터 허가를 받다
management 운영, 경영진, 관리실 perform ~을 행하다

You need to get permission from management before performing any major repairs.

(A) Yes, they are under major construction.
(B) It'll take two to three weeks to repair it.
(C) Oh, I didn't know that. Thank you for letting me know.

문제 해설

대규모 수리는 시행하기 전에 관리실로부터 허가를 받아야 한다는 내용의 평서문으로, 이에 모르는 사실을 알려 준 것에 대한 감사의 인사를 전달하고 있는 (C)가 정답이다.

토익 분석

(A)는 질문 속에 사용된 major를 반복 사용한 중복 단어 오류를 포함한 혼동 보기다. 대략적인 수리 기간을 밝히고 있는 (B)는 How long 의문문에 적절한 내용이자 질문의 repair를 반복적으로 들려 주는 동일 어휘 함정이 오답이라 할 수 있다.

11

★★ 선택의문문

일반 필름 카메라를 가지고 계신가요, 아니면 디지털 카메라를 가지고 계신가요?
(A) 아니요, 저는 이미 새로운 카메라를 구매했어요.
(B) 사실, 저는 둘 다 없습니다.
(C) 현상을 해야만 합니다.

어휘 regular 일반, 표준 either (부정문) ~도 그렇다
process 현상하다

Do you have a regular film camera or a digital one?

(A) No, I already bought a new one.
(B) Actually, I don't have either.
(C) It needs to be processed.

문제 해설

일반 카메라와 디지털 카메라 중 어느 것을 보유하고 있는지 묻는 단순 선택의문문으로, 이에 둘 다 가지고 있지 않다는 양자부정 형태의 답변을 제시하고 있는 (B)가 정답이다.

토익 분석

새로운 카메라를 구매했다는 (A)는 카메라 종류의 선택과 무관한 내용의 오답이며, 또한 선택의문문은 Yes/No로 답변할 수 없다는 사실을 기억해야 한다. 현상을 해야 한다고 답한 (C) 역시 카메라 종류의 선택과 관련이 없으며 또한 Part 2에서 'film-develop-process-director'의 조합은 언제나 오답을 구성하는 조합이라는 것도 기억해야 한다.

12

We got feedback on our new product from some customers, didn't we?

(A) No, I've got to renew my passport.
(B) Sales are up today.
(C) Yes, and it was very helpful.

문제 해설

일부 고객들에게 제품에 관한 의견을 받았는지 여부를 확인하는 부가의문문으로, 이에 제품에 관한 고객들의 의견을 수령했음을 뜻하는 Yes란 긍정 답변과 함께 그것이 큰 도움이 되었음을 밝히고 있는 (C)가 정답이 된다.

토익 분석

(A)는 질문 속에 사용된 new 의 변형인 renew 유사 단어 오류를 사용한 오답이다. 매출의 향상이 있음을 언급하고 있는 (B) 또한 고객들의 의견을 수령했는지 여부와 무관한 내용이자 질문의 product에서 연상할 수 있는 sales를 통한 연상 어휘 오답이 되겠다. 일반의문문과 부가의문문의 경우 Yes/No로 답을 하는 보기가 정답 확률이 90% 이상이 된다.

★★ 부가의문문

저희는 일부 고객들에게 제품에 관한 의견을 받았어요, 그렇지 않나요?
(A) 아니요, 저는 여권을 갱신해야만 합니다.
(B) 오늘 매출이 향상되었어요.
(C) 네, 그래서 그것은 큰 도움이 되었어요.

어휘 feedback 의견, 후기, 견해 renew 갱신하다 sales 매출 helpful 도움이 되는

13

Shouldn't we consider hiring the more experienced applicants?

(A) Yes, but I'm in no position to decide that.
(B) No, it could be a valuable experience for you.
(C) I was very impressed with her work experience.

문제 해설

더 많은 경력직 지원자의 채용을 고려해야 할지 여부를 묻는 Should 조동사로 시작되는 일반의문문으로, 이에 고려 중임을 뜻하는 Yes란 긍정 답변에 이어 자신은 그 부분을 결정할 수 있는 위치가 아님을 밝히고 있는 제한적 긍정 형태의 답변인 (A)가 정답이다.

토익 분석

(B)는 고려하고 있지 않다는 뜻을 지닌 부정 답변 No와 소중한 경험이 될 것이라는 부연 설명이 서로 연관이 없는 내용이자 experience와 experienced라는 파생어 관계를 이용한 파생어 오답이며, (C) 역시 그녀의 직장 경력에 대한 감명을 언급하는 내용이 더 많은 경력직 지원자의 채용 여부와 관련이 없을 뿐만 아니라 질문의 applicant에서 연상이 가능한 work experience를 이용한 연상 어휘 오답이다. 또한, 누구를 지칭하는지 알 수 없는 대명사인 she가 사용된 것도 눈여겨봐야 한다. Part 2에서 질문 속에 사용된 단어들과 비슷한 형태나 발음의 단어가 중복 사용되는 경우를 제외하고 질문에 관계없이 but이 포함된 보기는 정답 확률이 99%라는 점을 반드시 암기해 두자.

★★★ 일반의문문

더 많은 경력직 지원자의 채용을 고려해야 하지 않을까요?
(A) 네, 하지만 저는 그걸 결정할 수 있는 위치가 아니에요.
(B) 아니요, 그건 당신에게 소중한 경험이 될 겁니다.
(C) 그녀의 직장 경력에 상당히 감명을 받았어요.

어휘 consider ~을 고려하다 experienced 경력이 있는 applicant 지원자 be in no position to do ~을 할 수 있는 위치가 아니다 valuable 귀한, 소중한, 가치가 있는 be impressed with ~에 감명을 받다

14

Would you like me to complete the marketing report today, or can it wait until tomorrow?

(A) Because we're short staffed.
(B) I'll need it by the end of the day.
(C) I've already reported to him.

★★★ 선택의문문

제가 오늘 마케팅 보고서를 작성하길 원하세요, 아니면 내일 해도 될까요?
(A) 저희가 인력이 부족하기 때문에요.
(B) 오늘 퇴근 때까지는 그것이 필요합니다.
(C) 저는 이미 그에게 보고했습니다.

어휘 complete ~을 작성/완료하다 be short staffed 인력이 부족하다 by the end of the day 오늘 퇴근 때까지

마케팅 보고서를 오늘 작성해야 하는지, 아니면 내일 해도 되는지 묻는 선택의문문으로, 이에 오늘 퇴근 때까지 필요하다고 이야기하며 결과적으로 오늘 작성할 것을 요구하고 있는 (B)가 정답이다.

토익 분석

because란 접속사가 등장하고 있는 (A)는 Why 의문문에 적합한 내용의 오답이며, (C)는 질문 속에 사용된 report를 중복 사용한 오답이며 인칭대명사인 him을 사용한 오답 보기가 된다. Part 2에서 질문 속에 사람 이름이나 직책이 들리지 않거나 보기에 he, she, her, him이 등장할 경우 오답이므로 무조건 소거해야 한다.

15

★★ 부가의문문

그 회계 소프트웨어의 개정판은 사용하기가 매우 쉬워요, 그렇지 않나요?
(A) 아니요, 저는 그걸 다음에 입을 겁니다.
(B) 네, 저만 믿으세요.
(C) 네, 저도 그리 생각해요.

어휘 upgrade ~을 개정하다, ~을 향상시키다 count on 의지하다, 믿다

The upgraded version of the accounting software is very easy to use, isn't it?
(A) No, I'll wear it next time.
(B) Yes, you can count on me.
(C) Yes, I think so.

문제 해설

그 회계 소프트웨어의 개정판이 사용하기 쉽다는 사실을 확인하는 부가의문문으로, 이에 동의하는 Yes란 답변에 이어 본인도 그리 생각한다고 언급하고 있는 (C)가 정답이다.

토익 분석

(A)는 질문의 software의 일부분인 wear를 이용한 오답 보기다. (B) 질문 속 accounting을 변형한 count on을 활용한 오답이다. Part 2에서 일반의문문과 부가의문문에서 '당신 말이 맞다 you're right / 그럴 것이다 I think(guess, believe) so / 아닐 것이다 I don't think so'와 같은 표현들은 질문에 관계없이 100% 정답이 된다는 것을 기억해 두자.

16

★★★ 선택의문문

제가 이 새로운 프린터의 잉크를 교체해야 하나요, 아니면 조금 더 사용할 수 있을까요?
(A) 아니요, 출력이 아주 잘됩니다.
(B) 교체해야 한다고 생각해요.
(C) 그녀가 몇몇 대체 부품을 주문할 것입니다.

어휘 replace ~을 교체하다, ~을 대체하다 clearly 명백하게, 분명하게

Should I replace the toner in this printer with a new one now, or can we use it a bit more?
(A) No, it prints very well.
(B) I think you should change it.
(C) She will order some of the replacement parts.

문제 해설

새로운 프린터의 잉크를 교체해야 하는지, 혹은 좀 더 사용해야 하는지 선택할 것을 요청하는 선택의문문으로, 이에 교체하는 쪽을 선택하는 (B)가 정답이다.

토익 분석

(A)는 선택의문문에서 대체로 오답으로 제시되는 No라는 답변이 등장하고 있으며, printer의 변형인 print를 중복 사용한 오답 보기다. (C)는 질문의 동사 replace의 변형인 replacement parts가 사용된 오답 보기며 누구를 지칭하는지 알 수 없는 인칭대명사 her가 사용된 오답 보기다. Part 2에서 질문 속에 사람 이름이나 직책이 들리지 않을 경우 he, she, her, him 등의 인칭대명사가 사용되는 보기는 언제나 오답 보기라는 것을 기억해야 한다.

17

Would you please help me fill out this registration form?

(A) Sure, I'll be back in a minute.
(B) Yes, he works at a local accounting firm.
(C) To bid, you should register first.

문제 해설

등록 서류 작성에 대한 도움 여부를 묻는 권유, 제안, 요청 유형으로, 이를 수락하는 Sure이란 긍정 답변과 함께 곧 돌아올 것임을 언급하고 있는 (A)가 정답이다.

토익 분석

(B)는 질문에 등장한 적이 없는 남자를 지칭하는 인칭대명사 he가 제시된 대명사 오답이며, 등록부터 할 것을 권고하고 있는 (C)는 등록 서류 작성에 대한 도움을 요청하는 질문과 상충되는 내용의 답변이자 아울러 register와 registration이란 파생어 관계를 이용한 파생어 오답이라 할 수 있다. Part 2에서는 질문 속에 사용된 단어의 변형 또는 유사 발음의 단어가 반복 사용되는 보기는 항상 오답 보기다.

★★ 권유, 제안, 요청 유형

제가 이 등록 서류를 작성할 수 있도록 도와주시겠어요?
(A) 물론이에요, 곧 돌아오겠습니다.
(B) 네, 그는 지역에 있는 회계법인에서 근무해요.
(C) 입찰에 참여하시려면 등록부터 하셔야 해요.

어휘 fill out 서류를 작성하다 registration form 등록 서류 in a minute 곧, 바로 work at ~에서 근무하다 firm 업체, 회사 bid 입찰, 유치, 입찰을 하다, ~에게 명령하다 register 등록하다

18

Let's have lunch at the company cafeteria before the meeting.

(A) I'll have the one with red stripes.
(B) No, there are major issues that will be discussed.
(C) Sure, but don't forget that we should be back by twelve thirty.

문제 해설

회의 전에 회사 구내식당에 가서 점심을 먹자고 권고하는 권유, 제안, 요청 유형으로, 이를 수락하는 Sure이란 긍정 답변과 함께 12시 30분까지는 돌아와야 한다는 점을 상기시키는 제한적 긍정 답변 형태의 (C)가 정답이다.

토익 분석

(A)는 Which 직접의문문에 대한 일반적인 답변 형태이며, (B)는 점심 식사를 하러 갈 수 없다는 부정 답변 No와 그것들이 주요 안건들이라는 부연 설명이 서로 무관한 내용으로 구성되었을 뿐만 아니라 질문에는 they라는 인칭대명사가 지칭할 만한 복수 명사가 등장한 적이 없으므로 대명사 오류까지 포함된 오답이라 할 수 있다. 보기를 모두 이해해서 풀고자 한다면 어려울 수 있지만, Part 2에서 but이 포함된 보기가 중복 발음이나 단어가 없을 경우 정답 확률이 99%라는 것을 기억한다면 어렵지 않게 답을 찾을 수 있다.

★★★ 권유, 제안, 요청 유형

회의가 시작되기 전에 회사 구내식당에서 점심을 먹지요.
(A) 빨간 줄무늬가 있는 것으로 하겠습니다.
(B) 아니요, 논의될 주요 안건들이 있습니다.
(C) 네, 하지만 12시 30분까지 돌아와야 한다는 걸 잊지 맙시다.

어휘 have lunch 가서 점심을 먹다 company cafeteria 회사 구내식당 stripe 줄무늬 major issue 주요 안건, 주요 문제

19

It seems like years since you had your manufacturing equipment checked.

(A) No, he will check it tomorrow.
(B) Yes, we have a vegetarian menu.
(C) Yes, it's been a while.

★★ 평서문

귀하의 제조 공장에 있는 장비는 점검을 받은 지 수년이 지난 것 같네요.
(A) 아니요, 그는 그걸 내일 점검할 겁니다.
(B) 네, 저희는 채식주의자용 메뉴가 있어요.
(C) 네, 꽤 된 듯합니다.

어휘 seem like ~인 것처럼 보이다 equipment 장비 vegetarian 채식주의자

제조 공장 장비가 점검을 받은 후 수년이 지난 것 같다는 문제점을 지적하는 평서문으로, 이에 동의하는 Yes란 긍정 답변과 함께 꽤 된 것 같다고 추가 정보를 제시하고 있는 (C)가 정답이 된다.

토익 분석

(A)는 평서문에 등장하지 않은 특정 남자를 지칭하는 인칭대명사 he가 제시된 대명사 오답이 되겠으며, (B)는 장비 점검을 받고 수년이 지났음을 인정하는 Yes란 긍정 답변과 채식주의자용 메뉴를 보유하고 있다는 부연 설명이 서로 무관한 내용이자 질문에 등장한 manufacturing의 일부 어휘인 manu와 유사한 발음을 지닌 menu를 이용한 오답이 된다.

20

★★★ 일반의문문

당신은 혹시 유로화에 대한 캐나다 달러의 환율을 알고 계신가요?
(A) 네, 제가 잔돈을 구해 드릴 수 있습니다.
(B) 제가 알아볼게요.
(C) 현재 금리는 매우 낮아요.

어휘 happen to do 우연히 ~하다 current 지금, 현재의
exchange rate 환율 change 잔돈 look up ~을 찾아보다,
~을 조사하다 interest rate 금리, 이자율

Do you happen to know the current exchange rate for Canadian dollars to euros?
(A) Yes, I can get you some change.
(B) Let me look it up.
(C) The current interest rate is very low.

문제 해설

유로화에 대한 캐나다 달러의 환율을 알고 있는지 여부를 묻는 일반의문문으로, 이에 자신이 알아보겠다고 대답하며 궁극적으로는 자신도 아는 바가 없음을 밝히고 있는 (B)가 정답이다.

토익 분석

(A)는 질문 속에 사용된 exchange의 변형인 change를 활용한 중복 단어 오답이다. (C)는 질문의 rate를 중복하여 들려주는 동일 어휘 함정이 등장하고 있을 뿐, 환율과는 무관한 금리에 관해 언급하고 있는 오답이다. Part 2에서 질문에 관계없이 '알아보겠다, 확인해 보겠다'와 같은 내용의 표현은 무조건 정답으로 사용된다.

21

★★ 부가의문문

당신은 매일 통근하는데 한 시간 이상 걸리지요, 그렇지 않나요?
(A) 네, 하지만 회사 대부분의 직원들도 그 정도 걸려요.
(B) 아니요, 20분보다 조금 더 걸릴 것입니다.
(C) 네, 커뮤니케이션 기술에 관한 것입니다.

어휘 commute 통근하다 employee 직원
communication 대화

You commute more than an hour to work every day, don't you?
(A) Yes, but most employees in the company do.
(B) Yes, it will take a little over twenty minutes.
(C) Yes, it will be about communication skills.

문제 해설

매일 통근하는데 한 시간 이상 걸리는지 여부를 확인하는 부가의문문으로, 이에 통근이 한 시간 이상 걸리며 대부분의 직원들도 그 정도 걸린다는 부연 설명을 언급하고 있는 Yes, but ~ 형태의 제한적 긍정 답변인 (A)가 정답이다.

토익 분석

(B)는 1시간 이상 걸린다는 긍정 답변 Yes와 함께 20분 정도 걸린다고 했으니 대답과 뒤에 이어지는 부연 설명이 맞지 않다. (C)는 긍정하는 Yes란 답변과 커뮤니케이션 기술에 관한 것이라는 서로 무관한 내용으로 구성된 오답이 된다. 또한, 질문 속에 사용된 commute의 유사 단어인 communication이 활용된 오답 형태이기도 하다. Part 2에서는 질문에 관계없이 but을 포함한 보기의 경우 정답 확률이 매우 높다는 점을 기억해야 한다.

22

Mr. Smith is not going to be in the office this Thursday, is he?

(A) Yes, the new office is fully furnished.
(B) Right, he has a meeting with the suppliers.
(C) Yes, I'm going on a business trip on Thursday.

문제 해설

Smith 씨가 이번 주 목요일에 사무실을 비우는지 여부를 묻는 부가의문문이다. 이에 사무실을 비울 것이라는 긍정 답변 right에 이어 Smith 씨가 미팅이 있다고 부연 설명을 한 (B)가 정답이다.

토익 분석

(A)는 Smith 씨가 목요일에 사무실을 비운다고 긍정하는 Yes란 답변과 질문에서 등장한 적이 없는 새로운 사무실의 시설에 대해 언급하고 있으며 질문의 office를 반복하여 들려주는 동일 어휘 오답이며, (C) 역시 Smith 씨가 사무실을 비운다고 긍정하는 Yes란 답변과 자신이 목요일에 출장을 간다는 부연 설명이 서로 무관한 내용이자 질문의 going과 Thursday를 중복적으로 들려주는 동일 어휘 함정이 포함된 오답이다.

★★ 부가의문문

Smith 씨는 이번 주 목요일에 사무실에 없지요, 그렇지요?
(A) 네, 새로운 사무실은 모든 시설이 구비되어 있어요.
(B) 맞아요, 그는 공급 업체들과 미팅이 있습니다.
(C) 네, 저는 이번 주 목요일에 출장을 갑니다.

어휘 be fully furnished 모든 시설이 구비되다 go on a business trip 출장을 가다

23

Could you please tell me where the nearest office supplies store is?

(A) Yes, I went to a nearby store.
(B) Printer cartridges, notepads, and pens.
(C) There is one two blocks away from here.

문제 해설

간접의문문으로 문장 중간에 들리는 where에 대한 답을 찾아야 한다. 가장 가까운 사무용품점을 찾는 문제로 이곳에서 두 블록 떨어진 곳에 상점이 있다며 구체적인 위치를 언급하고 있는 (C)가 정답이다.

토익 분석

(A)는 가장 가까운 사무용품점의 위치를 알고 있다는 Yes란 답변과 자신이 근처에 있는 상점을 갔었다는 부연 설명은 가장 가까운 사무용품점의 위치와 무관한 내용이자 질문의 nearest 변형 단어인 nearby를 사용했으며 store를 중복하여 들려주는 동일 어휘 오답이다. (B)는 질문의 office supply를 통해 연상할 수 있는 여러 사무용품을 단순 열거하고 있는 오답이라 할 수 있다. 명사들의 열거는 주로 what 직접 의문문에 대한 답변이다.

★★ 간접의문문

여기서 가장 가까운 사무용품점이 어디에 있는지 알려 주시겠어요?
(A) 네, 저는 근처에 있는 상점으로 갔어요.
(B) 프린터용 잉크, 노트패드, 그리고 펜들이요.
(C) 이곳에서 두 블록 떨어진 곳에 상점이 있어요.

어휘 office supplies store 사무용품점 nearby 근처에 있는 cartridge 잉크 away from ~로부터 ~만큼 떨어져 있는

24

Please make sure that you turn off your cellular phone during the movie.

(A) She has postponed the meeting.
(B) Let's ask for directions to the theater.
(C) Actually, I already did.

★★ 권유, 제안, 요청

영화를 상영하는 동안, 귀하의 휴대 전화 전원을 필히 꺼주셔야 합니다.
(A) 그녀는 미팅을 연기했습니다.
(B) 극장으로 가는 길을 물어보도록 하지요.
(C) 사실, 저는 이미 껐어요.

어휘 make sure that 필히 ~하다 cellular phone 휴대 전화 during the movie 영화 상영하는 동안 postpone 연기하다 ask for ~을 요청하다

영화를 상영하는 동안 휴대 전화의 전원을 꺼야 한다고 요청을 하는 명령문이다. 이에 자신은 이미 휴대 전화를 껐다고 답한 (C)가 정답이다.

토익 분석

(A)는 누구를 지칭하고 있는지 알 수 없는 인칭대명사 she가 등장하고 있는 대명사 오답이며, (B)는 휴대 전화의 전원을 꺼달라는 요청에 대한 부적절한 답변이자 질문의 movie를 통해 연상할 수 있는 theater를 이용한 연상 어휘 오답이다.

25

★★★ 부정의문문

영업회의가 다음 주 수요일로 연기되었다는 사실을 모르셨나요?
(A) 네, 저희는 만난 적이 있어요.
(B) 몰랐어요, 저는 아직 전달받은 바 없어요.
(C) 네, 그 전화기를 항상 갖고 계세요.

어휘 be postponed until ~로 연기되다 inform 통보하다 keep ~을 유지하다, ~을 소유하다 at all times 늘, 항상

Didn't you know that the sales meeting was postponed until next Tuesday?

(A) Yes, we've met before.
(B) No, I haven't been informed yet.
(C) Yes, keep this phone with you at all times.

문제 해설

영업회의가 다음 주 수요일로 연기되었다는 사실을 알고 있는지 여부를 묻는 부정의문문으로, 이에 영업회의가 연기된 사실을 모른다는 부정 답변 No에 이어 아직 그에 대해 전달받은 바 없음을 밝히고 있는 (B)가 정답이다.

토익 분석

(A)는 질문 속에 사용된 meeting의 변형 단어인 met 활용한 오답 보기다. (C)는 영업회의가 연기된 사실을 알고 있다는 Yes란 긍정 답변과 항상 전화기를 지니도록 요청하고 있는 부연 설명이 서로 연관 없는 내용이자 질문의 postpone의 일부인 pone과 유사한 발음의 phone을 이용한 유사 발음 어휘 오답이다.

26

★★ 부가의문문

어젯밤에 식사가 아주 좋지 않았나요?
(A) 전 이곳이 처음이에요.
(B) 아니요, 오래 걸리지 않을 거예요.
(C) 네, 주요리가 아주 끝내줬어요.

어휘 meal 식사 last 지속되다 main dish 주요리 superb 최고의, 훌륭한

The meal was excellent last night, wasn't it?

(A) I'm new here.
(B) No, it won't last long.
(C) Yes, the main dish was superb.

문제 해설

식사에 대해 상대방의 의견을 묻는 부가의문문이다. 이에 대해 부가의문문의 빈출 정답 유형인 Yes로 답하고 주요리가 아주 좋았다고 부연 설명을 한 (C)가 정답이다.

토익 분석

(B)는 질문 속에 사용된 동사인 last를 다른 의미인 형용사로 반복 활용한 오답이다.

27

Would you rather have a meeting here or in my office?

(A) Yes, I prefer a window seat.
(B) It's up to you.
(C) That will be great.

문제 해설

미팅을 이곳과 사무실 어디에서 할지 묻는 선택의문문에 상대방이 알아서 결정하라고 답한 (B)가 정답이다.

토익 분석

(A)의 경우 Yes는 선택의문문에 사용할 수 없기에 오답이다. (C)는 상대방의 의견에 동의하는 표현으로 권유, 제안, 요청 질문 유형에 대한 대표적인 답변이다.

★ **선택의문문**

이곳에서 미팅할까요 아니면 제 사무실에서 할까요?
(A) 네, 저는 창가 자리를 선호합니다.
(B) 당신이 결정하세요.
(C) 좋습니다.

어휘 prefer 선호하다 window seat 창가 좌석 it's up to you 당신에게 달려 있다, 당신이 결정하세요

28

Why is the error message on the copy machine blinking?

(A) It might need a new toner.
(B) I'll go make some coffee.
(C) I need to check if they have any blankets left.

문제 해설

복사기에 왜 에러 메시지가 뜨는지 묻는 why 의문사로 시작하는 직접의문문이다. 이에 대해 토너가 필요한 것 같다고 이유를 설명한 (A)가 정답이다.

토익 분석

(B)는 질문 속에 사용된 copy의 유사 발음은 coffee를 활용한 유사 발음 오답이다. (C)는 질문 속 blink의 유사 단어인 blanket을 활용한 오답 보기다.

★★ **직접의문문**

복사기에 에러 메시지가 왜 깜박이나요?
(A) 새 토너가 필요한 듯해요.
(B) 제가 커피를 만들게요.
(C) 그들이 담요가 남은 게 있나 알아봐야 해요.

어휘 blink 깜박이다 blanket 담요 left 남다 (leave의 과거형)

29

Are you taking some time off anytime soon?

(A) I'm sorry, I don't think I can stay late.
(B) Next month, I think.
(C) Yes, I had a great time.

문제 해설

조만간 휴가 계획인 있는지 묻는 일반의문문에 다음 달 정도 휴가를 갈 것이라고 대답한 (B)가 정답이다.

토익 분석

(A) I'm sorry의 경우 뭔가를 제안하거나 요청했을 때 사용하는 대표적인 부정 답변이다. 그리고 질문 속에 사용된 time에서 연상 가능한 stay late를 활용한 오답이다. (C)는 일반의문문에 답변 형태지만 질문 속에 사용된 time을 반복 사용한 오답 보기가 된다.

★★ **일반의문문**

조만간 휴가를 낼 것인가요?
(A) 죄송하지만, 제가 늦게까지 있지 못할 것 같습니다.
(B) 아마, 다음 달쯤에요.
(C) 네, 아주 즐거웠어요.

어휘 take some time off 휴가를 가다 stay late 늦게까지 머물다 have a good time 즐거운 시간을 갖다

30

★★★ 직접의문문

얼마나 자주 마케팅 세미나를 개최하나요?
(A) 그는 일주일에 한 번 쇼핑을 갑니다.
(B) 확인해 봐야 합니다.
(C) 매일 마켓을 운전해 지나가요.

어휘 hold 개최하다 drive by 운전해 지나가다

How often do you hold marketing seminars?

(A) He goes shopping once a week.
(B) I'll have to check.
(C) I drive by the market every day.

문제 해설

얼마나 자주 세미나를 개최하는지 빈도를 묻는 how often 직접의문문이다. 이에 대해 확인을 해 봐야 한다고 답한 (B)가 정답이다

토익 분석

(A)의 경우 how often에 대한 대표적인 답변 형태인 once a week이 사용된 혼동 보기이지만 he로 시작하여 오답이다. 질문 속에 사람 이름이나 직책이 들리지 않을 경우 he, she, her, him을 포함한 보기는 오답이다. (C) 역시 every day를 이용한 혼동 보기가 된다. 그러나 질문 속에 사용한 marketing seminars를 변형하여 market을 활용했다는 것을 파악한다면 유사 단어 함정이 활용되었다는 것을 알 수 있다.

31

★★★ 선택의문문

국립 현대 박물관이 걸어갈 수 있는 거리인가요 아니면 먼가요?
(A) 그들은 서로 아주 친해요.
(B) 난 직장에 보통 걸어가요.
(C) 약 10분 운전 거리에요.

어휘 in walking distance 걸어갈 수 있는 거리에 close 가까운, 친한 walk to work 걸어서 출근하다

Is the National Modern Museum in walking distance or is it far?

(A) They are very close to each other.
(B) I usually walk to work.
(C) It's about a ten-minute drive.

문제 해설

박물관이 걸어갈 수 있는 거리에 있는지 여부를 묻는 선택의문문으로 약 10분 정도 운전해 가야 한다고 우회적으로 걸어갈 수 없는 거리임을 설명한 (C)가 정답이다.

토익 분석

(A)의 경우 close가 '거리가 가깝다'는 의미로 느껴지도록 만든 혼동 보기다. 오답 힌트는 they로 질문 속에 they가 받아줄 수 있는 대상이 없기에 오답이다. (B)의 경우 질문 속에 사용된 walking의 유사 발음은 work를 활용한 오답이다.

Questions 32-34 refer to the following conversation.

W   [32] I really enjoyed this year's seminar. All the speakers were excellent, and their topics were so timely.

M   I am glad that you had a good time. I hope you will spread the word about the event to your colleagues.

W   Of course. Oh, [34] by the way, could you tell me how I can obtain copies of the speakers' presentation slides? [33] I am especially interested in the keynote presentation and the one on supply chain management by the MK College professor. I also need to get a copy of the document that shows my registration for the seminar. I need to keep it for my files.

M   [34] I will have my secretary forward you what you need. Please give me your contact information.

어휘 conference 회의 timely 시기적절한 spread the word 입소문을 내다 soft copy 디지털 문서 keynote speech 기조연설 supply chain management 공급망 관리 original copies 원본 contact information 개인 연락처

여   [32] 저는 올해 세미나가 정말 좋았어요. 연설하신 모든 분들이 훌륭했고, 그들이 행한 연설 주제들도 아주 시기적으로 적절했고요.

남   좋은 시간을 보내셨다니 기뻐요. 저는 당신이 행사에 관해 동료들에게 잘 말씀해 주셨으면 합니다.

여   물론이죠. 오, [34] 그런데 당신은 제가 연설자들의 연설 내용을 어떻게 구할 수 있는지 말씀해 주실 수 있나요? [33] 저는 특히 기조 발표와 MK College 교수님이 말씀하셨던 공급망 관리에 관심이 있어요. 저는 또한 제가 세미나에 등록한 것을 보여 주는 서류 사본이 필요합니다. 제가 그 사본을 파일에 보관해 둘 필요가 있거든요.

남   [34] 제가 비서를 시켜 당신이 필요한 자료를 보내도록 하겠습니다. 제게 연락처를 알려 주세요.

32

What are the speakers talking about?

(A) A business course   **(B) An information event**
(C) A meeting schedule   (D) A confidential document

문제 해설

대화의 주제를 묻는 질문이므로 대화 초반부에서 집중적으로 언급되는 중심 소재를 파악하는 것이 관건이다. 여자는 대화 시작과 함께 'I really~so timely.'라고 말하며 올해 있었던 세미나가 훌륭했으며 연설자들과 주제들도 시의적절했다고 칭찬하는 내용을 통해 대화의 주제는 세미나임을 알 수 있다. 따라서 정답은 (B)가 되겠다. 다만 이는 선택지에서 information event라는 유사 표현으로 바뀌어 제시되고 있음에 유의해야 한다.

★★ 주제, 목적

화자들은 무엇에 관해 논의하는가?
(A) 경영학 과정
(B) 정보 관련 행사
(C) 회의 일정
(D) 기밀문서

어휘 confidential 비밀, 기밀의

토익 분석

주제는 언제나 첫 번째, 두 번째 대화 문장에 정답 힌트가 제시되어야 한다.

33

What topic is the woman interested in?

(A) Time management   (B) Data analysis
(C) Efficient communication skills   **(D) Supply chain management**

문제 해설

여자가 관심을 가지고 있는 주제를 묻고 있다. 여자의 대화 내용을 통해 단서를 파악하는 것이 바람직하다. 여자는 대화 후반부에서 'I am especially~MK College professor'라고 이야기하며 관심 사항들에 대해 언급하고 있다. 따라서 정답은 (D)가 되겠다.

★★ 세부 정보

여자가 관심을 갖는 주제는 무엇인가?
(A) 시간 관리   (B) 데이터 분석
(C) 효과적인 소통 기술   (D) 공급망 관리

어휘 analysis 분석 communication 소통

토익 분석

질문 속에 사용된 동사인 be interested가 키워드로 활용된 세부 정보 찾기 문제다.

34

What does the man say he will deliver to the woman?

(A) Several papers about value chain analysis
(B) Copies of the speakers' slides
(C) A guest speaker's contact information
(D) A complete set of conference presentations

문제 해설

남자가 여자에게 전달하기로 한 것이 무엇인지 묻는 질문으로, 여자가 'could you tell me how I can obtain copies of the speakers' presentation slides?'라고 이야기하며 이에 남자는 'I will have my secretary forward you what you need.'라고 말하며 비서를 통해 원하는 자료를 보내 주겠다고 대답하고 있다. 이를 통해 남자가 여자에게 전해 주겠다고 한 것은 궁극적으로 copies of the speakers' presentation slides임을 알 수 있다. 따라서 정답은 (B)이다.

★★★ 미래 행동

남자는 여자에게 무엇을 전달하기로 약속했는가?
(A) 몇몇 '가치 사슬 분석' 논문들
(B) 발표자들의 발표 원본들
(C) 명망 있는 학교의 초청 연사
(D) 회의 발표 자료 전체

어휘 guest speaker 초청 연사 prestigious 명망 있는

토익 분석

미래 행동이므로 대화 후반부에 I will~로 답이 제시되는 유형이다. 여자 대화 중 I need to가 정답 힌트이다.

여 안녕하세요. 저는 우리 창고 직원들이 착용할 회사의
새로운 로고와 슬로건이 담긴 모자를 주문하고 싶습
니다. 300개 정도의 모자가 필요한데요. 어떤 색상
과 디자인이 이용 가능한가요?

남 저희는 고객님을 위한 많은 디자인과 색상들을 보유
하고 있습니다. 35 귀사의 새로운 로고와 슬로건은 모
자에 단순 인쇄하거나, 저희 기술자가 수를 놓을 수
도 있습니다. 사실 대부분의 고객님들은 수로 놓은
로고와 슬로건이 더 전문가답게 보인다고들 하십니
다.

여 그렇군요. 저도 수놓은 로고와 슬로건 방식을 택하고
싶습니다. 36 이달 말까지 작업을 마무리하실 수 있겠
습니까?

남 문제없습니다. 시간은 충분합니다. 37 작업을 바로 시
작하기 위해 제게 이메일로 귀사의 로고와 슬로건이
담긴 이미지 파일을 보내셔서 저희가 그 디자인을 저
희 컴퓨터에 입력할 수 있도록 해 주시고요. 또한, 저
희 홈페이지, www.bestprinting.com을 방문하셔서
저희가 제공하는 다양한 형태의 모자들 중에서 어느
것을 원하시는지 선택해 주시길 바랍니다.

Questions 35-37 refer to the following conversation.

W Good morning. I want to order caps customized with my company's new logo and slogan for our warehouse men to wear. I think we need 300 caps. What kinds of designs and colors are available?

M We have many designs and colors for our customers. 35 Your company's new logo and slogan can be printed on the caps, or our technicians can have them embroidered. Most customers find the embroidered logo and slogan more professional looking.

W Right. I would like the logo and slogan to be embroidered. 36 Would you be able to get them finished by the end of this month?

M No problem. There should be enough time. To get started, 37 please e-mail me your company's logo and slogan image files so that we can get those designs put into our computer. You should also visit our Web site at www.bestprinting.com and make your choice among the various types of caps we offer.

어휘 customize 고객 맞춤형 warehouse 창고 technician 기술자 embroider 수를 놓다 professional 전문가

35

★★★ 세부 정보

남자는 여자에게 무엇을 비교해 주는가?
(A) 두 모자의 색상과 디자인
(B) 일부 고객층
(C) 대량 주문에 대한 할인
(D) 모자를 고객 맞춤형으로 제작하는 방법

어휘 bulk 다량의 personalize 개인 맞춤의

토익 분석

첫 번째 문제이므로 남자의 첫 번째 대화문에 집중한다.

What does the man compare for the woman?

(A) Two cap colors and designs　(B) Some of the customer bases
(C) Discounts for bulk orders　**(D) Cap personalization options**

문제 해설

남자가 여자에게 비교해 주는 것에 대해 묻고 있으므로 남자의 대화 내용에서 여자에게 구체적으로 비교해 주는 대상이 무엇인지 집중해야 할 필요가 있다. 남자는 여자에게 'Your company's~on the caps.'라고 말하며 모자에 회사의 새로운 로고와 슬로건을 인쇄하는 방식과 수를 놓는 방식이 있음을 언급하고 있으며, 추가로 'Most customers~professional.'이라고 말하며 대부분의 고객들은 수를 놓는 방식을 선호한다는 점을 전달하는 부분을 통해 남자가 비교하는 대상은 바로 모자를 고객 맞춤형으로 제작하는 방식임을 알 수 있다. 그러므로 정답은 (D)가 되겠다.

36

★★ 문제점

여자가 관심을 갖는 것은 무엇인가?
(A) 변경된 로고와 슬로건
(B) 총 제작비
(C) 여러 크기의 이용 가능성
(D) 그녀의 주문이 완료되는 일정

어휘 availability 유효성, 가능성 completion 완료, 완성

토익 분석

두 번째 문제이기에 정확한 위치 파악은 힘들지만 여자 대화 중 요청, 제안의 힌트 표현인 의문문 Would you ~?를 이용하여 문제점을 제시하고 있다.

What is the woman concerned about?

(A) The changed logo and slogan
(B) The total production costs
(C) The availability of several sizes
(D) The time schedule for the completion of her order

문제 해설

여자의 관심 사항에 대해 묻고 있으므로 여자의 대화 내용에서 여자가 관심(우려)하는 내용이 제시되는 부분을 사전에 노려 들어야 한다. 따라서 여자가 'Would you be able to get them finished by the end of this month?'라고 물으며 이달 말까지 주문한 모자에 대한 작업을 다 마무리할 수 있는지 여부를 묻는 부분을 통해 여자는 주문이 완료되는 시점에 관심이 있음을 알 수 있으므로 정답은 (D)가 되겠다.

37

★★ 요청, 제안

남자가 여자에게 요청하는 것은 무엇인가?
(A) 서류를 이메일로 보낼 것 (B) 로고 디자인을 선택할 것
(C) 그림 파일들을 보낼 것 (D) 계약금을 납부할 것

어휘 down payment 계약금, 착수금

토익 분석

요청, 제안의 답변을 이끄는 대표적인 힌트인 명령문 please~로 단서가 제시되고 있다.

What does the man ask the woman to do?

(A) E-mail him some documents　(B) Choose a logo design
(C) Send him some picture files　(D) Make a down payment

문제 해설

남자는 대화 후반부에서 'please e-mail me your company's new logo and slogan image files'라고 말하며 여자에게 회사의 새로운 로고와 슬로건이 담긴 이미지 파일을 보낼 것을 요청하고 있으므로 정답은 (C)임을 알 수 있다.

Questions 38-40 refer to the following conversation.

M [38] Hi, I'm calling to find out when the Ancient Japanese Sword Exhibit will run until.

W Let's see, [38] it will run until the last weekend in February, before the exhibit moves to another museum.

M Great, I'll be in town early February so that's perfect. How much are tickets?

W Well, we have a variety of reasonably priced packages available. [39] Can I ask how old you are? Tickets are usually $28, but seniors pay half price.

M I'm sixty-five, so I would only have to pay $14?

W Correct. I should also mention that you can get a bigger discount by booking a room at the Old Mill Hotel. [40] If you'd like, I can give you their Web site address.

M [40] Wonderful. I'll definitely do that.

W OK, do you have a pen?

어휘 find out ~을 알아보다 run (행사 등이) 진행되다 exhibit 전시(회) a variety of 다양한 reasonably-priced 저렴한 가격의 available 구매/이용 가능한 senior 연장자, 노인 half-price 반값 further 추가의 book ~을 예약하다

남 [38] 안녕하세요, 저는 고대 일본 검 전시회가 언제까지 진행되는지 확인하고자 전화 드렸습니다.

여 확인해 보겠습니다. [38] 이 전시회가 다른 박물관으로 옮기기 전까지는 2월 마지막 주말까지 열릴 것입니다.

남 좋습니다. 제가 2월 초에는 그 도시에 있을 것이기 때문에 딱 좋습니다. 티켓 값이 얼마인가요?

여 저, 구매 가능하신 저렴한 가격의 다양한 패키지가 있습니다. [39] 연세가 어떻게 되시는지 여쭤봐도 될까요? 티켓 값이 보통 28달러이지만 연세 드신 분들은 반값입니다.

남 저는 65세라서 14달러만 내면 되는 건가요?

여 맞습니다. 그리고 **Old Mill Hotel**에서 객실을 예약하시는 방법으로 더 많은 할인을 받으실 수 있다는 점도 알려 드립니다. [40] 괜찮으시다면 그곳의 웹 사이트 주소를 알려 드릴 수 있습니다.

남 [40] 좋습니다. 당연히 그렇게 해야죠.

여 알겠습니다. 펜 가지고 계셔요?

38

What type of business is the man calling?

(A) A movie theater (B) An opera house
(C) An art gallery **(D) A history museum**

문제 해설

남자가 전화를 거는 곳에 대해 유추할 것을 요구하는 첫 번째 질문이므로 대화 초반부에서 남자가 용건을 말하는 부분이나 대화 상대자인 여자가 하는 일과 관련해 직접적으로 언급되는 부분, 혹은 관련 어휘가 제시되는 부분에 집중해야 한다. 여자는 대화 초반부에 특정 전시회 일정에 대해 묻는 남자의 말에 대해 'it will~museum'이라는 말로 일정을 알려 주고 있는데, 해당 전시회 행사명과 함께 '다른 박물관'이라는 말로 대답하는 것으로 볼 때 여자가 일하는 곳으로 (D)가 적절하다는 것을 알 수 있다.

★ 도입부 정보

남자는 어떤 종류의 업체에 전화를 거는가?
(A) 극장 (B) 오페라 하우스
(C) 미술관 (D) 역사박물관

어휘 form 구성되다, 형성되다 protocol 규정, 규약

토익 분석

지문의 첫 번째 문제에서 발생한 사건을 묻는 것은 주제, 목적 문제이다. 언급된 남자의 첫 번째 대화문에 집중하자.

39

What information does the woman ask for?

(A) The man's travel arrangements (B) The man's credit card details
(C) The man's age (D) The man's preferred date

문제 해설

여자가 남자에게 요청하는 것이 무엇인지를 묻는 두 번째 문제이므로 대화의 중반부에서 들을 수 있는 여자의 말에서 요청 표현과 함께 제시되는 정보에 집중해 들어야 한다. 여자는 대화 중반부에 'Can I ~?'로 시작하는 요청 표현과 함께 'Can I ask~half-price.'라는 말로 나이를 알려 주도록 요청하면서 그 이유를 알리고 있으므로 (C)가 정답이다.

★★ 요청, 제안

여자는 무슨 정보를 요청하는가?
(A) 남자의 여행 준비 상황 (B) 남자의 신용카드 상세 정보
(C) 남자의 나이 (D) 남자가 선호하는 날짜

어휘 ask for ~을 요청하다 arrangement 준비 details 상세 정보 preferred 선호하는

토익 분석

조동사의 조합인 Can I~?가 정답 힌트를 제시하고 있다.

40

What will the man most likely do next?

(A) Fill out a form (B) Pick up a brochure
(C) Give his credit card information **(D) Visit a Web site**

문제 해설

남자의 추후 행동을 묻는 마지막 질문이며, 이에 대한 단서는 대화 후반부 또는 최종 화자의 말에서 제시되는 경우가 일반적이다. 대화의 후반부에 여자가 'If you'd like, I can give you their Web site address.'라는 말로 호텔 이용과 관련해 특정 웹 사이트 주소를 알려 주겠다고 말하자 남자가 이에 대해 'Wonderful. I'll definitely do that.'라는 말로 수락하고 있으므로 (D)가 남자가 대화에 이어 할 일을 나타내는 보기로 알맞다.

★★ 미래 행동

남자는 곧이어 무엇을 할 가능성이 가장 큰가?
(A) 양식을 작성한다. (B) 안내 책자를 가져간다.
(C) 신용카드 정보를 알려 준다. (D) 웹 사이트를 방문한다.

어휘 fill out ~을 작성하다 brochure 안내 책자

토익 분석

상대방 여자 대화 중 남자에게 무엇인가를 요청, 제안하는 If가정법~, I can~.문장이 힌트를 제시하고 있다.

여 일단 짐을 다 싸면 알려 주세요. [41] 제가 시설 관리부에 연락해서 시설 관리부 직원들이 당신의 상자들과 장비들을 옮길 수 있도록 조치를 취하겠습니다.

남 [41] 전 그저 이곳에서 이 건물과 같은 층의 서쪽 별관으로 옮겨 가는 겁니다. 누가 대신 옮겨 줄 사람들을 기다리기보다는 제가 직접 이 상자들을 옮겨 가는 것이 낫습니다.

여 그건 우리 주의 근로자 보상법과 관련이 있습니다. 네, 당신이 스스로 할 수 있을 만큼 단순하고 쉬워 보이긴 해요. 하지만 만약 짐을 옮기는 와중에 무슨 일이라도 발생하면요, 말하자면, [42] 만약 당신이 짐을 옮기다가 복도에서 넘어지거나 미끄러져서 다치면 당신은 홀로 짐을 옮겨야 했던 부분에 대한 회사의 보상을 요구하며 좀 더 적극적인 법적 조치를 취하게 될지도 모르잖아요.

남 그럼 시설 관리부에 연락해서 이 일을 빨리 처리해 달라고 해 주시겠습니까? [43] 제가 이 보고서 작업을 금요일 전에 마무리하려면 제가 최대한 빨리 이 컴퓨터를 설치해야 하거든요.

Questions 41-43 refer to the following conversation.

W Let me know once you complete your packing. [41] I will contact the Facilities Management Department so that they can move your boxes as well as your equipment.

M [41] I am moving from here to the west wing on the same floor of this building. I can just carry these boxes myself rather than wait for someone to move them for me.

W It has to do with the state workers compensation law. Yes, it is seemingly simple and easy to do it yourself, but if something happens on the way, I mean, [42] if you fall or slip on the floor and get injured while you are moving your stuff, you will demand compensation from the company for your own action and maybe take more aggressive legal action.

M Then could you have them take care of it quickly? [43] I need to set up my computer as soon as possible so that I can finalize this report before Friday.

어휘 once S+V 일단 ~가 ~하면 packing 짐 싸기 Facilities Management Department 시설 관리부 wing (건물의) 부속 건물 workers compensation law 근로자 보상법 seemingly 겉으로는 get injured 부상을 입다 stuff 재료, 물질 take an action 행동을 취하다 aggressive 공격적인 legal action 법적 조치 set up ~을 설치하다

41

★★ 주제, 목적

대화의 주제는 무엇인가?
(A) 사무실 이전　　(B) 사무실 도면
(C) 사무 용품 주문　(D) 사무기기

어휘 relocation 재배치 layout 배치 policy 정책, 규정 equipment 장비, 용품

토익 분석

대화 주제는 대화의 첫 번째, 두 번째 대화 문장에 단서가 제시된다.

What are the speakers mainly discussing?

(A) An office relocation　(B) An office layout
(C) An office supplies order　(D) Office equipment

문제 해설

대화의 주제를 묻는 문제이므로, 대화 초반부에서 중점적으로 취급하는 중심 소재를 파악하는 것이 관건이다. 여자는 대화 초반 남자에게 'I will contact~equipment.'라고 말하며 시설 관리부에 연락해서 시설 관리부 직원들이 당신의 상자들과 장비들을 옮길 수 있도록 조치를 취하겠다고 언급하는 내용을 통해 대화의 주제는 바로 사무실 이전임을 가늠할 수 있다. 그러므로 (A)가 정답이다.

42

★★★ 문제점

여자가 언급한 문제점은 무엇인가?
(A) 혼자서 처리하기에는 일이 너무 복잡하다.
(B) 그녀는 다음 주에 출장을 간다.
(C) 회사는 어떤 사고에 대해서든 법적인 책임이 있을 수 있다.
(D) 그녀는 야근하길 원하지 않는다.

어휘 complicated 복잡한 legally 법률상, 합법적 liable for ~에 대해 책임이 있는

토익 분석

여자의 대화 문장 중 문제점을 찾아야 한다. 요청, 제안에 대한 대표적인 힌트 문장 형태인 if 가정법~, you will~.구조가 정답으로 제시하고 있다.

What problem does the woman mention?

(A) The work will be too complicated to handle alone.
(B) She will go on a business trip next week.
(C) The company might be legally liable for an accident.
(D) She does not want to work overtime.

문제 해설

여자가 언급한 문제점이므로 여자의 대화 내용을 통해 단서를 파악해야 한다. 혼자 짐을 옮기겠다는 남자에게 여자는 'if you fall~own action'이라고 말하며 만약 남자가 부상을 입을 시 회사로 법적인 소송을 통한 보상 요구의 가능성을 자세하게 알려 주고 있으며, 이는 회사 내에서 발생하는 사고에 대해 회사도 책임이 있음을 남자에게 밝히는 내용이라 할 수 있다. 따라서 정답은 (C)가 되겠다.

43

★★ 문제점

남자가 걱정하는 것은 무엇인가?
(A) 그는 옮겨야 할 상자들이 너무 많다.
(B) 그는 자기 일을 좋아하지 않는다.
(C) 그는 맞춰야 할 마감 시한이 있다.
(D) 그는 노트북 컴퓨터를 갖고 있지 않다.

어휘 deadline 기한, 마감 meet (기한을) 지키다

토익 분석

의도나 미래 행동에 대한 답변을 제시하는 대표 힌트인 I need to가 단서를 제시하고 있다.

What is the man's concern?

(A) He has too many boxes to carry.　(B) He does not like his work.
(C) He has a deadline to meet.　(D) He doesn't have a laptop computer.

문제 해설

남자가 걱정하는 바를 묻고 있는 질문이므로 대화 후반부 남자의 대화 내용에서 단서를 파악하는 것이 현명하다. 남자는 대화 말미에서 'I need to~Friday.'라고 이야기하며 금요일 전까지 마무리해야 할 보고서 때문에 가능한 한 빨리 컴퓨터를 설치하길 원하고 있음을 밝히고 있는 부분을 통해 결국 남자는 지켜야 할 마감 시한이 있음을 알 수 있다. 따라서 (C)가 정답이다.

Questions 44-46 refer to the following conversation.

W   How did your interview with the BK Corporation go?

M   [44] It was tougher than I had expected! Their real-world scenario-type questions required very specific examples from my work experience, so I needed to articulate my answers in a very organized, detailed manner.

W   [45] I think I read about the company's interview methodology in a business periodical. [46] I am sure you did just fine. Even if you didn't, it's not the end of the world.

M   Yeah, I guess you're right. [44] I just wish I had been better prepared. That's all.

어휘 real-world 현실 세계 scenario-type 시나리오 유형 require 요구하다 specific 명확한 articulate (생각, 감정을) 분명하게 표현하다 in an organized and detailed manner 논리적이고 상세하게 methodology 방법론 periodical 정기 간행물, 잡지 even if 심지어 ~일지라도

44

What does the man think about the interview?

(A) He did very well.
(B) **He did poorly.**
(C) He was well-prepared.
(D) He had a great time.

문제 해설

면접에 대한 남자의 의견을 묻는 첫 번째 질문이므로, 대화 초반부 남자의 대화 내용을 통해 단서를 파악하는 것이 바람직하다. 남자는 면접이 어떠했는지 믿는 여자의 질문에 'it was tougher than I had expected'라며 자신의 예상보다 힘들었다고 표현하고 있다. 아울러 대화 후반부에서 남자는 'I just wish I had been better prepared'라고 말하며 면접에 대한 준비가 좀 더 잘되었다면 좋았을 것이란 후회를 언급하는 부분을 통해, 남자는 면접을 잘 보지 못했다는 점을 알 수 있다. 그러므로 정답은 (B)이다.

45

How did the woman find out BK's interview style?

(A) She had an interview with BK Corporation.
(B) She had heard from other interviewees.
(C) **She read a business magazine.**
(D) She has contacted the personnel department.

문제 해설

여자의 대화에서 'I think I read about the company's interview methodology in a business periodical.'라고 말하며 면접에 대해 잡지에서 읽었음을 밝히고 있다. 따라서, (C)를 정답으로 선택함이 옳다.

46

What is the woman trying to do?

(A) **Comfort the man**
(B) Critique the man's performance
(C) Persuade the man to keep his current job
(D) Provide the man with an analysis of his interview

문제 해설

여자는 하고자 하는 것을 묻는 마지막 질문이므로 대화 후반부에 등장하는 여자의 대화 내용을 통해 단서를 파악해야 한다. 여자는 대화 후반부에서 'I am sure you did just fine. Even if you didn't, it's not the end of the world'라고 이야기하며 상대가 면접을 잘 했을 것이며 설령 면접을 못 봤다고 하더라도 그것이 절망을 의미하지는 않는다고 이야기하는 부분을 통해 여자는 남자를 위로해 주려고 함을 알 수 있다. 그러므로 정답은 (A)가 되겠다.

여   BK 사와의 면접은 어땠습니까?
남   [44] 예상했던 것보다 힘들었습니다. 그들의 현실적인 시나리오가 담긴 질문들은 업무 경험에서 나오는 구체적인 예를 요구하는 것이어서요. 저는 아주 논리적이고 상세한 방식으로 똑 부러지게 대답해야만 했어요.
여   [45] 제가 그 회사의 인터뷰 방법론에 대해 어느 비즈니스 잡지에서 읽었던 것 같아요. [46] 분명히 당신은 잘 했을 겁니다. 설령 그렇지 못해도 세상이 끝난 것도 아닌데요.
남   네, 맞습니다. [44] 저는 그저 준비를 좀 더 잘했으면 싶었던 것이죠. 그게 다입니다.

★★★ 세부 정보

남자는 면접에 대해 어떻게 생각하는가?
(A) 그는 면접을 잘했다고 생각한다.
(B) 그는 면접을 못 했다고 생각한다.
(C) 그는 면접 준비가 잘 되었다고 생각한다.
(D) 그는 아주 즐거운 시간을 보냈다고 생각한다.

어휘 poorly 형편없이, 저조하게 well-prepared 잘 준비된

토익 분석

세부 정보 문제는 키워드를 활용해야 한다. interview가 키워드로 남자의 첫 번째 대화문에 정답이 제시되었다. 주의 사항으로 키워드가 의문문에 등장할 경우 보통 다음 화자의 대화문에 정답이 제시된다는 점을 기억해야 한다.

★ 세부 정보

여자가 BK사 면접 방식에 대해 어떻게 알았나?
(A) 그녀는 BK사와 면접을 했었다.
(B) 그녀는 다른 면접자들로부터 들었다.
(C) 그녀는 비즈니스 잡지를 읽었다.
(D) 그녀는 인사과에 연락을 취했었다.

어휘 interviewee 면접자 contact 연락을 취하다 personnel 인사과

토익 분석

세부 정보 문제로 키워드를 활용하는 문제다. 질문 속에 BK's interview style가 키워드다.

★★★ 의도 파악

여자는 무엇을 하려고 하는가?
(A) 남자를 위로해 준다.
(B) 남자의 실적을 비판한다.
(C) 남자가 현 직장에서 계속 근무하도록 설득한다.
(D) 남자에게 그의 면접에 대한 분석 내용을 제공한다.

어휘 comfort 위로하다 critique 비평하다 persuade 설득하다 current 현재의 analysis 분석

토익 분석

세 번째 문제이므로 후반부 여자 대화문에 집중해야 한다.

남 실례합니다만, 담당자분과 통화를 할 수 있을까요?
   ⁴⁷ 저는 이력서를 제출하려고 합니다. 상점 외부에 부
   착된 구인 광고를 봤어요.
여 제가 담당자입니다. ⁴⁸ 저희 구인 광고에 관심을 보여
   주셔서 감사 드립니다만, 이미 계산원을 충원한 상황
   이라 유감입니다. ⁴⁹ 만약에 일자리를 찾고 계신다면,
   저희 상점 옆에 있는 회계 사무실에서 현재 비서직을
   찾고 있거든요. 거기 지원하셔도 될 것 같은데요.
남 좋습니다, 감사 드려요. 제가 지금 바로 그 사무실을
   방문해도 될까요?

Questions 47-49 refer to the following conversation.

M   Excuse me. Can I talk to the person in charge? ⁴⁷ I would like to submit my resume. I read the job advertisement outside the store.

W   That would be me. ⁴⁸ Thanks for your interest in the position, but I'm afraid we've already found a cashier. ⁴⁹ If you are looking for a job, the accounting office next door needs a secretary. Maybe you could try there.

M   That would be great. Thanks. Do you think I can visit the office right now?

어휘 in charge 담당하는 submit ~을 제출하다 resume 이력서 job advertisement 구인 광고 cashier 계산원 secretary 비서

47

★ 주제, 목적

대화자들은 무엇에 관해 언급하는가?
(A) 회계 업무
(B) 일자리
(C) 인력 부족
(D) 새로운 비서

어휘 availability 유효성, 가능성 lack 부족 personnel 인력, 인사

토익 분석

대화의 주제는 첫 번째 문장에 의도 표현이나 미래 행동
표현이 중요하다. 의도 표현인 I would like to~가 정답 문
장을 제시하고 있다.

What are the speakers talking about?

(A) Accounting work
(B) The availability of a job
(C) The lack of personnel
(D) The new secretary

문제 해설

대화의 주제를 묻는 첫 번째 질문이니만큼 대화 초반부에서 집중적으로 언급되고 있는 중심 소재를
파악하는 것이 중요하다. 따라서 남자가 대화 초반 'I would like to submit my resume. I read the
job advertisement outside the store.'이라고 말하며 상점의 구인 광고를 보고 이력서를 제출하러 왔
음을 밝히는 부분을 통해 대화의 주제는 구직과 관련되어 있음을 알 수 있으므로 정답은 (B)가 되겠다.

48

★★ 세부 사항 / 여자가 남자의 채용을 거절한 이유

여자에 따르면, 여자가 남자를 채용할 수 없는 이유는 무
엇인가?
(A) 그녀는 이미 해당 직책에 충원을 했다.
(B) 그녀는 그가 경력이 부족하다고 생각한다.
(C) 그녀는 남자가 필요 이상의 자격 요건을 지녔다고 생
    각한다.
(D) 그녀는 그가 적합한 교육을 받지 못했다고 생각한다.

어휘 position 자리, 위치 overqualified 필요 이상의 자격
을 갖춘 suitable 적합한

토익 분석

여자가 채용을 하지 못하는 데는 무슨 문제(이유)가 있다
는 것. 여자 첫 번째 대화 문장에서 반전 표현을 찾는다.
반전 표현 but이 힌트이다.

According to the woman, why isn't she able to hire the man?

(A) She has already filled the position.
(B) She believes he lacks work experience.
(C) She thinks he is overqualified.
(D) She doesn't think he has the right education.

문제 해설

여자가 남자의 채용을 거절한 이유에 대해 묻는 마지막 질문이므로 여자의 대화 내용에서 여자가
남자의 채용을 거절하는 이유로 언급하는 내용에 집중해야 한다. 여자는 남자에게 'Thanks for your
interest in the position, but I'm afraid we've already found a cashier.'라고 말하며 구인에 대한
관심은 고마우나 이미 해당 직책에 인원을 충원했음을 밝히고 있다. 그러므로 이를 통해 남자를 채
용할 수 없는 이유는 이미 필요한 인력을 채용했기 때문임을 알 수 있으므로 정답은 (A)가 되겠다.

49

★★ 세부 정보

여자가 남자에게 제공한 정보는 무엇인가?
(A) 그는 할인 혜택을 받을 자격이 된다.
(B) 그는 이전 직장 경력을 보유한 사람이어야 한다.
(C) 그는 다른 곳에 취업 지원을 할 수 있다.
(D) 그는 추가 서류를 제출해야 한다.

어휘 be eligible for(to) ~을 할 수 있는 previous 이전
apply for ~에 지원하다

토익 분석

여자가 제공하는 정보는 세부 정보지만 무엇을 '제안'하
는 것과 관련된 사항일 수 있기에 요청, 제안 힌트 표현인
if가정법~문장이 단서를 제공하고 있다.

What information does the woman give the man?

(A) He is eligible for a discount.
(B) He is required to have previous work experience.
(C) He can apply for another job.
(D) He should submit additional documents.

문제 해설

남자가 제공한 정보가 무엇인지 묻는 질문이므로 남자의 대화 내용에서 여자에게 제공되는 정보의
내용을 사전에 대비한 상태에서 노려 들어야 할 필요가 있다. 따라서 여자가 상점에 취업을 지원하러
온 남자에게 'If you are looking for a job, the accounting office next door needs a secretary.'라
고 말하며 근처에 있는 회계 사무소에서 비서직에 적합한 인원을 구인하고 있다는 정보를 제시하는
부분을 통해 남자가 제공한 정보는 다른 곳의 취업 정보임을 알 수 있으므로 정답은 (C)가 되겠다.

Questions 50-52 refer to the following conversation.

M So what do you think about this joint venture proposal?

W It seems like an interesting opportunity for us. However, I am not in a position to make the final call. 50 I will carefully deliver your message to management.

M Please do. 51 The partnership will not only improve our revenue streams in the short term but will also pave the way to long-term dominance in the marketplace by our two companies.

W That sounds exciting. 52 But the number-one challenge is financing the entity. Investment banks are quite cautious when assessing deals these days.

남 그래서, 당신은 이 합작 투자 제안을 어떻게 생각합니까?

여 이 합작 투자 건은 저희에게 흥미로운 기회처럼 보입니다. 하지만 저는 최종 결정을 내릴 수 있는 위치에 있지 않습니다. 50 제가 경영진에게 당신의 생각을 신중하게 전달하도록 하겠습니다.

남 꼭 그렇게 해 주십시오. 51 이 제휴는 수익원을 단기적으로 증진시킬 뿐만 아니라 우리 두 회사에 의한 장기적인 시장 지배를 위한 토대를 마련하게 될 것입니다.

여 그렇습니다. 52 하지만 최고로 어려운 과제는 자금조달입니다. 최근 들어 투자 은행들은 합작 회사에 대한 대출 거래를 심사할 때 상당히 신중한 편이라서요.

어휘 joint venture 협동 벤처 사업, 합작 투자 사업 final call 최종 결정 management 운영, 경영진 pave the way ~을 용이하게 하다 dominance 지배, 우위 marketplace 시장 cautious 신중한 assess 평가하다

50

What is the woman likely going to do?

(A) Attend a board meeting   **(B) Talk to some executives about a proposal**

(C) Make a decision to launch a joint venture

(D) Complete a loan application

문제 해설

여자가 하게 될 행동에 대해 묻는 첫 번째 질문이므로 대화 초반부나 전반부에 등장하는 여자의 대화 내용에서 동사 중심으로 청취하는 것이 우선이며 여기서 단서가 제시되지 않는 경우 상대 대화자의 이야기에서 여자에게 요청, 제안, 명령, 권고하는 동사와 함께 제시되는 단서에 집중해야 한다. 여자는 대화 전반부에서 'I will carefully deliver your message to management.'라고 이야기하며 경영진에게 상대의 합작 사업 제안에 대해 알려줄 것임을 밝히고 있으므로 정답은 (B)가 되겠다.

★★ 의도 파악

여자는 무엇을 할 것 같은가?
(A) 이사회에 참석한다.
(B) 중역들에게 남자의 제안을 언급한다.
(C) 합작 사업을 시행할 것인지 결정한다.
(D) 대출 신청서를 작성한다.

어휘 board meeting 이사회 executives 경영진 make a decision 결정하다 loan application 대출 신청

토익 분석

여자의 의도를 묻고 있기에 여자의 첫 대화 문장에 집중해야 한다. 의도 표현인 I will~이 단서를 제시하고 있다.

51

What does the man mention about the joint venture proposal?

(A) It will be reviewed by the board next week.

(B) It will reduce costs to a great extent.

(C) It will be beneficial to both companies.

(D) It will encourage more joint ventures in the industry.

문제 해설

남자가 제안에 대해 언급한 내용을 묻고 있으므로 남자의 대화 내용에서 제안에 관해 구체적으로 다루고 있는 부분에 집중해야 할 필요가 있다. 남자는 'The partnership~our two companies.'라고 이야기하며 단기 수익을 증가시킬 수 있다는 것과 두 회사의 시장 지배를 공고히 할 수 있음을 밝히고 있다. 그러므로 이를 통해 이 제안은 양사에 모두 득이 될 것을 알 수 있으므로 정답은 (C)가 되겠다.

★★★ 세부 정보

남자가 이 제안에 대해 언급한 것은 무엇인가?
(A) 다음 주에 이사회에 의해 검토될 것이다.
(B) 비용이 상당 부분 감소될 것이다.
(C) 양사에 모두 이익이 될 것이다.
(D) 업계에 더 많은 합작 사업을 촉진할 것이다.

어휘 reduce cost 비용을 절감하다 extent (크기의) 정도, 규모 beneficial 이익의 encourage 격려하다

토익 분석

남자 대화에서 키워드 joint venture proposal를 the partnership으로 변형하여 단서를 제시했다.

52

What is the woman's concern about the situation?

(A) There are strict government regulations.

(B) Raising funds for the venture will be tough.

(C) The industry is very competitive.

(D) Both companies seem financially unsound.

문제 해설

여자가 현 상황에서 우려하는 것을 묻는 마지막 질문이므로 대화 후반부에서 등장하는 여자의 대화 내용에서 제시되는 여자의 관심/걱정/우려 관련 내용을 노려 들어야 할 필요가 있다. 여자는 대화 말미에서 But the number-one challenge is how we will finance the entity라고 이야기하며 자금 마련에 쉽지 않을 것임을 밝히고 있으므로, 이를 통해 여자는 현 상황에서 자금 마련의 어려움에 대해 우려하고 있음을 알 수 있다. 그러므로 정답은 (B)가 되겠다.

★★ 문제점

여자는 현 상황에 대해 무엇을 우려하는가?
(A) 엄격한 정부의 규제가 있다.
(B) 합작 사업에 대한 자금을 마련하는 것이 힘들다.
(C) 업계의 경쟁이 굉장히 치열하다.
(D) 양사는 모두 재정적으로 불건전하다.

어휘 regulation 통제 raising fund 기금 모집 competitive 경쟁력 있는 financially 재정적으로 unsound 부적절한

토익 분석

여자의 후반부 대화에서 반전 표현을 이용한 문제점을 찾아야 한다. 반전 표현 But이 정답을 제시하고 있다.

남 안녕하세요, **Wilson** 씨. 급하게 연락 드렸는데도 저희 회의에 참석해 주셔서 감사 드립니다. ⁵³ 제안한 광고 전략에 대해 어떻게 생각하시나요?

여 제 생각에는 그 전략대로 해야 할 것 같아요. 새로운 TV 광고가 우리의 고객층을 분명히 확대해 줄 것 같아요.

남 그 말씀을 들으니 기쁩니다. ⁵⁴ 더 자세한 의견 있으신가요?

여 ⁵⁴ 저, 제안된 광고 방송 시간이 더 다양한 연령층에 초점을 맞출 수 있도록 변경될 수 있다고 생각해요.

남 알겠습니다, 다음 주 목요일에 있을 부서장들과의 회의에 앞서 명심해 두도록 하겠습니다. 혹시 그 회의에 참석하실 건가요?

여 ⁵⁵ 수요일부터 금요일까지 경영 콘퍼런스에 가 있을 예정이라서 갈 수 없을 것 같아요. 하지만 그 전에는 어떤 회의에도 갈 수 있는 시간이 있습니다.

Questions 53-55 refer to the following conversation.

M Hi, Ms. Wilson. Thanks again for joining our meeting on such short notice. ⁵³ What are your thoughts on the proposed advertisement strategy?

W I think we should go ahead with it. I feel the new TV ads will definitely expand our customer base.

M I'm glad to hear that. ⁵⁴ Anything else?

W ⁵⁴ Well, I think the proposed air times could be changed to focus on a more diverse population.

M OK, I'll keep that in mind before my meeting with the corporate heads next Thursday. Will you be joining?

W ⁵⁵ I'm afraid I won't be able to make it as I'll be at a managerial conference from Wednesday to Friday. I'm available for any meetings before that, though.

어휘 on such short notice 급한 요청/공지에도 proposed 제안된 strategy 전략 go ahead with ~을 추진하다 ad 광고 (advertisement) definitely 분명히 expand ~을 확대하다 customer base 고객층 further 더 자세한 air time 방송 시간 focus on ~에 초점을 맞추다 diverse 다양한 population 인구, 주민 keep A in mind A를 명심하다 corporate 회사/기업의 head 책임자, 부서장 be able to do ~할 수 있다 make it managerial 경영의, 관리의

53

★ 주제, 목적

화자들은 주로 무엇에 관해 이야기하고 있는가?
(A) 비즈니스 회의 (B) 제품 주문
(C) 영업 콘퍼런스 (D) 광고 캠페인

토익 분석

주제를 찾는 문제로 대화의 도입부 중 첫 번째 문장이 가장 중요하다.

What are the speakers mainly discussing?
(A) A business meeting (B) A product order
(C) A sales conference **(D) An advertising campaign**

문제 해설

대화의 주제를 묻는 첫 번째 질문이므로 대화 초반부에서 중점적으로 언급하는 핵심 내용을 파악하는 것이 관건이다. 남자가 대화를 시작하면서 감사의 인사를 말한 후에 곧바로 'What are~strategy?'라는 말로 제안된 광고 전략에 대한 생각을 여자에게 묻고 있고 여자는 이에 대한 자신의 의견을 알리는 흐름으로 대화가 진행되고 있으므로 (D)가 정답임을 알 수 있다.

54

★★ 맥락 파악

남자가 "Anything else"라고 말할 때 무엇을 암시하는가?
(A) 여자가 마감 시한을 뒤로 미루기를 원하고 있다.
(B) 여자를 어딘가로 초청하고 싶어 한다.
(C) 여자가 회의 시간을 연장하기를 원하고 있다.
(D) 여자가 더 많은 상세 정보를 알려 주기를 원하고 있다.

어휘 push back ~을 뒤로 미루다 extend ~을 연장하다 details 상세 정보

토익 분석

맥락 파악 문제는 대화의 flow파악이 중요하지만 일부 구어체 표현들의 경우 단순히 사전적 의미만 알아도 답을 찾을 수 있는 경우가 있다.

What does the man imply when he says, "Anything else"?
(A) He wants the woman to push back a deadline.
(B) He wants to invite the woman somewhere.
(C) He wants to the woman to extend a meeting.
(D) He wants the woman to give more details.

문제 해설

남자가 말하는 "Anything else"라는 표현이 대화 속에서 어떤 의미로 사용되었는지를 묻는 두 번째 질문이므로 대화 중반부에 제시되는 남자의 말을 통해 해당 표현을 확인할 수 있어야 하며, 이때 앞뒤에 함께 제시되는 말들을 통해 의미의 흐름을 파악해 정답을 찾아야 한다. 남자는 대화 중반부에 여자의 의견을 들은 후 해당 표현으로 답변하고 있는데, 말 그대로 추가로 더 말해 줄 것이 있는지 묻는 표현이며, 이 표현 뒤에 여자도 구체적인 예시를 알려 주는 말로 답변하고 있으므로 (D)가 정답이 된다.

55

★★ 미래 행동

여자는 다음 주에 무엇을 할 것 같은가?
(A) 콘퍼런스에 참석한다. (B) 신입 사원들을 채용한다.
(C) 회의를 준비한다. (D) 휴가를 떠난다.

어휘 arrange 마련하다 take a vacation 휴가를 얻다

토익 분석

여자의 마지막 대화문에서 미래 행동에 대한 대표적인 힌트 표현인 I'll~이 단서를 제시하고 있다.

What will the woman probably do next week?
(A) Attend a conference (B) Hire new employees
(C) Arrange a meeting (D) Take a vacation

문제 해설

여자가 다음 주에 할 일을 묻는 세 번째 질문이므로 이에 대한 단서는 대화 후반부에서 찾아야 하며, 질문에 포함된 '다음 주'라는 시점 표현을 키워드로 삼아 해당 표현이 제시되는 부분에 특히 집중해 들어야 한다. 대화의 마지막에 여자는 'I'll be at a managerial conference from Wednesday to Friday.' 즉 경영 콘퍼런스에 갈 예정이라고 알리고 있으므로 (A)가 정답이 된다.

Questions 56-58 refer to the following conversation.

M   What do you think about introducing a new product targeting those who are retiring soon as well as those who already did?

W   What do you have in mind?

M   [57] In general, the retiree market category is still relatively underserved. [56] My idea is to come up with a portfolio mix of high-dividend stocks and bonds that pay stable interest so that our clients can receive a positive cash flow while enjoying a certain amount of appreciation.

W   Sounds like a good idea. [58] Why don't you put together a business plan for management? Let me know if you need my help.

어휘 as well as 뿐만 아니라 have in mind ~에 관해 생각하고 있다 in general 일반적으로 relatively 상대적으로 underserved 공급이 평균보다 못 미치는 come up with ~을 제안하다 high-dividend 높은 배당 stock 주식 bond 채권 pay stable interest 안정적인 이자를 지불하다 cash flow 현금 흐름 a certain amount of 일정량의 appreciation (가격의) 등귀, (수량의) 증가

남   이미 은퇴했거나 곧 은퇴할 사람들을 대상으로 신상품을 출시하는 것에 대해 어떻게 생각합니까?

여   뭔가 염두에 둔 것이 있습니까?

남   [57] 일반적으로 퇴직자 시장은 아직도 비교적 저평가되어 있거든요. [56] 제 생각은 안정적인 이자를 주는 고배당 주식이나 채권들의 포트폴리오 혼용하는 상품을 기획하는 겁니다. 그래서 우리 고객들이 일정한 수익을 즐기면서 원활한 현금 흐름을 누릴 수 있게끔 말이지요.

여   좋은 생각 같습니다. [58] 경영진에게 제출할 사업 계획서를 작성하는 것이 어떻겠습니까? 만약 도움이 필요하면 제게 알려 주세요.

56

What kind of business do the speakers most likely work for?

(A) A publishing company   **(B) A financial firm**
(C) A pharmaceutical company   (D) A healthcare service provider

문제 해설

대화자들이 근무하는 회사가 어떠한 업종의 회사인지 묻고 있으므로 화자의 직장이 직접 언급되는 부분이나 혹은 이를 추측할 수 있을 만한 관련 어휘나 표현에 집중해야 한다. 따라서 남자가 'My idea is to come up with a portfolio mix of high-dividend stocks and bonds that pay stable interest'라고 이야기하며 안정적인 이자를 주는 고배당 주식이나 채권들의 포트폴리오 혼용을 이용한 상품을 기획하자고 언급하는 부분을 통해 대화자들은 금융 회사에서 근무하고 있음을 가늠할 수 있다. 그러므로 정답은 (B)가 되겠다.

★★★ 도입부 정보

화자들은 어떠한 업종의 회사에서 근무할 것 같은가?
(A) 출판사   (B) 금융 기관
(C) 제약 회사   (D) 의료 서비스 제공 업체

어휘 firm 회사 pharmaceutical 약학의, 제약의 healthcare service 건강 관리 서비스

토익 분석

근무장소에 대한 힌트는 원래 도입부에 제시되지만, 간혹 대화의 전반적인 내용을 파악해야 답을 찾을 수 있는 문제들이 있다.

57

What does the man mention about the retiree market?

(A) It is extremely competitive.   **(B) It has been somewhat underserved.**
(C) It has been saturated.   (D) The regulatory hurdles are high.

문제 해설

퇴직자 시장에 대해 언급된 내용을 묻고 있으므로 대화 지문에서 퇴직자 시장, 즉, the retiree market이 소개되는 부분을 중심으로 관련 내용을 파악하는 것이 현명하다. 따라서 남자가 'In general, the retiree market category is still relatively underserved.'라고 이야기하는 부분을 통해 퇴직자 시장 분야가 상대적으로 저평가를 받고 있음을 알 수 있다. 그러므로 정답은 (B)이며 다만 대화 지문의 단서가 선택지에서는 undervalued라는 유사 표현으로 바뀌어 제시되고 있음에 주의해야 한다.

★★ 세부 정보

퇴직자 시장과 관련하여 언급된 내용은 무엇인가?
(A) 매우 경쟁력이 있다.   (B) 다소 저평가되었다.
(C) 포화 상태이다.   (D) 규제의 벽이 높다.

어휘 retiree 은퇴자, 퇴직자 underserved 서비스가 충분치 못한 saturated 포화된 regulatory 규제력을 지닌 hurdle 허들, 난관

토익 분석

남자 대화문에서 키워드 retiree market를 활용하는 세부 정보 찾기 문제다.

58

What does the woman suggest the man do?

(A) Start his own company   (B) Try hard to finalize the deal
(C) Write a new business proposal(D) Conduct more market research

문제 해설

여자가 남자에게 제안하는 것을 묻는 마지막 질문이므로 대화 후반부에 등장하는 여자의 이야기에 집중해야 하며 특히 동사 중심으로 청취해야 할 필요가 있다. 따라서 여자가 대화 말미에서 'Why don't you put together a business plan for management?'라고 말하며 남자에게 신규 사업 제안서를 작성하는 것이 어떠한지 권고하는 부분을 통해 정답은 (C)임을 알 수 있다.

★★ 요청, 제안

여자가 남자에게 제안하는 것은 무엇인가?
(A) 창업을 할 것
(B) 협상을 마무리할 수 있도록 노력할 것
(C) 신규 사업 제안서를 작성할 것
(D) 더 많은 시장조사를 할 것

어휘 finalize 마무리 짓다, 완결하다 conduct 행동하다, (활동을) 하다

토익 분석

여자의 후반부 대화문에서 요청, 제안 힌트 표현인 Why don't you ~가 힌트를 제시하고 있다.

여 안녕하세요, John. ⁵⁹ 당신이 부서장으로 승진되었다
　 는 얘기를 들었어요. 축하 드립니다!
남 고마워요, Mel! 지금까지 한동안 이렇게 되기 위해
　 노력해 왔어요. 회사 내에서 마침내 승진할 수 있게
　 되어 기분이 좋네요.
여 저, 당연히 그럴 자격이 있으시다고 생각해요. 축하
　 할 계획은 있으신가요? 저도 꼭 갈게요.
남 솔직히, 그것에 대해서는 아주 많이 생각해 보지 않
　 았어요. ⁶⁰ 퇴근 후에 저녁 식사를 하는 것은 어때요?
　 ⁶¹ 하지만 어디로 가야 할지는 잘 모르겠어요.
여 ⁶¹ 좋은 생각 같아요. 제가 한 번 생각해 볼게요.

Questions 59-61 refer to the following conversation.

W Hey, John. ⁵⁹ I heard that you have been promoted to manager.
   Congratulations!

M Thanks, Mel! I've been working towards this for a while now. It feels good
   to finally be able to move up in the company.

W Well, I think you deserve it. Do you have any plans to celebrate? I'll
   definitely join.

M I haven't really given it much thought, to be honest. ⁶⁰ How about we get
   dinner after work? ⁶¹ I'm not sure where to go, though.

W ⁶¹ That sounds good. I'll come up with something.

어휘 be promoted to ~로 승진되다 work towards ~을 위해 노력하다 be able to do ~할 수 있다 move up 승진/
진급하다 deserve ~을 받을 자격이 있다 celebrate 축하/기념하다 definitely 꼭, 분명히 give it much thought 많
이 생각해 보다 How about we ~? 우리 ~하는 건 어때요? where to go 가는 곳, 목적지 though (문장 끝이나 중간
에서) 하지만 come up with ~을 생각해 내다

59

★★ 세부 정보

여자는 왜 남자에게 축하 인사를 하는가?
(A) 남자가 자신의 사업을 시작했다.
(B) 남자가 승진되었다.
(C) 남자가 상을 받았다.
(D) 남자가 수상 후보자로 추천되었다.

어휘 win a prize 상을 받다 be nominated for ~에 대한
후보자로 추천되다

토익 분석

키워드 congratulate를 활용해 답을 찾는 문제다.

Why does the woman congratulate the man?

(A) He started his own business.　　(B) **He received a promotion.**
(C) He won a prize.　　(D) He was nominated for an award.

문제 해설

여자가 남자에게 축하 인사를 건네는 이유를 묻는 첫 번째 문제이므로 대화 시작 부분에서 축하 인
사가 언급되는 부분에서 함께 제시되는 정보를 파악해야 한다. 여자는 대화를 시작하면서 'I heard
that you have been promoted to manager. Congratulations!'라는 말로 승진된 사실과 함께 축하
인사를 하고 있으므로 (B)가 정답이 된다.

60

★★ 요청, 제안

남자는 여자에게 무엇을 하도록 제안하는가?
(A) 식사를 하러 가기 위해 만날 것
(B) 새로운 일자리에 지원할 것
(C) 자신과 함께 프로젝트 작업을 할 것
(D) 추천서를 써 줄 것

어휘 apply for ~에 지원하다 reference letter 추천서

토익 분석

남자의 대화에서 요청, 제안 힌트 표현을 찾아야 한다.
How about~?이라는 제안문이 답을 제시하고 있다.

What does the man suggest the woman do?

(A) Meet him for a meal　　(B) Apply for a new job
(C) Work with him on a project　　(D) Write a reference letter

문제 해설

남자가 제안하는 것이 무엇인지를 묻는 두 번째 문제이므로 대화의 중반부에서 들을 수 있는 남자
의 말에서 제안 관련 표현과 함께 제시되는 정보에 집중해 들어야 한다. 남자는 대화 중반부에 승진
을 기념하자는 여자의 말에 대해 'How about we get dinner after work?'라는 말로 식사를 하는 것
이 어떤지 제안하고 있으므로 (A)가 정답이 된다.

61

★★★ 맥락 파악

여자가 "I'll come up with something"이라고 말할 때 무엇
을 암시하는가?
(A) 남자에게 뭔가를 배송해 줄 것이다.
(B) 제안을 할 것이다.
(C) 남자에게 길을 가르쳐 줄 것이다.
(D) 남자를 위해 선물을 가져올 것이다.

어휘 make a suggestion 제안하다 give A directions A에
게 길을 가르쳐 주다

토익 분석

대화의 흐름을 파악해야 하므로 반드시 앞뒤 문장을 들어
야 한다. 남자가 I'm not sure where to go라고 한 부분이
단서가 된다.

What does the woman imply when she says, "I'll come up with something"?

(A) She will deliver something to the man.
(B) She will make a suggestion.
(C) She will give the man directions.
(D) She will bring a gift for the man.

문제 해설

여자가 말하는 "I'll come up with something"이라는 표현이 대화 속에서 어떤 의미로 사용되었는
지를 묻는 세 번째 질문이므로 대화 후반부에 제시되는 여자의 말을 통해 해당 표현을 확인할 수 있
어야 하며, 이때 앞뒤에 함께 제시되는 말들을 통해 의미의 흐름을 파악해 정답을 찾아야 한다. 여자
는 대화 후반부에 식사를 하자는 남자의 제안 및 어디로 가야 할지 모르겠다는 말에 대해 수락하는
표현과 함께 해당 표현으로 답변하고 있는데, 아직 장소가 결정된 상황이 아니므로 여자는 생각해
보고 제안을 하겠다는 의미로 해당 표현을 사용했음을 알 수 있다. 따라서 이와 같은 의미에 대해 언
급한 (B)가 정답이 된다.

Questions 62-64 refer to the following conversation with three speakers.

M　Hey, Jenn and Grace. ⁶² How is the work going for the new recruitment ad?

W1　We're almost finished. All we need to do is edit some of the final frames.

W2　⁶³ We should be able to finish it before our meeting with management tomorrow.

M　What time is your meeting? Would it be possible to have a look at it before you present it?

W1　The meeting is at nine o'clock in the morning, and sure, you can do that. It will be nice to get a fresh perspective on it.

W2　We should be finished this afternoon. ⁶⁴ Stop by then.

M　⁶⁴ Alright, great. I'll check my schedule and let you know when I'm free.

남　안녕하세요, Jenn 그리고 Grace. ⁶² 새로운 채용 광고에 대한 일을 어떻게 되어 가고 있나요?

여1　거의 끝나가요. 최종 테두리를 편집만 하면 됩니다.

여2　⁶³ 내일 있을 경영진과의 회의가 열리기 전에 끝낼 수 있을 거예요.

남　회의가 몇 시에 있죠? 그것을 발표하기 전에 한 번 확인해 보는 것이 가능할까요?

여1　회의는 아침 9시에 열리는데, 당연히 확인해 보실 수 있죠. 새로운 관점의 의견을 들어 보는 것은 좋을 거예요.

여2　오늘 오후에 끝낼 수 있을 거예요. ⁶⁴ 그때 잠깐 들르세요.

남　⁶⁴ 네, 좋습니다. 일정을 확인해 보고 시간이 날 때 알려 드릴게요.

어휘 recruitment 채용, 모집　edit ~을 편집하다　frame 테두리, 틀　be able to do ~할 수 있다　management 경영진, 운영진　Would it be possible to do? ~하는 것이 가능할까요?　have a look at ~을 한 번 보다　present ~을 발표하다, 제시하다　perspective 관점, 시각　stop by 잠깐 들르다　let A know A에게 알리다　free 시간이 나는

62

What is the main topic of the conversation?

(A) A job interview
(B) A recruitment event
(C) A workshop
(D) An advertisement

문제 해설

대화의 주제를 묻는 첫 번째 질문이므로 대화 초반부에서 중점적으로 언급하는 핵심 내용을 파악해야 한다. 남자가 대화를 시작하면서 'How is the work going for the new recruitment ad?'라는 말로 채용 광고에 대한 진행 상황을 묻고 있으므로 (D)가 정답이 된다.

★★ 주제, 목적

대화의 주제는 무엇인가?
(A) 구직 면접
(B) 채용 행사
(C) 워크숍
(D) 광고

토익 분석

주제는 도입부 대화문 중 첫 번째 문장에 대체로 단서가 제시된다.

63

When will the women meet with their manager?

(A) Later today
(B) Tomorrow morning
(C) Tomorrow afternoon
(D) In a few days

문제 해설

여자들이 소속 부서장을 만날 시점을 묻는 두 번째 질문이므로 대화 중반부에서 제시되는 여자들의 말에서 누군가를 만나는 일정 및 시점과 관련해 언급하는 부분에서 단서를 파악해야 한다. 대화 중반부에 여자들 중의 한 명이 'We should be able to finish it before our meeting with management tomorrow.'라는 말로 내일 경영진, 즉 소속 부서장과의 회의가 있다고 알리고 있으므로 (B)가 정답이 된다. 대화 속 남자의 직책은 언급되어 있지 않으므로 그를 부서장으로 혼동해서는 안 된다.

★★ 세부 정보

여자들은 언제 소속 부서장을 만날 것인가?
(A) 오늘 늦게
(B) 내일 아침
(C) 내일 오후
(D) 며칠 후에

토익 분석

세부 정보 문제의 경우 질문 속에서 적절한 키워드를 찾아야 한다. 이 문제의 경우 meet와 manager를 활용하여 정답을 제시했다.

64

What does a woman mean when she says, "Stop by then"?

(A) She wants the man to refrain from doing something.
(B) She is giving an invitation to the man.
(C) She is asking about the man's opinion.
(D) She is inquiring about the man's plans.

문제 해설

한 여자가 말하는 "Stop by then"이라는 표현이 대화 속에서 어떤 의미로 사용되었는지를 묻는 세 번째 질문이므로 대화 후반부에 제시되는 한 여자의 말을 통해 해당 표현을 확인할 수 있어야 한다. 남자가 발표 전에 확인해 보는 것에 대해 묻자 여자들 중의 한 명이 해당 표현으로 답변하고 있으며, 이에 대해 남자가 'Alright, great. I'll check my schedule and let you know when I'm free.'라는 말로 대답하는 것으로 볼 때 서로 만나는 일정에 대해 얘기하는 상황인 것으로 판단할 수 있다. 따라서 여자들 중의 한 명이 남자를 초대한 상황이라는 것을 알 수 있으므로 (B)가 정답이 된다.

★★★ 맥락 파악

한 여자가 "Stop by then"이라고 말할 때 무엇을 의미하는가?
(A) 남자가 뭔가 하는 것을 삼가기를 원하고 있다.
(B) 남자를 초대하고 있다.
(C) 남자의 의견에 대해 묻고 있다.
(D) 남자의 계획에 대해 문의하고 있다.

어휘 refrain from -ing ~하는 것을 삼가다　give an invitation to ~를 초대하다　ask about ~에 대해 묻다　opinion 의견　inquire about ~에 대해 문의하다

토익 분석

구어체 표현들의 사전적 의미를 학습하는 것도 중요하다. 방문하다 visit의 의미를 갖는 stop by의 뜻만 알아도 답을 찾을 수 있는 문제다.

남 ⁶⁵ Grace, 우리가 탄 버스가 곧 Selby Mountain Park
에 도착할 거예요. 어느 산길로 하이킹하고 싶은지
생각해 보셨어요?

여 저, 제가 배낭에 담아 가지고 온 이 안내 팸플릿을 확
인해 봐요. 여기 산길에 대한 정보가 있어요.

남 ⁶⁶ 좋아요, 하지만 제가 너무 멀리는 걸어갈 수 없다
는 점을 기억해 두세요. 지난주에 자전거에서 넘어진
후로 제 다리가 아직도 좀 뻐근해요.

여 알겠어요. 흠… ⁶⁷ 이 5.5 킬로미터 길이의 산길은 어
때요? 꽤 쉬워 보이는 데다 거리가 가장 긴 산길의
절반밖에 되지 않아요.

남 딱 좋은 것 같아요. 그러면 점심시간에 맞춰 끝날 거
예요.

도보 산길 – Selby Mountain Park	
Birch Trail	3.5 킬로미터
Oak Trail	5.5 킬로미터
Evergreen Trail	7.5 킬로미터
Valley Trail	11 킬로미터

Questions 65-67 refer to the following conversation and list.

M ⁶⁵ Grace, our bus will soon arrive at Selby Mountain Park. Do you have any idea which trail you'd like to hike?

W Well, let's check this information pamphlet I brought with me in my rucksack. It has some information about the trails.

M ⁶⁶ OK, but remember I can't walk too far. My leg is still a little sore after I fell off my bike last week.

W I know. Hmm… ⁶⁷ How about this 5.5 kilometer trail? It looks quite easy, and it's half the length of the longest trail.

M That sounds perfect. And we'll be finished in time for lunch.

Walking Trails – Selby Mountain Park	
Birch Trail	3.5 kilometers
Oak Trail	5.5 kilometers
Evergreen Trail	7.5 kilometers
Valley Trail	11 kilometers

어휘 arrive at ~에 도착하다　trail 산길, 오솔길　pamphlet 팸플릿　rucksack 배낭　too far 너무 멀리　a little 조금, 약간　sore 뻐근한, 아픈　fall off ~에서 떨어지다　look 형용사 ~한 것처럼 보이다　quite 꽤, 상당히　half the length 절반 길이　in time for ~의 시간에 맞춰

65

★ 도입부 정보

대화는 어디에서 이뤄지고 있는가?
(A) 차량 안에서
(B) 주차장에서
(C) 안내소에서
(D) 버스 터미널에서

어휘 vehicle 차량, 운송 수단　parking lot 주차장

토익 분석

장소를 묻는 도입부 정보 문제로 대화의 첫 번째, 두 번째
문장쯤에 힌트가 집중적으로 등장한다.

Where is the conversation taking place?

(A) In a vehicle
(B) In a parking lot
(C) In an information office
(D) In a bus terminal

문제 해설

대화 장소를 유추할 것을 요청하는 첫 번째 질문이므로 대화 초반부에서 언급되는 특정 주제와 관
련해 직접적으로 언급되는 부분, 혹은 두 화자가 하는 일을 측측할 수 있을 만한 관련 어휘가 제시
되는 부분에 집중해야 한다. 대화를 시작하면서 남자가 'Grace, our bus will soon arrive at Selby
Mountain Park.'라는 말로 버스가 곧 특정 장소에 도착할 예정임을 알리고 있는데, 이는 현재 버스
를 타고 어딘가로 이동 중이라는 것을 의미하므로 (A)가 정답이 된다.

66

What problem does the man mention?

(A) He forgot some equipment.

(B) He lost his rucksack.

(C) He hurt his leg.

(D) He does not have much time.

문제 해설

남자가 언급하는 문제점을 묻는 두 번째 질문이므로 대화 중반부에서 남자가 특정 문제점과 함께 걱정이나 우려 등을 나타내는 표현을 통해 언급하는 정보를 파악해야 한다. 대화 중반부에 남자는 하이킹을 하는 것과 관련해 'OK, but remember I can't walk too far. My leg is still a little sore after I fell off my bike last week.'라는 말로 과거 시점에 다리를 다쳤던 사실에 대해 걱정하는 말을 하고 있으므로 (C)가 정답이 된다.

★★ 문제점

남자는 무슨 문제점을 언급하는가?
(A) 장비를 깜빡 잊었다.
(B) 자신의 배낭을 잃어버렸다.
(C) 다리를 다쳤다.
(D) 시간이 많지 않다.

어휘 equipment 장비 hurt ~을 다치게 하다

토익 분석

문제점을 묻는 문제가 두 번째 문제로 등장할 경우 반드시 도입부에 답이 나오는 것은 아니다. 반전 표현을 찾는 데 집중해야 한다. 이 문제의 경우 남자 대화 중 반전 표현인 But이 정답 힌트를 제시하고 있다.

67

Look at the graphic. Which trail will the speakers probably choose?

(A) The Birch Trail

(B) The Oak Trail

(C) The Evergreen Trail

(D) The Valley Trail

문제 해설

질문에서 묻는 내용과 관련해 대화 속에 제시된 단서를 바탕으로 도표의 정보를 함께 확인해 정답을 찾아야 하는 문제이다. 이때 각 보기에 제시된 내용 외의 정보가 대화 속에서 단서로 제시될 것이므로 이에 집중해 대화를 들어야 한다. 각 보기에 산길 이름이 제시되어 있으므로 도표에 이와 함께 제시된 거리 정보에 집중해 들어야 한다. 대화 후반부에 여자가 'How about this 5.5 kilometer trail? It looks quite easy, and it's half the length of the longest trail.'라는 말로 5.5 킬로미터 길이의 산길을 제안하고 있고 남자도 이에 대해 동의하고 있으므로 이에 해당하는 산길인 (B)가 정답이 된다.

★★★ 그래픽

도표를 확인하시오. 화자들은 어느 산길을 선택할 것 같은가?
(A) The Birch Trail
(B) The Oak Trail
(C) The Evergreen Trail
(D) The Valley Trail

어휘 birch 자작나무 oak 오크 evergreen 상록수 valley 계곡, 골짜기

토익 분석

표에 트레일 종류와 거리 정보가 제시되었다. 따라서 트레일을 찾기 위해서는 대화에서 거리 정보를 들어야 한다. 요청, 제안 힌트 표현인 How about이 단서를 제공하고 있다.

남 ⁶⁸ 안녕하세요, 제가 이 병원에 오전 10시에 예약을 했는데요. 대기실에서 기다리면 되나요?

여 ⁶⁹ 아, 안녕하세요. 우선 신분증을 확인해야 합니다. 가져오셨나요?

남 네, 여기 있습니다. 하지만 지난번에 예약해서 왔을 때는 보여 드릴 필요가 없었는데요.

여 죄송합니다만, 저희 병원에 새로 생긴 정책입니다. 환자분들의 기록을 더 잘 정리해 두기 위해 노력하는 중입니다.

남 알겠습니다. 그럼, 제가 오늘 의사 선생님을 뵙는 데 오래 기다려야 할까요?

여 ⁷⁰ 실은, Brand 선생님은 지금 시간이 있으시기 때문에 진료하실 준비가 되어 있으십니다. 진료실까지 바로 가시면 됩니다.

Regis Health Clinic 레지던트 의사
1호실 – Torville 의사 선생님
2호실 – Brand 의사 선생님
3호실 – Owler 의사 선생님
4호실 – Mooney 의사 선생님

Questions 68-70 refer to the following conversation and sign.

M ⁶⁸ Hello, I have a 10 A.M. appointment here at the clinic. Shall I just wait in the waiting room?

W ⁶⁹ Oh, hello. First, I'll need to see your ID card. Did you bring it with you?

M Yes, here you are. But I didn't need to show it the last time I had an appointment here.

W I'm sorry, sir, but that's a new policy at our clinic. We're just trying to keep our patient records more organized.

M I see. So do you think I will have to wait long to see the doctor today?

W ⁷⁰ Actually, Dr. Brand is free now and ready to see you. Please go right through to her room.

Regis Health Clinic Resident Doctors		
Room 1 – Dr. Torville
Room 2 – Dr. Brand
Room 3 – Dr. Owler
Room 4 – Dr. Mooney

어휘 appointment 예약 the last time + 주어 + 동사 지난번에 ~했을 때 policy 정책, 방침 keep A 형용사 A를 ~한 상태로 유지하다 patient 환자 organized 정리된, 정돈된 will have to do ~해야 할 것이다 actually 실은, 사실은 free 시간이 나는 be ready to do ~할 준비가 되다 go right through to ~로 바로 쭉 가다

68

★★ 도입부 정보

여자는 누구일 가능성이 가장 큰가?
(A) 내과 의사
(B) 약사
(C) 병원 환자
(D) 접수 담당 직원

토익 분석

여자의 직업을 묻는 문제로, 도입부 중 첫 번째 대화문에서 힌트를 찾아야 한다.

Who most likely is the woman?

(A) A physician
(B) A pharmacist
(C) A clinic patient
(D) A receptionist

문제 해설

여자의 신분에 대해 유추할 것을 요구하는 첫 번째 질문이므로 담화 초반부에서 여자가 하는 일과 관련해 직접적으로 언급되는 부분, 혹은 이를 추측할 수 있을 만한 관련 어휘가 제시되는 부분에 집중해야 한다. 대화를 시작하면서 'Hello, I have a 10 A.M. appointment here at the clinic. Shall I just wait in the waiting room?' 바로 이 부분에서 여자의 직업이 안내 데스크 직원이라는 것을 추측할 수 있다. 따라서 여자의 신분으로 (D)가 가장 적절하다는 것을 알 수 있다.

69

What does the woman ask for?

(A) A prescription
(B) An appointment schedule
(C) An identification card
(D) A credit card

문제 해설

여자가 남자에게 요청하는 것이 무엇인지를 묻는 두 번째 문제이므로 대화의 중반부에서 들을 수 있는 여자의 말에서 요청 표현과 함께 제시되는 정보에 집중해 들어야 한다. 진료 예약 때문에 찾아온 남자에게 여자는 'First I'll need to see your ID card. Did you bring it with you?'라는 말로 신분증을 먼저 제시해 달라고 요청하고 있으므로 (C)가 정답이다.

★ 요청, 제안

여자는 무엇을 요청하는가?
(A) 처방전
(B) 예약 일정표
(C) 신분증
(D) 신용카드

토익 분석

여자 대화에서 요청, 제안을 찾는 문제다. 의도 표현인 **I need to~**,와 요청할 때 가장 많이 활용하는 의문문 **Did you~?**를 활용하여 정답을 제시하고 있다.

70

Look at the graphic. Which room will the man go to next?

(A) Room 1
(B) Room 2
(C) Room 3
(D) Room 4

문제 해설

질문에서 묻는 내용과 관련해 대화 속에 제시된 단서를 바탕으로 도표의 정보를 함께 확인해 정답을 찾아야 하는 문제이다. 이때 각 보기에 제시된 내용 외의 정보가 대화 속에서 단서로 제시될 것이므로 이에 집중해 대화를 들어야 한다. 각 보기에 방 호수가 쓰여 있으므로 도표에서 이와 함께 제시된 의사의 이름에 집중해 들어야 한다. 대화 후반부에 여자는 'Actually, Dr. Brand is free now and ready to see you. Please go right through to her room.'라는 말로 남자를 진료할 의사 이름을 'Dr. Brand'라고 알리고 있으므로 (B)가 정답임을 알 수 있다.

★★ 그래픽

도표를 확인하시오. 남자는 곧이어 어느 방으로 갈 것인가?
(A) 1호실
(B) 2호실
(C) 3호실
(D) 4호실

토익 분석

방 번호와 의사 이름의 조합으로 구성된 표다. 방번호를 찾기 위해서는 대화에서 의사의 이름을 들어야 한다.

여 MacArthur 의학 연구소는 의학 연구에 참여할 자원자들을 찾고 있습니다. ⁷¹ 이 연구는 몇 가지 간단한 운동을 통한 건강 효과를 조사를 목적으로 합니다. ⁷² 참석자들은 일상생활의 습관으로서 1년 동안 한 가지 운동을 50회씩 반복해야 합니다. 수면 방식, 식단 그리고 다른 운동들은 원래 하시던 대로 하시면 됩니다. ⁷³ 참석자들은 운동 후 수치를 측정하고 운동 결과를 추적할 수 있도록 매달 제공되는 온라인 설문지를 작성해 주시면 됩니다. 아울러 석 달마다 완전한 신체검사를 받아야 할 필요가 있습니다. 더 많은 정보를 원하시면 reg@mmr.com으로 이메일을 보내 주십시오.

Questions 71-73 refer to the following announcement.

W MacArthur Medical Research is looking for volunteers to participate in a medical study. ⁷¹ The study will investigate the effects of several simple exercises on health. ⁷² Participants will be asked to complete fifty reps of one exercise for one year as a part of their daily routine. Sleep patterns, diet, and other exercise should not be adjusted. ⁷³ Participants will be required to take measurements and to fill out an online survey every month to track their results. They will also need to have a complete physical every three months. For more information, e-mail reg@mmr.com.

어휘 volunteer 자원봉사자 participate in ~에 참석하다 medical study 의학 연구 investigate ~을 조사하다 effects 영향력 rep 반복 daily routine 일상생활 adjust ~을 조정/조절하다, ~에 적응하다 take measurements 수치를 재다 fill in ~을 작성하다 track ~을 추적하다 complete 완전한, 철저한 physical 신체검사, 신체적인

71

★ 세부 정보

화자에 따르면, 이 연구는 무엇에 관한 것인가?
(A) 신약의 효과
(B) 유기농 음식의 효과
(C) 운동이 건강에 미치는 효과
(D) 수면 방식의 효과

어휘 organic 유기농의 pattern 패턴, 유형

토익 분석

질문 속에 Study가 키워드로 사용된 세부 정보 문제다.

According to the speaker, what is the study mainly about?

(A) The effects of a new medicine
(B) The effects of organic food
(C) The effects of exercise on health
(D) The effects of sleeping patterns

문제 해설

연구의 주제에 대해 묻는 첫 번째 질문이므로 지문 초반부에서 연구가 소개되는 부분에 집중해야 할 필요가 있다. 따라서 화자가 지문 초반부에서 'The study will investigate the effects of several simple exercises on health.'라고 이야기하며 해당 연구는 몇 가지 운동이 건강에 미치는 효과에 대한 것임을 언급하고 있으므로 정답은 (C)임을 알 수 있다.

72

★★ 세부 정보

참석자들은 얼마 동안 참여해야 하는가?
(A) 1개월　　　　(B) 3개월
(C) 12개월　　　(D) 36개월

어휘 be involved 참여하다

토익 분석

세부 정보 문제는 대체로 질문 속에 사용된 단어가 지문에 반복 사용된다. 이러한 키워드를 듣는 것이 포인트로 이 문제의 경우 participants가 키워드로 사용되었다.

For how long will participants be involved?

(A) One month　　　　　　(B) Three months
(C) Twelve months　　　(D) Thirty-six months

문제 해설

참석자들의 참여 기간에 대해 묻고 있으므로 지문에서 참석자들, 즉, participants가 등장하는 부분을 전후하여 구체적인 참여 기간으로 제시되는 수치에 집중해야 한다. 화자는 'Participants will be asked to complete 50 reps of one exercise for one year as a part of their daily routine.'이라고 말하며 참석자들은 해당 운동을 1년간 지속적으로 해야 함을 밝히고 있다. 따라서 이를 통해 참석 기간은 1년, 즉 12개월임을 알 수 있으므로 정답은 (C)가 되겠다.

73

★★★ 세부 정보

참석자들은 매달 무엇을 해야 하는가?
(A) 의사를 방문해야 한다.
(B) 온라인 설문지를 작성해야 한다.
(C) 이메일로 보고서를 제출해야 한다.
(D) 몇 가지 운동을 해야 한다.

어휘 complete 작성하다, 기입하다 perform 행하다

토익 분석

시점이나 숫자의 경우 seven days는 a week, weekly로 12는 dozen과 같이 다른 형태의 단위로 변환될 수 있다는 점을 기억해야 한다. 이 문제는 monthly가 every month로 변환되었다.

What will participants do monthly?

(A) Visit the doctor　　　**(B) Complete an online survey**
(C) E-mail a report　　　(D) Perform some exercises

문제 해설

참석자들이 매달 해야 할 것을 묻는 마지막 질문이므로 지문에서 참석자들에게 요구되는 사항들이 열거되는 부분에 집중하되, 매달이란 시점이 등장하는 부분에 초점을 맞춰야 한다. 화자는 지문 후반부에서 'Participants will be required to take measurements and to fill out an online survey every month to track their results.'라고 이야기하며 참석자들은 매달 온라인 설문지를 작성해야 함을 요청하고 있다. 따라서 정답은 (B)임을 알 수 있다. 아울러 온라인 설문지를 매달 작성해야 한다는 내용을 월간 보고서를 작성하여 이메일을 통해 제출해야 한다는 의미의 (C)로 오해하지 않도록, 그리고 몇 가지 운동을 하는 것이지만 각 참석자는 하나의 운동만 행하므로 모든 참석자들이 몇 가지 운동을 모두 행하는 것으로 잘못 파악하지 않도록 주의해야 한다.

Questions 74-76 refer to the following telephone message.

M   Hi, Ms. Campbell. This is Michael Langdon. [74] I am sorry for the confusion my assistant caused you. She must have mixed up the dates of your and another patient's appointment. Your appointment is on the fourteenth at 2 P.M. [75] Since you came all the way from Langley for your physical therapy session but had to return, [76] your next appointment will be half the normal price. This time, I will personally take note of your appointment so there will be no confusion. I apologize again for the poor service you experienced.

어휘 confusion 혼동, 혼란 assistant 비서, 조수, 보조 인력 cause 원인, ~을 초래하다 must have V(p.p.) ~임에 틀림없다 appointment 예약 physical therapy session 물리 치료 normal price 정가 personally 개인적으로 take note of ~을 적다, ~을 필기하다 apologize for ~에 대해 사과하다

남   안녕하세요, **Campbell** 씨. 저는 **Michael Langdon**이라고 합니다. [74] 제 비서가 고객님을 헷갈리게 한 점에 대해 죄송스럽게 생각합니다. 그녀가 **Campbell** 씨의 예약일과 다른 고객님의 예약일을 혼동했었습니다. 고객님의 예약일은 14일 오후 2시입니다. [75] 고객님께서 물리 치료를 받으시러 **Langley**에서 이곳까지 오셨다가 다시 돌아가셨어야 했던 터라 [76] 다음 예약 때는 치료비의 절반만 받도록 하겠습니다. 이번에는 제가 개인적으로 고객님의 예약일을 기록해서 이와 관련하여 혼동을 겪는 일이 없도록 하겠습니다. 고객님께서 겪으셨던 부실한 서비스에 다시 한 번 사과의 말씀을 드립니다.

74

What is the speaker calling to discuss?

(A) An appointment problem   (B) A new medical treatment
(C) An accounting mistake   (D) An unpaid balance

문제 해설

화자가 연락해서 논의한 것을 묻는 첫 번째 질문이므로 지문 초반 화자가 중점적으로 언급하는 중심 소재를 파악하는 것이 관건이다. 화자는 인사말 및 자기소개 직후 'I am sorry for the confusion my assistant caused you. She must have mixed up the dates of your and another patient's appointment.'라고 말하며 비서가 실수로 Campbell 씨의 예약일과 다른 고객과의 예약일을 혼동했던 사실을 지적하고 있다. 따라서 이를 통해 화자는 예약상의 문제점에 대해 언급하고 있음을 알 수 있으므로 정답은 (A)가 되겠다.

★★ 전화 목적

화자가 연락해서 논의한 것은 무엇인가?
(A) 예약의 문제점   (B) 새로운 치료법
(C) 회계 실수   (C) 미납액

어휘 accounting 회계 unpaid 미납의 balance 잔액

토익 분석

전화 목적을 묻는 문제로 'this is 사람 이름' 형태의 자기소개 문장 다음에 답이 제시된다. I'm sorry와 같은 반전 표현이 힌트로 사용되었다.

75

Who most likely is the speaker?

(A) A receptionist   **(B) A physical therapist**
(C) A professional athlete   (D) A patient

문제 해설

화자의 정체를 유추해야 하는 질문이므로 지문에서 화자의 정체를 추측할 수 있을 만한 관련 어휘나 표현이 등장하는 부분에 주안점을 둬야 한다. 따라서 화자가 지문 중반부에서 'Since you came all the way from Langley for your physical therapy session'이라고 이야기하며 Campbell 씨에게 물리 치료를 받으시러 Langley에서 방문했음을 언급하는 부분을 통해 화자는 물리 치료사임을 유추할 수 있으므로 정답은 (B)가 되겠다.

★★ 도입부 정보 – 화자

화자는 누구일 것 같은가?
(A) 접수처 직원   (B) 물리 치료사
(C) 전문 운동선수   (D) 환자

토익 분석

화자 정보는 환영 인사 뒤 This is로 시작하는 부분에 답이 제시되어야 하지만, 이 문제의 경우 도입부를 포괄적으로 파악해야 유추가 가능한 문제다.

76

What is the listener offered as compensation?

(A) A free session   (B) A cash reward
(C) Complimentary gifts   **(D) A discount**

문제 해설

청자가 받게 되는 보상에 대해 묻는 마지막 질문이므로 지문 후반부에서 화자가 청자에게 제시하는 혜택을 노려 들어야 할 필요가 있다. 따라서 화자가 지문 후반부에서 'your next appointment will be half the normal price'라고 이야기하며 청자의 다음 예약은 치료비를 절반만 받을 것임을 언급하고 있으므로 정답은 (D)가 되겠다.

★★ 요청, 제안

청자는 보상으로 무엇을 제공받는가?
(A) 무료 치료   (B) 금전적 보상
(C) 무료 선물   (D) 할인

어휘 compensation 보상, 이득 session 기간, 시간 complimentary 무료의

토익 분석

요청, 제안 유형의 문제 중 무엇을 제공하는지 묻는 문제의 경우 '할인, 무료'와 관련된 표현들이 답을 제시한다. half the normal price가 힌트가 된다.

남 ⁷⁷ 안녕하세요. 저는 **Clinton Stationary**에서 전화 드리는 **John Paulson**입니다. 귀하께서 이전에 요청하셨던 프린터 카트리지가 현재 다시 재고가 확보되었다는 점을 알려 드리기 위해 전화 드립니다. 귀하의 프린터가 오래된 모델이기 때문에, ⁷⁸ 공급업체에서는 이번이 마지막 배송이 될 것이라고 저희에게 알려 주었는데, 올 연말쯤에 이 제품을 단종할 것이기 때문입니다. 이번이 마지막 기회일 수도 있습니다. 이제 귀하의 카트리지 제품을 구매하러 저희를 방문하실 때, 저를 찾아 주십시오. ⁷⁹ 제가 최신 프린터 모델들을 보여 드리고 새로운 기기로 바꾸시는 일을 도와 드리고 싶습니다. 감사 드리며, 곧 뵙겠습니다.

Questions 77-79 refer to the following telephone message.

M ⁷⁷ Good afternoon. This is John Paulson calling from Clinton Stationary. I'm just calling to let you know that the printer cartridges you previously requested are now back in stock. Because your printer is an outdated model, ⁷⁸ the supplier told us this will be the last shipment, as they will discontinue this product by the year's end. This might be your last chance. Now, when you visit us to purchase your cartridges, please ask for me. ⁷⁹ I'd love to show you some updated printer models and help you make the transition to a new device. Thanks, and see you soon.

어휘 let A know that A에게 ~라고 알리다 previously 이전에 request ~을 요청하다 in stock 재고가 있는 outdated 오래된, 구식의 supplier 공급업체 shipment 배송, 선적 discontinue ~을 단종하다 updated 최신의 help A do A가 ~하는 것을 돕다 make A 형용사 A를 ~하게 만들다 transition 이전, 갈아탐, 옮겨 감 device 기기

77

★ 도입부 정보 – 화자 근무 장소

화자는 어디에서 근무하고 있을 가능성이 가장 큰가?
(A) 지역 신문사에서　　(B) 서점에서
(C) 사무용품 매장에서　　(D) 인쇄소에서

토익 분석

환영 인사 다음에 화자 소개 부분인 **this is~**, 문장과 **I'm~**. 이하 문장에서 화자가 근무하는 장소에 대한 단서가 제시되었다.

Where does the speaker most likely work?
(A) At a local newspaper　　(B) At a bookstore
(C) At an office supplies store　　(D) At a print shop

문제 해설

화자의 근무 장소를 유추할 것을 요청하는 첫 번째 질문이므로 담화 초반부에서 언급되는 소개 인사와 함께 직접적으로 언급되는 회사명이나 부서명, 혹은 화자가 하는 일을 추측할 수 있을 만한 관련 어휘가 제시되는 부분에 집중해야 한다. 화자는 담화를 시작하면서 'Good afternoon~in stock.'라는 말로 자신이 속한 회사 및 취급 물품을 언급하고 있는데, 프린터 카트리지를 취급하는 곳으로 (C)가 가장 적절하다.

78

★★★ 맥락 문제

화자는 왜 "This might be your last chance"라고 말하는가?
(A) 청자가 제품을 구입하도록 권하기 위해서
(B) 청자에게 결정한 것을 알리기 위해서
(C) 청자가 비용을 송금하도록 요청하기 위해서
(D) 청자에게 매장이 문을 닫는다는 것을 알리기 위해서

어휘 encourage A to do A가 ~하도록 권하다, 장려하다 inform A of B A에게 B에 대해 알리다 decision 결정 request that ~할 것을 요청하다 notify A that A에게 ~라고 알리다

토익 분석

제시된 표현 전후 문장의 흐름을 파악해야 하는 문제다. 이 문제의 경우 제시된 표현 바로 전 문장 **as they will~**에 단서가 존재한다.

Why does the speaker say, "This might be your last chance"?
(A) To encourage the listener to buy an item
(B) To inform the listener of a decision
(C) To request that the listener send a payment
(D) To notify the listener that a store is closing

문제 해설

화자가 말하는 "This might be your last chance"라는 표현이 담화 속에서 어떤 의미로 사용되었는지를 묻는 두 번째 질문이므로 담화 후중반부에 제시되는 이 표현 및 앞뒤에 함께 제시되는 말들을 통해 의미의 흐름을 파악해 정답을 찾아야 한다. 우선 이 표현은 말 그대로 '이번이 마지막 기회일 것이다'라는 뜻인데, 담화 중반부에서 화자가 'the supplier~year's end'라는 말로 해당 제품이 단종될 예정이라는 말과 함께 사용된 것으로 보아 마지막이 될 기회를 살려 꼭 제품을 구입하도록 유도하기 위한 표현임을 알 수 있다. 따라서 이와 같은 의미에 대해 언급한 (A)가 정답이 된다.

79

★★ 요청, 제안

화자는 무엇을 하겠다고 하는가?
(A) 길을 알려 주는 일
(B) 추가 주문을 하는 일
(C) 할인을 제공하는 일
(D) 새로운 프린터들을 추천하는 일

어휘 directions 길, 방향 place an order 주문하다

토익 분석

요청, 제안의 대표 힌트 표현인 **I'd like to**와 같은 의미인 **I'd love to**가 정답을 제시하고 있다.

What does the speaker offer to do?
(A) Provide directions　　(B) Place another order
(C) Give a discount　　**(D) Recommend new printers**

문제 해설

화자가 해 주겠다는 의도를 나타내는 일이 무엇인지를 묻는 세 번째 문제이므로 담화의 후반부에서 화자가 언급하는 제안 관련 표현과 함께 제시되는 정보를 파악해야 한다. 화자는 담화 후반부에 'I'd love to ~'라는 제안 표현을 사용해 'I'd love to show you some updated printer models and help you make the transition to a new device as easy as possible.'라는 말로 새로운 프린터 모델들을 보여 주고 기기를 새로운 것으로 바꾸는 일을 돕겠다고 알리고 있으므로 (D)가 정답이 된다는 것을 알 수 있다.

Questions 80-82 refer to the following recorded message.

W   Hello. [80] Thank you for calling the Trust Bank Employee Information Center. [81] The following locations will be closed today due to the blizzard: the Berryville location, the Winchester location north of Weems Lane, and the Warrenton Mountain Road location. All other employees should report to work at their scheduled times. [82] We will be putting this announcement on our company Web site as well as sending out an e-mail to all our customers to keep them informed.

여   안녕하세요. [80] Trust 은행 직원 정보 센터에 연락을 주셔서 감사합니다. [81] 이후에 언급되는 지점들은 눈보라로 인해 오늘 영업을 하지 않는 지점들입니다. Berryville 지점, Weems Lane 북쪽에 위치한 Winchester 지점, Warrenton Mountain Road 지점. 이 외 다른 지점에서 근무하는 모든 직원들은 정시에 출근해야 합니다. [82] 저희는 모든 고객님들에게 이메일을 발송하여 해당 내용을 공지할 것이며 또한 회사 홈페이지에도 이 안내문을 게재할 것입니다.

어휘 following 이후에, 이어지는 due to ~로 인해 blizzard 눈보라 report to work 출근하다, 근무를 보고하다 scheduled times 정해진/예정된 시간 B as well as A A 뿐만 아니라 B도 keep sby informed ~가 알도록 하다, ~에게 알리다

80

Who is this message intended for?

(A) Bank investors
(B) Customers
(C) Bank personnel
(D) Weather reporters

문제 해설

녹음 메시지의 청자에 대해 묻고 있으므로 지문 초반부에서 청자의 정체가 직접적으로 언급되는 부분에 집중해야 한다. 따라서 화자가 지문 시작과 함께 'Thank you for calling the Trust Bank Employee Information Center.'이라고 말하며 Trust 은행 직원 정보 센터에 연락을 주셔서 감사하다는 인사말을 전달하는 부분을 통해 청자는 은행 직원임을 알 수 있으므로 정답은 (C)임을 알 수 있다.

★ 도입부 정보 – 청자

이 메시지는 누구를 의도하고 있는가?
(A) 은행 투자가
(B) 고객
(C) 은행 직원
(D) 기상 예보관

어휘 intend 의도하다, 생각하다 investor 투자자

토익 분석

지문에서 청자 힌트는 지문이 시작하자마자 등장하는 환영 인사 부분에 제시된다.

81

According to the speaker, what caused the closures?

(A) Road resurfacing
(B) Building construction
(C) Adverse weather
(D) A national holiday

문제 해설

폐쇄를 초래한 원인을 묻는 질문이므로 지문에서 폐쇄와 관련된 내용이 제시되는 부분을 중심으로 폐쇄를 초래한 원인을 노려 들어야 한다. 따라서 화자가 지문 초반 'The following locations will be closed today due to the blizzard'이라고 말하며 심한 눈보라로 인해 이후 언급되는 지점들은 오늘 영업을 하지 못한다는 내용을 안내하는 부분을 통해 폐쇄를 초래한 원인은 바로 악천후 때문임을 알 수 있으므로 정답은 (C)가 되겠다.

★ 세부 정보

화자에 따르면, 폐쇄를 초래한 원인은 무엇인가?
(A) 도로포장
(B) 건물 공사
(C) 악천후
(D) 국가 공휴일

어휘 resurfacing 재포장 construction 건설, 공사 adverse 부정적인, 불리한

토익 분석

세부 정보 문제 중 open/close관련 문제는 언제나 open/close가 키워드로 활용된다. 이 문제는 질문 속 closure의 변형인 closed가 키워드로 사용되었다.

82

How does the speaker say the information will be shared?

(A) By personal phone calls
(B) By electronic mail
(C) By text messages
(D) By social networking services

문제 해설

구체적인 정보 공유 방법을 묻는 마지막 질문으로 지문 후반부에서 화자가 제시하는 구체적인 정보 공유 방법에 집중해야 한다. 따라서 화자가 지문 종료 직전 'We will be putting this announcement on our company Web site as well as sending out an e-mail to all our customers to keep them informed.'이라고 말하며 고객에게 지점 휴무 내용을 이메일을 통해 전달할 것이며 또한 회사의 홈페이지에도 해당 안내문을 게재할 것임을 밝히는 부분을 통해 정답은 (B)임을 알 수 있다.

★ 세부 정보

화자는 정보가 어떤 방법을 통해 공유될 것이라 언급하는가?
(A) 개별 전화
(B) 이메일
(C) 문자 메시지
(D) 사회 관계망 서비스

어휘 social networking service (= SNS) 소셜 네트워킹 서비스

토익 분석

추가 정보 제공 방법은 언제나 지문의 가장 후반부에 제시된다.

남 저는 우리 모두가 굉장히 바쁜 한 주를 앞두고 있으
며 헛되이 쓸 시간조차 없다는 사실을 너무 잘 알고
있어서, 이 월요일 오전 회의를 굉장히 빠르고 신속
하게 처리하려고 합니다. 몇 가지 전달 사항이 있습
니다. ⁸⁴ 우리는 수요일에 각자 음식을 가지고 와서
함께 점심 식사를 하려고 하니, 음식을 가지고 와서
수요일 점심을 준비해 주세요. 또한, 시설 관리부의
Bob 씨가 남자 화장실을 더럽게 사용한 만행이 있었
다고 언급하더군요. 만약 누군가 이러한 극악한 행위
를 범하는 모습을 본다면 제게 바로 보고해 주셨으면
합니다. 마지막으로, 이번 주에 우리는 경쟁을 벌이
게 될 겁니다. ^{83, 85} 우리 케이블 상품에 등록하는 신
규 고객들을 가장 많이 유치한 직원은 Fishbone Grill
에서 2인용 저녁 식사권을 얻게 될 겁니다. 자, 업무
를 시작합시다!

Questions 83-85 refer to the following talk.

M   I know we all have a very busy week ahead of us and don't have any time to waste, so I'll make this Monday morning meeting as quick as possible. Just a few announcements: ⁸⁴ We are going to have a potluck lunch on Wednesday, so please bring a dish to share to work on Wednesday. In addition, Bob from maintenance mentioned there has been some vandalism in the men's bathroom. If you see anyone committing this type of crime, please report it directly to me. Finally, we're going to have a competition this week: ^{83, 85} The person to get the most new customers to sign up for a cable package will win a dinner for two at the Fishbone Grill! Now, get to work!

어휘 waste 폐기물, ~을 낭비하다 as quickly as possible 최대한 빨리 announcement 발표 potluck 일상적인 음식, 각자 음식을 가져와서 하는 파티 dish 요리 maintenance 보수, 유지, 시설 관리부서 vandalism 만행 commit ~을 저지르다, ~을 범하다 crime 범죄, 극악한 행위 competition 경쟁 sign up for ~에 등록하다 get to work 일을 하다

83

★★★ 도입부 정보 – 화자

화자는 어느 분야의 산업에 종사하는 것 같은가?
(A) 케이블 TV 서비스   (B) 스포츠 마케팅
(C) 소매 금융   (D) 식품 생산

어휘 finance 재정, 돈 production 생산

토익 분석

화자 정보는 대체로 지문의 가장 초반부 자기소개 문장에
제시되지만 이 문제의 경우 도입부를 전반적으로 이해해
야 유추가 가능한 문제다.

What industry does the speaker most likely work in?

(A) Cable TV service   (B) Sports marketing
(C) Personal finance   (D) Food production

문제 해설

화자가 종사하는 분야를 유추해야 하는 질문이므로 지문에서 화자가 종사하는 분야를 추측할 수 있
을 만한 관련 어휘나 표현이 제시되는 부분을 파악하는 것이 관건이다. 지문 말미에서 화자는 'The
person~Fishbone Grill!'이라고 이야기하며 케이블 패키지 상품에 가장 많은 고객들이 등록하도록
하는 직원이 Fishbone Grill에서의 2인용 저녁 식사권을 획득하게 될 것임을 밝히고 있다. 그러므로 이
를 통해 화자는 케이블 TV 서비스를 제공하는 업계에 종사하는 사람임을 추측할 수 있으므로 정답은
(A)가 되겠다. 무엇보다 지문 초반부에서 단서가 제시되는 유형의 질문임에도 불구하고 단서가 지문
말미에서 등장한다는 점에서 동형의 여느 문제들에 비해 난이도가 높다고 할 수 있다.

84

★★ 세부 정보

화자는 수요일에 어떠한 일이 벌어질 것이라 언급하는가?
(A) 사무실이 늦게 연다.
(B) 음식을 공유할 것이다.
(C) 몇몇 새로운 패키지 상품들이 출시될 것이다.
(D) Fishbone Grill에서 점심을 제공할 것이다.

어휘 share 나누다, 공유하다 release 공개(발표) 하다

토익 분석

Wednesday가 이 문제의 키워드로 정답을 제시한다.

What does the speaker say will happen on Wednesday?
(A) The office will open late.   **(B) Food will be shared.**
(C) Some new packages will be released.   (D) The Fishbone Grill will provide lunch.

문제 해설

수요일에 발생할 일에 대해 묻고 있으므로 지문에서 수요일이란 시점이 제시되는 부분을 중심으로
단서를 파악하는 것이 현명하다. 따라서 화자가 지문 초반부에서 'We are going to have a potluck
lunch on Wednesday.'라고 말하며 수요일에 각자 음식을 가지고 와서 함께 점심 식사를 하고자 한
다는 계획을 밝히는 부분을 통해 정답은 (B)임을 알 수 있다.

85

★★ 세부 정보

화자에 따르면, 어떻게 해야 직원들이 경쟁에서 이길 수
있는가?
(A) 가장 많은 시간을 근무한다.
(B) 가장 창조적인 제품을 생산한다.
(C) 가장 많은 고객을 등록시킨다.
(D) 가장 많은 추천을 받는다.

어휘 enroll 등록하다 recommendation 추천

토익 분석

질문 속에 사용된 동사 win이 결정적인 키워드로 답을 제
시하고 있다.

According to the speaker, how can employees win the competition?
(A) By working the most hours
(B) By making the most creative product
(C) By enrolling the most customers
(D) By receiving the most recommendations

문제 해설

경쟁에서의 승리 방법에 대해 묻는 마지막 질문이므로 지문에서 경쟁, 즉, competition이 언급되는
부분을 중심으로 제시되는 경쟁에서의 승리 방식을 노려 들어야 할 필요가 있다. 따라서 화자가 지
문 종료 직전 'The person~Fishbone Grill!'이라고 이야기하며 케이블 패키지 상품에 가장 많은 고
객들이 등록하도록 하는 직원이 Fishbone Grill에서의 2인용 저녁 식사권을 획득하게 될 것임을 밝
히는 부분을 통해 정답은 (C)임을 알 수 있다.

Questions 86-88 refer to the following excerpt from a meeting.

W I just heard from the client, and it sounds like we will be able to give a presentation next week. Don't forget that we need to win their hearts this time. [86] The advertisement we made last time was too casual for them. [87] I think we should focus on sounding clear and professional this time. Instead of consulting with famous social media users, I think we should consult with people related to business marketing. [88] If anyone knows someone or has examples of work that sound like what I just described, send me an e-mail so we can talk about it at our meeting next week.

어휘 win one's hearts ~의 마음을 얻다 advertisement 광고 casual 평이한 focus on ~에 집중하다 consult with ~와 협의/논의하다 related to ~와 관련이 있는 describe ~을 묘사/표현하다

여 제가 고객님에게 막 이야기를 들었습니다만, 우리는 다음 주에 그들에게 발표하는 것이 가능할 것 같습니다. 잊지 마십시오, 우리는 이번에 그들의 마음을 얻어야만 합니다. [86] 우리가 지난번에 제작한 그 광고는 그들에게 너무 평이하다는 평가를 받았습니다. [87] 이번에는 명료하고 전문적인 메시지를 전달하는 광고를 제작하는 것에 집중해야 한다고 생각합니다. 유명한 소셜 미디어 사용자들과 논의하기에 앞서 비즈니스 마케팅과 관련이 있는 사람들과 논의해야 한다고 봅니다. [88] 만약 누군가 제가 방금 언급한 것과 같은 사람이나 작품을 알고 계신다면 제게 이메일을 보내주셔서 다음 주에 있을 회의에서 그 부분에 관해 의견을 나눌 수 있도록 말이지요.

86

What kind of company does the speaker work for?

(A) A marketing firm
(B) A furniture design firm
(C) An advertisement agency
(D) An Internet service company

문제 해설

화자가 근무하는 회사를 유추해야 하는 첫 번째 질문이므로 지문 초반부에서 화자의 직장을 추측할 수 있을 만한 관련 어휘나 표현이 제시되는 부분에 집중해야 한다. 지문 조반 화자는 'The advertisement we made last time was too casual for them.'이라고 이야기하며 지난번에 제작한 광고가 그들에게 너무 평이했음을 언급하고 있으므로 이를 통해 화자는 광고 회사에서 근무하고 있음을 가늠할 수 있다. 따라서 정답은 (C)임을 알 수 있다.

★★ 도입부 정보 – 화자 근무 장소

화자는 어떠한 회사에서 근무할 것 같은가?
(A) 마케팅 회사
(B) 가구 디자인 회사
(C) 광고 회사
(D) 인터넷 서비스 회사

어휘 work for 을 위해 일하다 agency 대리점, 대행사

토익 분석

화자가 근무하는 장소는 환영 인사 다음에 this is~로 시작하는 화자 소개 문장에 제시되거나 주제문에서 유추를 해야만 한다. 이 문제의 경우 주제문에서 화자 근무 장소를 유추해야 하는 문제다.

87

According to the speaker, what will be different for this project?

(A) It will look flashier.
(B) It will look more casual.
(C) It will look more professional.
(D) It will be more appropriate for social media.

문제 해설

이번 프로젝트의 차이점에 대해 묻는 질문이므로 선택지에 있는 형용사를 먼저 살펴본 이후 지문에서 이번 프로젝트의 구체적인 특징으로 제시되는 형용사가 언급되는 부분에 집중해야 한다. 따라서 화자가 'I think we should focus on sounding clear and professional this time.'이라고 이야기하며 이번에는 명료하고 전문적인 메시지를 전달할 수 있는 광고 제작에 집중해야 함을 요청하고 있으므로 이를 통해 정답은 (C)임을 알 수 있다.

★★ 세부 정보

화자에 따르면 이번 프로젝트는 어떠한 차이점이 있어야 하는가?
(A) 좀 더 화려하게 보여야 한다.
(B) 좀 더 평이하게 보여야 한다.
(C) 좀 더 전문적으로 보여야 한다.
(D) 소셜 미디어에 좀 더 적합해야 한다.

어휘 flashy 화려한, 호화스러운 appropriate 적절한

토익 분석

세부 정보 문제지만 키워드가 사용되지 않은 문제로 I think we should~와 같은 요청, 제안 답변 힌트가 단서를 제시하고 있다.

88

What does the speaker ask the listeners to do before the next meeting?

(A) Respond to a survey
(B) Send related information
(C) E-mail a proposal
(D) Work additional hours

문제 해설

화자가 다음 회의 이전에 청자들에게 요청하는 것을 묻는 마지막 질문이므로 지문 후반부에서 다음 회의 이전이란 시점이 제시되는 부분을 중심으로 화자의 요청 사항과 관련된 정보를 파악하는 것에 집중해야 한다. 화자는 지문 말미에서 'If anyone knows someone or examples of work that sound like what I just described, send an e-mail to me so we can talk about it at our meeting next week.'라고 말하며 누군가 자신이 방금 언급한 것과 같은 사람이나 작품을 알고 있다면 이메일을 보내줄 것을 요청하고 있다. 따라서 화자는 청자들이 알 수도 있는 관련 정보를 전달받기 원하고 있으므로 정답은 (B)가 되겠다.

★★★ 요청, 제안

화자는 다음 회의 이전에 청자들에게 무엇을 요청하고 있는가?
(A) 설문 조사에 응답하기
(B) 관련 정보 보내기
(C) 이메일로 제안서 보내기
(D) 추가 근무하기

어휘 proposal 제안서 additional 추가의

토익 분석

요청, 제안에 대한 답변을 이끌어 주는 힌트 표현인 if가정법~, 명령문. 구조 문장이 단서를 제시하고 있으며 질문 속에 시점 표현인 next meeting 또한 키워드로 사용되었다.

여 안녕하세요, 그리고 우리 격월 회의에 오신 것을 환영합니다. [89] 저는 이 시간을 빌어 연단에 모실 다음 연설자를 소개하고자 합니다. 우리는 Richard Wolfstein 교수님의 연설을 듣게 될 것입니다. 교수님께서는 성인이 된 이후의 삶 전체를 경제학을 가르치는 선생님으로 살아오셨으며, 현재 뉴욕에 있는 New School University에서 강의를 하고 계십니다. [90] 오늘 밤, 교수님께서는 현시대에 살고 있는 일반 사람들이 맞닥뜨리고 있는 충격적인 경제 상황에 대해 이야기하실 예정입니다. 여러분께서는 귀를 의심하시게 될 것입니다. [91] 저는 주요 연설 후에 로비에 우리가 마련해 둔 테이블로 모든 분을 초대합니다. 그곳에서 여러분은 저희 월간 소식지를 신청하실 수 있으며, 우리가 계획해 둔 추가 행사에 대한 정보도 얻으실 수 있습니다. 자, Wolfstein 교수님을 환영해 주시기 바랍니다.

Questions 89-91 refer to the following excerpt from a meeting.

W Good evening, and welcome to our bimonthly meeting. [89] I'd like to take this time to introduce our next speaker to the podium. We will be hearing from Professor Richard Wolfstein. He has been a teacher of economics for his entire adult life, and he currently teaches at the New School University in New York. [90] Tonight he'll be discussing the shocking economic situation regular people face in current times. You'll not believe your ears. [91] I invite everyone to visit the table we have set up in the lobby after the main talk. There, you can sign up for our monthly newsletter and become informed of further events we have planned. Now, please welcome Professor Wolfstein.

어휘 bi-monthly 격월의 I'd like to take this time to do 이 시간을 빌어 ~하고자 합니다 introduce ~을 소개하다 podium 연단 economics 경제학 entire 전체의 currently 현재 discuss ~을 이야기/논의하다 economic 경제의 situation 상황 face 마주하다 current 현재의 invite ~을 초대하다 set up ~을 마련하다, 설치하다 sign up for ~을 신청/등록하다 monthly 월간의, 달마다의 become informed of ~에 대한 정보를 얻다 further 추가의

89

★★ 주제, 목적

담화의 목적은 무엇인가?
(A) 문제점을 논의하는 것   (B) 과정을 설명하는 것
(C) 연설자를 소개하는 것   (D) 행사 일정을 알리는 것

어휘 explain ~을 설명하다 process 과정

토익 분석

주제문은 의도 표현 및 미래 행동 표현들이 답을 이끌어준다. 이 문제는 **I'd like to~**가 정답 문장을 제시하고 있다.

What is the purpose of the talk?

(A) To discuss a problem   (B) To explain a process
(C) To introduce a speaker   (D) To give a schedule of events

문제 해설

담화의 목적을 묻는 첫 번째 질문이므로 담화 초반부에서 중점적으로 언급하는 핵심 내용을 파악하는 것이 관건이다. 화자는 담화를 시작하는 인사를 하면서 'I'd like to take this time to introduce our next speaker to the podium.'라는 말로 연설자를 소개하겠다는 말과 함께 해당 인물에 대해 간략히 설명하는 것으로 담화를 진행하고 있으므로 (C)가 정답이 된다.

90

★★★ 맥락 문제

화자는 왜 "You'll not believe your ears"라고 말하는가?
(A) 강연이 놀라울 것이라고 생각하고 있다.
(B) 볼륨이 너무 크다고 생각하고 있다.
(C) 라디오 방송을 추천하고 있다.
(D) 제공된 헤드폰을 사용하도록 권하고 있다.

어휘 radio broadcast 라디오 방송 advise -ing ~하도록 권하다 provided 제공된

토익 분석

제시된 표현이 나오기 바로 전 문장에 답에 대한 힌트가 제시되고 있다. 특히 시점 표현 **Tonight**과 미래 행동 표현인 **he'll**이 이끄는 문장이 중요한 단서가 된다.

Why does the speaker say, "You'll not believe your ears"?

(A) He thinks a talk will be surprising.
(B) He believes the volume is too loud.
(C) He is recommending a radio broadcast.
(D) He advises using the provided headphones.

문제 해설

화자가 말하는 "You'll not believe your ears"라는 표현이 담화 속에서 어떤 의미로 사용되었는지를 묻는 두 번째 질문이므로 담화 후중반부에 제시되는 이 표현 및 앞뒤에 함께 제시되는 말들을 통해 의미의 흐름을 파악해 정답을 찾아야 한다. 이 표현을 해석해 보면 '당신의 귀를 믿지 못할 것이다'라는 의미이므로 무언가 놀라운 일에 대해 사용하는 말이라는 것을 알 수 있는데, 담화 중반부에 화자가 연설 내용과 관련해 'Tonight~our current times.'라고 말하면서 해당 표현을 사용하고 있으므로 뭔가 놀라운 사실을 듣게 될 것이라는 점을 알 수 있다. 따라서 이와 같은 의미에 대해 언급한 (A)가 정답이 된다.

91

★★ 요청, 제안

청자들은 담화 후에 무엇을 하도록 요청 받고 있는가?
(A) 다과를 즐길 것   (B) 경품 추첨 행사에 참여할 것
(C) 연설자를 만날 것   (D) 소식지를 신청할 것

어휘 be invited to do ~하도록 요청 받다 refreshment 다과 prize raffle 경품 추첨 (행사)

토익 분석

요청/제안 문제의 답을 이끄는 동사인 **invite**가 사용된 문장에 정답에 대한 단서가 제시되고 있다. 특히 질문 속에 사용된 **after the talk**는 시점관련 키워드로 활용되었다.

What is the audience invited to do after the talk?

(A) Enjoy some refreshments   (B) Enter a prize raffle
(C) Meet the speaker   **(D) Sign up for a newsletter**

문제 해설

청자들이 담화 후에 하도록 요청 받는 일이 무엇인지를 묻는 세 번째 문제이므로 담화의 후반부에서 들을 수 있는 화자의 말에서 요청 표현과 함께 제시되는 정보에 집중해 들어야 한다. 특히 특정 시점을 나타내는 'after the talk'라는 말이 키워드이므로 이 시점 표현이 제시되는 부분에 집중해야 한다. 화자는 담화 마지막에 'I invite~we have planned.'라는 말로 연설 후에 로비에 있는 테이블로 올 것을 알리면서 그 자리에서 할 수 있는 일로 월간 소식지를 신청할 수 있다는 점과 추후 행사 계획에 대해 들을 수 있다는 점을 말하고 있다. 이 중에서 소식지 신청에 대해 언급한 (D)가 정답이다.

Questions 92-94 refer to the following broadcast and schedule.

M   Welcome back to Hit Songs dot FM. I'm sorry to tell you this, but I have bad news regarding the Late Night Festival in Grand Stadium. [92, 93] There's an unexpected repair to Main Boulevard planned for August 14 to August 18. Three parking lots will be forced to close down, and it'll be impossible to get to the Grand Stadium while the construction is taking place. Unfortunately, [93] the DJ performance that's scheduled that week is going to be moved to a different week. We are trying our best to reschedule it to September. [94] Please call us for more information about the concert schedule.

Late Night Festival Schedule	
DJ Momo	August 2
DJ Doom	August 10
DJ Chan	August 16
DJ Summer	September 4

어휘 regarding ~와 관련해 unexpected 예기치 못한 repair 수리 therefore 따라서, 그러므로 parking lot 주차장 be forced to do 어쩔 수 없이 ~하다, ~할 수밖에 없다 close down 폐쇄되다 get to ~로 가다 while ~하는 동안 take place 발생되다, 일어나다 unfortunately 안타깝게도 try one's best 최선의 노력을 다하다 reschedule ~의 일정을 재조정하다

남   다시 **Hit Songs dot FM**을 찾아 주신 것을 환영합니다. 이런 말씀 드리게 되어 죄송하지만, **Grand Stadium**에서 열리는 **Late Night Festival**과 관련된 좋지 않은 소식이 있습니다. [92, 93] **Main Boulevard**에 예기치 못한 수리 작업이 생겼으며, 이는 8월 14일부터 18일까지 있을 계획입니다. 세 곳의 주차장들이 피치 못하게 폐쇄될 것이며, 공사가 진행되는 동안 **Grand Stadium**으로 진입하는 것이 불가능할 것입니다. 안타깝게도, [93] 해당 주에 예정되어 있던 **DJ** 공연이 다른 주로 계획될 것입니다. 이 공연의 일정을 9월로 재조정하기 위해 최선의 노력을 다하고 있습니다. [94] 콘서트 일정과 관련해 더 많은 정보가 필요하신 분은 저희에게 전화 주시기 바랍니다.

Late Night Festival 일정표	
DJ Momo	8월 2일
DJ Doom	8월 10일
DJ Chan	8월 16일
DJ Summer	9월 4일

92

What problem does the speaker mention?

(A) A road needs to be repaired.
(B) An artist is unavailable.
(C) The venue is overbooked.
(D) Wrong information was announced.

문제 해설

화자가 언급하는 문제점을 찾는 첫 번째 질문이므로 담화 시작 부분에서 문제점과 관련된 부정적인 정보를 찾는 것이 관건이다. 담화 초반부에 화자는 'There's an unexpected repair to Main Boulevard which is planned on August 14th to August 18th.'라는 말로 특정 도로에 예기치 못한 수리 작업이 발생되었음을 알리고 있으므로 이에 대해 언급한 (A)가 정답이다.

★★ 문제점

화자는 무슨 문제를 언급하는가?
(A) 도로가 수리 되어야 한다.
(B) 한 예술가가 참석할 수 없다.
(C) 행사 장소가 초과 예약되었다.
(D) 잘못된 정보가 알려졌다.

어휘 be unable to do ~할 수 없다 attend ~에 참석하다 venue 행사 장소 overbooked 초과 예약된 announce ~을 알리다

토익 분석

교통방송의 문제점은 바로 방송의 주제문, 즉 '화자 소개 및 방송명' 다음 문장에 답이 제시된다.

93

★★★ 그래픽

도표를 확인하시오. 화자의 말에 따르면, 어느 DJ의 공연 일정이 재조정될 것인가?
(A) DJ Momo
(B) DJ Doom
(C) DJ Chan
(D) DJ Summer

어휘 performance 연주회, 공연 reschedule 일정 변경

토익 분석

그래픽 문제는 문제 보기에 정보와 짝을 이루는 간접 정보가 중요하다. 이 문제의 경우 DJ이름과 일정의 조합이다. DJ를 찾기 위해서는 일정 정보를 들어야 한다.

Look at the graphic. According to the speaker, which DJ's performance will be rescheduled?
(A) DJ Momo
(B) DJ Doom
(C) DJ Chan
(D) DJ Summer

문제 해설

공연 일정이 재조정되는 DJ의 공연을 찾는 두 번째 문제이므로 담화 중반부에 일정 변경과 관련된 정보가 제시될 것임을 예상하고 들어야 한다. 화자는 초반부에 언급한 공사 기간인 on August 14th to August 18th와 관련해, 'the DJ performance that's scheduled that week is going to be planned on a different week'라는 말로 해당 주에 있을 DJ 공연이 다른 주로 계획될 것이라고 알리고 있다. 도표에서 이 기간에 해당되는 날짜인 8월 16일에 공연이 예정된 DJ가 DJ Chan이므로 (C)가 정답이다.

94

★★ 요청, 제안

화자는 청자들에게 무엇을 하도록 권하는가?
(A) 환불을 받을 것
(B) 문의를 위해 전화할 것
(C) 예약 일정을 재조정할 것
(D) 우편물을 확인할 것

어휘 refund 환불 inquiry 문의 appointment 예약 mail 우편물

토익 분석

요청, 제안 문제에 대한 대표적인 힌트 표현인 'please 명령문'이 답변을 제시하고 있다.

What does the speaker recommend the listeners do?
(A) Get a refund
(B) Call for questions
(C) Reschedule an appointment
(D) Check an e-mail

문제 해설

화자가 권하는 일을 묻는 마지막 질문이므로 담화 후반부에서 권고나 제안 등을 나타내는 표현을 중심으로 단서를 찾아야 한다. 화자는 담화 마지막 부분에 'Please call us to ask more information about the concert schedule.'라는 말로 추가 정보를 얻을 수 있도록 전화하라고 권하고 있는데, 이는 전화를 통해 문의하라는 말과 같으므로 (B)가 정답임을 알 수 있다

Questions 95-97 refer to the following public announcement and boarding pass.

W　Passengers on Flight KA816, there's an important announcement. **95 There has been a critical mechanic problem detected on the aircraft.** We are moving all passengers to other flights. You will be called to the counter to find your new flight information. **96 Please check the zone number on your boarding pass and pay attention to the announcements.** When your zone number is called, come to the counter and present your passport. We are sorry for the inconvenience. **97 We'll also be offering you free airport lounge coupon after a while. In order to use the luxury lounge for free, please wait for a separate announcement about where to claim it.** Thank you.

Passenger	Carly Fine	
Flight	**Seat**	**Gate**
KA816	3B	I19
Boarding Zone	3	

어휘　announcement 안내 (방송), 공지　critical 중대한　mechanic 기계의, 기계적인　detect ~을 발견하다　pay attention to ~에 귀 기울이다, 주목하다　inconvenience 불편함　free 무료의　after a while 잠시 후에　in order to do ~하기 위해　for free 무료로　separate 별도의, 따로 하는　claim ~을 요청하다

여　KA816 항공편 탑승객 여러분, 중요한 안내 사항이 있습니다. **95 항공기에서 발견된 중요한 기술적 문제점이 있습니다.** 모든 승객 여러분을 다른 비행편으로 이동시키고자 합니다. 여러분 모두 새로운 항공편 정보를 위해 카운터로 호출이 될 것입니다. **96 항공권에 구역 번호를 확인하시고 안내방송에 귀 기울여 주십시오.** 여러분의 탑승 구역 번호가 불리면, 카운터에 오셔서 여권을 제시해 주십시오. 불편을 끼쳐 드린 점에 대해 사과 드립니다. **97 저희는 또한 잠시 후에 무료 공항 라운지 이용 쿠폰을 제공해 드릴 것입니다. 고급 라운지를 무료로 이용하실 수 있도록, 쿠폰 요청 장소에 관한 별도의 안내 방송을 기다려 주시기 바랍니다.** 감사합니다.

탑승객	Carly Fine	
항공편	**좌석**	**탑승구**
KA816	3B	I19
탑승 구역	3	

95

What is the announcement about?

(A) A flight delay
(B) A boarding zone change
(C) A plane problem
(D) A lost child

문제 해설

안내 방송의 주제를 묻는 첫 번째 문제이므로 담화 시작 부분에 집중해 언급되는 핵심 정보를 파악하는 것이 관건이다. 화자는 담화를 시작하면서 'There has been a critical mechanic problem detected on the aircraft.'라는 말로 항공기에서 기계적인 문제가 발견되었음을 알리고 있으므로 (C)가 정답이다. 뒤이어 해결책으로 다른 항공편 일정(other flight schedule)을 제공하고 있다고 알리고 있으므로 (A)에 제시된 '항공편 지연'은 오답임을 알 수 있다.

★★ 주제, 목적

안내 방송은 무엇에 관한 것인가?
(A) 항공편 지연
(B) 탑승 구역 변경
(C) 비행기 문제
(D) 미아

어휘　delay 지연, 지체　lost 잃어버린, 분실한

토익 분석

공항 안내방송의 주제 목적은 언제나 '문제점'에 대한 안내방송이다. 지문 도입부 청자 정보 다음에 바로 답이 제시된다.

96

★★ 주제, 목적

도표를 확인하시오. Carly Fine 씨는 현재 어느 번호에 주목해야 하는가?
(A) KA816
(B) I19
(C) 3B
(D) 3

어휘 pay attention to 주목하다, 집중하다

토익 분석

제시된 항공권에 정보들을 미리 파악해야 한다. 요청, 제안 표현인 'please 명령문~' 형태로 정답을 제시하고 있다.

Look at the graphic. Which number should Carly Fine pay attention to now?
(A) KA816
(B) I19
(C) 3B
(D) 3

문제 해설

Carly Fine 씨가 주목해야 하는 정보를 찾는 두 번째 문제이므로 담화 중반부에서 특정 항목에 해당되는 정보가 제시될 것임을 예상하고 들어야 한다. 화자는 담화 중반부에 'Please check the zone number on your boarding passes and pay attention to the announcements.'라는 말로 탑승 구역 번호를 확인하고 안내 방송에 귀 기울이라고 알리고 있으며, 도표에 쓰여 있는 탑승 구역 번호가 '3'이므로 (D)가 정답이다.

97

★★ 미래 행동

화자는 나중에 무엇을 알릴 것인가?
(A) 쿠폰을 받는 곳
(B) 가장 가까운 호텔로 가는 방법
(C) 항공기가 지연된 이유
(D) 탑승이 시작되는 때

어휘 where to do ~하는 곳 how to do ~하는 법 get to ~로 가다 nearest 가장 가까운 boarding 탑승

토익 분석

화자의 미래 행동은 언제나 지문의 가장 마지막 문장에 제시된다. 요청, 제안 형태인 'please 명령문~' 구조로 화자가 무엇을 제시할지 단서를 제공하고 있다.

What will the speaker announce later?
(A) Where to get a coupon
(B) How to get to the nearest hotel
(C) Why the flight was delayed
(D) When the boarding will start

문제 해설

화자가 나중에 알리는 정보를 묻는 마지막 문제이므로 담화 후반부에서 언급되는 '추가 정보'와 관련된 단서를 찾아야 한다. 화자는 담화 후반부에 'We'll also be offering you free airport lounge coupon after a while. In order to use the luxury lounge for free, please wait for separate announcement about where to claim it.'라는 말로 무료 공항 라운지 쿠폰을 제공한다고 알리면서 그것을 요청할 수 있는 곳과 관련해 별도로 안내한다고 밝히고 있다. 따라서 쿠폰을 받는 장소를 나중에 알린다는 것을 알 수 있으므로 (A)가 정답이다.

Questions 98 to 100 refer to the following talk and menu.

W   I'd like to congratulate all of you who work here at Flora's Restaurant. 98 As you know, I write a regular food column in the *Washington Times*, and my job here today was to review this business and the food it serves. I'm pleased to say that I really enjoyed my meal and the level of service. 99 It was disappointing that the blue crab cakes were unavailable, but the alternative appetizer was excellent. The salmon was also fantastic, and 100 most of all, the dessert was the best I ever had. I totally understand why it was featured on the cover of Food *Guru Magazine*. Thank you for the pleasant dining experience. I hope to return sometime soon.

**Flora's Restaurant
- Set Lunch Menu -**

Appetizer
Blue Crab Cakes

Main Dish
Poached Salmon

Side Dish
Greek Salad

Dessert
Cherry Cheesecake

어휘 congratulate ~에게 축하 인사를 하다 regular 정기적인 column (신문 등의) 칼럼 기사 review ~을 평가하다, ~의 후기를 작성하다 serve (음식 등) ~을 제공하다 be pleased to do ~해서 기쁘다 meal 식사 It is disappointing that ~해서 실망스럽다 unavailable 이용할 수 없는 alternative 대체하는, 대안의 appetizer 전채 요리 salmon 연어 taste ~의 맛을 보다 totally 전적으로, 완전히 feature ~을 특집으로 싣다 pleasant 기쁜 dining 식사 experience 경험

여   저는 우리 Flora's Restaurant에서 근무하시는 여러분 모두에게 축하 인사를 드리고자 합니다. 98 아시다시피, 저는 Washington Times에 음식과 관련된 정기 칼럼을 작성하고 있으며, 오늘 여기서 제가 할 일은 이 레스토랑 및 제공되는 음식에 대한 평가를 작성하는 것입니다. 저는 정말로 제가 맛본 음식과 서비스 수준이 마음에 들었다고 말씀 드리게 되어 기쁘게 생각합니다. 99 블루 크랩 케이크를 맛볼 수 없어서 실망스러웠지만, 그 음식을 대체한 전채 요리는 훌륭했습니다. 연어도 환상적이었으며, 100 무엇보다도 디저트는 제가 맛본 것들 중에서 최고였습니다. 이 음식이 왜 Food Guru Magazine의 표지에 특집으로 실렸는지 전적으로 이해가 됩니다. 즐거운 식사 경험에 대해 감사 드립니다. 조만간 다시 찾아올 수 있기를 바랍니다.

**Flora's Restaurant
– 점심 세트 메뉴 –**

전채 요리
Blue Crab Cakes

주요리
Poached Salmon

곁들임 요리
Greek Salad

디저트
Cherry Cheesecake

98

Who most likely is the speaker?

(A) A restaurant owner
(B) A head chef
(C) A food critic
(D) A waiter

문제 해설

화자의 신분에 대해 유추할 것을 요구하는 첫 번째 질문이므로 담화 초반부에서 화자가 하는 일과 관련해 직접적으로 언급되는 부분, 혹은 이를 추측할 수 있을 만한 관련 어휘가 제시되는 부분에 집중해야 한다. 화자는 담화를 시작하면서 'As you know, I write a regular food column in the Washington Times, and my job here today was to review this business and the food it serves.'라는 말로 자신이 하는 일을 알리고 있는데, 음식에 대한 칼럼을 작성하는 사람이며 현재 화자가 와 있는 곳에서 제공하는 음식에 대해 평가한 것을 말하고 있으므로 (C)가 화자의 신분으로 알맞다는 것을 알 수 있다.

★★ 도입부 정보 – 화자

화자는 누구인가?
(A) 레스토랑 소유주
(B) 수석 요리사
(C) 음식 평론가
(D) 웨이터

어휘 critic 평론가, 비평가

토익 분석

지문 도입부 화자 소개 부분을 들어야 한다. 문두 부사구인 as you know가 힌트 표현이다. as you know는 화자, 청자 정보 또는 주제문에 대한 힌트를 지시하는 표현 중 하나다.

99

★★ 문제점

화자는 무슨 문제점을 언급하는가?
(A) 서비스가 매우 느렸다.
(B) 한 가지 음식이 차갑게 제공되었다.
(C) 직원들이 불친절했다.
(D) 한 가지 음식이 이용 불가능했다.

어휘 be served cold 차갑게 제공되다 impolite 불친절한 unavailable (획득)할 수 없는, 만날 수 없는

토익 분석

문제점은 대체로 반전 표현이 정답 힌트로 사용되지만, 이 문제의 경우 반전 표현 없이 부정적인 내용을 암시하는 disappointing이 사용되었다.

What problem does the speaker mention?

(A) Service was very slow.
(B) A dish was served cold.
(C) Staff members were impolite.
(D) An item was unavailable.

문제 해설

화자가 언급하는 문제점을 묻는 두 번째 질문이므로 담화 중반부에서 화자가 특정 문제점과 함께 걱정이나 우려 등을 나타내는 부정적인 표현 등을 통해 언급하는 정보를 파악해야 한다. 담화 중반부에 화자는 'It was disappointing that ~'이라는 부정적인 감정을 나타내는 표현과 함께 'It was disappointing that the blue crab cakes were unavailable, but the alternative appetizer was excellent.'라는 말로 특정 음식을 맛볼 수 없었던 것에 대해 언급하고 있으므로 이를 item과 unavailable이라는 단어를 포함해 바꿔 표현한 (D)가 정답이다.

100

★★★ 그래픽

도표를 확인하시오. 어느 음식이 잡지에 특집으로 실렸는가?
(A) 블루 크랩 케이크
(B) 주요리
(C) Greek 샐러드
(D) 체리 치즈케이크

어휘 be featured in ~에 등장/방영하다 (feature: 특징, 신문/TV 특집 기사/방송)

토익 분석

메뉴에 각 코스별 음식 이름이 적혀 있다. 음식 이름을 찾기 위해서는 지문에서 코스명을 확인해야 한다. 문두 부사구 Most of all은 강조 표현으로 언제나 중요한 정보를 제시한다.

Look at the graphic. Which menu item was featured in a magazine?

(A) Blue Crab Cakes
(B) Poached Salmon
(C) Greek Salad
(D) Cherry Cheesecake

문제 해설

질문에서 묻는 내용과 관련해 담화 속에 제시된 단서를 바탕으로 도표의 정보를 함께 확인해 정답을 찾아야 하는 문제이다. 이때 각 보기에 제시된 내용 외의 정보가 담화 속에서 단서로 제시될 것이므로 이에 집중해 담화를 들어야 한다. 화자는 담화 후반부에 'Most of all, the dessert was the best I ever had. I totally understand why it was featured on the cover of Food Guru Magazine.'이라는 말로 디저트에 대해 극찬을 하면서 잡지에 실린 이유를 알 것 같다고 말하고 있으므로 디저트 항목에 쓰여 있는 음식인 (D)가 정답이다.

ACTUAL TEST
4

해설서

1

★ 1인 중심 + 사람 동작

(A) 그녀는 바지들을 물에 담그고 있다.
(B) 그녀는 빨래를 건조시키기 위해 널고 있다.
(C) 그녀는 빨래 바구니 뚜껑을 들고 있다.
(D) 그녀는 세탁기에 옷을 채워 넣고 있다.

어휘 soak 물에 담그다 hang 걸다 laundry 빨래 lid 뚜껑 fill A with B A를 B에 채우다 basket 바구니

(A) She is soaking some pants.
(B) She is hanging up the laundry to dry.
(C) She is holding the lid of the laundry basket.
(D) She is filling the laundry basket with clothes.

문제 해설

1인 중심의 사진이므로 여자의 행동과 외모적 특징부터 살펴봐야 하며 특히 사람이 도구나 기기와 함께 등장하는 경우 해당 도구나 기기를 사용하고 있는 동작을 묘사하는 정답이 제시되는 경우가 일반적이다. 따라서 여자가 옷을 쥐고 있는 행동과 여자가 옷을 꺼내고 있는 듯한 행동에 집중해야 하며, 이 중 여자가 세탁기에서 옷을 꺼내는 동작을 표현하고 있는 (D)가 정답이다.

토익 분석

동작 문제의 경우 사진 속에 등장하는 동작과 잘못된 사물을 매칭시켜 오답을 만드는 경우가 일반적이다. (C)의 경우 동작 포인트인 holding과 lid를 잘못 매칭시킨 예이다.

2

★ 2인 이상 + 사람 동작

(A) 여자는 휴대 전화기를 들고 있다.
(B) 여자가 가방 안을 보고 있다.
(C) 여자가 사무실에서 전화 통화를 하고 있다.
(D) 여자가 큰 가방을 메고 있다.

어휘 mobile phone 휴대 전화기 look into 안을 들여다보다 talk on a phone 전화상으로 통화하다 carry a bag 가방을 들다(메다)

(A) She is holding a mobile phone.
(B) She is looking into a bag.
(C) She is talking on a phone in the office.
(D) She is carrying a large bag.

문제 해설

다수의 인물이지만 사진 중앙에 남녀 각 1명씩이 강조된 사진이므로 여자와 남자의 행동과 외모적 특징부터 살펴봐야 하며 특히 사람이 도구나 기기와 함께 등장하는 경우 해당 도구나 기기를 사용하고 있는 동작을 묘사하는 정답이 제시되는 경우가 일반적이다. 여자가 공중전화를 사용하고 가방을 메고 있는 상태 그리고 남자가 앉아 전화기를 사용하는 동작이 중요하다. 이 중 여자가 가방을 메고 있는 동작을 묘사하고 있는 (D)가 정답이다.

토익 분석

(A)와 (B)처럼 사람의 행동은 정확하게 표현하되, 남녀 주어를 잘못 사용하거나 잘못된 사물을 매칭 시켜 오답을 유도하는 함정에 주의해야 한다.

3

(A) The shop attendant is arranging the products in the showcase.
(B) Price tags have been placed on each item.
(C) The sales clerk is showing an item to the customers.
(D) The customers are looking at the goods in the display case.

(A) 상점 직원이 진열장 안에 있는 제품들을 배열하고 있다.
(B) 각 제품마다 가격표가 부착되어 있다.
(C) 상점 판매 직원이 고객들에게 제품을 보여 주고 있다.
(D) 고객들은 진열장에 있는 상품들을 보고 있다.

어휘 showcase 진열장　price tag 가격표　shop attendant 상점 직원　sales clerk 상품 판매 직원　item 제품, 상품　goods 제품, 상품　display case 진열장

문제 해설

2인 이상 등장하는 사진이므로 이들의 공통된 행동 및 외모적 특징을 살펴본 후, 이들의 개별적 행동과 외모적 특징을 파악해야 하며, 이어서 사물의 위치와 상태에 초점을 맞춰야 한다. 따라서 한 남자가 남녀에게 제품을 소개하는 행동, 제품을 보고 있는 남녀의 행동, 그리고 벽면에 TV들이 진열되어 있는 상태와 관련된 부분에서 정답이 제시될 가능성이 높으며, 이 중 직원이 고객들에게 제품을 보여 주고 있는 동작을 묘사하고 있는 (C)가 정답이다.

토익 분석

사람의 동작과 짝을 이루는 사물을 꼼꼼히 들어야 한다. (D)의 경우 고객들이 바라보고 있는 것은 맞지만 진열장 안에 상품들을 보고 있는 것은 아니다.

4

(A) The woman is handing a credit card to the cashier.
(B) The woman is purchasing some machinery.
(C) A couple is exchanging business cards.
(D) The woman is browsing inside the store.

(A) 여자가 계산원에게 신용카드를 건네주고 있다.
(B) 여자가 기계를 구매하고 있다.
(C) 남녀가 명함을 교환하고 있다.
(D) 여자가 상점 내부를 구경하고 있다.

어휘 hand A to B A를 B에게 건네주다　cashier 계산원　machinery 기계류　business card 명함　browse ~을 구경하다

문제 해설

2인 이상 등장하는 사진이므로 이들의 공통된 행동 및 외모적 특징을 살펴본 후, 이들의 개별적 행동과 외모적 특징을 파악해야 하며, 이어서 사물의 위치와 상태에 집중해야 한다. 그러므로 남녀가 카운터를 사이에 두고 서로 마주 보고 있는 상태, 직원에게 신용카드를 건네 있는 행동, 한 남자가 손에 기기를 쥐고 신용카드를 받는 행동, 그리고 남자 직원이 앞치마를 착용하고 있는 상태와 관련된 정답이 제시될 가능성이 높으며 이 중 여자가 직원에게 신용카드를 전달하고 있는 동작을 설명하고 있는 (A)가 정답이다.

토익 분석

(B)는 여자가 물건을 구매하고 있지만, 기계류인지 알 수 없는 사진이다. 항상 사진 속에 명확히 보이는 경우가 아니라면 추측성 보기로 답이 될 수 없음을 기억하자.

★★★ 2인 이상 + 실내 상태

(A) 몇몇 책상들 위에 서류가 쌓이고 있다.
(B) 모두들 창문들을 보고 있다.
(C) 업무 공간들이 칸막이로 나눠져 있다.
(D) 몇몇 사람들이 메뉴판을 보고 있다.

어휘 be stacked with ~가 쌓이다 workstation 업무 공간 partition 칸막이 be separated by ~로 분류되다, ~로 나눠지다 study ~을 집중해서 보다, ~을 학습하다

(A) Some desks are being stacked with papers.
(B) They are all looking at the windows.
(C) The workstations are separated by partitions.
(D) Some people are studying the menu.

문제 해설

작업 공간을 배경으로 여러 사람이 등장하는 사진이므로 이들의 공통된 행동 및 개별적 행동, 그리고 외모적 특징을 살펴본 후 이어서 실내 정경을 구성하는 주요 사물의 위치와 상태를 파악하는 것이 중요하다. 따라서 사람들이 자신의 업무 공간에 착석한 상태, 사람들이 컴퓨터를 조작하며 업무를 보는 행동, 칸막이로 나눠진 업무 공간의 상태와 일부 좌석이 비어 있는 상태에 집중해야 하며, 이 중 업무 공간들이 칸막이로 나눠진 상태를 묘사하고 있는 (C)가 정답이다.

토익 분석

사람들이 등장하는 사진이라도 이들의 행동이나 외모적 특징이 아닌 주변 사물의 위치나 상태와 관련된 정답이 제시될 수도 있다는 점을 필히 숙지해야 한다. (A)의 경우 주의해야 할 혼동 보기다. 사물 주어일 경우 행동을 취할 수 있는 입장이 아니기에 display나 arrange와 같은 단어를 제외하고 being이 등장할 경우 대체로 오답이 된다.

★★ 2인 이상 + 사람 동작

(A) 그들은 작은 소규모 집단으로 나눠져 있다.
(B) 화자 옆에 많은 좌석들이 비어 있다.
(C) 여자는 벽에 스크린을 가리키고 있다.
(D) 남자가 사람들에게 발표를 하면서 몸짓을 취하고 있다.

어휘 be divided into ~로 나눠지다 seat 좌석 available 이용 가능한, 사용 가능한 beside ~옆에 point to ~을 가리키다 gesture 몸짓을 하다, 손짓을 하다 address 연설하다, 발표하다

(A) They are divided into small groups.
(B) Many seats are available beside the speaker.
(C) The woman is pointing at the large screen on the wall.
(D) The man is gesturing as he is addressing the people.

문제 해설

2인 이상 여러 사람이 등장하는 사진이므로, 이들의 공통된 행동 및 개별적 행동, 그리고 옷차림이나 장신구 착용과 관련된 외모적 특징을 중시해야 한다. 그러므로 손짓하며 발표 중인 한 남자의 행동, 착석한 상태에서 이를 경청하는 사람들의 행동, 그리고 테이블 위에 놓인 노트북과 빈 좌석과 연관된 표현이 정답으로 등장할 가능성이 높다는 점을 알 수 있으며, 이 중 남자가 발표하며 손짓을 취하고 있는 동작을 언급하고 있는 (D)를 정답이다.

토익 분석

여러 명의 사람이 등장하는 경우 동사를 올바로 쓰고 주어의 수 일치나 짝을 이루는 사물이나 사람 장소 등을 잘못 연결한 혼동 보기가 등장할 수 있다. (B)는 many seats가 아니고 (C)는 주어가 여자가 아니라 남자다.

7

What time is the presentation for the new project?

(A) On the fifth floor.
(B) She will leave at 2 P.M.
(C) It will begin in half an hour.

문제 해설

프로젝트 발표 시간을 묻는 What time 의문문에 대해 미래 시제 동사와 함께 '30분 후에'라는 말로 미래 시점을 언급하는 (C)가 정답이다.

토익 분석

(A)는 위치 표현이므로 Where 의문문에 어울리는 답변이며, (B)에는 시간 표현이 쓰여 있기는 하지만 발표 시간이 아니라 대상을 알 수 없는 She가 떠나는 시간을 알리는 말이므로 질문의 핵심에서 벗어난 오답이다.

★★ 직접의문문 **What time**

새로운 프로젝트에 대한 발표가 몇 시에 있죠?
(A) 5층에서요.
(B) 그녀는 오후 2시에 출발합니다.
(C) 30분 후에 시작될 겁니다.

어휘 presentation 발표 leave 출발하다, 떠나다, 나가다 in half an hour 30분 후에

8

Who's organizing the picnic this time?

(A) I thought it was you.
(B) Almost everyone signed up.
(C) At the local organic stores.

문제 해설

야유회를 준비하는 사람이 누구인지를 묻는 Who 의문문에 대해 그 당사자가 상대방인 줄 알았다는 말로 답변하는 (A)가 정답이다.

토익 분석

(B)는 행사 준비 담당자가 아닌 참가자 규모와 관련된 답변이므로 어울리지 않는 반응이며, (C)는 장소 표현이므로 Where 의문문에 어울리는 반응이다.

★★ 직접의문문 **Who**

이번에는 누가 야유회를 준비하고 있나요?
(A) 저는 당신인 줄 알았어요.
(B) 거의 모든 사람이 신청했습니다.
(C) 지역의 유기농 매장들에서요.

어휘 organize ~을 준비하다, 조직하다 sign up 신청하다, 등록하다 local 지역의, 현지의 organic 유기농의

9

Why is Rebecca out of the office today?

(A) Because they are all sold out.
(B) She has a meeting with clients.
(C) Yes, it is out of order.

★★ 직접의문문 **Why**

Rebecca 씨가 왜 오늘 사무실 밖에 나가 계신 거죠?
(A) 그것들이 모두 매진되었기 때문입니다.
(B) 고객들과 회의가 있으십니다.
(C) 네, 그것은 고장 나 있습니다.

어휘 out of ~ 밖에 있는 sold out 매진된, 품절된 out of order 고장 난

문제 해설

Rebecca 씨가 오늘 사무실 밖에 나가 있는 이유를 묻는 Why 의문문에 대해 Rebecca 씨를 She로 지칭해 고객들과 회의가 있다는 말로 그 이유를 알리는 (B)가 정답이다.

토익 분석

(A)는 Why와 짝을 이루는 Because가 사용된 답변이지만 질문에 나타나 있지 않은 대상을 지칭하는 they를 활용한 오답이며, out까지 반복 사용되어 혼동을 유발하는 답변이지만 물품의 판매 상태와 관련된 말이므로 어울리지 않는다. (C)는 의문사 의문문에 어울리지 않는 Yes로 대답하는 오답이다.

10

★★ 일반의문문

새로운 환불 정책에 관해 들어 보셨어요?
(A) 네, 그것은 각각 약 25유로입니다.
(B) 아무도 제게 얘기해 주지 않았어요. 뭔가요?
(C) 저는 다음 주 월요일이나 되어야 이곳에 있을 겁니다.

어휘 hear about ~에 관해 듣다 refund 환불 policy 정책, 방침 about 약, 대략 not A until B B나 되어야 A하다

Did you hear about the new refund policy?

(A) Yes, it's about 25 euros each.
(B) No one has told me. What is it?
(C) I won't be here until next Monday.

문제 해설

새로운 환불 정책에 관해 들어 봤는지를 확인하기 위한 의문문이므로 아무도 말해 주지 않았다는 말로 들어 보지 못했음을 언급한 후에 새 정책이 무엇인지를 되묻는 (B)가 정답이다.

토익 분석

(A)는 긍정을 나타내는 Yes와 policy를 지칭하는 것으로 생각할 수 있는 it으로 답변이 시작되고 있지만, 뒤에 이어지는 내용이 물품의 가격에 해당되는 말이므로 어울리지 않는 반응이다. (C)는 hear와 발음은 같지만, 의미가 다른 here를 활용해 혼동을 유발하는 오답으로, 환불 정책과는 전혀 관련 없는 내용이므로 오답이다.

11

★★ 직접의문문 When

언제 본사를 방문하실 예정이신가요?
(A) 곧이요, 아마도.
(B) 저는 Boston에 있을 겁니다.
(C) 네, 그는 어제 방문했어요.

어휘 be supposed to do ~할 예정이다, ~하기로 되어 있다 head office 본사 soon 곧, 머지않아

When are you supposed to visit the head office?

(A) Soon, I think.
(B) I'll be in Boston.
(C) Yes, he visited yesterday.

문제 해설

본사를 방문하기로 되어 있는 시점을 묻는 When 의문문에 대해 가까운 미래를 의미하는 Soon으로 답변하는 (A)가 정답이다.

토익 분석

(B)는 시점이 아닌 장소와 관련된 답변이므로 Where 의문문에 어울리는 반응이며, (C)는 의문사 의문문에 어울리지 않는 Yes로 답변하는 오답이다.

12

Can I make an important announcement before the play begins?

(A) Of course, it comes in five different colors.
(B) Sure, you will play an important role.
(C) OK, but please keep it brief.

문제 해설

연극이 시작되기 전에 자신이 공지 사항을 말해도 되는지를 묻는 요청의문문이므로 이에 대해 긍정을 나타내는 OK와 함께 간단히 말하라는 의미를 뜻하는 조건을 함께 제시하는 (C)가 정답이다.

토익 분석

(A)는 긍정을 나타내는 Of course로 대답이 시작되고 있지만, 뒤에 이어지는 내용이 이용 가능한 제품 색상에 해당되는 내용이므로 어울리지 않는 반응이며, (B)도 마찬가지로 긍정을 의미하는 Sure로 답변이 시작되고 있지만, play가 동사로 사용될 경우에 해당되는 의미를 활용해 혼동을 유발하는 오답일 뿐, 공지 사항을 말하는 것과는 전혀 관련이 없는 내용이다.

★★ 권유 제안 요청

연극이 시작되기 전에 제가 중요한 공지를 말해도 될까요?
(A) 물론이죠, 그것은 5가지 다른 색상으로 나옵니다.
(B) 그럼요, 당신은 중요한 역할을 할 겁니다.
(C) 좋아요, 하지만 간단히 하시기 바랍니다.

어휘 make an announcement 공지하다, 발표하다 play 연극 play an important role 중요한 역할을 하다 keep A 형용사 A를 ~한 상태로 유지하다 brief 간단한, 짤막한

13

Have the new posters arrived yet?

(A) I haven't seen them.
(B) Have you confirmed your arrival time?
(C) I need some stamps and envelops.

문제 해설

포스터들이 도착했는지를 확인하기 위한 일반의문문이므로 이에 대해 posters를 them으로 지칭해 보지 못했다는 말로 도착했는지 알 수 없다는 의미를 나타내는 (A)가 정답이다.

토익 분석

(B)는 arrived와 발음이 유사한 arrival을 활용해 혼동을 유발하는 오답으로, 포스터의 도착 시간이 아닌 상대방의 도착 시간을 확인했는지를 되묻는 말이므로 어울리지 않는 반응이다. (C)는 poster와 연관성 있게 들리는 stamps와 envelops를 활용해 혼동을 유발하는 오답이며, 포스터 도착 여부가 아닌 자신이 필요로 하는 물품을 언급하는 답변이다.

★★ 일반의문문

새로운 포스터들이 이미 도착했나요?
(A) 저는 아직 보지 못했습니다.
(B) 당신의 도착 시간을 확인해 주셨나요?
(C) 저는 우표와 봉투가 좀 필요합니다.

어휘 arrive 도착하다 yet (의문문에서) 이미, 벌써 confirm ~을 확인해 주다 arrival 도착 stamp 우표 envelop 봉투

14

Do you want me to reschedule the meeting or just cancel it?

(A) I need to talk to my supervisor first.
(B) Yes, it should work out fine.
(C) I want to see him later today.

★★ 선택의문문

제가 회의 일정을 재조정해 드릴까요, 아니면 그냥 취소할까요?
(A) 제 상사와 먼저 얘기해 봐야 합니다.
(B) 네, 그 일은 잘 될 겁니다.
(C) 저는 오늘 이따가 그를 만나고 싶습니다.

어휘 want A to do A가 ~하기를 원하다 reschedule ~의 일정을 재조정하다 cancel ~을 취소하다 supervisor 상사, 책임자 work out fine 잘 되어 가다

자신이 회의 일정을 재조정하기를 원하는지, 아니면 취소하기를 원하는지를 묻는 선택의문문에 대해 한 가지를 선택하는 대신 선택에 필요한 조건으로 상사에게 먼저 얘기해 봐야 한다고 알리는 (A)가 정답이다.

(B)는 두 가지 선택 사항이 제시되는 선택의문문에 어울리지 않는 Yes로 답변하는 오답으로, 일정 재조정 또는 취소 중에서 어느 것과도 어울리지 않는 반응이다. (C)는 회의 일정과 연관성 있게 들리는 later today를 활용한 오답으로, 대상을 알 수 없는 him을 언급해 그 사람을 만나는 일정을 말하는 보기이므로 질문의 핵심에서 벗어난 답변이다.

15

★★★ 평서문

등록 양식을 작성하시는 것을 제가 도와 드릴 수 있습니다.
(A) 제가 직접 할 수 있을 것 같습니다.
(B) 그것은 냉동실에 있습니다.
(C) 도움을 받으셨나요?

어휘 help A do A가 ~하는 것을 돕다 fill out ~을 작성하다 registration 등록 form 양식 manage (어떻게든) 해내다 oneself (부사적으로) 직접, 스스로 freezer 냉동실

I can help you fill out the registration form.

(A) I think I can manage myself.
(B) It is in the freezer.
(C) Have you been helped?

상대방이 등록 양식을 작성하는 일을 도와줄 수 있다는 의미를 나타내는 일종의 제안에 해당되는 평서문이므로 이에 대해 자신이 직접 할 수 있다는 말로 거절의 의사를 나타내는 (A)가 정답이다.

(B)는 장소와 관련된 의미를 나타내는 답변이므로 제안을 의미하는 평서문에 대한 반응으로 어울리지 않는 답변이며, (C)는 help가 반복 사용되어 혼동을 유발하는 답변으로, 도움을 제안 받은 입장에 있는 사람이 말할 수 있는 반응으로 적절하지 않다.

16

★★ 직접의문문 How

그 레스토랑이 어떠셨나요?
(A) 네, 그는 아주 흥미로웠습니다.
(B) 저는 그것들이 매우 유익하다고 생각했습니다.
(C) 당신 말이 맞았어요. 음식이 아주 훌륭했습니다.

어휘 How did you like A? A는 어떠셨나요? interesting 흥미로운 find A 형용사 A가 ~하다고 생각하다 informative 유익한

How did you like the restaurant?

(A) Yes, he was so interesting.
(B) I found them very informative.
(C) You were right. The food was excellent.

특정 레스토랑이 마음에 들었는지를 묻는 How 의문문에 대해 상대방의 말이 맞았다는 말과 함께 음식이 아주 맛있었음을 의미하는 말로 답변하는 (C)가 정답이다.

(A)는 의문사 의문문에 어울리지 않는 Yes로 답변하는 오답이며, (B)는 자신의 의견을 말하는 답변이기는 하지만 질문에 나타나지 않은 대상을 지칭하는 복수 대명사 them에 대한 의견이므로 어울리지 않는 반응이다.

17

Was it Mr. Kayman who came up with the new project?

(A) Well, I'm not really sure.
(B) I've already renewed the lease.
(C) Yes, she came by earlier.

문제 해설

새로운 프로젝트를 제안한 사람이 Kayman 씨였는지를 묻는 의문문에 대해 잘 모르겠다는 말로 답변하는 (A)가 정답이다. '잘 모르겠다, 확인해 봐야 한다, 결정되지 않았다' 등과 같은 회피성 답변들은 대부분의 문제에서 정답 가능성이 높다는 점도 함께 기억해 두는 것이 좋다.

토익 분석

(B)는 new와 발음이 유사하게 들리는 renewed를 활용해 혼동을 유발하는 오답으로, 프로젝트를 제안한 당사자와는 전혀 관련이 없는 임대 계약 갱신에 관련된 말이므로 어울리지 않는 반응이다. (C)는 긍정을 나타내는 Yes로 답변이 시작되기는 하지만 남성을 나타내는 Mr. Kayman에 맞지 않는 she가 포함되어 있으므로 오답이다.

★★ 일반의문문

새로운 프로젝트를 제안한 사람이 Kayman 씨였나요?
(A) 저, 저는 잘 모르겠습니다.
(B) 저는 이미 임대 계약을 갱신했습니다.
(C) 네, 그녀가 아까 들렀습니다.

어휘 come up with (아이디어 등) ~을 제안하다, 내놓다 renew ~을 갱신하다 lease 임대 계약(서) come by 들르다

18

You'll be at the company banquet, won't you?

(A) Yes, but I might be a little late.
(B) I will come to the bank.
(C) He wanted you to attend the workshop.

문제 해설

상대방이 연회에 참석하는 것이 맞는지를 확인하는 부가의문문에 대해 긍정을 나타내는 Yes와 함께 늦게 도착할 수도 있음을 알리는 말을 덧붙인 (A)가 정답이다.

토익 분석

(B)는 banquet과 일부 발음이 유사하게 들리는 bank를 활용해 혼동을 유발하는 오답으로, 연회 참석과는 전혀 관련이 없는 정보를 언급하는 답변이다. (C)는 질문을 받는 자신이 아닌 대상을 알 수 없는 He에 대해 말하는 오답이다.

★★ 부가의문문

회사 연회에 오실 예정이신 것이 맞죠?
(A) 네, 하지만 조금 늦을 수도 있습니다.
(B) 저는 은행으로 갈 겁니다.
(C) 그는 당신이 워크숍에 참석하기를 원했어요.

어휘 banquet 연회 a little 조금, 약간 want A to do A가 ~하기를 원하다 attend ~에 참석하다

19

Which office is Mr. Park working at?

(A) I'll just walk home.
(B) Let's ask at the front desk.
(C) No, mine is on the second floor.

★★ 직접의문문 Which

Park 씨가 어느 사무실에서 근무하고 계시죠?
(A) 저는 그냥 집에 걸어서 갈게요.
(B) 프런트 데스크에 물어봅시다.
(C) 아뇨, 제 사무실은 2층에 있습니다.

어휘 walk home 집으로 걸어가다 mine 나의 것

문제 해설

Park 씨의 사무실 위치를 묻는 Which 의문문에 대해 프런트 데스크에 물어보자는 말로 해당 사무실을 확인할 수 있는 방법을 언급하는 (B)가 정답이다.

토익 분석

(A)는 working과 발음이 유사하게 들리는 walk를 활용해 혼동을 유발하는 답변으로, Park 씨의 사무실 위치가 아닌 자신의 이동 방법을 언급하는 오답이다. (C)는 의문사 의문문에 어울리지 않는 No로 답변하는 오답이다.

20

★★★ 평서문

여기 교육 설명서 10부가 있습니다.
(A) Ono 씨께서도 어제 신청하셨어요.
(B) 제가 커피를 좀 더 만들겠습니다.
(C) 그 기차는 매시 정각에 출발합니다.

어휘 copy 1부, 1장, 1권, 사본 training 교육 manual 설명서, 안내서 sign up 신청하다, 등록하다 leave 출발하다, 떠나다 every hour on the hour 매시 정각에

Here are ten copies of the training manual.

(A) Mr. Ono also signed up yesterday.
(B) I'll make some more coffee.
(C) The train leaves every hour on the hour.

문제 해설

물건을 건네줄 때 자주 쓰이는 표현인 'Here are ~'와 함께 교육 설명서 10부를 건네주는 상황에 해당되는 평서문에 대해 Ono 씨도 어제 신청했다는 말로 Ono 씨 또한 해당 자료를 필요로 한다는 의미를 나타내는 (A)가 정답이다.

토익 분석

(B)는 copies와 발음이 유사하게 들리는 coffee를 활용해 혼동을 유발한 오답으로, 교육 설명서를 건네주는 상황과 전혀 관련 없는 반응이다. (C)는 training과 일부 발음이 유사하게 들리는 train을 활용한 혼동 보기이며, 마찬가지로 교육 설명서를 건네주는 상황과 전혀 관련 없는 기차 출발 시간을 알리는 답변이므로 오답이다.

21

★★ 권유 제안 요청

시상식 만찬에서 연설을 해 주시겠습니까?
(A) 그럼요, 저는 정말로 기뻤어요.
(B) 제 생각에 그녀는 행사 장소에 제시간에 올 것 같습니다.
(C) 이번에는 어디에서 개최되는 거죠?

어휘 give a speech 연설을 하다 awards dinner 시상식 만찬 pleased 기쁜, 만족한 venue 행사 장소 in time 제시간에 be held 개최되다, 열리다

Would you please give a speech at the awards dinner?

(A) Sure, I was so pleased.
(B) I think she'll be at the venue in time.
(C) Where is it being held this time?

문제 해설

시상식 만찬에서 연설을 해 줄 수 있는지를 묻는 요청의문문에 대해 긍정 또는 부정에 해당되는 답변을 말하기에 앞서 결정을 내리는 데 필요한 조건으로서 개최 장소를 되묻는 (C)가 정답이다.

토익 분석

(A)는 긍정을 의미하는 Sure로 답변이 시작되고 있지만, 뒤에 이어지는 말에 과거 시제 동사가 쓰여 있으므로 앞으로의 일에 대해 요청하는 의미를 나타내는 질문과 시점이 맞지 않는 오답이다. (B)는 요청을 받는 자신의 의견이 아니라 대상을 알 수 없는 she의 행사 참석과 관련된 내용이므로 어울리지 않는 반응이다.

22

Should we try out the new burger place that just opened?

(A) Yeah, I heard the food there is excellent.
(B) I think you should try on a smaller one.
(C) We'll launch the new product soon.

문제 해설

새로운 햄버거 매장에 한 번 가 보자고 제안하는 의문문에 대해 긍정을 나타내는 Yeah와 함께 해당 음식점을 there로 지칭해 그곳의 음식이 뛰어나다는 말을 들었다는 의미에 해당되는 (A)가 정답이다.

토익 분석

(B)는 질문에 포함된 should try가 반복 활용된 답변으로, 식당이 아닌 의류 등을 착용해 보는 상황에 어울리는 말이므로 오답이다. (C)는 new를 반복 활용한 오답으로, 식당에 가 보는 것과는 관련 없는 신제품 출시를 언급하는 말이므로 어울리지 않는 반응이다.

23

The vending machine was fixed yesterday, right?

(A) It should be working now.
(B) I'm expecting an urgent fax.
(C) Yes, there will be a live band.

문제 해설

자판기가 어제 수리된 것이 맞는지를 확인하기 위한 부가의문문에 대해 해당 작업을 It으로 지칭해 지금쯤 작동될 것이라는 말로 답변하는 (A)가 정답이다.

토익 분석

(B)는 fixed와 발음이 유사한 fax를 활용한 오답으로, 기계 수리와 관련 없는 팩스 문서를 기다리고 있다는 의미를 나타내는 답변이므로 어울리지 않는다. (C)는 긍정을 나타내는 Yes로 답변이 시작되고 있지만, 뒤에 vending과 발음이 유사한 band를 활용한 오답으로, 마찬가지로 기계 수리와 관련 없는 답변에 해당된다.

24

Do you know how late the food court stays open?

(A) It opens at nine in the morning.
(B) It will close in ten minutes.
(C) I'm not sure how he did it.

푸드 코트가 얼마나 늦게까지 문을 여는지를 알고 있는지 묻는 의문문이므로 가까운 미래 시점에 문을 닫는다는 의미를 나타내는 (B)가 정답이다. 'in + 시간/기간'은 미래 시점을 나타내는 표현임을 기억해 두는 것이 좋다.

토익 분석

(A)는 open이 반복 활용된 답변으로, 질문이 문을 닫는 시점과 관련된 것인 반면에 문을 여는 시간을 알리는 말이므로 어울리지 않는 반응이다. (C)는 푸드 코드가 아니라 대상을 알 수 없는 he를 언급한 오답이다.

25

★★ 직접의문문 Why

저는 왜 인터넷에 연결되지 않는 거죠?
(A) 제가 한 번 확인해 볼게요.
(B) 중간 휴식 시간 동안에요.
(C) 아뇨, 그것들을 직접 바로잡으셔야 합니다.

어휘 connect to ~에 연결되다　take a look 한 번 보다　during ~ 동안, ~ 중에　intermission (연극 등의) 중간 휴식 시간　correct ~을 바로잡다, 수정하다　oneself (부사적으로) 직접, 스스로

Why can't I connect to the Internet?
(A) Let me take a look.
(B) During the intermission.
(C) No, you should correct them yourself.

문제 해설

인터넷에 접속할 수 없었던 이유를 묻는 Why 의문문에 대해 '한 번 확인해 보겠다'는 말로 자신이 그 원인을 파악해 보겠다는 의미에 해당되는 (A)가 정답이다.

토익 분석

(B)는 internet과 일부 발음이 유사한 intermission을 활용한 오답으로, 인터넷 접속과는 전혀 관련이 없는 '중간 휴식 시간'을 언급하는 답변이므로 어울리지 않는다. (C)는 의문사 의문문에 어울리지 않는 No로 답변하는 오답이다.

26

★★ 일반의문문

우리가 전화번호부에서 찾은 파티 공급 업체들에게 연락하실 건가요?
(A) 그에게 길을 좀 알려 주시겠어요?
(B) 네, 저는 정말로 놀랐어요.
(C) Brian 씨에게 그 일을 하도록 요청했어요.

어휘 contact ~에게 연락하다　supplier 공급업체　phone directory 전화번호부　directions 찾아가는 길, 방향　surprised 놀란　ask A to do A에게 ~하도록 요청하다

Will you contact the party suppliers we found in the phone directory?
(A) Can you give him directions?
(B) Yes, I was so surprised.
(C) I asked Brian to do it.

문제 해설

전화번호부에서 찾은 파티 공급 업체에 연락해 볼 것인지를 묻는 의문문에 대해 그와 같은 일을 it으로 지칭해 자신이 아닌 다른 사람에게 부탁했다는 의미를 나타내는 (C)가 정답이다.

토익 분석

(A)는 대상을 알 수 없는 him을 언급한 오답으로, directory와 발음이 유사한 directions를 활용해 혼동을 유발하는 답변이다. (B)는 긍정을 나타내는 Yes로 답변이 시작되고 있지만, suppliers와 발음이 유사하게 들리는 surprised를 활용해 혼동을 유발하는 답변으로 자신의 감정을 말하는 내용이므로 오답이다.

27

Who's going to be the new manager for accounting?

(A) Sure, I can finish counting them.
(B) It will be announced tomorrow.
(C) Don't worry! I'm used to it.

문제 해설

회계부의 신임 부서장이 누가 될 것인지를 묻는 Who 의문문에 대해 해당 직책을 It으로 지칭해 내일 발표될 것이라는 말로 아직 알 수 없다는 의미에 해당되는 (B)가 정답이다.

토익 분석

(A)는 긍정을 나타내는 Sure로 답변이 시작되고 있으므로 Yes와 마찬가지로 의문사 의문문에 어울리지 않는 반응이다. (C)는 Who와 관련 없는 답변으로 걱정하지 말라는 말로 상대방을 안심시킬 때 쓰이는 표현이므로 오답이다.

★★ 직접의문문 Who

누가 회계부의 신임 부서장이 되실 예정인가요?
(A) 그럼요, 그것들을 세는 일을 완료할 수 있습니다.
(B) 그건 내일 발표될 겁니다.
(C) 걱정하지 마세요! 저는 그것에 익숙합니다.

어휘 accounting 회계(부) finish -ing ~하는 것을 완료하다, 끝내다 announce ~을 발표하다 be used to ~에 익숙하다

28

Teddy gave us one more day to complete the remaining work.

(A) Really? I walk home too.
(B) You should enter the competition.
(C) Great, let's finish the rest tomorrow then.

문제 해설

남은 작업을 완료할 수 있도록 하루의 시간이 더 생겼다는 의미를 나타내는 평서문에 대해 그에 따른 결과로 나머지 작업을 내일 하자고 제안하는 (C)가 정답이다.

토익 분석

(A)는 놀라움을 나타내는 Really?로 답변이 시작되고 있지만, work와 발음이 유사하게 들리는 walk를 활용한 오답으로 이동 방식을 나타내는 말이므로 어울리지 않는 반응이다. (B)는 complete과 일부 발음이 유사하게 들리는 competition를 활용한 오답으로, 마찬가지로 작업 일정과 전혀 어울리지 않는 반응이다.

★★★ 평서문

남은 작업을 완료할 수 있도록 Teddy 씨가 우리에게 하루를 더 주셨어요.
(A) 정말인가요? 저도 집에 걸어 다녀요.
(B) 당신은 대회에 참가해야 합니다.
(C) 잘됐네요, 그럼 남은 일은 내일 끝냅시다.

어휘 complete ~을 완료하다 remaining 남아 있는 walk home 집에 걸어가다 enter ~에 참가하다 competition 대회, 경연 대회 rest 나머지, 남은 것 then 그럼, 그렇다면

29

Why didn't you finish the paperwork first?

(A) Thank you, that would be really helpful.
(B) I'm sorry, I forgot.
(C) Yes, we can do that.

★★ 직접의문문 Why

왜 문서 작업을 먼저 끝내지 않으신 거죠?
(A) 감사합니다, 그렇게 해 주시면 정말로 도움이 될 겁니다.
(B) 죄송합니다, 제가 깜빡 잊었습니다.
(C) 네, 그렇게 해 드릴 수 있습니다.

어휘 finish ~을 완료하다, 끝내다 paperwork 문서 작업 helpful 도움이 되는 forget 깜빡 잊다

문제 해설

문서 작업을 먼저 끝내지 않은 이유를 묻는 Why 의문문에 대해 사과의 의미를 나타내는 말과 함께 깜빡 잊었다는 말로 그 이유를 언급하는 (B)가 정답이다.

토익 분석

(A)는 감사의 표현과 함께 도움이 될 것이라는 의미를 나타내는 말이므로 문서 작업이 먼저 완료되지 않은 이유를 묻는 질문에 어울리지 않는 반응이며, (C)는 의문사 의문문에 맞지 않는 Yes로 답변하는 오답이다.

30

★★★ 평서문

공항으로 가는 셔틀버스가 곧 이곳으로 올 겁니다.
(A) 그 버스는 20분마다 한 번씩 운행합니다.
(B) 그는 항공편 일정을 재조정하기를 원했어요.
(C) 제가 Yamamoto 씨께 알려 드릴게요.

어휘 soon 곧, 머지않아 run (교통편이) 운행되다 every twenty minutes 20분마다 한 번씩 reschedule ~의 일정을 재조정하다 flight 항공편 let A know A에게 알리다

The shuttle bus to the airport will be here soon.

(A) The bus runs every twenty minutes.
(B) He wanted to reschedule the flight.
(C) I'll let Mr. Yamamoto know.

문제 해설

공항으로 가는 셔틀버스가 곧 도착한다는 의미를 나타내는 평서문에 대해 이와 같은 정보를 다른 사람에게도 알려 주겠다는 뜻에 해당되는 (C)가 정답이다.

토익 분석

(A)는 bus를 반복 활용해 버스의 운행 주기를 언급하는 답변으로서, 일반적인 운행 빈도를 나타내는 말이므로 가까운 미래 시점에 도착할 셔틀버스에 대해 알리는 평서문에 어울리지 않는 반응이다. (B)는 대상을 알 수 없는 He를 언급하는 답변으로, airport와 연관성 있게 들리는 flight를 활용한 오답이다.

31

★★★ 평서문

저는 그 레스토랑에 관한 아주 좋은 후기를 읽었어요.
(A) 네, 저희에게는 멋진 바다 경관을 지닌 객실이 있습니다.
(B) 면접이 아주 잘 진행되었습니다.
(C) 저도 그랬어요.

어휘 review 이용 후기, 의견, 평가 view 경관, 풍경 go well 잘 진행되다 So do I 저도 그렇습니다

I read some great reviews of the restaurant.

(A) Yes, we had a room with a nice ocean view.
(B) The interview went very well.
(C) So did I.

문제 해설

특정 레스토랑에 관한 이용 후기를 읽어 봤다는 의미를 나타내는 평서문에 대해 자신도 그랬다는 의미에 해당되는 표현으로 공감을 나타내는 (C)가 정답이다.

토익 분석

(A)는 reviews와 일부 발음이 유사한 view를 활용한 오답으로, 레스토랑 이용 후기가 아닌 객실의 경관을 언급한 답변이므로 어울리지 않는 반응이다. (B)도 reviews와 일부 발음이 유사한 interview를 활용한 오답으로, 마찬가지로 레스토랑 이용 후기가 아닌 면접 진행 상황을 알리는 답변이므로 어울리지 않는 반응이다.

PART 3

Questions 32-34 refer to the following conversation.

M   Hello, Penny. 32 Congratulations on your new position at Wilson Contractors. How is it going over there? We all miss you back at the office.

W   Hi, Marcus. Everything is going pretty well so far. But things aren't as organized as they are back at Scully Corporation.

M   Oh, really? I thought Wilson would be a very professionally run company

W   33 There have been a few problems. For example, I received my pay late for my first two months.

M   34 Oh, you don't say. I am sorry to hear that. Did you complain about it?

W   Not yet, but I certainly will if it happens again this month.

어휘 miss ~을 그리워하다 go well 잘 되어 가다 pretty 매우, 아주 so far 지금까지 organized 체계적인, 정리된 professionally-run 전문적으로 운영되는 for example 예를 들어 receive ~을 받다 pay 급여 you don't say 설마 그럴까요 complain about ~에 대해 불평하다 not yet 아직 아니다 certainly 분명히 happen 발생하다

남   안녕하세요, Penny. 32 Wilson Contractors 사에서 새로 맡은 직책에 대해 축하 드립니다. 그곳에서는 어떻게 지내고 계세요? 우리는 모두 당신이 사무실에 있던 때를 그리워하고 있어요.

여   안녕하세요, Marcus. 지금까지는 모든 일이 아주 잘 되어 가고 있어요. 하지만 Scully Corporation에서만큼 일들이 체계적이지는 않아요.

남   아, 그래요? 저는 Wilson 사가 매우 전문적으로 운영되는 회사일 거라고 생각했어요.

여   33 몇몇 문제가 있었어요. 예를 들면, 근무를 시작한 지 첫 두 달 동안은 급여를 늦게 받았어요.

남   34 아, 설마 그런 일이 있을 줄은 몰랐어요. 그 얘기를 듣게 되어 유감입니다. 그 일에 대해 불만을 제기했었나요?

여   아직이요, 하지만 이번 달에 같은 일이 다시 일어나면 분명 그렇게 할 겁니다.

32

What has the woman recently done?

(A) Trained some staff   (B) Moved overseas
(C) Started a new job   (D) Requested a promotion

문제 해설

여자가 최근에 한 일을 묻는 첫 번째 질문이므로 대화 초반부에서 '최근'이라는 과거 시점과 관련해 여자가 한 일로 제시되는 정보를 파악해야 한다. 남자가 'Congratulations on your new position at Wilson Contractors.'라는 말로 축하 인사를 건네고 있는데, 새로운 회사에서의 직책에 대해 축하하는 것이므로 여자는 최근에 이직했음을 알 수 있다. 따라서 이에 대해 언급한 (C)가 정답이 된다.

★★ 세부 정보

여자는 최근에 무엇을 했는가?
(A) 일부 직원 교육했다.   (B) 해외로 이주했다.
(C) 새로운 일을 시작했다. (D) 승진을 요청했다.

어휘 overseas 해외로 request ~을 요청하다 promotion 승진

토익 분석

첫 번째 문제인 만큼 최근에 여자에게 일어난 일이 대화의 주제가 된다. 주제가 대화 초반부 첫 번째, 두 번째 문장에 제시된다는 것을 기억해야 한다.

33

What problem does the woman mention?

(A) Her workspace is untidy.   (B) Her Internet connection is slow.
(C) Her supervisor is inexperienced. **(D) Her salary was paid late.**

문제 해설

여자가 언급하는 문제점을 묻는 두 번째 질문이므로 대화 중반부에서 여자가 특정 문제점과 함께 걱정이나 우려 등을 나타내는 표현을 통해 언급하는 정보를 파악해야 한다. 대화 중반부에 여자는 'There have been a few problems. For example, I have received my pay late for my first two months of working.'라는 말로 자신이 겪은 문제점에 대해 언급하고 있는데, 여기서 핵심은 급여가 늦게 지급된 것이므로 (D)가 정답임을 알 수 있다.

★ 문제점

여자는 무슨 문제점을 언급하는가?
(A) 자신의 근무지가 지저분하다.
(B) 자신의 인터넷 연결이 느리다.
(C) 자신의 상사가 경험이 없다.
(D) 자신의 급여가 늦게 지급되었다.

어휘 untidy 지저분한, 정리가 안 된 supervisor 상사, 책임자, 부서장 inexperienced 경험이 없는

토익 분석

여자 대화에서 problem이 키워드로 반복 사용되었다. 문두 부사구 for example 역시 답을 제시하는 힌트다.

34

Why does the man say, "Oh, you don't say"?

(A) He is surprised by the information.
(B) He thinks the woman is exaggerating.
(C) He misheard the woman's response.
(D) He would like to discuss something in more detail.

문제 해설

남자가 말하는 "Oh, you don't say"이라는 표현이 대화 속에서 어떤 의미로 사용되었는지를 묻는 세 번째 질문이므로 대화 후반부에 제시되는 남자의 말을 통해 해당 표현을 확인할 수 있어야 하며, 이때 앞뒤에 함께 제시되는 말들을 통해 의미의 흐름을 파악해 정답을 찾아야 한다. 남자는 대화 후반부에 'Oh, you don't say. I am sorry to hear that. Did you complain about it?'라는 말로 앞서 여자가 급여를 받지 못했던 상황에 대해 말한 것에 반응하고 있는데, 유감이라는 말과 함께 불만을 제기해 봤는지 묻는 것으로 볼 때, 해당 상황에 대한 놀라움을 나타내기 위해 'Oh, you don't say'라고 말했음을 알 수 있다. 따라서 이와 같은 의미에 대해 언급한 (A)가 정답이 된다.

★★★ 맥락 파악

남자는 왜 "Oh, you don't say"라고 말하는가?
(A) 정보에 대해 놀라고 있다.
(B) 여자가 과장하고 있다고 생각한다.
(C) 여자의 반응을 잘못 알아들었다.
(D) 뭔가를 더 자세히 논의하고 싶어 한다.

어휘 be surprised by ~에 대해 놀라다 exaggerate 과장하다 mishear ~을 잘못 알아듣다 discuss ~을 논의하다

토익 분석

앞뒤 문장의 flow 파악이 중요하다. 또한 구어체 표현의 사전적 의미를 알면 답을 찾는데 도움이 된다. you don't say 는 설마(그럴 리가)의 뜻이다.

남 안녕하세요. ³⁵ 제가 새로운 차를 찾고 있는데, 되도록 연비가 정말로 좋은 것이면 좋겠어요. 그러한 차를 보유하고 계신가요?

여 물론입니다. 최근 유가로 인해, 모든 분이 이곳에 오셔서 경제적인 연비에 관해 문의하고 계세요. 바로 이쪽에 있는 것들이 저희가 보유하고 있는 연비가 가장 좋은 모델입니다. 여기 있는 Selena는 성인 다섯 명이 편안하게 앉을 수 있을 만큼 충분한 공간이 있는 자동 변속기 모델입니다. 연비에 관해서라면 저희 재고 차량 중의 그 어느 것보다 가장 높은 등급을 받았습니다. ³⁶ 또한, 차량 제조업체로부터 1,500달러의 환급을 받으실 수 있습니다.

남 아주 멋져 보이는 자동차네요. 내부 인테리어도 아주 마음에 들고요. ³⁷ 그런데 차량이 조금 많이 크네요. 저희는 두 명뿐이라서, 이렇게 큰 차량은 필요하지 않거든요. 이것보다 약간 더 작은 차량도 있을까요?

여 그럼요, 저희는 모든 분을 위한 모든 종류의 차량들을 보유하고 있습니다. 바로 이쪽을 보시면 기본적으로 같은 차량이지만 좀 더 크기가 작으면서 스포티한 모델이 있습니다. 소규모 가족에게 이상적인 차량입니다.

Questions 35-37 refer to the following conversation.

M Hi. ³⁵ I'm looking for a new car, preferably something that is really fuel efficient. Do you have anything like that?

W Of course. With the price of gas today, everyone is in here asking about fuel economy. Right over here are our most fuel-efficient models. This one, the Selena, is an automatic with enough room for five adults to sit comfortably. It has the highest rating of any car on the lot in terms of fuel efficiency. ³⁶ There is also a manufacturer's rebate of $1,500.

M It's a very nice-looking car. I like the interior a lot ³⁷ but It's a bit too big though. There are only two of us, and we don't need such a large vehicle. Do you have anything that is a bit smaller?

W Sure, we have all kinds of cars for all kinds of people. Over here is basically the same car but in a smaller and sportier design. It's ideal for small families.

어휘 look for ~을 찾다 preferably 가급적이면 fuel efficient 연비가 좋은 right over here 바로 이쪽에 automatic 자동 변속기 차량 enough 충분한 seating 좌석 (공간) comfortably 편안하게 rating 등급, 순위, 평가 lot 부지, 주차장 in terms of ~에 관해서라면 rebate 환불, 환급 basically 기본적으로 sporty 스포티한 ideal 이상적인

35

★ 의도 파악

남자는 자동차의 주로 어떤 부분을 찾아보고 있는가?
(A) 디자인 독창성 　　(B) 인테리어 공간
(C) 시장 가치 　　(D) 연비 효율성

어휘 value 가치, 값어치 fuel 연료 efficiency 효율성

토익 분석

첫 번째 문제로 남자의 초반 대화에 집중해야 한다. 의도를 설명하는 I'm looking for~가 답의 단서를 제시하는 표현이다.

What is the man mainly looking for in a car?

(A) Design originality 　　(B) Interior space
(C) Market value 　　**(D) Fuel efficiency**

문제 해설

남자가 중시하는 자동차의 특성을 묻는 첫 번째 질문이므로 대화 초반부 남자의 말에서 특히 중점을 두고 있는 특성이 있음을 예상하고 들어야 한다. 남자는 대화 시작과 함께 'I'm looking for a new car, preferably something that is really fuel efficient.'라고 말하며 연비가 좋은 신차를 찾고 있음을 밝히고 있으므로 (D)가 정답임을 알 수 있다.

36

★★ 요청, 제안

여자에 따르면, 현재 자동차 구매자들에게 제공되는 혜택은 무엇인가?
(A) 상품권 　　(B) 부분적인 환불
(C) 무료 자동차 보험 　　(D) 무이자 대출

어휘 currently 현재 gift certificate 상품권 refund 환불 insurance 보험 zero-percent loan 무이자 대출

토익 분석

뭔가 제공을 하는 offer유형의 문제는 언제나 할인이나 무료 관련 표현이 등장한다. 이 문제 역시 rebate이 언급되었고 반전 표현 also도 답의 단서를 제공한다.

According to the woman, what is currently being offered to car buyers?

(A) A gift certificate 　　**(B) A partial refund**
(C) Free auto insurance 　　(D) A zero-percent loan

문제 해설

자동차 구매자에게 제공되는 혜택이 무엇인지 묻는 두 번째 질문이므로 대화 중반부에서 언급되는 특정 혜택이나 이점 등과 관련된 정보를 파악하는 데 집중해야 한다. 여자가 대화 중반부에 Selena라는 자동차를 소개하면서 'There is also a manufacturer's rebate of $1,500'이라는 말로 제조업체가 1,500달러를 환급해 준다는 정보를 제공하고 있으므로 '부분적인 환불'을 뜻하는 (B)가 정답이다. 참고로, rebate는 비용의 환급을 의미하는 말이므로 할인(discount), 부분 환불(partial refund), 또는 보상(reward) 등으로 바뀌어 표현될 수 있다.

37

★★ 의도 파악

남자가 여자에게 다른 자동차 모델을 보여 달라고 요청하는 이유는 무엇인가?
(A) 고급 차량을 원한다.
(B) 디자인이 멋진 도시형 차량을 원한다.
(C) 좀 더 저렴한 차량을 원한다.
(D) 좀 더 작은 크기의 차량을 원한다.

어휘 urban 도시적인 less expensive 덜 비싼

토익 분석

반전 표현 but이 요청에 대한 이유를 제공하고 있다. 이어지는 문장에 의문문 Do you~?가 요청 문장이다.

Why does the man ask the woman to show another car model?

(A) He wants a luxury car. 　　(B) He wants a stylish urban car.
(C) He wants a less expensive car. 　　**(D) He wants a car in a smaller size.**

문제 해설

남자가 다른 차량을 보여 달라고 요청하는 이유를 묻는 마지막 문제이므로 대화 후반부에서 이와 같은 요청 사항과 함께 그 이유가 언급될 것임을 예상하고 들어야 한다. 남자는 대화 후반부에 'It's a bit too big though. There are only two of us, and we don't need such a large vehicle. Do you have anything that is a bit smaller?'라는 말로 크기가 더 작은 차량이 있는지 묻고 있으므로 차량 크기에 대해 언급한 (D)가 정답이다.

Questions 38-40 refer to the following conversation.

M Thanks for calling Jim's Supplement Outlet. This is Jim. What can I do for you today?

W [38] Hi, Jim. This is May from City Health Club on Heaton Road. [51] You made a delivery of protein powder to us yesterday and some of the tubs seem to be damaged.

M [39] Are you serious? I'm sorry to hear that. How many are damaged?

W There are eight of them. They are unsellable.

M OK. [40] We actually hire another company to make deliveries for us, so I'll go ahead and give them a call. I'll contact you when I figure out what went wrong.

어휘 make a delivery of ~을 배송하다 protein 단백질 tub 통 seem to do ~한 것 같다 damaged 손상된 unsellable 판매할 수 없는 actually 실은, 사실은 hire ~을 고용하다 go ahead 어서 하다 give A a call A에게 전화하다 contact ~에게 연락하다 figure out ~을 알아내다 go wrong 잘못되다

남 Jim's Supplement Outlet에 전화 주셔서 감사합니다. 저는 Jim입니다. 오늘 무엇을 도와 드릴까요?
여 [38] 안녕하세요, Jim. 저는 Heaton Road에 있는 City Health Club의 May입니다. [51] 어제 저희에게 단백질 파우더를 배송해 주셨는데, 몇몇 통이 손상된 것 같아요.
남 [39] 정말인가요? 그 말씀을 들으니 유감이네요. 몇 개나 손상되었나요?
여 총 8개에요. 판매할 수 없게 됐어요.
남 알겠습니다. [40] 실은 저희를 위해 배송을 해 주는 회사를 새로 고용한 상태라서 제가 어서 그 회사에 전화해 보겠습니다. 무엇이 잘못됐는지 확인해 보고 연락 드리겠습니다.

38

Where does the woman work?

(A) At a restaurant
(B) At a theater
(C) At a health food store
(D) **At a fitness center**

문제 해설

여자의 근무 장소에 대해 유추할 것을 요구하는 첫 번째 질문이므로 대화 초반부에서 여자가 하는 일과 관련해 직접적으로 언급되는 부분, 혹은 이를 추측할 수 있을 만한 관련 어휘가 제시되는 부분에 집중해야 한다. 여자는 대화 초반부에 'Hey, Jim. This is May from City Health Club on Heaton Road.'라는 말을 통해 자신이 일하는 곳을 밝히고 있는데, 'City Health Club'의 업체 종류에 해당하는 보기가 (D)이다.

★ **도입부 정보**

여자는 어디에서 근무하는가?
(A) 레스토랑에서 (B) 극장에서
(C) 건강식품 매장에서 (D) 피트니스 센터에서

어휘 real estate agent 부동산 중개업자 professor 교수

토익 분석

여자가 근무하는 장소이므로 여자의 첫 번째 대화문에 답이 나오는 유형이며, 이 부분에 언급된 업체명이 정답의 단서다.

39

Why does the man say, "Are you serious"?

(A) To show appreciation
(B) **To express disbelief**
(C) To agree with a statement
(D) To change the topic

문제 해설

남자가 말하는 "Are you serious"라는 표현이 대화 속에서 어떤 의미로 사용되었는지를 묻는 두 번째 질문이므로 대화 중반부에 제시되는 남자의 말을 통해 해당 표현을 확인할 수 있어야 하며, 이때 앞뒤에 함께 제시되는 말들을 통해 의미의 흐름을 파악해 정답을 찾아야 한다. 이 표현은 '정말인가요?'라는 뜻으로 쓰이는데, 대화의 중반부에 여자가 'You made a delivery of protein powder to us yesterday and some of the tubs seem to be damaged.'라고 알리는 말에 대해 해당 표현을 사용해 대답하고 있으므로 제품이 손상됐다는 말에 대해 놀라움을 표현하고 있음을 알 수 있다. 따라서 '믿기지 않음을 표현하고 있다'라는 의미로 쓰인 (B)가 정답이 된다.

★★★ **맥락 파악**

왜 남자가 "Are you serious"라고 말하는가?
(A) 감사를 하기 위해
(B) 믿기지 않음을 표현하기 위해
(C) 여자의 말에 동의하기 위해
(D) 화제를 바꾸기 위해

어휘 make an apology 사과하다 express ~을 표현하다 disbelief 믿기지 않음, 불신감 agree with ~에 동의하다 statement 말, 진술

토익 분석

'Are you serious?'는 '놀라움'이나 '불신' 등을 의미한다.

40

What will the man probably do next?

(A) Make a delivery
(B) Refund an order
(C) Visit a supplier
(D) **Make a phone call**

문제 해설

남자의 추후 행동을 묻는 마지막 질문이며, 이에 대한 단서는 대화 후반부 또는 최종 화자의 말에서 제시되는 경우가 일반적이다. 대화의 마지막에 남자는 'We actually hire another company to make deliveries for us, so I'll go ahead and give them a phone call.'라는 말로 새로 고용한 회사에 전화해 보겠다는 뜻을 나타내고 있으므로 (D)가 정답임을 알 수 있다.

★★ **미래 행동**

남자는 곧이어 무엇을 할 것 같은가?
(A) 물품 배송을 한다. (B) 주문품에 대해 환불해 준다.
(C) 공급업체를 방문한다. (D) 전화를 건다.

어휘 refund ~을 환불해 주다 order 주문(품) supplier 공급업체 make a phone call 전화하다

토익 분석

남자의 가장 후반부 대화에서 의도나 미래 행동 답변을 이끌어 주는 표현을 찾아야 한다. I'll~이 정답에 대한 단서가 되었으며 반전 표현 So 역시 답을 찾는데 도움이 되었다.

남 안녕하세요, Hoffman 씨. ⁴¹ 저는 London에 위치한 미국 대사관에서 연락 드리는 Joshua Pack이라고 합니다. 저는 귀하의 비자가 발급되었음을 알려 드리고자 합니다. ⁴² 내일 방문하셔서 수령해 가시기 바랍니다.

여 네, 전화 주셔서 감사합니다. ⁴² 그런데 제가 내일은 일정이 많아서 방문이 어려울 것 같습니다. 제 남편이 대신 가서 수령해도 괜찮겠습니까?

남 네, 남편께서 하셔도 됩니다만, 귀하와의 관계를 입증할 수 있는 일종의 법적인 서류를 가져오셔야 합니다. ⁴³ 또한, 이미 아실지도 모르겠지만, 소정의 수수료를 내시면, 저희가 귀하께 비자를 배송해 드릴 수도 있습니다.

여 그렇게 해 주시면 정말 좋겠어요. ⁴³ 그 배송 서비스를 이용하려면 얼마를 지불해야 하는지 알려 주세요.

Questions 41-43 refer to the following conversation.

M Hello, Ms. Hoffman. ⁴¹ It's Joshua Pack calling from the US Embassy in London. I just want to let you know that your visa has been issued. ⁴² Please visit us and pick it up tomorrow.

W OK, thank you for calling. ⁴² But I have a full schedule tomorrow. Would it be OK if my husband came and picked it up?

M Yes, he can, but he should bring some sort of legal document proving his relationship to you. ⁴³ In addition, I don't know if you already know this, but for a small fee, we can have it delivered to you.

W That would be really good. ⁴³ Please let me know how much I need to pay for your delivery service.

어휘 visa 사증, 비자 issue ~을 발급하다 pick A up A를 가져 가다/오다 Would it be ok if ~? ~해도 괜찮을까요? sort 종류 legal 법적인 document 서류 prove ~을 입증/증명하다 relationship 관계 small fee 소정의 비용 have A p.p. A가 ~되게 하다 deliver ~을 배송하다 pay for ~에 대한 비용을 지불하다

41

★ 도입부 정보

남자는 어디에서 근무하는가?
(A) 우체국에서
(B) 항공사에서
(C) 외교 기관에서
(D) 소매점에서

어휘 diplomatic 외교의 institution 기관, 협회

토익 분석

남자가 근무하는 장소이므로 남자의 첫 번째 대화 문장에 힌트가 등장한다.

Where does the man work?

(A) At a post office
(B) At an airline
(C) At a diplomatic institution
(D) At a retailer

문제 해설

남자의 근무지가 어디인지 묻는 첫 번째 질문이므로 대화 초반부에서 남자가 근무하는 곳의 이름이나 업무적 특성 등과 관련된 정보를 찾아야 한다. 남자는 대화 초반부에 인사말과 함께 'It's Joshua Pack calling from the U.S. Embassy in London.'이라는 말로 런던에 위치한 미국 대사관에서 근무하는 사람임을 밝히고 있으므로 이와 같은 곳을 지칭하는 보기에 해당되는 (C)가 정답이다.

42

★★ 문제점

여자가 우려하는 것은 무엇인가?
(A) 예산을 초과하는 것
(B) 면접에 늦게 도착하는 것
(C) 방문할 수 없다는 것
(D) 비자를 받지 못하는 것

어휘 be worried about ~에 대해 걱정하다 exceed ~을 초과하다 budget 예산 be unable to do ~할 수 없다 fail to do ~하지 못하다

토익 분석

여자의 대화 문장에서 반전 표현인 but과 요청, 제안 힌트인 would it be ok if~?가 문제점에 대한 단서를 제시하고 있다.

What is the woman worried about?

(A) Exceeding a budget
(B) Arriving late for an interview
(C) Being unable to visit
(D) Failing to get a visa

문제 해설

여자의 우려하는 내용에 대해 묻는 두 번째 문제이므로 대화 중반부 여자의 말에서 걱정이나 문제점 등과 같이 부정적인 말이 제시되는 부분이 있음을 예상하고 들어야 한다. 남자가 연락한 이유를 들은 여자는 'But I have a full schedule tomorrow. Would it be ok if my husband came and picked it up?'이라는 말로 자신을 대신해 남편이 수령해도 되는지 묻고 있으므로 자신이 방문할 수 없다는 점을 걱정하고 있음을 알 수 있으므로 (C)가 정답임을 알 수 있다.

43

★ 요청, 제안

여자가 남자에게 물어본 것은 무엇인가?
(A) 등록 절차
(B) 유효 기간
(C) 배송 시간
(D) 서비스 요금

어휘 registration 등록 expiration date 유효 기간 fee 요금

토익 분석

질문 속에 ask가 등장할 경우 요청, 제안 유형의 문제다. '의문문'이나 정보 요청 '명령문'이 정답 단서를 제시한다. please let me know~가 정답 힌트로 사용되었다.

What does the woman ask the man about?

(A) A registration procedure
(B) An expiration date
(C) A delivery time
(D) A service fee

문제 해설

여자 후반부 대화에 명령문 'Please let me know how much I need to pay for your delivery service.'에서 여자는 남자에게 배송 서비스 비용에 관해 문의하고 있으니 (D)가 정답이다.

Questions 44-46 refer to the following conversation.

W   Hi. ⁴⁴ I bought one of your toasters a while ago. It was working fine until now. I think there is something wrong with the timer.

M   Sorry to hear that. You have two options. ⁴⁵ You can return the product and get a refund if it has been less than a month since you purchased it. Or we can send someone that can help you with the toaster. The latter will cost you a fee.

W   I see. ⁴⁶ I think I purchased it less than a month ago, but I am not really sure. I don't think I kept the receipt for it, so I can't check.

M   If you are registered in our system, you may have received an e-mail when you purchased it. Why don't you check that? If you need a technician, I can transfer you to our aftersales department.

어휘 a while ago 얼마 전에 work fine 잘 작동되다 option 선택 사항 return ~을 반품/반납하다 get a refund 환불을 받다 less than ~미만의 since ~이후로, ~이기 때문에 help A with B B에 대해 A를 돕다 the latter 후자 cost A B A에게 B의 비용이 들게 하다 fee 요금, 수수료 receipt 영수증, 수령 register ~을 등록시키다 may have p.p. ~했을 수도 있다 transfer A to B (전화상에서) A를 B로 연결시켜 주다

여   안녕하세요. ⁴⁴ 제가 얼마 전에 귀사의 토스터기를 구매했어요. 지금까지 잘 작동되고 있었어요. 타이머에 뭔가 문제가 있는 것 같아요.

남   그 말씀을 듣게 되어 유감입니다. 두 가지 선택 사항이 있습니다. ⁴⁵ 만약 제품이 구매하신 후 한 달 미만이 된 것이라면 제품을 반납하시고 환불을 받으실 수 있습니다. 또는 저희가 토스터기 문제를 도와 드릴 직원을 보내 드릴 수 있습니다. 후자의 경우 비용이 발생될 수 있습니다.

여   알겠습니다. ⁴⁶ 구매한 지 아직 한 달이 안 된 걸로 알고 있는데, 정확히는 모르겠습니다. 제가 영수증을 보관한 것 같지 않아서 확인할 수가 없네요.

남   만약 고객님께서 저희 회사 시스템에 등록되어 있으시다면, 고객님께서 제품을 구매하셨을 때 이메일을 수신하셨을 수도 있습니다. 그것을 한 번 확인해 보시겠습니까? 만약 기술자가 필요하면, 제품 관리 부서로 전화를 연결해 드리도록 하겠습니다.

44

What problem does the woman mention?

(A) The repair costs are too high.
(B) An item she purchased is not working properly.
(C) Her repair request has not been processed yet.
(D) Her product is too complicated to operate.

문제 해설

여자가 언급하고 있는 문제점에 대해 묻고 있으므로 대화 초반부 여자의 말에서 제시되는 문제점을 노려 들어야 한다. 여자는 대화 시작과 함께 'I bought~the timer.'라고 말하며 얼마 전에 구매한 토스터기의 타이머에 뭔가 문제가 있음을 언급하고 있다. 따라서 제대로 작동하지 않는다는 의미를 나타내는 (B)가 정답이다.

★ **문제점**

여자가 언급하고 있는 문제점은 무엇인가?
(A) 수리비가 너무 비싸다.
(B) 자신이 구매한 상품이 제대로 작동하지 않는다.
(C) 자신의 수리 신청이 아직도 처리되지 않았다.
(D) 자신의 제품이 작동하기가 너무 복잡하다.

어휘 repair 수리 properly 제대로, 적당히 process ~을 처리하다 too A to do ~하기에는 너무 A하다 complicated 복잡한 operate ~을 작동/가동하다

토익 분석

'남자 또는 여자의 문제점'을 묻는 경우 대화의 남자 또는 여자의 첫 번째 문장에 답이 등장한다.

45

Why does the man need to know the purchase date?

(A) To record the incident   (B) To check out the inventory
(C) To find out the average life span of the product
(D) To determine if the woman can get her money back

문제 해설

남자가 구매 일자를 알아야 하는 이유에 대해 묻고 있으므로 대화 중반부 남자의 말에서 구매 일자 혹은 제품 구매와 관련된 내용이 제시되는 부분에 집중해야 한다. 남자는 대화 중반부에 'You can return the product and get a refund if it has been less than a month since you purchased it.'라는 말로 구매한 지 한 달이 되지 않았으면 제품을 반납하고 환불받을 수 있음을 알리고 있다. 따라서 제품 환불을 위해 구매 일자를 확인하려는 것임을 알 수 있으므로 (D)가 정답이다.

★★ **세부 정보**

남자가 구매 일자를 알아야 하는 이유는 무엇인가?
(A) 사고를 기록하기 위해서 (B) 재고를 확인하기 위해서
(C) 제품의 평균 수명 기간을 파악하기 위해서
(D) 여자가 환불을 받을 수 있는지를 결정하기 위해서

어휘 incident 사고 check out ~을 확인하다 inventory 재고(품) average 평균의 life span 수명 determine ~을 결정하다 get A back A를 돌려받다

토익 분석

답의 단서를 요청, 제안의 힌트가 되는 'You can~, if 가정법 ~'이 제시하고 있다. purchase 역시 키워드로 활용되었다.

46

Why does the woman say she doesn't remember when she bought the product?

(A) She has a poor memory.   (B) She didn't check her e-mail.
(C) She received it as a gift.   **(D) She lost her receipt.**

문제 해설

여자가 제품 구매 일자를 기억하지 못하는 이유에 대해 묻는 마지막 질문이므로 대화 후반부 여자의 말에서 구매 일자를 기억하지 못한다는 사실과 그 이유가 언급될 것임을 예상하고 들어야 한다. 여자는 대화 후반부에 'I think~I can't check.'라는 말을 통해 영수증을 보관하지 않아서 확인할 수가 없음을 밝히고 있다. 따라서 이에 대해 언급한 (D)가 정답이다.

★★ **세부 정보**

여자가 언제 제품을 구매했는지를 왜 기억하지 못한다고 말하는가?
(A) 기억력이 좋지 않다. (B) 이메일을 확인하지 않았다.
(C) 그것을 선물로 받았다. (D) 영수증을 분실하였다.

어휘 poor memory 좋지 않은 기억력

토익 분석

반전 표현인 but을 사용하여 답에 대한 단서를 제시하고 있다. 반전 표현들은 언제나 중요한 정보를 제시한다.

남 Bales 씨, 인사부에서 온 이메일을 읽어 봤어요? ^{47, 48} 보아하니, 다음 주에 회사에 대규모 인사이동이 있을 것 같네요. 유럽 지점 개설에 관한 소문이 사실인 것 같아요.

여 네, 인사부에 근무하는 제 동료 한 명이 일주일 전에 그 소식에 대해 알려 줬어요. 이사회에서 이미 누가 유럽에 개설되는 지점들을 담당하게 될지 결정했어요. 조만간, 이사진은 유럽 지점들로 전근을 갈 지원자들을 물색할 겁니다. 사실 저는 그 지점들 중의 한 곳으로 전근하는 요청서를 제출하는 것에 대해 고려 중이에요.

남 행운을 빌어요. 저는 누가 유럽 지점들을 담당하게 될지 궁금하네요. ⁴⁹ 만약 저희 부서의 Welch 부장님께서 지점장 중의 한 분으로 내정되어 있다면, 저 또한, 유럽 지점으로 전근 가는 것을 생각해 봐야 할 것 같아요. 저는 그분이 가장 유능한 관리자들 중의 한 분이라고 생각하기 때문에 그분과 같은 사무실에서 근무하고 싶어요.

Questions 47-49 refer to the following conversation.

M Ms. Bales, did you read the e-mail from human resources? ^{47, 48} Apparently, there will be some major transfers in the company next week. I guess the rumor about branch openings in Europe is true.

W Yes, one of my colleagues in HR told me about it a week ago. The board of directors already decided who will be taking over the European branches. Soon, they will be looking for volunteers that want to transfer to the European branches. I'm actually considering submitting a request to transfer to one of them.

M I wish you good luck on that. I wonder who will be taking over those European branches. ⁴⁹ If my department head, Mr. Welch, has been designated as one of the branch managers, I should think about transferring to a branch in Europe as well. I think he is one of the most competent managers, and I want to work with him in the same office.

어휘 Human Resources 인사부 apparently 보아하니, 듣자 하니 transfer n. 전근, 이동 v. 전근 가다 rumor 소문 branch openings 지점 개설 colleague 동료 직원 decide ~을 결정하다 take over ~을 맡다, ~을 인수하다 look for ~을 찾다 volunteer 지원자 consider -ing ~하는 것을 고려하다 submit ~을 제출하다 request 요청(서) department head 부서장 be designated as ~로 지정되다 as well 또한, 마찬가지로 competent 유능한

47

★★★ 세부 정보

남자에 따르면, 회사는 무엇을 했는가?
(A) 새로운 직원들 채용   (B) 자사의 사업 확장
(C) 본사를 유럽으로 이전 (D) 규모가 더 작은 곳을 인수

어휘 expand ~을 확장/확대하다 headquarters 본사

토익 분석

부사인 apparently가 정답의 단서를 이끄는 포인트가 되며 세부 정보 문제이므로 company가 키워드로 사용되었다.

According to the man, what did the company do?

(A) Hired some new staff members   **(B) Expanded its business**
(C) Moved its headquarters to Europe   (D) Took over a smaller one

문제 해설

회사가 한 일을 묻는 첫 번째 질문으로 대화 전반부에 제시되는 남자의 말을 통해 회사가 한 일이 소개되는 부분에 집중해야 한다. 남자는 대화 초반부에 'Apparently~next week.'라는 말로 인사이동을 언급하고 있으며, 이어서 'I guess the rumor~'라고 말하며 유럽의 지점 개설에 대해 알리고 있다. 이와 같은 일들은 회사가 사업을 확장하는 상황에 가능한 것들이므로 이에 대해 언급한 (B)가 정답이다.

48

★★★ 세부 정보

조만간 회사에서 무슨 일이 있을 것인가?
(A) 유럽의 여러 지점들이 폐쇄될 것이다.
(B) 사내 행사를 위해 몇몇 자원봉사자들이 필요하게 될 것이다.
(C) 대규모 인사 개편이 발생할 것이다.
(D) 몇몇 직원들이 전근 요청서를 제출할 것이다.

어휘 corporate 회사의, 공동의 personnel 인사(부), 직원들 reshuffle 개편, 재편 take place 발생되다, 일어나다

토익 분석

company가 키워드로 사용되었으며, 질문의 soon이라는 시점 표현이 next week이라는 표현으로 등장했다.

What will happen at the company soon?

(A) Several branches in Europe will be closed.
(B) Some volunteers will be needed for a corporate event.
(C) A large personnel reshuffle will take place.
(D) Some employees will hand in transfer requests.

문제 해설

조만간 회사에서 발생하게 될 일에 대해 묻고 있으므로 soon에 해당되는 가까운 미래 시점에 있을 일이 언급되는 부분이 있다는 것을 예상하고 들어야 한다. 남자가 대화 초반부에 'Apparently, there will be some major transfers in the company next week.'라는 말로 대규모 인사이동이 있을 것임을 밝히고 있으므로 이와 같은 의미에 해당되는 A large personnel reshuffle로 표현한 (C)가 정답이다.

49

★★★ 의도 파악

여자가 다른 지점으로의 전근을 원할 수도 있는 이유는 무엇인가?
(A) 일부 동료 직원들과 사이가 좋지 않다.
(B) 유럽의 고전 문화에 관심이 많다.
(C) 더 많은 보수와 나은 혜택을 받게 될 것이다.
(D) 유능한 사람의 감독하에 근무하길 원한다.

어휘 get along with 잘 지내다 get paid 급여를 받다

토익 분석

의도 및 미래 행동의 I want to~가 단서를 제시한다.

Why might the woman want to transfer to another branch office?

(A) She doesn't get along with some of her colleagues.
(B) She is interested in classical European culture.
(C) She can get paid more and receive better benefits.
(D) She wants to work under competent direction.

문제 해설

여자가 전근을 원할 수도 있는 이유를 묻는 마지막 질문이므로 대화 후반부 여자의 말에서 전근과 관련해 언급하는 부분에 집중해야 한다. 여자는 대화 마지막에 자신의 부서장을 언급하면서 'I think~same office.'라고 말하는 부분을 통해 자신의 상사가 굉장히 유능하기 때문에 함께 근무하고 싶다는 의사를 밝히고 있으므로 유능한 사람의 감독하에 근무하고 싶다는 의미로 쓰인 (D)가 정답이다.

Questions 50-52 refer to the following conversation.

M   Sally, [50] we really need to discuss the Summer Job Exposition, which our company will be attending. It's only a month away.

W   Well, I think we can use the same materials we used last year. [51] But the thing is that the booth is a bit more spacious than last year.

M   I heard that too. [52] Have you talked to the head of HR? I'm sure we can get some posters and product samples from him.

W   No, I haven't. [52] I'll get back to you after checking with him.

어휘 discuss ~을 논의하다 attend ~에 참석하다 only a month away 불과 한 달밖에 남지 않은 material 자료, 재료 booth 부스, 칸막이 공간 a bit 조금, 약간 spacious (공간이) 넓은 HR department 인사부 get back to ~에게 다시 연락하다, 답신하다 check with ~에게 확인해 보다

남   Sally, [50] 우리 회사가 참석할 예정인 하계 구인 박람회에 관해 꼭 논의해 봐야 합니다. 불과 한 달밖에 남지 않았어요.

여   저, 제 생각엔 우리가 작년에 사용했던 동일한 자료를 사용할 수 있을 것 같아요. [51] 하지만 문제는 부스가 작년보다 조금 더 넓다는 점이에요.

남   저도 그 부분에 대해 들었어요. [52] 인사부장님께 말씀드려 보셨나요? 그분으로부터 몇몇 포스터와 제품 샘플들을 받을 수 있을 거라고 확신해요.

여   아뇨, 아직이요. [52] 그분께 확인해 보고 다시 말씀 드릴게요.

50

What does the man say will take place in a month?

(A) A talent show
(B) A client meeting
(C) A product launch
(D) A career fair

문제 해설

남자가 한 달 후에 있을 것이라고 말하는 일을 묻는 첫 번째 문제이므로 대화 초반부에서 남자가 '한 달 후'라는 미래 시점과 함께 언급하는 일이 있을 것임을 예상하고 들어야 한다. 대화는 시작하면서 남자가 'we really need to discuss Summer Job Exposition that our company will be attending. It's only a month away.'라는 말로 구인 박람회 행사가 한 달밖에 남지 않았다고 언급하고 있으므로 이 행사와 같은 의미에 해당되는 '채용 박람회'를 뜻하는 (D)가 정답이다.

★★ 세부 정보

남자는 한 달 후에 무슨 일이 있을 것이라고 말하는가?
(A) 오디션 행사
(B) 고객과의 회의
(C) 제품 출시 행사
(D) 채용 박람회

어휘 take place 발생되다 talent show 오디션 행사 launching 출시(회), 공개 career fair 채용 박람회

토익 분석

남자 대화에서 키워드 in a month를 이용하는 문제다. 시점이나 숫자 표현은 언제나 최고의 키워드로 활용된다. 이 문제의 경우 의도 및 미래 행동 힌트를 제시하는 we (really) need to가 정답의 단서를 이끌고 있다.

51

What does the woman say she is concerned about?

(A) The duration of the event
(B) The location of the show
(C) The size of the booth
(D) The number of participants

문제 해설

여자가 걱정하는 일을 묻는 두 번째 문제이므로 대화 중반부 여자의 말에서 걱정되는 사항을 언급하는 부분에 집중해서 들어야 한다. 여자는 대화 중반부에 자신이 신경 쓰여 하는 일을 'But the thing is that the booth is a bit more spacious than last year.'와 같이 언급해 걱정하는 일을 알리고 있는데, 부스의 공간이 더 넓다는 의미이므로 부스의 크기를 뜻하는 (C)가 정답이다.

★★ 문제점

여자는 무엇에 대해 걱정된다고 말하는가?
(A) 행사의 기간
(B) 쇼가 개최되는 장소
(C) 부스의 크기
(D) 참가자들의 수

어휘 be concerned about ~에 대해 걱정하다 duration (지속) 기간 location 장소, 위치 participant 참가자

토익 분석

여자 대화에서 문제점을 찾아야 한다. 문제점은 반전 표현이 단서를 제시하는 경우가 많다. 이 문제 역시 반전 표현 but이 단서를 제공한다.

52

What will the woman do next?

(A) Make a suggestion
(B) Check the stock
(C) Print out some posters
(D) Talk to a manager

문제 해설

여자가 곧이어 할 일을 묻는 마지막 문제이므로 대화 후반부 여자의 말에서 앞으로의 계획이나 미래 시점의 일을 언급하는 부분이 있을 것임을 예상하고 들어야 한다. 여자는 대화 마지막 부분에 'I'll get back to you after checking with him.'라는 말로 누군가에게 확인해 보고 남자에게 알려 주겠다고 말하고 있는데, 이는 앞서 남자가 'Have you talked to the head of HR department?'라는 말로 언급한 인사부장에게 확인해 보겠다는 의미이다. 따라서 한 책임자와 이야기한다는 말로 표현한 (D)가 정답이다.

★★ 미래 행동

여자는 곧이어 무엇을 할 것인가?
(A) 제안을 한다.
(B) 재고를 확인한다.
(C) 일부 포스터를 출력한다.
(D) 한 책임자와 이야기한다.

어휘 make a suggestion 제안하다 stock 재고(품) print out ~을 출력하다

토익 분석

세 번째 문제로 미래 행동을 묻고 있으니 여자의 마지막 대화에 답이 나오게 된다. 의도 및 미래 행동의 단서를 제시하는 표현들을 기억해야 한다. 이 문제의 경우 I'll~이 결정적인 단서가 된다.

남 안녕하세요, Jill 그리고 Jina. ⁵³ 오늘 근무 시간표가
　나왔다는 것을 알게 되었는데, 제가 금요일에 근무할
　예정이지만, 그날 제 아들의 졸업식에 참석해야 합니
　다.
여1 지금 우리들 중의 한 명이 당신 근무를 대신해 줄 수
　있는지 물어보시는 거죠?
남 네, 그게 가능하시다면요.
여2 죄송해요, 대신해 드리고 싶지만 저는 이미 근무하기
　로 예정되어 있어요.
여1 ⁵⁴ 제가 그날 휴무라서 대신 기꺼이 일하러 올게요.
　근무 시간이 어떻게 되죠?
남 ⁵⁴ 9시부터 4시예요. 와우, 제가 무슨 말씀을 드려야
　할지 모르겠어요.
여2 ⁵⁵ 그저 고맙다고 말씀하시고 나서 지금 저희와 함께
　Dino's Deli로 식사하러 가시면 될 것 같은데요.
남 좋습니다. 제 재킷을 가져올게요. 그리고 점심은 제
　가 낼게요.

Questions 53-55 refer to the following conversation with three speakers.

M　Hi, Jill and Gina. ⁵³ I noticed the hours came out today and I'm scheduled to work on Friday, but I have to attend my son's graduation ceremony that day.
W1　Are you asking if one of us would be able to cover for you?
M　Yes, if that's possible.
W2　Sorry, I would, but I'm already scheduled to work.
W1　⁵⁴ I have the day off, so I will gladly come in for you. What are the hours?
M　⁵⁴ From nine to four. Wow, I don't know what to say.
W2　^{55.} You should probably just say thank you and join us now for lunch at Dino's Deli.
M　Sounds great. Let me grab my jacket. And lunch is on me.

어휘 notice (that) ~임을 알게 되다 hours 근무 시간(표) come out 나오다, 발표되다 be scheduled to do ~할 예정이다 attend ~에 참석하다 graduation ceremony 졸업식 ask if ~인지 묻다 be able to do ~할 수 있다 cover for ~을 대신하다 if that's possible 그게 가능하다면 have a day off 하루 쉬다 gladly 기꺼이, 기쁘게 probably 아마도 join A for B A와 함께 B하러 가다 grab ~을 가져오다 A is on me A의 값은 제가 내겠습니다

53

★★ 문제점

남자의 문제점은 무엇인가?
(A) 일정이 겹치는 문제가 있다.
(B) 정책의 변화에 대해 통보받지 못했다.
(C) 일부 정보를 이용할 수 없다.
(D) 자신이 받은 메시지에 관해 혼란스러워하고 있다.

어휘 scheduling conflict 일정의 겹침 be notified of ~에 대해 통보받다 policy 정책 access n. ~을 이용하다, ~에 접근하다 be confused about ~에 대해 혼란스러워하다

토익 분석

남자 대화에 반전 표현 but이 단서를 제공하는 힌트다.

What is the man's problem?

(A) He has a scheduling conflict. 　(B) He was not notified of a policy change.
(C) He is unable to access some information.
(D) He is confused about a message he received.

문제 해설

남자의 문제점에 대해 묻는 첫 번째 질문이므로 대화 초반부에 언급되는 남자의 말에서 들을 수 있는 부정적인 내용을 파악하는 것이 관건이다. 남자는 대화를 시작하면서 'I noticed~ceremony that day.'라는 말로 자신이 근무하기로 예정된 날에 아들의 졸업식에 가야 한다는 문제점을 말하고 있는데, 이는 일정이 겹치는 문제에 해당하므로 이를 'scheduling conflict'라는 말로 바꿔 표현한 (A)가 정답이다.

54

★★ 맥락 파악

남자는 왜 "I don't know what to say"라고 말하는가?
(A) 연설을 하는 것에 대한 우려를 설명하기 위해
(B) 감사함을 표현하기 위해 (C) 좌절감을 나타내기 위해
(D) 여자들에게 의견을 요청하기 위해.

어휘 be worried about ~에 대해 걱정하다 give a speech 연설하다 express ~을 표현하다 gratitude 감사(하는 마음) frustration 좌절(감) ask A for B A에게 B를 요청하다

토익 분석

맥락 파악 문제로 상대방 여자 대화 중 반전 표현 So~가 중요한 단서를 제시하고 있다.

Why does the man say, "I don't know what to say"?

(A) To explain his worries about giving a speech

(B) To express his gratitude

(C) To show his frustration 　　(D) To ask the women for their opinion

문제 해설

남자가 말하는 "I don't know what to say"라는 표현이 대화 속에서 어떤 의미로 사용되었는지를 묻는 두 번째 질문이므로 대화 중반부에 제시되는 남자의 말을 통해 해당 표현을 확인할 수 있어야 하며, 이때 앞뒤에 함께 제시되는 말들을 통해 의미의 흐름을 파악해 정답을 찾아야 한다. 이 표현은 말 그대로 '무슨 말을 해야 할지 모르겠다'라는 의미인데, 바로 앞에서 여자들 중의 한 명이 'I have~the hours?'라는 말로 자신을 대신해 근무할 수 있다고 알리는 말에 대한 반응으로 사용한 표현이므로 감사의 뜻을 나타내는 말이라는 것을 알 수 있다. 따라서 (B)가 정답이 된다.

55

★★ 미래 행동

화자들은 곧이어 무엇을 할 것 같은가?
(A) 레스토랑에 간다. 　　(B) 일정표를 확인한다.
(C) 기념행사에 참석한다. (D) 옷을 쇼핑하러 간다.

어휘 attend ~에 참석하다 ceremony 기념행사, 축하 행사 shop for ~을 쇼핑하다 clothing 옷, 의류

토익 분석

미래 행동 문제는 I'll과 같은 의도 및 미래 행동 단서나 요청, 제안 단서들이 답을 제시한다.

What will the speakers likely do next?

(A) Go to a restaurant 　　(B) Check a schedule
(C) Attend a ceremony 　　(D) Shop for some clothing

문제 해설

화자들의 추후 행동을 묻는 마지막 질문이며, 이에 대한 단서는 대화 후반부 또는 최종 화자의 말에서 제시되는 경우가 일반적이다. 여자들 중의 한 명이 대화 후반부에 'You should~Dino's Deli.'라는 말로 다 같이 식사하는 것에 대해 제안하고 있고, 뒤이어 남자도 이에 동의하고 있으므로 (A)가 정답임을 알 수 있다.

Questions 56-58 refer to the following conversation.

W [56] Did you check out East Village Apartment on Lloyd Street? I heard that one of the tenants there is looking for someone to sublease the place for the remaining year.

M Yes, I heard about that. [57] It sounds like a decent option, but it's too far from work. I want to live somewhere near work. I have been commuting two hours a day from New Jersey to my workplace in Manhattan since last year, and I can't stand the long commute anymore.

W I see. [58] In that case, you should try searching the company's community Web site. There are many rental advertisements in some areas close to Manhattan you can check out.

여 [56] Lloyd 가에 있는 East Village 아파트는 확인해 봤어요? 그곳 주민 중 한 사람이 올해 남은 기간 동안 자신의 아파트를 임대해서 쓸 사람을 찾고 있다고 들었어요.

남 네, 저도 그곳에 대해 들었어요. [57] 좋은 선택 사항인 것 같은데, 제 직장에서 너무 멀리 있어요. 저는 직장 근처에서 거주하고 싶거든요. 저는 작년 이후로 New Jersey에서 Manhattan에 있는 제 집까지 하루에 2시간씩 통근해 왔는데, 더 이상 긴 통근 시간을 견딜 수가 없네요.

여 알겠어요. [58] 그런 경우라면, 회사 직원용 웹 사이트를 한번 검색해 보세요. Manhattan과 가까운 지역에 당신이 확인해 볼 만한 임대 광고들이 많이 올라와 있거든요.

어휘 check out ~을 확인해 보다 tenant 거주/입주자 sublease ~을 재임대하다 remaining 남은, 남아 있는 decent 품위 있는, 좋은 too far from ~에서 너무 멀리 있는 commute 통근하다 workplace 직장 stand ~을 견디다, 참다 long commute 긴 통근 거리 not ~ any more 더 이상 ~ 않다 in that case 그런 경우라면 rental advertisement 임대 광고 close to ~와 가까운

56

Why does the woman talk to the man?

(A) To sublease her house
(B) To discuss some tenants' complaints
(C) To renew a rental agreement
(D) To inform him about some available housing

문제 해설

여자가 남자에게 말을 건네는 이유를 묻는 문제는 주제 문제와 동일한 유형에 해당되므로 대화 초반부 여자의 말에 제시되는 핵심 정보를 파악하는 것에 주력해야 한다. 대화 시작과 함께 여자가 남자에게 'Did you check out East Village Apartment on Lloyd Street?'라는 말로 특정 아파트를 확인해 봤는지 물으면서, 'I heard that~remaining year.'라는 말로 해당 주민이 아파트를 재임대할 사람을 찾고 있음을 밝히고 있다. 이는 남자에게 아파트 임대 관련 정보를 제공하려는 것이므로 (D)가 정답이다.

★★ 주제, 목적

여자가 남자에게 말을 건네는 이유는 무엇인가?
(A) 자신의 집을 재임대하기 위해서
(B) 몇몇 세입자들의 불만 사항을 논의하기 위해서
(C) 임대 계약서를 갱신하기 위해서
(D) 그에게 이용 가능한 주택에 대해 알리기 위해서

어휘 complaint 불만 renew ~을 갱신하다 inform A about B B에 대해 A에게 알리다

토익 분석

방문 목적이나 전화 목적은 언제나 주제에 해당한다. 따라서 초반부 대화 중 첫 번째 문장이 답을 찾는데 있어 가장 중요하다.

57

Why is the man looking for a new place to live?

(A) He started a new job.
(B) He has a long commute.
(C) His lease will expire soon.
(D) The apartment where he currently lives is very old.

문제 해설

남자가 새로운 거주지를 물색한 이유에 대해 묻는 두 번째 질문이므로 대화 중반부 남자의 말에서 집을 찾는 일과 관련된 정보가 제시될 것임을 예상하고 들어야 한다. 여자의 말을 들은 남자는 자신이 원하는 집의 조건과 관련해 'I want to live~any more.'라는 말로 더 이상 긴 통근 시간을 감당할 수 없음을 언급하고 있으므로 (B)가 정답이다.

★★ 의도 파악

남자가 새로운 거주지를 찾는 이유는 무엇인가?
(A) 새로운 직장에서 일을 시작했다.
(B) 통근 거리가 멀다.
(C) 임대 계약이 곧 만료된다.
(D) 현재 거주하고 있는 아파트가 노후하다.

어휘 lease 임대 (계약) expire 만료되다 currently 현재

토익 분석

남자 대화에서 의도 및 미래 행동의 단서를 제시하는 표현을 찾아야 한다. I want to~가 단서가 된다.

58

What does the woman suggest that the man do?

(A) Contact a real estate agent
(B) Look for a different house on Lloyd Street
(C) Search through the company's online database
(D) Take a tour of a new apartment

문제 해설

여자가 남자에게 제안하는 내용에 관해 묻는 세 번째 문제이므로 대화 후반부 여자의 말에 제시되는 제안 표현을 중심으로 단서를 찾아야 한다. 여자는 대화 마지막에 남자에게 'In that case, you should try searching the company's community Web site.'라고 이야기하며 회사의 홈페이지에서 관련 정보를 검색할 것을 제안하고 있으므로 이에 해당되는 보기인 (C)가 정답임을 알 수 있다.

★★ 요청, 제안

여자가 남자에게 무엇을 하도록 제안하는가?
(A) 부동산 중개업자에게 연락할 것
(B) Lloyd가에 있는 다른 주택을 물색할 것
(C) 회사 온라인 데이터베이스를 통해 검색할 것
(D) 새로운 아파트를 둘러볼 것

어휘 real estate agent 부동산 중개업자 through ~을 통해 take a tour of ~을 둘러보다, 견학하다

토익 분석

여자의 후반부 대화문에서 전형적인 요청, 제안 힌트 표현인 you should~ 정답 단서를 제시하고 있다.

남 ⁵⁹ 안녕하세요, Gruber Sports에 오신 것을 환영합니다. 무엇을 도와 드릴까요?

여 안녕하세요, 제가 일전에 ⁶⁰ 새로운 S-시리즈 야구 배트가 도착했다고 알려 주는 메시지를 받았는데, 찾을 수 없는 것 같아요.

남 ⁶⁰ 죄송합니다만, 어제 그 제품이 품절되었습니다. 그 메시지를 언제 받으셨죠?

여 수요일이요. 직원 분께서 20개를 주문하셨다고 말씀하셔서 미리 하나를 예약할 생각을 하지 못했어요.

남 네, 저희도 그렇게 빨리 판매될 거라고 전혀 예상하지 못했습니다.

여 알겠습니다. ⁶¹ 다시 주문하셔서 저를 위해 2개를 예약해 주실 수 있으세요?

남 물론이죠. 이번 일로 인해 발생된 불편함에 대해 약간 할인도 해 드리겠습니다.

여 잘됐네요. 정말로 감사합니다.

Questions 59-61 refer to the following conversation.

M ⁵⁹ Hello, and welcome to Gruber Sports. How can I help you?

W Hi, I got a message the other day informing me that ⁶⁰ the new S-series baseball bats had arrived, but I can't seem to find them.

M ⁶⁰ Sorry, but we sold out of them yesterday. When did you receive the message?

W On Wednesday. I didn't think to reserve one in advance as the employee told me you had ordered twenty.

M Yes, we really didn't expect them to go so quickly.

W I see. ⁶¹ Could you make another order and hold two for me?

M No problem. We'll even give you a small discount for the inconvenience this has caused.

W That's great. I really appreciate it.

어휘 the other day 일전에 inform A that A에게 ~라고 알리다 sold out of ~가 품절/매진되다 receive ~을 받다 think to do ~할 생각을 하다 reserve ~을 예약하다 in advance 미리, 사전에 order ~을 주문하다 expect A to do A가 ~할 것으로 예상/기대하다 quickly 빠르게 make another order 또 다시 주문하다 even 심지어 discount 할인 inconvenience 불편함 cause ~을 초래하다, 발생시키다 appreciate ~에 대해 감사하다

59

★★ 도입부 정보

대화는 어디에서 이뤄지고 있을 가능성이 가장 큰가?
(A) 슈퍼마켓 (B) 피트니스 센터
(C) 스포츠 용품 매장 (D) 건강식품 매장

어휘 sporting goods 스포츠 용품

토익 분석

대화 초반부 첫 번째 두 번째 문장에서 장소와 관련된 표현들을 찾아야 한다. 업체 이름 Gruber Sports과 baseball bat이 단서가 된다.

Where most likely does the conversation take place?

(A) In a supermarket (B) In a fitness center
(C) In a sporting goods store (D) In a health food store

문제 해설

대화 장소에 관해 묻는 첫 번째 질문이므로 대화 초반부에서 대화 장소를 직접적으로 밝히는 부분, 혹은 대화 장소를 유추할 수 있는 단서가 제시되는 부분에 집중해야 한다. 남자가 대화를 시작하면서 'Hello, and welcome to Gruber Sports.'라는 말로 매장 이름을 포함한 인사말을 건네고 있으며, 뒤이어 야구 배트 제품에 관한 이야기가 이어지고 있으므로 (C)가 정답임을 알 수 있다.

60

★★ 문제점

여자의 문제점은 무엇인가?
(A) 엉뚱한 물품을 배송 받았다.
(B) 자신이 원하는 물품이 구매 불가능하다.
(C) 너무 많은 금액을 청구 받았다.
(D) 잘못된 곳에 가 있다.

어휘 wrong 잘못된 item 물품 available 구매 가능한 be charged 비용을 청구 받다

토익 분석

여자 대화에 반전 표현 but과 남자 대화에 반전 표현 (I'm) sorry, but~이 정답 힌트를 제시하고 있다.

What is the woman's problem?

(A) She was sent the wrong items. **(B) The items she wants are not available.**
(C) She was charged too much. (D) She is in the wrong place.

문제 해설

여자의 문제점에 대해 묻는 두 번째 질문이므로 대화 중반부에 언급되는 여자의 말에서 들을 수 있는 부정적인 내용을 파악하는 것이 관건이다. 대화 중반부에 여자는 자신이 원하는 야구 배트 제품을 찾을 수 없다고 알리자 남자가 'Sorry, but we sold out of them yesterday.'라는 말로 품절되었다고 밝히고 있다. 이는 해당 제품을 구매할 수 없음을 의미하는 것이므로 이를 'not available'로 표현한 (B)가 정답이 된다.

61

★★ 요청, 제안

여자는 남자에게 무엇을 하도록 요청하는가?
(A) 물품을 재주문할 것 (B) 배송을 할 것
(C) 매니저에게 전화할 것 (D) 할인을 해 줄 것

어휘 reorder 재주문하다 make a delivery 배송하다

토익 분석

여자 후반부 대화에서 요청, 제안, 단서 표현인 could you~?가 정답을 제시하고 있다.

What does the woman ask the man to do?

(A) Reorder some items (B) Make a delivery
(C) Call a manager (D) Give her a discount

문제 해설

여자가 남자에게 요청하는 일을 파악하도록 요구하는 세 번째 문제이므로 대화 후반부에 제시되는 요청, 요구, 추천, 권고 등의 표현에 집중해 들어야 한다. 여자는 자신이 원하는 제품을 구매할 수 없다는 말을 듣고 대화 후반부에 Could you ~? 라는 요청 표현을 통해 'Could you make another order and keep hold of two for me?'라고 묻고 있으므로 (A)가 정답임을 알 수 있다. 이 문장의 핵심 내용인 'make another order'가 정답 보기에서는 'Reorder some items'라는 말로 바뀌어 제시되었다.

Questions 62-64 refer to the following conversation and list.

M Sarah, are you all prepared for our trip this weekend? [62] I've planned a great biking route to the mountain.

W I think so! [63] The only thing that worries me is the rain we are supposed to get this weekend.

M Oh, I think it'll be just a light shower. I wouldn't worry about it.

W You're probably right. Did you finally buy a new bike for our trip?

M [64] I've been looking at some Sureshot bikes. I'm planning to just get the cheapest one. I don't think I need anything fancy.

W Right. We won't be biking on any difficult routes or anything. Just get one that's reliable and affordable.

Sureshot Bicycles	
Sureshot Sierra	$430
Sureshot Trek	$460
Sureshot Glide	$490
Sureshot Blizzard	$520

어휘 be prepared for ~에 대한 준비가 되다 plan ~을 계획하다 biking route 자전거 경로 be supposed to do ~할 예정이다 light shower 약한 소나기 worry about ~에 대해 걱정하다 probably 아마 finally 결국, 마침내 look at ~을 보다 cheapest 가장 싼 fancy 고급스러운, 멋진 or anything ~ 같은 것/곳 reliable 믿을 만한 affordable 가격이 적절한

남 Sarah, 이번 주말에 있을 여행 준비가 전부 되었나요? [62] 제가 산으로 가는 멋진 자전거 경로를 계획했어요.

여 그런 거 같아요! [63] 저를 걱정하게 만드는 유일한 일은 이번 주말에 내릴 예정인 비예요.

남 아, 저는 그게 약한 소나기일 거라고 생각해요. 저라면 걱정하지 않을 거예요.

여 당신 말이 맞을 수도 있어요. 이번 여행에 사용할 새 자전거를 결국 구입했나요?

남 [64] 제가 몇몇 Sureshot 자전거들을 확인해 봤어요. 저는 그냥 가장 싼 걸로 구입할 계획입니다. 고급스러운 것은 필요치 않을 것 같아요.

여 맞아요. 우리는 다니기 어려운 경로 같은 곳에서 자전거를 타지는 않을 테니까요. 믿을 만하고 가격이 적절한 것으로 구입하세요.

Sureshot 자전거	
Sureshot Sierra	430달러
Sureshot Trek	460달러
Sureshot Glide	490달러
Sureshot Blizzard	520달러

62

Where are the speakers planning to go?

(A) To a beach
(B) To a mountain
(C) To an amusement park
(D) To a historical site

문제 해설

화자들이 어디에 갈 것인지를 묻는 첫 번째 문제이므로 대화의 초반부에서 목적지나 이동 방법과 함께 제시되는 도착 장소 등에 집중해 들어야 한다. 대화 초반부에 남자는 주말여행 준비가 되었는지 물으면서 'I've planned a great biking route to the mountain.'라는 말로 산으로 가는 길을 계획해 뒀다고 알리는 것으로 볼 때 화자들의 목적지는 '산'이라는 것을 알 수 있으므로 (B)가 정답이다.

★ **주제, 목적**

화자들은 어디에 갈 계획인가?
(A) 해변으로
(B) 산으로
(C) 놀이공원으로
(D) 역사적인 장소로

어휘 historical 역사적인 site 장소

토익 분석

첫 번째 문제로 화자들의 공통된 계획을 묻는 것은 대화의 주제와 같다. 따라서 첫 번째 또는 두 번째 문장에 정답의 단서가 제시된다. 질문 속에 사용된 plan을 키워드로 반복 사용한 것도 정답의 단서가 된다.

63

★★ 문제점

여자는 무엇에 대해 걱정하는가?
(A) 여행 일정
(B) 자전거 경로
(C) 일기 예보
(D) 업무 마감 시한

어휘 be concerned about ~에 대해 걱정하다 deadline 마감 시한

토익 분석

여자 대화문에 문제점을 암시하는 The only thing that worries me~가 정답의 단서를 제공하는 표현이다.

What is the woman concerned about?

(A) A travel schedule
(B) A bicycle route
(C) A weather forecast
(D) A work deadline

문제 해설

여자가 걱정하는 일을 묻는 두 번째 질문이므로 대화 중반부에서 여자가 특정 문제점과 함께 걱정이나 우려 등을 나타내는 표현을 통해 언급하는 정보를 파악해야 한다. 대화 중반부에 여자는 'The only thing that worries me ~'라는 말로 걱정하는 일이 있음을 나타내는 표현과 함께 'The only thing that worries me is the rain we are supposed to get this weekend.'라는 말로 비가 내릴 것에 대해 걱정하고 있음을 알리고 있으므로 이를 '일기 예보'라는 말로 바꿔 제시한 (C)가 정답이 된다.

64

★★ 그래픽

도표를 확인하시오. 남자는 어느 자전거를 구입할 가능성이 가장 큰가?
(A) Sureshot Sierra
(B) Sureshot Trek
(C) Sureshot Glide
(D) Sureshot Blizzard

토익 분석

제시된 표에 자전거 종류와 가격 정보가 포함되어 있다. 자전거 종류를 찾기 위해서 대화 내용 중 언급되는 가격 정보에 집중해야 한다.

Look at the graphic. Which bicycle will the man probably purchase?

(A) Sureshot Sierra
(B) Sureshot Trek
(C) Sureshot Glide
(D) Sureshot Blizzard

문제 해설

질문에서 묻는 내용과 관련해 대화 속에 제시된 단서를 바탕으로 도표의 정보를 함께 확인해 정답을 찾아야 하는 문제이다. 이때 각 보기에 제시된 내용 외의 정보가 대화 속에서 단서로 제시될 것이므로 이에 집중해 대화를 들어야 한다. 각 보기에 자전거 제품명이 쓰여 있으므로 도표에서 함께 제시된 가격 정보에 집중해 들어야 한다. 남자는 대화 후반부에 자전거 구입 조건을 'I've been looking at some Sureshot bikes. I'm planning to just get the cheapest one.'라는 말로 알리고 있는데, '가장 싼 것'이 남자가 원하는 조건이므로 도표에서 가격이 가장 저렴한 제품에 해당하는 (A)가 정답임을 알 수 있다.

Questions 65-67 refer to the following conversation and chart.

M   I have the results of the company vote here. 34% of the staff voted for the company workshop to be held in the Erasmus Resort.

W   ⁶⁵ Well, Mr. Rogers, you're the personnel manager, so the final decision is yours.

M   To be honest, I don't think the Erasmus Resort is worth the money. ⁶⁶ Let's go to the one with 28% of the votes.

W   ⁶⁷ OK, I'll get in touch with the resort and arrange rooms for all staff members. And we should probably make a formal announcement at the weekly meeting tomorrow morning.

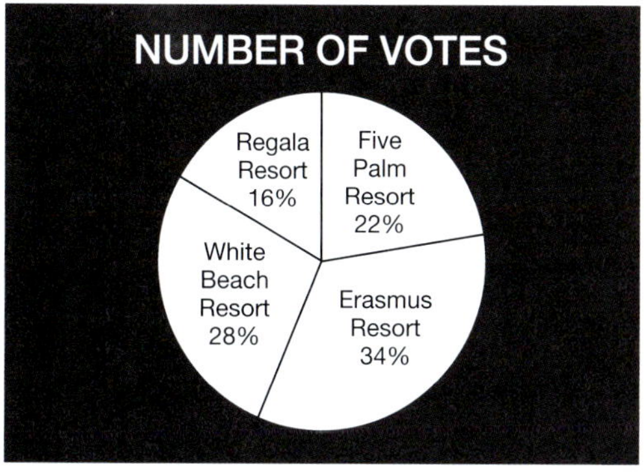

어휘 result 결과 vote 투표 be held in ~에서 열리다, 개최되다 personnel manager 인사부장 final decision 최종 결정 to be honest 솔직히 worth the money 비용에 대한 값어치가 있는 get in touch with ~에게 연락하다 arrange ~을 준비/마련하다 probably 아마 make an announcement 발표하다 formal 공식적인, 정식의

남 여기 회사 내 투표 결과를 갖고 있습니다. 직원들 중의 34%가 회사의 워크숍이 Erasmus Resort에서 열려야 한다고 투표했어요.

여 ⁶⁵ 저, Rogers 씨, 당신이 인사부장이시니까 최종 결정은 당신에게 달려 있습니다.

남 솔직히, 저는 Erasmus Resort가 비용에 대한 값어치가 있다고 생각하지 않아요. ⁶⁶ 28%의 표를 얻은 곳으로 가시죠.

여 ⁶⁷ 좋아요, 제가 그 리조트에 연락해서 모든 직원들을 위한 객실을 준비할게요. 그리고 아마 내일 있을 주간 회의에서 공식적으로 발표해야 할 겁니다.

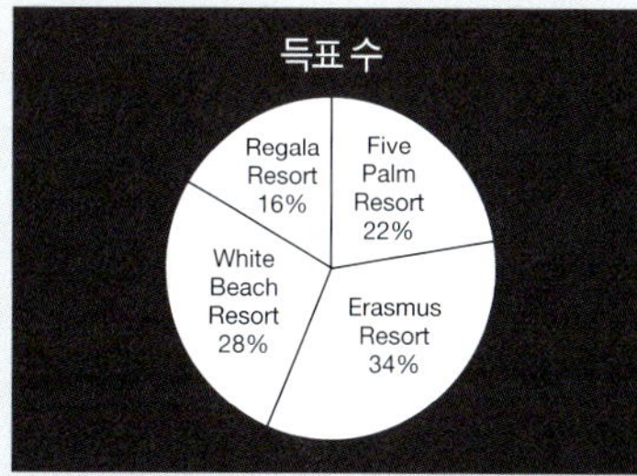

65

What department do the speakers work in?

(A) Accounting
(B) Marketing
(C) Personnel
(D) Sales

문제 해설

화자들의 근무 장소를 유추할 것을 요청하는 첫 번째 질문이므로 대화 초반부에서 언급되는 소개 인사와 함께 직접적으로 언급되는 회사명이나 부서명, 혹은 화자가 하는 일을 추측할 수 있을 만한 관련 어휘가 제시되는 부분에 집중해야 한다. 대화 초반부에 남자가 워크숍 장소에 대한 투표 결과 정보를 언급하는 말에 대해 여자가 'Well, Mr. Rogers, you're the manager of Personnel, so the final decision is up to you.'라는 말로 남자의 직책을 알리고 있는데, '인사부장'이라고 말하는 것으로 볼 때 (C)가 정답임을 알 수 있다.

★ 도입부 정보

화자들은 무슨 부서에서 근무하는가?
(A) 회계부
(B) 마케팅부
(C) 인사부
(D) 영업부

토익 분석

근무 장소는 초반부 대화 중 첫 번째, 두 번째 문장에 관련 단서가 제시된다.

66

★★★ 그래픽

도표를 확인하시오. 남자는 어느 리조트를 선택할 것 같은가?
(A) Regala Resort
(B) Five Palm Resort
(C) White Beach Resort
(D) Erasmus Resort

어휘 choose ~을 선택하다

토익 분석

그래프상에 리조트 종류와 득표수 정보가 포함되어 있다. 리조트를 찾기 위해서 득표 정보를 대화에서 들어야 한다. 요청, 제안 표현 let's ~ 28%~ 문장이 정답의 단서다.

Look at the graphic. Which resort will the man probably choose?

(A) Regala Resort
(B) Five Palm Resort
(C) White Beach Resort
(D) Erasmus Resort

문제 해설

질문에서 묻는 내용과 관련해 대화 속에 제시된 단서를 바탕으로 도표의 정보를 함께 확인해 정답을 찾아야 하는 문제이다. 이때 각 보기에 제시된 내용 외의 정보가 대화 속에서 단서로 제시될 것이므로 이에 집중해 대화를 들어야 한다. 각 보기에 리조트 이름이 쓰여 있으므로 도표에서 이와 함께 제시된 정보, 즉 득표율이 대화에 언급될 것임을 예상하며 대화를 들어야 한다. 남자는 대화 중반부에 자신이 원하는 장소와 관련해 'Let's go to the one with 28% of the votes.'라는 말로 '28%의 표를 얻은 곳으로 가자'고 알리고 있으므로 도표에서 해당 득표율을 보이는 (C)가 정답이 된다.

★★ 미래 행동

여자는 곧이어 무엇을 할 것인가?
(A) 직원들에게 계획을 발표한다.
(B) 항공편 일정을 확인한다.
(C) 여행사를 방문한다.
(D) 객실을 예약한다.

어휘 announce ~을 발표하다 travel agency 여행사 reserve ~을 예약하다

토익 분석

여자의 후반부 대화문에서 미래 행동 및 의도 문제의 단서를 제시하는 I'll~이 정답을 이끌고 있다.

What will the woman do next?

(A) Announce plans to the staff
(B) Check a flight schedule
(C) Visit a travel agency
(D) Reserve some rooms

문제 해설

여자의 추후 행동을 묻는 마지막 질문이며, 이에 대한 단서는 대화 후반부 또는 최종 화자의 말에서 제시되는 경우가 일반적이다. 대화의 마지막에 여자는 남자가 원하는 리조트와 관련해 'OK, I'll get in touch with the resort and arrange rooms for all staff.'라는 말로 자신이 그곳에 연락해 객실을 준비하겠다고 알리고 있으므로 (D)가 정답임을 알 수 있다.

Questions 68-70 refer to the following conversation and sign.

W [68] Hello. I'm new in town, and I'd like to become a member of the library.

M No problem. I can help you sign up right now and issue you a library card.

W Great! Do I need to show you any identification? I brought a bill and my passport.

M That's perfect. [69] And please complete this application form for our records.

W OK. [70] Oh, I'd also like to check out some DVDs from your collection while I'm here. Can you show me where the elevator is?

M Certainly. It's right over there. Let me know if you need any assistance.

Dundee Public Library
1st Floor – General Books Section
2nd Floor – Reference Section
3rd Floor – DVDs & CDs
4th Floor – Journals & Periodicals

어휘 new 새로 이사 온 help A do A가 ~하는 것을 돕다 sign up 등록/신청하다 issue ~을 발급하다 identification 신분증 bill 고지서, 청구서 passport 여권 complete ~을 완료하다 application form 신청서, 지원서 records 기록 (보관) check out ~을 대여/대출하다 collection 소장품, 수집품 while ~하는 동안 Certainly 물론입니다, 맞습니다 right over there 바로 저쪽에 let A know A에게 알리다 assistance 도움 reference 참고 도서/자료 periodical 정기 간행물

여 [68] 안녕하세요. 제가 이 도시에 새로 이사를 왔는데, 도서관 회원이 되고 싶어요.

남 좋습니다. 지금 바로 등록하시도록 도와 드리고 도서관 카드를 발급해 드릴 수 있습니다.

여 잘됐네요! 제가 어느 신분증이든 보여 드려야 하나요? 제가 고지서 한 장이랑 여권을 가져 왔어요.

남 아주 좋습니다. [69] 그리고 기록 보관을 위해 이 신청서를 작성 완료해 주시기 바랍니다.

여 알겠어요. [70] 아, 여기 온 김에 보유 중이신 DVD도 좀 대여해 가고 싶어요. 엘리베이터가 어디 있는지 알려 주시겠어요?

남 물론입니다. 바로 저쪽에 있습니다. 도움이 필요하시면 알려 주시기 바랍니다.

Dundee 공공 도서관
1층 – 일반 도서 구역
2층 – 참고 도서 구역
3층 – DVD와 CD
4층 – 저널 및 정기 간행물

68

What is the conversation mainly about?

(A) Borrowing a book
(B) Replacing a lost library card
(C) Applying for a position
(D) Obtaining a membership

문제 해설

대화의 주제를 묻는 첫 번째 질문이므로 대화 초반부에서 중점적으로 언급하는 핵심 내용을 파악하는 것이 관건이다. 여자가 대화를 시작하면서 'Hello. I'm new in town and I'd like to become a member of the library.'라는 말로 도서관 회원이 되고 싶다고 알리고 있고 뒤이어 회원 가입 절차에 대해 이야기하고 있으므로 (D)가 정답임을 알 수 있다.

★★ 주제, 목적

대화는 주로 무엇에 관한 것인가?
(A) 도서를 대출하는 일
(B) 분실한 도서관 카드를 교체하는 일
(C) 한 직책에 지원하는 일
(D) 회원 자격을 얻는 일

어휘 borrow ~을 빌리다, 대여하다 replace ~을 교체하다 lost 분실한 apply for ~에 지원하다 obtain ~을 얻다

토익 분석

주제가 첫 번째 대화 문장에 빈출 힌트 표현인 I'd like to~로 제시되고 있다.

★★ 요청, 제안

남자는 여자가 무엇을 하도록 요청하는가?
(A) 요금을 지불할 것
(B) 자료를 반납할 것
(C) 서류를 복사할 것
(D) 양식을 작성할 것

어휘 fee 요금 return ~을 반납하다 material 자료, 재료 photocopy ~을 복사하다 document 문서, 서류 fill out ~을 작성하다 form 양식

토익 분석

요청, 제안 문제의 단서가 되는 Please 명령문~이 답을 제시하고 있다

What does the man ask the woman to do?

(A) Pay a fee
(B) Return some materials
(C) Photocopy a document
(D) Fill out a form

문제 해설

남자가 여자에게 요청하는 것이 무엇인지를 묻는 두 번째 문제이므로 대화의 중반부에서 들을 수 있는 남자의 말에서 요청 표현과 함께 제시되는 정보에 집중해 들어야 한다. 남자는 대화 중반부에 'Please ~'라는 요청 표현을 활용해 'And please complete this application form for our records.' 라는 말로 신청서를 작성하도록 요청하고 있으므로 'complete'와 같은 의미로 쓰이는 'Fill out'과 함께 해당 요청 사항을 바꿔 표현한 (D)가 정답이 된다.

70

★★★ 그래픽

도표를 확인하시오. 여자는 곧이어 몇 층으로 갈 것 같은가?
(A) 1층
(B) 2층
(C) 3층
(D) 4층

토익 분석

각 층별 특징이 언급되어 있다. 층 정보를 찾기 위해 층별 특징을 찾아야 한다. 빈출 의도 및 미래 행동 단서인 I'd also like to가 답을 제시했다.

Look at the graphic. Which floor will the woman probably go to next?

(A) The first floor
(B) The second floor
(C) The third floor
(D) The fourth floor

문제 해설

질문에서 묻는 내용과 관련해 대화 속에 제시된 단서를 바탕으로 도표의 정보를 함께 확인해 정답을 찾아야 하는 문제이다. 이때 각 보기에 제시된 내용 외의 정보가 대화 속에서 단서로 제시될 것이므로 이에 집중해 대화를 들어야 한다. 각 보기에 층에 대한 정보가 쓰여 있으므로 도표에 이와 함께 제시된 층별 특징에 집중해 들어야 한다. 여자는 대화 후반부에 'Oh, I'd also like to check out some DVDs from your collection while I'm here.'라는 말로 DVD를 대여해 가고 싶다고 알리고 있으므로 이 일을 할 수 있는 층으로 제시된 (C)가 정답이다.

PART 4

Questions 71-73 refer to the following excerpt from a speech.

M Welcome, everyone, to an evening of celebration. 71 Mr. Mark Andrews started the Beagle Corporation when he was only eighteen years old. Already at such a young age, he had a desire to make a living while also giving back to his community, his country, and the world. 72 Now, the Beagle Corporation has over five hundred patented products on the market that range from home appliances to manufacturing machines and even baked goods. At the same time, the Beagle Corporation has donated almost 15% of its manufactured baked goods to needy people, communities, and countries around the world. All of our employees earn decent salaries, and over half of them donated to charity every year. 73 All of this started with the vision of a young Mark Andrews forty-two years ago, and 71 that is why we are here tonight to celebrate his vision and the vision of his son and successor, Mr. Adams Andrews. At the ripe age of thirty-two, Mark is ready to continue down his father's path.

남 오늘 저녁 축하연에 참석해 주신 여러분께 환영 인사를 드립니다. 71 Mark Andrews 씨는 18세의 나이로 Beagle 사를 설립하였습니다. 아주 젊은 나이였지만, 그는 자신이 속한 지역 사회, 국가, 그리고 세계에 환원하며 삶을 살아가고자 하는 바람이 있었습니다. 72 현재, Beagle 사는 가전제품에서 제조용 기기, 그리고 심지어는 제과 제품에 이르기까지 5백 개가 넘는 특허 제품들을 시장에 출시한 상태입니다. 동시에, Beagle 사는 불우한 이웃, 지역 사회, 그리고 전 세계 여러 국가에 자사에서 제조한 제과 제품의 거의 15%를 기부해 왔습니다. 모든 우리 직원들은 남부럽지 않은 연봉을 받고 있으며, 그들의 절반 이상이 해마다 자선 단체에 기부했습니다. 73 이 모든 것은 바로 42년 전 젊은 Mark Andrews 씨의 비전에서 시작되었고, 71 이는 오늘 밤 우리가 그의 비전과, 그의 아들이자 후계자인 Adams Andrews 씨가 지닌 앞으로의 비전을 축하하기 위해 이곳에 모인 이유이기도 합니다. 성숙한 32세의 나이로, Mark 씨는 계속하여 아버지의 전철을 밟아 나갈 준비가 되어 있습니다.

어휘 celebration 축하, 축하연 desire 바람, 희망 make a living 삶을 영위하다 give back to ~에게 환원하다 community 지역 사회 patented 특허를 받은 on the market 시장에 출시된 range from A to B A에서 B에 이르다 home appliances 가전제품 manufactured goods 제조품 needy people 불우한/가난한 사람 decent 품위 있는, 보기 좋은 donate to ~에 기부하다 charity 자선 단체 successor 후계자 ripe 성숙한, 농익은 down one's path ~의 길을 따라

71

Where is this speech probably being given?

(A) At a new-hire training session   **(B) At a retirement dinner**
(C) At a press conference   (D) At a charity fundraiser

★★★ 암시 추론

연설은 어디에서 이뤄지고 있을 것 같은가?
(A) 신입 직원 연수에서   (B) 은퇴 만찬에서
(C) 기자 회견에서   (D) 자선기금 마련 행사에서

어휘 new hire 신입 사원 training session 교육 연수 retirement 은퇴 press conference 기자 회견 charity 자선 (단체) fundraiser 모금 행사

문제 해설

연설문의 장소를 유추하는 질문이므로 담화 초반부에서 연설문의 장소를 추측할 수 있을 만한 관련 어휘나 표현이 제시되는 부분에 집중하는 것이 우선이다. 화자는 담화 초반부에 'Mr. Mark Andrews~18 years old.' 부분을 통해, 18세에 Beagle 사를 설립했다는 약력을 언급하고 있다. 그리고 담화 마지막에 가서 'that is why~Mr. Adams Andrews'라는 말로 Mark Andrews 씨와 그의 아들이자 후계자인 Adams Andrews 씨의 비전을 축하하고자 모였음을 밝히는 부분을 통해 바로 Mark Andrews 씨의 은퇴 기념식임을 가늠할 수 있으므로 (B)가 정답이다.

토익 분석

행사 종류는 및 목적은 도입부에 정확한 행사명이 제시되는 쉬운 유형과 환영 인사와 주제문에서 유추를 해야 한다.

72

What products does the Beagle Corporation probably manufacture?

(A) Vehicles   **(B) Microwaves**
(C) Ceramic objects   (D) Semiconductor chips

★★ 세부 정보

Beagle 사에서 제조하는 제품은 무엇일 것 같은가?
(A) 자동차   (B) 전자레인지
(C) 도자기 제품   (D) 반도체 칩

어휘 ceramic 도자기 semiconductor 반도체

토익 분석

세부 정보 문제로 Beagle Corporation를 키워드로 답을 찾는 문제다.

문제 해설

Beagle 사의 제조품에 대해 묻는 두 번째 문제이므로 담화 중반부에 화자가 해당 회사의 제품을 소개하는 부분이 있을 것임을 예상하고 들어야 한다. 화자는 담화 중반부에 'Now, the Beagle~baked goods.'라는 말로 가전제품에서 제조 장비 그리고 심지어는 제과 제품에 이르기까지 제조한다고 알리고 있다. 따라서 이 품목들 중 가전제품에 해당되는 (B)가 정답이다.

73

How long has the Beagle Corporation been in business?

(A) 18 years   (B) 32 years
(C) 42 years   (D) 60 years

★★★ 세부 정보

Beagle 사는 얼마나 오랫동안 사업을 해왔는가?
(A) 18년   (B) 32년
(C) 42년   (D) 60년

어휘 be in business 사업/영업을 하고 있다

토익 분석

회사소개 문장에서 답을 찾아야 한다. 이어지는 문장들 중 기간 표현에 집중해야 한다.

문제 해설

Beagle 사가 지금까지 사업을 해 온 기간을 묻는 마지막 문제이므로 담화 후반부에 Beagle 사의 정보와 관련해 제시되는 기간에 집중해야 한다. 화자는 담화 후반부에서 'All of this~42 years ago'라고 말하며 42년 전 젊은 Mark Andrews 씨의 비전에서 비롯되었음을 밝히고 있다. 이는 42년 전에 회사가 시작되었음을 알리는 것이므로 (C)가 정답이 된다.

여 **74** 비가 오는데도 불구하고 이 자리에 참석하신 모든 분에게 매우 감사 드립니다. 거의 모든 분께서 이미 아시다시피, **75** 오늘 저녁의 첫 연례 자선 공연은 주거지가 절실히 필요한 사람들을 위한 기금을 마련하기 위해 자선 연주가들에 의해 마련됐습니다. 이 연례 자선 행사는 따뜻한 잠자리가 필요한 아이들을 돕는 것뿐만 아니라, 그들에게 우리가 반드시 생활에 필요한 것들로 당연하게 받아들이는 교육과 음식을 제공하기 위한 것입니다. 따라서 **76** 피아니스트 Susan Kang 씨와 함께 오늘 저녁의 행사를 시작하는 동안 여러분 모두 편안하고 즐거운 시간이 되셨으면 합니다.

Questions 74-76 refer to the following speech.

W **74** I am so grateful for all of you coming here today despite the rainy weather. As most of you already know, **75** this evening's first annual charity performance was put together by volunteer performers to raise money for those who desperately need shelter. This yearly event will not only help children who need warm beds but will also go toward their education and food, the necessities of life we all take for granted. So everyone relax and have a great time as **76** we'll begin this evening's event with pianist Susan Kang.

어휘 grateful 고마워하는 despite ~에도 불구하고 annual 연례의 charity performance 자선 공연 put together ~을 준비하다 volunteer 자원봉사자 raise money 기금을 마련하다, 돈을 모으다 those who ~하는 사람들 desperately 필사적으로, 절실하게 shelter 주거지, 은신처 yearly event 연례행사 not only A but B A뿐만 아니라 B도 go toward ~을 목적으로 하다 necessity 필수품 take A for granted ~을 당연하게 여기다 relax 긴장을 풀다

74

★ 세부 정보

화자에 따르면, 외부의 날씨는 어떠한가?
(A) 화창하다.
(B) 바람이 분다.
(C) 구름이 끼어 있다.
(D) 비가 온다.

토익 분석

첫 번째 문제이므로 초반부 지문에서 날씨관련 표현에 집중해야 하는 문제다.

According to the speaker, how is the weather outside?

(A) It's sunny.
(B) It's windy.
(C) It's cloudy.
(D) It's rainy.

문제 해설

날씨에 관해 묻는 첫 번째 문제이므로 담화 초반부에서 화자가 날씨 상태를 언급하는 부분에 초점을 맞춰야 한다. 화자가 담화 시작과 함께 'I am so grateful for all of you coming here today despite the rainy weather.'라고 언급하는 부분에서 비가 오는 날씨임을 알 수 있으므로 (D)가 정답이다.

75

★★ 세부 정보

모금된 돈은 어느 지출 부분을 충당하는 데 사용될 것인가?
(A) 의료 서비스 (B) 주거지
(C) 장난감 선물 (D) 교통

어휘 cover ~을 충당하다 living allowances 생활비 transportation 교통

토익 분석

질문 속에 사용된 **money**와 **raise**가 키워드로 사용되는 문제다.

Which expense will the money raised be used to cover?

(A) Medical services **(B) Housing**
(C) Toy presents (D) Transportation

문제 해설

모금액의 용도에 대해 묻는 두 번째 문제이므로 담화의 중반부에 화자가 구체적인 용도를 알리는 부분이 있음을 예상하고 들어야 한다. 화자가 담화 중반부에 'this evening's first annual charity performance was put together by volunteer performers to raise money for those who desperately need shelter'라는 말로 주거지가 필요한 사람들을 돕기 위한 기금을 마련하는 행사임을 밝히고 있으므로 (B)가 정답이다.

76

★ 세부 정보

Susan Kang은 누구인가?
(A) 기부자
(B) 자선 행사 주최자
(C) 연주자
(D) 초청 연사

어휘 donor 기부자 organizer (행사 등의) 주최자, 조직자 guest speaker 초청 연사

토익 분석

특정 인물의 직업은 언제나 '이름'이 등장하는 문장에 제시되므로 '이름'이 키워드가 된다.

Who is Susan Kang?

(A) A donor (B) A charity organizer
(C) A performer (D) A guest speaker

문제 해설

Susan Kang 씨의 정체를 묻는 마지막 문제이므로 담화 후반부에서 Susan Kang이라는 이름이 제시되는 부분에 함께 들을 수 있는 직책이나 관련 업무 등의 정보를 찾아야 한다. 담화 마지막에 화자가 'we'll begin this evening's event with pianist Susan Kang'이라는 말로 피아니스트임을 알리고 있으므로 '연주자'를 뜻하는 (C)가 정답이다.

Questions 77-79 refer to the following radio broadcast.

W   Hello, listeners! [77, 78] My name is Lisa McGowan, and I'd like to thank Today's Health Tour Show for inviting me to speak about relationship management today. As a psychologist, I have counseled hundreds of married couples and families to improve their relationships and communication. Communication really is the key to a good relationship with anyone, whether at home or at work. The first thing you must learn is how to be a good listener. To become a better communicator, you must be willing to listen so you can understand the other person's perspective. [79] Communicating and listening to others are the most important relationship skills you can ever learn to bridge the gap between you and another person.

여 안녕하세요? 청취자 여러분! [77, 78] 제 이름은 Lisa McGowan이며, 대인 관계 유지에 대해 이야기할 수 있도록 저를 초대해 주신 점에 대해 Today's Health Tour Show 측에 감사를 표하고 싶습니다. 심리학자로서, 저는 수백 명의 부부와 가족들이 그들의 관계와 의사소통 방법을 개선할 수 있도록 상담을 해 왔습니다. 의사소통은 집에서든 직장에서든 그 누구와도 좋은 관계를 맺기 위해선 아주 중요합니다. 우선 여러분이 꼭 배워야 하는 것은 타인의 이야기를 잘 들어주는 사람이 되는 방법입니다. 의사소통을 더 잘하는 사람이 되기 위해서, 타인의 이야기를 경청하겠다는 의지가 있어야 하며, 그로 인해 타인의 관점을 잘 이해할 수 있도록 해야 합니다. [79] 타인과 의사소통을 하고 타인의 말을 경청하는 것이 여러분과 타인 사이의 간극을 연결하기 위해 배울 수 있는 제일 중요한 대인 관계 능력입니다.

어휘 relationship 대인 관계 psychologist 심리학자 counsel ~와 상담하다 married couple 부부 improve ~을 개선하다 communication 의사소통 whether A or B A이든 B이든 상관없이 how to do ~하는 법 communicator 의사소통하는 사람 be willing to do ~할 의향이 있다, 기꺼이 ~하다 perspective 관점, 견해 bridge ~을 연결하다, 가교 역할을 하다 gap 간격, 사이 between A and B A와 B 사이에

77

Who most likely is Ms. McGowan?

(A) A language specialist   (B) A public speaking trainer
(C) A radio show host   **(D) A relationship therapist**

문제 해설

Lisa McGowan이라는 사람의 정체에 대해 묻는 첫 번째 질문이므로 담화 초반부에서 Lisa McGowan이라는 이름과 신분 관련 정보가 제시될 것임을 예상하고 들어야 한다. 화자는 'I'd like~today.'라는 말로 자신이 대인 관계 관리에 대해 이야기하러 나온 초대 손님일 뿐만 아니라 as a psychologist와 같이 심리학자라고 소개하고 있으므로 화자는 대인 관계 치료를 전문으로 하는 심리학자임을 알 수 있다. 따라서 (D)가 정답이다. (A) psychiatrist는 정신과 의사를 의미하므로 유의해야 한다.

★★★ 암시 추론

McGowan 씨는 누구일 것 같은가?
(A) 언어 전문가   (B) 화술 트레이너
(C) 라디오 프로그램 진행자 (D) 대인 관계 치료사

어휘 psychiatrist 정신과 의사 host (프로그램 등의) 진행자 therapist 치료사

토익 분석

질문에서 알 수 있듯 most likely가 포함되어 있다는 것은 사람 이름과 함께 명확한 직책이 등장하지 않는 문제다. 이름이 언급된 문장에서 유추를 해야 하는 유형이다.

78

What is the main topic of Ms. McGowan's talk?

(A) How to find a business partner   (B) How to become a psychologist
(C) How to avoid divorce   **(D) How to communicate better**

문제 해설

McGowan 씨가 하는 이야기의 주제를 묻는 두 번째 문제이므로 담화 중반부에 이야기 주제가 언급된다는 것을 예상하고 들어야 한다. 화자는 담화 중반부에 'I'd like to~relationships and communication.'라는 말로 자신이 수백 명의 부부와 가족들이 의사소통을 개선할 수 있도록 상담했다는 점을 밝히면서 의사소통의 중요성을 언급하는 것으로 담화를 이어가고 있으므로 (D)가 정답임을 알 수 있다.

★★ 세부 정보

McGowan 씨가 하는 이야기의 주제는 무엇인가?
(A) 사업 파트너를 찾는 방법 (B) 심리학자가 되는 방법
(C) 이혼을 피하는 방법   (D) 의사소통을 잘하는 방법

어휘 avoid ~을 피하다 divorce 이혼

토익 분석

초대 연사의 연설 주제는 discuss, talk about, share, explain등과 같은 표현들이 힌트로 등장한다. 주제문은 의도 및 미래 행동 표현이 자주 등장한다. I'd like to와 speak about가 힌트로 활용되었다.

79

According to the speaker, which is the most critical to successful relationships?

(A) Understanding human psychology
(B) Showing respect for the opposition
(C) Listening to other people's opinions
(D) Winning the favor of one's colleagues

문제 해설

성공적 관계에서 가장 중요한 것을 묻는 마지막 문제이므로 지문 후반부에서 화자가 성공적 관계, 즉, successful relationships에 대해 언급하는 부분이 있음을 예상하고 들어야 한다. 화자가 담화 후반부에 'communicating and listening to others are the most important relationship skills'이라고 말하며 의사소통에서 어떻게 타인의 이야기를 들어야 하는지가 성공적 대인 관계 능력에 있어 가장 중요하다고 언급하고 있으므로 정답은 (C)임을 알 수 있다.

★★ 세부 정보

화자에 따르면, 성공적인 대인 관계에 있어 가장 중요한 것은 무엇인가?
(A) 인간의 심리를 이해하는 것
(B) 반대 의견을 존중하는 것
(C) 타인의 의견을 들어주는 것
(D) 동료들의 호감을 얻는 것

어휘 critical 아주 중요한 psychology 심리 show respect for ~을 존중하다 win the favor of ~의 호감을 얻다

토익 분석

질문 속에 most critical to successful relationship을 키워드로 활용한 문제로 most important relationship skills가 정답의 단서가 된다.

남 저는 진행자 Bill Jones이며, 다음으로 지역 소식을
전해 드리겠습니다. Carford 시의 연례 스테이크 축
제가 이번 주말에 열리며, 여러 레스토랑이 특별 행
사를 개최할 예정입니다. 이 행사는 지역 주민들과
여행객들 모두에게 인기 있는 행사이며, 행사 장소
들은 매우 분주할 가능성이 큽니다. 80 전체 일정표를
보시려면 저희 웹 사이트를 확인해 보십시오. 81 이번
주말에 가장 기대되는 행사들 중의 하나가 Lavender
Bistro에서 있을 예정이며, 이곳에서 빨리 먹기 대회
가 토요일에 개최될 것입니다. 큰 상금을 탈 수 있는
기회가 제공되는데 참가자들에게는 5개의 스테이크
를 먹는 데 오직 1분의 시간이 주어집니다. 또한, 당
일 밤에 라이브 음악 공연 및 특별 판촉 행사도 있을
것입니다. 82 이 행사는 많은 사람을 유치할 것이 분
명하므로 예약하시기 바라며, Lavender Bistro에는
좀처럼 빈 테이블이 나지 않습니다.

Questions 80-82 refer to the following news report.

M I'm your host, Bill Jones, and next I have your local news. Carford City's
Annual Steak Festival is this weekend, and several restaurants will be
hosting special events. This event is popular with both local residents and
tourists, and venues are likely to be very busy. 80 Check our Web site for a
full schedule. 81 One of the most anticipated events of the weekend will be
at the Lavender Bistro, where an eating contest will be held on Saturday.
Participants will have only one minute to eat five steaks for a chance
to win big prizes. There will also be live music and special promotions
throughout the night. 82 Make a booking in advance, as this event is sure
to draw a big crowd, and Lavender Bistro rarely has an empty table.

어휘 several 여럿의 host ~을 주최하다 be popular with ~에게 인기가 있다 both A and B A와 B 둘 다 resident
주민 venue 행사 장소 be likely to do ~할 가능성이 있다 anticipated 기대되는 eating contest 빨리 먹기 대회
participant 참가자 a chance to do ~할 기회 win (상 등) 받다 prize 상금 promotion 판촉 행사 make a booking 예
약하다 in advance 미리 be sure to do 분명 ~하다 draw 끌어들이다 crowd 사람들 rarely 좀처럼 ~ 않다

80

★★ 세부 정보

청자들은 웹 사이트에서 무슨 정보를 찾아야 하는가?
(A) 운전해서 가는 방법   (B) 행사 일정
(C) 티켓 비용   (D) 여행 일정표

어휘 directions 길, 방향 itinerary 여행 일정(표)

토익 분석

세부 정보 문제로 키워드를 활용해야 한다. Web site가 키
워드가 되며 요청, 제안 힌트인 Check~과 같은 명령문 문
장도 답을 찾는데 중요한 단서가 된다.

What information should the listeners look for on a Web site?

(A) Driving directions   **(B) An event schedule**
(C) Ticket costs   (D) A tour itinerary

문제 해설

웹 사이트에서 찾아야 하는 정보를 묻는 첫 번째 문제이므로 담화 초반부에 웹 사이트와 관련된 내
용이 제시될 것임을 예상하고 들어야 한다. 화자는 담화 초반부에 스테이크 축제가 열린다는 사실
을 언급하면서 'Check our Web site for a full schedule'라는 말로 행사의 전체 일정표를 웹 사이트
에서 확인하라고 알리고 있으므로 (B)가 정답임을 알 수 있다.

81

★★ 세부 정보

Lavender Bistro에서의 행사는 왜 인기 있을 것으로 예상
되는가?
(A) 새로운 음식 메뉴가 출시될 것이다.
(B) 그 레스토랑이 좋은 평가를 받았다.
(C) 대회가 열릴 것이다.
(D) 광고 캠페인이 성공적이었다.

어휘 be expected to do ~할 것으로 예상되다 launch ~
을 출시하다 review 평가, 의견 competition (경연) 대회

토익 분석

Lavender Bistro가 키워드로 활용되는 문제다. most
anticipated events와 같은 최상급 표현들 역시 언제나 중요
한 정보를 제시한다.

Why is the event at Lavender Bistro expected to be popular?

(A) A new menu item will be launched.
(B) The restaurant has received good reviews.
(C) A competition will be held.
(D) An advertising campaign was successful.

문제 해설

Lavender Bistro에서의 행사가 인기 있을 것으로 생각되는 이유를 묻는 두 번째 문제이므로 담화
중반부에 Lavender Bistro라는 명칭과 함께 인기 있는 행사 및 그 이유로 언급되는 정보를 찾아야
한다. 화자는 담화 중반부에 'One of the~on Saturday.'라는 말로 가장 기대되는 행사가 Lavender
Bistro에서 열리는데 그 행사가 빨리 먹기 대회라고 알리고 있다. 따라서 contest와 같은 의미를 나
타내는 competition과 함께 대회가 열린다는 의미로 쓰인 (C)가 정답이다.

82

★★★ 맥락 파악

화자가 왜 "Lavender Bistro rarely has an empty table"라
고 말하는가?
(A) 한 지역 레스토랑의 실내 배치를 비판하기 위해
(B) 한 업체에서 제공되는 음식을 칭찬하기 위해
(C) 청자들에게 다른 장소를 선택하도록 조언하기 위해
(D) 예약을 하도록 권하기 위해

어휘 criticize ~을 비판하다 layout 배치 praise ~을 칭
찬하다 make a reservation 예약하다

토익 분석

제시된 표현의 바로 전 문장 Make a booking in advance
가 명령문 형태로 답을 찾는데 중요한 단서가 되고 있다.

Why does the speaker say, "Lavender Bistro rarely has an empty table"?

(A) To criticize the layout of a local restaurant
(B) To praise the food served at a business
(C) To advise listeners to choose a different venue
(D) To recommend making a reservation

문제 해설

"Lavender Bistro rarely has an empty table"라는 문장을 미리 확인해 둔 후 해당 문장이 제시되는
부분의 앞뒤에 함께 언급되는 정보 및 담화의 흐름을 함께 확인하는 것이 관건이다. 화자는 담화 마
지막에 'Make a booking~empty table.'라는 말로 예약을 하라고 당부하면서 해당 문장을 언급하
고 있으므로, 테이블이 좀처럼 나지 않는다는 말은 예약을 해야 한다는 것을 강조하는 의미임을 알
수 있다. 따라서 이와 같은 의미에 해당되는 (D)가 정답이다.

Questions 83-85 refer to the following announcement.

W   Good morning, everyone, and welcome to this market research study. My name is Melissa, and during this morning's session, ⁸³ I'll be asking you to use some of my company's new fitness machines to test whether they function well and are easy to use. ⁸⁴ Please be aware that you shouldn't be afraid to speak your mind here. We want to make sure our products are the best ones on the market, so we appreciate all your comments, even the negative ones. ⁸⁵ Before we get started, I'd like you to change into these workout outfits. It's important that you all feel comfortable while using the treadmills and bikes. Thanks.

여   안녕하세요, 여러분, 그리고 시장 조사 연구를 위해 와 주셔서 환영합니다. 제 이름은 Melissa이며, 오늘 아침의 이 시간 동안, ⁸³ 저희 회사의 새로운 피트니스 기계들이 잘 작동되고 사용하기 쉬운지 테스트해 보시도록 여러분께 요청 드릴 것입니다. ⁸⁴ 이곳에서 여러분의 생각을 거리낌 없이 말씀해 주셔야 한다는 점에 유의해 주시기 바랍니다. 저희는 저희 제품이 반드시 시장에서 최고의 제품이 되기를 원하고 있기 때문에 심지어 부정적인 것이더라도 여러분의 모든 의견에 대해 감사히 여길 것입니다. ⁸⁵ 시작하기에 앞서, 이 운동복으로 갈아입으시기 바랍니다. 러닝 머신과 자전거를 이용해 보시는 동안 여러분 모두가 편안함을 느끼는 것이 중요합니다. 감사합니다.

어휘 market research 시장 조사 study 연구, 조사 session (특정 활동을 위한) 시간 ask A to do A에게 ~하도록 요청하다 whether ~인지 (아닌지) function 작동되다 be aware that ~임에 유의/인식하다 be afraid to do ~하기를 두려워하다 mind 생각, 마음 make sure (that) 반드시 ~하도록 하다 on the market 시장에서 appreciate ~에 대해 감사하다 comment 의견 even 심지어 negative 부정적인 get started 시작하다 workout outfit 운동복 feel comfortable 편안함을 느끼다 treadmill 러닝 머신

83

What are the listeners scheduled to do?

(A) Sample some foods   **(B) Test out some machines**
(C) Perform some repairs   (D) Survey some customers

문제 해설

청자들이 하게 될 일을 묻는 첫 번째 문제이므로 담화 초반부에서 청자들에게 요청하는 일이나 부탁하는 일로 제시되는 정보를 찾는 것이 관건이다. 화자는 담화 초반부에 'I'll be asking you to use some of my company's new fitness machines to test whether they function well and are easy to use.'라는 말로 새로운 피트니스 운동 기계들이 잘 작동되고 사용하기 쉬운지 테스트해 보도록 요청할 것이라고 알리고 있다. 따라서 기계를 시험해 보는 일을 뜻하는 (B)가 정답이다.

★★ 세부 정보

청자들은 무엇을 할 예정인가?
(A) 음식을 시식하는 일   (B) 기계들을 시험해 보는 일
(C) 수리 작업을 실시하는 일
(D) 고객들에게 설문 조사를 하는 일

어휘 sample ~을 시식하다 test out ~을 테스트해 보다 perform ~을 실시/수행하다 repair 수리

토익 분석

청자의 행동은 화자의 요청, 제안에 의해 이루어진다는 것을 기억해야 한다. 따라서 요청, 제안의 단골 힌트인 ask를 활용한 I'll be asking you가 정답 힌트다.

84

What does the speaker imply when she says, "you shouldn't be afraid to speak your mind here"?

(A) The listeners should discuss an issue among themselves.
(B) The listeners can leave the room whenever necessary.
(C) The listeners will listen to a talk by an expert.
(D) The listeners should feel free to say negative things.

문제 해설

"you shouldn't be afraid to speak your mind here"라는 문장을 미리 확인해 둔 후 해당 문장이 제시되는 부분의 앞뒤에 함께 언급되는 정보 및 담화의 흐름을 함께 확인하는 것이 관건이다. 화자는 담화 중반부에 해당 문장과 함께 'We want to make sure our products are the best ones on the market, so we appreciate all your comments, even the negative ones.'라는 말로 부정적인 의견까지 모두 말해 주기를 권하고 있으므로 (D)가 정답임을 알 수 있다.

★★★ 맥락 파악

화자가 "you shouldn't be afraid to speak your mind here"라고 말할 때 무엇을 암시하는가?
(A) 청자들이 서로 한 가지 사안을 논의해야 한다.
(B) 청자들이 필요할 때마다 방에서 나갈 수 있다.
(C) 청자들이 한 전문가의 연설을 들을 것이다.
(D) 청자들이 부정적인 것들을 마음껏 얘기해야 한다.

어휘 whenever necessary 필요할 때마다 expert 전문가 feel free to do 마음껏 ~하다

토익 분석

제시된 표현에 이어지는 문장에 의도 및 미래 행동 힌트인 We(I) want to~와 반전 표현 So~가 정답의 단서가 된다.

85

What are the listeners asked to do next?

(A) Review some guidelines   (B) Go to another room
(C) Complete a form   **(D) Change their clothes**

문제 해설

청자들이 곧이어 하도록 요청 받는 일을 묻는 마지막 문제이므로 담화 후반부에서 앞으로의 계획이나 순서 등과 관련된 정보를 찾는 데 집중해야 한다. 화자는 담화 마지막에 'Before we get started, I'd like you to change into these workout outfits.'라는 말로 시작하기 전에 운동복으로 갈아입으라고 부탁하고 있으므로 이에 대해 언급한 (D)가 정답이다.

★★ 요청, 제안

청자들은 곧이어 무엇을 하도록 요청 받는가?
(A) 가이드라인을 검토할 것 (B) 다른 방으로 갈 것
(C) 양식을 작성 완료할 것 (D) 그들의 옷을 갈아입을 것

어휘 review ~을 검토하다 complete ~을 작성 완료하다

토익 분석

청자의 행동은 바로 화자의 요청 또는 제안이다. 따라서 요청, 제안 단서인 I'd like you to가 정답을 이끌고 있다.

여 주간 회의를 마무리하기에 앞서 마지막으로 간단한 전달 사항을 언급하고자 합니다. **86, 87** 이사진에서 내일 우리 부서의 모든 직원들이 사무실에 있는 각자의 컴퓨터에 새로운 관리 프로그램을 설치해 달라는 요청 사항을 전달해 왔습니다. 이 프로그램은 여러분의 활동, 근무 시간, 그리고 생산성을 파악하기 위해 개발되었습니다. 이 프로그램은 새로운 계획의 첫 번째 단계로서 오직 우리 부서에서만 사용될 예정입니다. **88** 저는 여러분에게 매주 금요일 자동적으로 이메일로 발송되는 주간 통계 자료를 자세히 검토하는 것과 함께 일치하지 않는 통계 자료가 보고된 것과 관련하여 어떤 의견이든 기술 지원팀에게 제시해 주실 것을 당부 드립니다. 자, 그러면 다시 일하도록 합시다.

Questions 86-88 refer to the following announcement.

W I have one final, quick announcement before we finish our weekly meeting. **86, 87** The board has passed down a request that all employees in our department should install a new management program on their office computers tomorrow. The program was developed to track your activities, work hours, and productivity. This is a new initiative that is going to be used only in our department for its initial phases. **88** I encourage you to examine the weekly statistics that will be automatically e-mailed to you each Friday and to give our technical support team any feedback about inconsistent statistics that are reported. OK, let's get back to work.

어휘 pass down ~을 전달하다 request 요청 install ~을 설치하다 develop ~을 개발하다 track ~을 파악/추적하다 work hours 근무 시간 productivity 생산성 initiative 계획 initial 초기/최초의 phase 국면, 단계 encourage A to do A에게 장려하다 examine ~을 점검/검토하다 statistics 통계, 통계 자료 automatically 자동적으로 technical support 기술 지원 feedback 의견 inconsistent 불일치하는 get back to ~로 다시 돌아가다

86

★★ 주제, 목적

공지는 무엇에 관한 것인가?
(A) 생산성 증대 (B) 새로운 컴퓨터 과정 프로그램
(C) 근무 시간의 변경 (D) 새로운 업무 관리 프로그램

어휘 increase 증대, 증가 performance 업무 능력, 실적

토익 분석

announcement이라는 단어가 반복되고 시점 관련 표현 before we finish our weekly meeting이 답을 찾는 단서다. ~하기 전에, ~한 후에 와 같은 표현들은 언제나 중요한 정보를 제공한다.

What is the announcement about?

(A) A productivity increase (B) A new computer course
(C) A change in business hours
(D) New performance management software

문제 해설

공지의 주제를 묻는 첫 번째 문제이므로 담화 초반부에서 언급되는 핵심 주제를 파악하는 것이 관건이다. 화자는 지문 초반부에 'The board~office computers tomorrow.'라는 말로 새로운 관리 프로그램을 컴퓨터에 설치해 달라는 요청을 받았음을 알리고 있으므로 (D)가 정답이다.

87

★★ 요청, 제안

직원들은 내일 무엇을 해달라는 요청을 받는가?
(A) 새로운 프로그램을 사용할 것
(B) 새로운 컴퓨터 시스템을 설치할 것
(C) 컴퓨터의 전원을 끌 것
(D) 생산성에 관한 통계 자료를 수집할 것

어휘 turn off ~을 끄다 gather ~을 모으다

토익 분석

요청, 제안 문제지만 질문 속에 등장한 tomorrow와 같은 시점 표현은 언제나 결정적인 키워드가 된다.

What are the employees asked to do tomorrow?

(A) Use a new program (B) Install a new computer system
(C) Turn off their computers (D) Gather statistics on productivity

문제 해설

직원들에게 내일 해달라고 요청 받는 것이 무엇인지 묻는 두 번째 문제이므로 '내일'이라는 시점이 제시되는 부분을 중심으로 단서를 파악하는 것이 우선이다. 화자는 지문 초반부에 'The board~office computers tomorrow.'이라고 이야기하며 부서 내 모든 직원들이 새로운 관리 프로그램을 컴퓨터에 설치해야 한다고 알리고 있다. 따라서 이를 통해 직원들은 내일 새로운 관리 프로그램을 설치하여 사용해야 함을 알 수 있으므로 (A)가 정답이다.

88

★★★ 요청, 제안

화자에 따르면, 기술 지원부에 연락해야 하는 이유는 무엇인가?
(A) 새로운 소프트웨어를 개발하게 하려고
(B) 비판적 의견을 제시하기 위해서
(C) 창의적인 아이디어를 논의하기 위해서
(D) 컴퓨터 네트워크의 문제점을 보고하기 위해서

어휘 have A do A에게 ~하게 하다 submit ~을 제출하다 criticism 비판(적인 의견) creative 창의적인

토익 분석

요청 제안 단서인 encourage가 포함된 I encourage you to가 답의 단서가 된다. technical support는 키워드로 사용되고 있다.

According to the speaker, why should the technical support team be contacted?

(A) To have them develop new software
(B) To submit criticism
(C) To discuss some creative ideas with them
(D) To report problems with the computer network

문제 해설

기술 지원부에 연락해야 하는 이유를 묻는 마지막 질문이므로 담화 후반부에서 기술 지원부라는 부서명이 등장하는 부분을 중심으로 해당 부서에 연락해야 하는 이유를 파악해야 한다. 따라서 화자가 담화 후반부에 'I encourage~that are reported.'라고 이야기하며 직원의 이메일로 발송되는 주간 통계 자료를 자세히 검토하고 실제와 일치하지 않는 통계 자료에 대해 기술 지원팀에게 의견을 제시할 것을 요청하는 부분을 통해 (B)가 정답임을 알 수 있다.

Questions 89-91 refer to the following excerpt from a meeting.

M Good afternoon and thank you for showing up early for this staff meeting. [89] We want to show you some items that are going to be new to our menu starting tonight. [90] Our new menu items are in response to a customer survey, where we found out our clientele would like to see seasonal items rotating in our menu throughout the year. You will have the opportunity to watch the kitchen staff make the food, to ask questions, and to taste each item. [91] If any of you have peanut allergies, you will not be able to sample the new shrimp spring roll as it contains nuts.

남 안녕하세요, 오늘 직원회의에 일찍 와 주셔서 감사드립니다. [89] 우리는 여러분께 오늘 밤부터 메뉴에 새롭게 제공되는 제품들을 보여 드리고자 합니다. [90] 새로운 메뉴 제품들은 고객 설문 조사에 따른 것이며, 이 조사에서 우리는 고객님들께서 우리의 한 해 메뉴에서 계절에 따른 음식들을 번갈아 접하실 수 있기를 원하신다는 점을 확인했습니다. 여러분께서는 주방 직원들이 음식을 조리하는 모습을 보신 후에 궁금한 점에 대해 질문하시고 각 제품의 맛을 보실 기회를 갖게 되실 것입니다. [91] 여러분 중 누구라도 견과류 알레르기가 있으실 경우, 견과류가 포함된 새로운 Shrimp Spring Roll은 시식하실 수 없습니다.

어휘 show up 나타나다, 모습을 드러내다 staff meeting 직원회의 have the opportunity to do ~할 기회를 갖다 watch A do A가 ~하는 것을 보다 allergy 알레르기 반응 be able to do ~할 수 있다 sample ~을 시식/시음하다 contain ~을 포함하다 nut 견과류 be in response to ~에 대응/반응하여 survey 설문 조사 find out (that) ~임을 확인하다, 알아내다 clientele 고객, 고객층 seasonal item 계절 음식 rotate ~이 돌고 돌다, ~이 순환하다 throughout the year 한 해 동안, 1년 동안

89

What kind of business does the speaker probably work for?

(A) A courier service　　　　　(B) A supermarket
(C) A restaurant　　　　　(D) A kitchen appliance manufacturer

문제 해설

화자가 근무하는 업체를 유추해야 하는 첫 번째 문제이므로 담화 초반부에서 화자가 근무하는 업체를 추측할 수 있는 관련 어휘나 표현이 제시되는 부분에 집중해야 한다. 화자는 지문 초반부에 'We want to show you some items that are going to be new to our menu starting tonight.'이라는 말로 새로 제공되는 메뉴를 보여 주겠다고 언급하고 있으므로 (C)가 정답임을 알 수 있다.

★ 도입부 정보 – 화자

화자는 무슨 종류의 업체에서 근무할 것 같은가?
(A) 택배 서비스　　　　(B) 슈퍼마켓
(C) 식당　　　　(D) 주방 기기 제조업체

어휘 courier service 택배 서비스 appliance (가전) 기기 manufacturer 제조사 vary 다르다, 차이가 나다

토익 분석

화자와 관련된 정보는 도입부 환경 인사 다음 부분이다. We(I) want to는 의도 및 미래 행동의 단서로 Part 4에서 주제문을 이끄는 중요한 표현이다.

90

What do some customers want the business to offer?

(A) Options that vary　　　　(B) Gourmet recipes
(C) Longer business hours　　　　(D) Better customer service

문제 해설

고객들이 업체에 바라는 것을 묻는 질문이므로 무엇보다 담화에서 고객과 관련된 내용이 어느 부분에서 등장하는지에 집중해야 한다. 화자는 담화 중반부에 'Our new menu items are in response to a customer survey, where we found out our clientele would like to see seasonal items rotating through our menu throughout the year.'라고 말하며 한 해 메뉴에서 계절에 따른 음식들을 접할 수 있길 바란다는 고객 설문 조사 결과를 언급하고 있다. 이는 계절마다 특화된 음식들을 접할 수 있길 바란다는 말과 같으므로 기간에 따라 다른 선택 사항을 의미하는 (A)가 정답이다.

★★★ 세부 정보

일부 고객들은 업체에서 무엇을 제공하길 원하는가?
(A) 다양한 선택 사항
(B) 고급 음식의 조리법
(C) 더 긴 영업시간
(D) 더 향상된 고객 서비스

어휘 over time 기간에 따라 gourmet 고급 요리 recipe 조리법

토익 분석

일단 고객들이 무엇을 원하는지 찾아야 한다. 주체가 customer이므로 customer는 키워드가 된다. 원하는 것을 설명하기 위해 our clientele would like to 와 같은 요청, 제안 표현이 사용된 것이다.

91

What will the listeners probably do next?

(A) Fill out a questionnaire　　　　**(B) Sample some products**
(C) Enter a cooking contest　　　　(D) Ask for a discount

문제 해설

청자들의 미래 행동에 대해 묻는 마지막 문제이므로 담화에서 청자들이 하게 되는 일과 관련된 계획이나 일정 등을 언급하는 부분에 집중해야 한다. 화자는 담화 후반부에 'If any of you have peanut allergies, you will not be able to sample the new shrimp spring roll as it contains nuts.'라고 이야기하며 견과류 알레르기가 있는 경우 새로운 shrimp spring roll을 시식하지 말 것을 요청하고 있다. 이는 청자들이 이후에 제품을 시식할 것임을 암시하는 말이므로 (B)가 정답이다.

★★ 미래 행동

청자들은 곧이어 무엇을 할 것 같은가?
(A) 설문지를 작성한다.　　　(B) 제품을 시식한다.
(C) 요리 경연 대회에 참가한다.　(D) 할인을 요청한다.

어휘 fill out ~을 작성하다 questionnaire 설문지 enter ~에 참가하다 ask for ~을 요청하다

토익 분석

미래 행동은 언제나 지문의 가장 후반부에 등장한다. if 가정법 ~, you will~ 구조 문장이 정답의 단서를 제시하고 있다.

여 안녕하세요, 그리고 92 이렇게 오래 기다리게 해서 죄송합니다. 제가 도시의 외곽 지역에 거주하고 있는데, Benton Boulevard가 현재 공사 중에 있습니다. 어쨌든, 견학을 시작해 보겠습니다. 일단 공사가 완료되고 나면, 이 쇼핑몰은 전 세계에서 가장 큰 곳이 될 것입니다. 푸드 코트 및 공연 구역은 모두 완공된 상태이므로 우선 이 구역들을 먼저 둘러보시도록 안내해 드리겠습니다. 93 1층에는 놀이공원이 있지만, 아직 어느 놀이기구도 작동되고 있지 않습니다. 이 기구들은 3개월 후에 운영되기 시작할 것입니다. 아, 시작하기 전에, 94 오늘 견학의 특별 손님이신 Joseph Kilmer 씨를 소개해 드리겠습니다. Kilmer 씨께서 이 새로운 쇼핑몰을 설계하셨으며, 이곳에 관한 여러분의 질문에 기꺼이 답변해 드릴 것입니다.

Questions 92-94 refer to the following announcement.

W Good afternoon, and 92 I'm sorry I kept you waiting so long. I live on the outskirts of town, and Benton Boulevard is under construction right now. Anyway, let's start the tour. Once it's finished, this shopping mall will be the biggest one in the entire world. The food court and performance area are fully constructed, so I'll guide you around those areas first. 93 There is an amusement park on the first floor, but none of the rides work yet. They will begin operating in three months. Oh, before we begin, 94 I'd like to introduce Joseph Kilmer, who will be our special guest on this tour. Mr. Kilmer designed this new shopping mall, and he'll be happy to answer your questions about it.

어휘 keep A do A가 ~하게 만들다 on the outskirts of ~의 외곽에, 교외에 under construction 공사 중인 entire 전체의 fully 완전히, 모두 guide ~을 안내하다 amusement park 놀이공원 ride 놀이기구 work (기계 등이) 작동되다 operate 운영/가동되다 introduce ~을 소개하다 design ~을 설계/고안하다 be happy to do 기꺼이 ~하다

92

★★★ 맥락 파악

화자는 왜 "Benton Boulevard is under construction right now"라고 말하는가?
(A) 소음에 대해 불만을 제기하기 위해
(B) 대중교통을 추천하기 위해
(C) 지연된 것에 대해 해명하기 위해
(D) 다른 경로를 제안하기 위해

어휘 public transportation 대중교통 explain ~을 해명/설명하다 delay 지연, 지체 suggest ~을 제안하다 route 경로

토익 분석

앞뒤 문장의 흐름을 파악해야 한다. 바로 앞 문장에 제시된 반전 표현 I'm sorry ~가 정답의 단서가 되고 있다.

Why does the speaker say, "Benton Boulevard is under construction right now"?
(A) To complain about noise
(B) To recommend public transportation
(C) To explain a delay
(D) To suggest a different route

문제 해설

"Benton Boulevard is under construction right now"라는 문장을 미리 확인해 둔 후 해당 문장이 제시되는 부분의 앞뒤에 함께 언급되는 정보 및 담화의 흐름을 함께 확인하는 것이 관건이다. 화자는 담화 초반부에 'I'm sorry I kept you waiting so long.'라는 말로 오래 기다리게 한 것에 대해 사과하는 말을 전하면서 해당 문장을 말하고 있다. 따라서 늦은 것에 대한 사과와 함께 그 이유를 설명하는 것임을 알 수 있으므로 '지연된 것에 대해 해명하기 위해'라는 의미로 쓰인 (C)가 정답이다.

93

★★ 세부 정보

화자는 놀이공원에 대해 무슨 말을 하는가?
(A) 현재 운영되지 않고 있다.
(B) 오늘 일찍 문을 닫을 것이다.
(C) 3개월째 영업을 해 오고 있다.
(D) 여러 상을 받았다.

어휘 currently 현재 operational 운영 중인 award 상

토익 분석

질문에 amusement park가 키워드로 활용되어 정답의 단서를 제시하고 있다.

What does the speaker say about the amusement park?
(A) It is not currently operational.
(B) It will close early today.
(C) It has been open for three months.
(D) It has won awards.

문제 해설

화자가 놀이공원에 대해 하는 말을 찾는 두 번째 문제이므로 담화 중반부에 놀이공원 및 관련 정보가 제시될 것임을 예상하고 들어야 한다. 화자는 담화 중반부에 'There is an amusement park on the first floor, but none of the rides work yet. They will begin operating in three months.'라는 말로 놀이공원이 있지만, 현재 어느 놀이기구도 작동되지 않고 있으며, 3개월 후에 운영되기 시작할 것이라고 알리고 있다. 이는 현재 운영되지 않고 있다는 의미이므로 (A)가 정답임을 알 수 있다.

94

★★ 세부 정보

화자는 특별 손님으로 누구를 소개하는가?
(A) 업체 소유주
(B) 저널리스트
(C) 건축가
(D) 투자자

어휘 architect 건축가 investor 투자자

토익 분석

세부 정보 문제이므로 질문에서 적절한 키워드를 찾아야 한다. 지문 속에서 special guest가 키워드로 정답 문장을 이끌어 주고 있다.

Whom does the speaker introduce as a special guest?
(A) A business owner
(B) A journalist
(C) An architect
(D) An investor

문제 해설

화자가 소개하는 사람을 묻는 마지막 문제이므로 담화 후반부에 화자가 소개하는 사람이 있다는 것을 알 수 있으며, 이 사람의 직업이나 업무적 특성 등과 관련된 정보를 파악해야 한다. 담화 마지막에 화자는 'I'd like~new shopping mall'라는 말로 Joseph Kilmer 씨를 소개하겠다고 알리면서 쇼핑몰을 설계한 사람임을 언급하고 있다. 따라서 건축가를 소개하려 한다는 것을 알 수 있으므로 (C)가 정답이다.

Questions 95-97 refer to the following telephone message and calendar.

M   Hi, Kristina, it's your manager, James. I'm calling about scheduling your live performance at Gold Soundz Record Store. [95] I think you should perform the day after your radio interview, so you can promote the performance to radio listeners. [96] The record store owner sent me a contract that he wants you to sign before the performance. I already forwarded that to you by e-mail. I know you have an important studio session on Wednesday, so do you mind playing at the record store the day before? I don't want you to get too tired, but I think it's the best day. [97] I apologize for a number of appointments you have scheduled that week. Let me know what you think.

MON	TUE	WED	THU	FRI	SAT
Radio Interview		Studio Session		CD Launch Party	

어휘 schedule ~의 일정을 정하다 performance 공연, 연주 perform 공연/연주하다 promote ~을 홍보하다 owner 소유주 contract 계약(서) want A to do A가 ~하기를 원하다 forward A to B A를 B에게 전송하다 studio session 스튜디오 녹음 일정 Do you mind -ing? ~해도 괜찮으시겠어요? the day before 그 전날에 get too tired 너무 피곤해지다 apologize for ~에 대해 사과하다 appointment 약속, 예약 let A know A에게 알리다

남   안녕하세요, Kristina, 매니저 James예요. Gold Soundz Record Store에서 있을 당신의 라이브 공연 일정을 정하는 것과 관련해 전화 드려요. [95] 저는 당신이 라디오 인터뷰 다음 날에 공연해야 한다고 생각하는데, 그래야 라디오 청취자들에게 공연을 홍보할 수 있거든요. [96] 해당 음반 매장의 소유주가 공연 전에 당신이 서명하기를 원하는 계약서를 제게 보내 주셨어요. 이는 이미 이메일로 당신께 전송했고요. 수요일에 중요한 스튜디오 녹음 일정이 있는 것으로 알고 있는데, 그 전날에 음반 매장에서 공연하시는 것이 괜찮으실까요? 너무 피곤해지시는 것을 원하지는 않지만, 그날이 가장 좋은 날인 것 같아요. [97] 그 주에 많은 일정을 잡아 둔 것에 대해 사과 드립니다. 어떻게 생각하시는지 제게 알려 주세요.

월	화	수	목	금	토
라디오 인터뷰		스튜디오 녹음 일정		CD 출시 기념 파티	

95

Look at the graphic. On which day does the speaker want to schedule the live performance?

(A) Tuesday
(B) Wednesday
(C) Thursday
(D) Saturday

문제 해설

화자가 원하는 공연 요일을 묻는 첫 번째 문제이므로 담화 초반부에 화자가 공연 일정을 언급한다는 것을 알 수 있으며, 이와 관련해 도표의 일정이 함께 제시될 것임을 예상하고 들어야 한다. 화자는 담화 초반부에 'I think you should perform the day after your radio interview, so you can promote the performance to radio listeners.'라는 말로 라디오 인터뷰 다음 날에 공연해야 홍보를 하기 좋다고 알리고 있다. 도표에 라디오 인터뷰가 있는 요일이 월요일이므로 화자가 원하는 공연 요일로 (A)가 정답임을 알 수 있다.

★★★ 그래픽

도표를 보시오. 화자는 어느 요일에 공연 일정을 잡고 싶어 하는가?
(A) 화요일
(B) 수요일
(C) 목요일
(D) 토요일

토익 분석

표에 요일 별 **performance** 정보가 제공되고 있다. 요일 정보를 찾기 위해 지문에서 '공연 정보'를 들어내야 한다. 요청, 제안 표현인 **I think you should**가 정답의 단서를 이끌어 주고 있다.

96

★★ 세부 정보

화자는 청자에게 무엇을 보냈는가?
(A) 지도
(B) 인터뷰 질문들
(C) 계약서
(D) 콘서트 티켓

토익 분석

세부 정보 문제로 키워드를 먼저 찾아야 한다. 질문 속에 적절한 명사 키워드가 없으므로 동사 send가 키워드가 되었다.

What did the speaker send to the listener?

(A) A map
(B) Interview questions
(C) A contract
(D) Concert tickets

문제 해설

화자가 보낸 것을 묻는 두 번째 문제이므로 담화 중반부에 화자가 뭔가를 보낸 사실을 언급하는 부분이 있음을 예상하고 들어야 한다. 화자는 담화 중반부에 'The record store owner sent me a contract that he wants you to sign before the performance. I already forwarded that to you by e-mail.'라는 말로 자신이 받은 계약서를 청자에게 이메일로 전송했다고 밝히고 있으므로 (C)가 정답이다.

★★ 세부 정보

화자는 무엇에 대해 사과하는가?
(A) 공연 입장료
(B) 바쁜 일정
(C) 업체의 위치
(D) 행사의 취소

어휘 fee 요금 location 위치, 지점 cancelation 취소

토익 분석

역시 세부 정보 문제로 키워드가 활용되는 유형이다. 질문 속에 apologize가 지문 속에 키워드로 반복 사용되었다.

What does the speaker apologize for?

(A) The performance fee
(B) The busy schedule
(C) The location of a business
(D) The cancelation of an event

문제 해설

화자가 사과하는 이유를 묻는 마지막 문제이므로 담화 후반부에 사과 관련 표현과 함께 그 이유가 언급될 것임을 예상하고 들어야 한다. 화자는 담화 마지막에 'I apologize for how many appointments you have scheduled that week.'라는 말로 많은 일정이 잡힌 것에 대해 사과한다고 밝히고 있으므로 (B)가 정답임을 알 수 있다.

Questions 98-100 refer to the following broadcast and map.

W Greetings, listeners. You're tuned in to WRPK Radio, and this is your local news report. [98] Today, Mark Forster, the president of Urbana Construction Company, held a press conference to give details about the plan to widen certain downtown roads. Mr. Forster told journalists that [99] the project would begin next week with the closure of Stratford Road, so drivers should be aware that they need to find a different route. Other nearby streets will be closed in the months to follow. Mr. Forster mentioned that [100] a detailed schedule for the road construction work can be found on the city council's Web site at www.ashfordcity.gov.

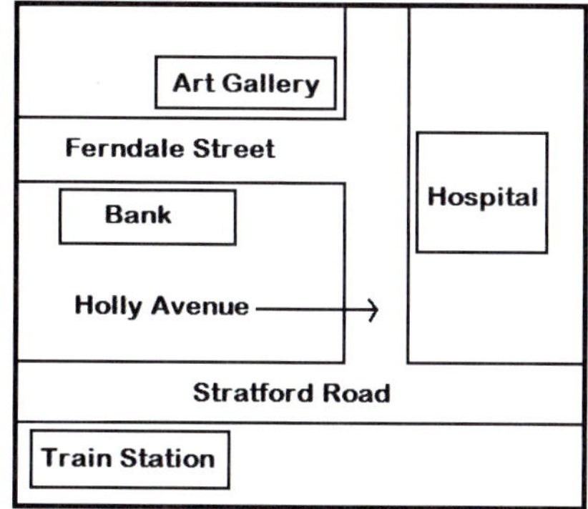

여 안녕하세요, 청취자 여러분. 여러분께서는 WRPK Radio를 청취하고 계시며, 지금은 지역 소식을 보도해 드리는 시간입니다. [98] 오늘, Urbana Construction Company의 Mark Forster 대표 이사가 기자 회견을 열어 시내의 특정 도로들을 확장하는 계획에 관한 세부 사항을 발표했습니다. Forster 대표 이사는 기자들에게 [99] 이 프로젝트가 Stratford Road의 폐쇄와 함께 다음 주에 시작될 것이라고 알렸으므로, 차량 운전자들께서는 다른 경로를 찾으셔야 한다는 점에 유의하시기 바랍니다. 근처의 다른 거리들도 이후의 기간 동안 폐쇄될 것입니다. Mark Forster 대표 이사는 [100] 이 도로 공사 작업에 대한 상세 일정이 시의회 웹 사이트인 www.ashfordcity.gov에서 찾아볼 수 있다고 언급했습니다.

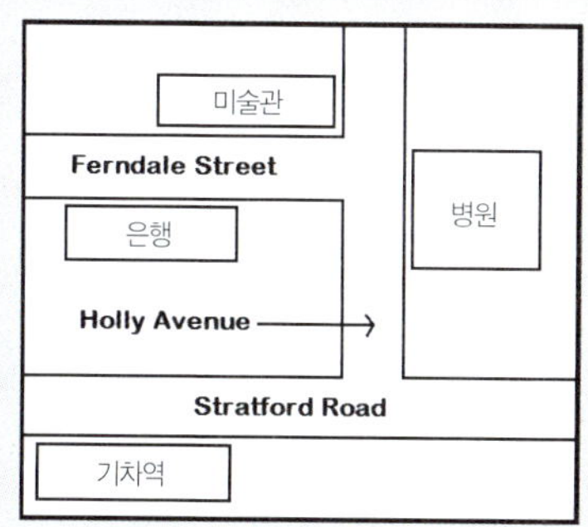

어휘 be tuned in to ~을 청취하다, ~에 채널을 맞추다 hold ~을 개최하다, 열다 press conference 기자 회견 details 상세 정보, 세부 사항 plan to do ~하는 계획 widen ~을 확장하다 certain 특정한 downtown 시내의 tell A that A에게 ~라고 말하다 closure 폐쇄 be aware that ~임을 인식/유의하다 route 경로 nearby 근처의 in the months to follow 뒤따르는 기간 동안 mention that ~라고 언급하다 detailed 상세한 city council 시의회

98

Who gave a press conference today?

(A) A local celebrity
(B) A community group leader
(C) A council member
(D) A company president

문제 해설

기자 회견을 연 사람을 묻는 첫 번째 문제이므로 담화 초반부에 기자 회견이 열린 사실과 함께 그 당사자가 언급된다는 점을 예상하고 들어야 한다. 담화 시작 부분에 화자는 'Today, Mark Forster, the president of Urbana Construction Company, held a press conference to give details about the plan to widen certain downtown roads.'라고 밝히면서 Urbana Construction Company의 대표인 Forster 씨가 기자 회견을 열었다고 알리고 있으므로 (D)가 정답이다.

★★ 세부 정보

누가 오늘 기자 회견을 열었는가?
(A) 지역의 유명 인사
(B) 지역 사회 단체의 대표
(C) 시의회 의원
(D) 회사의 대표

어휘 celebrity 유명 인사 council 의회

토익 분석

질문 속에 사용된 press conference가 키워드가 된다. 그리고 시점 표현인 today 역시 결정적인 키워드가 된다.

★★★ 그래픽

도표를 보시오. 어느 건물이 첫 도로 폐쇄에 의해 영향을
받을 것인가?
(A) 기차역
(B) 은행
(C) 미술관
(D) 병원

어휘 be affected by ~에 영향을 받다 gallery 갤러리

토익 분석

건물명과 도로명이 표시된 지도에서 건물을 찾기 위해서
는 지문에서 '도로명'이 언급되는 문장을 집중해서 들어야
한다.

Look at the graphic. Which building will be affected by the first road closure?

(A) The train station
(B) The bank
(C) The art gallery
(D) The hospital

문제 해설

처음으로 폐쇄되는 도로에 따라 영향을 받는 건물을 찾아야 하므로 담화에서 도로 폐쇄 일정 및 해
당 도로의 이름이 언급될 것임을 예상하고 들어야 한다. 담화 중반부에 화자는 'the project would
begin next week with the closure of Stratford Road'라는 말로 다음 주에 Stratford Road가 폐쇄
되면서 프로젝트가 시작된다고 알리고 있으므로 이 도로에서 가장 가까운 건물인 기차역이 영향을
받을 것으로 생각할 수 있다. 따라서 (A)가 정답이다.

100

★ 세부 정보

화자는 웹 사이트에서 무슨 정보를 찾을 수 있다고 말하
는가?
(A) 한 건물로 찾아가는 길
(B) 한 행사에 대한 상세 정보
(C) 공사 일정
(D) 의견 제출 양식

어휘 detail 세부 사항 construction 공사, 건설 feedback
피드백

토익 분석

정보 제공, 요청 등과 관련된 정보는 언제나 지문의 가장
후반부에 등장한다. 질문 속에 Web site는 키워드로 활용
되거나 실제 웹 주소가 지문에 등장할 수 있다.

What information does the speaker say can be found on the Web site?

(A) Directions to a building
(B) Details about an event
(C) A construction schedule
(D) A feedback form

문제 해설

웹 사이트에서 찾을 수 있는 정보를 묻는 마지막 문제이므로 담화 후반부에 웹 사이트가 언급될 때
를 놓치지 않고 들어야 한다. 화자는 담화 마지막에 'a detailed schedule for the road construction
work can be found on the city council's Web site at www.ashfordcity.gov'라고 알리는 부분에
서 공사에 대한 상세 일정을 웹 사이트에서 확인할 수 있다고 알리고 있으므로 (C)가 정답이다.

해설서

1

★★ 1인 중심 + 사람 동작

(A) 여자는 기계 옆을 지나쳐 걸어가고 있다.
(B) 여자는 서류를 검토하고 있다.
(C) 여자는 커피를 만들고 있다.
(D) 여자는 기계의 사진을 찍고 있다.

어휘 walk by 지나쳐 걸어가다 examine 검토하다 make coffee 커피를 만들다 photograph 사진, ~의 사진을 찍다

(A) The woman is walking by the machine.
(B) The woman is examining some documents.
(C) The woman is making some coffee.
(D) The woman is photographing a machine.

문제 해설

한 사람이 등장하는 사진이므로 여자의 행동과 외모적 특징 그리고 실내 정경을 구성하는 주요 사물인 복사기의 위치와 상태부터 눈여겨봐야 한다. 따라서 여자가 서류를 검토하며 복사기 앞에 서 있는 행동, 그리고 복사기가 창가에 위치하고 있는 상태와 관련된 정답이 제시될 가능성이 높으며, 이 중 여자가 서류를 검토하는 동작을 묘사하고 있는 (B)가 정답이다.

토익 분석

사람 문제의 경우 동작 포인트와 관련된 유사 발음이나 유사 단어 보기를 이용해 오답을 만든다. (A)는 작업하다 work on과 유사한 walk by를 활용한 오답 보기이며 (C)의 경우 make a copy(복사하다)와 유사한 make some coffee를 활용한 혼동 보기이다.

2

★★★ 실외 풍경

(A) 일련의 건물들이 물을 따라 늘어서 있다.
(B) 물가에 파도가 치고 있다.
(C) 몇몇 배들이 강가에 닻을 내리고 있다
(D) 많은 차들이 도로를 따라 세워져 있다.

어휘 stretch ~이 뻗다, ~이 이어지다, ~을 늘리다 crash on ~에 부딪히다 shore 해안 be anchored at ~에 닻을 내리고 있다 edge 가장자리 park 주차하다 along ~를 따라

(A) A row of buildings stretches along the water.
(B) Waves are crashing on the shore.
(C) Some boats are anchored at the river's edge.
(D) Many vehicles are parked along the street.

문제 해설

실외 풍경 중심의 사진이므로 풍경을 구성하는 주요 사물들의 위치와 상태를 집중적으로 살펴보는 것이 적절하다. 따라서 여러 건물들이 강을 따라 일렬로 늘어선 상태와 하늘에 구름이 떠 있는 상태 그리고 배경으로 고층 건물이 보이는 상태가 중요하다. 이 중 건물들이 강을 따라 늘어서 있는 모습을 묘사하고 있는 (A)가 정답이다.

토익 분석

사람이나 사물이 한 줄 또는 여러 줄로 배열된 상태는 정답으로 자주 등장하는 경향이 있으니 유의해야 한다.

3

(A) A worker is climbing the ladder.
(B) A man is working on the electrical cables.
(C) Some electrical cables are being loaded onto the truck.
(D) The truck is being parked on the sidewalk.

★★ 1인 + 사람 동작

(A) 작업자가 사다리에 올라가고 있다.
(B) 남자가 전선 작업을 하고 있다.
(C) 몇몇 케이블들이 트럭에 실려지고 있다.
(D) 트럭이 인도에 주차가 되고 있다.

어휘 climb ~를 오르다 ladder 사다리 work on ~에 대한 작업을 하다, ~을 수리하다 electrical cable 전선 load A onto B A를 B에 싣다

문제 해설

사람이 등장하는 사진이므로 행동 및 외모적 특징을 살펴본 후, 외모적 특징을 파악해야 하며, 이어서 사물인 송전탑의 상태에 초점을 맞춰야 한다. 따라서 송전탑에서 전선 작업 중인 행동, 인부가 안전모를 착용하고 있는 상태, 그리고 송전탑에 많은 전선들이 위치하고 있는 모습과 관련된 표현에서 정답이 제시될 것임을 가늠할 수 있으며, 이 중 전선 작업 중 인부의 동작을 표현하고 있는 (B)가 정답이다.

토익 분석

사물이 주어인 보기 문장의 경우 사물이 행동을 취할 수 있는 입장이 아니기에 보기에 being이 사용될 경우 display나 arrange와 같은 상태를 의미하는 동사를 제외하고 대체로 오답이 된다. (D)의 경우 being이 포함되어 오답이 된다. 이미 주차가 된 상태로 주차가 되는 동작을 설명할 수 없다.

4

(A) The landscape is dry and rocky.
(B) A pathway encircles a lake.
(C) Sunshine is streaming through the trees.
(D) Trees have lost all their leaves.

★★★ 실외 풍경

(A) 풍경이 건조하고 돌투성이다.
(B) 오솔길이 호수를 둘러싸고 있다.
(C) 햇살이 나무들 사이로 비치고 있다.
(D) 나무에서 나뭇잎들이 모두 떨어졌다.

어휘 rocky 돌투성이의 pathway 오솔길, 소로 encircle ~을 둘러싸다, ~을 에워싸다 sunshine 햇볕, 햇살 stream through ~을 통해 비치다, ~을 통해 흐르다 leaf 낙엽

문제 해설

실외 풍경 사진이므로 풍경을 구성하는 주요 사물들의 위치와 상태를 파악하는 것이 우선이다. 그러므로 나무들 사이로 뻗은 오솔길, 오솔길 양쪽으로 위치하고 있는 나무들의 배열 형태, 그리고 나무들 사이로 비치고 있는 햇살의 상태에서 정답이 제시될 것임을 가늠할 수 있으며, 이 중 나무 사이로 햇살이 흐르는 상태를 묘사하고 있는 (C)가 정답이라 할 수 있다.

토익 분석

사진 속에 보이지 않는 사물이 포함된 보기는 먼저 소거해야 한다. 그리고 all이 포함된 보기의 경우 대체로 오답으로 사용된다는 점도 기억해야 한다.

5

★★★ 2인 이상 + 사람 동작

(A) 그들은 바닥을 가로지르며 카트를 움직이고 있다.
(B) 몇몇 박스들이 안으로 운반되고 있다.
(C) 그들은 트럭 뒤에서 물건을 조립하고 있다.
(D) 한 물건이 경사로 위로 운반되고 있다.

어휘 wheel 바퀴, 바퀴를 굴려서 움직이다 across ~을 가로지르는, ~을 건너서 assemble 조립하다 ramp 경사로, 고속 도로 진입로

(A) They are wheeling a cart across the floor.
(B) Some boxes are being carried into a room.
(C) They are assembling an item in the back of the truck.
(D) An object is being carried up the ramp.

문제 해설

2인 이상이 등장하는 사진이므로 공통 행동과 외모적 특징 그리고 등장하는 사물의 위치에 집중해야 한다. 따라서 경사로를 이용하여 물건을 끌고 올리는 동작과 반바지를 착용하고 있는 사람들의 상태에 초점을 맞춰야 하며, 이 중 경사로를 통해 물건을 이동하고 있는 동작을 표현하고 있는 (D)가 정답이다.

토익 분석

사진 속에 등장하지 않는 단어가 포함된 보기는 우선 소거해야 하며 사람이 주가 되는 사진이라 해도 난이도가 높은 문제의 경우 사물을 주어로 동작을 수동태로 묘사하는 경우가 있다.

6

★★ 사물 위치

(A) 서류들이 책상 위에 펼쳐져 있다.
(B) 펜들이 파일 폴더 위에 놓여 있다.
(C) 고객들에게 식사가 제공될 준비가 되어 있다.
(D) 몇몇 파일 폴더들이 서류가방 위에 놓여 있다.

어휘 spread ~이 확산되다, ~이 퍼지다, ~을 펴다
a meal 식사 be set on ~위에 놓여 있다

(A) Papers have been spread out across the desk.
(B) Some pens have been placed on the file folder.
(C) A meal is ready to be served to clients.
(D) Some file folders have been set on a briefcase.

문제 해설

사물의 위치 및 상태에 집중해야 하는 문제다. 따라서 책상 위에 많은 서류가 널려 있는 상태와 책상 위에 여러 가지 사무용품들이 놓여 있는 상태와 관련된 표현이 정답으로 언급될 가능성이 높으며, 이 중 책상 위에 많은 서류가 넓게 펼쳐져 있는 상태를 설명하고 있는 (A)가 정답이다.

토익 분석

(D)의 경우 파일 폴더들이 놓여 있는 상태를 이용한 혼동 보기로 사진 속에 briefcase가 보이지 않기에 오답이다.

7

Could you pass me the salt?

(A) They are sold out.
(B) Here it is.
(C) No thanks. I'll pass this time.

문제 해설

소금은 자신에게 건네 달라고 부탁하는 의문문에 대해 물건을 전달할 때 사용되는 '여기 있습니다' 라는 의미를 지닌 표현으로 대답하는 (B)가 정답이다.

토익 분석

(A)는 질문에 사용된 salt와 발음이 유사하게 들리는 sold를 활용한 오답이며, They가 지칭하는 복수 명사도 나타나 있지 않으므로 어울리지 않는 답변이다. (C)는 거절을 의미하는 No thanks로 시작되고 있지만, 뒤에 이어지는 내용이 소금을 건네는 일과는 전혀 관련이 없으며, 단순히 pass의 다른 의미를 활용해 혼동을 유발하는 오답 보기이다.

★★ 권유, 제안, 요청

소금 좀 건네주시겠어요?
(A) 그것들은 품절되었습니다.
(B) 여기 있습니다.
(C) 괜찮습니다, 이번엔 그냥 넘어가겠습니다.

어휘 pass ~을 건네주다, (하지 않고) 그냥 넘어가다 **sold out** 품절된, 매진된 **Here it is** (물건을 건넬 때) 여기 있습니다

8

How do I get to Dr. Wilson's lab from here?

(A) It's right next to the elevator.
(B) No, he's not here.
(C) I think it's your turn.

문제 해설

get to는 이동을 의미하는 표현이므로 방법을 묻는 How 의문문임을 알 수 있으며, 이동 방법과 관련해 이용 가능한 엘리베이터의 위치를 알려 주는 (A)가 정답이다.

토익 분석

(B)는 의문사 의문문에 어울리지 않는 No로 대답하는 오답이며, (C)는 이동 방법을 묻는 질문에서 연상 가능한 turn을 활용한 오답으로, turn이 명사로 쓰여 '차례, 순서'를 의미하는 답변이므로 질문에서 묻는 핵심에서 벗어난 답변이다.

★★ 직접의문문 How

여기서 Wilson 박사님의 실험실까지 어떻게 가죠?
(A) 엘리베이터 바로 옆에 있습니다.
(B) 아뇨, 그분은 여기에 계시지 않습니다.
(C) 당신 차례인 것 같습니다.

어휘 lab 실험실, 연구실

9

Why did you take the smaller room?

(A) He needs a lot of space.
(B) No, this is enough.
(C) Because it has better view.

★★ 직접의문문 Why

왜 더 작은 방을 선택하신 거죠?
(A) 그는 많은 공간을 필요로 합니다.
(B) 아뇨, 이곳이면 충분합니다.
(C) 경관이 더 좋기 때문이죠.

어휘 take ~을 선택하다, 차지하다 enough 충분한 view 경관, 전망

더 작은 방을 선택한 이유를 묻는 Why 의문문에 대해 Why와 짝을 이루는 Because와 함께 경관이 더 좋다는 말로 답변하는 (C)가 정답이다.

(A)는 대상을 알 수 없는 He에 대해 말하고 있어 어울리지 않는 데다 room과 연관 지을 수 있는 space를 활용해 혼동을 유발하는 오답이다. (B)는 의문사 의문문에 어울리지 않는 No로 답변하는 오답이다.

10

★★ 일반의문문

Yusuf 씨가 언제 Paris로 떠나셨는지 아시나요?
(A) 정오쯤인 것 같아요.
(B) 저는 그게 어디 있는지 모릅니다.
(C) 서랍 안에 있지 않나요?

어휘 leave 떠나다, 출발하다　around ~쯤에, ~경에
drawer 서랍

Do you know when Yusuf left for Paris?

(A) Around noon, I think.
(B) I don't know where it is.
(C) Isn't it in the drawer?

문제 해설

Yusuf 씨가 언제 Paris로 떠났는지를 알고 있는지 묻고 있으므로 when에 해당되는 시점 표현으로 답변하는 (A)가 정답이다.

토익 분석

(B)는 질문에 포함된 when과 관련 없는 where에 해당되는 답변이며, 사람을 대신할 수 없는 대명사 it이 쓰였으므로 어울리지 않는 오답이다. (C)도 마찬가지로 위치와 관련해 되묻는 질문이며, 사람이 아닌 사물에 초점을 맞춘 내용이므로 질문과 어울리지 않는 답변이다.

11

★★ 직접의문문 What

그 삽화를 위로 옮겨서 왼쪽 구석으로 놓으면 어떨까요?
(A) 네. 오늘 이따가 그분을 뵐 수 있습니다.
(B) 그렇게 하는 게 가장 좋겠어요.
(C) 이사 전문 회사에 연락해 보셨나요?

어휘 move A up to B A를 위로 올려 B로 옮기다
illustration 삽화, 도해　left corner 왼쪽 구석　contact ~에
게 연락하다　moving company 이사 전문 회사

What if we move the illustration up to the left corner?

(A) Yes. You can see him later today.
(B) That would be best.
(C) Have you contacted the moving company?

문제 해설

What if로 시작하는 의문문은 '~하면 어떨까요?, ~하면 어떻게 될까요?' 등의 의미를 나타내므로 삽화를 옮기는 일을 That으로 지칭해 그렇게 하는 게 가장 좋겠다는 말로 동의를 나타내는 (B)가 정답이다.

토익 분석

(A)는 의문사 의문문에 어울리지 않는 Yes로 대답하는 오답이다. (C)는 삽화를 이동하는 일과 관련 없는 답변으로 질문에 포함된 move와 발음이 유사한 moving을 이용해 혼동을 유발하는 오답이다.

12

When will the ceremony be over?

(A) Not for another hour.
(B) He's coming at two o'clock.
(C) Third Avenue and Central Street.

문제 해설

기념식이 언제 끝날지를 묻는 When 의문문이므로 앞으로의 시점과 관련해 '1시간은 더 있어야 한다'는 의미로 쓰이는 (A)가 정답이다.

토익 분석

(B)는 시간 표현이 제시되기는 하지만, 기념식이 아니라 대상을 알 수 없는 He가 도착하는 시간을 말하는 내용이므로 질문에 맞지 않는 오답이며, (C)는 장소를 나타내는 표현이므로 Where 의문문에 어울리는 대답이다.

★★ 직접의문문 When

기념식이 언제 끝날까요?
(A) 1시간은 더 있어야 합니다.
(B) 그는 2시에 올 예정입니다.
(C) Third Avenue와 Central Street이에요.

어휘 ceremony 기념식, 의식 over 끝난, 종료된 Not for another hour 1시간은 더 있어야 한다

13

The new K6 cell phone is waterproof, right?

(A) You can reach me at this number.
(B) That's what I heard.
(C) Yes. With some ice, please.

문제 해설

새로 나온 휴대 전화기가 방수 제품이 맞는지를 확인하려는 부가의문문이므로 해당 사실을 That으로 지칭해 자신도 그렇게 들었다는 말로 답변하는 (B)가 정답이다.

토익 분석

(A)는 질문에 포함된 cell phone과 연관성 있게 들리는 this number를 활용해 혼동을 유발하는 오답으로, 제품의 기능에 대한 확인을 해 주는 것이 아니라 자신에게 연락할 방법을 알려 주는 답변이므로 어울리지 않는다. (C)는 긍정을 나타내는 Yes로 답변하고 있지만, 뒤에 이어지는 내용이 음식과 관련된 것이므로 오답이다.

★★ 부가의문문

새로 나온 K6 휴대 전화기는 방수 제품이죠, 그렇죠?
(A) 이 번호로 제게 연락하실 수 있습니다.
(B) 그게 제가 들은 바입니다.
(C) 네. 얼음을 넣어서 주세요.

어휘 waterproof 방수의 reach ~에게 연락하다

14

Can you please help me carry this box to the storeroom?

(A) Sure. What's in it?
(B) It's on the second floor.
(C) We don't carry that model anymore.

★★ 권유, 제안, 요청

제가 이 상자를 보관실로 옮길 수 있게 도와주시겠어요?
(A) 그럼요. 안에 뭐가 들어 있죠?
(B) 그건 2층에 있습니다.
(C) 저희는 더 이상 그 모델을 취급하지 않습니다.

어휘 help A do A가 ~하는 것을 돕다 carry ~을 옮기다, 나르다, (매장 등에서) ~을 취급하다 storeroom 보관실 not ~ anymore 더 이상 ~ 않다

상자를 옮기는 일을 도와 달라고 요청하는 의문문에 대해 긍정을 나타내는 Sure와 함께 box를 it으로 지칭해 그 안에 무엇이 들어 있는지를 추가로 묻는 (A)가 정답이다.

토익 분석

(B)는 위치를 나타내는 말이므로 Where 의문문에 어울리는 답변이며, 요청에 대한 대답으로 맞지 않는다. (C)는 질문에 포함된 carry의 다른 의미를 활용해 혼동을 유발하는 오답으로, 매장에서 제품 취급 여부를 말할 때 잘 쓰이는 표현이다.

15

★★ 일반의문문

이미 지원서를 제출하셨나요?
(A) 그것들을 하루에 두 번씩 바르셔야 합니다.
(B) 저희에게 많은 구직 지원자들이 있습니다.
(C) 지금 막 하려는 참입니다.

어휘 submit ~을 제출하다 application form 지원서, 신청서 apply ~을 바르다, 적용하다 twice a day 하루에 두 번 job applicant 구직 지원자 be about to do 막 ~하려 하다

Have you already submitted the application form?
(A) You should apply it twice a day.
(B) We had many job applicants.
(C) I'm about to do it now.

문제 해설

이미 지원서를 제출했는지를 확인하기 위한 의문문에 대해 제출하는 일을 it으로 지칭해 '지금 하려 한다'는 말로 답변하는 (C)가 정답이다.

토익 분석

(A)는 질문에서 그 대상을 찾을 수 없는 복수 대명사 them을 활용한 오답이며, application과 발음이 유사한 apply를 통해 혼동을 유발하는 오답이다. apply 다음에 목적어가 바로 이어지는 경우 '~을 바르다, 적용하다' 등의 의미를 나타낸다는 것도 함께 기억해 두자. (B)도 질문에 포함된 application과 발음이 유사한 applicants를 활용한 오답으로, 지원서 제출 여부를 묻는 질문의 핵심에서 벗어난 답변이다.

16

★★★ 평서문

지난주에 모든 지원자들을 면접하는 일을 마무리했습니다.
(A) 영업을 해 보신 경험이 있으신가요?
(B) 그럼, 누가 가장 뛰어나다고 생각하세요?
(C) 알겠습니다. 제가 그것을 당장 이메일로 보내겠습니다.

어휘 finish -ing ~하는 것을 끝내다 applicant 지원자 sales 영업, 판매, 매출 right away 당장, 곧장

I finished interviewing all the applicants last week.
(A) Do you have any experience in sales?
(B) So who do you think is the best?
(C) OK. I'll e-mail it right away.

문제 해설

지원자들을 면접하는 일을 지난주에 끝낸 사실을 언급하는 평서문에 대해 그에 따른 결과로 누가 가장 뛰어난 사람이라고 생각하는지를 묻는 (B)가 정답이다.

토익 분석

(A)는 평서문에 포함된 interviewing과 연관성 있게 들리는 내용으로, 특정 업무에 대한 경험을 묻는 것으로 면접 상황과 관련된 답변인 것처럼 혼동을 유발하는 오답이다. (C)는 대상을 알 수 없는 it을 활용한 오답으로, 이메일로 전송 가능한 대상이 평서문에 언급되어 있지 않으므로 어울리지 않는 답변이다.

17

Do you like white meat or dark meat?

(A) What would you recommend?
(B) Yes, they were delicious.
(C) Sure, with some sugar.

문제 해설

두 가지 고기 형태 중에서 마음에 드는 것이 무엇인지를 묻는 선택의문문에 대해 어느 것을 추천해 줄 수 있는지를 되묻는 (A)가 정답이다. 이렇게 선택의문문에서는 미리 언급된 대상들 중에서 하나를 선택하지 않고 오히려 상대방에게 선택권을 되묻는 답변이 정답 가능성이 높다.

토익 분석

(B)는 두 가지 선택 대상 중에서 하나를 고르도록 묻는 선택의문문에 어울리지 않는 Yes로 답변하는 오답이며, 고기의 색상이 아닌 맛을 언급하고 있으므로 어울리지 않는다. (C)도 마찬가지로 긍정을 나타내는 Sure로 답변이 시작되고 있어 어울리지 않으며, 첨가물을 언급하고 있으므로 질문의 의도에 맞지 않는 반응이다.

★★ 선택의문문

흰 살 고기가 좋으세요, 아니면 짙은 색 고기가 좋으세요?
(A) 어느 것을 추천해 주시겠어요?
(B) 네, 그것들을 맛이 좋습니다.
(C) 그럼요, 설탕을 넣어서요.

어휘 meat 고기 recommend ~을 추천하다 delicious 맛이 좋은

18

How did the interview go?

(A) I took a taxi.
(B) You should apply for it.
(C) I think it went well.

문제 해설

How did A go?는 'A는 어떻게 되었나요?'라는 의미로 일의 진행 상황을 물을 때 잘 쓰이는 질문이다. 따라서 과거 시점의 진행 상황과 관련해 '잘 된 것 같다'라는 의미를 지닌 답변인 (C)가 정답이다.

토익 분석

(A)는 방법을 나타내는 How와 연관 지을 수 있는 답변으로, 일의 진행 상황이 아니라 교통수단을 언급하는 답변이므로 어울리지 않으며, (B)는 interview와 연관성 있게 들리는 apply를 활용한 오답으로 과거의 일이 아닌 앞으로 있을 일에 대한 권유에 해당되는 말이므로 어울리지 않는 반응이다.

★★ 직접의문문 How

면접은 어떻게 되셨나요?
(A) 저는 택시를 탔습니다.
(B) 당신을 그 자리에 지원해 보셔야 합니다.
(C) 제 생각엔 잘 진행된 것 같습니다.

어휘 How did A go? A는 어떻게 되었나요? apply for ~에 지원하다 go well 잘 진행되다

19

Where did you put the tumbler I used yesterday?

(A) You can get them at the post office.
(B) Isn't it in the dishwasher?
(C) Well, I'm not used to it.

★★ 직접의문문 Where

제가 어제 사용했던 텀블러는 어디에 두셨나요?
(A) 그것들을 우체국에서 받으실 수 있습니다.
(B) 식기 세척기에 있지 않나요?
(C) 저, 저는 그것에 익숙하지 않습니다.

어휘 put ~을 놓다, 두다 tumbler 텀블러 dishwasher 식기 세척기 be used to ~에 익숙하다

자신이 사용했던 텀블러를 어디에 두었는지를 묻는 Where 의문문이므로 텀블러를 it으로 지칭해 식기 세척기에 있는 것이 아닌지 되묻는 (B)가 정답이다.

토익 분석

(A)는 질문에 나타나지 않는 복수 명사를 대신하는 them을 활용한 오답이며, '우체국에서'라는 장소 표현이 사용되었지만, 텀블러 위치를 묻는 질문과 어울리지 않는 반응이다. (C)의 경우 used가 반복되어 혼동을 유발하는 오답으로, used의 또 다른 의미(익숙한)를 활용한 답변이므로 질문의 핵심에서 벗어난 답변이다.

20

★★★ 평서문

저는 제 여름 휴가 전체를 Tokyo에서 보낼 예정입니다.
(A) 둘 중 어느 것이든 좋습니다.
(B) 제가 함께 가도 될까요?
(C) 그는 조금 늦을 겁니다.

어휘 spend (시간) ~을 보내다, 들이다, (돈) ~을 쓰다, 소비하다 whole 전체의 either 둘 중 어느 것이든 a bit 조금, 약간

I'm going to spend my whole summer vacation in Tokyo.

(A) Either will be fine.
(B) Can I come with you?
(C) He will be a bit late.

문제 해설

자신의 휴가 계획과 관련해 어디에서 휴가를 보낼 생각인지를 밝히는 평서문에 대해 함께 갈 수 있는지를 확인하기 위해 되묻는 (B)가 정답이다.

토익 분석

(A)는 미리 제시된 두 가지 사항에 대해 선택하는 상황에 어울리는 답변이며, (C)는 대상을 알 수 없는 He를 활용한 답변이므로 평서문의 내용과 어울리지 않는 오답이다.

21

★★ 직접의문문 How often

제가 얼마나 자주 재고품을 확인해야 하나요?
(A) 직무 안내서에 쓰여 있습니다.
(B) 우리는 먼저 호텔에 체크인해야 합니다.
(C) 그것을 항상 착용하셔야 합니다.

어휘 inventory 재고(품) staff manual 직무 안내서, 직무 설명서 at all times 항상

How often will I need to check the inventory?

(A) It's in the staff manual.
(B) We should check in at the hotel first.
(C) You have to wear it at all times.

문제 해설

How often으로 시작하는 의문문은 빈도를 묻는 것인데, 재고품 확인 빈도와 관련해 관련 정보를 확인할 방법을 알려 주는 (A)가 정답이다. 의문사 의문문에서는 이렇게 직접적인 답변이 아닌 관련 정보를 알고 있는 사람이나 확인 가능한 방법 등을 알려 주는 답변이 정답이 되는 경우가 많다.

토익 분석

(B)는 질문에 포함된 check를 활용해 혼동을 유발하는 오답으로, 재고품 확인과는 전혀 관련성이 없는 호텔 체크인이 언급된 답변이므로 오답이다. (C)는 특정 의류나 장비를 항상 착용하도록 당부하는 상황에 쓰이는 말이므로 재고품 확인 빈도와 관련 없는 오답이다.

22

Enrollment in the speech class starts next month, doesn't it?

(A) Yes, he is a great speaker.

(B) I prefer Yoga class.

(C) Why? Are you going to sign up?

문제 해설

특정 강좌에 대해 등록하는 시점을 확인하는 부가의문문에 대해 등록하려는 이유를 묻는 Why와 함께 등록할 예정인지를 되묻는 (C)가 정답이다.

토익 분석

(A)는 긍정을 나타내는 Yes로 답변이 시작되고 있지만, 뒤에 이어지는 내용이 등록 시점이 아니라 대상을 알 수 없는 He에 관련된 것이므로 어울리지 않는 반응이며, (B)는 등록 시점이 아니라 자신이 선호하는 강좌를 언급하고 있으므로 질문의 핵심에서 벗어난 오답이다.

★★ 부가의문문

연설 교육 강좌에 대한 등록이 다음 달에 시작되지 않나요?
(A) 네. 그는 뛰어난 연사입니다.
(B) 저는 요가 수업을 더 좋아합니다.
(C) 왜요? 등록하실 건가요?

어휘 enrollment in ~에 대한 등록 speech class 연설 교육 강좌 speaker 연사 prefer ~을 더 좋아하다, 선호하다 sign up 등록하다, 신청하다

23

Do you have time to proofread my term paper?

(A) Have you seen today's paper?

(B) I don't think it's waterproof.

(C) Sure, let me see.

문제 해설

자신의 학기말 과제를 교정해 줄 시간이 있는지를 확인하기 위한 일반의문문이므로 이에 대해 긍정을 나타내는 Sure와 함께 자신이 한 번 보겠다는 말로 답변하는 (C)가 정답이다.

토익 분석

(A)는 term paper의 paper가 반복 사용되어 혼동을 유발하는 오답으로, paper가 신문으로 사용되는 경우를 활용한 말이므로 어울리지 않는다. (B)는 proofread와 일부 발음이 유사한 waterproof를 활용해 혼동을 유발하는 오답으로, 단순히 유사한 소리가 포함된 단어가 활용되었을 뿐, 의미적인 관계는 전혀 어울리지 않는 반응이다.

★★ 일반의문문

제 학기말 과제를 교정해 주실 시간이 있으신가요?
(A) 오늘 신문 보셨어요?
(B) 저는 그것이 방수라고 생각되지 않네요.
(C) 그럼요, 제가 한 번 볼게요.

어휘 proofread ~을 교정 보다 term paper 학기말 과제 paper 신문 waterproof 방수의

24

I'd like to make an appointment with Mr. Miles sometime next week.

(A) Actually, he'll be out of town next week.

(B) You made a very good point.

(C) The result was disappointing.

★★★ 평서문

저는 다음 주중으로 Miles 씨와 예약을 잡고자 합니다.
(A) 실은, 그분께서는 다음 주에 다른 지역에 가 계실 겁니다.
(B) 아주 좋은 지적을 해 주셨습니다.
(C) 그 결과는 실망스러웠습니다.

어휘 make an appointment 예약하다, 약속하다 sometime next week 다음 주중으로 actually 실은, 사실은 out of town 다른 지역에 가 있는 make a good point 좋은 지적을 하다 result 결과 disappointing 실망시키는

다음 주중으로 Miles 씨와 예약을 잡기를 원한다는 의미를 나타내는 평서문에 대해 Miles 씨를 he 로 지칭해 다음 주에 시간이 나지 않는 이유를 설명하는 (A)가 정답이다. Actually는 일종의 반전 표현으로 상대방이 말한 정보와 반대되는 경우를 언급할 때 자주 사용되며, 정답 가능성이 높은 보기에 해당된다.

토익 분석

(B)는 appointment와 일부 발음이 비슷한 point를 활용한 오답으로, '좋은 지적을 했다'는 의미를 나타내는 말이므로 어울리지 않는 반응이며, (C) 또한 appointment와 일부 발음이 비슷한 disappointing을 활용한 오답으로서 결과의 실망스러움을 나타내는 말이므로 오답이다.

25

★★★ 평서문

서두르세요! 오늘 밤 쇼를 보실 수 있는 티켓이 조금 남아 있습니다.
(A) 저는 남아 있는 어떤 음식도 원하지 않습니다.
(B) 저는 과속으로 딱지를 뗐습니다.
(C) 저는 오늘 밤에 갈 수 없을 것 같습니다.

어휘 There is A left A가 남아 있다 leftover food 남은 음식 be ticketed for speeding 과속으로 딱지를 떼다 I'm afraid (that) (부정적인 일에 대해) ~인 것 같습니다 make it 가다, 오다

Hurry! There are some tickets left for tonight's show.

(A) I don't want any leftover food.
(B) I have been ticketed for speeding.
(C) I'm afraid I can't make it tonight.

문제 해설

쇼를 보실 수 있는 티켓이 조금 남아 있어서 서두르라는 의미를 나타내는 평서문에 대해 오늘 밤에 갈 수 없다는 말로 표를 구입할 필요가 없음을 나타내는 (C)가 정답이다.

토익 분석

(A)는 left와 일부 발음이 유사한 leftover를 활용해 혼동을 유발하는 오답으로, 티켓 구매가 아닌 음식과 관련된 말이므로 어울리지 않는 반응이며, (B)는 ticket이 동사로 사용되는 경우를 활용한 오답으로, 과속에 대해 딱지를 뗐다는 의미를 나타낼 때 사용하는 표현이므로 마찬가지로 어울리지 않는 답변이다.

26

★★ 직접의문문 Why

Lao 씨가 왜 우리의 제안을 거절하신 거죠?
(A) 네. 그것을 월요일까지 반환하셔야 합니다.
(B) 당신이 그것에 대한 비용을 지불하기만 하시면요.
(C) 더 좋은 거래 조건을 찾으셨어요.

어휘 turn down ~을 거절하다 proposal 제안(서) return ~을 반환하다, 반납하다 by (기한) ~까지 as long as ~하기만 하면, ~하는 한 pay for ~에 대한 비용을 지불하다 deal 거래 (조건)

Why did Mr. Lao turn down our proposal?

(A) Yes. You should return it by Monday.
(B) As long as you pay for it.
(C) He found a better deal.

문제 해설

Lao 씨가 제안을 거절한 이유를 묻는 Why 의문문에 대해 Lao 씨는 He로 지칭해 더 나은 거래 조건을 찾았다는 말로 그 이유를 알리는 (C)가 정답이다.

토익 분석

(A)는 의문사 의문문에 어울리지 않는 Yes로 대답하는 오답이며, (B)는 상대방이 비용을 지불하는 조건을 나타내는 말이므로 Lao 씨가 제안을 거절한 이유로 어울리지 않는 답변이다.

27

I can go over the material after lunch if you'd like.

(A) It will be over soon.
(B) Why don't you wait until he comes out?
(C) Great, that will be a great help.

문제 해설

자신이 특정 자료를 검토할 수 있다는 말로 대신 검토해 주겠다는 제안을 나타내는 평서문이므로 이에 대해 긍정을 나타내는 Great와 함께 검토하는 일을 that으로 지칭해 큰 도움이 될 것이라고 답변하는 (C)가 정답이다.

토익 분석

(A)는 go over의 over를 반복 활용해 혼동을 유발하는 오답으로, over가 지니는 또 다른 의미(끝난)를 활용한 답변이며, (B)는 대상을 알 수 없는 he를 언급해 핵심에서 벗어난 오답이다.

★★★ 평서문

괜찮으시다면 제가 점심 식사 후에 그 자료를 검토할 수 있습니다.
(A) 곧 끝날 겁니다.
(B) 그가 나올 때까지 기다리는 건 어때요?
(C) 좋습니다, 그렇게 해 주시면 큰 도움이 될 거예요.

어휘 go over ~을 검토하다, 살펴보다 material 자료, 재료 if you'd like 괜찮으시다면 over 끝난, 종료된 soon 곧, 머지않아 Why don't you ~? ~하는 게 어때요? until (지속) ~할 때까지

28

How did you hear about the job openings?

(A) I believe it opens at nine thirty.
(B) I'm not really satisfied with the job.
(C) Through the Internet.

문제 해설

공석인 자리에 대해 어떻게 알게 되었는지를 묻는 How 의문문에 대해 정보를 얻을 수 있었던 방법으로 '인터넷을 통해서'라는 말로 답변하는 (C)가 정답이다.

토익 분석

(A)는 openings와 발음이 유사한 opens를 활용해 혼동을 유발하는 오답으로, 공석에 대해 알게 된 방법이 아니라 한 매장의 영업이 시작되는 시간을 말하는 내용이므로 어울리지 않는다. (B)는 job을 반복 활용한 오답으로, 공석에 대해 알게 된 방법이 아닌 자신의 업무 만족도를 언급하는 말이므로 마찬가지로 어울리지 않는 반응이다.

★★ 직접의문문 How

그 직책의 공석에 대해 어떻게 알게 되셨죠?
(A) 그곳이 9시 30분에 문을 여는 것 같아요.
(B) 저는 일자리에 그렇게 만족하지 않습니다.
(C) 인터넷을 통해서요.

어휘 How did you hear about A? A에 대해 어떻게 알게 되셨죠? job opening 공석, 빈자리 be satisfied with ~에 만족하다 through ~을 통해

29

Is the weather in England always this bad?

(A) It gets even worse during the winter season.
(B) I'm not sure whether he is coming.
(C) I prefer summer to winter.

★★ 일반의문문

England의 날씨는 항상 이렇게 좋지 않은가요?
(A) 겨울철 동안에는 훨씬 더 나빠집니다.
(B) 저는 그가 오는 건지 모르겠어요.
(C) 저는 겨울보다 여름을 선호합니다.

어휘 this 이렇게, 이만큼 get worse 더 나빠지다 even (비교급 수식) 훨씬 whether ~인지 (아닌지) prefer A to B B보다 A를 선호하다, 더 좋아하다

England의 날씨가 항상 좋지 않은 것인지를 확인하는 일반의문문이므로 이에 대해 겨울철 날씨가 더 좋지 않다는 말로 현재의 날씨가 오히려 좋은 편이라는 의미를 나타내는 (A)가 정답이다.

토익 분석

(B)는 weather와 발음은 같지만, 의미가 전혀 다른 whether를 활용해 혼동을 유발하는 오답으로, 날씨가 아니라 대상을 알 수 없는 he의 도착 여부를 말하는 내용이므로 어울리지 않는 반응이다. (C)는 단순히 자신이 선호하는 계절을 말하는 내용이므로 England의 날씨 상태를 확인하는 질문에 전혀 어울리지 않는 말이다.

30

★★ 직접의문문 Which

지난주에 어느 영화가 가장 높은 예매율을 기록했나요?
(A) 웹 사이트에서 기록을 확인해 보실 수 있습니다.
(B) 네. 그것은 아주 성공적이었습니다.
(C) 그것을 조금 더 높이 옮겨 주시겠어요?

어휘 booking 예약 rate 비율, 등급, 요금, 속도 on the Web 웹 페이지에서 successful 성공적인 a little 조금, 약간

Which movie had the highest booking rate last week?
(A) You can check the record on the Web.
(B) Yes. It was very successful.
(C) Can you move it a little higher?

문제 해설

가장 높은 예매율을 보인 영화가 어느 것인지를 묻는 Which 의문문에 대해 직접적인 답변 대신 관련 정보를 확인할 방법을 알려 주는 (A)가 정답이다.

토익 분석

(B)는 의문사 의문문에 어울리지 않는 Yes로 답변하는 오답이며, (C)는 movie와 발음이 유사한 move 및 highest와 관련성 있게 들리는 higher를 활용해 혼동을 유발하는 오답으로, 영화 예매와 전혀 관련 없는 위치 이동에 대해 묻는 질문이므로 어울리지 않는 답변이다.

31

★★ 부가의문문

제가 A 두 개짜리 배터리를 5상자 주문하지 않았었나요?
(A) 그것들은 여전히 고장 난 상태입니다.
(B) 제가 갈색 가방을 갖다 드릴 수 있습니다.
(C) 죄송합니다, 제가 실수를 했습니다.

어휘 order ~을 주문하다 double A batteries A 표시가 두 개인 배터리 out of order 고장 난 get A B A에게 B를 사 주다, 갖다 주다 make a mistake 실수를 하다

I ordered five boxes of the double A batteries, didn't I?
(A) They are still out of order.
(B) I can get you a brown bag.
(C) I'm sorry, I made a mistake.

문제 해설

자신이 주문한 물품의 수량을 확인하기 위한 부가의문문으로 주문한 수량과 관련해 실수를 했다는 말로 주문 사항이 제대로 이행되지 않았음을 나타내는 (C)가 정답이다.

토익 분석

(A)는 They가 batteries를 지칭하는 것으로 생각할 수 있지만, 뒤에 이어지는 내용이 수량이 아니라 제품의 작동 여부와 관련된 내용이므로 어울리지 않는 반응이며, (B)는 boxes와 연관성 있게 들리는 bag을 활용해 혼동을 유발하는 오답으로, 마찬가지로 주문 수량과 관련 없는 답변이다.

Questions 32-34 refer to the following conversation.

M   Excuse me. [32, 33] I want to get some information on one of your vacation homes that you have for rent. I was looking at the property at 101 Park Avenue. Is that one of your properties?

W   [33] Yes, that's one of our new properties. It's been very popular because of its great location. It looks like the house is rented out for most of the summer. It is only available for the first two weeks in August. Is that going to work for you?

M   That might just work, but I need to talk to my colleagues before making a decision. We're all taking a vacation together. Do you know how many people that property accommodates?

W   It's a big property, so it sleeps ten comfortably. Let me give you a rental brochure to show to your colleagues. [34] I will say you should make up your minds soon, though, because it's not likely to stay available for much longer.

어휘 vacation home 별장 for rent 임대용으로 property 건물, 부동산 because of ~ 때문에 location 위치 be rented out 임대가 완료되다 available 이용 가능한 work for ~에게 괜찮다, 적합하다 colleague 직장 동료 make a decision 결정하다 accommodate ~을 수용/포함하다 comfortably 편안하게 brochure 안내 책자 make up one's mind 결정하다 though 하지만 be likely to do ~할 것 같다 stay + 형용사 ~한 상태로 있다

남   실례합니다. [32, 33] 저는 임대용으로 보유 중이신 귀하의 별장들 중의 한 곳에 관한 정보를 얻고자 합니다. 저는 Park Avenue 101번지에 있는 주택을 봤습니다. 그곳도 귀하의 건물들 중 한 곳인가요?

여   [33] 네, 새로운 제 건물들 중 한 곳이에요. 위치가 아주 좋아서 인기가 많았고요. 그 주택은 여름 대부분의 기간 동안 임대가 확정된 곳입니다. 오직 8월의 첫 2주 동안만 이용하실 수 있어요. 그래도 괜찮으신가요?

남   괜찮을 겁니다, 하지만 결정을 내리기 전에 제 직장 동료들과 이야기해 봐야 합니다. 저희가 함께 휴가를 갈 예정이거든요. 그 건물은 몇 명을 수용할 수 있는지 알고 계신가요?

여   큰 주택이라 10명이 편안하게 잘 수 있습니다. 직장 동료들께 보여 드릴 수 있는 임대 안내 책자를 드리겠습니다. [34] 하지만 이용 가능한 상태로 오래 있지 않을 가능성이 크기 때문에 빨리 결정하셔야 한다는 말씀을 드려야겠네요.

32

What does the man want to do?

(A) Use a moving service　　(B) **Rent a house**
(C) Visit a property　　(D) Purchase an office building

문제 해설

남자가 원하는 것을 묻는 첫 번째 문제이므로 대화 초반에 남자가 원하는 바를 언급하는 부분이 있다는 것을 예상하고 들어야 한다. 남자는 대화 시작과 함께 'I want to~for rent'라고 말하며 상대방 소유의 임대 주택에 대한 정보를 구하고자 하는 의사를 밝히고 있다. 뒤이어 'I was looking at the property at 101 Park Avenue. Is that one of your properties?'라고 말하며 특정 임대 주택에 대한 관심을 표명하는 부분을 통해 (B)가 정답임을 알 수 있다.

★★ **의도 파악**

남자는 무엇을 하길 원하는가?
(A) 이사 서비스를 이용하기　(B) 집을 임대하기
(C) 부지에 방문하기　　　(D) 사무용 건물을 구입하기

어휘 moving service 이사 서비스 purchase 구입하다

토익 분석

남자의 첫 번째 대화문에서 의도 및 미래 행동 표현을 찾아야 한다. I want to~가 정답을 이끌고 있다.

33

Who most likely is the woman?

(A) **A property manager**　(B) An architect
(C) A travel agent　　　(D) An office worker

문제 해설

여자의 정체를 추측할 수 있을 만한 관련 어휘나 표현이 제시되는 부분에 집중해야 한다. 남자가 대화 시작과 함께 'I want to get some information on one of your vacation homes that you have for rent.'라고 말하며 임대 주택에 대한 정보를 구하고자 하는 의사를 밝히는 부분, 그리고 남자가 문의한 임대 주택에 대해 여자가 'Yes, that's one of our new properties.'라고 대답하며 새로 임대를 놓는 주택임을 밝히는 부분을 통해 여자는 부동산 관리자임을 알 수 있으므로 (A)가 정답이다.

★★ **도입부 정보**

여자는 누구일 것 같은가?
(A) 부동산 관리자　　　(B) 건축가
(C) 여행사 직원　　　　(D) 사무직 직원

어휘 property 부동산, 재산 architect 건축가 travel agent 여행사 직원

토익 분석

여자의 직업은 도입부에 첫 번째 또는 두 번째 대화 문장에 직업과 관련된 표현이 반드시 등장한다.

34

What does the woman advise the man to do?

(A) Look at a map　　　(B) **Make a quick decision**
(C) Start a meeting without her　(D) Take his key to the security office

문제 해설

여자의 권장 사항을 묻는 마지막 문제이므로 대화 후반부 여자의 말에서 제시되는 권고 표현을 중심으로 단서를 찾아야 한다. 여자는 대화 종료 직전 남자에게 'I will say~much longer.'라고 말하며 임대를 할 것인지 여부를 빨리 결정해야 한다고 권하고 있으므로 (B)가 정답임을 알 수 있다.

★★★ **요청, 제안**

여자는 남자에 무엇을 하도록 권하는가?
(A) 지도를 볼 것　　　(B) 빠른 결정을 내릴 것
(C) 자기 없이 회의를 시작할 것
(D) 열쇠를 경비실로 가지고 올 것

어휘 make a decision 결정하다

토익 분석

요청, 제안 표현인 (I will say) you should가 정답을 이끌고 있다.

여1 안녕하세요, 여러분. 제가 노트북을 빌리기 위해 두
　 분을 찾고 있었어요. 아침 내내 어디에 계셨나요?
남　 ³⁷ Susan과 저는 회의 때문에 나가 있었는데, 지금 저
　 희에게 노트북이 없습니다. ³⁵ 제가 사무실로 가서 가
　 져다 드릴까요?
여1 아뇨, 그러실 필요는 없습니다. ³⁶ 제 고객들 중의 한
　 분께 이메일을 보내려고 했었는데, 제 노트북이 작동
　 되지 않았어요. 어쨌든 제 노트북을 수리 받아야 할
　 거예요.
남　 있잖아요, ³⁷ 전화기로 이메일을 보내실 수 있을 거예
　 요.
여2 네, 맞아요. ³⁷ 그렇게 어렵지 않아요. 그 방법을 알지
　 못하시면, 제가 알려 드릴 수 있습니다.

Questions 35-37 refer to the following conversation with three speakers.

W1　Hi, guys. I've been looking for you two to borrow a laptop. Where were you all morning?

M　³⁷ Susan and I went out for a meeting, and we don't have the laptops with us now. ³⁵ Do you want me to go to the office and get one?

W1　No, that won't be necessary. ³⁶ I just wanted to send an e-mail to one of my clients, but my laptop wasn't working. I'll have to get my laptop repaired anyway.

M　You know, ³⁷ you can send an e-mail with your phone.

W2　Yes, that's right. ³⁷ It's not that hard. If you don't know how to do it, I can show you.

어휘 look for ~을 찾다 borrow ~을 빌리다 go out for ~하러 나가다 want A to do A가 ~하기를 원하다 necessary 필요한, 필수의 work (기계 등) 작동되다 get A p.p. A가 ~되게 하다 repair ~을 수리하다 that 그렇게, 그만큼 how to do ~하는 법

35

★★ 요청, 제안

남자는 무엇을 하겠다고 제안하는가?
(A) 회의에 참석하는 일
(B) 기기를 수리하는 일
(C) 사무실에 전화하는 일
(D) 노트북 컴퓨터를 가져오는 일

어휘 offer to do ~하겠다고 제안하다 attend ~에 참석하다 fix ~을 고치다, 수리하다 device 기기

토익 분석

남자 대화문에서 요청, 제안 힌트 표현인 Do you want me to~?가 정답 단서를 제시하고 있다.

What does the man offer to do?

(A) Attend a meeting
(B) Fix a device
(C) Call the office
(D) Get a laptop

문제 해설

남자가 제안하는 것을 묻는 첫 번째 문제이므로 대화 초반부 남자의 말에서 제안 사항을 언급하는 부분이 있다는 것을 예상하고 들어야 한다. 남자는 대화 초반부에 'Do you want me to go to the office and get it?'라는 말로 뭔가를 갖다 주는 것을 제안하고 있는데, 이는 앞서 여자 한 명이 언급한 a laptop, 즉 노트북 컴퓨터를 가리키는 것이므로 (D)가 정답임을 알 수 있다.

36

★★ 의도 파악

한 여자가 왜 노트북 컴퓨터를 필요로 하는가?
(A) 프로젝트 작업을 하기 위해　(B) 일정을 확인하기 위해
(C) 이메일을 보내기 위해　　　 (D) 예약을 하기 위해

어휘 laptop 노트북

토익 분석

여자들의 대화에 집중하여 의도 및 미래 행동 표현을 들어야 한다. I (just) wanted to~가 단서를 제시하고 있다. 질문 속에 사용된 laptop 역시 결정적인 키워드로 사용되었다.

Why does one woman need a laptop?

(A) To work on a project
(B) To check a schedule
(C) To send an e-mail
(D) To make an appointment

문제 해설

한 여자가 노트북 컴퓨터를 필요로 하는 이유를 묻는 두 번째 문제이므로 대화 중반부 한 여자의 말에서 노트북 컴퓨터를 필요로 하는 이유를 언급하는 부분이 있다는 것을 예상하고 들어야 한다. 여자 한 명이 대화 중반부에 노트북 컴퓨터와 관련해 'I just wanted to send an e-mail to one of my clients, but my laptop wasn't working.'라는 말로 고객에게 이메일을 보내야 하지만 자신의 노트북 컴퓨터가 작동되지 않는 상황임을 알리고 있다. 따라서 (C)가 정답임을 알 수 있다.

37

★★★ 요청, 제안

Susan은 무엇을 하겠다고 제안하는가?
(A) 이메일을 보내는 방법을 설명해 주는 일
(B) 고객과의 약속을 잡는 일
(C) 노트북 컴퓨터를 구입하는 일
(D) 이메일을 회송하는 일

어휘 make an appointment 예약하다, 약속을 잡다 forward ~을 회송/전송하다

토익 분석

Susan의 대화문에서 요청, 제안 힌트인 'If가정법~, I can'이 정답을 제시하고 있다.

What does Susan offer to do?

(A) Explain how to send an e-mail (B) Make an appointment with the clients
(C) Buy a laptop computer　　(D) Forward an e-mail

문제 해설

Susan이 제안하는 것을 묻는 세 번째 문제이므로 Susan이라는 이름을 지닌 한 여자가 제안 사항을 언급하는 부분이 있다는 것을 예상하고 들어야 한다. Susan이라는 이름은 대화 중반부에 남자가 하는 말에서 들을 수 있고, 대화 후반부에 남자가 'you can send an e-mail with your phone'이라는 말로 전화기를 이용해 이메일을 보낼 수 있다는 사실을 언급하는 것에 대해 'If you don't know how to do it, I can show you.'라고 말하면서 그 방법을 알려 줄 수 있다고 말하고 있다. 따라서 이메일을 보내는 방법을 가르쳐 주겠다고 제안하는 것이므로 (A)가 정답이다.

Questions 38-40 refer to the following conversation.

W [38] Hello, this is Veronica Cooks calling from room 701. [39] I need a cab this afternoon, and I'm wondering if you can assist me with that.

M Of course, Ms. Cooks. [38] If you let me know the time you would like to depart and your intended destination, I will have a driver waiting for you in front of our hotel. There's a covered pickup area right outside.

W Thank you. [40] I'll need to leave here at 2 P.M., and I'm going to the Olympic Stadium. I've been invited to take some photographs of the team during one of their practices.

어휘 cab 택시 wonder if ~인지 궁금하다 assist A with B B에 대해 A를 돕다 let A know A에게 알리다 depart 출발하다, 떠나다 intended 계획/의도된 destination 목적지 have A -ing A가 ~하고 있도록 하다 covered 지붕이 설치된 pick-up area 손님을 태우는 곳 right (강조) 바로 be invited to do ~하도록 요청 받다 take a photograph 사진 촬영을 하다 during ~ 중에 practice 연습

여 [38] 안녕하세요, 저는 701호실에서 전화 드리는 **Veronica Cooks**입니다. [39] 제가 오늘 오후에 택시가 필요한데, 저 좀 도와주실 수 있는지 궁금합니다.

남 물론입니다, **Cooks** 씨. [38] 출발하고자 하시는 시간과 원하시는 목적지를 제게 알려 주시면, 저희 호텔 앞에 기사를 대기시켜 드리겠습니다. 바로 바깥쪽에 지붕이 설치된 탑승 구역이 있습니다.

여 감사합니다. [40] 제가 여기서 오후 2시에 출발해야 하는데, **Olympic Stadium**으로 갈 예정입니다. 그곳에서 팀이 연습하는 시간 중에 사진을 촬영하도록 요청을 받았습니다.

38

Where does the man most likely work?

(A) At a taxi company   (B) At a furniture store
(C) At a hotel   (D) At a restaurant

문제 해설

대화가 시작하자 마자 연자가 'Hello, this is Veronica Cooks calling from room 701.'라고 말하고 있다 동시에 남자의 첫 번째 대화 문 속에 'If you let me know the time you would like to depart and your intended destination, I will have a driver waiting for you in front of our hotel.'라는 말로 자신이 근무하는 호텔 앞에 택시를 대기시켜 줄 수 있음을 언급하는 부분을 통해 호텔 직원임을 알 수 있으므로 (C)가 정답이다.

★★ 도입부 정보

남자는 어디에서 근무하고 있을 것 같은가?
(A) 택시 회사에서   (B) 가구 매장에서
(C) 호텔에서   (D) 레스토랑에서

토익 분석

남자의 근무 장소를 묻는 첫 번째 문제이므로 대화 중에 특정 직책이나 회사 이름, 업무적 특성 등과 관련된 정보가 제시된다는 점을 예상하고 들어야 한다. 남자의 첫 번째 대화문이 중요하다.

39

What is the purpose of the woman's call?

(A) To make a complaint
(B) To cancel a request
(C) To inquire about a bill
(D) To arrange transportation

문제 해설

여자가 전화하는 목적을 묻는 두 번째 문제이므로 여자의 말에서 전화를 거는 특정한 이유가 언급된다는 것을 예상하고 그 정보를 파악하는 데 집중해야 한다. 여자는 대화를 시작하면서 'I need a cab this afternoon, and I'm wondering if you can assist me with that'이라는 말로 자신이 이용할 택시가 필요하다고 알리고 있으므로 교통편을 마련하기 위해서라는 의미로 쓰인 (D)가 정답이 된다.

★★ 주제, 목적

여자가 전화를 거는 목적은 무엇인가?
(A) 불만을 제기하기 위해 (B) 요청을 취소하기 위해
(C) 청구서에 관해 문의하기 위해
(D) 교통편을 마련하기 위해

어휘 make a complaint 불만을 제기하다 request 요청 inquire about ~에 관해 문의하다 bill 청구서 arrange ~을 마련/조치하다 transportation 교통편

토익 분석

전화의 목적은 언제나 전화건 사람의 첫 번째 대화문에 정답이 제시된다. 의도 및 미래 행동의 힌트인 I need (to)와 요청 제안 표현인 If가정법 + you can이 정답을 이끌고 있다.

40

What does the woman plan to do this afternoon?

(A) Practice an instrument   (B) View a photography exhibit
(C) Visit a sports venue   (D) Meet a friend

문제 해설

여자의 오늘 오후 계획을 묻는 마지막 문제이므로 여자의 말에서 '오늘 오후'에 해당되는 시점 표현과 함께 자신의 계획을 언급하는 부분이 있다는 것을 예상하고 들어야 한다. 여자는 대화 마지막에 'I'll need to leave here at 2 P.M., and I'm going to the Olympic Stadium. I've been invited to take some photographs of the team during one of their practices.'라는 말로 자신이 오후에 경기장에서 한 팀의 사진을 촬영하도록 요청 받은 일을 알리고 있으므로 해당 경기장을 방문할 계획임을 알 수 있다. 따라서 이에 대해 언급한 (C)가 정답이다.

★★ 세부 정보

여자는 오늘 오후에 무엇을 할 계획인가?
(A) 악기를 연습한다.   (B) 사진 전시회를 본다.
(C) 스포츠 경기장을 방문한다. (D) 친구를 만난다.

어휘 practice ~을 연습하다 instrument 악기 exhibit 전시(회) venue (행사) 장소

토익 분석

여자의 후반부 대화문에서 여자의 미래 행동 또는 의도를 나타내는 힌트를 찾아야 한다. I'll + need to~가 정답을 제시하고 있다. 또한 시점 키워드 this afternoon가 2 P.M.으로 변형되어 활용된 점도 확인하자.

여 문구 제품 배송 서비스에 대해 다시 한 번 감사 드려요, Phil.

남 별말씀을요, Harvey 씨. [41] 다시 한 번, 어젯밤에 주문하셨던 컬러 용지 묶음을 가져다 드리는 걸 잊은 것에 대해 진심으로 사과 드립니다.

여 괜찮습니다. 금요일 오후나 되어야 필요할 텐데요. [42] 토요일에 있을 대규모 여름 세일 행사에 대한 표지를 만들 계획이에요. 그전에 다시 오시는 건가요?

남 네, 저는 이번 주에 제 정규 배송 구역을 돌 예정이라서, 목요일 오전에 다시 오겠습니다.

여 잘됐네요. [43] 어쩌면 창고에 전화를 하셔서 미리 물품을 준비시키시면 좋을 거예요, 그러면 잊지 않으실 겁니다.

남 [43] 좋은 생각입니다. 제가 지금 돌아가기 전에 하겠습니다.

Questions 41-43 refer to the following conversation.

W Thanks again for your stationery delivery service, Phil.

M No problem, Ms. Harvey. [41] Again, I'm so sorry that I forgot to bring the packets of colored paper you ordered last night.

W That's OK. We won't be needing them until Friday afternoon. [42] We're planning to make some signs for the big summer sale on Saturday. You'll be back before then?

M Yes, I'm running my regular delivery route this week, so I'll be back on Thursday morning.

W Great. [43] Maybe you can give the warehouse a call and have them get the goods ready in advance so you don't forget them.

M [43] Good idea. I'll do that now before I head off.

어휘 stationery 문구 제품 delivery 배송, 배달 forget to do ~하는 것을 잊다 packet 묶음 not A until B B나 되어야 A하다 plan to do ~할 계획이다 then 그때 run one's delivery route 배달 구역을 돌다 regular 정규의, 일반적인 give A a call A에게 전화하다 warehouse 창고 have A do A에게 ~하게 하다 get A ready A를 준비하다 in advance 미리, 사전에 head off 가다, 향하다

41

★★ 세부 정보

남자는 무엇에 대해 사과하는가?
(A) 엉뚱한 곳으로 주문품을 보낸 것
(B) 문서에 실수를 한 것
(C) 일부 물품을 가져오는 일을 잊은 것
(D) 약속에 늦은 것

어휘 order n. 주문(품) make an error 실수하다 document 문서, 서류 appointment 약속, 예약

토익 분석

첫 번째 문제이므로 남자의 첫 번째 대화문에 집중해야 한다. 세부 정보 힌트를 반전 표현인 I'm sorry가 제시하고 있다.

What does the man apologize for?

(A) Sending an order to the wrong location
(B) Making an error in a document
(C) Forgetting to bring some items
(D) Being late for an appointment

문제 해설

남자는 사과하는 이유를 묻는 첫 번째 질문이므로 대화의 초반부에서 남자가 사과하는 표현과 함께 제시되는 이유에 집중해 들어야 한다. 남자는 대화 초반부에 감사의 인사를 전하는 여자에게 'Again, I'm so sorry that I forgot to bring the packets of colored paper you ordered last night.'라는 말로 사과를 하고 있는데, 자신이 깜빡 잊고 물품을 가져오지 않은 것을 언급하고 있으므로 (C)가 정답임을 알 수 있다.

42

★ 세부 정보

토요일에 매장에서 무슨 일이 있을 것인가?
(A) 직원 파티가 열릴 것이다.
(B) 신입 직원들이 근무를 시작할 것이다.
(C) 배송이 이뤄질 것이다.
(D) 세일 행사가 시작될 것이다.

어휘 staff 직원, 스태프 hold ~을 열다, 개최하다

토익 분석

질문 속에 사용된 시점 표현 Saturday가 키워드로 활용된다.

What will happen at the store on Saturday?

(A) A staff party will be held.
(B) New employees will start working.
(C) A delivery will be made.
(D) A sale will begin.

문제 해설

토요일에 매장에서 있을 일을 묻는 두 번째 질문이므로 대화의 중반부에서 '토요일'이라는 시점 표현과 함께 언급되는 일을 파악하는 것이 관건이다. 여자는 대화 중반부에 'We're planning to make some signs for the big summer sale on Saturday.'라는 말로 토요일이라는 시점 표현과 함께 그날 있을 세일 행사를 언급하고 있으므로 (D)가 정답이 된다.

43

★★ 미래 행동

남자는 곧이어 무엇을 할 것 같은가?
(A) 창고를 청소한다.　(B) 물품을 배달한다.
(C) 상품을 가져간다.　(D) 전화를 건다.

어휘 goods 상품 make a phone call 전화하다

토익 분석

남자의 후반부 대화 속에 I'll~문장이 정답 힌트다. 여자 대화 속에 요청, 제안 표현인 Maybe you can~ 역시 결정적인 힌트다.

What will the man likely do next?

(A) Clean a warehouse
(B) Deliver some items
(C) Pick up some goods
(D) Make a phone call

문제 해설

남자의 추후 행동을 묻는 마지막 질문이며, 이에 대한 단서는 대화 후반부 또는 최종 화자의 말에서 제시되는 경우가 일반적이다. 대화 후반부에 여자가 'Maybe you can give the warehouse a call and have them get the goods~'라는 말로 전화를 해서 미리 물품을 준비시키라고 제안하는 것에 대해 남자가 'Good idea. I'll do that now before I head off.'라는 말로 동의하면서 바로 하겠다고 대답하고 있으므로 (D)가 정답임을 알 수 있다.

Questions 44-46 refer to the following conversation.

W Good evening, sir. I'm Joan Park, the owner of this restaurant. One of the waitresses informed me that you wished to speak with me. Was there an issue with your food?

M No. Actually, [45] the food was fantastic, and I was wondering if you cater for off-site events. [44] My company often needs meals for training sessions or special occasions. I think my employees would love your food.

W Thank you for the compliment. Unfortunately, we only serve our food here in the restaurant. However, [46] I have a few friends in the industry that I could recommend to you.

여 안녕하세요, 고객님. 저는 이 레스토랑의 소유주인 **Joan Park**입니다. 저희 여종업원들 중의 한 명이 손님께서 저와 이야기하고 싶어 하신다고 알려 주었습니다. 음식에 문제가 있으셨나요?

남 아뇨. 사실, [45] 음식은 아주 환상적이었는데, 외부 행사에 대해 출장 요리를 제공해 주시는지 궁금했어요. [44] 제 회사가 종종 교육 연수나 특별 행사에 음식을 필요로 합니다. 저희 직원들이 이곳의 음식을 아주 마음에 들어 할 것 같아서요.

여 칭찬해 주셔서 감사합니다. 안타깝게도, 저희는 오직 이곳 레스토랑에서만 음식을 제공해 드리고 있습니다. 하지만 [46] 제가 추천해 드릴 만한 몇몇 동료들이 업계에 종사하고 있습니다.

어휘 owner 소유주 waitress 여종업원 inform A that A에게 ~라고 알리다 wish to do ~하고 싶어 하다 issue 문제, 사안 actually 실은, 사실은 wonder if ~인지 궁금하다 cater 출장 요리를 제공하다 off-site event 외부의 행사, 야외 행사 meal 식사 training session 교육 연수 occasion 행사, 경우 compliment 칭찬, 찬사 unfortunately 안타깝게도 serve (음식 등) ~을 제공하다, 내오다 industry 업계 recommend ~을 추천하다

44

Who is the man?

(A) A restaurant manager   (B) A waiter
(C) A business owner   (D) A caterer

문제 해설

남자의 정체를 묻는 첫 번째 문제이므로 대화 중에 특정 직책이나 회사 이름, 업무적 특성 등과 관련된 정보가 제시된다는 점을 예상하고 들어야 한다. 대화 중에 남자가 'My company often needs meals for training sessions or special occasions. I think my employees would love your food.' 라고 말하는 부분에서 자신의 회사 및 소속 직원들에게 필요한 것을 언급하고 있으므로 사업체 소유주를 뜻하는 (C)가 정답임을 알 수 있다.

★★ 도입부 정보

남자는 누구인가?
(A) 레스토랑 매니저   (B) 종업원
(C) 사업체 소유주   (D) 출장 요리업자

어휘 caterer 출장 요리업자

토익 분석

직업은 대화 도입부에서 관련 단어를 찾아야 한다.

45

What does the man inquire about?

(A) Getting a discount on his meal   (B) Reserving a table
(C) Using a catering service   (D) Interviewing the chef

문제 해설

남자가 문의하는 것을 묻는 두 번째 문제이므로 대화 중반부에 남자가 뭔가에 대해 문의하는 부분이 있다는 것을 예상하고 해당 정보를 파악하는 데 집중해야 한다. 대화 중반부에 남자가 'the food was fantastic, and I was wondering if you cater for off-site events'라는 말로 궁금한 부분을 묻는 내용이 있는데, 음식 맛이 좋아서 외부 행사에 대한 출장 요리 서비스를 제공하는지를 묻는 것이므로 (C)가 정답임을 알 수 있다.

★★ 요청, 제안

남자는 무엇에 관해 문의하는가?
(A) 자신의 음식에 대해 할인을 받는 일
(B) 테이블을 예약하는 일
(C) 출장 요리 서비스를 이용하는 일
(D) 주방장을 인터뷰하는 일

어휘 inquire about ~에 관해 문의하다 get a discount on ~에 대해 할인 받다 reserve ~을 예약하다

토익 분석

남자가 남자 대화에서 요청, 제안 힌트인 '(I was wondering) if 가정법~'이 정답을 제시하고 있다.

46

What does the woman offer to do?

(A) Make a recommendation
(B) Create a price list
(C) Waive a fee
(D) Attend an event

문제 해설

여자가 이 제안하는 것을 묻는 세 번째 문제이므로 대화 후반부에 제시되는 여자의 말에서 제안 관련 표현과 함께 언급되는 정보를 파악해야 한다. 여자는 대화 마지막에 레스토랑에서만 음식을 제공한다고 알리면서 'I have a few friends in the industry that I could recommend to you.'라는 말로 다른 동료를 추천해 줄 수 있다고 밝히고 있으므로 (A)가 정답이다.

★★ 요청, 제안

여자는 무엇을 하겠다고 제안하는가?
(A) 추천해 주는 일
(B) 가격 목록을 만드는 일
(C) 요금을 적용하지 않는 일
(D) 행사에 참석하는 일

어휘 offer to do ~하겠다고 제안하다 make a recommendation 추천하다 create ~을 만들어 내다 waive 철회하다, 보류하다 fee 요금 attend ~에 참석하다

토익 분석

여자 후반부 대화 속에 요청, 제안 힌트 표현인 I could~가 활용된 문제다.

여 안녕하세요, [47] 항구 건설 프로젝트에 대해 엉뚱한 파일들을 보내 드려서 정말로 죄송합니다. 실수로 제가 작업해 오던 발표 슬라이드를 이메일로 보내 드렸습니다.

남 괜찮습니다. 그런 것 같다고 생각했습니다. 그런데 그 프로젝트 파일들이 준비되어 있는지 궁금합니다. [48] 그 프로젝트에 대한 설계도가 늦어도 5월 17일까지는 완료되어야 합니다.

여 네, 지금 준비되어 있습니다. 그것을 검토해 보시고 제게 어떤 변경 사항이든지 요청하실 것이 있으신지 알려 주실 수 있도록 보내 드리겠습니다.

남 실은, 제가 지금 고객과의 회의에 가는 중입니다. [49] 제 상사인 Christina 씨께 바로 보내 주시겠습니까?

Questions 47-49 refer to the following conversation.

W Hi, [47] I'm really sorry that I sent you the wrong files for the harbor construction project. I accidentally e-mailed you the presentation slides I've been working on.

M That's OK. I figured it was something like that. But I'm wondering if you have the project files ready. [48] The blueprints for the project need to be done no later than May 17.

W Yes, they are ready now. I'll send them to you so you can review them and let me know if you require any changes.

M Actually, I'm on my way to a client meeting now. [49] Can you send them directly to my supervisor Christina?

어휘 harbor 항구 construction 건설, 건축 accidentally 실수로, 잘못하여 presentation 발표 work on ~에 대한 작업을 하다 figure (that) ~라고 생각하다, ~임을 알다 wonder if ~인지 궁금하다 have A ready A를 준비하다 blueprint 설계도 no later than 늦어도 ~까지 review ~을 검토하다 let A know if A에게 ~인지 알리다 require ~을 요청하다, 필요로 하다 actually 실은, 사실은 on one's way to ~로 가는/오는 중인 supervisor 상사, 책임자

47

★★ 주제, 목적

여자는 왜 남자에게 전화를 거는가?
(A) 실수에 대해 사과하기 위해
(B) 한 고객에 대한 새로운 정보를 얻기 위해
(C) 남자의 이메일 주소를 요청하기 위해
(D) 남자가 한 일에 대해 칭찬하기 위해

어휘 apologize for ~에 대해 사과하다 get an update on ~에 대한 새로운 정보를 얻다 ask for ~을 요청하다 praise A for B B에 대해 A를 칭찬하다

토익 분석

여자가 전화를 건 목적은 언제나 여자의 첫 번째 대화문에 답이 나온다. 반전 표현 I'm (really) sorry~가 힌트다.

Why is the woman calling the man?

(A) To apologize for an error (B) To get an update on a client
(C) To ask for his e-mail address (D) To praise him for some work he did

문제 해설

여자가 전화하는 이유를 묻는 첫 번째 문제이므로 대화 시작 부분에 제시되는 여자의 말에서 전화를 거는 특정한 이유가 언급된다는 것을 예상하고 그 정보를 파악하는 데 집중해야 한다. 여자는 대화를 시작하면서 'I'm really sorry that I sent you the wrong files for the harbor construction project. I accidentally e-mailed you the presentation slides I've been working on.'이라는 말로 자신이 잘못 보낸 파일에 대해 사과하고 있으므로 실수에 대해 사과한다는 의미로 쓰인 (A)가 정답이다.

48

★★ 세부 정보

남자의 말에 따르면, 5월 17일까지 무엇이 준비되어야 하는가?
(A) 설계 도면   (B) 성과 평가서
(C) 발표 슬라이드   (D) 카탈로그

어휘 prepare ~을 준비하다 by (기한) ~까지 floor plan 설계 도면, 평면도 performance 성과, 실적 evaluation 평가(서) catalogue (제품 등의) 카탈로그

토익 분석

질문 속 시점 포인트는 언제나 결정적인 키워드다. May 17 포함된 문장이 정답을 제시하고 있다.

According to the man, what should be prepared by May 17?

(A) Some floor plans
(B) Some performance evaluations
(C) Some presentation slides
(D) Some catalogues

문제 해설

5월 17일까지 준비되어야 하는 것을 묻는 두 번째 문제이므로 대화 중반부에 해당 시점 표현과 함께 언급되는 정보를 파악하는 데 집중해야 한다. 대화 중반부에 남자가 'The blueprints for the project need to be done no later than May 17.'라는 말로 설계도가 5월 17일까지 완료되어야 한다는 사실을 알리고 있으므로 blueprints와 유사한 의미를 나타내는 (A)가 정답이다.

49

★★ 요청, 제안

여자는 무엇을 하도록 요청 받는가?
(A) 회의 일정을 재조정할 것   (B) 발표를 할 것
(C) 보조 직원을 고용할 것   (D) 상사에게 연락할 것

어휘 deliver a presentation 발표하다 hire ~을 고용하다 assistant 보조 contact ~에게 연락하다

토익 분석

남자 후반부 대화 속에 요청, 제안 표현인 Can you~가 정답을 제시했다.

What is the woman asked to do?

(A) Reschedule the meetings   (B) Deliver a presentation
(C) Hire an assistant   **(D) Contact the supervisor**

문제 해설

여자가 요청 받는 것을 묻는 마지막 문제이므로 대화 후반부 남자의 말에서 여자에게 요청하는 사항이 있음을 예상하고 들어야 한다. 대화 마지막에 남자가 'Can you send them to my supervisor Christina directly?'라는 말로 자신의 상사에게 직접 보내라고 요청하고 있다. 이는 그 상사에게 직접 연락하는 것과 같으므로 (D)가 정답임을 알 수 있다.

Questions 50-52 refer to the following conversation.

W ⁵⁰ Hi, I just moved to the area, and I am interested in joining a country club. What are the membership costs at Silver Horse Grounds?

M Hello. New members have to pay a one-time membership fee of $2,000. After that, members pay $250 a month.

W OK. That sounds reasonable. What do you have available at your club?

M Basic membership comes with access to our renowned golf course, premier tennis courts, and our world-class swimming pool.

W You mentioned that it's a basic membership. What would a VIP membership include?

M VIP membership, in addition to everything else, gives access to the Prestige Lounge. ⁵¹ In fact, there will be a discount on VIP membership next month.

W ⁵¹ I have good timing then. I think I'd like to have access to the Prestige Lounge.

M Great. But before signing up, ⁵² I would recommend taking a tour of the club to see our facilities and meet some members.

W Yes, I suppose I should start by meeting other members. Thank you for your help.

어휘 membership fee 회비　reasonable 합리적인　have A available A가 이용 가능하다　come with ~가 딸려 있다

여 ⁵⁰ 안녕하세요, 제가 막 이 지역으로 이사를 왔는데, 컨트리클럽에 가입하는 데 관심이 있어요. Silver Horse Grounds의 회비는 얼마인가요?

남 안녕하세요. 신입 회원들은 1회만 지불하면 되는 2,000달러의 회비를 내셔야 합니다. 그 후에는 회원들은 한 달에 250달러를 냅니다.

여 알겠습니다. 합리적인 것 같네요. 이 클럽에서는 무엇이 이용 가능한가요?

남 기본적인 회원 가입에 딸린 서비스는 유명한 저희 골프 코스와 최고의 테니스 코트, 그리고 세계 최상급의 수영장이 있습니다.

여 그게 기본적인 회원 서비스라고 말씀하셨는데요. 그럼 VIP 회원 서비스에는 무엇이 있나요?

남 다른 모든 것들에 더해, VIP 회원 서비스는 프레스티지 라운지에 대한 이용권을 제공해 드립니다. ⁵¹ 사실, 다음 달에 VIP 회원 서비스에 대한 할인이 있을 겁니다.

여 ⁵¹ 그럼 저는 타이밍이 좋은 거네요. 제 생각에 저는 프레스티지 라운지 이용권을 갖고 싶습니다.

남 좋습니다. 하지만 등록하시기 전에, ⁵² 저희 시설을 확인해 보시고 다른 회원들을 만나 보실 수 있도록 클럽 내를 견학해 보시기를 권해 드립니다.

여 네, 제 생각에 다른 회원들을 만나는 것으로 시작해야 할 것 같네요. 도와주셔서 감사합니다.

50

Why is the woman calling?

(A) To ask about membership costs　(B) To request an interview

(C) To contact a manager　(D) To schedule a meeting

문제 해설

여자가 전화를 거는 목적을 묻는 첫 번째 질문이므로 대화 초반부에서 전화 용건과 관련해 중점적으로 언급하는 핵심 내용을 파악하는 것이 관건이다. 여자는 대화를 시작하면서 'Hi~Silver Horse Grounds?'라는 말로 컨트리클럽에 가입하는 데 관심이 있다는 말과 함께 회비가 얼마인지 묻고 있으므로 (A)가 정답임을 알 수 있다.

★★ 주제, 목적

여자는 왜 전화를 거는가?
(A) 회비에 대해 물어보기　(B) 면접 요청하기
(C) 매니저에게 연락하기　(D) 회의 일정을 정하기

어휘 request ~을 요청하다　contact ~에게 연락하다

토익 분석

여자가 전화건 목적이므로 여자의 첫 번째 대화 문에 정답이 등장한다. What~? 의문문이 결정적인 힌트다.

51

What does the woman imply when she says, "I have good timing then"?

(A) She can stay longer than expected.

(B) She can take advantage of a new deal.

(C) She has a very busy schedule.　(D) She plans to revisit another time.

문제 해설

여자가 말하는 "I have good timing then"이라는 표현이 대화에서 어떤 의미로 사용되었는지를 묻는 두 번째 질문으로 대화 중반부에 제시되는 여자의 말을 통해 해당 표현을 확인할 수 있어야 한다. 이 말을 그대로 해석하면, '나는 타이밍이 좋다'라는 뜻인데, 이는 앞서 남자가 VIP 회원 서비스에 대해 다음 달에 할인이 제공된다고 말하는 것에 대해 해당 표현과 함께 'I have good timing~Prestige Lounge.'라는 말로 VIP 회원 서비스를 통해 제공되는 혜택을 이용하고 싶다고 알리므로 해당 거래 조건을 이용할 수 있다는 말로 바꿔 표현한 (B)가 정답이 된다.

★★★ 맥락 파악

여자가 "I have good timing then"이라고 말할 때 무엇을 암시하는가?
(A) 예상보다 더 오래 머무를 수 있다.
(B) 새로운 거래 조건을 이용할 수 있다.
(C) 매우 바쁜 일정이 있다.
(D) 다음번에 다시 방문할 계획이다.

어휘 than expected 예상보다　take advantage of ~을 이용하다　deal 거래 (조건)　revisit ~을 다시 방문하다

토익 분석

대화의 흐름을 파악해야 한다. 의도 및 미래 행동 표현인 I think I'd like가 힌트를 제시한다.

52

What does the man recommend?

(A) Visiting the Web site　(B) Contacting other locations

(C) Taking a tour　(D) Attending a luncheon

문제 해설

남자가 여자에게 추천하는 것이 무엇인지를 묻는 세 번째 문제이므로 대화의 후반부에서 들을 수 있는 남자의 말에서 뭔가를 추천하거나 권하는 표현과 함께 제시되는 정보에 집중해 들어야 한다. 남자는 I would recommend~라는 표현과 함께 'I would recommend~some members.'라는 말로 해당 컨트리클럽을 견학해 볼 것을 추천하고 있으므로 (C)가 정답이 된다.

★ 요청, 제안

남자는 무엇을 추천하는가?
(A) 웹사이트를 방문할 것　(B) 다른 지점에 연락할 것
(C) 견학을 할 것　(D) 오찬 행사에 참석할 것

어휘 location 지점　attend ~에 참석하다　luncheon 오찬

토익 분석

힌트 표현으로 I would recommend~가 사용되었다.

남 안녕하세요. ⁵³ 귀하의 영업 기술 워크숍에 제 직원들
　　몇 명을 등록하기 위해 전화 드립니다. 다음 달에 시
　　작될 때 해당 강좌에 참석하기를 원하는 15명의 직
　　원이 있습니다.

여 죄송합니다만, 전화상으로는 등록해 드릴 수 없습니
　　다. ⁵⁴ 저희 웹 사이트에서 등록하셔야 합니다. 양식
　　을 작성하셔서 제출 버튼을 누르시기만 하시면 됩니
　　다.

남 사실, 이미 세 번이나 시도해 봤는데, 그 과정을 진행
　　할 수가 없었습니다. 제가 양식을 제출할 때마다, 에
　　러 메시지가 떴습니다.

여 이상한 일이네요! ⁵⁵ 괜찮으시다면, 제가 귀하의 이
　　름, 이메일 주소, 그리고 전화번호를 받아 적은 다음
　　에 가능한 한 빨리 저희 기술 지원부 직원에게 다시
　　연락 드리도록 요청하겠습니다.

Questions 53-55 refer to the following conversation.

M　Hi. ⁵³ I'm calling to enroll some of my staff in your sales technique
　　workshop. I have fifteen people who want to join the class when it starts
　　next month.

W　I'm sorry, I can't enroll them over the phone. ⁵⁴ You have to register on our
　　Web site. You can just fill out the form and hit the submit button.

M　Actually, I've already tried three times, but I couldn't go through the
　　process. Every time I submitted the form, I got an error message.

W　That's strange! ⁵⁵ If you don't mind, I'll take down your name, e-mail,
　　and phone number, and then I'll have someone in our technical support
　　department get back to you as soon as possible.

어휘 enroll A in B A를 B에 등록시키다 join ~에 참가하다, 함께하다 over the phone 전화상으로 register 등록
하다 fill out ~을 작성하다 form 양식 hit (버튼 등) ~을 누르다 submit 제출하다 actually 실은, 사실은 try 시도
해 보다 go through ~을 거치다 process 과정 take down ~을 받아 적다 have A do A에게 ~하게 하다 technical
support 기술 지원 get back to ~에게 다시 연락하다 as soon as possible 가능한 한 빨리

53

★★ 주제, 목적

남자는 왜 전화를 거는가?
(A) 예약을 확인하기 위해
(B) 행사에 관한 정보를 얻기 위해
(C) 직원들을 한 워크숍에 등록시키기 위해
(D) 영업직에 지원하기 위해

어휘 confirm ~을 확인하다 reservation 예약 apply for
~에 지원하다

토익 분석

전화를 건 목적이다. 남자의 첫 번째 대화문에 정답이 나
오는 유형이다. I'm calling~이 정답 힌트다.

Why is the man calling?

(A) To confirm a reservation
(B) To get information about an event
(C) To register employees for a workshop
(D) To apply for a sales position

문제 해설

남자가 전화하는 이유를 묻는 첫 번째 문제이므로 대화 시작 부분에 제시되는 남자의 말에서 전화
를 거는 특정한 이유가 언급된다는 것을 예상하고 그 정보를 파악하는 데 집중해야 한다. 남자는 대
화를 시작하면서 'I'm calling to enroll some of my staff in your sales technique workshop.'라는
말로 자신의 직원들을 워크숍에 등록하려 한다고 알리고 있으므로 (C)가 정답임을 알 수 있다.

54

★★ 요청, 제안

여자의 말에 따르면, 남자는 무엇을 해야 하는가?
(A) 안내 부스를 방문해야 한다.
(B) 온라인으로 등록해야 한다.
(C) 계정 번호를 제공해야 한다.
(D) 우편 주소를 확인해 줘야 한다.

어휘 booth 부스 sign up 등록/신청하다 online 온라인
으로 account 계정, 계좌 verify ~을 확인해 주다

토익 분석

남자의 행동을 여자가 통제한다. 여자 대화문에서 요청,
제안 표현을 들어야 한다. 요청, 제안 표현 You have to~
와 You can~이 단서를 제시했다.

According to the woman, what does the man have to do?

(A) Visit an information booth
(B) Sign up online
(C) Provide an account number
(D) Verify an e-mail address

문제 해설

여자는 대화 중반부에 남자가 해야 할 일을 알리기 위해 'You have to register on our Web site.
You can just fill out the form and hit the submit button.'라는 말로 정보를 제공하고 있다. 따라
서 웹 사이트에서 등록하는 것과 동일한 의미를 나타내는 (B)가 정답이다.

55

★★ 요청, 제안

여자는 무엇을 요청하는가?
(A) 연락처　　　　　(B) 참석자들의 이름
(C) 회사의 주소　　　(D) 지원서

어휘 contact information 연락처 attendee 참석자
application form 지원서

토익 분석

여자의 후반부 대화에서 요청, 제안 표현을 찾아야 한다.
'if가정법~, I'll~' 문장이 정답을 제시한다.

What does the woman request?

(A) Contact information　　　(B) The names of attendees
(C) The address of a company　　(D) Application forms

문제 해설

여자의 요청 사항을 묻는 문제이므로 대화 후반 요청 관련 표현이 언급되는 부분을 통해 단서를
찾아야 한다. 여자는 대화 후반부에 'If you don't mind, I'll take down your name, e-mail, and
phone number ~'라는 말로 상대방에게 이름과 이메일 주소, 그리고 전화번호를 알려 달라는 의미
를 지닌 말을 하고 있다. 이는 연락처를 가르쳐 달라고 요청하는 것이므로 (A)가 정답이다.

Questions 56-58 refer to the following conversation with three speakers

M Hi, ladies. [56] I'm on a strict deadline to finish up the monthly sales report, but I'm supposed to meet some clients from Montegro at 2 P.M. Do you think one of you could go instead?

W1 Sorry, but I have too much work to do. I wish I could. [57] How about you, Rosemary?

W2 [57] Mmm… Let me see when I'm free.

W1 By the way, what's the meeting about?

M They're going to introduce a new product line, and we're considering stocking it.

W2 My schedule says I'm free, so I'll go. What should I take to the meeting?

M [58] You'll just need a copy of our current inventory. I'll print it off and bring it to your office.

남 여러분, 안녕하세요. [56] 제가 월간 매출 보고서를 끝내야 하는 엄격한 마감 기한에 걸려 있는데, 오후 2시에 Montegro에서 오시는 고객들을 만나기로 되어 있어요. 혹시 두 분 중의 한 분이 대신 가 주실 수 있으세요?

여1 죄송하지만, 저는 해야 할 일이 너무 많아요. 제가 갈 수 있으면 좋겠어요. [57] 당신은 어때요, Rosemary?

여2 [57] 음… 제가 언제 시간이 있는지 볼게요.

여1 그건 그렇고, 회의가 무엇에 관한 것인가요?

남 그들이 신제품 라인을 소개하려고 하는데, 우리 회사가 그것을 재고로 받아들이는 것을 고려하고 있어요.

여2 제 일정표를 보니 시간이 나니까 제가 갈게요. 회의에 뭘 가져가야 하죠?

남 [58] 현재 우리 회사의 재고 목록이 한 부 필요할 거예요. 제가 출력을 해서 당신 사무실로 가져갈게요.

어휘 on a strict deadline 엄격한 마감 기한에 걸려 있는 finish up ~을 끝내다 monthly 월간의, 매달의 sales 매출, 판매(량), 영업 be supposed to do ~하기로 되어 있다 instead 그 대신 too much A to do 해야 할 너무 많은 A I wish I could ~할 수 있었으면 좋겠다 free 시간이 나는 by the way (화제 전환 시) 그건 그렇고, 그런데 introduce ~을 소개하다 product line 제품 라인 consider -ing ~하는 것을 고려하다 stock v. ~을 재고로 갖추다 a copy of ~ 1부, ~의 사본 current 현재의 inventory 재고 (목록) print A off A를 출력하다 bring ~을 가져가다/오다

56

What are the women asked to do?

(A) Order some materials   (B) Call some clients
(C) Submit a report   **(D) Attend a meeting**

문제 해설

대화를 시작하면서 남자는 'I'm on a strict deadline to finish up the monthly sales report, but I'm supposed to meet some clients from Montegro at 2 P.M. Do you think one of you could go instead?'라는 말로 자신이 시간이 나지 않아 회의에 갈 수 없을 것 같으니 여자들 중에서 대신 갈 수 있는 사람이 있는지 묻고 있으므로 (D)가 정답임을 알 수 있다.

★★ 요청, 제안

여자들은 무엇을 하도록 요청 받는가?
(A) 물품을 주문할 것   (B) 고객들에게 전화할 것
(C) 보고서를 제출할 것   (D) 회의에 참석할 것

어휘 material 물품, 재료 submit ~을 제출하다

토익 분석

대화 초반부 남자의 말에서 요청이나 부탁 등을 나타내는 표현을 찾아야 한다. 의문이자 you can이 사용된 Do you think one of you could~가 정답 힌트다.

57

Why does the woman say, "Let me see when I'm free"?

(A) She is offering a service for no charge.
(B) She is checking her availability.
(C) She wants to know about some costs.
(D) She would like to change her work shift.

문제 해설

여자가 말하는 "Let me see when I'm free"라는 표현이 대화 속에서 어떤 의미로 사용되었는지를 묻는 두 번째 질문이므로 대화 중반부에 제시되는 여자의 말을 통해 해당 표현을 확인할 수 있어야 한다. 이 표현은 대화 중반부에 한 여자가 시간이 되지 않는다고 말한 다음에 제시되고 있는데, 말 그대로 '언제 시간이 있는지 확인해 보겠다'라는 의미이므로 이를 '시간이 나는지의 여부'를 뜻하는 availability로 바꿔 제시한 (B)가 정답이다.

★★★ 맥락 파악

여자는 왜 "Let me see when I'm free"라고 말하는가?
(A) 무료로 서비스를 제공하고 있다.
(B) 자신이 시간이 나는지를 확인하고 있다.
(C) 비용에 관해 알고 싶어 한다.
(D) 자신의 근무 조를 바꾸고 싶어 한다.

어휘 for no charge 무료로 availability 시간이 날 가능성 cost 비용 shift 교대 근무(조)

토익 분석

맥락 파악 문제의 경우 대화의 전후 내용을 이해하여 흐름을 파악해야 한다. 물론 단순히 제시된 표현의 사전적 의미가 답이 되는 경우도 많다.

58

What does the man say he will send the woman?

(A) A client's contact details   **(B) An inventory report**
(C) An event schedule   (D) A product catalog

문제 해설

남자가 보내 주겠다고 말하는 것이 무엇인지를 묻는 세 번째 문제이므로 대화 후반부에 제시되는 남자의 말에서 뭔가를 전달하는 것과 관련된 상황이 언급되는 부분에 집중해 들어야 한다. 남자는 대화 마지막에 'You'll~your office.'라는 말로 자신이 주려고 하는 것을 알리고 있고 그 대상으로 언급된 것이 'a copy of our current inventory'이므로 (B)가 정답임을 알 수 있다.

★★ 미래 행동

남자는 여자에게 무엇을 보내 주겠다고 말하는가?
(A) 고객의 연락처   (B) 재고 목록 보고서
(C) 행사 일정표   (D) 제품 카탈로그

어휘 contact details 연락처

토익 분석

남자 후반부 대화에 남자의 미래 행위를 설명하는 힌트 표현인 I'll~이 정답을 이끌고 있다.

여 ⁵⁹ 안녕하세요. 저는 저희의 월간 서비스에 대해 전화 드렸습니다. 저는 저희가 월간 정기 점검 서비스에 가입했다고 생각하고 있는데, 지금이 7월 말이지만 해충 구제 담당자가 아직도 저희를 방문하지 않았어요.

남 제가 도와 드릴 수 있습니다. 우선, 일반 주택 고객이신가요, 아니면 기업 고객이신가요?

여 저는 Sandy Florists에서 전화 드리는 겁니다. 저희는 석 달 전에 귀사와의 계약을 시작했어요.

남 아, 알겠습니다. 잠시 저희 일정을 확인해 보겠습니다. 여기 있네요. 저희 해충 구제 담당자들 중의 한 명이 지난주에 귀사를 방문하기로 되어 있었다고 나오네요.

여 저는 이곳에 매일 나와 있는데, 아무도 온 적이 없었어요. 저희가 아무런 문제가 없기는 했지만, 그래도 저희는 비용을 지불할 것에 대한 서비스를 받기를 기대하고 있습니다.

남 ⁶⁰ 대단히 죄송합니다, 고객님. 제가 그 직원과 얘기해 보겠습니다. 자신의 목록에서 귀사를 빠뜨린 것이 분명합니다.

여 그럼, 같은 일 다시 일어나지 않게 해 주세요. 그리고 보상을 좀 해 주셨으면 좋겠어요.

남 물론입니다. ⁶¹ 지금 바로 직원을 보내 드리고, 다음 달에 대한 청구 비용을 10% 할인해 드리겠습니다. 다시는 같은 일이 일어나지 않을 것입니다.

Questions 59-61 refer to the following talk.

W ⁵⁹ Hi. I'm calling about our monthly service. I believe we signed up for a monthly checkup, but it's the end of July and an exterminator still hasn't visited us.

M I can help you. First, are you a residential or business client?

W I am calling from Sandy Florists. We started a contract with you three months ago.

M Ah, I see. Just give me a moment to check our schedule. There we go. It says one of our exterminators was supposed to visit you last week.

W I was here every day, and nobody ever came. We haven't had any problems, but still, we expect to get what we paid for.

M ⁶⁰ I am deeply sorry, ma'am. I will speak with the employee. I'm sure he skipped you on his list.

W Well, please don't let it happen again. Also, I expect some kind of compensation.

M Of course. ⁶¹ I will send someone over right now, and I will lower your bill for next month by 10%. It won't happen again.

어휘 monthly 월간의, 달마다의 sign up for ~을 신청/등록하다 check-up 정기 점검 exterminator 해충 구제 담당자 residential 주거의, 거주에 관한 contract 계약(서) There we go (뭔가를 찾았을 때) 여기 있군요 be supposed to do ~하기로 되어 있다, ~할 예정이다 still 여전히, 그래도 expect to do ~할 것을 기대하다 pay for ~에 대한 값을 지불하다 deeply 깊이 employee 직원 skip ~을 빠트리다 let A do A가 ~하게 하다 compensation 보상 send A over A를 보내다 right now 지금 바로 lower ~을 낮추다, 내리다 bill 청구서, 계산서 by (정도) ~ 만큼

59

★★ 암시 추론

남자는 누구일 가능성이 가장 큰가?
(A) 정비사
(B) 변호사
(C) 해충 구제 담당자
(D) 조경사

토익 분석

직업은 언제나 대화의 초반부에 집중한다 질문에 **most likely**가 있으므로 남자의 직업을 유추해야 한다. 따라서 반드시 남자 대화에만 힌트가 있다 생각하면 안 된다.

Who most likely is the man?

(A) A mechanic
(B) An attorney
(C) An exterminator
(D) A landscaper

문제 해설

남자의 신분에 대해 유추할 것을 요구하는 첫 번째 질문이므로 대화 초반부에서 남자가 하는 일과 관련해 직접적으로 언급되는 부분, 혹은 이를 추측할 수 있을 만한 관련 어휘가 제시되는 부분에 집중해야 한다. 대화를 시작하면서 여자가 'Hi~visited us.'라는 말로 'exterminator(해충 구제 담당자)'가 오지 않은 것에 대해 문의하기 위해 남자에게 전화하는 상황임을 알리고 있으므로 (C)가 정답임을 알 수 있다.

60

★★ 의도 파악

남자는 왜 사과하는가?
(A) 비용 지불 실수가 있었다.
(B) 예정된 방문이 이뤄지지 않았다.
(C) 계약을 취소하고 있다. (D) 매장이 일찍 문을 닫는다.

어휘 apologize 사과하다 payment 비용 지불 scheduled 예정된 occur 일어나다, 발생되다 contract 계약

토익 분석

초반부 대화에서 반전 표현인 I am (deeply) sorry~와 의도 및 미래 행동 힌트인 I will~ 이 정답을 제시했다.

Why does the man apologize?

(A) There was a payment error.
(B) A scheduled visit didn't occur.
(C) He is cancelling a contract.
(D) The store is closing early.

문제 해설

남자가 사과하는 이유를 묻는 두 번째 질문이므로 대화 중반부에서 남자의 말을 통해 사과 표현이 제시되는 부분에 집중해 정보를 파악해야 한다. 대화 중반부에 남자는 'I am deeply sorry~on his list.'라는 말로 사과를 하면서 담당 직원이 빠트린 것에 대해 언급하고 있으므로 여자가 원했던 방문이 이뤄지지 않은 것에 대해 사과하는 상황임을 알 수 있다. 따라서 (B)가 정답이 된다.

61

★★ 요청, 제안

남자는 여자에게 무엇을 제안하는가?
(A) 무료 제품
(B) 할인
(C) 회원권
(D) 상품권

어휘 certificate 증서, 자격증

토익 분석

여자의 후반부 대화에서 의도 및 미래 행동 힌트인 I will~ 이 정답을 이끌고 있다.

What does the man offer the woman?

(A) A free item
(B) A discount
(C) A membership
(D) A gift certificate

문제 해설

여자에게 권하는 일이 무엇인지를 묻는 세 번째 문제이므로 대화의 후반부에서 들을 수 있는 남자의 말에서 권유나 제안 관련 표현과 함께 제시되는 정보에 집중해 들어야 한다. 대화 후반부에 남자는 'I will send~by 10%.'라는 말로 청구 비용을 낮춰 주겠다고 알리고 있는데, 이는 곧 비용을 할인해 주겠다는 뜻이므로 (B)가 정답이 된다.

Questions 62-64 refer to the following conversation and map.

W   Welcome to Capaldi Art Gallery. Do you need some help?

M   [62] I'm here to meet one of the artists in the sculpture hall to interview him for my magazine. Can you tell me where to go?

W   Here, take this brochure. You can find a map of the gallery inside.

M   Thanks! And [63] I heard that there's a drawing class this evening. Can I stay and join that?

W   Sure, we still have some spaces available for that. Can I have your name, please?

M   Yes, it's Joshua Park. OK, I'd better go. The artist will be waiting for me.

W   No problem. Oh, and [64] you should use the west door to enter the hall. It's just around the corner here. It would take you too long to go around to the east door.

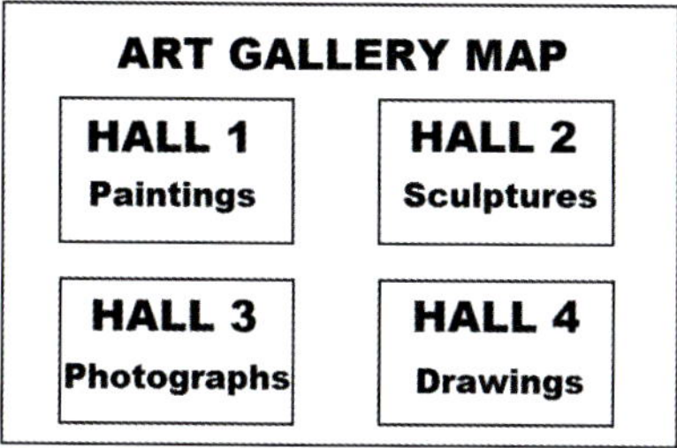

어휘 sculpture 조각 interview ~을 인터뷰하다 where to go 가야 하는 곳 brochure 안내 책자 inside 안에 drawing 소묘 join ~에 참석하다, ~와 함께하다 available 이용 가능한 had better + 동사 원형 ~하는 게 낫다 enter ~에 들어가다, 입장하다 just around the corner 모퉁이를 바로 돈 곳에 있는 take A B to do A가 ~하는 데 B 만큼의 시간이 들게 하다 go around 돌아가다 painting 그림

여   Capaldi Art Gallery에 오신 것을 환영합니다. 도움이 필요하신가요?

남   [62] 제 잡지를 위해 조각품 전시장에서 미술가들 중의 한 분을 만나 인터뷰하기 위해 왔습니다. 어디로 가야 하는지 알려 주시겠습니까?

여   여기, 이 안내 책자를 가져가세요. 그 안에 저희 미술관 지도를 찾아보실 수 있습니다.

남   감사합니다! 그리고 [63] 오늘 저녁에 소묘 강좌가 있다고 들었습니다. 머물렀다가 그 강좌에 참석해도 될까요?

여   물론입니다. 여전히 이용 가능하신 자리가 남아 있습니다. 성함 좀 알려 주시겠습니까?

남   네, Joshua Park입니다. 그럼, 이제 가 봐야겠네요. 그 미술가께서 저를 기다리고 계시거든요.

여   알겠습니다. 아, 그리고 [64] 그 홀에 들어가시려면 서쪽 출입문을 이용하셔야 합니다. 이쪽 모퉁이를 돌아가시면 바로 있습니다. 동쪽 출입문까지 돌아서 가시기에는 너무 오래 걸리실 겁니다.

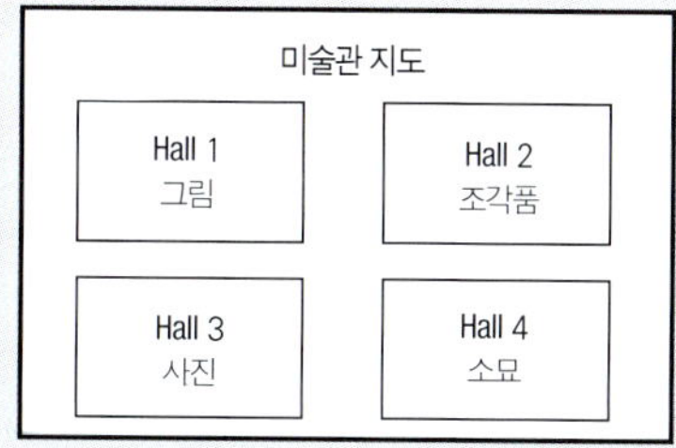

62

Look at the graphic. In which hall will the man meet the artist?

(A) Hall 1
(B) Hall 2
(C) Hall 3
(D) Hall 4

문제 해설

남자가 미술가를 만나는 곳을 묻는 첫 번째 문제이므로 대화 초반부 남자의 말에서 미술가를 만나려는 일정이 언급된다는 것을 예상하고 들어야 하며, 이때 도표에 제시된 각 장소의 특성을 함께 파악하고 들어야 한다. 대화 시작 부분에 남자가 'I'm here to meet one of the artists in the sculpture hall to interview him for my magazine.'라는 말로 조각품 전시장에서 미술가 한 명을 만나러 왔다고 알리고 있으므로 조각품 전시장인 (B)가 정답임을 알 수 있다.

★★ 그래픽

도표를 보시오. 남자는 어느 홀에서 미술가를 만날 것인가?

(A) 전시홀 1
(B) 전시홀 2
(C) 전시홀 3
(D) 전시홀 4

토익 분석

그림에 hall번호와 각 hall에서 전시되는 내용이 표시되어 있다. Hall을 찾기 위해서는 전시 내용에 관한 정보를 들어야만 한다.

63

★★ 세부 정보

오늘 저녁에 미술관에서 무슨 일이 있을 것인가?
(A) 미술 강좌가 열릴 것이다.
(B) 연설이 있을 것이다.
(C) 전시회가 시작될 것이다.
(D) 공연이 열릴 것이다.

어휘 hold ~을 개최하다, 열다 give a talk 연설하다
exhibition 전시회 performance 공연, 연주(회)

토익 분석

질문 속에 시점 표현인 this evening가 키워드로 활용되는
문제다.

What will happen at the gallery this evening?

(A) An art class will be held.
(B) A talk will be given.
(C) An exhibition will begin.
(D) A performance will take place.

문제 해설

오늘 저녁에 미술관에서 있을 일을 묻는 두 번째 문제이므로 대화 중반부에 '오늘 저녁'에 해당되는
시점 표현이 제시될 것임을 예상하고 함께 언급되는 관련 정보를 파악하는 데 집중해야 한다. 대화
중반부에 남자가 'I heard that there's a drawing class this evening.'이라는 말로 저녁에 소묘 강좌가
있음을 언급하는 부분이 있으므로 (A)가 정답임을 알 수 있다.

★★ 요청, 제안

여자는 왜 서쪽 문을 이용하도록 제안하는가?
(A) 유일하게 잠겨 있지 않은 문이다.
(B) 덜 붐빈다.
(C) 선물 매장 옆에 있다.
(D) 가장 가까운 출입문이다.

어휘 suggest -ing ~하도록 제안하다 unlocked 잠겨 있
지 않은 less 덜하게, 더 적게 crowded 붐비는 next to ~
옆에 closest 가장 가까운

토익 분석

여자의 후반부 대화에서 요청, 제안 힌트인 you should~
가 정답 힌트를 이끌고 있다.

Why does the woman suggest using the west door?

(A) It is the only unlocked door.
(B) It is less crowded.
(C) It is next to a gift shop.
(D) It is the closest entrance.

문제 해설

여자가 서쪽 문을 이용하도록 제안하는 이유를 묻는 마지막 문제이므로 대화 후반부에 '서쪽 문'과
관련된 정보가 제시된다는 것을 예상하고 들어야 한다. 대화 마지막에 여자가 'you should use the
west door to enter the hall. It's just around the corner here. It would take you too long to go
around to the east door'라는 말로 서쪽 문을 이용하도록 권하고 있는데, 동쪽 문으로 가는 것이 너
무 멀기 때문이라고 알리고 있다. 따라서 서쪽 문이 가깝기 때문에 이와 같이 권하는 것임을 알 수
있으므로 (D)가 정답이 된다.

Questions 65-67 refer to the following conversation and list.

W ⁶⁵ How's the doctor's new waiting room coming along? Are you finished preparing it?

M ⁶⁵ I'm almost finished. The carpet and curtains are installed, and I just finished arranging the furniture. ⁶⁶ The only thing left to do is to buy some entertainment and lifestyle magazines for our patients to read. Do you have any good suggestions for what to buy?

W ⁶⁷ In the past, we bought a variety through the Magazine Portal Web site. The doctor has a subscription to the site, so we can get a discount. I'll give you the account details so that you can go online and buy some.

---

www.magazineportal.com/categories

Magazine Categories

1 - Sports and Fitness

2 - Entertainment and Culture

3 - Computers and Technology

4 - Cooking and Home Improvement

여 ⁶⁵ 의사 선생님의 새로운 대기실 작업은 어떻게 되어 가고 있나요? 준비하시는 일을 완료하셨나요?

남 ⁶⁵ 거의 끝나 갑니다. 카펫과 커튼을 설치되어 있고, 가구 배치 작업을 막 완료했습니다. ⁶⁶ 유일하게 남은 일은 환자들이 읽을 만한 연예 및 라이프스타일 잡지들을 구입하는 것입니다. 무엇을 사야 할지 좋은 생각이 있으신가요?

여 ⁶⁷ 과거에, **Magazine Portal** 웹 사이트를 통해서 여러 가지를 구입했어요. 의사 선생님께서 그 사이트 이용권을 가지고 계시기 때문에 할인을 받을 수 있습니다. 온라인에서 구입하실 수 있도록 제가 계정 상세 정보를 알려 드릴게요.

---

www.magazineportal.com/categories

잡지 항목

1 – 스포츠와 피트니스
2 – 연예 및 문화
3 – 컴퓨터와 기술
4 – 요리와 주택 개조

어휘 How's A coming along? A를 어떻게 되어 가고 있나요? waiting room 대기실 be finished -ing ~하는 것을 완료하다 prepare ~을 준비하다 install ~을 설치하다 finish -ing ~하는 것을 완료하다 arrange ~을 배치/정렬하다 the only thing left to do 남아 있는 유일한 일 patient 환자 suggestion 생각, 아이디어, 제안 what to do ~할 것 in the past 과거에 a variety 다양한 것 through ~을 통해 subscription 이용/구독권 get a discount 할인을 받다 account 계정, 계좌 details 상세 정보 so that ~할 수 있도록 go online 온라인에 접속하다 category 항목, 범주 home improvement 주택 개조

65

What project is the man busy doing?

(A) Preparing a room
(B) Filing some documents
(C) Updating a Web site
(D) Contacting patients

문제 해설

남자가 바쁜 이유를 묻는 첫 번째 문제이므로 대화 초반부에 남자가 하는 일이 언급되는 부분이 있음을 예상하고 들어야 한다. 대화를 시작하면서 여자가 'How's the doctor's new waiting room coming along? Are you finished preparing it?'라는 말로 새로운 대기실을 준비하는 일을 완료했는지 묻는 것을 통해 남자가 그 대기실 작업을 하는 중이라는 것을 알 수 있으므로 (A)가 정답이다.

★★ 의도 파악

남자는 무슨 프로젝트를 하느라 바쁜가?
(A) 공간을 준비하는 일
(B) 문서를 파일로 정리하는 일
(C) 웹 사이트를 업데이트하는 일
(D) 환자들에게 연락하는 일

어휘 prepare ~을 준비하다 file ~을 파일로 정리하다 document 문서, 서류 contact ~에게 연락하다

토익 분석

의도는 대화 초반부에 등장한다. 여자 첫 번째 대화의 의문문들이 중요한 힌트로 활용된 문제다.

★★ 그래픽

도표를 보시오. 남자는 어느 항목을 검색할 것 같은가?
(A) 항목 1
(B) 항목 2
(C) 항목 3
(D) 항목 4

토익 분석

그림에는 카테고리 별 내용이 제시되어 있다. 카테고리를 찾기 위해서는 대화 속에 언급되는 '항목에 대응하는 세부 내용'을 들어야 한다.

Look at the graphic. Which category will the man most likely search?

(A) Category 1
(B) Category 2
(C) Category 3
(D) Category 4

문제 해설

남자가 검색할 항목을 묻는 두 번째 문제이므로 대화 중반부에서 검색 항목이 언급된다는 것을 예상하고 들어야 하며, 이때 도표에 제시된 각 주제 내용을 미리 파악하고 들어야 한다. 대화 중반부에 남자가 'The only thing left to do is to buy some entertainment and lifestyle magazines for our patients to read. Do you have any good suggestions for what to buy?'라는 말로 연예 및 라이프스타일 잡지를 구매하는 것에 대해 여자에게 좋은 생각이 있는지 묻고 있으므로 이 주제에 해당하는 항목인 (B)가 정답임을 알 수 있다.

★★★ 요청, 제안

여자는 왜 **Magazine Portal**에서 잡지를 구매하도록 권하는가?
(A) 잡지들이 수준이 높다.
(B) 환자들이 그 잡지들을 가장 즐겨 읽는다.
(C) 그 웹 사이트가 가장 선택권이 많다.
(D) 자신들의 업체가 할인을 받는다.

어휘 recommend -ing ~하도록 권하다, 추천하다 high quality 수준이 높은, 품질이 좋은 the most 가장 많이 selection (제품 등의) 선택(권), 모음

토익 분석

여자의 후반부 대화에서 반전 표현 so 와 요청, 제안 힌트 we can~이 정답을 제시했다.

Why does the woman recommend buying magazines from Magazine Portal?

(A) The magazines are high quality.
(B) The patients enjoy them the most.
(C) The Web site has the largest selection.
(D) The business receives a discount.

문제 해설

여자가 Magazine Portal에서 잡지를 구매하도록 권하는 이유를 묻는 마지막 문제이므로 대화 후반부 여자의 말에서 'Magazine Portal'라는 명칭과 함께 언급되는 정보를 파악하는 데 집중해야 한다. 여자는 대화 후반부에 'In the past, we bought a variety through the Magazine Portal Web site. The doctor has a subscription to the site, so we can get a discount.'라고 알리면서 Magazine Portal을 이용해야 하는 이유로 할인을 받는 것을 언급하고 있으므로 (D)가 정답이 된다.

Questions 68-70 refer to the following conversation and signs.

M Good morning. [68] I just noticed the sign that says I need to check in at the security office. So here I am. My name is George Mulder.

W Good morning, Mr. Mulder. Do you have an appointment with someone here at the construction site?

M [69] Actually, I'm here to inspect the site and make sure that safety guidelines are being followed.

W Oh, of course! I forgot that you were coming today.

M That's not a problem. So can I just go on inside?

W Sure. [70] And here… take this map of the construction site. You can go straight to the office and speak with the construction manager. He'll give you all the safety gear you need.

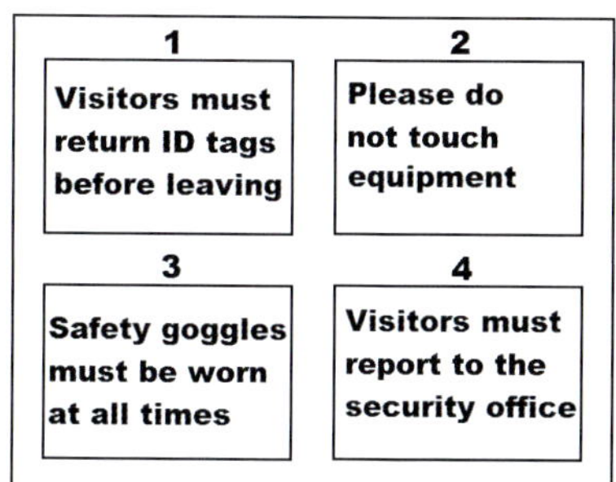

어휘 notice ~을 알아차리다 sign 표지(판) check in 체크인하다, 수속을 밟다 appointment 약속, 예약 construction site 공사장 actually 실은, 사실은 inspect ~을 점검하다 site 현장, 부지 make sure that ~하는 것을 확실히 하다, 반드시 ~하도록 하다 follow ~을 따르다, 준수하다 forget that ~임을 잊다 go on inside 계속해서 안으로 들어가다 go straight to ~로 곧장 가다 safety gear 안전 장비 return ~을 반납하다 leave 나가다, 떠나다 equipment 장비 safety goggles 보호 안경 at all times 항상 report to ~로 가다, ~에 알리다

남 안녕하세요. [68] 경비실에서 출입 절차를 밟고 들어가야 한다는 안내 표지를 방금 봤습니다. 그래서 왔습니다. 제 이름은 George Mulder입니다.

여 안녕하세요, Mulder 씨. 이 공사장에서 약속하신 분이 있으신가요?

남 [69] 실은, 현장을 점검하고 안전 가이드라인이 준수되고 있는지 확실히 해 두기 위해 왔습니다.

여 아, 그러시군요! 오늘 오신다는 것을 잊고 있었습니다.

남 괜찮습니다. 그럼, 그냥 안으로 들어가면 되나요?

여 물론입니다. [70] 그리고 여기… 이 공사 현장 안내도를 가져가세요. 사무실로 곧장 가셔서 현장 감독관께 이야기하시면 됩니다. 그분께서 필요하신 모든 안전 장비를 챙겨 드릴 겁니다.

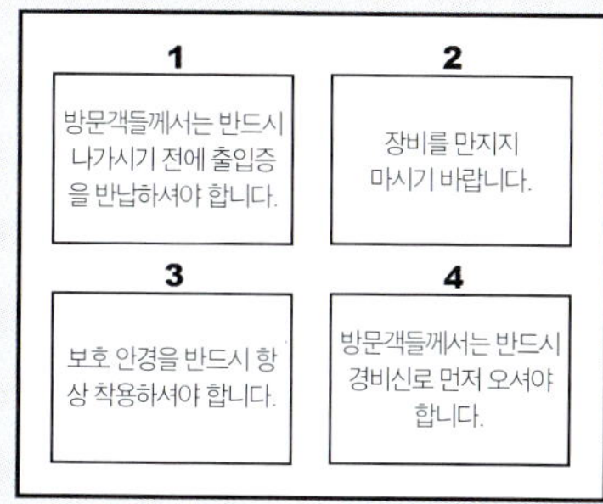

68

Look at the graphic. Which sign does the man refer to?

(A) Sign 1
(B) Sign 2
(C) Sign 3
(D) Sign 4

문제 해설

남자가 참고한 표지판을 묻는 첫 번째 문제이므로 대화 초반부에 남자가 각 표지판 내용 중의 하나를 언급하는 부분이 있음을 예상하고 들어야 하며, 이때 도표에 제시된 각 표지판의 핵심 내용을 미리 파악하고 들어야 한다. 남자는 대화를 시작하면서 'I just noticed the sign that says I'll need to check in at the security office.'라는 말로 경비실을 거쳐 들어가야 한다는 표지판을 봤다고 알리고 있으므로 이 내용에 해당되는 표지판인 (D)가 정답이다.

★★ 그래픽

도표를 확인하시오. 남자는 어느 표지판을 참고했는가?
(A) 표지판 1
(B) 표지판 2
(C) 표지판 3
(D) 표지판 4

어휘 refer to ~을 참고하다

토익 분석

항상 보기에 주어진 정보를 찾기 위해서는 대화 속에서 보기의 내용에 해당하는 간접정보를 들어야 한다. 따라서 이 문제의 경우 sign의 내용을 파악해야만 한다. 의도 및 미래 행동 힌트인 **I'll need to~**가 결정적인 단서다.

★★ 세부 정보

남자는 왜 공사 현장에 있는가?
(A) 자재를 가져가기 위해
(B) 점검을 실시하기 위해
(C) 장비를 설치하기 위해
(D) 일자리에 대해 면접을 보기 위해

어휘 pick up ~을 가져가다 material 자재, 재료 perform ~을 실시/수행하다 install ~을 설치하다 equipment 장비 interview for ~에 대해 면접을 보다

토익 분석

남자 대화에 반전 표현인 **Actually**가 힌트로 활용되었다.

Why is the man at the construction site?

(A) To pick up some materials
(B) To perform an inspection
(C) To install some equipment
(D) To interview for a job

문제 해설

남자가 공사 현장에 있는 이유를 묻는 두 번째 문제이므로 대화 중반부 남자의 말에서 공사 현장을 찾은 이유가 언급된다는 것을 예상하고 들어야 한다. 대화 중반부에 남자가 'Actually, I'm here to inspect the site and make sure that safety guidelines are being followed.'라는 말로 공사 현장 점검을 위해 왔다고 알리고 있으므로 (B)가 정답임을 알 수 있다.

70

★★ 세부 사항

여자는 남자에게 무엇을 주는가?
(A) 출입증
(B) 주차 허가증
(C) 보호 안경
(D) 현장 안내도

어휘 parking permit 주차 허가증

토익 분석

세 번째 문제이므로 여자의 후반부 대화에 집중한다. '명령문' 문장인 take this map가 힌트다.

What does the woman give to the man?

(A) An ID tag
(B) A parking permit
(C) Safety goggles
(D) A site map

문제 해설

여자가 남자에게 주는 것을 묻는 마지막 문제이므로 대화 후반부 여자의 말에서 물품을 전달하는 행위를 나타내는 표현이 제시된다는 것을 예상하고 그 물품을 파악하는 데 집중해야 한다. 대화 마지막에 여자가 'And here… take this map of the construction site.'라는 말로 공사 현장 안내도를 가져가라고 알리는 부분에서 (D)가 정답임을 알 수 있다.

Questions 71-73 refer to the following advertisement.

W **71** If you are looking for your forever home, your search has ended because Harmony Park Village has everything any family could ever want. Not only are our houses built with the modern family in mind—each complete with a loft area, a spacious living room, a high-end kitchen, a top-floor laundry room, and a great basement—but the neighborhood also has countless perks. **72** Your homeowner's association (HOA) fee will grant you access to a private golf course, a swimming pool, tennis courts, basketball courts, and a fully equipped fitness center. Harmony Park Village is located just blocks from **73** the high-end downtown area of Kensington, where many restaurateurs offer exquisite food that will tickle your fancy. The avid shopper there will find countless delights, and even your dog will be panting at the dog park and full-service puppy boutique.

여 **71** 만약 여러분께서 영구히 거주하고자 하는 주택을 찾고 계신다면, 저희 Harmony Park Village가 어느 가족이든 원하는 모든 것을 갖추고 있는 주택이니만큼 여러분은 더 이상 주택을 알아보실 필요가 없습니다. 저희 주택은 현대 가족이 염두에 두는 2층 공간, 넓은 거실, 최고급 주방, 꼭대기 층의 세탁 시설, 그리고 훌륭한 지하와 함께 지어졌을 뿐만 아니라 인근에 수많은 특혜까지 있습니다. **72** 여러분께서 주택 조합 회비를 납부하시면 개인 골프 코스, 수영장, 테니스 코트, 농구장, 그리고 모든 시설을 완벽하게 구비하고 있는 휘트니스 시설을 이용하실 수 있습니다. Harmony Park Village는 **73** 많은 식당 소유주들이 여러분의 기호를 충족시켜줄 수 있는 훌륭한 음식을 제공하는 Kensington의 부유한 시내 지역에서 불과 몇 블록 떨어지지 않은 곳에 위치해 있습니다. 그곳의 생기 넘치는 쇼핑객들은 수없이 많은 즐길 거리를 찾게 되며, 심지어는 여러분의 애완견이 전용 공원과 완벽한 서비스를 제공하는 애완견 전문 부티크에서 즐거워하며 숨을 헐떡일 수 있습니다.

어휘 not only A but also B B뿐만 아니라 A도 with A in mind A를 마음에 두고 있는 complete 완전한, 마무리된 loft 다락방, 2층 공간 spacious 넓은 high-end 최고급의 neighborhood 인근, 주변 환경, 주변 지역 countless 셀 수 없는, 많은 perks 장점, 특혜 grant A B A에게 B를 주다 access to ~로의 접근, ~의 이용 fully equipped 모든 설비를 갖춘 downtown area 시내 restaurateur 식당 소유주 exquisite 우아한, 정교한, 훌륭한 tickle ~을 간지럽게 하다, ~을 기쁘게 하다 fancy 기호, 취미 avid 열심인, 열망하는 delight 기쁨, 즐거움 pant 숨을 헐떡거리다

71

What is the speaker advertising?

(A) A new residential complex (B) A shopping mall
(C) An architectural firm (D) An athletic complex

문제 해설

광고의 주제를 묻는 첫 번째 문제이므로 광고 대상이나 광고 주제가 가장 잘 드러나는 초반부에 집중해 들어야 한다. 화자가 지문 시작과 함께 'If you are~ever want.'라고 말하며 Harmony Park Village 가 어느 가족이든 원하는 바를 모두 갖추고 있는 주택이니만큼 더 이상 주택을 알아볼 필요가 없다고 언급하는 부분을 통해 주택을 광고하고 있음을 알 수 있으므로 (A)가 정답이다.

★★ 도입부 정보 – 광고 대상

화자는 무엇을 광고하고 있는가?
(A) 새로운 거주 단지 (B) 쇼핑몰
(C) 건축 사무소 (D) 스포츠 종합 단지

어휘 residential 거주/주거의 complex 복합 단지 architectural 건축의 athletic complex 스포츠 종합 단지

토익 분석

광고 대상은 지문이 시작하자마자 등장하는 가정법 또는 의문문에서 유추 가능하다.

72

What benefit does the speaker mention?

(A) A clean environment (B) Discounts at local restaurants
(C) Access to exclusive facilities (D) Special prices on memberships

문제 해설

화자가 언급하고 있는 혜택에 대해 두 번째 문제이므로 담화 중반부에 화자가 구체적인 혜택을 설명하는 부분이 있음을 예상하고 단서를 찾아야 한다. 화자가 담화 중반부에 'Your homeowner's~fitness center.'라는 말로 개인 골프 코스, 수영장, 테니스 코트, 농구장 그리고 시설이 완비된 체육관을 모두 이용할 수 있다고 언급하는 부분을 통해 화자는 전용 시설에 대한 이용을 알리고 있으므로 (C)가 정답이다.

★★★ 세부 정보

화자는 어떠한 혜택에 대해 언급하는가?
(A) 깨끗한 환경 (B) 지역 식당에서의 할인
(C) 전용 시설에 대한 이용 (D) 회원에 대한 특별 가격

어휘 environment 환경 exclusive 독점적인 facility 시설

토익 분석

광고에서 제품이나 서비스에 대한 혜택은 세부 정보로 주제문 다음에 부가 설명 부분에 등장한다.

73

According to the advertisement, what is located in downtown Kensington?

(A) A golf course (B) Luxury accommodations
(C) Animal amenities (D) An underground shopping center

문제 해설

Kensington 시내에서 발견할 수 있는 시설에 대해 묻는 마지막 문제이므로 담화 후반부에서 downtown Kensington이라는 지명이 제시되는 부분을 중심으로 단서를 파악해야 한다. 담화 후반부에 화자가 'the high-end~puppy boutique'라고 언급하는 부분에서 애완견들을 위한 시설을 알리고 있으므로 이에 대해 말한 (C)가 정답이다.

★★★ 세부 정보

광고에 따르면, Kensington 시내에 무엇이 위치해 있는가?
(A) 골프 코스 (B) 고급 숙박 시설
(C) 동물 편의 시설 (D) 지하 쇼핑센터

어휘 accommodation 숙박 시설 amenities 편의 시설

토익 분석

세부 정보 문제로 질문 속 고유 명사인 Kensington가 키워드로 활용된 문제다.

남 ⁷⁴ 우리 매출이 새로운 TV 광고의 성공으로 인해 급격하게 증가해 오고 있습니다. 지난달 초에 광고가 시작된 이후로 이번 달에 우리 주문이 3배나 늘어났으며, 올해 남은 기간에도 판매가 증가할 것으로 예상하고 있습니다. 이런 이유로, ⁷⁵ 회사는 시간제 직원들을 좀 더 채용하고 정규 직원들에게는 초과 근무를 하도록 요청하기로 했습니다. ⁷⁶ 초과 근무를 원하시는 분들께서는 오늘 퇴근 전까지 인사부장이신 John Allen 씨에게 말씀해 주십시오. 초과 근무는 선착순으로 배분될 것입니다. 초과 근무를 하시는 모든 직원들은 초과 근무 수당을 지급 받게 되실 것입니다. 감사 드리며, 좋은 하루 되십시오.

Questions 74-76 refer to the following announcement.

M ⁷⁴ Our sales have been dramatically increasing due to the success of our new television advertisement. Our orders this month have tripled since the ad started running at the beginning of last month, and we anticipate climbing sales for the remainder of the year. For this reason, ⁷⁵ the company has decided to hire more part-time workers and to ask full-timers to work overtime. ⁷⁶ For those who wish to work overtime, please speak to our personnel manager, Mr. John Allen, before the end of the day. Overtime hours will be distributed on a first-come, first-served basis. All of the employees who work overtime will get paid extra. Thank you and have a nice day.

어휘 sales 매출, 판매, 영업 dramatically 급격하게 due to ~로 인해 triple 3배로 늘다 run 운영/진행되다 anticipate ~을 기대/예상하다 climbing 상승하는 remainder 나머지 decide to do ~하기로 결정하다 part-time worker 시간제 근로자 ask A to do A에게 ~하도록 요청하다 full-timer 정규직 work overtime 초과 근무/야근을 하다 those who ~하는 사람들 distribute ~을 배부하다, ~을 나눠주다 on a first-come, first-served basis 선착순으로 get paid extra 추가 수당을 지급받다

74

★ 세부 정보

무엇이 매출 증가로 이어졌는가?
(A) 낮은 가격　　(B) 호황을 이룬 수출
(C) 성공적인 광고　　(D) 높은 품질

어휘 lead to ~로 이어지다, ~의 결과를 낳다 booming 호황인 export 수출 quality 질, 품질

토익 분석

첫 번째 문제로 지문의 도입부에 답이 제시된다. increase와 sales가 키워드로 활용된 문제다. 원인은 주로 due to, because으로 설명한다.

What led to the increase in sales?

(A) Low prices　　(B) Booming exports
(C) Successful advertising　　(D) High quality

문제 해설

매출 상승의 원인을 묻는 첫 번째 질문으로 담화 초반부에서 매출 상승이 언급되는 부분을 중심으로 제시되는 원인에 집중해 들어야 한다. 화자가 지문 시작과 함께 'Our sales have been dramatically increasing due to the success of our new television advertisement.'라고 말하며 성공적인 TV 광고로 인해 매출이 급격하게 상승하고 있음을 밝히고 있으므로 (C)가 정답임을 알 수 있다.

75

★ 세부 정보

화자에 따르면, 회사는 무엇을 하기로 결정했는가?
(A) 구인 광고를 게시하는 일
(B) 오래된 재고를 처분하는 일
(C) 임시 직원들을 채용하는 일
(D) 직원들에게 보너스를 지급하는 일

어휘 post ~을 게시하다 remove ~을 없애다, 치우다 inventory 재고(품) temporary 임시의

토익 분석

주체가 되는 company와 decide 역시 키워드로 사용되었다.

According to the speaker, what has the company decided to do?

(A) Post a job advertisement　　(B) Remove the old inventory
(C) Employ temporary workers　　(D) Pay bonuses to employees

문제 해설

회사의 결정 사항에 대해 묻는 두 번째 문제이므로 담화 중반부에 동사 decide를 중심으로 회사가 결정 내린 사항이 언급된다는 점을 예상하고 들어야 한다. 화자가 지문 중반부에 'the company has decided to hire more part-time workers'라고 말하는 부분을 통해 시간제 직원들을 더 채용하기로 결정했음을 알 수 있으므로 이에 해당되는 의미를 지닌 (C)가 정답이다.

76

★★★ 요청, 제안

청자들이 초과 근무를 원하는 경우 무엇을 하도록 지시 받고 있는가?
(A) 먼저 신청할 것
(B) 신청서를 제출할 것
(C) 공장 책임자에게 이야기할 것
(D) 등록 데스크로 갈 것

어휘 be instructed to do ~하도록 지시/안내 받다 submit ~을 제출하다 application 신청(서) registration 등록

토익 분석

요청, 제안 힌트가 되는 명령문 please speak to~ 문장이 힌트가 되고 질문 속에 if they want to work overtime 가정법 문장은 언제나 키워드의 역할을 한다.

What are the listeners instructed to do if they want to work overtime?

(A) Sign up first　　(B) Submit an application
(C) Talk to the plant manager　　(D) Go to the registration desk

문제 해설

청자들이 초과 근무를 원할 시 어떻게 하도록 지시 받고 있는지 묻는 마지막 문제이므로 지문 후반부에서 화자가 초과 근무와 관련해 제공하는 정보에 집중해 들어야 한다. 화자는 지문 후반부에 'For those who wish to work overtime, please speak to our personnel manager, Mr. John Allen, before the end of the day'라는 말로 초과 근무를 원하는 경우 인사부장인 John Allen 씨에게 이야기할 것을 언급하고 있다. 이어서 'Overtime hours will be distributed on a first-come, first-served basis'와 같이 초과 근무는 선착순으로 배정된다는 정보를 추가로 안내하고 있다. 그러므로 초과 근무를 하기 위해서는 다른 이들보다 먼저 인사부장에게 신청해야 함을 알 수 있으므로 (A)가 정답임을 알 수 있다.

Questions 77-79 refer to the following introduction.

W   Hello, and welcome to Stillwell Biochemicals. [77] As I guide you around the laboratories during today's tour, you'll see all the ways that we conduct our scientific research and experiments. Now, [78] it'll take at least three hours, so as we walk around the facility, we'll stop from time to time to rest and get some refreshments. Also, because we work on many very important projects here, our security is very tight. So [79] make sure you hold on to your ID tags, as you'll need to present these to the security guards when entering and exiting certain laboratories.

여   안녕하세요, 그리고 Stillwell Biochemicals에 오신 것을 환영합니다. [77] 제가 오늘 견학 시간에 여러분을 실험실로 안내해 드리는 동안, 여러분께서는 저희가 과학 연구 및 실험을 실시하는 모든 방식을 확인해 보시게 될 것입니다. 자, [78] 이 견학은 최소 3시간이 걸릴 것이므로 시설물을 둘러 보며 다니는 동안, 때때로 휴식과 다과를 위해 잠시 쉴 것입니다. 또한, 저희가 이곳에서 매우 중요한 여러 프로젝트에 대한 작업을 하기 때문에, 저희 보안이 매우 엄격합니다. 따라서, [79] 특정 실험실에 출입하실 때 보안 담당 직원들에게 제시하셔야 하므로 여러분의 출입증을 반드시 소지하고 계시기 바랍니다.

어휘 guide A around B A가 B를 둘러 보도록 안내하다 laboratory 실험실 way 방식, 방법 conduct ~을 실시하다 research 연구, 조사 experiment 실험 at least 최소한 walk around ~ 주변을 걸어 다니다 facility 시설(물) from time to time 때때로 rest 휴식 refreshments 다과 security 보안 tight 엄격한, 빈틈 없는 make sure (that) 반드시 ~하도록 하다 present ~을 제시하다 enter ~에 들어가다 exit ~에서 나오다 certain 특정한

77

Where does the talk most likely take place?

(A) At a factory
(B) At a tourist information center
(C) At a science museum
(D) At a research facility

★★ 도입부 정보 – 장소

담화는 어디에서 이뤄지고 있을 것 같은가?
(A) 공장에서
(B) 관광객 안내 센터에서
(C) 과학박물관에서
(D) 연구 시설물에서

어휘 take place 발생되다, 일어나다

토익 분석

담화가 이루어지는 장소는 지문의 도입부에 힌트가 등장한다.

문제 해설

담화 장소를 묻는 첫 번째 문제이므로 담화 시작 부분에 장소와 관련된 특성을 알리는 정보가 제시된다는 것을 예상하고 들어야 한다. 화자는 담화를 시작하면서 'As I guide you around the laboratories during today's tour, you'll see all the ways that we conduct our scientific research and experiments.'라는 말로 실험실을 안내하는 견학이 진행된다는 것을 언급하면서 연구와 실험을 한다는 말이 있으므로 (D)가 정답임을 알 수 있다.

78

Why does the speaker say, "It'll take at least three hours"?

(A) To tell the listeners to be prepared
(B) To apologize for a schedule change
(C) To arrange a meeting time
(D) To correct some details

★★★ 맥락 파악

화자는 왜 "It'll take at least three hours"라고 말하는가?
(A) 청자들에게 대비하도록 이야기해 주기 위해
(B) 일정 변경에 대해 사과하기 위해
(C) 회의 시간을 조정하기 위해
(D) 일부 세부 사항을 바로잡기 위해

어휘 tell A to do A에게 ~하도록 이야기하다 prepare ~에 대비/준비하다 apologize for ~에 대해 사과하다 arrange ~을 조정하다 correct ~을 수정하다 details 세부 사항, 상세 정보

토익 분석

제시된 표현 전후 관계를 파악해야 한다. 반전 표현 so~ 와 의도 및 미래 행동 힌트인 we'll~이 단서를 제시하고 있다.

문제 해설

"It'll take at least three hours"라는 문장을 미리 확인해 둔 후 해당 문장이 제시되는 부분의 앞뒤에 함께 언급되는 정보 및 담화의 흐름을 함께 확인하는 것이 관건이다. 화자는 담화 중반부에 해당 문장과 함께 'it'll take at least three hours, so as we walk around the facility, we'll stop from time to time for a rest and refreshments'라고 알리고 있다. 최소 3시간이 걸리는 것과 관련해 중간에 휴식을 취하고 다과를 먹는다는 말은 미리 대비시키기 위한 것임을 알 수 있으므로 이와 같은 의미로 쓰인 (A)가 정답이다.

79

According to the speaker, what should the listeners keep in their hands?

(A) Their guide books
(B) Their ID tags
(C) Their notepads
(D) Their security keycards

★★ 요청, 제안

화자의 말에 따르면, 청자들은 무엇을 각자 소지하고 있어야 하는가?
(A) 가이드북
(B) 출입증
(C) 메모장
(D) 보안용 카드키

어휘 keep A in one's hands A를 소지하다 notepad 메모장

토익 분석

Part 4에서 청자의 행동은 화자의 요청, 제안에 의한 것이다. 따라서 요청, 제안 힌트인 명령문 make sure you keep~이 단서가 되고 있다.

문제 해설

청자들이 소지해야 하는 것을 묻는 마지막 문제이므로 담화 후반부에 청자들에게 소지하도록 당부하는 내용이 제시된다는 것을 예상하고 들어야 한다. 담화 마지막에 화자는 'make sure you keep a hold on your ID tags, as you'll need to present these to the security guards when entering and exiting certain laboratories'라는 말로 필요 시 제시할 수 있도록 출입증을 꼭 소지하라고 알리고 있으므로 (B)가 정답임을 알 수 있다.

여 안녕하세요, **Kyle** 씨. 저는 **Kristen Miller**라고 합니다. 저는 **Cary's** 신발 매장의 고객 서비스 직원입니다. ⁸⁰ 저희는 이틀 전에 저희 홈페이지를 통해 귀하께서 제출하신 **Vince Gouchi** 블랙 드레스 슈즈 한 쌍에 대한 주문 신청을 접수했습니다. ⁸¹ 안타깝게도, 이 제품은 현재 재고가 없는 상태인 것으로 드러났습니다. 제조업체로부터 들어오는 새로운 공급 물량이 이 달 말까지 매장으로 입고될 예정이라, ⁸¹ 그때가 되어야 저희가 귀하의 주문을 처리해 드릴 수 있을 것입니다. ⁸² 하지만 현재 매장에서 동일한 신발의 갈색 상품은 구매 가능하십니다. 만약 고객님께서 이 변경 사항에 대해 허락하신다면 오늘이라도 제품을 배송해 드릴 수 있습니다. 저희에게 692-9815로 전화 주셔서 귀하께서 선호하시는 바를 알려 주셨으면 합니다. 대단히 감사 드리며 좋은 하루 보내십시오.

Questions 80-82 refer to the following telephone message.

W Hello, Mr. Kyle. This is Kristen Miller. I am a customer service representative at Cary's Shoe Store. ⁸⁰ We received the order for a pair of Vince Gouchi black dress shoes that you submitted through our Web site two days ago. ⁸¹ Unfortunately, it turns out that they are out of stock at the moment. The new supply from the manufacturer is scheduled to arrive at the store by the end of this month, ⁸¹ so we will not be able to process your order until then. ⁸² However, we have the same shoes in brown available at the store right now. We can ship them today if you are to approve the change. Please call us at 692-9815 and let us know what your preference is. Thank you very much and have a nice day.

어휘 customer service representative 고객 서비스 직원 receive ~을 받다 submit ~을 제출하다 through ~을 통해 unfortunately 안타깝게도 turn out that ~임이 드러나다, ~으로 판명되다 be out of stock 재고가 없다 at the moment 지금, 현재 supply 공급(품) be scheduled to do ~할 예정이다 by (기한) ~까지 not A until B B나 되어야 A하다 be able to do ~할 수 있다 process ~을 처리하다 available 구매 가능한 ship ~을 배송하다 be to do ~해야 하다, ~할 예정이다 approve ~을 승인/허락하다 preference 선호(하는 것)

80

★ 세부 정보

메시지에 따르면, 이틀 전에 무슨 일이 있었는가?
(A) 몇몇 제품들이 단종되었다.
(B) 온라인으로 주문이 이뤄졌다.
(C) 신상품이 매장에 도착했다.
(D) 인터넷 거래가 취소되었다.

어휘 discontinue ~을 단종하다 place an order 주문하다 transaction 거래

토익 분석

질문 속에서 키워드를 찾아야 한다. 시점 표현 **two days ago**가 결정적인 키워드로 활용되었다.

According to the message, what happened two days ago?

(A) Some items were discontinued.
(B) An order was placed online.
(C) New products arrived at the store.
(D) Internet transactions were cancelled.

문제 해설

이틀 전에 발생한 일에 관해 묻는 첫 번째 문제이므로 담화 초반부에 'two days ago'라는 시점이 제시되는 부분을 중심으로 단서를 파악해야 한다. 화자가 담화 초반부에 'We received ~two days ago.'라고 말하며 이틀 전에 인터넷을 통한 Kyle 씨의 주문을 접수했음을 밝히고 있으므로 (B)가 정답임을 알 수 있다.

81

★★ 문제점

화자는 왜 현재 Kyle 씨의 주문을 처리하지 못한다고 말하는가?
(A) 그녀가 그의 주문서를 분실했다.
(B) 컴퓨터 시스템이 고장 났다.
(C) 제품이 현재 재고가 없는 상태이다.
(D) 그가 아직 구매 제품에 대한 비용을 지불하지 않았다.

어휘 order form 주문서 out of order 고장 난, 작동되지 않는 out of stock 재고가 없는 purchase 구매(품)

토익 분석

여자가 언급하는 문제점을 찾아야 한다. 문제점은 대체로 반전 표현이 힌트로 등장한다. **Unfortunately**가 단서가 되었다.

Why does the speaker say she cannot process Mr. Kyle's order now?

(A) She lost his order form.   (B) The computer system is out of order.
(C) An item is currently out of stock.   (D) He hasn't paid for his purchase yet.

문제 해설

현재 Kyle 씨의 주문이 처리되지 못하는 이유에 대해 묻는 두 번째 문제이므로 담화 중반부에 Kyle 씨의 주문 처리가 불가하다는 내용과 그 이유가 제시될 것임을 예상하고 들어야 한다. 화자는 담화 중반부에 'Unfortunately, it turns out that they are out of stock at this moment.'이라고 이야기하며 Kyle 씨가 원하는 제품이 현재 재고가 없는 상태임을 밝힌 후에 'so we will not be able to process your order until then'이라는 말로 주문 처리가 불가한 상황임을 언급하고 있다. 따라서 재고가 없는 것이 주문 처리를 할 수 없는 이유임을 알 수 있으므로 (C)가 정답이다.

82

★★★ 요청, 제안

화자가 Kyle 씨에게 알려 주고자 하는 것은 무엇인가?
(A) 대체 상품이 구매 가능하다.
(B) 가격 정보가 부정확하다.
(C) 그의 주문이 막 처리되었다.
(D) 일부 상품은 할인가로 제공된다.

어휘 alternative 대체의 accurate 정확한

토익 분석

however ~로 시작하는 문장이 단서가 되었으며 요청, 제안 힌트인 'we can~ if가정법~' 문장이 추가 정보를 제공한다.

What does the speaker want Mr. Kyle to know?

(A) An alternative product is available.
(B) The pricing information was not accurate.
(C) His order has just been processed.
(D) Some products are being offered at discounted prices.

문제 해설

화자가 Kyle 씨에게 알려주고자 하는 것을 묻는 마지막 문제이므로 담화 후반부에 화자가 상대방에게 알리는 정보를 파악하는 데 집중해야 한다. 화자는 담화 후반부에 'However~right now.'라는 말로 동일한 제품을 다른 색상으로 구매하는 것이 가능함을 알리고 'We can ship~the change.'라는 말로 오늘 발송이 가능하다고 했으니 대체 상품 구매가 가능하다는 의미로 쓰인 (A)가 정답이다.

Questions 83-85 refer to the following excerpt from a meeting.

M Welcome, council members. The first item on our agenda today is the expansion of the space for parking near the city library. [83] As you all know, the project has been put on hold due to budget problems. [84] It is my proposal to use the income the city earned from ticket sales at the recent food festival and other events for the parking project. [85] In order to proceed, we need a majority vote from the council members who are present today. Please raise your hand if you support this initiative.

어휘 agenda 안건, 의제 expand ~을 확장하다, ~을 늘리다 be put on hold ~이 보류/지연되다 due to ~로 인해 budget 예산 proposal 제안 income 수익 earn ~을 벌어 들이다 recent 최근의 in order to do ~하기 위해 proceed 진행하다, 나아가다 majority vote 과반수 의결, 다수결 present 참석한 raise ~을 들어 올리다 support ~을 지지하다 initiative (문제 해결, 목적 달성을 위한) 계획

남 환영합니다, 시 의원 여러분. 오늘 우리의 첫 번째 안건은 시립 도서관 근처에 주차 공간을 확장하는 것입니다. [83] 여러분 모두 아시겠지만, 이 공사는 예산 문제로 인해 보류된 상태입니다. [84] 저는 최근의 음식 축제 및 기타 행사들에서 입장권 판매를 통해 우리 시가 얻은 수익을 이 주차장 프로젝트에 대해 사용하도록 제안합니다. [85] 이 안건을 계속 진행시키기 위해서는, 오늘 회의에 참석해 주신 시 의원 여러분들의 과반수 의결이 필요합니다. 이 계획을 지지하시는 분께서는 손을 들어 주시기 바랍니다.

83

According to the speaker, what caused the project delay?

(A) A land shortage
(B) Weather conditions
(C) Insufficient funds
(D) Some mechanical problems

문제 해설

프로젝트의 지연 이유에 대해 묻는 첫 번째 문제이므로 담화 초반부에서 화자가 프로젝트를 언급하면서 지연된 상황 및 이유를 함께 제시한다는 점을 예상하고 들어야 한다. 화자가 지문 초반부에 'As you all know, the project has been put on hold due to budget problems.'라는 말로 프로젝트가 예산 문제로 인해 보류되었음을 밝히는 부분을 통해 자금 부족이 가장 큰 이유임을 알 수 있으므로 (C)가 정답이다.

★ 문제점

화자에 따르면, 프로젝트의 지연을 초래한 것은 무엇인가?
(A) 부지의 부족
(B) 기상 상태
(C) 부족한 자금
(D) 몇몇 기계적인 문제점

어휘 cause ~을 초래하다 shortage 부족 lack 부족 sufficient 충분한 fund 자금, 기금 mechanical 기계적인

토익 분석

지문의 초반부 주제문에 답이 제시된다. 문두 부사구 As you all know와 같은 표현은 중요한 힌트를 제시한다.

84

What does the speaker propose the city do to continue the project?

(A) Raise property taxes
(B) Use profits from events
(C) Hold a fundraising event
(D) Recruit volunteers for the project

문제 해설

화자가 프로젝트 지속을 위해 제안하는 것에 대해 묻는 두 번째 문제이므로 담화 중반부에 화자의 제안 사항이 언급될 것임을 예상하고 들어야 한다. 화자는 담화 중반부에 'It is my proposal to use the income the city earned from ticket sales at the recent food festival and other events for the parking project.'라고 말하며 음식 축제 및 여러 행사에서 입장권 판매를 통해 얻은 수익을 주차장 프로젝트에 이용할 것을 제안하고 있다. 따라서 행사 수익금을 활용하는 방안을 언급한 (B)가 정답이다.

★★ 세부 정보

그 도시가 프로젝트를 지속하기 위해서 무엇을 제안하고 있는가?
(A) 재산세를 인상해야 한다.
(B) 행사를 통해 얻은 수익금을 이용해야 한다.
(C) 기금 마련 행사를 개최해야 한다.
(D) 프로젝트를 위해 자원봉사자를 모집해야 한다.

어휘 raise ~을 인상하다, 올리다 property tax 재산세 profit 수익 hold ~을 개최하다, 열다 fundraising 기금 마련 recruit ~을 모집하다 volunteer 자원봉사자

토익 분석

세부 정보 문제는 키워드를 최대한 활용해야 한다. 질문 속에 동사 propose가 키워드로 반복 사용되었고 명사 city와 project 역시 키워드로 활용되었다.

85

What is required to proceed with the speaker's proposal?

(A) A vote from all residents
(B) A review by the government
(C) The approval of the mayor
(D) A majority vote by the council members

문제 해설

화자의 안건을 지속하기 위해 요구되는 것을 묻는 마지막 문제이므로 담화 후반부에 '진행하다, 지속하다'를 뜻하는 proceed가 등장하는 부분을 중심으로 제시되는 해당 단서에 초점을 맞춰야 한다. 화자는 담화 후반부에 'In order to proceed, we need a majority vote from the council members who are present today.'라고 말하며 제안 사항을 계속 진행하기 위해서는 회의에 참석한 시 의원들의 다수결이 필요함을 직접적으로 밝히고 있다. 따라서 이와 같은 조건에 대해 언급한 (D)가 정답이다.

★★ 세부 정보

화자의 제안이 계속 진행되기 위해서는 무엇이 요구되는가?
(A) 모든 주민의 투표
(B) 정부에 의한 심의
(C) 시장의 승인
(D) 시 의원들의 다수결

어휘 proceed with ~을 진행하다 resident 주민 review 심의, 검토 approval 승인 mayor 시장

토익 분석

세부 정보 문제이므로 키워드를 활용해야 한다. 동사 proceed가 키워드로 활용되었다.

여 ⁸⁷ 고급 전자 제품에 관한 우리 워크숍의 첫째 날에 오신 것을 환영합니다. ⁸⁶ 여러분의 지점장님께서 제게 여러분의 수리 작업에 대한 속도와 성공률을 개선하는 데 도움을 드리도록 요청해 주셨습니다. 여러분께서 기기들을 빠르고 효과적으로 수리하실 수 있다면, 여러분께서는 매일 더 많은 고객들을 도와 드리실 수 있습니다. ⁸⁷ 우선, 우리는 일반적인 기기 오작동과 이를 해결하는 방법들에 초점을 맞출 것입니다. 그런 다음, 여러분께서는 여러분의 기술적인 작업의 속도를 높이는 방법을 배우실 것입니다. 12시 30분에는 점심 식사를 할 예정입니다. ⁸⁸ 보통, 우리 구내 직원 식당으로 가시도록 권해 드리지만, 오늘은 문을 닫은 것 같습니다. 그러나 아마 아시겠지만, 길 바로 건너편에 카페가 하나 있습니다.

Questions 86-88 refer to the following talk.

W ⁸⁷ Welcome to the first day of our workshop on advanced electronics. ⁸⁶ Your branch manager has asked me to help you improve the speed and success rate of your repairs. If you can repair devices quickly and effectively, you can assist more customers per day. ⁸⁷ First, we'll be focusing on common device malfunctions and ways to solve them. Then, you'll learn how to speed up your technical work. At twelve thirty, we'll take a break for lunch. ⁸⁸ Normally, we'd suggest that you go to our staff cafeteria, but I'm afraid it's closed today. But as you probably noticed, there is a café just across the road.

어휘 advanced 고급의, 진보한 electronics 전자 제품 branch manager 지점장 ask A to do A에게 ~하도록 요청하다 improve ~을 개선하다, 향상시키다 success rate 성공률 repair ~을 수리하다 device 기기 effectively 효과적으로 per day 매일, 하루마다 focus on ~에 초점을 맞추다 common 일반적인, 흔한 malfunction 오작동 way to do ~하는 방법 solve ~을 해결하다 how to do ~하는 법 speed up ~의 속도를 높이다 take a break for lunch 점심 식사 시간을 갖다 normally 보통, 일반적으로 suggest that ~하도록 제안하다 staff cafeteria 구내 직원 식당 notice 알아차리다 across the road 길 건너편에

86

★★ 암시 추론

청자들은 누구일 것 같은가?
(A) 전화 교환원들
(B) 영업 사원들
(C) 수리 기술자들
(D) 광고 책임자들

어휘 telephone operator 전화 교환원
sales representative 영업 사원 advertising 광고

토익 분석

직업은 도입부 정보에 해당하지만 질문에 most likely가 포함되어 있으니 지문의 도입부를 듣고 유추해야 하는 유형의 문제다.

Who most likely are the listeners?

(A) Telephone operators
(B) Sales representatives
(C) Repair technicians
(D) Advertising managers

문제 해설

청자들의 정체를 묻는 첫 번째 문제이므로 담화 시작 부분에 상대방의 업무적 특성이 언급되는 부분이 있다는 것을 예상하고 들어야 한다. 화자는 담화 시작 부분에 'Your branch manager has asked me to help you improve the speed and success rate of your repairs.'라는 말로 청자들이 수리 업무를 담당하는 사람들이라는 것을 언급하고 있으므로 (C)가 정답임을 알 수 있다.

87

★★ 주제, 목적

담화의 목적은 무엇인가?
(A) 새로운 업무 정책을 발표하는 것
(B) 신입 사원들을 소개하는 것
(C) 워크숍 일정을 설명하는 것
(D) 고객 불만 사항들을 설명하는 것

어휘 policy 정책, 방침 introduce ~을 소개하다 explain ~을 설명하다 describe ~을 설명하다 complaint 불만

토익 분석

환영인사 welcome~ 다음이 주제문이다. 문두 부사 중 순서를 나타내는 First와 같은 표현은 매우 중요하다.

What is the purpose of the talk?

(A) To announce a new work policy
(B) To introduce new staff members
(C) To explain a workshop schedule
(D) To describe some customer complaints

문제 해설

담화의 목적을 묻는 첫 번째 문제이므로 담화에 언급되는 인사말이나 안내 정보 등의 핵심을 파악하는 데 집중해야 한다. 화자는 담화를 시작하면서 화자는 담화 시작 부분에 'Welcome to the first day of our workshop on advanced electronics.'라는 인사말로 워크숍 행사 온 것을 환영하면서, 중반부에 가서는 'First~solve them.'라는 말 이후로 순서대로 발생될 일을 알리고 있다. 이는 일정을 설명하는 것에 해당되므로 이와 같은 의미로 쓰인 (C)가 정답임을 알 수 있다.

88

★★★ 맥락 파악

화자가 "There is a café just across the road"라고 말할 때 무엇을 암시하는가?
(A) 커피 매장들이 있지 않다는 점에 대해 청자들이 틀렸다.
(B) 청자들이 한 장소를 찾는 데 어려움을 겪을 수 있다.
(C) 청자들이 카페에서 점심 식사를 해야 한다.
(D) 청자들이 하루 일과를 마칠 때 카페에서 만날 것이다.

어휘 have difficulty -ing ~하는 데 어려움을 겪다

토익 분석

요청, 제안 힌트인 we'd suggest와 반전 표현 but~과 I'm afraid가 결정적인 단서가 되었다.

What does the speaker imply when she says, "There is a café just across the road"?

(A) The listeners are wrong about there being no coffee shops.
(B) The listeners might have difficulty finding a location.
(C) The listeners should have lunch at the café.
(D) The listeners will meet in the café at the end of the day.

문제 해설

"There is a café just across the road"라는 문장을 미리 확인해 둔 후 해당 문장이 제시되는 부분의 앞뒤에 함께 언급되는 정보 및 담화의 흐름을 함께 확인하는 것이 관건이다. 화자는 담화 후반부에 'Normally, we'd suggest that you go to our staff cafeteria, but I'm afraid it's closed today.'라고 알린 후에 해당 문장을 언급하고 있다. 이는 구내식당이 문을 닫은 것에 따른 조치를 알리는 것이므로 카페에서 식사하도록 공지하는 내용임을 알 수 있다. 따라서 (C)가 정답이다.

Questions 89-91 refer to the following excerpt from a meeting.

M ⁸⁹ I'm delighted to tell you that we'll be expanding our office area after the marketing department moves to the third floor. I should have made the announcement earlier this month. However, I was away from the office to attend client meetings. Some of you will be moving over to the area where the marketing department used to work. ⁹⁰ So we'll be rearranging the desks and getting extra office furniture this Friday. ⁹¹ I think those of you in the design team are going to be happy with the spacious shelves available to keep the files. Now, feel free to ask any questions regarding this matter.

남 ⁸⁹ 마케팅부가 3층으로 옮긴 후에 우리의 사무 공간을 확장할 예정이라는 점을 여러분께 알려 드리게 되어 기쁩니다. 이 공지 사항을 이달 초에 알려 드렸어야 했습니다. 하지만 제가 고객 회의에 참석하기 위해 멀리 가 있어야 했습니다. 여러분 중의 일부는 마케팅부가 근무하던 공간으로 자리를 옮기게 될 것입니다. ⁹⁰ 따라서 우리는 이번 주 금요일에 책상들을 재배치하고 추가 사무 가구를 들여놓을 것입니다. ⁹¹ 제 생각에 디자인 팀에 속한 여러분께서는 파일들을 보관하는 데 사용될 수 있는 널찍한 선반에 대해 기뻐하실 것 같습니다. 자, 이 사안과 관련된 어떤 질문이든지 마음껏 해 주시기 바랍니다.

어휘 be delighted to do ~해서 기쁘다 expand ~을 확장하다 move to ~로 옮기다, 이사하다 should have p.p. ~했어야 했다 make an announcement 공지/발표/안내하다 had to do ~해야 했다 stay away from ~에서 멀리 가 있다 attend ~에 참석 used to do (과거에) ~하곤 했다 rearrange ~을 재배치하다 extra 추가/별도의 spacious 널찍한 shelf 선반 available 이용 가능한 feel free to do 마음껏 ~하세요 regarding ~와 관련해 matter 사안, 문제

89

What is the talk mainly about?

(A) Meetings with clients
(B) Reports about marketing strategy
(C) Plans on expanding a working area
(D) The efficiency of documentation

문제 해설

담화의 목적을 묻는 첫 번째 문제이므로 담화에 언급되는 인사말이나 안내 정보 등의 핵심을 파악하는 데 집중해야 한다. 화자는 담화를 시작하면서 'I'm delighted to let you know that we'll be expanding our office area after the Marketing Department moves to the 3rd floor.'라는 말로 사무 공간을 확장한다는 것을 알리고 있으므로 업무 공간 확장 계획을 의미하는 (C)가 정답임을 알 수 있다.

★★ 주제, 목적

담화는 주로 무엇에 관한 것인가?
(A) 고객들과의 미팅들
(B) 마케팅 전략에 관한 보고서들
(C) 업무 공간을 확장하는 것에 대한 계획
(D) 서류 작업의 효율성

어휘 strategy 전략 efficiency 효율성 documentation 서류 작업

토익 분석

주제문을 찾아야 한다. '~기쁘다, ~유감이다, ~알리다' 등은 주제문을 이끄는 대표적인 힌트다. I'm delighted to let you know~가 정답을 제시했다.

90

What will the listeners probably do this Friday?

(A) Reorganize the office area
(B) Move to third floor
(C) Arrange a client meeting
(D) Attend a workshop

문제 해설

이번 주 금요일에 있을 일을 묻는 두 번째 문제이므로 담화 중반부에 '이번 주 금요일'이라는 시점 표현과 함께 언급되는 정보를 파악하는 데 집중해야 한다. 화자는 담화 중반부에 'So, we'll be rearranging the desks and get extra office furniture this Friday.'라는 말로 이번 주 금요일에 책상을 재배치하고 가구를 추가로 들이는 일을 한다고 알리고 있으므로 사무 공간 재정리를 의미하는 (A)가 정답이다.

★ 세부 정보

청자들은 이번 주 금요일에 무엇을 할 것 같은가?
(A) 사무 공간을 재정리하는 일
(B) 3층으로 옮기는 일
(C) 고객 회의 일정을 잡는 일
(D) 워크숍에 참석하는 일

어휘 reorganize ~을 재정리/재편하다 arrange ~의 일정을 잡다, 준비하다 attend ~에 참석하다

토익 분석

세부 정보 문제로 키워드 this Friday를 활용하는 문제다. 동시에 반전 표현 so와 의도 및 미래 행동 표현 we'll~역시 단서가 되었다.

91

What does the speaker think the designers will like?

(A) The choice of programs to use   **(B) The wide space for documents**
(C) The decreased workload   (D) The technical support service

문제 해설

디자이너들이 좋아하는 것을 묻는 마지막 문제이므로 담화 후반부에 디자이너와 관련된 정보가 제시될 것임을 예상하고 들어야 한다. 담화 후반부에 화자는 'I think those of you in Design team are going to be happy with the spacious shelves available to keep the files.'라고 알리면서 디자인 팀 사람들이 파일 보관에 필요한 넓은 선반에 대해 기뻐할 것이라고 알리고 있으므로 이에 대해 언급한 (B)가 정답이다.

★★ 세부 정보

화자는 디자이너들이 무엇을 좋아할 것이라고 생각하는가?
(A) 사용할 프로그램들에 대한 선택권
(B) 서류들을 놓을 넓은 공간
(C) 줄어든 업무량
(D) 기술 지원 서비스

어휘 choice 선택(권) decreased 감소된, 줄어든 workload 업무량 technical support 기술 지원

토익 분석

질문 속에 designers를 변형한 those of you in Design team가 키워드가 되었다.

여 안녕하세요, Frank, 저는 Veronica입니다. 회사의 회장님께서 다음 주에 Los Angeles에서 열리는 식음료 컨벤션 행사에서 우리 Zinger Snack Foods 사가 진열 테이블을 확보하기를 원하고 계시며, 행사에 필요한 진열품을 만들어 그것을 보여주기를 바랍니다. ⁹³ 우리가 이번 주에 신제품에 대한 광고 캠페인에 초점을 맞추기로 되어 있다는 것을 알고 있기는 하지만, 이 업무가 막 생겨났는데, 좀 긴급한 일입니다. 이것이 제 아이디어는 아니었습니다. ^{92, 94} 어쨌든, 제가 마케팅팀의 다른 직원들에게도 도와 달라고 요청하겠습니다. 하지만 진열 테이블을 확보하는 것과 관련해 컨벤션 주최 측에 연락해 주시겠습니까? 감사 드리며, 그쪽에서 뭐라고 하는지 제게 알려 주십시오.

Questions 92-94 refer to the following telephone message.

W Hi, Frank. It's Veronica. The company chairman wants Zinger Snack Foods to have a display table at the food and beverage convention in Los Angeles next week, and he needs us to create a display for the event and present it. ⁹³ I know we are supposed to be focusing on the ad campaign for our new products this week, but this task just came up, and it's rather urgent. It wasn't my idea. ^{92, 94} Anyway, I'll ask other members of the marketing team to help out as well. But would you mind contacting the convention organizers about getting a display table? Thanks, and let me know what they say.

어휘 want A to do A가 ~하기를 원하다 display 진열(품), 전시(품) food and beverage 식음료 need A to do A가 ~하기를 원하다 create ~을 만들어 내다 present ~을 보여주다, 제시하다 be supposed to do ~하기로 되어 있다 focus on ~에 초점을 맞추다 ad campaign 광고 캠페인 task 업무, 일 come up 생겨나다, 나타나다 rather 좀, 약간, 다소 urgent 긴급한 help out 도움을 주다 as well 또한, 마찬가지로 contact ~에게 연락하다 organizer 주최자, 조직자

92

★★★ 전화 목적

화자는 왜 전화를 거는가?
(A) 컨벤션에 등록하기 위해
(B) 한 가지 업무에 대해 도움을 요청하기 위해
(C) 광고 캠페인에 관해 문의하기 위해
(D) 찾아가는 길을 알아내기 위해

어휘 register for ~에 등록하다 ask for ~을 요청하다 inquire about ~에 관해 문의하다 find out ~을 알아내다

토익 분석

반전 표현 anyway와 의도 및 미래 행동 힌트인 I'll~그리고 요청 제안에 답변이 되는 동사 ask가 정답 문장을 제시했다.

Why is the speaker calling?
(A) To register for a convention **(B) To ask for help with a task**
(C) To inquire about an ad campaign (D) To get some directions

문제 해설

화자가 전화를 거는 목적을 묻는 첫 번째 문제이므로 담화 시작 부분에 언급되는 정보에 특히 집중해 들어야 한다. 또한 종종 배경 설명 후에 후반부에 가서 핵심 목적이 제시되는 경우도 있으므로 이에 함께 유의하면서 들어야 한다. 화자는 담화를 시작하면서 회장의 요청 사항과 관련해 먼저 설명한 후, 후반부에 가서 'Anyway~display table?'라는 말로 자신이 도움을 요청할 일과 상대방에게 부탁하는 일을 함께 언급해 도와 달라고 요청하는 상황임을 알 수 있다. 따라서 (B)가 정답이 된다.

93

★★★ 맥락 파악

화자가 "It wasn't my idea"라고 말할 때 무엇을 암시하는가?
(A) 한 가지 변경 사항이 불편하다는 것을 이해한다.
(B) 청자가 자랑스러워해야 한다고 생각한다.
(C) 팀이 의사소통을 잘 하고 있어서 기뻐하고 있다.
(D) 청자가 몇몇 선택권들을 제안해 주기를 원하고 있다.

어휘 inconvenient 불편한 communicate 의사소통하다 option 선택권

토익 분석

지문의 흐름을 이해할 수 있어야 한다. 반전 표현을 포함하고 있는 we are supposed to ~, but~ 문장이 정답을 찾는데 힌트가 된다.

What does the speaker imply when she says, "It wasn't my idea"?
(A) She understands a change is inconvenient.
(B) She thinks the listener should be proud.
(C) She is pleased that the team is communicating well.
(D) She wants the listener to suggest some options.

문제 해설

"It wasn't my idea"라는 문장을 미리 확인해 둔 후 해당 문장이 제시되는 부분의 앞뒤에 함께 언급되는 정보 및 담화의 흐름을 함께 확인하는 것이 관건이다. 화자는 담화 중반부에 'I know we are~rather urgent.'라는 말로 원래 하려던 일이 있는 상황에서 긴급한 다른 일이 생긴 것을 언급하면서 해당 문장을 말하고 있다. 이는 업무 순서가 변경되는 것에 따른 불편함이 발생되는 것을 염두에 두고 한 말이므로 이와 같은 의미에 해당되는 (A)가 정답이다.

94

★★ 요청, 제안

화자는 청자에게 무엇을 하도록 요청하는가?
(A) 광고를 낼 것 (B) 회사의 회장님께 연락할 것
(C) 직원 회의를 열 것 (D) 진열 테이블을 요청할 것

어휘 place an advertisement 광고를 내다 hold ~을 열다, 개최하다 request ~을 요청하다

토익 분석

요청 제안 힌트 표현인 would you mind -ing~가 정답 문장을 이끌고 있다.

What does the speaker ask the listener to do?
(A) Place an advertisement (B) Contact the company chairman
(C) Hold a staff meeting **(D) Request a display table**

문제 해설

화자가 요청하는 일을 묻는 마지막 문제이므로 담화 후반부에 제시되는 요청 관련 표현을 중심으로 단서를 파악해야 한다. 화자는 담화 마지막에 'would you mind contacting the convention organizers about getting a display table?'라는 말로 진열 테이블을 확보하는 일과 관련해 주최 측에 연락하도록 요청하고 있으므로 (D)가 정답임을 알 수 있다.

Questions 95-97 refer to the following broadcast and schedule.

M   You're listening to Whizz Radio, your local entertainment station. I have some news about the upcoming fall movie series at Maple Lake. [95, 96] We just learned that Morrow Road will be closed for repairs from September 10 to September 18. This means that the movie screen next to the lake will be inaccessible during that time. Unfortunately, the movie that was supposed to be shown during that time will need to be postponed until October. The organizers of the movie series are very sorry about the inconvenience. [97] If you're interested in seeing the full movie schedule and finding out how to purchase tickets, you should log on to our Web site.

```
┌──────────────────────────────────────────────┐
│  Movies by the Lake: Fall Schedule           │
│                                              │
│  September 4th    -    Golden Years          │
│                                              │
│  September 15th   -    A Brief Romance        │
│                                              │
│  September 25th   -    The Outlaw            │
│                                              │
│  October 2nd      -    Space Quest III       │
└──────────────────────────────────────────────┘
```

어휘 entertainment station 연예 방송(국) upcoming 다가오는, 곧 있을 learn that ~임을 알다 closed 폐쇄된 repair 수리 mean that ~임을 의미하다 next to ~ 옆의 inaccessible 이용할 수 없는, 접근할 수 없는 unfortunately 안타깝게도 be supposed to do ~할 예정이다, ~하기로 되어 있다 show ~을 상영하다 postpone ~을 연기하다 organizer 주최자, 조직자 inconvenience 불편함 be interested in ~하는 데 관심이 있다 find out ~을 알아내다 how to do ~하는 법 purchase ~을 구입하다 log on to ~에 로그인/접속하다

남 여러분께서는 지역 연예 방송 프로그램인 Whizz Radio을 청취하고 계십니다. Maple Lake에서 열리는 다가오는 가을 영화 시리즈에 관한 소식이 있습니다. [95, 96] 저희는 9월 10일부터 18일까지 수리 작업을 위해 Morrow Road가 폐쇄된다는 소식을 막 접했습니다. 이는 호수 옆에 설치되는 영화 스크린이 해당 기간 동안 이용할 수 없음을 의미하는 것입니다. 안타깝게도, 해당 기간 동안 상영될 예정이었던 영화는 10월로 연기되어야 할 것입니다. 이 영화 시리즈 행사의 주최 측에서는 이와 같은 불편함에 대해 대단히 유감으로 생각하고 있습니다. [97] 전체 영화 상영 일정을 확인해 보시는 것과 입장권 구매 방법을 알아보시는 데 관심이 있으신 분은, 저희 웹 사이트에 접속하시기 바랍니다.

```
┌──────────────────────────────────────┐
│        호반 영화 시리즈: 가을 일정        │
│                                      │
│  9월 4일 – Golden Years               │
│  9월 15일 – A Brief Romance            │
│  9월 25일 – The Outlaw                │
│  10월 2일 – Space Quest III           │
└──────────────────────────────────────┘
```

95

What problem does the speaker mention?

(A) A road will be temporarily closed.
(B) Inclement weather is expected.
(C) A guest speaker is unavailable.
(D) Some equipment has been damaged.

문제 해설

화자가 언급하는 문제점을 묻는 첫 번째 문제이므로 담화 초반부에 문제점과 관련된 부정적인 정보가 제시된다는 것을 예상하고 들어야 한다. 화자는 담화 초반부에 'We just learned that Morrow Road will be closed for repairs from September 10th to September 18th.'라는 말로 특정 기간에 폐쇄되는 도로가 있음을 언급하고 있으므로 이와 같은 문제점에 해당되는 (A)가 정답이다.

★★ 문제점

화자는 무슨 문제를 언급하는가?
(A) 도로가 일시적으로 폐쇄될 것이다.
(B) 악천후가 예상되고 있다.
(C) 초청 연사가 시간이 나지 않는다.
(D) 일부 장비가 손상되었다.

어휘 temporarily 일시적으로 inclement weather 악천후 expect ~을 예상하다 unavailable (사람이) 시간이 나지 않는 equipment 장비 damaged 손상된, 피해를 입은

토익 분석

첫 번째 문제로 등장하는 문제점은 주제문에 답이 제시된다.

96

★★★ 그래픽

도표를 보시오. 화자의 말에 따르면, 어느 영화 상영 일정이 연기될 것인가?
(A) Golden Years
(B) A Brief Romance
(C) The Outlaw
(D) Space Quest III

어휘 brief 짧은, 간략한 outlaw n. 도망자 v. 불법의, 금하다

토익 분석

제시된 정보가 날짜와 영화 제목이다. 보기에 영화 제목들이 열거되어 있으니 지문에서 날짜 정보를 집중해서 들어야 한다.

Look at the graphic. According to the speaker, which film showing will be postponed?

(A) Golden Years
(B) A Brief Romance
(C) The Outlaw
(D) Space Quest III

문제 해설

연기되는 영화 상영 일정을 묻는 두 번째 문제이므로 담화 중에 화자가 일정이 연기되는 일을 언급한다는 것을 알 수 있으며, 이와 관련해 도표에 쓰여 있는 날짜와 관련된 기간이 제시될 것임을 예상하고 들어야 한다. 화자는 담화 초반부에 'We just learned that Morrow Road will be closed for repairs from September 10th to September 18th.'라는 말로 9월 10일에서 18일 사이에 도로가 폐쇄된다고 알리면서, 중반부에 'the movie that was supposed to be shown during that time will need to be postponed until October'라고 밝히면서, 이에 해당되는 행사가 10월로 연기되어야 한다고 알리고 있다. 따라서 해당 기간에 속한 날짜인 9월 15일로 표기된 (B)가 정답이다.

★★ 요청, 제안

화자는 청자들에게 무엇을 하도록 권하는가?
(A) 환불을 요청할 것
(B) 웹 사이트를 방문할 것
(C) 행사 주최자에게 연락할 것
(D) 다른 행사에 참석할 것

어휘 request ~을 요청하다 refund 환불 contact ~에게 연락하다 attend ~에 참석하다

토익 분석

요청, 제안 힌트 표현을 찾아야 한다. 'if가정법~, you should~' 문장이 정답 문장이다.

What does the speaker recommend the listeners do?

(A) Request a refund
(B) Visit a Web site
(C) Contact an event organizer
(D) Attend a different event

문제 해설

화자가 권하는 일을 묻는 마지막 문제이므로 담화 후반부에 제시되는 권고 관련 표현을 중심으로 단서를 파악해야 한다. 화자는 담화 마지막에 'If you're interested in seeing the full movie schedule and finding out how to purchase tickets, you should log on to our Web site.'라는 말로 특정 정보를 확인하려면 웹 사이트에 접속하라고 권하고 있으므로 (B)가 정답임을 알 수 있다.

Questions 98-100 refer to the following excerpt from a meeting and pie chart.

W Good morning, everyone, and thanks for attending this management meeting. [98] I'm sure you all got the memo that I sent out yesterday, so you must have read that sales of our kitchen appliances are much lower than we had hoped. [99] This is partly because our recent advertising campaign turned out to be quite unpopular with consumers. In an effort to cut our expenses, we are considering closing one of our branches and moving some employees to different branches. [100] I discussed this issue with our CEO, and we think the branch that contributes 22% of total sales should be the one that is shut down. So let's take a look at which employees we can relocate to other branches.

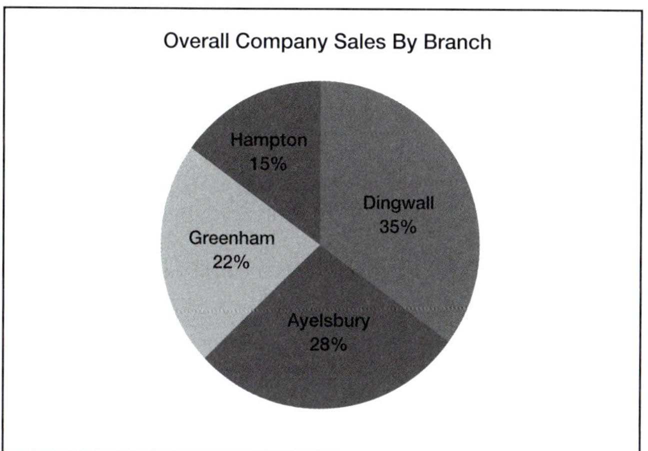

여 안녕하세요, 여러분, 그리고 이번 경영진 회의에 참석해 주셔서 감사 드립니다. [98] 여러분 모두 제가 어제 보내 드린 메모를 받으셨으리라 확신하고 있으므로 여러분께서는 우리의 주방 기기 매출이 희망했던 것보다 훨씬 더 낮다는 점을 틀림없이 읽어 보셨을 겁니다. [99] 이는 우리의 최근 광고 캠페인이 소비자들에게 상당히 인기가 없는 것으로 드러난 점에 일부 원인이 있습니다. 우리의 지출 비용을 줄이기 위한 노력의 일환으로, 우리는 지점들 중의 한 곳을 폐쇄하고 일부 직원들을 다른 지점들로 옮기는 것을 고려하고 있습니다. [100] 제가 이 사안을 대표 이사님과 논의했으며, 총 매출의 22%에 기여하고 있는 지점이 폐쇄되어야 하는 곳이라고 생각합니다. 따라서, 어떤 직원들을 우리가 다른 지점으로 이전시켜야 하는지 한 번 살펴보겠습니다.

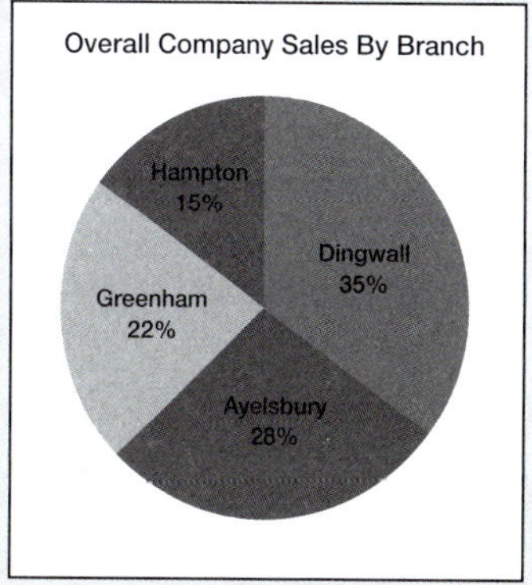

어휘 attend ~에 참석하다 management 경영(진) must have p.p. ~했음에 틀림없다 sales 매출, 판매, 영업 appliance (가전) 기기 much (비교급 수식) 훨씬 partly 일부, 부분적으로 recent 최근의 turn out to be ~한 것으로 드러나다, 판명되다 quite 상당히, 꽤 unpopular with ~에게 인기 없는 consumer 소비자 in an effort to do ~하기 위한 노력의 일환으로 cut ~을 줄이다, 삭감하다 expense 지출 비용 consider -ing ~하는 것을 고려하다 branch 지점, 지사 discuss ~을 논의하다 issue 사안, 문제 contribute ~을 기여/공헌하다 shut down ~을 닫다, 폐쇄하다 take a look at ~을 한 번 보다 relocate ~을 이전하다, 옮기다 overall 전반적인

98

According to the speaker, what was mentioned in the memo?

(A) The company will release new products.
(B) Employees must attend a training session.
(C) Sales are lower than expected.
(D) Some managers have been promoted.

문제 해설

메모에 언급된 것을 묻는 첫 번째 문제이므로 담화 초반부에 화자가 메모 및 그 안에 포함된 정보를 언급하는 내용이 있다는 것을 예상하고 들어야 한다. 화자는 담화를 시작하면서 'I'm sure you all got the memo that I sent out yesterday, so you must have read that sales of our kitchen appliances are much lower than we had hoped.'라는 말로 자신이 보낸 메모를 통해 매출이 바라던 것보다 낮은 상황임을 알게 되었으리라고 언급하고 있다. 따라서 매출의 저조함을 언급한 (C)가 정답이다.

★★ 세부 정보

화자의 말에 따르면, 메모에 무엇이 언급되어 있었는가?
(A) 회사가 신제품들을 출시할 것이다.
(B) 직원들이 반드시 교육 연수에 참석해야 한다.
(C) 매출이 예상보다 더 낮다.
(D) 일부 부서장들이 승진되어야 한다.

어휘 release ~을 출시하다, 내놓다 training session 교육 연수 than expected 예상보다 promote ~을 승진시키다

토익 분석

세부 정보 문제이므로 키워드를 이용해야 한다. memo가 키워드로 활용되었다.

★★ 문제점

화자는 무슨 문제를 언급하는가?
(A) 경쟁사에서 자사의 시장 점유율을 높였다.
(B) 한 광고 캠페인이 성공적이지 못했다.
(C) 고객들이 한 제품에 대해 불만을 제기했다.
(D) 생산비가 증가했다.

어휘 competitor 경쟁사, 경쟁자 market share 시장 점유율 unsuccessful 성공하지 못한 complain about ~에 대해 불만을 제기하다 production costs 생산비 increase 증가하다

토익 분석

문제점의 원인을 찾는 문제. 문제점의 원인은 due to, because, owing to 등이 단서를 제시한다.

What problem does the speaker mention?

(A) A competitor has increased its market share.

(B) An advertising campaign was unsuccessful.

(C) Customers have complained about a product.

(D) Production costs have increased.

문제 해설

화자가 언급하는 문제점을 묻는 두 번째 문제이므로 담화 중반부에 문제점과 관련된 부정적인 정보가 제시된다는 것을 예상하고 들어야 한다. 화자는 담화 중반부에 매출이 저조한 이유와 관련해 'This is partly because our recent advertising campaign turned out to be quite unpopular with consumers.'와 같이 광고 캠페인이 인기가 낮았음을 알리고 있으므로 성공적이지 못한 광고 캠페인을 언급한 (B)가 정답이다.

100

★★ 그래픽

도표를 보시오. 어느 지점이 폐쇄될 수 있는가?
(A) Hampton
(B) Dingwall
(C) Ayelsbury
(D) Greenham

토익 분석

지사 이름과 매출 비율이 그래프에 나타나 있다. 지사를 찾기 위해서는 지문에서 '매출 비율'관련 정보를 들어야 한다.

Look at the graphic. Which branch may be closed?

(A) Hampton

(B) Dingwall

(C) Ayelsbury

(D) Greenham

문제 해설

폐쇄되는 지점을 묻는 마지막 문제이므로 담화 후반부에 화자가 지점 폐쇄와 관련된 정보를 언급한다는 것을 알 수 있으며, 이와 관련해 도표에 쓰여 있는 매출 비율이 제시될 것임을 예상하고 들어야 한다. 화자는 담화 마지막에 'I discussed this issue with our CEO, and we think the branch that contributes 22% of total sales should be the one that is shut down.'라는 말로 22%를 차지한 곳이 폐쇄되어야 한다고 알리고 있으므로 도표에서 이 비율에 해당되는 곳인 (D)가 정답임을 알 수 있다.

Answer Sheet

응시일자 :

TOEIC Actual Test

성명	한글	
	한자	
	영문	

Listening Comprehension

No.	ANSWER	No.	ANSWER	No.	ANSWER	No.	ANSWER	No.	ANSWER
1	Ⓐ Ⓑ Ⓒ Ⓓ	21	Ⓐ Ⓑ Ⓒ	41	Ⓐ Ⓑ Ⓒ Ⓓ	61	Ⓐ Ⓑ Ⓒ Ⓓ	81	Ⓐ Ⓑ Ⓒ Ⓓ
2	Ⓐ Ⓑ Ⓒ Ⓓ	22	Ⓐ Ⓑ Ⓒ	42	Ⓐ Ⓑ Ⓒ Ⓓ	62	Ⓐ Ⓑ Ⓒ Ⓓ	82	Ⓐ Ⓑ Ⓒ Ⓓ
3	Ⓐ Ⓑ Ⓒ Ⓓ	23	Ⓐ Ⓑ Ⓒ	43	Ⓐ Ⓑ Ⓒ Ⓓ	63	Ⓐ Ⓑ Ⓒ Ⓓ	83	Ⓐ Ⓑ Ⓒ Ⓓ
4	Ⓐ Ⓑ Ⓒ Ⓓ	24	Ⓐ Ⓑ Ⓒ	44	Ⓐ Ⓑ Ⓒ Ⓓ	64	Ⓐ Ⓑ Ⓒ Ⓓ	84	Ⓐ Ⓑ Ⓒ Ⓓ
5	Ⓐ Ⓑ Ⓒ Ⓓ	25	Ⓐ Ⓑ Ⓒ	45	Ⓐ Ⓑ Ⓒ Ⓓ	65	Ⓐ Ⓑ Ⓒ Ⓓ	85	Ⓐ Ⓑ Ⓒ Ⓓ
6	Ⓐ Ⓑ Ⓒ Ⓓ	26	Ⓐ Ⓑ Ⓒ	46	Ⓐ Ⓑ Ⓒ Ⓓ	66	Ⓐ Ⓑ Ⓒ Ⓓ	86	Ⓐ Ⓑ Ⓒ Ⓓ
7	Ⓐ Ⓑ Ⓒ	27	Ⓐ Ⓑ Ⓒ	47	Ⓐ Ⓑ Ⓒ Ⓓ	67	Ⓐ Ⓑ Ⓒ Ⓓ	87	Ⓐ Ⓑ Ⓒ Ⓓ
8	Ⓐ Ⓑ Ⓒ	28	Ⓐ Ⓑ Ⓒ	48	Ⓐ Ⓑ Ⓒ Ⓓ	68	Ⓐ Ⓑ Ⓒ Ⓓ	88	Ⓐ Ⓑ Ⓒ Ⓓ
9	Ⓐ Ⓑ Ⓒ	29	Ⓐ Ⓑ Ⓒ	49	Ⓐ Ⓑ Ⓒ Ⓓ	69	Ⓐ Ⓑ Ⓒ Ⓓ	89	Ⓐ Ⓑ Ⓒ Ⓓ
10	Ⓐ Ⓑ Ⓒ	30	Ⓐ Ⓑ Ⓒ	50	Ⓐ Ⓑ Ⓒ Ⓓ	70	Ⓐ Ⓑ Ⓒ Ⓓ	90	Ⓐ Ⓑ Ⓒ Ⓓ
11	Ⓐ Ⓑ Ⓒ	31	Ⓐ Ⓑ Ⓒ	51	Ⓐ Ⓑ Ⓒ Ⓓ	71	Ⓐ Ⓑ Ⓒ Ⓓ	91	Ⓐ Ⓑ Ⓒ Ⓓ
12	Ⓐ Ⓑ Ⓒ	32	Ⓐ Ⓑ Ⓒ Ⓓ	52	Ⓐ Ⓑ Ⓒ Ⓓ	72	Ⓐ Ⓑ Ⓒ Ⓓ	92	Ⓐ Ⓑ Ⓒ Ⓓ
13	Ⓐ Ⓑ Ⓒ	33	Ⓐ Ⓑ Ⓒ Ⓓ	53	Ⓐ Ⓑ Ⓒ Ⓓ	73	Ⓐ Ⓑ Ⓒ Ⓓ	93	Ⓐ Ⓑ Ⓒ Ⓓ
14	Ⓐ Ⓑ Ⓒ	34	Ⓐ Ⓑ Ⓒ Ⓓ	54	Ⓐ Ⓑ Ⓒ Ⓓ	74	Ⓐ Ⓑ Ⓒ Ⓓ	94	Ⓐ Ⓑ Ⓒ Ⓓ
15	Ⓐ Ⓑ Ⓒ	35	Ⓐ Ⓑ Ⓒ Ⓓ	55	Ⓐ Ⓑ Ⓒ Ⓓ	75	Ⓐ Ⓑ Ⓒ Ⓓ	95	Ⓐ Ⓑ Ⓒ Ⓓ
16	Ⓐ Ⓑ Ⓒ	36	Ⓐ Ⓑ Ⓒ Ⓓ	56	Ⓐ Ⓑ Ⓒ Ⓓ	76	Ⓐ Ⓑ Ⓒ Ⓓ	96	Ⓐ Ⓑ Ⓒ Ⓓ
17	Ⓐ Ⓑ Ⓒ	37	Ⓐ Ⓑ Ⓒ Ⓓ	57	Ⓐ Ⓑ Ⓒ Ⓓ	77	Ⓐ Ⓑ Ⓒ Ⓓ	97	Ⓐ Ⓑ Ⓒ Ⓓ
18	Ⓐ Ⓑ Ⓒ	38	Ⓐ Ⓑ Ⓒ Ⓓ	58	Ⓐ Ⓑ Ⓒ Ⓓ	78	Ⓐ Ⓑ Ⓒ Ⓓ	98	Ⓐ Ⓑ Ⓒ Ⓓ
19	Ⓐ Ⓑ Ⓒ	39	Ⓐ Ⓑ Ⓒ Ⓓ	59	Ⓐ Ⓑ Ⓒ Ⓓ	79	Ⓐ Ⓑ Ⓒ Ⓓ	99	Ⓐ Ⓑ Ⓒ Ⓓ
20	Ⓐ Ⓑ Ⓒ	40	Ⓐ Ⓑ Ⓒ Ⓓ	60	Ⓐ Ⓑ Ⓒ Ⓓ	80	Ⓐ Ⓑ Ⓒ Ⓓ	100	Ⓐ Ⓑ Ⓒ Ⓓ

Reading Comprehension

No.	ANSWER	No.	ANSWER	No.	ANSWER	No.	ANSWER	No.	ANSWER
101	Ⓐ Ⓑ Ⓒ Ⓓ	121	Ⓐ Ⓑ Ⓒ Ⓓ	141	Ⓐ Ⓑ Ⓒ Ⓓ	161	Ⓐ Ⓑ Ⓒ Ⓓ	181	Ⓐ Ⓑ Ⓒ Ⓓ
102	Ⓐ Ⓑ Ⓒ Ⓓ	122	Ⓐ Ⓑ Ⓒ Ⓓ	142	Ⓐ Ⓑ Ⓒ Ⓓ	162	Ⓐ Ⓑ Ⓒ Ⓓ	182	Ⓐ Ⓑ Ⓒ Ⓓ
103	Ⓐ Ⓑ Ⓒ Ⓓ	123	Ⓐ Ⓑ Ⓒ Ⓓ	143	Ⓐ Ⓑ Ⓒ Ⓓ	163	Ⓐ Ⓑ Ⓒ Ⓓ	183	Ⓐ Ⓑ Ⓒ Ⓓ
104	Ⓐ Ⓑ Ⓒ Ⓓ	124	Ⓐ Ⓑ Ⓒ Ⓓ	144	Ⓐ Ⓑ Ⓒ Ⓓ	164	Ⓐ Ⓑ Ⓒ Ⓓ	184	Ⓐ Ⓑ Ⓒ Ⓓ
105	Ⓐ Ⓑ Ⓒ Ⓓ	125	Ⓐ Ⓑ Ⓒ Ⓓ	145	Ⓐ Ⓑ Ⓒ Ⓓ	165	Ⓐ Ⓑ Ⓒ Ⓓ	185	Ⓐ Ⓑ Ⓒ Ⓓ
106	Ⓐ Ⓑ Ⓒ Ⓓ	126	Ⓐ Ⓑ Ⓒ Ⓓ	146	Ⓐ Ⓑ Ⓒ Ⓓ	166	Ⓐ Ⓑ Ⓒ Ⓓ	186	Ⓐ Ⓑ Ⓒ Ⓓ
107	Ⓐ Ⓑ Ⓒ Ⓓ	127	Ⓐ Ⓑ Ⓒ Ⓓ	147	Ⓐ Ⓑ Ⓒ Ⓓ	167	Ⓐ Ⓑ Ⓒ Ⓓ	187	Ⓐ Ⓑ Ⓒ Ⓓ
108	Ⓐ Ⓑ Ⓒ Ⓓ	128	Ⓐ Ⓑ Ⓒ Ⓓ	148	Ⓐ Ⓑ Ⓒ Ⓓ	168	Ⓐ Ⓑ Ⓒ Ⓓ	188	Ⓐ Ⓑ Ⓒ Ⓓ
109	Ⓐ Ⓑ Ⓒ Ⓓ	129	Ⓐ Ⓑ Ⓒ Ⓓ	149	Ⓐ Ⓑ Ⓒ Ⓓ	169	Ⓐ Ⓑ Ⓒ Ⓓ	189	Ⓐ Ⓑ Ⓒ Ⓓ
110	Ⓐ Ⓑ Ⓒ Ⓓ	130	Ⓐ Ⓑ Ⓒ Ⓓ	150	Ⓐ Ⓑ Ⓒ Ⓓ	170	Ⓐ Ⓑ Ⓒ Ⓓ	190	Ⓐ Ⓑ Ⓒ Ⓓ
111	Ⓐ Ⓑ Ⓒ Ⓓ	131	Ⓐ Ⓑ Ⓒ Ⓓ	151	Ⓐ Ⓑ Ⓒ Ⓓ	171	Ⓐ Ⓑ Ⓒ Ⓓ	191	Ⓐ Ⓑ Ⓒ Ⓓ
112	Ⓐ Ⓑ Ⓒ Ⓓ	132	Ⓐ Ⓑ Ⓒ Ⓓ	152	Ⓐ Ⓑ Ⓒ Ⓓ	172	Ⓐ Ⓑ Ⓒ Ⓓ	192	Ⓐ Ⓑ Ⓒ Ⓓ
113	Ⓐ Ⓑ Ⓒ Ⓓ	133	Ⓐ Ⓑ Ⓒ Ⓓ	153	Ⓐ Ⓑ Ⓒ Ⓓ	173	Ⓐ Ⓑ Ⓒ Ⓓ	193	Ⓐ Ⓑ Ⓒ Ⓓ
114	Ⓐ Ⓑ Ⓒ Ⓓ	134	Ⓐ Ⓑ Ⓒ Ⓓ	154	Ⓐ Ⓑ Ⓒ Ⓓ	174	Ⓐ Ⓑ Ⓒ Ⓓ	194	Ⓐ Ⓑ Ⓒ Ⓓ
115	Ⓐ Ⓑ Ⓒ Ⓓ	135	Ⓐ Ⓑ Ⓒ Ⓓ	155	Ⓐ Ⓑ Ⓒ Ⓓ	175	Ⓐ Ⓑ Ⓒ Ⓓ	195	Ⓐ Ⓑ Ⓒ Ⓓ
116	Ⓐ Ⓑ Ⓒ Ⓓ	136	Ⓐ Ⓑ Ⓒ Ⓓ	156	Ⓐ Ⓑ Ⓒ Ⓓ	176	Ⓐ Ⓑ Ⓒ Ⓓ	196	Ⓐ Ⓑ Ⓒ Ⓓ
117	Ⓐ Ⓑ Ⓒ Ⓓ	137	Ⓐ Ⓑ Ⓒ Ⓓ	157	Ⓐ Ⓑ Ⓒ Ⓓ	177	Ⓐ Ⓑ Ⓒ Ⓓ	197	Ⓐ Ⓑ Ⓒ Ⓓ
118	Ⓐ Ⓑ Ⓒ Ⓓ	138	Ⓐ Ⓑ Ⓒ Ⓓ	158	Ⓐ Ⓑ Ⓒ Ⓓ	178	Ⓐ Ⓑ Ⓒ Ⓓ	198	Ⓐ Ⓑ Ⓒ Ⓓ
119	Ⓐ Ⓑ Ⓒ Ⓓ	139	Ⓐ Ⓑ Ⓒ Ⓓ	159	Ⓐ Ⓑ Ⓒ Ⓓ	179	Ⓐ Ⓑ Ⓒ Ⓓ	199	Ⓐ Ⓑ Ⓒ Ⓓ
120	Ⓐ Ⓑ Ⓒ Ⓓ	140	Ⓐ Ⓑ Ⓒ Ⓓ	160	Ⓐ Ⓑ Ⓒ Ⓓ	180	Ⓐ Ⓑ Ⓒ Ⓓ	200	Ⓐ Ⓑ Ⓒ Ⓓ

Answer Sheet

응시일자 :

TOEIC Actual Test

성명 | 한글
 | 한자
 | 영문

Listening Comprehension

Reading Comprehension

Answer Sheet

응시일자 :

TOEIC Actual Test

성명	한글	
	한자	
	영문	

Listening Comprehension

No.	ANSWER	No.	ANSWER	No.	ANSWER	No.	ANSWER	No.	ANSWER
	A B C D		A B C D		A B C D		A B C D		A B C D
1	ⓐ ⓑ ⓒ ⓓ	21	ⓐ ⓑ ⓒ	41	ⓐ ⓑ ⓒ ⓓ	61	ⓐ ⓑ ⓒ ⓓ	81	ⓐ ⓑ ⓒ ⓓ
2	ⓐ ⓑ ⓒ ⓓ	22	ⓐ ⓑ ⓒ	42	ⓐ ⓑ ⓒ ⓓ	62	ⓐ ⓑ ⓒ ⓓ	82	ⓐ ⓑ ⓒ ⓓ
3	ⓐ ⓑ ⓒ ⓓ	23	ⓐ ⓑ ⓒ	43	ⓐ ⓑ ⓒ ⓓ	63	ⓐ ⓑ ⓒ ⓓ	83	ⓐ ⓑ ⓒ ⓓ
4	ⓐ ⓑ ⓒ ⓓ	24	ⓐ ⓑ ⓒ	44	ⓐ ⓑ ⓒ ⓓ	64	ⓐ ⓑ ⓒ ⓓ	84	ⓐ ⓑ ⓒ ⓓ
5	ⓐ ⓑ ⓒ ⓓ	25	ⓐ ⓑ ⓒ	45	ⓐ ⓑ ⓒ ⓓ	65	ⓐ ⓑ ⓒ ⓓ	85	ⓐ ⓑ ⓒ ⓓ
6	ⓐ ⓑ ⓒ ⓓ	26	ⓐ ⓑ ⓒ	46	ⓐ ⓑ ⓒ ⓓ	66	ⓐ ⓑ ⓒ ⓓ	86	ⓐ ⓑ ⓒ ⓓ
7	ⓐ ⓑ ⓒ	27	ⓐ ⓑ ⓒ	47	ⓐ ⓑ ⓒ ⓓ	67	ⓐ ⓑ ⓒ ⓓ	87	ⓐ ⓑ ⓒ ⓓ
8	ⓐ ⓑ ⓒ	28	ⓐ ⓑ ⓒ	48	ⓐ ⓑ ⓒ ⓓ	68	ⓐ ⓑ ⓒ ⓓ	88	ⓐ ⓑ ⓒ ⓓ
9	ⓐ ⓑ ⓒ	29	ⓐ ⓑ ⓒ	49	ⓐ ⓑ ⓒ ⓓ	69	ⓐ ⓑ ⓒ ⓓ	89	ⓐ ⓑ ⓒ ⓓ
10	ⓐ ⓑ ⓒ	30	ⓐ ⓑ ⓒ	50	ⓐ ⓑ ⓒ ⓓ	70	ⓐ ⓑ ⓒ ⓓ	90	ⓐ ⓑ ⓒ ⓓ
11	ⓐ ⓑ ⓒ	31	ⓐ ⓑ ⓒ	51	ⓐ ⓑ ⓒ ⓓ	71	ⓐ ⓑ ⓒ ⓓ	91	ⓐ ⓑ ⓒ ⓓ
12	ⓐ ⓑ ⓒ	32	ⓐ ⓑ ⓒ ⓓ	52	ⓐ ⓑ ⓒ ⓓ	72	ⓐ ⓑ ⓒ ⓓ	92	ⓐ ⓑ ⓒ ⓓ
13	ⓐ ⓑ ⓒ	33	ⓐ ⓑ ⓒ ⓓ	53	ⓐ ⓑ ⓒ ⓓ	73	ⓐ ⓑ ⓒ ⓓ	93	ⓐ ⓑ ⓒ ⓓ
14	ⓐ ⓑ ⓒ	34	ⓐ ⓑ ⓒ ⓓ	54	ⓐ ⓑ ⓒ ⓓ	74	ⓐ ⓑ ⓒ ⓓ	94	ⓐ ⓑ ⓒ ⓓ
15	ⓐ ⓑ ⓒ	35	ⓐ ⓑ ⓒ ⓓ	55	ⓐ ⓑ ⓒ ⓓ	75	ⓐ ⓑ ⓒ ⓓ	95	ⓐ ⓑ ⓒ ⓓ
16	ⓐ ⓑ ⓒ	36	ⓐ ⓑ ⓒ ⓓ	56	ⓐ ⓑ ⓒ ⓓ	76	ⓐ ⓑ ⓒ ⓓ	96	ⓐ ⓑ ⓒ ⓓ
17	ⓐ ⓑ ⓒ	37	ⓐ ⓑ ⓒ ⓓ	57	ⓐ ⓑ ⓒ ⓓ	77	ⓐ ⓑ ⓒ ⓓ	97	ⓐ ⓑ ⓒ ⓓ
18	ⓐ ⓑ ⓒ	38	ⓐ ⓑ ⓒ ⓓ	58	ⓐ ⓑ ⓒ ⓓ	78	ⓐ ⓑ ⓒ ⓓ	98	ⓐ ⓑ ⓒ ⓓ
19	ⓐ ⓑ ⓒ	39	ⓐ ⓑ ⓒ ⓓ	59	ⓐ ⓑ ⓒ ⓓ	79	ⓐ ⓑ ⓒ ⓓ	99	ⓐ ⓑ ⓒ ⓓ
20	ⓐ ⓑ ⓒ	40	ⓐ ⓑ ⓒ ⓓ	60	ⓐ ⓑ ⓒ ⓓ	80	ⓐ ⓑ ⓒ ⓓ	100	ⓐ ⓑ ⓒ ⓓ

Reading Comprehension

No.	ANSWER	No.	ANSWER	No.	ANSWER	No.	ANSWER	No.	ANSWER
	A B C D		A B C D		A B C D		A B C D		A B C D
101	ⓐ ⓑ ⓒ ⓓ	121	ⓐ ⓑ ⓒ ⓓ	141	ⓐ ⓑ ⓒ ⓓ	161	ⓐ ⓑ ⓒ ⓓ	181	ⓐ ⓑ ⓒ ⓓ
102	ⓐ ⓑ ⓒ ⓓ	122	ⓐ ⓑ ⓒ ⓓ	142	ⓐ ⓑ ⓒ ⓓ	162	ⓐ ⓑ ⓒ ⓓ	182	ⓐ ⓑ ⓒ ⓓ
103	ⓐ ⓑ ⓒ ⓓ	123	ⓐ ⓑ ⓒ ⓓ	143	ⓐ ⓑ ⓒ ⓓ	163	ⓐ ⓑ ⓒ ⓓ	183	ⓐ ⓑ ⓒ ⓓ
104	ⓐ ⓑ ⓒ ⓓ	124	ⓐ ⓑ ⓒ ⓓ	144	ⓐ ⓑ ⓒ ⓓ	164	ⓐ ⓑ ⓒ ⓓ	184	ⓐ ⓑ ⓒ ⓓ
105	ⓐ ⓑ ⓒ ⓓ	125	ⓐ ⓑ ⓒ ⓓ	145	ⓐ ⓑ ⓒ ⓓ	165	ⓐ ⓑ ⓒ ⓓ	185	ⓐ ⓑ ⓒ ⓓ
106	ⓐ ⓑ ⓒ ⓓ	126	ⓐ ⓑ ⓒ ⓓ	146	ⓐ ⓑ ⓒ ⓓ	166	ⓐ ⓑ ⓒ ⓓ	186	ⓐ ⓑ ⓒ ⓓ
107	ⓐ ⓑ ⓒ ⓓ	127	ⓐ ⓑ ⓒ ⓓ	147	ⓐ ⓑ ⓒ ⓓ	167	ⓐ ⓑ ⓒ ⓓ	187	ⓐ ⓑ ⓒ ⓓ
108	ⓐ ⓑ ⓒ ⓓ	128	ⓐ ⓑ ⓒ ⓓ	148	ⓐ ⓑ ⓒ ⓓ	168	ⓐ ⓑ ⓒ ⓓ	188	ⓐ ⓑ ⓒ ⓓ
109	ⓐ ⓑ ⓒ ⓓ	129	ⓐ ⓑ ⓒ ⓓ	149	ⓐ ⓑ ⓒ ⓓ	169	ⓐ ⓑ ⓒ ⓓ	189	ⓐ ⓑ ⓒ ⓓ
110	ⓐ ⓑ ⓒ ⓓ	130	ⓐ ⓑ ⓒ ⓓ	150	ⓐ ⓑ ⓒ ⓓ	170	ⓐ ⓑ ⓒ ⓓ	190	ⓐ ⓑ ⓒ ⓓ
111	ⓐ ⓑ ⓒ ⓓ	131	ⓐ ⓑ ⓒ ⓓ	151	ⓐ ⓑ ⓒ ⓓ	171	ⓐ ⓑ ⓒ ⓓ	191	ⓐ ⓑ ⓒ ⓓ
112	ⓐ ⓑ ⓒ ⓓ	132	ⓐ ⓑ ⓒ ⓓ	152	ⓐ ⓑ ⓒ ⓓ	172	ⓐ ⓑ ⓒ ⓓ	192	ⓐ ⓑ ⓒ ⓓ
113	ⓐ ⓑ ⓒ ⓓ	133	ⓐ ⓑ ⓒ ⓓ	153	ⓐ ⓑ ⓒ ⓓ	173	ⓐ ⓑ ⓒ ⓓ	193	ⓐ ⓑ ⓒ ⓓ
114	ⓐ ⓑ ⓒ ⓓ	134	ⓐ ⓑ ⓒ ⓓ	154	ⓐ ⓑ ⓒ ⓓ	174	ⓐ ⓑ ⓒ ⓓ	194	ⓐ ⓑ ⓒ ⓓ
115	ⓐ ⓑ ⓒ ⓓ	135	ⓐ ⓑ ⓒ ⓓ	155	ⓐ ⓑ ⓒ ⓓ	175	ⓐ ⓑ ⓒ ⓓ	195	ⓐ ⓑ ⓒ ⓓ
116	ⓐ ⓑ ⓒ ⓓ	136	ⓐ ⓑ ⓒ ⓓ	156	ⓐ ⓑ ⓒ ⓓ	176	ⓐ ⓑ ⓒ ⓓ	196	ⓐ ⓑ ⓒ ⓓ
117	ⓐ ⓑ ⓒ ⓓ	137	ⓐ ⓑ ⓒ ⓓ	157	ⓐ ⓑ ⓒ ⓓ	177	ⓐ ⓑ ⓒ ⓓ	197	ⓐ ⓑ ⓒ ⓓ
118	ⓐ ⓑ ⓒ ⓓ	138	ⓐ ⓑ ⓒ ⓓ	158	ⓐ ⓑ ⓒ ⓓ	178	ⓐ ⓑ ⓒ ⓓ	198	ⓐ ⓑ ⓒ ⓓ
119	ⓐ ⓑ ⓒ ⓓ	139	ⓐ ⓑ ⓒ ⓓ	159	ⓐ ⓑ ⓒ ⓓ	179	ⓐ ⓑ ⓒ ⓓ	199	ⓐ ⓑ ⓒ ⓓ
120	ⓐ ⓑ ⓒ ⓓ	140	ⓐ ⓑ ⓒ ⓓ	160	ⓐ ⓑ ⓒ ⓓ	180	ⓐ ⓑ ⓒ ⓓ	200	ⓐ ⓑ ⓒ ⓓ

Answer Sheet

TOEIC Actual Test

성명	한글	
	한자	
	영문	

응시일자 :

Listening Comprehension

No.	ANSWER A B C D	No.	ANSWER A B C D	No.	ANSWER A B C D	No.	ANSWER A B C D	No.	ANSWER A B C D
1	ⓐ ⓑ ⓒ ⓓ	21	ⓐ ⓑ ⓒ	41	ⓐ ⓑ ⓒ ⓓ	61	ⓐ ⓑ ⓒ ⓓ	81	ⓐ ⓑ ⓒ ⓓ
2	ⓐ ⓑ ⓒ ⓓ	22	ⓐ ⓑ ⓒ	42	ⓐ ⓑ ⓒ ⓓ	62	ⓐ ⓑ ⓒ ⓓ	82	ⓐ ⓑ ⓒ ⓓ
3	ⓐ ⓑ ⓒ ⓓ	23	ⓐ ⓑ ⓒ	43	ⓐ ⓑ ⓒ ⓓ	63	ⓐ ⓑ ⓒ ⓓ	83	ⓐ ⓑ ⓒ ⓓ
4	ⓐ ⓑ ⓒ ⓓ	24	ⓐ ⓑ ⓒ	44	ⓐ ⓑ ⓒ ⓓ	64	ⓐ ⓑ ⓒ ⓓ	84	ⓐ ⓑ ⓒ ⓓ
5	ⓐ ⓑ ⓒ ⓓ	25	ⓐ ⓑ ⓒ	45	ⓐ ⓑ ⓒ ⓓ	65	ⓐ ⓑ ⓒ ⓓ	85	ⓐ ⓑ ⓒ ⓓ
6	ⓐ ⓑ ⓒ ⓓ	26	ⓐ ⓑ ⓒ	46	ⓐ ⓑ ⓒ ⓓ	66	ⓐ ⓑ ⓒ ⓓ	86	ⓐ ⓑ ⓒ ⓓ
7	ⓐ ⓑ ⓒ	27	ⓐ ⓑ ⓒ	47	ⓐ ⓑ ⓒ ⓓ	67	ⓐ ⓑ ⓒ ⓓ	87	ⓐ ⓑ ⓒ ⓓ
8	ⓐ ⓑ ⓒ	28	ⓐ ⓑ ⓒ	48	ⓐ ⓑ ⓒ ⓓ	68	ⓐ ⓑ ⓒ ⓓ	88	ⓐ ⓑ ⓒ ⓓ
9	ⓐ ⓑ ⓒ	29	ⓐ ⓑ ⓒ	49	ⓐ ⓑ ⓒ ⓓ	69	ⓐ ⓑ ⓒ ⓓ	89	ⓐ ⓑ ⓒ ⓓ
10	ⓐ ⓑ ⓒ	30	ⓐ ⓑ ⓒ	50	ⓐ ⓑ ⓒ ⓓ	70	ⓐ ⓑ ⓒ ⓓ	90	ⓐ ⓑ ⓒ ⓓ
11	ⓐ ⓑ ⓒ	31	ⓐ ⓑ ⓒ	51	ⓐ ⓑ ⓒ ⓓ	71	ⓐ ⓑ ⓒ ⓓ	91	ⓐ ⓑ ⓒ ⓓ
12	ⓐ ⓑ ⓒ	32	ⓐ ⓑ ⓒ ⓓ	52	ⓐ ⓑ ⓒ ⓓ	72	ⓐ ⓑ ⓒ ⓓ	92	ⓐ ⓑ ⓒ ⓓ
13	ⓐ ⓑ ⓒ	33	ⓐ ⓑ ⓒ ⓓ	53	ⓐ ⓑ ⓒ ⓓ	73	ⓐ ⓑ ⓒ ⓓ	93	ⓐ ⓑ ⓒ ⓓ
14	ⓐ ⓑ ⓒ	34	ⓐ ⓑ ⓒ ⓓ	54	ⓐ ⓑ ⓒ ⓓ	74	ⓐ ⓑ ⓒ ⓓ	94	ⓐ ⓑ ⓒ ⓓ
15	ⓐ ⓑ ⓒ	35	ⓐ ⓑ ⓒ ⓓ	55	ⓐ ⓑ ⓒ ⓓ	75	ⓐ ⓑ ⓒ ⓓ	95	ⓐ ⓑ ⓒ ⓓ
16	ⓐ ⓑ ⓒ	36	ⓐ ⓑ ⓒ ⓓ	56	ⓐ ⓑ ⓒ ⓓ	76	ⓐ ⓑ ⓒ ⓓ	96	ⓐ ⓑ ⓒ ⓓ
17	ⓐ ⓑ ⓒ	37	ⓐ ⓑ ⓒ ⓓ	57	ⓐ ⓑ ⓒ ⓓ	77	ⓐ ⓑ ⓒ ⓓ	97	ⓐ ⓑ ⓒ ⓓ
18	ⓐ ⓑ ⓒ	38	ⓐ ⓑ ⓒ ⓓ	58	ⓐ ⓑ ⓒ ⓓ	78	ⓐ ⓑ ⓒ ⓓ	98	ⓐ ⓑ ⓒ ⓓ
19	ⓐ ⓑ ⓒ	39	ⓐ ⓑ ⓒ ⓓ	59	ⓐ ⓑ ⓒ ⓓ	79	ⓐ ⓑ ⓒ ⓓ	99	ⓐ ⓑ ⓒ ⓓ
20	ⓐ ⓑ ⓒ	40	ⓐ ⓑ ⓒ ⓓ	60	ⓐ ⓑ ⓒ ⓓ	80	ⓐ ⓑ ⓒ ⓓ	100	ⓐ ⓑ ⓒ ⓓ

Reading Comprehension

No.	ANSWER A B C D	No.	ANSWER A B C D	No.	ANSWER A B C D	No.	ANSWER A B C D	No.	ANSWER A B C D
101	ⓐ ⓑ ⓒ ⓓ	121	ⓐ ⓑ ⓒ ⓓ	141	ⓐ ⓑ ⓒ ⓓ	161	ⓐ ⓑ ⓒ ⓓ	181	ⓐ ⓑ ⓒ ⓓ
102	ⓐ ⓑ ⓒ ⓓ	122	ⓐ ⓑ ⓒ ⓓ	142	ⓐ ⓑ ⓒ ⓓ	162	ⓐ ⓑ ⓒ ⓓ	182	ⓐ ⓑ ⓒ ⓓ
103	ⓐ ⓑ ⓒ ⓓ	123	ⓐ ⓑ ⓒ ⓓ	143	ⓐ ⓑ ⓒ ⓓ	163	ⓐ ⓑ ⓒ ⓓ	183	ⓐ ⓑ ⓒ ⓓ
104	ⓐ ⓑ ⓒ ⓓ	124	ⓐ ⓑ ⓒ ⓓ	144	ⓐ ⓑ ⓒ ⓓ	164	ⓐ ⓑ ⓒ ⓓ	184	ⓐ ⓑ ⓒ ⓓ
105	ⓐ ⓑ ⓒ ⓓ	125	ⓐ ⓑ ⓒ ⓓ	145	ⓐ ⓑ ⓒ ⓓ	165	ⓐ ⓑ ⓒ ⓓ	185	ⓐ ⓑ ⓒ ⓓ
106	ⓐ ⓑ ⓒ ⓓ	126	ⓐ ⓑ ⓒ ⓓ	146	ⓐ ⓑ ⓒ ⓓ	166	ⓐ ⓑ ⓒ ⓓ	186	ⓐ ⓑ ⓒ ⓓ
107	ⓐ ⓑ ⓒ ⓓ	127	ⓐ ⓑ ⓒ ⓓ	147	ⓐ ⓑ ⓒ ⓓ	167	ⓐ ⓑ ⓒ ⓓ	187	ⓐ ⓑ ⓒ ⓓ
108	ⓐ ⓑ ⓒ ⓓ	128	ⓐ ⓑ ⓒ ⓓ	148	ⓐ ⓑ ⓒ ⓓ	168	ⓐ ⓑ ⓒ ⓓ	188	ⓐ ⓑ ⓒ ⓓ
109	ⓐ ⓑ ⓒ ⓓ	129	ⓐ ⓑ ⓒ ⓓ	149	ⓐ ⓑ ⓒ ⓓ	169	ⓐ ⓑ ⓒ ⓓ	189	ⓐ ⓑ ⓒ ⓓ
110	ⓐ ⓑ ⓒ ⓓ	130	ⓐ ⓑ ⓒ ⓓ	150	ⓐ ⓑ ⓒ ⓓ	170	ⓐ ⓑ ⓒ ⓓ	190	ⓐ ⓑ ⓒ ⓓ
111	ⓐ ⓑ ⓒ ⓓ	131	ⓐ ⓑ ⓒ ⓓ	151	ⓐ ⓑ ⓒ ⓓ	171	ⓐ ⓑ ⓒ ⓓ	191	ⓐ ⓑ ⓒ ⓓ
112	ⓐ ⓑ ⓒ ⓓ	132	ⓐ ⓑ ⓒ ⓓ	152	ⓐ ⓑ ⓒ ⓓ	172	ⓐ ⓑ ⓒ ⓓ	192	ⓐ ⓑ ⓒ ⓓ
113	ⓐ ⓑ ⓒ ⓓ	133	ⓐ ⓑ ⓒ ⓓ	153	ⓐ ⓑ ⓒ ⓓ	173	ⓐ ⓑ ⓒ ⓓ	193	ⓐ ⓑ ⓒ ⓓ
114	ⓐ ⓑ ⓒ ⓓ	134	ⓐ ⓑ ⓒ ⓓ	154	ⓐ ⓑ ⓒ ⓓ	174	ⓐ ⓑ ⓒ ⓓ	194	ⓐ ⓑ ⓒ ⓓ
115	ⓐ ⓑ ⓒ ⓓ	135	ⓐ ⓑ ⓒ ⓓ	155	ⓐ ⓑ ⓒ ⓓ	175	ⓐ ⓑ ⓒ ⓓ	195	ⓐ ⓑ ⓒ ⓓ
116	ⓐ ⓑ ⓒ ⓓ	136	ⓐ ⓑ ⓒ ⓓ	156	ⓐ ⓑ ⓒ ⓓ	176	ⓐ ⓑ ⓒ ⓓ	196	ⓐ ⓑ ⓒ ⓓ
117	ⓐ ⓑ ⓒ ⓓ	137	ⓐ ⓑ ⓒ ⓓ	157	ⓐ ⓑ ⓒ ⓓ	177	ⓐ ⓑ ⓒ ⓓ	197	ⓐ ⓑ ⓒ ⓓ
118	ⓐ ⓑ ⓒ ⓓ	138	ⓐ ⓑ ⓒ ⓓ	158	ⓐ ⓑ ⓒ ⓓ	178	ⓐ ⓑ ⓒ ⓓ	198	ⓐ ⓑ ⓒ ⓓ
119	ⓐ ⓑ ⓒ ⓓ	139	ⓐ ⓑ ⓒ ⓓ	159	ⓐ ⓑ ⓒ ⓓ	179	ⓐ ⓑ ⓒ ⓓ	199	ⓐ ⓑ ⓒ ⓓ
120	ⓐ ⓑ ⓒ ⓓ	140	ⓐ ⓑ ⓒ ⓓ	160	ⓐ ⓑ ⓒ ⓓ	180	ⓐ ⓑ ⓒ ⓓ	200	ⓐ ⓑ ⓒ ⓓ

Answer Sheet

응시일자 :

TOEIC Actual Test

성명	한글
	한자
	영문

Listening Comprehension

(Answer grid for Nos. 1–100, columns A B C D)

Reading Comprehension

(Answer grid for Nos. 101–200, columns A B C D)

백형식 저 | 520쪽 | 170×250
| 16,800원 | 본문 MP3 파일 다운로드

기본 무장 + 유형 정비 + 정답 연결 풀이 비법

LC 막귀도, RC 어휘 문법 역대급 포기자도 100점 올리는 건 일도 아닙니다!

짠내 나는 토익 점수, 대체 언제까지 맞을 거죠? 단짠단짠이 대세인 요즘, 달달한 점수도 맞아 봐야 하지 않겠습니까? 그래서 〈TOEIC 누추한 점수에 던지는 기특한 풀이 비법〉이 나왔습니다. 비법이라서 요령만 알려 줄 것 같다고요? NO! 이 책의 정체는 기본서 + 비법서. 그렇기에 토익을 샅샅이 파헤치고 분석해서 토익 문제를 읽고 이해하는 데 필요한 필수 학습 분량을 명확히 제시합니다. 이렇게 기본기가 쌓이게 하면서 파트별 문제 유형마다 풀이 과정을 제시해 단시간 내에 정답 찾기 회로가 머릿속에 콕 박히게 하죠. 이것만으로도 안 풀릴 때를 대비해, 최후에 쓸 수 있는 풀이 tip까지 꽉꽉 채워 넣었습니다. 이 한 권이면 꿈쩍 않던 토익 앞자리 숫자가 확 바뀝니다.

국가대표급 영포자도 점수를 올릴 수 있는 핵심 학습법

- 최신 경향 파악, 빈출 유형부터 공략하라!
- 문법은 최대한 기본적인 것 위주로 간결하게 끝내라!
- 어휘 공부에 더 많은 시간을 투자하라!